DATE			
MAY 24 '89			
MAY 9 '90			
[illegible]			
MAY 20			
JUL 31			

Speaking for You

Speaking for You

THE VISION OF RALPH ELLISON

Edited by
Kimberly W. Benston

Howard University Press
Washington, D.C. 1987

Printed in the United States of America

Library of Congress Cataloging-in-Publication Data

Speaking for you.

Bibliography: p.
Includes index.
1. Ellison, Ralph—Criticism and interpretation.
I. Benston, Kimberly W. II. Title.
PS3555.L625Z88 1987 818′.5409 87–17019
ISBN 0–88258–169–4

Contents

Acknowledgments

Acknowledgment is gratefully extended to the following for permission to reprint from copyrighted works:

The Modern Language Association for "To Move Without Moving: An Analysis of Creativity and Commerce in Ralph Ellison's Trueblood Episode," by Houston Baker, Jr., from *PMLA* 98 (1983). Reprinted by permission of the Modern Language Association of America. Copyright © 1983 by the Modern Language Association of America.

The University of Illinois Press for "Chaos, Complexity, and Possibility: The Historical Frequencies of Ralph Waldo Ellison," by John F. Callahan, from *Chant of Saints: A Gathering of Afro-American Literature, Art, and Scholarship*, eds. Michael S. Harper and Robert B. Stepto, 1979. Copyright © 1979 by John F. Callahan; Poems from *Healing Song for the Inner Ear* by Michael S. Harper, 1985. Copyright © 1985 by Michael S. Harper; "Literacy and Hibernation: Ralph Ellison's *Invisible Man*," by Robert B. Stepto, from *From Behind the Veil: A Study of Afro-American Narrative*, 1979. Copyright © 1979 by Robert B. Stepto.

Jeanne Davis for "The Mixed Heritage of the Modern Black Novel: Ralph Ellison and Friends," by Charles T. Davis, from *Black Is the Color of the Cosmos*, 1982. Copyright © 1982 by Charles T. Davis.

Random House for "Remembering Richard Wright," from *Going to the Territory* by Ralph Ellison. Copyright © 1971 by Ralph Ellison.

The Carleton Miscellany for "Luminosity from the Lower Frequencies," by Leon Forrest, from *The Carleton Miscellany* 18, No. 3, Winter 1980. Copyright © 1980 by Leon Forrest; "Shadowing Ellison," by John S. Wright, from *The Carleton Miscellany* 18, No. 3, Winter 1980. Copyright © 1980 by John S. Wright.

Prentice-Hall, Inc. for "'A Completion of Personality," by John Hersey, from *Ralph Ellison: A Collection of Critical Essays*, ed. John Hersey, 1970. Copyright © 1974, 1986 by John Hersey.

Desiré A. Kent for "Ralph Ellison and Afro-American Folk and Cultural Tradition," by George E. Kent, from *Blackness and the Adventure of Western Culture*, 1972. Copyright © 1972 by George E. Kent.

The New York Review of Books for ''Ellison's Essays,'' by R. W. B. Lewis, from *The New York Review of Books*, January 28, 1964. Copyright © 1964 by Nyrev, Inc.

The Atlantic Monthly for ''Indivisible Man,'' by James Alan McPherson, from *The Atlantic Monthly*, December 1970. Copyright © 1970, Epilogue © 1984 by James Alan McPherson.

Evelyn Neal for ''Ellison's Zoot Suit,'' by Larry Neal, from *Black World* 20, 1970. Copyright © 1970 by Larry Neal.

The Massachusetts Review for ''The Wright Interpretation: Ellison and the Anxiety of Influence,'' by Joseph T. Skerrett, Jr., from *The Massachusetts Review* 21, No. 1, Spring 1980. © 1980 by The Massachusetts Review, Inc.

Interpretations: Studies in Language and Literature for ''Ellison's 'Usable Past': Toward a Theory of Myth,'' by Hortense Spillers, from *Interpretations: Studies in Language and Literature*, Vol. IX, No. 1, 1977. © 1977 by Hortense Spillers.

The Washington Post for ''Through a Writer's Eyes,'' by Hollie West, from *The Washington Post*, August 19, 20, 21, 1973. Copyright © 1973 by *The Washington Post*.

Speaking for You

Introduction: The Masks of Ralph Ellison

KIMBERLY W. BENSTON

I could hear him: "Stephen's problem, like ours, was not actually one of creating the uncreated conscience of his race, but of creating the uncreated features of his face. . . . *We create the race by creating ourselves and then to our great astonishment we will have created something far more important: We will have created a culture."*

Ralph Ellison
Invisible Man

Face/Race—such is the essential dialectic of Ralph Ellison's vision. Ellisonian "culture" is formed in the creative and continuous struggle between individual impulse and traditional imperative, between freedom and order, difference and identity. And so the process of self-delineation is for Ellison inextricably interwoven with the avowed "end" of that process, a tradition of achieved selfhood. If, as Ellison has said, we must recognize the lesson from the blues tradition that "there is no scapegoat but the self,"[1] so must we engage the paradoxical obligations of our exotically colored "familial past" (*S&A*, 148).

Ellison is both the most traditional of modern American writers (insofar as he demands our constant attention to the details and wisdom of Afro-American and Euro-American culture) and the most revisionist critic of tradition (in that he constantly focuses our attention on the ambiguities inherent in any embrace of the past). In both fiction and criticism, Ellison has exhorted us not only to assimilate the past but also to acquire it, to *appropriate* it by interested engagement, in the context of the present. Whether reading the blues in(to) Hemingway or blackness in(to) the American Renaissance, Ellison's construct of a "usable past" is primarily a record of how he (and, he implies, we with him) got to where he is (and we are). "Tradition" thus emerges in Ellison's meditations as not merely a residue of material but also as an authorizing model of both the potential for self-articulation and the formulation of that "something far more important" of culture. The past for him is not a static, prescriptive ideal form but a protean idea freshly rethought and revalued by the artist's consciousness. Hence, Ellison at every phase of his career has written of the individual's multiform encounters with the living past, and in so doing he has provided a radical critique and revision of every convention his art explores.

Ellison, then, has sought to forge a unique cultural instrument, one consonant with this flexible conception of Afro-American identity. Toward this end, he has espoused an aesthetic of inclusion, in which influences are "chosen" freely from all available traditions:

> I felt that I would have to make some sort of closer identification with the tradition of American literature, if only by way of finding out why I was *not* there—or better, by way of finding how I could use that very powerful literary tradition by way of making literature my own, and by way of using literature as a means of clarifying the peculiar and particular experience out of which I came.[2]

Ellison's eclecticism, while often misread as an espousal of aestheticism, is oriented toward elevation of the self in relation to a given image of culture. Although Ellison absorbs influences (e.g., Marxist, nationalist, existentialist) more openly than his detractors would wish, his critique of tradition is perhaps the most radical among all modern American writers—but one which, because of Ellison's simultaneous engagement and revision of borrowed material, provokes our alternating impulses to idealize and then demystify his achievements. For it is the fluctuating, unstable relation of Ellison's characters and patterns to their enabling conventions that makes his art at once captivating and elusive.

The complexity of Ellison's vision is evident in many aspects of *Invisible Man*.[3] Using a wealth of folkloristic material, Ellison shows us black *and* white characters enacting the same archetypical roles. For example, Bledsoe, Peter Wheatstraw, and Brockway are cast as guileful tricksters of contrasting moral value. Yet the insidious Brother Jack is also a trickster, a rabbit (his "movements" are "those of a lively small animal" [*IM*, 219]) who ensnares the bearish narrator. At the same time, the Brotherhood leader is "Jack the Bear" as prefigured in the hero's meeting with the rabbit Wheatstraw. A similar subtlety in the use of folk motifs is evident when the narrator, having entered a drugstore lunch counter, is repelled by the "special" menu of pork chops, grits, and hot biscuits, which a white man then orders (*IM*, 135–36). As with the blues, Ellison seems to be asserting that the meaning of inherited patterns is not given but determined by function, content, and imagination. If the purveyors of folk culture are the "bearers of something precious" (*IM*, 333), this "something" cannot be uncritically imposed on life but must be shaped into currently meaningful forms, and this (again, as in the blues) is the individual's responsibility.

Ellison structures into his narrative several exemplars of false and proper uses of tradition. Homer A. Barbee—himself a complex amalgam of European (blind Homer) and Afro-American roots—manipulates the details and techniques of black sermon and classical mythmaking traditions to create a deleterious historical allegory (that of the legendary Founder's struggle up from slavery). Tod Clifton, in contrast, employs the worst aspect of minstrel tradition, the Sambo image, only to transcend its stereotypical implications. He refuses to allow the image to control his identity; instead, with his invisible puppeteer's thread, he controls the Sambo doll.

Of all the paradigmatic artists in *Invisible Man*, however, Jim Trueblood best exemplifies the individual's acceptance and creative transformation of tradition. Having fomented chaos in his home, Trueblood becomes a wounded outcast caught in the tragic web of absurd circumstance ("I had to move without movin'" [*IM*, 46]). As a suffering figure cast in the mold of classic tragedy, Trueblood faces the paradox of inevitable sin: "I thinks and thinks, until I thinks my brain go'n bust, 'bout how I'm guilty and how I ain't guilty" (*IM*, 51). Yet soon, he creates form where chaos had reigned, ordering the warring details of his past by accepting their ambiguities and his own isolated identity. To the tragic protagonist's ability to suffer and question his fate, Trueblood adds the comic lyricism that mitigates and structures experience. He becomes, in other words, what Ellison has termed the *tragicomic* bluesman who, in recognizing his necessary distinction from society, simultaneously reshapes tradition and reconnects his personal voice with the community's:

> Finally, one night, way early in the mornin', I looks up and sees the stars and I starts singin'. I don't mean to. I didn't think 'bout it, just start singin'. I don't know what it was, some kinda church song, I guess. All I know is I *ends up* singin' the blues. I sings me some blues that night ain't never been sang before, and while I'm singin' them blues I makes up my mind that I ain't nobody but myself and ain't nothin' I can do but let whatever is gonna happen, happen. I made up my mind that I was goin' back home and face Kate; yeah, and face Matty Lou too. (*IM*, 51)

Trueblood's narrative effectively combines the Afro-American idioms of blues singing and tale telling with the cross-cultural themes of incest and tragic suffering. Yet even these traditions are, as Ellison would say, "distorted in the interest of a design" (*IM*, 380). For Trueblood's riveting tale of incest, which mirrors Norton's need and the hero's guilty innocence, undermines the expectations of minstrel narrative that Norton—like the hero—brings to Trueblood's performance. In addition, the incest tale's standard function of establishing taboo is undermined by Trueblood's blues-inspired acceptance of his absurd predicament. Trueblood, then, uses the trappings of venerated custom to transcend the bonds they would impose on life.

The blues tradition (which, from Louis Armstrong's lament in the Prologue to the Epilogue's final line, is evoked throughout the novel) serves as a thematic mirror to the quasi-picaresque chronicle of the hero's quest. It also provides a crucial ethical perspective on that quest. The hero learns that he must become a kind of Trueblood, first sifting through the contradictory details of the past (as embodied by such models as his grandfather, Bledsoe, Trueblood, Barbee, Mary Rambo, Wheatstraw, and Brockway) and then forging anew the "possibilities" of selfhood. His bumbling journey from darkness to light and back again is, in effect, a tour through the collective history of his race during which he meets and chooses from among his ancestors. Yet when, near the novel's end, the hero burns the contents of his briefcase—among them his diploma, Clifton's doll, and the paper on which Jack had written his new name—he renounces any specific claims of the past. Through this exorcistic act he accepts the lesson of the blues that there is "no scapegoat but the self," for this rejection of prefabricated models points, by its simultaneous invocation of multiple contradictory authorities, to the ultimate necessity of self-orientation.

It would be a mistake, however, to take this scene as a final dismissal of acquired symbols and modes. Ellison is careful to point out the functionality of the hero's fire: it initiates his understanding of the underground passageway. The past is not destroyed but rather transmuted into a form useful in the present. After all, the figure of Rinehart, whose fluid purity of possibility is equivalent to *faceless* chaos, has already made the hero realize that some form, some defining pattern, must be imposed on one's experience (*IM*, 376–77). The value of the past, for Ellison, is that it provides us with tested and pliable patterns that facilitate formation of our unique features. If the value of the gifts of the past is ambiguous, it is only because those gifts manifest the curious splendor of human complexity. And if, as Trueblood claimed, "I ain't nobody but myself," that "I" gives birth to itself by choosing its fathers: "I yam what I am!" (*IM*, 201).

Like Trueblood singing the blues alone, Ellison's hero goes underground to write his "memoirs," to organize his past as prerequisite for reassimilation into society as a presumably named and visible entity. He is creating the features of his face and the many styles he employs to do so reflect not only creativity in the presence of chaos but an appreciation for the variety of alternatives supplied by a variety of traditions.

Ellison has urged all of us to join his hero and "make up our faces and our minds" (*S&A*, 156). A major motif throughout *Invisible Man* and the critical works is the metaphor of *masking* implicit in this appeal, a metaphor that can be highlighted as an emblem of Ellison's vision per se. For Ellison, "masking is a play upon possibility" that gives man an "ironic awareness of the joke that always lies between appearance and reality, between the discontinuity of social tradition and that sense of the past which clings to the mind" (*S&A*, 53).

The narrator of *Invisible Man* is constantly made the butt of this joke. While he discovers that Bledsoe is villainously deceptive behind his mask (''his face twitched and cracked like the surface of dark water'' [*IM*, 108]), he also learns that Trueblood is heroically shrewd ''behind his eyes'' (*IM*, 47). He encounters the ambiguously ''veiled'' statue of the Founder (a former slave) and both good and bad masked tricksters (Wheatstraw and Jack, respectively, with Rinehart, like his prototype, Melville's confidence-man, embodying a bit of both ''good'' and ''bad''). Even the Sambo minstrel mask takes on conflicting values when placed on Mary Rambo's antique coin bank or Clifton's doll (whose ''dance . . . was completely detached from the black, mask-like face'' [*IM*, 326]).

The narrator calls the image on Mary's bank ''self-mocking,'' and Ellison's critics (from Irving Howe to Amiri Baraka)[4] would agree. Yet Ellison's hero suffers precisely because he does not perceive the bridge erected by the mask between the violence of social history and the beauty of his people's continual transcendence within that history. The mask, for Ellison, is a formal response to experience and tradition. It may be stifling sham (Bledsoe, Jack) or, like the blues, a liberating self-creation (Trueblood, Wheatstraw). Ellison suggests that the Sambo image is more valuable controlled than rejected. He might say, to rephrase Mary Rambo's attitude toward Harlem, ''I may shape the mask but it doesn't shape me.''

Ellison's ultimate mask, like that of his hero, is that of the writer, and Trueblood, Barbee, Rine, Ras, Tod, and all the other variously disguised performers in the masquerade of *Invisible Man* are the many figures through which Ellison can occupy all possible positions of creation and critique. His esteem for craftmanship, style, discipline, and intellectual sophistication is but one version of the mask; his celebration of human willfulness and the comic unpredictability of experience yet another. Above all, Ellison affirms not so much one guise or another but the freedom and compulsion to *choose* our ''selves'' endlessly. It is in this sense, finally, that he offers himself and his art as a mask in dialectical relation to our own emergent identities, a ritual *persona* of our grand and complex culture: Who knows but that, on the lower frequencies, I speak for you?

* * *

Since the publication of *Invisible Man* in 1952, scholarship on Ellison's masterpiece has been abundant indeed. Scores of articles, dissertations, book chapters, and the like have delineated aspects of the novel's narrative structure, imagistic texture, and thematic design; at the same time, Ellison's own essays and interviews (collected chiefly in *Shadow and Act*)[5] have provided lucid authorial perspectives on these and similar issues. And yet, while reviewing this impressive interpretive activity a few years ago, I found that the criticism tended to collect at either of two extremes: descriptive-aesthetic and prescriptive-ideological. This volume reflects an effort to redress this schism by suggesting an image of a more complex and coherent career.

The essays in this collection have been chosen and organized to reflect the dynamic *interplay* of aesthetic practice and cultural perception which I take to be the cornerstone of Ellison's vision. Indeed, nothing unites the essays gathered here more than the collective intuition of Ellison's central "moral" ideal: the dialectical mutuality of conscience and craft that enables the artist to dare "speak for you."

Many of the essays presented here were commissioned especially to engage the complexities of this Ellisonian vision.[6] Several essays from recent years have been added to enrich the insights generated by the newer commentaries. The volume begins with the widest concerns (biography, sense of place, general aesthetics), then moves to increasingly focused matters of practice (instances of interaction between Ellison and his forebears) and, finally, to readings of *Invisible Man* illuminated by consideration of Ellison's cultural vision at large. Each section begins with Ellison's own reflections: it seems only proper that even as we speak for him he speaks, in turn, for himself! We hope the book will stimulate and prepare readers to explore further the map and terrain, the vision and act, of Ellison's distinctive cultural territory.

NOTES

1. Ralph Ellison, *Shadow and Act* (New York: Random House, 1964), 94. Subsequent references are cited in text as *S&A*.

2. Ellison, "On Initiation Rites and Power: Ralph Ellison Speaks at West Point," *Contemporary Literature* 15 (Spring 1974): 167.

3. Ellison, *Invisible Man*, 30th Anniversary Edition (New York: Random House, 1982), 268.

4. Elsewhere in this volume, Baraka's first name appears as "Imamu," reflecting usage current at the time a given essay was written.

5. Ellison's most recent collection of essays, *Going to the Territory* (New York: Random House, 1986), appeared as this volume was going to press.

6. These pieces, a few of which have also appeared in various journals, include those by Reilly, Harris, Tate, Bigsby, Fabre, Frank, O'Meally, Baker, Burke, Whitaker, and Dixon, as well as the addenda to the contributions by McPherson and Hersey.

PART ONE

Going to the Territory

BIOGRAPHY, GEOGRAPHY, TOPOGRAPHY

Growing Up Black in Frontier Oklahoma . . . From an Ellison Perspective

HOLLIE WEST

Q: We were talking earlier about your growing up in Oklahoma City, and you said that your parents came from South Carolina and Georgia. Oklahoma was part of the frontier shortly before you were born. Did this create any special meaning for people growing up there at that time?

A: I think so. I think that the people were aggressive. They had a sense of what it meant to come to the frontier because they had come looking for better conditions for themselves and for their children. They were quite aware—those who had come early—of the struggle to keep the new state of Oklahoma as liberal as possible. They had actively fought against the adoption of the Texas segregationist laws as a model for the Oklahoma constitution; and they had failed in that. But someone has said geography is fate, and it is fate for black Americans as well as for white.

The people who went out there were trying to determine their fate. And they did this quite actively. There were such all-black towns as Boley, as an example of a place where they were trying to determine that fate. In Oklahoma City you had constant struggles to keep the bigoted whites—and not all were bigoted—from imposing the old patterns of the segregationist South upon the racial relationships there. I know that a great number of the people I grew up with were armed, and during the 1920s, when there was a lot of trouble, I've seen them produce those arms and stand waiting.

A man was lynched in Chickasha, and his body was brought over to Oklahoma City for burial. The members of the white mob telephoned to Oklahoma City that they were coming over to drag this body back. And the Negroes sent word: "Come on. We'll be waiting." And they were waiting. Jack Walton was mayor at the time. I was out there when he came out and took a stand with the Negroes to keep this thing from exploding.

You had segregation in Oklahoma City. But you had no tradition of slavery. So those old patterns were not imposed as successfully as they might have been. There was never a time that we didn't have white friends. The neighborhood was mixed. But there were friends of my father who would come by to see him, and he'd go by to see them.

Q: Did this spirit pervade the entire Southwest—Texas and Arkansas?

A: It did not pervade Texas or Arkansas because both states were older and they had been involved in the Civil War and had a tradition of slavery. But Oklahoma was rather fresh and had been conceived of by various Negro leaders as an all-black state. Sojourner Truth thought of the old Indian Territory as an all-black state. It was feared that Negroes were actively trying to convert it into such an entity—early, in fact, just before statehood (1907).

Q: Wasn't there a duality of sorts in Oklahoma? The state was both South and West. It had some of the traditions of the South, but it was also a frontier state. Did this cause any conflict?

A: It caused conflict. But when you speak of something like tradition, you must remember that tradition is not something abstract. Tradition is within the attitudes of individuals, especially on a frontier. Say, in the South—the traditions of the slave South are inspirited in buildings, patterns of movement about the cities, in manners, in signs, in monuments, in all kinds of things. And especially in the memories and attitudes of people.

But on a frontier the tradition—at a given point—is apt to be more in the attitudes and memories of individuals. When you run into a person who has an antiblack tradition, and you meet some black who isn't going to accept it, who has determined to confront it head-on—then you have conflict. Certainly it made for a conflict, but what was good about it was the constant jockeying to assert a different pattern of relationships: and that was very, very important for the people that I grew up with. And certainly it was important for me.

In the atmosphere of the place there was a sense that you had to determine your own fate, and that you had a chance to do it.

Q: Does this mean that there was a special set of circumstances surrounding Oklahoma because it was a frontier state? I don't know if I had that same feeling growing up in Oklahoma in the fifties. Maybe the frontier tradition had dried up by that time?

A: Well, what did you have by the fifties? My God, man, what did you have? Just consider what was happening during the forties. The tremendous changes that occurred when they were building liberty ships out that way. You know, in parts—then shipping them to a sea coast and riveting them together.

The influx of labor, of different traditions, the growth of the business community with its investment in maintaining discrimination and so on. You would get changes. Also, you got a great influx of people who had not shared that sense of promise that your people and my people had shared. They were in Oklahoma but Oklahoma was not in them.

We have to look at this thing in the perspective of time. Given the late 1890s and the early 1900s, you had a heck of a period there—say, thirty years in which to feel enthusiastic and hopeful and during which you could build something for yourself.

For instance, people are surprised when I tell them I knew a few millionaires who were black. Some had made their fortunes in farming, one man in making cosmetics. There were a number of wealthy doctors who were land poor and then had oil discovered. People who traveled and had a lifestyle that was rather elegant considering that they lived much better than many of the whites and they possessed a higher degree of culture than many of the whites who had an opportunity to make more money, because you did have discrimination and you did have whites who were trying to keep Negroes under control.

Q: Were there any literary developments in Oklahoma that made any impact on you?

A: No. Where literature came into my life, I guess, was through my father's having been a reader; he read all the time and I don't even remember when I learned to read. I learned to read very early. I loved books. One year after my father died, the members of the church decided that my mother would work as the janitor of Avery Chapel Church and that since the new minister had his own home, we would live in the parsonage.

So for a couple of years, maybe three years, I lived in the church parsonage, the Methodist parsonage, and there were plenty of books there that had been left. Some of these were novels. I remember reading Rex Beach, such people, and then at some point a black Episcopalian priest went to the library to work on some sermons and was told it was against the law, that it was segregated. And he said, "Who says so?" and they looked around and discovered there was no ordinance refusing admittance to Negroes. It was just a custom. So immediately they rented a couple of rooms, big rooms out in the Slaughter Building, and put in some shelves, and dumped all kinds of books in there, and appointed a lady as librarian. So we had a library and I quickly began to read through those books, along with a few of my friends.

Incidentally, last year, last fall, I got word that the city council had voted six to one to name a new branch library after me.

Q: Is that right. Did they follow through with that?

A: Well, they are going to. They haven't broken the ground, but we had a letter from the mayor recently saying that when the ceremony comes he wants us to come out, and of course we will, if at all possible.

But I'm saying this puts things in perspective. I should also say that as early as the fifties when I went home after publishing a book, I was given a reception in the big downtown library and the segregation was over. One reason that segregation and certain of its aspects ended so easily in Oklahoma was that it was in the Deep South. [Segregation] hadn't been practiced so long, nor were there the social structures that would support it in the same way.

Q: Did you know Roscoe Dunjee, the editor of the *Black Dispatch* [a black weekly newspaper in Oklahoma City]?

A: I knew Roscoe Dunjee. I used to sell the papers when I was going barefoot and I used to talk with him a lot. It never occurred to me that I would be a writer or anything, so I didn't know him or hadn't been interested in him in that way. I was a musician, I thought. But I used to see him daily. He used to come across the street to Randolph's Drugstore where I worked. I jerked sodas and was the delivery boy.

Dunjee was very well known for his attitudes, his forthrightness, and his leadership. He was one of those men in the neighborhood—the community we would call it now—who was always stressing the political. He was a constitutionalist and understood the possibilities of the Constitution long before the forties and fifties, when we got around to tackling the thing head-on. His paper would carry on editorial controversy with the writers and editors of the *Daily Oklahoman* and the *Oklahoma City Times*.

He was always involved in politics and he was always writing editorials about the historical implications of events and the historical background of the black struggle. So he was very important to me in terms of putting events into perspective.

He was an example of a man who did not approach events in some sort of stylized, second-class citizen's way but who spoke to the main issue, always fighting for us but seeing that his responsibility went far beyond the racial aspect. What was good for Oklahoma was good for us.

He had a tremendous impact because he was very articulate and a number of white people read what he had to say. He was handicapped because for a good while Negroes did not have the vote in Oklahoma.

Indivisible Man

JAMES ALAN McPHERSON

July 1969

Ralph Ellison, a pair of high-powered binoculars close to his eyes, sits by the window of his eighth-floor Riverside Drive apartment, looking down. Across the street, in the long strip of green park which parallels the Hudson River, two black boys are playing basketball. "I watch them every afternoon," he says, and offers the binoculars to me. I look down and recognize the hope of at least two major teams, ten years hence, developing. Perhaps future sociologists will say that they possess superior athletic abilities because of biological advantages peculiar to blacks; but perhaps by then each of these black boys will have gained enough of a sense of who he is to reply: "I'm good at what I do because I practiced it all my life." The encouragement of this sort of self-definition has become almost a crusade with Ellison. But I also recognize that if I ran down and waved my arms and shouted to them: "Did you know that Ralph Ellison watches you playing every afternoon?" they would continue to shoot at the basket and answer: "Who is Ralph Ellison?"

* * *

"He spoke at Tougaloo last year," a black exchange student at Santa Cruz told me. "I can't stand the man."

"Why?"

"I couldn't understand what he was saying. He wasn't talking to *us*."

"Did you read his book?"

Originally published in *Atlantic Monthly*, 226, December 1970, 45–60. The remarks in the Epilogue were delivered by James Alan McPherson at the first Langston Hughes Festival at the City College of New York on April 11, 1984, and appear in print for the first time here.—Ed.

"No. And I don't think I will, either. I can't stand the man."

If you ask him about the Tougaloo experience, Ellison will laugh and then tell an anecdote about the stuttering black student who said: "Mr. E-l-li-s-s-s-*on*, I r-r-*ead* your b-b-o*ok The* Inv-v-v-si-b-b-*ble* M-m-*man*. B-b-but after he-e-e-ar*ing* you tonight I f-f-*feel* like I j-j-ju-*us*t hear-r-*rd* J-j-je-*sus* C-c-ch-r-r-*rist* d-d-d-runk on *Thunderbird Wine!*" And if you laugh along with him, and if you watch Ellison's eyes as you laugh, you will realize that he is only testing a deep scar to see if it has healed.

* * *

Ellison's difficulty, one cause of all the cuts, is that matter of self-definition. At a time when many blacks, especially the young, are denying all influences of American culture, Ellison, as always, doggedly affirms his identity as a Negro American, a product of the blending of both cultures. But more than this, he attempts to explore most of the complex implications of this burden in his fiction, his essays, his speeches, and his private life. He is nothing as simple as a "brown-skinned aristocrat" (as Richard Kostelanetz characterized him in a *Shenandoah* essay-portrait); rather, he is a thinking black man who has integrated his homework into the fabrics of his private life. "I don't recognize any white culture," he says. "I recognize no American culture which is not the partial creation of black people. I recognize no American style in literature, in dance, in music, even in assembly-line processes, which does not bear the mark of the American Negro." And he means it. For this reason he has difficulty reconciling some of the ideas of black nationalists, who would view black culture as separate from the broader American culture. To these people he says: "I don't recognize any black culture the way many people use the expression." And Ellison is one of the few black intellectuals who have struggled to assess the influence of the black on American culture and the relationships between the two. But, until fairly recently, not many blacks—perhaps even college-educated blacks—knew that he existed.

In 1952 he published his first novel, *Invisible Man*, which won a National Book Award, and this at a time when the white critical establishment was less eager to recognize literary achievement by black Americans. Now, almost nineteen years later, he is still the only black American who has received this honor. The novel has gone through twenty paperback printings and was judged, in a 1965 *Book Week* poll of two hundred authors, critics, and editors, "the most distinguished single work published in the last twenty years." A second book, a collection of essays and interviews called *Shadow and Act*, was published in 1964 and is essential reading for any attempt at understanding Ellison, the man or the artist. While *Invisible Man* is a story of one man's attempt to understand his society and himself, the essays outline Ellison's own successful struggle to master the craft of the writer and to understand, and then affirm, the complexities of his own rich cultural experience.

He likes to call himself a college dropout because he completed only three years of a music major at Tuskegee Institute before coming to New York in 1936. Before that he was a shoeshine boy, a jazz musician, a janitor, a freelance photographer, and a man who hunted game during the Depression to keep himself alive.

Today he is a member, and a former vice president, of the National Institute of Arts and Letters; a member of New York's Century Club and the American Academy of Arts and Sciences; and a trustee of the John F. Kennedy Center for the Performing Arts. He is a former teacher at Bard, Rutgers, and Chicago and was Albert Schweitzer Professor in the Humanities at New York University. He has an interest in noncommercial television, which began with his work on the Carnegie Commission on Educational Television, and continues with his trusteeships in the Educational Broadcasting Corporation, and the National Citizens' Committee for Broadcasting. Among his awards are listed the Russwurm Award, the Medal of Freedom (awarded by President Johnson), five honorary Ph.D.'s, and one of the highest honors which France can bestow on a foreign writer: Chevalier de l'Ordre des Arts et Lettres, awarded to him in 1970 by the French Minister of Cultural Affairs, André Malraux. But all these experiences seem to have equal weight in his mind; all seem to have given equal access to information, equal opportunity for observation of the culture. And he is as likely to begin a discussion with some observation made when he was a shoeshine boy as he is to mention the first names of some of America's most respected writers and critics.

His success does not prove, as one writer says, that "a fatherless American Negro really does have the opportunity to become the author of one of America's greatest novels as well as an aristocratic presence and an all but universally respected literary figure." Ellison's achievements are too enormous to be reduced to a sociological cliché, a rhetorical formulation. If anything, his success proves that intelligence, perseverance, discipline, and love for one's work are, together, too great a combination to be contained, or even defined, in terms of race.

Although he lives in New York and has access to literary and intellectual areas, Ellison seems to have very limited contact with the black writers who also live there. Yet his shadow lies over all their writers' conferences, and his name is likely to be invoked, and defamed, by any number of the participants at any conference. One man has said that he would like to shoot Ellison. Another, whom Ellison has never met, has for almost ten years blamed Ellison for his not receiving the last Prix de Rome Award, given by the American Academy of Arts and Letters. On the other hand, a growing number of young black writers, among them Ernest J. Gaines, Cecil Brown, Michael Harper, Ishmael Reed, and Al Young, are quick to admit their respect for him.

He reads the work of black writers, dismisses some of it, and is always willing to give an endorsement. And although he is very protective of his time, his telephone number is listed in the Manhattan directory, and he will usually grant an interview or a few hours of conversation in the afternoon (his working day usually ends at 4:00 P.M.) to anyone who is insistent.

"A fellow called me one morning," Ellison chuckles, lighting up a cigar, "said he just had to see me. So I consented. I went to the door, and there was a brown-skinned fellow from the Village. He brought a bottle of wine, several records, and four attempts at short stories. I looked at these things, and they weren't really stories. So I asked: 'What do you want me to tell you?' He said: 'Well, what I want you to do is to tell me, should I just write, or should I tell the truth?'" Ellison pauses to laugh deep in his chest, "I said: 'Tell the truth.'"

* * *

"He came to Oberlin in April of 1969," a black girl in Seattle recalled. "His speech was about how American black culture had blended into American white culture. But at the meeting with the black caucus after the speech, the black students said: 'You don't have anything to tell us.'"

"What did he say?"

"He just accepted it very calmly. One girl said to him: 'Your book doesn't mean anything because in it you're shooting down Ras the Destroyer, a rebel leader of black people.'"

"What was his answer?"

"He said: 'Remember now, this book was written a long time ago. This is just one man's view of what he saw, how he interpreted what he saw. I don't make any apologies for it.' Well, she went on to tell him: 'That just proves that you're an Uncle Tom.'"

* * *

Another of Ellison's problems, one peculiar to any black who attempts to assert his own individuality in his own terms, is that he challenges the defense mechanisms of the black community. Because of a history of enforced cohesiveness, some blacks have come to believe in a common denominator of understanding, even a set number of roles and ideas which are assumed to be useful to the community. Doctors, lawyers, teachers, social workers, some orthodox thinkers, some orthodox writers are accepted—as long as they do not insist on ideas which are foreign to the community's own sense of itself. But when a black man attempts to think beyond what has been thought before, or when he asserts a vision of reality which conflicts with or challenges the community's conception, there is a movement, sometimes unconscious, to bring him back into line or, failing that, to ostracize him. The "mass man" of sociological terminology is the "right-on man" of black slang, gliding smoothly and simplistically, and perhaps more comfortably, over questionable assumptions, and reducing himself to a cliché in the process. For a black thinker, such as Ellison, this assertion of individual vision is especially painful because the resultant ostracism carries with it the charge of "selling out" or "trying to be white." Yet a white thinker who challenges assumptions held by whites about themselves is not charged with "trying to be black." The underlying assumption is that whites have a monopoly on individuality and intelligence, and in order for a black man to lay claim to his own he must, necessarily, change color.

In response to charges by attackers that he is a "token Negro" because he is very often the only black serving on cultural commissions, Ellison says: "All right, if you don't want me on, I'll resign. But you had better put a *cardboard Negro* in my place because when decisions are made which will affect black people you had better make sure that those people who make the decisions remember that you exist and are forced to make sure that some of your interests are being met."

This impulse toward leveling, however, is not confined to the black community. It is a minority-group reaction. And while Ellison remembers a black professor at Tuskegee who tore up a leather-bound volume of Shakespeare's plays to discourage his interest in literature, he also remembers a white professor friend who said: "Ah, here's Ralph again, talking about America. There's no goddamn America out there."

* * *

"At Oberlin," the Seattle girl said, "one of the ideas they couldn't accept was Ellison's statement that black styles had historically been incorporated into American life. He went on to say that in the future, don't be surprised if white people begin to wear Afros because that's now a part of American popular culture. Well, the kids went out screaming, 'Who is he to insult what we wear? No honky could wear an Afro. They're stealing what is ours.'"

One year later disenchanted white youth, on both coasts and in between, are sporting their versions of the Afro. . . .

* * *

He is as practiced a listener as he is a speaker, and gives even the most naively put question thorough consideration before responding. He is a bit guarded at first, perhaps unwinding from a day at his desk, perhaps adjusting to the intellectual level of his guest. Then he begins talking, occasionally pausing to light a cigar, occasionally glancing out the window at the street, the park, the river beyond. After a while you both are trading stories and laughing while Mrs. Ellison makes noises in the kitchen, just off the living room. A parakeet flutters into the room. Ellison calls it, imitating its chirps, and the bird comes and hovers near his hand. "Have you ever heard a dog talk?" he asks.

"No."

We go into his study, and he plays a tape of a dog clearly imitating the rhythm and pitch of a human voice saying "hello." We listen again, and laugh again. Mrs. Ellison calls us to dinner. It is difficult enjoying the food and digesting his conversation at the same time.

"Ralph, stop talking and let him eat," Mrs. Ellison says.

After dinner we move back into the living room and continue the conversation. Finally Ellison's dog, Tucka Tarby, comes into the room and walks back and forth between us. Then you realize that it is well after midnight and that you have put a serious dent in the essential personal rhythm of a writer's day. Tucka has been patient, waiting for his evening walk. Ellison puts on an army jacket, and we go down in the elevator. This is an old building, just on the edge of Harlem, and most of the tenants are black. The lobby has colored tiles, a high ceiling, and live flowers protected by glass. "I've lived here for eighteen years," he says. "But it wasn't until 1964 that some of the people found out I was a writer." Tucka pulls us up 150th Street toward Broadway. We shake hands, and he and the dog walk off into the Harlem night.

* * *

"I think that what made it hard for him," the Seattle girl said, "was that LeRoi Jones was coming to Oberlin that next day. The kids figured that Jones the Master is coming, so let's get rid of this cat. But I think he's very gutsy, in a day like today with all these so-called militants trying to run him into the ground, coming to Oberlin saying to the kids: 'You are American, not African.'"

"Did anyone come to his defense?"

"One of the teachers stopped the meeting at one point and said: 'Would you please listen to what the man has to say? You're sitting here criticizing, and some of you haven't even read the damn book.'"

* * *

Among his peers Ellison's presence or even the mention of his name causes the immediate arming of intellectual equipment. There can be no soft-pedaling, no relaxation of intellect where he is involved. At Brown University in November of 1969, novelists and critics gathered at the annual Wetmore Lecture to discuss form, the future of the novel, and each other. Critic Robert Scholes opened one discussion on form by reading from Ellison's acceptance speech before the National Book Award Committee. "Ah, Ellison," Leslie

Fiedler said, throwing his arm out in a gesture of dismissal. ''He's a black Jew.''

Ellison chuckles. ''Leslie's been trying to make me a Jew for years,'' he says. ''I have to look at these things with a Cold Oklahoma Negro Eye. But someone should have said that *all* us old-fashioned Negroes are Jews.''

* * *

Ellison is not only interested in the fiction written by young black writers; he is concerned about young black people in general: what they are thinking, what they are doing, what their ambitions are. But his knowledge of them is limited to sessions during speaking engagements, letters, and what he hears from the media. ''A hell of a lot of them are reading my book,'' he observes with obvious pleasure. ''I have a way of checking this. And for a long time they didn't read much of anything.''

Yet he worries that despite the increased educational opportunities available to them, young black people are becoming too involved in, and almost symbolic of, the campus reactions against intellectual discipline, the life of the mind. ''It's too damn bad,'' he says. ''You see that men are now analyzing the song of the whales, the talk of dolphins, planning to go to the moon; computer technology is becoming more and more humanized and miniaturized; great efforts are being made to predetermine sex, to analyze cells, to control the life process in the human animal. And all of this is done with the *mind*. And indeed,'' he goes on, ''the irony is that we've never really gotten away from that old *body* business; the Negro as symbolic of *instinctual* man. Part of my pride in being what I am is that as a dancer, as a physical man''—and again that distant chuckle comes from deep within his chest—''I bet you I can outdance, outriff most of these intellectuals who're supposed to have come back.'' Now he is serious again. ''*But that isn't the problem, dammit!* I was *born* doing *this!* It's a glorious thing to know the uses of the body and not to be afraid of it. But *that has to be linked to the mind.* I don't see any solution for literary art. If you're a dancer, fine. If you're a musician, fine. But what are you going to do as a writer, or what are you going to do as a critic?'' He sighs, as if he were weighed down by these considerations.

''I find this very interesting,'' he continues, ''but not new. When I think about Tuskegee and people with whom I went to school, I know that over and over again they really did not extend themselves because they didn't have the imagination to look thirty years ahead to a point where there would be a place for them in the broader American society, had they been prepared.''

He says: ''I understand ambition; I understand the rejection of goals because they're not self-fulfilling. I've turned down too many things starting as a youngster.''

He looks out the window toward the Hudson, then continues in a lower tone. ''I was married once before, and one reason that marriage came to an end was that my in-laws were disgusted with me, thought I had no ambition, because I didn't want a job in the Post Office. And here I was with a dream of myself writing the symphony at twenty-six which would equal anything Wagner had done at twenty-six. This is where my ambitions were. So I can understand people getting turned off on that level. But what I can't understand is people who do not master a technique or discipline which will get them to a point where they can actually see that it's not what they want or that something else is demanded. But over and over again I see black kids who are dropping out or rejecting intellectual discipline as though what exists now will always exist and as though they don't have the possibility of changing it by using these disciplines as techniques to affirm *their* sense of what a human life should be. It's there where I get upset."

He has a habit of pausing whenever the discussion begins to touch areas pregnant with emotion, as if careful of remaining within a certain context. But on some subjects he is likely to continue. "I also get upset when I see announcements of prizes and medical discoveries and scientific advances, and I don't see any black names or black faces. I believe that we are *capable*," he says. "I believe that there are enough unique features in our background to suggest solutions to problems which seem very, very far removed from our social situation."

The duality of cultural experience which Ellison insists on in his writing is acted out in his professional and personal life. He is just as much at home, just as comfortable, in a Harlem barbershop as he is as a panelist before the Southern Historical Association exchanging arguments with C. Vann Woodward, Robert Penn Warren, and William Styron. He is a novelist well respected by his peers (when his name is mentioned in almost any literary circle, there will invariably be an inquiry about his current project), and he brings to bear the same respect for craft in an introduction to the stories of Stephen Crane as he uses to evaluate the work of black artist Romare Bearden. Yet, precisely because of his racial identity, he is also the leading black writer in American letters. And while he disclaims this position as "an accident, part luck and part a product of the confusion over what a black writer is and what an American writer is," the reality is there, nevertheless, and has to be coped with.

Before he accepted the professorship at New York University, Ellison earned a good part of his income from college speaking engagements. He accepted around twenty each year. He tends to favor the East Coast or Midwest and avoids the West Coast, partially because of the great distance and partially because of the political nature of the West. He is very much in demand, although his fee is usually $1,500 to $2,000. In the past year he has spoken at such colleges as Millsaps, East Texas State, Rockland, Illinois, West Point, and Iowa State University at Ames.

He takes pride in being able to deliver a ninety-minute speech without the aid of notes. He will make some few digressions to illuminate his points, but will always pick up the major thread and carry it through to its preconceived end.

* * *

March 1970

Ralph Ellison stands on a stage broad enough to seat a full symphony orchestra. Before him, packed into a massive new auditorium of gray concrete and glass and deep red carpets, 2,700 Ames students strain to hear the words of the man billed as ''Ralph Ellison: Writer.'' Ames is almost an agricultural school, and its students still have fraternity rows, beer parties, frat pins and ties, white shirts and jackets. Most of them are the beardless sons of farmers and girls whose ambitions extend only as far as engagement by the senior year. The American Dream still lingers here, the simple living, the snow, the hamburgers and milk shakes, the country music and crickets and corn. This is the breadbasket of the country, the middle of Middle America. And yet, ninety miles away in Iowa City, students torn from these same roots are about to burn buildings. ''When the pioneers got to your part of the country,'' he tells them, speaking again of the vernacular, the functional level of the American language, ''there was no word for 'prairie' in the *Oxford English Dictionary*.'' His speech is on ''The Concept of Race in American Literature.'' And he delivers just that. But it is abstract, perhaps over the heads of many of the students there (even though parts of it later appeared as a *Time* essay in the issue on ''Black America''). Still, the students are quiet, respectful, attempting to digest. Speaking of the ethnic blending which began with the formation of the country, he says: ''And, to make it brief, there was a whole bunch of people from Africa who were not introduced by the British, but quite some time before were introduced into what later became South Carolina by the Spanish. Whereupon they immediately began to revolt—'' Here loud applause floats down to the lower audience from black students in the second balcony. Ellison pauses. Then continues: ''—and went wild, and started passing for Indians. I hear a lot about black people passing for white, but remember, they first started passing for Indians.'' There is some giggling and laughter at this. But, behind me, I notice a black student cringing.

During the question-and-answer session afterwards, the students ask the usual things: the conflict between Richard Wright and James Baldwin, the order of symbols in *Invisible Man*. One girl wants to know if racial miscegenation is a necessary ingredient of racial integration. He laughs. ''Where'd you get that word?'' he says. And answers: ''I don't think that any of us Americans wants to lose his ethnic identity. This is another thing which has been used to manipulate the society in terms of race. Some few people might want to lose their identities; this has happened. But I would think that the very existence of such strong Negro American influences in the society, the style, the way things are done, would indicate that there's never been the desire to lose that. There's just too much self-congratulation in so much of Negro American expression. They wouldn't want to give that up.'' He says: ''The thing that black people have been fighting for for so long was the opportunity to decide whether they *wanted* to give it up or not. And the proof is that in this period when there is absolutely more racial freedom than has ever existed before, you have the most militant rejection of integration. These are individual decisions which will be made by a few people. But if I know anything about the human being, what *attracts* a man to a woman has usually been picked up very early from the first woman he's had contact with. There is enough of a hold of tradition, of ways of cooking, of ways of just relaxing, which comes right out of the family circle, to keep us in certain groups.''

At the reception after the speech, the whites dominate all three rooms; the few black students cluster together in one. Ellison moves between the two, sometimes almost tearing himself away from the whites. He talks to the black students about books, LeRoi Jones, Malcolm X, color, their personal interests. They do not say much. A white woman brings a book for his autograph; a professor gives a nervous explanation of the source of the miscegenation question: the girl has been reading Norman Podhoretz's essay ''My Negro Problem and Ours'' in his course. Ellison smiles and shifts back and forth on his feet like a boxer. Everyone is pleasantly high. The black students, still in a corner, are drinking Coke. I am leaving, eager to be out in the Iowa snow. We shake hands. ''This is awkward,'' he says. ''Call me Ralph and I'll call you Jim.''

Santa Cruz, California
April 1970

Dear Amelia:

I was very pleased to have met you during my stay in Ames. Now, before the Spring Holidays begin, I wish you would tell me your impressions of Ellison as an artist, as a black man in touch with young black people, as a man of ideas. . . .

There are thousands and thousands of books in the rooms of his apartment; and besides the pieces of sculpture, paintings, African violets, self-designed furniture, and other symbols of a highly cultivated sensibility, are deep drawers and file cabinets which, if opened, reveal thick sheaves of notes and manuscripts. Ellison's huge desk, which sits in a study just off the living room, is covered with books, a red electric typewriter, well-thumbed manuscripts, and tape equipment. In conversation he always sits in the leather-strap chair by the window, looking out on the Hudson and the street below.

He is a very direct and open man, even though there are silent levels of intimidating intelligence and unexpressed feeling beneath much of what he says. And he tends to approach even the most abstract idea from a personal point of view, usually including in any observation some supportive incident drawn from his own experience.

He talks freely of his mother, who died when he was in his early twenties, his relatives in Oklahoma, his professional relationships with other writers and critics, conversations with people on the subway or in the streets of Harlem; a recent chance meeting with Kurt Vonnegut in the streets of Manhattan; his respect for Saul Bellow as an extremely well-read novelist. And there is not an unkind, unprofessional, or imperceptive word for anyone, not even his most rabid critics. But he does become irritated if you question too closely his sense of identity as an American writer as opposed to a black writer, and he is likely to react when he senses a too containing category being projected onto him. "Let's put it this way, Jim," he says, irritation in his voice. "You see, I *work* out of American literature. In order to write the kind of fiction that I write I would *have* to be in touch with a broader literary culture than our own particular culture." He pauses, and then says: "This is not to denigrate what we have done, but in all *candor* we haven't begun to do what we can do or what we should have done. I think one reason why we haven't is that we've looked at our relationship to American literature in a rather negative way. That is, we've looked at it in terms of our trying to break into it. Well, damn it"—and his voice rises, and his hand hits the arm of the chair—"*that literature is built off our folklore to a large extent!*" And then he laughs that deep honest chuckle, and says: "I ain't conceding that to *nobody!*"

Ames, Iowa
April 1970

Dear James:

As an artist the man is beautiful. I think that is what was so captivating about his book. The symbolism that he uses and the combination of literary mechanics that he employs will probably make his work much more lasting than that of his black contemporaries. *Invisible Man* is a classic, and to say any more or less about it would be an understatement.

As for being in touch with the ideas of young people today, I think that he is quite aware, but he doesn't have the charisma that one would expect after hearing his reputation as a speaker and taking into account the acclaim his book has received. Part of my feeling is due to the disappointment of hearing him explain the figure in *Invisible Man*. So many concerned blacks had read the plight of the Afro-American into this figure with no face and no name. So many people saw the author riding to champion the cause of the black man. Those same people heard him say that the symbol was representative of a universal man. I found that most disheartening.

We are unfortunate at Ames, as well as at many other places across this nation, to have a group of young people who have been introduced to new ideologies and a new rhetoric and are attempting to adopt both when they do

> not understand either. Therefore, when they see or hear anyone who does not speak in their rhetoric they cannot, do not, and will not try to communicate with him. This was very true of Ellison.
>
> He has a lot to say to a people who will listen to him. Today's youth are angry, and many times this anger closes their ears to a different rationale. Ellison's language and approach, I fear, attach to him the stigma of black bourgeois and conservatism. This figure does not communicate well with the vocal black youth.

Ellison is still a first-novelist, despite his reputation. And that one novel was published over eighteen years ago. He contributes a steady flow of articles to intellectual journals and periodicals, and scholars and critics are rapidly making a permanent place for him in the archives of American literary criticism. But while students continue to read and his critics continue to write, there is the expectation of his long-awaited second novel. So far he has read from it in universities and on public television, published sections of it in intellectual journals, allowed a few close friends to read some of it, and has remained strangely silent about publication of the rest. Inestimable numbers of people, black and white, in and out of universities, friends and enemies, await the publication of the complete novel. Whenever his name is mentioned among a group of writers or literati, the immediate response is: "When is his novel coming out?" One man has heard that he has pulled it back from his publisher again for more revisions; another says that Ellison worries about its being dated, a third man says he has heard that Ellison cannot finish it.

Concerning that novel there are many other stories. Perhaps the best one is that which some friends of the Ellisons supposedly heard from the writer's wife. "She says she hears him in his study at night turning pages and laughing to himself. He enjoys the book so much that he isn't in a hurry to share it with the public."

Whether or not this is true, Ellison is extremely reluctant, at first, to discuss the book. A fire in his summer home in Plainfield, Massachusetts, destroyed a year's worth of revisions, he says, and he is presently in the process of revising it again. "I want what I do to be good," he says.

"Are you worried about the quality of it?"

"No," he says. "But you want to be sure when you write so slowly, because if it's not good, if it's just passable, they'll be terribly disappointed."

He has enough typed manuscripts to publish three novels, but is worried about how the work will hold up as a total structure. He does not want to publish three separate books, but then he does not want to compromise on anything essential. "If I find that it is better to make it a three-section book, to issue it in three volumes, I would do that as long as I thought that each volume had a compelling interest in itself. But it seems to me that one of the decisions one has to make about long fiction is whether the effect of *reading* it is lengthy. If you don't get the impression that you're reading a long thing, then you've licked the problem of the battle of time.''

The setting of the novel, he says, is roughly around 1955. The form of it, he says, chuckling to himself, is in the direction of a ''realism extended beyond realism.'' There are several time schemes operating within it, and the sections already published heavily suggest that it is complexly involved with the Negro church and its ritual. In fact, three of its major characters, Bliss, Eatmore, and Hickman, are ministers.

On an afternoon, after a martini and before dinner, if the flow of conversation has been relaxing, and if the mood is right, Ellison might read a few sections from the book. It may take him a while to thumb through several huge black-bound manuscripts, perhaps numbering thousands of pages, to find an appropriate section. But when he does begin to read there is the impression, from the way the rhythms rise and fall and blend and flow out of him, that he is proud of every word. He chuckles as he reads, stops to explain certain references, certain connections, certain subtle jokes about the minister whose sermon he is reading. And in those sermons his voice becomes that of a highly sophisticated black minister, merging sharp biblical images with the deep music of his voice, playing with your ears, evoking latent memories of heated southern churches and foot-stomping and fanning ladies in long white dresses, and sweating elders swaying in the front rows. And suddenly the sermons are no longer comic, and there is no writer reading from his work. You see a minister, and you feel the depth of his religion, and you are only one soul in a huge congregation of wandering souls hearing him ask, over and over: ''*Oh Yes, Yes, Yes, Yes, Yes. DO You Love, Ah DO You Love?*''

''Stephen's [Dedalus] problem,'' he wrote in *Invisible Man*, ''like ours, was not actually one of creating the uncreated conscience of his race, but of creating the *uncreated features of his face*.'' Ellison is fifty-six. His face does not show very much of it, but enough is visible. He has a receding hairline, a broad forehead, and deep curved lines on either side of his nose running down to the corners of his mouth. It is a handsome brown face, from either point of view, and there is a healthy stubbornness, besides all else inside that forehead, which helps him to protect it. The face can be cold, severe, analytical, pensive, even smiling. But it is not going to change.

Epilogue

In the early 1970s I gained access to the Langston Hughes papers, then just acquired by the Sterling Library at Yale University. One letter in particular I remember. It was from Ralph Ellison, written sometime in the 1940s. ''Dear Lang,'' it began, and went on to describe the beauty of the intellectual experience Ellison had just derived from his reading of Thomas Mann's *Joseph and His Brothers*. Hughes had apparently encouraged Ellison to read the novel. In many respects, it was a love letter to the ideas of Thomas Mann. What struck me was the great importance that Ellison, and possibly Hughes, must have placed on the life of the intellect. This was, after all, in the 1940s, a time when, given certain social and economic realities, ideas must have seemed of little use to an American classified as black.

I had met Ralph Ellison, and Fanny, several years before. My interest, during that highly polarized time, was in incorporating into my own thinking some of his insights into the relationship of black Americans to what is sometimes called, with embarrassment, American Culture. Statements by him such as ''Uncle Remus was teaching that white boy calculus'' would embarrass my imagination into action. He would force me to make imaginative leaps.

For fifteen years now I have been trying to complete the reading necessary for such leaps of the imagination. I assure you that such insights, such creative ideas as his, are of fundamental importance. They chart new directions, for individuals and for nations. But they are, unfortunately, the stock and trade of a very few—an elite, if you will. The average person will not and cannot be comfortable with abstractions. He demands something close to his own experience, something concrete. And yet the idea, the imaginative shadow, is an essential prelude to the *act*. For example, but for the creative use of ideas derived from Roman Civil Law by a man named Charles Hamilton Houston, there might not have been a Civil Rights Movement in this country or a Thurgood Marshall. But for the imaginative leap made by Martin Luther King, Jr., there would be no practical platform on which Jesse Jackson could run. Good ideas, no matter how wild they seem at first, have a way of making their practical impression.

Rome, in Julius Caesar's time, was content with the tradition of the city-state inherited from the Greeks. Rome was said to be ''blind'' to the future because it could not move forward without first looking back for a precedent. Caesar's genius led him to *imagine* that by making the provinces equal with the city of Rome, authority would no longer have to flow outward from the city square. The concept of the nation-state appeared first in Caesar's imagination. The price he paid for his imaginative leap was assassination. It was left to Augustus to impose, consciously, the psychological habits that made ideas and institutions, and not blood, the basis of membership in a community. Perry Miller has remarked that only two nations in the history of the world—Rome under Augustus and America under Jefferson—came consciously into existence. He also noted that black Americans and Indians were the only wild cards in the *ethnic* equation. The cultural factors imposed by these two groups were the only elements that kept this country from becoming a mere extension of Europe. Of these two, black Americans made up the only group that *could not* look back to a time before the very earliest colonial period, the only group on this continent which created itself, consciously, out of the raw materials indigenous to this country's basic tradition: European, African, and Indian.

I admire Ralph Ellison because he had the courage, when it was not fashionable, to stick to his guns to affirm the complexity of his ethnic and cultural background. Sometimes I wish we were merely Africans. Life would be easier and romances are fun to write. And I am aware of the price, political and personal, that must be paid for this stance. One runs the risk of not seeming "pure" to all other ideologies and "races." And allies are few and far between. Worse, one runs the risk of alienating one's own group, often on the merest chance that someone, sometime in the future, will understand the implications of one's thought. It is to Ralph Ellison's credit that he has stood up for the complexity and the integrity of an entire culture that has sometimes been too "blind" to appreciate the universal implications of his thought. He has very painstakingly cultivated the psychological habits that could help make his countrymen something more than mere expressions of this group or that. His work has been involved with exploring the cultural foundations of a nation-state. Perhaps it is ironic that the implications of his work are just beginning to be realized, at a time when the institution of the nation-state is becoming obsolete.

Much has been said about Ralph's projected novel. I expect that much more will be said about it. I have never read the book, but I remember one night, back in the summer of 1969, when he read a section of it to me. The prose was unlike anything I had ever heard before, a combination of Count Basie's sense of time and early American minstrelsy and Negro Baptist preaching. And the narrator was riffing everything, from coffins to the Book of Numbers. I have been thinking about those five or ten minutes for many years now, and what I think is that, in his novel, Ellison was trying to solve the central problem of American literature. He was trying to find forms invested with enough familiarity to reinvent a much broader and much more diverse world for those who take their provisional identities from groups. I think he was trying to *Negro-Americanize* the novel form, at the same time he was attempting to move beyond it. There are a lot of us who are waiting, patiently, for him to make that leap.

An old friend of his, a man named Virgil Branam, who grew up with Ellison in Oklahoma, told me once, "Ralph's the same way he was when he was a boy. He ain't changed." I think that, for a long time now, he has been trying to teach all of us a little calculus.

A Meditation on the Life and Times of Ralph Waldo Ellison

MICHAEL S. HARPER

1

GOIN' TO THE TERRITORY

"The prayers of both could not be answered—
that of neither has been answered fully."
A. Lincoln

Ethical schizophrenia you called it:
come back to haunt the cattle-drive,
Indians coming into blacktown
because it's home; your father's will
lies uncontested, his blood welling up in oil;
"Deep Second" hones its marks in Jimmy Rushing;
Charlie Christian's father leads the blind.

Such instruments arrange themselves
at Gettysburg, at Chickamauga;
the whites in Tulsa apologize
in the separate library,
all the books you dreamed of,
fairy tales and Satchmo jesting
to the Court of St. James,
infirmary is the saints already home.

The hip connected to the thigh
converges in tuberculosis; your mother's
knees spank the planks of rectory,

From *Healing Song for the Inner Ear* (University of Illinois Press, 1985) by Michael S. Harper.

your father's imago sanctified
in documents, in acts won out
on hallelujahs of "A" train,
nine Scottsboro Boys spun upward
over thresholds of Duke's dance.

Dance and mask collect their greasepaint,
idioms stand on bandstand, in stove-
pipe pants of riverman, in gambling shoes,
his gold-toothed venom vexing sundown,
the choir at sunrise-service cleansing
a life on a Jim Crow funeral car.

The first true phrase sings out in barnyard;
the hunt in books for quail.

2
THE PEN

"The artifact is the completion of personality."

The Big E. is still making up
complexity;
he can't be stolen
from—his long black tongue
isn't nearly as deadly
as his memory
which is of the frontier,
the fiber and floor covering,
the blossom and elixir of bhang
and hashish, and the pen is quick:
the seeds are used as food for caged birds

and so the Big E. enjoys a shared delight,
a feast.

The Big E. don't like theft—
he got powerful arms, a scarred
eyelid, and a pocketknife
that has a fast safety and quick release—
it has a double-edge sword,
it is as black
as gunpowder, as red as a hieroglyphic
rose; the Big E. is a gangplank

with nettles on either side
                                        the berry sweet
enough for the nightingale to eat,
jam of the crow.
                                The Big E. has orchestration—
his patterns of the word fling out into destiny
as a prairie used to when the Indians
were called Kiowa, Crow, Dakota, Cheyenne.

The Big E. ain't in love with Indian hating;
he don't like phony dance—he's got his problems
with terrain in Mississippi—
                                        the great slab
of stone on the Mississippi makes you swim—
The Big E. likes hawks;
                                he's got time for deer—
he can seed watermelon, pumpkins, canteloupe—
he got problems with theft,
                                        highway robbery—
his own name—and he likes the source
of things, deeds, and the snakeskin well-wrought
and finely earned; he likes the sentiment
of defanging—he got two teeth with poison
in between, got a hot, tested lip,
                                        a sense of ease
at the break—he's got a tinker bell
likes radio equipment, got tapes in his closet,
old coats still in style from the haberdashery
shop—has a sense of honor on the dancefloor,
don't step on nobody's feet, brings his own smoke,
can tan a hide, fish in the stream of the dream,
the big dream—looks for the possible in things
unwritten; and when it comes to rite, jokes, jokes bad!

3
THE BODY POLITY

A half-century ago the Scottsboro Boys
jackknifed into vectors of the runagate
dream, and not the dream of Anglican
vice, when act hid shadow, shadow act.

Decatur relatives and neighbors,
not too far from Chehaw Station and Tuskegee,
flight squadrons and turkey regiments
peopled medical corps, Jim Crow'd Tuxedo Junction.

I saw the oldest son of any slave hide his thought
in Latin-English treasury books of Apuleius,
saw the roots of Constitution and the family Bible,
tree and joist of history, and the self: democracy.

A sterling beacon tintype or a worksong;
thumbed eight-ball English, elegiac blues, on any
continental shelf.

PART TWO

Slipping the Yoke

THE "FREQUENCIES" OF *SHADOW AND ACT*

Travels with Ralph Ellison Through Time and Thought

HOLLIE WEST

Q: You once wrote that American literature was built partly from Negro folklore.

A: Yes. There's never been a time when we—our expression, our symbols, our turns of face—were not finding our way into the products of other Americans who were consciously or unconsciously creating. After all, "Turkey in the Straw" is a Negro tune, but it is identified with whites just as is "Carry Me Back to Ole Virginny," by a black Virginia composer. Very early, I guess in the 1830s, Whitman was suggesting that in the dialect of the American Negro was a basis of an American form of grand opera. You see, this is overlooked. Americans had to create themselves. We had to be conscious of language in a way that English people did not have to be. It was their mother tongue. It was our mother tongue but we were in rebellion against it—against the values on which it was based, which were those of kinship. We didn't reject the great traditions of British literature, the King James version of the Bible, Shakespeare or the great poets, but we rejected the values which enspirited that language and we began to try to discover how to create an American literature. This was consciously stated over and over by many people. What was more American than Mose, and who was more expressive, more artistically inventive in dancing, making jokes, telling stories? Mark Twain delighted in telling Negro ghost stories and used to do it on public stage, public platforms. He knew very consciously that he was using the moral predicament surrounding the racial conflict in this country to give structure to his imagination and his stories. This was inescapable. So when I say that we are always there, it isn't just an idle assertion. All you have to do is look and say, My God, when would the white man have had that particular insight?

"Through a Writer's Eyes," a series by Hollie West, from *The Washington Post*, August 19, 20, 21, 1973.

How could he have had the insight if there had been no racial conflict? How could he have had this particular kind of conception of humanity if there had been no blacks within the society?

Q: Well, much of this sort of thing is oral. Much of folklore, for that matter, is oral.

A: The study of folklore tends to be literary, but folklore is usually the expression of a preliterate society. Of course it continues even after literature develops because it's tradition.

Q: In that connection, do you see the study of oral history as a valid way of interpreting and understanding American history?

A: I would think that a great part of American history has been lost precisely because those people who wrote the history structured it to their own conceptions. We could just take the Negro part of American history. Much of that was lost because it was not written down but passed along from individual to individual.

Yet there doubtless still remains a lot of correspondence written by blacks as they moved about the country, which would tell us quite a lot about American history as it actually unfolded. But until recently historians haven't bothered with this material. Quite a lot of work was done during the WPA [Works Progress, later Works Projects Administration] days when many ex-slaves were interviewed. I was reading recently some accounts collected during the Writers Project in Oklahoma. I read the statement of this man and looked at his name and then realized that I had known him. He was in his eighties when I was a little kid out there, but he was very much alive. And it had never occurred to me that he had been a slave. In fact, many of the people who went to Oklahoma had had some slavery experience.

Q: In a sense you saw folklore developing in Oklahoma, and by that I mean you saw certain lifestyles and traditions being created. Was this crucial to the development of your later interest in folklore, and how it was interwoven into culture generally?

A: Well, folklore was interwoven. I wasn't aware that I was seeing it develop. I was just a part of a community in which you had an extension of folklore patterns from the South and into the Southwest. After all, many of the people came from Alabama, North Carolina, Mississippi, South Carolina, and Georgia. And they brought along stories. As with any situation where folkloristic pattern is adapted to new situations, the people who were involved with it were not aware of it unless they were scholars. I was not a scholar, but I delighted in stories and lyrics. As one who wanted to be a musician and a composer I was getting it on all sides: classical music as well as jazz and the blues and spirituals. But one thing I can say that was important in this connection was that I very early began to read Shaw. I was reading Shaw when I was ten, and I came across a number of these Haldeman Julius blue and gray books, and I read some of Nietzsche, and I understood the relationship between Nietzsche and Shaw. Nietzsche was, of course, concerned not with folklore but with the underlying ritual patterns. Years later when I began to try to understand Eliot and Pound, and so on, to see how they worked putting these things together, I began to look back and understand, "Oh yes, I was involved with folklore," but this was the result of certain sorts of conscious experience based upon literature. I discovered the folklore because I had become a literary person.

Q: Sterling Brown has written that the urbanization of blacks is helping to break up rural folk culture. Is there such a thing as urban folklore?

A: Yes, I think so. But it isn't a thing in itself. The traditions are modified in the city. I worked on a folklore project here in New York City under WPA collecting children's rhymes and things. But I went beyond that to get older people to tell me stories, and very often a word or a concept would have just become a mumble. Usually a word becomes some nonsense phrase because it was out of the rural context in which the rhyme or story had originated. It continued because that's what the people have to work out of. This tradition goes way back to the South, and some of it goes back to Africa.

Q: The tradition may continue, may be modified in the urban setting, but is some of the vitality lost?

A: The vitality is lost in some ways. Some patterns drop out. But what is it that gives life to folklore or any kind of literature? It's the experience of people. And as the experience maintains a continuity where issues and motives remain alive and there's an audience for it, you get a vitality. You're not going to keep life from changing. You can't do that. One of the things that tends to throw people off is that they don't go looking for folklore, they don't go places where folklore is still alive. I'm sure that the Afro [hair style] has killed off more folklore than anything else, because guys don't have to go to the barbershop or stay there long enough for the lying to start. But there're still plenty of people around who know the stories.

Q: I'm not asking that life stand still, but I have questions about whether much of the vitality of Negro life is being retained.

A: I think the vitality is maintained, but you just have to know where it is. Here the great emphasis is on writing. I'd like to feel that all my fiction has themes, motives, and images from folklore. That's my way of keeping it alive. I'm just conscious of literature generally, to see how to structure it with similar patterns. And I think that that's happening with a number of the younger writers. I think that they realize that this heritage is a valuable one. But the trick is how to use it.

I might write a decent blues lyric, but for me to write a blues lyric is quite different from some guy who knows no other form of expression. You can see that it is more immediately native to him than it is to me, although it is my tradition, too.

Q: In a sense you took direct part in some folk traditions: the tradition of hoboing, for one.

A: Well, that sure ain't Negro—that's American! Yes, I did. But you must remember this: My father's people built railroad trestles for the Southern Railroad during the Reconstruction period, and my people were railroad people to an extent. That's part of it. So much of folklore is mixed up with traveling, with freight trains, with the sounds of trains and so on. That's the advantage of having lived close to the railroads. One reason I live here [on Riverside Drive in Upper Manhattan] is that there's a railroad track right down there. I've got a river, a highway, and a railroad track. I like to hear those cars bumping along there.

Yes, I did hobo. That's how I got to school during the Depression. I was able to get to Tuskegee by riding freight trains rather than going across Arkansas where they were pretty rough on you. They had chain gangs. I went north—went up to East St. Louis, over to Evansville, got the L & N, and went down south. I was taken off the train at Decatur when the Scottsboro case was being tried. They were just shaking the train down. They didn't bother us. I ran and got away from whatever was going to happen.

Q: Do you miss the trains?

A: Yes, I do, because they were a vehicle of folklore. I miss them very much. Mark Twain understood the importance of the Mississippi River (as did T.S. Eliot and others) to the fluidity of American literature and folklore. Where you get people going back and forth you get literature, art. Kansas City and Chicago were great towns for jazz because they were great railroad towns. People would come up and tell their stories. Sometimes they would go back. The Pullman porter was a great agent of that type of culture, the waiter and so on. You miss that. You miss the sound, the romance of the railroad. There's something very valuable that has been lost.

Q: I've been told that someone taught you to hobo, to hop freights. Is that right?

A: Yes, I made notes on that, and I will write about it. It was a friend of my parents, a little white-looking, blue-eyed, light-haired Negro fellow. Whenever he was outside Oklahoma he was a white man. He used to come back and forth, stay a few days, and take off. He happened to be there when I had the scholarship at Tuskegee.

They needed a trumpet player, but I got word that I'd have to be there at a certain time and I didn't have the money to do it because I was buying clothing and I was buying a horn, and so on. So I approached him and said, "Charlie, why don't you teach me to hobo?" I got my mother's reluctant permission and we took off. I had thirty-two bucks and he had very little. He taught me who to avoid, how to get on trains, and how to protect myself. It was quite a nice thing to have done.

Q: Was it an involved technique?

A: You had to be able to read a manifest which was nailed on the side of the car to know where a train was going and when it was scheduled to be there. You had to know how to avoid railroad bulls [detectives]. You had to know what to do when a train got into town where there were difficult police or sheriffs. You had to know where you could buy things in a racial situation. It was quite a bit involved.

You had to know the best route to take. I wouldn't have known to have gone north. And as it was, I was taken off the train. I wasn't allowed to go into St. Louis. I was stopped because they were turning boys around who were going up to the World's Fair. Charlie went across into East St. Louis. He told me to see what I could do with the guard. I walked across the Mississippi River bridge and convinced the guard that I wasn't going to the fair, that I was going to college, and this was the only way I could do it. And he let me through.

Q: Do you see any special problems in the study of Negro folklore, distinguishing it from the folklore of white America—say, Appalachian whites or whites in the Ozarks?

A: Well, you just have to find out where Negroes are and you have to give up the idea that culture exists in neat pockets. Culture is exchange. A slave could be in the yard looking in at whites dancing and come out and imitate that dance, and then put his own riffs to it, and you've got something else. That's how American choreography developed.

Remember there was an exchange. Just as they looked at polite forms of dancing, European dancing as adopted by American whites—many of whom were going back and forth to Europe during colonial times—those slaves looked at that, they learned from that and put something of their own with it, and later on whites looked at what the [slaves] did and put something of their own to it, and you get this interchange.

It's a dialectical process. You tell me a story, or I hear you telling your child a story. I'm a cook or a maid or a butler. I go back home and tell my kids the story. Since there's an element of rhetoric involved, I change it to fit in with the background of my child, and then I enspirit it with my own motives for freedom or my own sense of humanity, my own sense of the complexity of human experience. And so you've got a modification.

You can look and say, "This is a Negro story." You look at "John Henry"—that seems absolutely black. But you look a little closer and you remember the tales of Hercules, you recognize the modification. I'm not saying it's not ours. But I'm saying it was not created out of the empty air but out of the long tradition of storytelling, out of myth.

Q: I know that you have laid great emphasis on the give-and-take process in our culture. Do you see it working as effectively now as it was when the main thrust of blacks was to integrate with whites?

A: It isn't an arbitrary matter. You cannot control integration by setting up an ideological structure and saying, "We're separatists." I still watch the guys walking around. They may be wearing dashikis, but who makes the cloth? They don't. The Africans don't, for the most part. Maybe a few do.

It's too damn expensive to cloak a political movement. They're still looking at American TV, listening to American news, using European cameras, American cameras, drinking the best Scotch whiskey. You see, that's to kid themselves. But to get back to the question.

I think there is a more conscious interchange of cultural styles between the races in this country now than ever before. When did you ever hear blonde, blue-eyed white girls shouting like Holy Roller sisters and making millions out of it? When did you ever see young white boys singing in the style that used to be common to backwoods Negro entertainers? This, too, was in churches: all that falsetto singing and shrieking and going on. This is being exploited not simply by people in show business but by middle-class kids who have heard it and liked it, and decided it was easy to do. They couldn't do that with jazz, and it got so for a while there you couldn't hear any decent music, even on an FM station.

In literature, and I'm not going to call any names, but we have our guys who—in the name of black power—are picking up some of the sleaziest attitudinizing of whites.

Q: Let's consider one of your statements from an essay in *Shadow and Act*. You said you feared the commercialization and banalization of Negro culture.

A: I still do. And I wish there could be some control of it, but there cannot be control of it, except in this way: through those of us who write and who create using what is there to use in a most eloquent and transcendent way. You cannot control Tin Pan Alley—too many people are making money off it—any more than you can control a tenor saxophone player who, instead of playing music, found he could make more money and go further commercially by rolling on the floor and shrieking. And we had quite a lot of that.

But at the same time Johnny Hodges and Coleman Hawkins and God knows who else just kept on developing the possibilities which were implicit in the style of saxophone jazz from way, way back, beyond Sidney Bechet. It's one thing for a commercial group to go out and exploit the possibilities of gospel music and quite a different thing for a serious composer who sees something which is valuable in that style and uses it to realize his own artistic vision.

Q: But what you mentioned earlier—the blue-eyed blonde wearing her hair in Afro style, shrieking and shouting like a backwoods Baptist—is happening more frequently than a serious composer utilizing the resources of Negro music.

A: It always does. The vulgar tongue is spoken by more people than the refined tongue. The task of the artist is always to refine that which is the vulgar speech—to make it sharper and make it more transcendent and more eloquent. As I said, Negroes cannot control that any more than we can control the economy. But we don't have to play the game and we can set our own fashions as we did with jazz.

Back in the twenties and thirties most white people were not dancing to jazz. And the musicians did not need great commercial success among whites to determine artistic values for them, I suppose, because that avenue was closed to them. They determined their own artistic values in the academy of the dance hall and jam session. That's the kind of self-determination which is needed to preserve not only the artistic values of jazz but all American culture.

Q: I'd like to go back to your earlier statement about there being more cultural exchange than before. You cite the example of young whites taking on the lifestyles of blacks. But I don't see young blacks being influenced so much by the lifestyle of young whites. Take rock music. Many blacks have been reluctant to embrace it. But there have been some: Jimi Hendrix, for one.

A: I was going to say that. Keep on talking.

Q: But I think he's more of an exception than a Janis Joplin or many of the other young white rock performers.

A: What about Chuck Berry? You see, here you have to watch the circling—the back-and-forth play. Chuck Berry was doing some of this stuff a long time ago. They took it up and did their version of it. He's done his version of it. He fits into that slot.

Q: We spoke earlier about the commercialization and banalization of Negro-American cultural expression. You said this was happening, but at the same time in the portion of *Shadow and Act*, "Some Questions and Some Answers," you said at one point that you did not believe that as we win our struggle for full participation in American life we abandon our group expression. Do you still believe that today, in light of what's happened since. . . ?

A: No. I don't think that we will abandon it. That's all we have. You see, you might have people on a certain cultural level who will seek to abandon our expression, but tradition is more devious than that. It isn't an arbitrary matter.

You watch a little Negro kid try to dance. He's going to dance like a little Negro American kid. And why is that? Beyond any physical question or articulation of the limbs there is a spirit of the dance which is around him, and he observes and absorbs it before he is aware of what he is absorbing. It's very interesting to watch little white and Negro kids dance on television and observe the difference between them. Now some of those little white kids can dance and some of them have been very much influenced by Negro American style, but I think that this is a part of the culture that moves from individual to individual in the context of the community and you don't have to be altogether aware of it. You are doing what comes naturally.

You are not going to lose a certain way with words because it is built into the way we speak. What we call rapping or riffing—you are going to hear your daddy talking or your uncle or your older brothers and sisters. This is preserved in speech and its informed attitudes, which can range from the most explicit to that which is implicit and subtle. So you're not going to get away from that. What will happen, I think, is that as you become conscious as an artist, you will begin to exploit it consciously. You will work it in terms of what others have done in other cultures. You will abstract motives from there and impose them within your own scheme.

But it's a give-and-take human thing rather than a racial thing, and at some point we're going to have to realize that simply by having the same skin we're not all the same people. There are many cultural levels within the Negro group. There are people who are on the folk level in their cultural lives, even though they might be operating computers. And there are people who shine shoes who, in their cultural lives, are on the high level of articulate culture.

Q: It's this give-and-take that's so important, I suppose. This reminds me of something that Duke Ellington said to me in an interview. He said the pull of American culture was so strong that no one could resist it.

A: Not only that, but it's in artifacts, you see. You put on a pair of shoes, a hat. Negroes thought they were going to isolate themselves by putting on an Afro. The Jewish kids, the blonde kids—they're wearing them too. Why? Because it's irresistible. It's a style. It's a new way of making the human body do something; and that operates over and beyond any question of race.

Ellison's Essays

R.W.B. LEWIS

Shadow and Act contains Ralph Ellison's real autobiography—in the form of essays and interviews—as distinguished from the symbolic version given in his splendid novel of 1952, *Invisible Man*. Some of the twenty-odd items in it were written as early as 1942, and not all of them have been published before. One or two were rejected by liberal periodicals, apparently because Ellison insisted on saying that Negro American life was not everywhere as hellish or as inert or as devastated by hatred and self-hatred as it was sometimes alleged; it is not unlikely that liberal criticism will be equally impatient with this new book. Most of the pieces, were, however, written after *Invisible Man* and in part are a consequence of it. They may even help to explain the long gap of time between Ellison's first novel and its much awaited successor. There have been other theories about this delay: for example, an obituary notice by LeRoi Jones who, in a recent summary of the supposedly lethal effect of America upon its Negro writers, referred to Ellison as "silenced and fidgeting away in some college." But he has not been silent, much less silenced—by white America or anything else. The experiences of writing *Invisible Man* and of vaulting on his first try "over the parochial limits of most Negro fiction" (as Richard G. Stern says in an interview), and, as a result, of being written about as a literary and sociological phenomenon, combined with sheer compositional difficulties, seem to have driven Ellison to search out the truths of his own past. Inquiring into his experience, his literary and musical education, Ellison has come up with a number of clues to the fantastic fate of trying to be at the same time a writer, a Negro, an American, and a human being.

It is hard at the best of times to be even two of those things; the attempt to be all four must be called gallant. For even those among us who consent to Negroes' being accepted as human beings, don't really want them to be writers. We want them to be warriors, and wounded warriors at that: with their creative talents enlisted in the (great and real) struggle for racial justice. This is our curious contemporary device for keeping the Negro in his place, which, when it is not on the actual battlefield, is thought to be in some immitigable psychological hell. When a Negro like Ellison says, "Why, this is not *altogether* hell, after all," and then goes on to talk about the role and responsibility of the writer, his remarks are resented as mere aestheticism, or worse, as a kind of betrayal. A good many pages of *Shadow and Act* describe Ellison's patient effort to explain the organic relation between his personal sense of life, his racial and national identity, and his chosen artistic vocation: to explain, not how he sought to escape or deny his Negroness by fleeing into the colorless domain of art, but how it has been essentially as a writer that he managed to discover what it means for him to be a Negro American and a human being. It is obviously a tough point to get across.

Ellison works toward that point from several directions and in various modes. In interviews with Richard Stern and the editors of the *Paris Review*, he reflects on the origins of *Invisible Man*, on the devious craft of fiction, and on the usual failure of dialogue between Negro writer and white reader. In an exchange with Stanley Edgar Hyman he argues for the "specificity" of literary works, including his own, and questions the value of "archetype-hunting," especially since, with Negro writing, it tends to reimpose the stereotypes Negroes are most anxious to shake off. On the question of a "Negro culture," Ellison rejects the notion of African antecedents. "I know of no valid demonstration," he says, "that culture is transmitted through the genes. . . . The American Negro people is North American in origin . . . its spiritual outlook is basically Protestant, its system of kinship is Western, its time and historical sense are American." In essays on twentieth-century fiction and on Stephen Crane, and in a speech in 1953 accepting the National Book Award, Ellison evinces just that outlook and sense of kinship, though, as I'll suggest, in beguilingly specialized terms.

It is above all in an autobiographical lecture called "Hidden Name and Complex Fate," and in a long reply to an essay by Irving Howe, that Ellison confronts these intertwining issues with full intellectual and imaginative authority. Elsewhere the book's central argument is at times spotty and groping, and once in a while gummy; but these two pieces have an assurance and a truth that are bound to unsettle and dismay all those whose minds have grown rigid with the fixed concept of the American Negro as trapped agony incarnate.

The Oklahoma of Ellison's childhood had joined the Union long after the Emancipation, and hence had no tradition of slavery except for the ancestral memories brought into it by the descendants of slaves. Even those memories were effectively diverse; for while "slavery was a most vicious system and those who endured and survived it a tough people," Ellison observes, a person born into slavery might look forward to becoming "a coachman, a teamster, a cook, the best damned steward on the Mississippi, the best jockey in

Kentucky, a butler, a farmer, a stud, or, hopefully, a free man!" In Oklahoma, there was segregation, to be sure; though perhaps less thirty years ago than now; but there was always a certain amount of elbowroom. The experience of precarious freedom within carefully defined limits made Ellison aware of a similar phenomenon in the music of the southwestern jazzmen of the day. Their music expressed for him "the freedom lying within the restrictions of their musical traditions as within the limitations of their social background." The sense of that twofold possibility—artistic and social—remained with Ellison when he moved on later to the Deep South and then to New York City. He is aware that Oklahoma was not Harlem: that is just his point. His point, too, is that Harlem—particularly Harlem as currently imagined—is not Oklahoma; and that there is a variety that adds spice and vigor and even a sort of battered enjoyment to American Negro life, and that those qualities should be added to the anguish and the appalling humiliations in any account of it.

There were separate but equal moviehouses back in Oklahoma, standing shoulder to shoulder and entered from the same doorway. But, Ellison remarks dryly, "I went to the movies to see pictures, not to be with whites." He also went to the library. Ellison seems to have known what every aspiring writer has to know: that his apprenticeship can take place only in literature. In "Black Boys and Native Sons," Irving Howe, while admiring *Invisible Man*, accused Ellison of forgetting the urgencies of the Negro cause in the interests of mere "literature," and of failing in particular to continue along the savage polemical path mapped out by Richard Wright. In reply, Ellison argues that, quite apart from the frozen inaccuracy of Howe's and Wright's appraisal of the Negro situation, Negro writers do not and cannot descend from Negroes, but from writers. "James Baldwin," he goes on, "is the product not of a Negro store-front church but of the library, and the same is true of me." It is depressing to realize that this is a daring statement. (But it is the kind of insight that distinguishes a genuine writer.)

As a novelist, Ellison was drawn to the novels of Dostoevski and Conrad, and much more to those of Malraux (though not, oddly enough, to Silone, with whom he has much in common, attempting, like Silone, to convert political violence into poetry, from the periphery of the culture into which he is moving). But as a Negro American writer, he was drawn to the classical period of American literature—and exactly because he found there "the conception of the Negro as the symbol of Man." I am not quite convinced that slavery and the Negro were as central to the imagination of Whitman, Emerson, Thoreau, Melville, and Mark Twain as Ellison makes out. But his reading of these writers, like Eliot's Protestant American reading of Donne and Dante, is the critical paraphrase by which every authentic writer creates a new literary tradition for himself, to suit his artistic needs and abilities. Melville and Mark Twain and other writers showed Ellison how to give shape to his subject: that is, to his experience, as a Negro in modern America.

Drawing on earlier treatments of the Negro as the symbol of Man, Ellison found ways not only to articulate, but to universalize his own complex identity—and to celebrate its pain-wracked, eternally wondering and comical nature. Writers after Mark Twain have been mainly useful to him because of their technical skills; for, except in the novels of Faulkner, Ellison finds that "the human Negro" has to a large extent disappeared from American fiction, has been replaced by Jim Crow (whose late arrival in fiction Ellison describes in a manner similar to C. Vann Woodward's account of the belated rise of Jim Crow in historic fact).

Ellison had originally expected to make a career in music, as a composer of symphonies and as a jazz trumpeter. He abandoned the notion, but almost a third of *Shadow and Act* consists of luxuriantly written and affectionate recollections of jazzmen and singers of blues and spirituals. There is also a review of LeRoi Jones's book, *Blues People*, in which Ellison contends characteristically that, by treating his subject sociologically, Jones failed to see that music was what slaves had instead of freedom and that, later, the blues were what Negroes had instead of religion. In both epochs, he suggests, music was the vehicle by which an otherwise powerless black people could profoundly influence, could indeed enthrall or counter-enslave, the white people. This section of Ellison's book contains the least intimidating, because the most unpretentious and humane, descriptions of Negro musical expression that I have read. And when Ellison defines the blues as the "chronicle of personal catastrophe expressed lyrically," and as "an impulse to keep the painful details and episodes of a brutal experience alive in one's aching consciousness . . . and to transcend it, not by the consolations of philosophy but by squeezing from it a near-tragic, near-comic lyricism"—he makes the same connection between art and experience that he makes in the essays on literature and his autobiographical memoir. One can also make out a fairly exact summary of the themes of *Invisible Man*.

This may be the worst possible moment for an attempt at dialogue between or about Negroes and whites in America. But Ellison's demonstration of his identity had a singular effect upon me. The more he invoked the phrase "Negro American," the more I found myself mumbling to myself the phrase "white American"—not in pride nor shame, but with a shock of recognition. Ellison's identity, because of the power and wisdom and stubborn sanity of its pronouncement, serves to limit mine, to establish its boundaries and focus its intermixing elements. No experience is more to be cherished; for Ellison is not only a self-identifier but the source of self-definition in others. At just that point, a falsely conceived integration (the melting of indistinguishable persons) ceases, and the dialogue can begin.

The Testament of Ralph Ellison

JOHN M. REILLY

Suppose we take Ralph Ellison at his word when he tells us that the basic significance of the essays and occasional pieces collected in *Shadow and Act* is autobiographical.[1] Then, despite the omission from this version of a life writing of dates and particularized events that would mark it as an objective chronicle of the passage from youth to maturity and obscurity to fame, the reader's expectation that the autobiography will depict a destiny is met by Ellison's repeated mention of the essential experience that forms the condition for his life's project.

The dominant feature emerging from his reflective viewpoint is the good fortune he had being brought up in Oklahoma, whose settlement by black and white Americans hardly more than a generation before his birth exempted its society, for a time, from the equilibrium of rigid caste relationships prevalent in the Old South and the fixed systems of power characteristic of the capitalist industrial sectors of the United States. It was a newer America where he was born, and, though soon enough it fastened upon itself the rites of racial segregation and the forms of a class society, during the early years of its statehood and Ellison's life, Oklahoma recapitulated in the minds of its citizens, if not entirely in the circumstances of their material lives, the situation of the American frontier. Exhilarated by the sense of possibility in a loosely structured community, the young Ellison and his confrères could imaginatively transcend the categories of race, thinking of themselves as the "Renaissance men" of an American comedy rather than as victims in a racist melodrama.

Through the selections of memory and the emphases of rhetoric, Ellison invests the musicians who created the vernacular idiom of the region's native music—Southwestern jazz—with the authority of practical philosophers on his latter-day frontier. In the outlaw status earned by their exclusion and willed separation from the company of respectable judges, ministers, and politicians who were the agents of repressive "civilization," the jazzmen embodied in the art for which they lived the attributes of popular archetype. Their versatility and improvisational style evinced the idealized individualism of American legend and evoked the witty triumphs of Afro-American folk heroes, while in the processions of their art they performed a kind of democratic enactment, singing the self in musical phrases that combined in an utterance *en masse*. True jazz, Ellison writes

> is an art of individual assertion within and against the group. Each true jazz moment . . . springs from a contest in which each artist challenges all the rest; each solo flight, or improvisation, represents (like the successive canvases of a painter) a definition of his identity; as individual, as member of the collectivity and as a link in the chain of tradition. (*S&A*, 234)

The climax of Ellison's projection of the importance of the frontier in his life is, of course, his own emergence as an artist. Exuberance and ambition allied with incontestable talent impelled him, as it did the jazzmen, to creative expression as a means of self-definition. It diminishes his accomplishment not at all to say that this was a result of personality more than of conviction that he possessed prodigious abilities. Taking up writing, he says, depended upon the chance of Richard Wright's asking him to do a review and then a short story for *New Challenge* magazine. Even so, writing "was a reflex of reading, an extension of a source of pleasure, escape and instruction" (*S&A*, xii). And before that, the composition of music for which he originally hoped to prepare himself appears to have signified less an immersion in a process than the hope of achieving a state of being, as in *being* another Richard Wagner by composing a great symphony before the age of twenty-six. Furthermore, there was a good deal of serendipity and scarcely any sense of determinism bringing him to New York and within the reach of Wright's literary suggestions before he completed the prescribed course of formal study at Tuskegee Institute. A problem about his scholarship and the lure of the city he knew from Alain Locke's *The New Negro* as the setting of a contemporary "Renaissance" led him to yet another frontier.

Ellison's mention in *Shadow and Act*, and elsewhere, of writers from whose friendship and example he learned something of craft—Eliot, Hemingway, Malraux, Wright—has unquestionable interest, but not because they constitute a list of influences to be discerned in his writing. Rather, these references complete the imaginative paradigm of the inceptive autobiography by introducing his companions in the free republic of letters, an environment whose inhabitants define themselves through works undertaken individually, as members of the collectivity, and as links in the chains of tradition. A life of literature can be a difficult, combative one, but it is lived, Ellison tells us, in a zone of undiscovered possibilities that is the natural home and destiny of a man formed and conditioned by the historical and cultural environment of America's last physical frontier.

Intriguing as the factual details Ellison provides us of his life may be, they are insufficient to satisfy fully our curiosity. In "The World and the Jug" (*S&A*, 141), he asks Irving Howe to remember that an act of Chekhov's "was significant only because Chekhov was *Chekhov*, the great writer.'' So, because Ralph Ellison is Ralph *Ellison*, we should like to know all manner of things about his life in the hope that they could ''explain'' him, and, if not that, at least give us the fullest possible description of the man. But *Shadow and Act* offers a truncated autobiography. Even with the addition of writings not collected in that volume, we have only the framework of a life, and a subjectively rendered framework, at that. Ellison has situated his life for us within a broadly outlined episode of history resonant of the schemes of Frederick Jackson Turner and the images of popular culture. It is a generalized, a priori picture that will not reveal how the unique Ralph Ellison, equipped with certain predispositions, actually became the particular man. ''Negroness'' is nothing like a metaphysical condition, he says.

> It is not skin color which makes a Negro American but cultural heritage as shaped by the American experience, the social and political predicament, a sharing of that ''concord of sensibilities'' which the group expresses through historical circumstances. . . . (*S&A*, 131)

What, then, are the features of person, the experiences in family and intimate relationships that particularized Ellison's assumption of the Afro-American cultural heritage and, thus, individualizes him within the group? He does not say.

It might be objected that this is a querulous response to the casual remark Ellison makes about the autobiographical significance of *Shadow and Act*. Perhaps. But to note that the plot of a life we glimpse only in fragments dispersed throughout his essays is an abstract representation of the self establishes two crucial points for understanding his nonfiction. The first point is that Ellison presents himself as a symbolic figure in whose portrayal the absence of particularized data encourages us to see a typical product of the American frontier. Moreover, in delineating his experience among a people who intentionally left the realm of slavery to make a new way, he indicates that the frontier effects the necessary rupture in the repetitive order of social oppression that gives birth to history. Like the protagonist of *Invisible Man*, who claims to speak for all of us on one frequency or another, Ellison the essayist stands at the beginning of self-determining Afro-American history. The second crucial point to observe about the generalized autobiography is that its broad frontiersman scheme is obviously a fiction, not in the sense that it bears no relationship to a reality that can be documented from other sources, but rather it is like fiction in the selectivity it uses to enforce the compelling significance of a single, unqualified feature of Ellison's life: his certain and intuitive resolve to achieve the birthright of a free citizen of a democracy.

So the apparent autobiography in *Shadow and Act* is an exemplum; yet, in its purpose it is more than that. It provides the authenticating image for a volume of writing devoted to exploration of classical issues in American social philosophy. As it discusses democracy from the unusual vantage point of an aesthetic concept of self-realization, Ellison's fragmentary autobiography certifies that the source of discussion is a representative Afro-American.

The Afro-American, as citizen and artist, engages in a continual struggle against reductive stereotype, not merely the Negrophobic characterizations of vicious racists, but also the interpretations of black life advanced by a social science that describes its object almost entirely by reference to the dominant white majority. Nineteenth-century students of the "Negro problem" applied their supposed science to demonstration of the black's comparative inferiority, thereby creating a justification for continued exploitation. More "progressive" thought in the twentieth century has redefined the condition once perceived as subhuman as a situation wherein blacks are the victims of whites. In either interpretation Afro-Americans are conceived as existing in dependency. Even the corrective work of Gunnar Myrdal, whose influential study *An American Dilemma* earns Ellison's praise for discrediting the "non-scientific nonsense that has cluttered our sociological literature" (*S&A*, 305), must be eventually disqualified as a truthful or useful tool for understanding, because despite its microscopic empirical analyses it retains in conclusion the reductive idea that "the Negro's entire life and, consequently, also his opinions on the Negro problem are, in the main, to be considered as secondary reactions to more primary pressures from the side of the dominant white majority" (*S&A*, 315). Ellison's displeasure with this conclusion would seem to be phrased moderately enough to suit the decorum of an academic journal, but in 1944, when the review failed to be published in the *Antioch Review*, maybe it was a different story. Nevertheless, it took twenty years before Ellison could explain the point of difference between that famous study of the Negro and the perspective of the critic whose source of knowledge is the living of a Negro life. "Can a people," Ellison asks,

> live and develop for over three hundred years simply by *reacting*? Are American Negroes simply the creation of white men, or have they at least helped to create themselves out of what they found around them? Men have made a way of life in caves and upon cliffs, why cannot Negroes have made a life upon the horns of the white man's dilemma? (*S&A*, 316)

Ellison could easily be bringing ethical proof to his commentary on Myrdal and the traditions of American social science. Common sense dictates that he ought to be qualified by "Negroness" to evaluate discussions of Afro-American social reality. The common-sense assumption will not pertain, however, in the face of the closed systems erected on the premises of stereotypes. These systems hold that opinions of Negroes are products of dependency, too, and Ellison has no inclination to counter with an invocation of racial mysticism. The counterattack would be as irrational as the view it meant to rebut is absurd. In any case, the contest with stereotypes is not a simple matter of posing truth, even the truth of personal testimony, against falsity. The "struggle over the nature of reality" (*S&A*, 26) does not concern data. Nor does it involve contrary perceptions. What the struggle is about is conceptions, the patterns and forms men and women construct from their observations and by their actions to give life a shape.

The function of stereotypes is instrumental. Arising "from an internal psychological state . . . from an inner need to believe" (*S&A*, 28), bigotry seizes upon the stock ideas current in social exchange to sanction irrational needs with the plausible appearance of overgeneralized evidence. To complicate the matter, other intellectual structures spring from personal needs by a similar process. Ellison's explicit example is art, which psychologically

> represents the socialization of some profoundly personal problem involving guilt (often symbolic murder—parricide, fratricide—incest, homosexuality, all problems at the base of personality) from which by expressing them along with other elements (images, memories, emotions, ideas) he [the artist] seeks transcendence. To be effective as personal fulfillment, if it is to be more than dream, the work of art must simultaneously evoke images of reality and give them formal organization. And it must, since the individual's emotions are formed in society, shape them into socially meaningful patterns. (*S&A*, 39)

Somewhere between the pathology of bigotry and the sublimation of profound art occurs the use of stereotype that amounts to a linguistic redundancy, the repetition of customary formulas without examination of their implications. The continuum of conceptions interests Ellison much less for its genesis hidden in the fog of singular psyches than for its significance in fostering or obstructing the progress of democracy. The instrumentality of concepts working in relation to democracy he images as a dialectic of texts.

During his literary apprenticeship among left-wing American writers, Ralph Ellison was familiar with the plan of the Communist party of the United States to establish a black republic in the South ("Study," 421). Although the plan has been criticized by anti-Communists as an alien notion, it attracted the interest of Richard Wright and other blacks who viewed it as a synthesis of nationalism and socialism. The program for the autonomous republic was built upon an analysis of the lower South, where blacks had been historically a majority in certain contiguous counties, had shared a common life in agricultural production, and had evolved distinctive institutions;[2] thus, the Black Belt, by this analysis, met Stalin's definition of a nation as "a historically evolved, stable community of language, territory, economic life and psychological make-up manifested in a community of culture."[3] Apart from the political campaign in which it was used, Stalin's description of a nation is hardly remarkable. It is in fact consistent with a current of American thought beginning in Crevecoeur's *Letters from an American Farmer* and continuing to the present to define American character by association with a unique social and physical environment. Yet the truly remarkable thing is that Ellison offers his conception of the origin of the American nation without regard to material and social history or to a current in American writing with which in other contexts he shows unquestionable sympathy:

> We began as a nation not through the accidents of race or religion or geography . . . but when a group of men, *some* of them political philosophers, put down, upon what we now recognize as quite sacred papers, their conception of the nation which they intended to establish on these shores. They described, as we know, the obligations of the state to the citizen, of the citizen to the state; they committed themselves to certain ideas of justice, just as they committed us to a system which would guarantee all of its citizens equality of opportunity. (*S&A*, 163–64)

Again, when he speaks in a later essay, "The Little Man at Chehaw Station," of the struggle to define the corporate American identity, he establishes the site of conflict as intellectual:

> The terrain upon which we struggle is itself abstract, a terrain of ideas that, although man-made, exert the compelling force of the ideal, of the sublime; ideas that draw their power from the Declaration of Independence, the Constitution, and the Bill of Rights. We stand, as we say, united in the name of these sacred principles. But, indeed, it is in the name of these same principles that we ceaselessly contend, affirming our ideals even as we do them violence. ("Little Man," 34)

According to these definitions, America, and especially the American character, are voluntarist creations, the dialectic of their development abstracted from the circumstances of material processes to the level of the word.

In its search for an essence, Ellison's image of etiology endows America with the characteristics of intentional documents. Assuming the aura of philosophical principles, the history of America, which is to say a history of texts, is all consequential to their appearance. For documents of universal significance there can be no point to an inquiry into the recesses of the authors' psychology or even the particular circumstances that made up their original context. Instead, what is pertinent is a history from the point of view of efforts to realize, or evade, the meaning of those sacred documents, a history that is a record of intended effects and that is apprehensible through the symbolic actions and cross references of succeeding texts. Such a history becomes the primary theme of Ralph Ellison's nonfiction.

Among the most important works succeeding upon the axiomatic democratic documents are novels, instances of a literary genre that in America has always been tied up with the idea of nationhood, because it is "a form which deals with change in human personality and human society," that is, with individual and social life that has broken the cake of custom. In treating its inevitable subject the American novel brings "to the surface those values, those patterns of conduct, those dilemmas, psychological and technological, which abide within the human predicament," thereby proposing answers to the questions: What are we? Who are we? ("Novel," 1023). The tentative and open form of the novel associates with democratic philosophy; its morality confirms an identity between democracy and fiction. "The novel," Ellison explains in an interview, "is a complex agency for the symbolic depiction of experience, and it demands that the writer be willing to look at both sides of characters and issues. . . . You might say that the form of the novel imposes its morality upon the novelist by demanding a complexity of vision and an openness to the variety and depth of experience" ("Study," 428).

Ellison sees the discussion of the nature of democratic life taking place in texts, but this is not to say he believes reality is exclusively linguistic, or that the texts embodying the varied concepts of democratic life exist autonomously. Using his exemplary autobiography to illustrate the origins of an outlook, he offers an ample listing in "Hidden Name and Complex Fate" of the materials he gathered for art in his formative years. In addition to weather, the sounds of black people's voices, and experiences of the physical world reminiscent of the catalogued responses of Richard Wright's sensibility that impressed him when he reviewed *Black Boy* (*S&A*, 81), Ellison cites the characters of players of the "dozens," fortunetellers, bootleggers, "men who did anything well," blind blues singers, "Negroes who were part Indian . . . and Indians who had children who lived in towns as Negroes, . . . certain Jews, Mexicans, Chinese cooks, a German orchestra conductor and an English grocer who owned a Franklin touring car. And certain Negro mechanics . . . who had so assimilated the automobile that they seemed to be behind a steering wheel even as they walked the streets or danced with girls. And there were the whites who despised us and the others who shared our hardships and our joys" (*S&A*, 158–59). Each figure independently suggests an anecdote that might develop as a story of uniqueness; collectively they defy the expectations of categorization by race, class, or type. Like the legendary jazzmen they imply a transcendence of the limits upon the self. Their lives, too, might be art, and, in telling of their diversity, the writer like Ellison would appropriate from life the sense of human potentiality and plasticity that links the values of fiction with the principles of democracy.

"The novel," Ellison declares, "is a way of possessing life, of slowing it down, and giving it the writer's own sense of values in a deliberately and subtly structured way" ("Novel," 1023), which is another way of saying that art objectifies the subjective experiences, making available to the audience the substance of a consciousness that through the discipline of art—its morality and techniques—has acquired a way of seeing and feeling, summoning and directing the imagination (*S&A*, 162).

Ellison's faith in the novel depends upon a further point that is implicit in his adoption of a speaking voice in some of his writings, his evident interest in readings of the classic American novels, and the metaphor for audience he presents as the little man at Chehaw Station. Fiction is social communication. It exists only as it is read. The reader's subjectivity is equally important as the writer's consciousness objectified in the text. The novel is a product of the self and, at the same time, becomes something different from the self, namely, an object in the world. The reader who discerns and participates in the writer's intention by recovering the transmuted world in art freely chooses to enter a contract with the writer by the terms of which art becomes a collective enterprise. Thus, writer and reader form a community of free equals offering by their relationship a prevision of a fuller democracy. In the works of Mark Twain, Herman Melville, Stephen Crane, *and* Ralph Ellison, the prevision gains added sanction from the direct attention given to democracy by writers with an abiding faith in it, but even writers who ignore democratic obligations altogether participate in the community of freedom that distinguishes the aesthetic dimension of life. They can not choose to do otherwise. Nothing could be more important, then, than creating structures of reality that are consistent with their artistic medium, and no recognition could be more significant to the artist than that he or she engages in the democratic culture.

Ellison's dislike of hard-boiled individualistic writers grows out of a belief that their techniques and outlook contradict the quality of aesthetic community, but criticism of hard-boiled mannerism is comparatively easy. Much more difficult is developing a criterion to distinguish the stereotype on a philosophical level from the profound structures of democratically enhancing art that arise, we recall, in similarly subjective ways. Complexity of reference is one measure but not a sufficient one, because Ellison's own concepts often display a simplified eloquence echoing the "self-evident" declarations of eighteenth-century political writing. The inadequacy of stereotypes, starkly asserted or embedded in complex writing, is to be discerned in their employment of false resolutions to the basic contradictions of American experience.

America's "founders asserted the noble idea of creating a free, open society while retaining slavery, a system in direct contradiction to their rhetorically inclusive concept of freedom. Thus, from the beginning, racism has mocked the futuristic dream of democracy" ("Essential," 137). Stereotypes confront this contradiction with "symbolic magic" by which "the white American seeks to resolve the dilemma arising between his democratic beliefs and certain antidemocratic practices, between his acceptance of the sacred democratic belief that all men are created equal and his treatment of every tenth man as though he were not" (*S&A*, 28). Patently ridiculous representations of blacks as biologically unfit to participate in democratic fraternity resolve the contradiction between practice and belief with racist myth. Yet, even among those made queasy by overt racism, a racial segregation persists within the mind, as though the reconciliation of North and South that provided the dénouement to the Civil War and Reconstruction by effectively excluding blacks from the national economic and political life also erased them from white public memory.

According to Ellison's reading, the black once served as the inevitable symbol of humanity in literature written by the generation that spanned the time of the Civil War, and the rebelliousness of authors repulsed by the conventional evil of "civilization" projected fraternal association of blacks and whites as their social ideal (*S&A*, 32–33). Alas, by the mid-twentieth century it was no longer true. The Negro remained resident in the American consciousness to the extent that "it is practically impossible for the white Americans to think of sex, of economics, his children or womenfolk, or of sweeping socio-political changes, without summoning . . . fear-flecked images of black men." But now the white American, even the literary artist, rejects his own consciousness "discarding an ambiguous substance which the artists of other cultures would confront boldly and humanize into the stuff of tragic art" (*S&A*, 100). Legalized racism of the past was an outrageous denial of human community, but the evasion of the significance of the black in contemporary public discourse is equally outrageous, for it is an act of bad faith, positing a separation of white and black that cannot, and did not, in fact, ever exist. Failing to confront the existence of black Americans even for the purpose of constructing a myth to resolve the contradiction between pragmatic morality and the creed that supposedly informs our institutional life, the new segregationists of the intellect invalidate their own conceptions of reality and can produce only more stereotypes.

Finally, in addition to exposing the stereotypes of racists and the segregationists of the intellect, there is the more subtle problem of judging and describing the inadequacy of the social science Ellison deplores. This sort of writing on the Afro-American does not conspicuously evade the contradiction between professions of Americanism and its practices; still, as his review of Myrdal and his response to Irving Howe indicate, Ellison sees in the sociological habit of thought no chance of texts that will be worthy of the democratic literary tradition. Melville or Twain could emplot their fictions as tragedy because of their conceptions of the black in society, but no tragedy can pertain when the actors are defined as objects of history disabled by their exterior circumstances from imitating the legendary figures of the Oklahoma frontier and leaping the boundaries of the enclosing circle that enforcers of practical order think they can draw about the alien blacks. Ellison is probably convinced that most of the new "friends of the Negro" mean well, but in their own way, he might say, the concepts embodying and expressing their concern for blacks are still little better than segregationist, because they do not acknowledge human kinship beneath outward circumstances.

Those who struggle over the definition of American reality are united in a dialectic that replicates the reciprocal relationships that characterize America. Particularly on the level of culture there is an irrepressible movement toward integration illustrated, among other ways, by the three examples of cultural pluralism in "The Little Man at Chehaw Station": (1) a recollection of the Tuskegee teacher who taught Ellison never to substitute mere technique for artful structure of emotion—that teacher, Hazel Harrison, had been a successful concert performer, a student of Ferruccio Busoni, and a friend of world-renowned figures in music, including Sergei Prokofiev, who presented her with a signed manuscript; (2) his observations of "a light-skinned, blue-eyed, Afro-American-featured young man" clad in dashiki and English riding clothes who set up a reflex camera on Riverside Drive to photograph himself in histrionic poses beside a customized Volkswagen Beetle; and (3) his anecdote of a startling encounter in a basement of the formerly black section of New York City called San Juan Hill, with coal heavers who carried on an expert discussion of operatic technique they had learned by years of appearances as extras at the Metropolitan Opera in the southern idiomatic vernacular of formally uneducated Afro-American workingmen. The latter occurrence especially seemed a great "American joke . . . centered on the incongruities of race, economic status, and culture" that vastly extended his "appreciation of the arcane ways of American cultural possibility" ("Little Man," 48).

Any comprehensive study of American music, dance, language, costume, cuisine, or, for that matter, mating practices might provide the evidence to substantiate Ellison's impressionistic anecdotes and put the lie to the notion that the races are separate. Useful as such proof of syncretism might be as further illustration of democratic exchange, Ellison's main interest in culture remains disclosure of the motive for creation. "Who wills to be a Negro?" he asks at one point in *Shadow and Act*. "*I* do!" (*S&A*, 132). And so do the musicians who play black music and the storytellers whose tales project their Afro-American identity in an improvised vernacular that is the equivalent of jazz. Again and again he proclaims that cultural expression comes from the urge to control reality. The blues, he says in explanation, is "an assertion of the irrepressibly human over all circumstances whether created by others or by one's own human failings" (*S&A*, 246). The voice of his long-time friend Jimmy Rushing carries a "rock-bottom sense of reality, coupled with our sense of the possibility of rising above it" (*S&A*, 242). And although the blues is not obvious political protest, it is "an art form and thus a transcendence of those conditions created within the Negro community by the denial of social justice" (*S&A*, 257). No wonder Jimmy Rushing, Charlie Christian, and Mahalia Jackson appear in the essays as leaders of ritual in the community. Their performance draws the audience into a sacred rite celebrating the musician-hero and affirming the presence within their ceremony of the central principle of collective Afro-American life—the control of destiny by aesthetic will that was once the slaves' means of humanizing their servitude.

Ellison has been criticized for weighing the material circumstances of oppression too lightly in the balance with his convictions about this power of Afro-American cultural initiative. Apart from his sympathetic exposition of Richard Wright's "almost unrelieved picture of a personality corrupted by brutal environment" (*S&A*, 81), Ellison writes only twice at length about the bleakness of oppression. Once is the essay "The Way It Is," originally printed in *New Masses*. In this reconstructed interview, a Harlem woman voices the bitterness she feels about sacrificing for the war effort of a country that evidently intends to do nothing about "all the little Hitlers over here" (*S&A*,

289). This is the closest Ellison may have ever come to the familiar mode of protest writing. Just as unique in the Ellison canon is the piece titled "Harlem is Nowhere," unprinted before *Shadow and Act*. In a discussion of the Lafargue Clinic's psychiatric treatment of patients without defense against the chaos that threatens their personalities, he comes nearer than anywhere else to attempting a total analysis of the Afro-American condition. The report mentions that "talented youths . . . leap through the development of decades in a brief twenty years" (*S&A*, 296), but its burden is description of the people who stumble through anxiety and alienation because their abrupt arrival in the modern world has stripped them of the supports of traditional folk culture, while for the old reasons of racial discrimination they are denied a place in a new institutional life that might nurture them through change. In a rare combination of the approach of historical anthropology and the philosophy of democratic idealism, Ellison limns *this* Harlem as an area of perverse freedom, the home base, perhaps, of Bliss Proteus Rinehart.

These exceptional departures of Ellison's from his usual stance in nonfiction point up the genuine need for a defense of his work against the charge that it takes too sanguine a view of Afro-American life, because it ordinarily minimizes the effects of material reality. For all his concern with combating the vicious and dehumanizing stereotypes, his struggle over the nature of reality takes place on the level of concept; and despite the undoubted attraction of the frontiersman's autobiography and the celebratory characterizations of black artists, these portrayals may be said to be just momentary pauses between the beats of day-to-day living.

There is no possibility of converting the criticism into a depiction of Ellison as an ingenuous optimist. On the contrary, he has no doubt that evil will always define the plot of the American story and some form of victimization will always be with us, although he aims to see that racial prejudice will not determine the designation of evil or scapegoat (*Interviews*, 69–70). Whether we call that conservatism or realism, Ellison's nonfiction still must be seen as conducting its campaign on a site that even by analogy cannot be identified with the location of the socioeconomic conflict that necessarily preoccupies the mass of black people.

Nevertheless there is a ready defense to be made, and it is not sophistically tricky, equivocal, or dependent upon establishing culture as a superior reality. Ralph Ellison is not evasive or casuistic. In a paraphrase of Kenneth Burke, his favorite theorist, he says that the words evoking democratic principles are

> charismatic terms for transcendent order. . . . Being forms of symbolic action, they tend, through their nature as language, to sweep us in tow as they move by a process of linguistic negation toward the ideal. As a form of *symbolic* action, they operate by negating nature as a given and amoral condition, creating endless series of man-made or man-imagined positives. . . . In this way . . . man uses language to moralize both nature and himself. ("Little Man," 35)

So, of course, these words are involved in a search for a system of aesthetics and they influence our expositions in the area of artistic form, but precisely how do they actually become active influences in the realm of sociopolitical life? Here the argument needs a development that must be inferred from the tone and total effect of Ellison's nonfiction.

The subsystem of language in art is social as well as symbolic action, social for the reasons explained in the discussion of the community of writer and reader as a prevision of democracy, active because the qualitative difference of aesthetic language from the immediate physical world generates new behavior. Detaching themselves from the empirical world in order to apprehend the recreated world of art, writers, performers, and their audiences experience reality with its shape and underlying principles laid open by virtue of art's conceptual structures. The world in art presents a more complete entity than the empirical world; thus, it becomes an engaging totality without mystification, yet at the same time a totality possessing the power to enhance life through appropriation of the significance of reality to consciousness. The processes of art, its creation and reception, found a zone of freedom, even for the oppressed. The audience recognizes human intention, a piece of deliberate work, in the creation of the aesthetic artifact. Collaborating in the task of completing the work or artifact, the reader or listener finds immanent his or her own freedom and possibility of intentional action. Moreover, the substance of art induces reflection, perhaps through recognition of plausibility in the story, admiration of technique, or identification with a character to accompany identification with the artist. That reflection experienced as discovery redresses the sense of powerlessness and alienation previously felt amid the welter of routine events. Set free, however briefly, by the aid of art, the audience is prepared to abandon spontaneous or reflexive behavior and to act with the same deliberate intention as the artists toward the world. For example, in the communion of the blues the audience joins with the singer to supplant suffering with the splendid control of tragicomic lyricism, or readers of *Invisible Man* who join the protagonist in his quest realize that because their own identity, like his, entails no obligation to the expectations of others, they have achieved a decisive moment of self-knowledge and are free to make themselves in action.

Shadow and Act has much further use, too, as a guide to Ellison's fiction. As he points out in his *Paris Review* interview, each section of *Invisible Man* "begins with a sheet of paper; each piece of paper is exchanged for another and contains a definition of his identity, or the social role he is to play as defined by others" (*S&A*, 177). In other words, a contest of concepts regarding American reality conducted through textual relations and interrelations forms an armature for the novel's plot, and not only in the representation of literal texts, but also through the associations of simulated speeches and metaphoric descriptions that read as texts of commentary about approximations and departures from the intent of the principal documents that founded the ideal of

American democracy. Together this intertextuality within the complex enveloping form of the novel constitutes Ellison's assessment of the contradictions in which the possibility of making history is born.

The making of history—Ellison's ultimate subject—has subjective significance, for the freedom to act intentionally and humanize the world arises in consciousness. One becomes an historical actor by coming to know one can transcend the conditions made by others. The anecdotes and selective memories we receive as Ellison's inchoate autobiography in the nonfiction take their tone and form from the need to represent the first emergence of what philosophers would call his project. We feel the episodes are fragmentary, because doubtless the sense of the possibility of becoming one's own product could only have been seen in glimpses, at first. Acquaintance with purposive life awaited his meeting with musicians in the black community whose witness he celebrates in the essays grouped under the rubric "Sound and Mainstream." The discipline enabling Ellison to initiate his own transcendent project he discovered through literature, the art whose semantic and referential nature can synthesize the entire range of human experience. Finally, through the happy accident of living in the culture of a nation preoccupied with its social novelty, Ellison located in the founding texts of America the words that addressed his emergence as a writer as well as a citizen. Thus, the subtext of *Shadow and Act* charts the evolution of its author's conscious motive. Here are the particulars that will be overlooked if the reader looks for a conventionally drawn autobiography, particulars that explain the necessity to counter stereotypes that would deny his capacity, because of his race, to enter history as a conscious player. As a self-determining figure, then, he writes his primary text—the evidently topical discussions—out of devotion to confronting the American contradiction of race and democracy with a theory meant to surpass the contradiction, a theory explaining the appearance of a synthetic democratic culture that acquires its requisite vigor from the Afro-American arts.

Let us, therefore, take Ralph Ellison at his word when he tells us that the significance of *Shadow and Act* is basically autobiographical, not because he tells us things that can interest us only because he is a famous writer, but because this autobiographer addresses the fundamental literary question: Why write? In the answer he gives, we find both the essential Ralph Ellison and his compelling democratic testament.

NOTES

1. Ralph Ellison, in the Introduction to *Shadow and Act*, xviii. All subsequent citations of this source appear in text as *S&A*.

2. The position was developed most fully in James S. Allen, *The Negro Question in America*.

3. Joseph Stalin, *Marxism and the National and Colonial Question* (London: n.d.), 8. [A paperback edition of this work was printed in the U.S.]

WORKS CITED

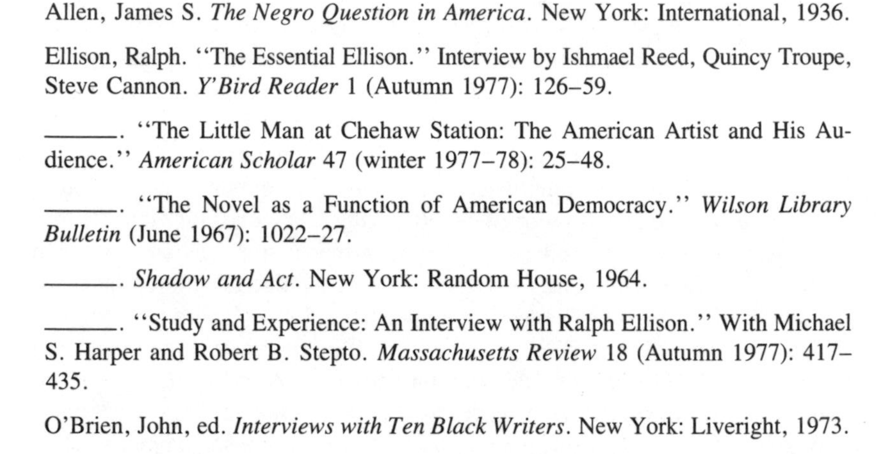

Allen, James S. *The Negro Question in America*. New York: International, 1936.

Ellison, Ralph. "The Essential Ellison." Interview by Ishmael Reed, Quincy Troupe, Steve Cannon. *Y'Bird Reader* 1 (Autumn 1977): 126–59.

______. "The Little Man at Chehaw Station: The American Artist and His Audience." *American Scholar* 47 (winter 1977–78): 25–48.

______. "The Novel as a Function of American Democracy." *Wilson Library Bulletin* (June 1967): 1022–27.

______. *Shadow and Act*. New York: Random House, 1964.

______. "Study and Experience: An Interview with Ralph Ellison." With Michael S. Harper and Robert B. Stepto. *Massachusetts Review* 18 (Autumn 1977): 417–435.

O'Brien, John, ed. *Interviews with Ten Black Writers*. New York: Liveright, 1973.

Stalin, Joseph. *Marxism and the National and Colonial Question*. London: n.d. Also: San Francisco: Proletarian Pubs., 1975.

Shadowing Ellison

JOHN WRIGHT

Nicknaming is a deadly art in black communities, Ralph Ellison taught us some years ago in a time of trial, an art much practiced in a tightly pressed but voluble social world supremely aware of the power of words to mask, to reveal, to assault, or to embrace whatever human beings do and are that warrants being codified. Streetcorner raconteurs have made nicknaming an analogical and hyperbolic art devoted to sizing up the ludicrous and the laudable, to extracting essences; and masters at "capping" simultaneously wreak havoc and do homage with simple sobriquets. So it suits vernacular tradition that poet Michael Harper's testamental riffs have bestowed "The Big E" on Ellison himself. For such a monicker evokes the muscular skill and grace of some Harlem hoopster or the vital force of some streetlife magnifico as an analogue for the expressive energy of a major literary intellect. It unmasks the bodacious homeboy in a heady man of words. And of that coming-to-terms with articulate elders which the communal will to continuity and memory requires, it makes a celebration.

A grimmer spectacle, though, has hypnotized the public eye during the past decade and a half through the literary politics which, Ellison himself admits, turned him for a moment in history into "a hateful straw man" targeted by radical discontent.[1] There has been in this an unwitting rehearsal of those ancient rituals of sacrifice and exculpation around a scapegoat king that Ellison, ironically, anatomized years earlier in a provocative review essay on the private torments and public fate of fabled, waggishly monickered jazzman Charlie "Yardbird" Parker.[2] Little of the orgiastic excesses and frenzied cult worship that ultimately maimed and martyred Bird has surfaced in Ralph Ellison's experience as a writer. But in the much pandered images of Ellison

Reprinted by permission of the author. This article is an abridged version of a longer essay, "Dedicated Dreamer, Consecrated Acts: Shadowing Ellison," which originally appeared in *Carleton Miscellany* 18, No. 3 (Winter 1980): 142–99.

as literary lion playing scarecrow to an irreverent, besieging throng of the black-plumed disaffected, there is *more* than a little of the spectacle he had so wryly described of the darktown rebel artist become, in reverse proportion to the intensity of his own creative struggles, a white hero-victim and black reprobate picked clean and picked again—like jazz lore's Poor Robin—before a culturally disoriented and divided public which has but the dimmest notion of his real significance.

But with the savant's grasp of social ritual—and his entanglement in it—Ellison, unlike Bird, marshalled the fortitude he cites as essential equipment for any vital man or artist and endured patiently the rites of political assault that threatened for a while to reduce the debate on his work and life "to the level of the dirty dozens" ("Study," 427). That same fortitude has sustained forty years of battlefield maneuvers in the literary career he has long conceived of as "a guerrilla action in a larger war, in which I found some of the most treacherous assaults against me committed by those who regarded themselves either as neutrals, as sympathizers, or as disinterested military advisers" (*S&A*, 128). Ellison traces his schooling in stylish forbearance to the Georgia-born, plantation-bred mother whose frontier odyssey in turn-of-the-century Oklahoma produced, among other things, a son whose passion for reading, dreams of faraway places, and drive to excel she nourished with the rich texture of her own limit-defying personal and political experience, and with her counterbalancing "tolerance for the affairs of the world."[3] He credits too, more obliquely, the father who named him and then died when he was three—the ex-soldier, construction foreman, and lover of books who bequeathed his infant son the hidden name and complex fate of a poet and philosopher, which a recalcitrant, music-minded Ralph Waldo Ellison would, through a first unconscious, then mysterious, then consuming process, discipline his life to achieve. And in dedicating the collection of essays which still comprises the most profound statement of the pluralist position in Afro-American letters, to one Morteza Sprague, "A Dedicated Dreamer in a Land Most Strange," Ellison has acknowledged his indebtedness also to the idealistic black teachers who, by their own example, helped him see that dreamers could function responsibly and durably even in a nightmare world.

That the dreamer's bent might be transformed by literary technique into consecrated acts of staggering power, Ellison claims first to have glimpsed through his Tuskegee confrontation with T.S. Eliot's *Waste Land* in 1935. And, decades later, from Eliot's "Hollow Men," he gleaned a title for the American drama of power and pathos his gathered fugitive essays tried to name: "Between the idea / and the reality / Between the motion / and the act / Falls the Shadow." To return to *Shadow and Act* now, when many of the specific issues the essays addressed are faint, at best, in the popular imagination, must be justified by a focus on what it is they hold of enduring relevance, and on what—when their chronology is straightened somewhat and the broader context in which they originally appeared sketched out—

they can reveal about the movement to maturity of one of the nation's most important literary minds. Despite Ellison's longevity in the public eye, we still know little about these things.

Ralph Ellison's fiction, essays, interviews, and speeches have been characteristically canny and complex. And both white and black readers of *Invisible Man* and *Shadow and Act* have routinely, even ritually, approached the politics, the art, and the "racial" values these books codify in terms narrower than those Ellison himself proposes. In consequence, the body of "conscious thought" he has erected since the late 1930s has been left in shadow, artificially isolated from its intellectual roots in Afro-American tradition, and almost invariably denied a critical context as pluralistic in its techniques and cultural references as Ellison's extraordinary eclecticism demands.

The central drama of his work is the unraveling imaginative confrontation with the chimeric forms of power and of freedom. Drawn initially into writing, he has told us, by the desire to understand "the aesthetic nature of literary power" and the devices through which literature commands the mind and emotions, he found himself, "like a sleepwalker searching for some important object," seized with a sense of mission to preserve in art, as codified in Afro-American experience, "those human values which can endure by confronting change" (*S&A*, 35, 39–40). The essays and interviews of *Shadow and Act* are his witness to a shift of role and strategy in a continuing quest for power and possibility. They chronicle his "slow precarious growth of consciousness" and the related effort "to confront, to peer into, the shadow of my past and to remind myself of the complex resources for imaginative creation that are my heritage" (xix). From the early, doctrinaire jottings in his collected and uncollected articles, reviews, and short fiction, through the proliferating series of recent interviews, speeches, and profiles that have marked the anxious watch for his second novel, Ellison has been formulating his own "program" for a black literary initiative. And he has enlisted himself "for the duration" in what he agreed with Wright was the pivotal political battle of American culture—the struggle between black people and white over the very nature of reality. Contrary to Wright's spartan ideological perception, however, for Ellison this is not the unrelievedly grim and morally unambiguous confrontation of a group and its allies challenging the defenders of an existing horror, but rather a tragicomic battle royal, the painful joke of which squares off two interbred, interdependent peoples each of whom knows *its* experience is the real American experience, knows the other group knows as much, and cannot understand why they won't admit it.

From Ellison's effort to carry on the combat, what has emerged in the course of forty-odd years of writing is a dynamic but self-consistent body of "conscious thought" devoted to transforming the themes, the enigmas, the contradictions of character and culture native to the Afro-American predicament, into literary capital. The Du Boisian echoes of Ellison's opening paragraphs in *Shadow and Act* —the Icarian image of himself "with these thin essays for wings . . . launched full flight into the dark" where "beyond the veil of consciousness" he seeks to function responsibly, "to range widely and, sometimes, even to soar" (ix, xi)—mark the visionary and poetic mode in Ellison's essays. Though more muted than in Du Bois and largely unremarked by critics, it signals a shared thrust beyond the attractive but reductive materialism of Marxist political theory to a more humane and liberating vision animated both by classical humanism and by the cultural ethos and spiritual strivings of black folk.

This liberating vision in Ellison's work reveals at least four major organizing impulses, four intermingled disciplining strategies for divining order in the experience he knows and for converting that experience into potent symbolic action: the *syncretic* impulse in his "passion to link together all I loved within the Negro community and all those things I felt in the world which lay beyond" (*S&A*, 31); the *celebratory* impulse to explore "the full range of American Negro humanity" and to affirm the attitudes and values which give Afro-American life "its sense of wholeness and which render it bearable and human, and when measured by our own terms, desirable" (xviii, 36); the *dialectical* impulse behind his "ceaseless questioning of those formulas through which historians, politicians, sociologists, and an older generation of Negro leaders and writers—those of the so-called Negro Renaissance—had evolved to describe my group's identity, its predicament, its fate and its relation to the larger society and the culture which we share" (xvii); and finally the *demiurgic* impulse to seek cultural power and personal freedom through art, to propose "an idea of human versatility and possibility which went against the barbs or over the palings of almost every fence which those who controlled social and political power had erected to restrict our roles in the life of the country" (xii). The object ultimately was to dominate reality by a willed projection of cultural personality nourished on the highly developed Afro-American ability to abstract desirable qualities even from enemies and on the "yearning to make any and everything of quality *Negro American*; to appropriate it, possess it, recreate it in our own group and individual images" (*S&A*, xiv).

The literary imagination, as a comprehensive way of perceiving and controlling, as "a form of energy through which experience is transformed into consciousness,"[4] became Ellison's agency for guiding these impulses and for answering the questions: "Who am I, what am I, how did I come to be? What shall I make of the life around me, what celebrate, what reject, how confront the snarl of good and evil which is inevitable? What does American society *mean* when regarded out of my *own* eyes, when informed by my own sense of the past and viewed by my *own* complex sense of the present?" (*S&A*, xix). From his vantage point in culture, regional geography and the social hierarchy, and out of his commitment to a wry Cartesian doubting of all negative definitions imposed on him by others, Ralph Ellison has tested and sifted and remolded the prevailing concepts of man, of culture, of the national experience, of high art and popular traditions, of the links between art and freedom, in order to fashion a credo capable of comprehending that experience in all its mystery, contradiction, and plurality. The syncretic, the celebratory, the dialectical, and the demiurgic impulses that shape his critical vision mediate the tensions between the concepts he confronts and the experience he knows in the same way that technique—ever the key to creative freedom for Ellison—mediates the tension between human desire and human ability.

Ellison's syncretic drive to combine, reconcile, and reintegrate competing cultural realities is amply evident throughout his work, but nowhere more suggestively than in his theories of Afro-American and American character and nowhere more unexpectedly than in his resurrection of Renaissance Man. In order to reveal the truths of his own experience and those around him, Ralph Ellison quite early discovered the need for a concept of man and a concept of culture that could illuminate that blind spot of irrationality Americans called "The Negro problem"—that site in psychic geography where he saw theologians and humanists and social scientists alike stumble, and "where Marx cries out for Freud and Freud for Marx" (*S&A*, 297).

* * *

The conceptual keys for distilling fragmentary patterns of sense, memory, imagination, and rite into a new codification of Afro-American ethos and world view Ellison discovered, in part, in the philosophic criticism of Kenneth Burke. Decades ahead of the anthropologists who have turned to Ernest Cassirer and to Burke for a semiotic concept of culture, Ralph Ellison appropriated the theories of symbolic action after first hearing Burke's critique of Adolph Hitler's *Mein Kampf* in 1937.[5] Ellison saw that to approach Afro-American culture simply as patterned behavior or as a model in the mind, or even as a mixture of the two, failed to get at the true import of a way of life whose profound, inescapable material constraints and compensatorily muscular subjective structures implied beings who defined themselves, and dealt with the existential dilemmas of living, through the medium of symbolic actions. Neither material reflex or disengaged ideation, symbolic action gave ritual form to the attitudes people worked out, in solitude or in concert, for coping with real situations. And though we hardly recognized it, much of human "reality" consisted of such systems of gyroscopic meanings. For Man, as Burke conceived him, was quintessentially a symbol-making, self-fabricating being who struggled compulsively for order amid the clutter of self-propagated signs and metaphors that constituted human culture. Humanity's cultural creations—myths, religion, folklore, music, dance, visual art, science, and literature—were all symbolic "equipments for living," stylized strategies for naming or prescribing attitudes toward recurring human problems. And the pattern of black life especially, as Burke pictured it, embodied a "complex, subtle, and gratifying" symbolicity that, under intense pressure, mediated aesthetically between the beleaguered life of the body and the processes of spiritual gratification (Burke, 366–67).

As Ellison employed it, such a view made visible and dynamic black cultural patterns that had been shrouded by the concept of race or misinterpreted mechanistically as impassive artifacts, traits, and survivals. Ellison saw Afro-American life expressed "in a body of folklore, in the musical forms of the spirituals, jazz, and the blues; in an idiomatic version of American speech . . .; a cuisine; a body of dance forms and even a dramaturgy which is generally unrecognized as such because still tied to the more folkish Negro churches" (*S&A*, 254). But the culture itself consisted of actions, symbolic actions, that were no less real for often being checked, diverted, or concealed. Again, his accolade to Richard Wright's blues-toned autobiography, even as it marked the maturation of Ellison's prose style and offered penetrating literary insights, also provoked a cultural redefinition and a new awareness of covert black symbol systems. Besides presenting the now classic definition of the blues as a complex, cathartic symbolic strategy, Ellison attempted to describe in "Richard Wright's Blues" how, crucial for self-definition, black people always had had a margin of freedom to choose the cultural means and ends with which they would confront the destiny white oppression had prepared for them.

That the resultant symbolic maneuvering might distort the "inner world" or be maladaptive was evident to Ellison in the "homeopathic" intrafamilial violence and "pre-individualistic" values southern black communities employed, in the face of organized terrorism, to deflect the individual will from dangerous self-assertion (*S&A*, 94, 96). It was evident also in the deceptively "physical" character of black expressive culture, where music and dance were frenziedly erotic; religious ceremony violently ecstatic; speech rhythmical, gestural, and imagistic. But this sensuousness, Ellison admonished, did not "mean" the simple spontaneity of primitives and peasants that whites often interpreted it to be. For Afro-American life existed "in the seething vortex of those tensions generated by the most industrialized of Western nations," and the physicality offered as evidence of the black man's primitive simplicity was "actually the form of his complexity." In response to social conditions that drove the self in turn from comatose to hysterical states, black dance, for instance, had become a symbolic strategy for creating an alternative form of consciousness that approximated a reverse cataleptic trance: "Instead of his consciousness being lucid to the reality around it while the body is rigid, here it is the body which is alert, reacting to pressures which the constricting forces of Jim Crow block off from the transforming, concept-creating activity of the brain.The 'eroticism' of Negro expression springs from much the same conflict as that displayed in the violent gesturing of a man who attempts to express a complicated concept with a limited vocabulary;

thwarted ideational energy is converted into unsatisfactory pantomime, and his words are overburdened with meanings they cannot convey'' (*S&A*, 99–100). Ideas and concepts which the intellect could not or dare not formulate, Ellison hypothesized, were literally being, in Burke's terms, ''danced out,'' albeit unsatisfactorily. And because the defensive character of black life transmuted the human ''will toward organization'' into a ''will to camouflage, to dissimulate,'' the public meanings symbolized in such cultural forms were so distorted ''as to render their recognition as difficult as finding a wounded quail against the brown and yellow leaves of a Mississippi thicket'' (*S&A*, 103–104). Deciphering the covert symbolic meanings of Afro-American culture required the methodology of a quail hunt, then, Ellison hinted metaphorically, and hunters sympathetic enough with the quarry to be able to ask themselves and to answer: ''Where would I hide if *I* were a wounded quail?''

That this mode of cultural inquiry would be neither an inspiring jaunt nor a pilgrimage for wound-worshipers, Ellison made clear in another essay unpublished before *Shadow and Act*, written in 1948 while he was hard at work on *Invisible Man*. ''Harlem is Nowhere'' presented his existentialist reading of Afro-American culture at its bleakest and most nearly deterministic, although this meditation on a visit to a psychiatric clinic for Harlem's underprivileged acknowledged both the ''mark of oppression'' and the possibility of transcendence for men and women who had momentarily become confused before chaos. Sanity more than simple physical survival was the object of human action here, and the field for symbolic maneuver had shifted from the feudal darkness of Wright's southern nightmare world to a garish northern urban surreality. Its wastage, grotesqueries, and masquerades diverted the major energy of the imagination from creating an orienting art to overcoming the frustrations of discrimination, and to locating an alienated self in ''a labyrinthine existence among streets that explode monotonously skyward with the spires and crosses of churches and clutter underfoot with garbage and decay'' (*S&A*, 283). The Harlem Ellison portrayed here was not the New Negro Mecca and culture capital it had been to James Weldon Johnson and Alain Locke in the 1920s, but instead a wasteland ruin, ''the scene and symbol of the Negro's perpetual alienation in the land of his birth,'' and a site where symbolic possibilities proliferated even as personality became more fragmented. Here the traditional symbolic linkages between black culture and personality had been disrupted so that the symbology of transcendence was that by which the talented grandchildren of peasants who believed in magic and possessed no written literature had come to master technology and ''examine their lives through the eyes of Freud and Marx, Kierkegaard and Kafka, Malraux and Sartre'' (*S&A*, 284). The symbology of prophylaxis was that word-magic through which songs like the ''Blow Top Blues'' and vernacular expressions like ''frantic,'' ''buggy,'' and ''mad'' were conjured to neutralize the states they named: Harlemites answered the greeting, ''How are you?'' with a formulaic ''I'm nowhere, man'' that ritually objectified their feelings of homelessness and facelessness and their status as "displaced persons" (*S&A*, 287).

In the Harlem Ellison dissected here, the supports of southern black rationality—the protective peasant cynicism, the sense of rootedness, the authoritative religion, the gyroscopic folklore—had been largely surrendered and not replaced through migration northward, as "the near themeless technical virtuosity of bebop" did not replace the lyrical, ritual elements of folk jazz. So, black people had lost many of the symbolic bulwarks they had placed between themselves and the threat of chaos. The patients at the Lafargue Clinic had succumbed to "irrational, incalculable forces that hover about the edges of human life like cosmic destruction lurking within an atomic stockpile" (*S&A*, 286), and for them the last-ditch symbology of survival was the white man's frustrated psychic science, deflected from the treatment of a sick social order, and incapable of dispelling the unreality that haunted Harlem, but modestly attuned to helping bewildered black patients understand themselves and their environment enough to "reforge the will to endure in a hostile world" (*S&A*, 289).

Against the backdrop of this tragic adaptation of symbolic action to social pathology, the concept of Renaissance Man that Ellison reclaimed from his boyhood for *Shadow and Act* by his own admission "seems a most unlikely and even comic concept to introduce" (x). But he did so, and with a straight face, because, as taken over and transformed by his "wild free outlaw tribe" of Oklahoma boys, Renaissance Man became a potent symbol of that cultural playing with possibility and that potentially subversive processing of dream and reality which Ellison believes to be the saving dynamic of Afro-American culture. Transmitted originally "from some book or from some idealistic Negro teacher, some dreamer," and suggesting a surreptitious sociology of ideas that intellectual historians have only begun to contemplate, Renaissance Man as elaborated by Ellison's youthful cadre functioned as a projective father-surrogate for boys who, like Ellison himself, were often fatherless (*S&A*, xi, xiii). It offered, he reflected, a way to fuse symbolically the black middle-class faith in education, and the idea of self-cultivation, with a notion of aristocratic elegance that was fervently populist and full of roguish style. A strategic antidote to self-hate and defensiveness, it formulated an ideal image of intellectual competence and verve which was neither foppish nor effete. It encouraged self-discipline and expansive growth. And it "violated all ideas of social hierarchy and order and all accepted conceptions of the hero handed down by cultural, religious, and racist tradition": "Gamblers and scholars, jazz musicians and scientists, Negro cowboys and soldiers from the Spanish-American and First World Wars, movie stars and stunt men, figures from the Italian Renaissance and literature, both classical and popular, were combined with the special virtues of some local bootlegger, the eloquence of some Negro preacher, the strength and grace of some local athlete, the ruthlessness of some businessman-physician, the elegance in dress and manners of some headwaiter or hotel doorman" (*S&A*, xiii).

* * *

The relation of this conception of communal style and ideal character to Ellison's encompassing view of the national culture is clear enough: Renaissance Man is an analogue, a metaphor for the broader cultural processes and national character as historically evolved. Ellison's theories of American national culture cast aside completely "the sterile concept of race" (while conceding that the relations between culture and biology remain "mysterious") and carefully distinguish the forms of the nation's inner "spiritual" life, as projected in the imagination, from the forms of material compulsion. Like American literary nationalists from Emerson onward, Ellison's is the "organic" theory, Herderian in origin, that national culture is, or ought to be, a crystallization in language, music, dance, architecture, art, and literature, of the character of the people as a whole and the contours of the land. The radical heterogeneity of a population compressed together through colonial conquest, slavery, and immigration, and through the democratic principles that rationalized revolution, is the prime support, in Ellison's construct, of the cultural pluralism and the egalitarian "folk ideology" which he has inherited and extended. His roguish Renaissance Man, though, supplants Emerson's Representative Man as a projection of national possibility; and the jazz, folk blues, city/country, cinematic, and vernacular folk/classical amalgam he personifies represents a new pluralism, philosophical and cultural, revived and progressively indigenized by Ellison's integrative use of the Emerson-Whitman legacy, the theories of Constance Rourke, the literary works of Melville, Twain, and Faulkner, the critical insights of Kenneth Burke and Stanley Edgar Hyman, and the social thought of W.E.B. Du Bois and Alain Locke.

The strain of pluralist social thought in Ellison's speculations about the national culture has its broader antecedents in Thomas Paine's Quakerism and immigrant Hector St. John de Crèvecoeur's agrarian cultural ecumenism; in Emerson's and Whitman's and Margaret Fuller's transcendentalist advocacy of a "spiritual" fusion of the races; in William James's pluriverse and John Dewey's promulgation of the "Freedom to Be One's Best Self"; in Randolph Bourne's image of a "Trans-National America"; and in the ideas of philosophers Horace Kallen and Alain Locke. Always at war with racism, with nativist xenophobia, and with the antiamalgamation doctrine of racial purists, it has characteristically been a submerged, antinomian current in our intellectual and imaginative life, championed in its fullest implications mainly by out-groups and radical democrats. For Ellison, the pluralist outlook afforded the only version of the past that could explain the complex present, and offered the only prospect for a livable future. To him, the misnamed "Negro problem" has been the most potent symbol of the issues raised in America by the plurality of races and cultures. And the enduring relevance and power for him of the nineteenth-century works of Whitman, Emerson, Thoreau, Hawthorne, Melville, and Twain is that, for them, he argues, the question of the Negro and other races in the development of an American literature was an "organic" part of the debate (49).

And the question of slavery—it was not termed a "Negro problem" then, he tells us—was "a vital issue in the American consciousness, symbolic of the condition of man, and a valid aspect of the writer's reality" (108). But one of Ellison's most recurrent themes, elaborated earliest and most fully in the 1945 and 1946 essays "Beating That Boy" and "Twentieth-Century Fiction and the Black Mask of Humanity," is that the post-Civil War betrayal of Reconstruction exacerbated in the white American mind an ethical schizophrenia and a guilty need to "force the Negro down into the deeper level of his consciousness" (*S&A*, 109). Sterling Brown's scholarship in the late 1930s had demonstrated that the American literary imagination had historically been obsessed with the symbolic figure of the Negro—multivariously stereotypic—and Brown had initiated a critical war on literary stereotypy in support of which Ellison, with telling originality, now marshalled the psychoanalytic insights of Freud.[6] The borders between the white world and the black, Ellison argued, were not spatial or merely social, but psychological and ritual. Racial oppression's social symbiosis had a psychic counterpart which made it "practically impossible for the white American to think of sex, of economics, of crime, his children or womenfolk, or of sweeping sociopolitical changes, without summoning into consciousness fear-flecked images of black men" (*S&A*, 109). The black man in the white mind had become an ambivalently attractive and repulsive image of "the unorganized, irrational forces of American life," and the black stereotype in literature became part of a ritual of exorcism, sacrifice, and consolation that sublimated white men's guilt, confirmed obversely the "white" identity, and systematically evaded human reality. The American writer, who, Ellison insisted, could be "no freer than the society in which he lives," was inescapably but uncalculatedly tied to the currents of popular belief; and in suppressing in the moral imagination, since Reconstruction, the organic national tragedy of race, American writers, with rare exception, routinely evaded their responsibility for the health of democracy. They had "formed the habit of living and thinking in a culture that is opposed to the deep thought and feeling necessary to profound art; hence its avoidance of emotion, its fear of ideas, its obsession with mere physical violence and pain, its overemphasis of understatement, its precise and complex verbal constructions for converting goatsong into carefully modulated squeaks" (*S&A*, 110).

* * *

What Ellison has found, in the face of radical despair, to celebrate in the dream and nightmare psychopathology of American life is, first of all, the democratic principle that rebel slavemasters birthed in contradiction and which, *Jack-the-Bear* tells us, had been "dreamed into being out of the chaos and darkness of the feudal past, [then] violated and compromised to the point of absurdity'' (*IM*, 30th Anniversary Edition, 561). Beyond this unretractable promise of a future, it is not the material, technological, or institutional achievements of American civilization he exalts—its ordering forces—but rather the qualities that most closely approximate chaos and disorder: the formlessness, the fluidity, the instability, and the diversity of American life—precisely those features that American writers like Hawthorne and Henry James found cause to lament. Again, this is in Ellison not so much the obsecration of an anarchist for whom chaos is a subversive god, but the revelation of an artist for whom chaos is possibility in life as in literature. For when Ellison turns to explore the broad continuum of Afro-American experience and to affirm its enduring values, it is the ordering, stabilizing, controlling qualities he celebrates most expansively: style, discipline, technique, abstractive and assimilative powers, and will. This is no contradiction but an Hegelian corollary of Ellison's belief that ''the mixture of the marvelous and the terrible is a basic condition of human life'' and of the American experience (*S&A*, 39). As in a fairy tale, ''here the terrible represents all that hinders, all that opposes human aspiration, and the marvelous represents the triumph of the human spirit over chaos.'' And as in Marx's Hegelian phenomenology, here those who dominate through force and a contempt for human life exercise a destructive freedom that breeds death and chaos, while the dominated, forced to struggle with the world's intractability, learn its secrets and infuse it with mind. So, whether he is describing the intricate vocal pyrotechnics of Mahalia Jackson's priestly art or upholding that ''American Negro tradition which teaches one to deflect racial provocation and to master and contain pain,'' Ellison perceives black people defining and creating themselves against the background of America's chaotic mixture of the marvelous and the terrible. And though admitting that he ''would be hard put to say where the terrible could be localized in our national experience,'' he sees ''in so much of American life which lies beyond the Negro community the very essence of the terrible'' (*S&A*, 39).

This is hardly the unqualified optimism often attributed to Ellison, hardly the nonpartisan relativism that the liberal imagination embraced as supposedly separating him from Baldwin and Baraka and other black artists whose ''aggressive'' assertions of black moral and cultural superiority were allegedly inimical to the pluralist ideal. For Ellison does believe, qualifiedly, in the moral and cultural superiority of the oppressed—in a complex cultural ''secret'' wherein ''the weak do something to correct the wrongs of the strong.''[7] And he conceives of pluralism not as a passive idealism but, like his ideal prose, as ''confronting the inequalities and brutalities of our society forthrightly, but yet thrusting forth its images of hope, human fraternity and individual self-realization'' (*S&A*, 113). As a writer he rejected the idea that novels are either ''weapons'' or public relations vehicles, for the view that ''true novels, even when most pessimistic and bitter, arise out of an impulse to celebrate human life and therefore are ritualistic and ceremonial at their core'' (*S&A*, 121). The riddle posed to him by his dual commitment to the black struggle for human freedom and to the celebration of human fraternity-in-difference has been this: What values conditioned by oppression but opposed to it can be celebrated both by those who oppress and by those who are oppressed?

His answer has been to assert, first, that the condition of oppression is not the whole, or even the most salient, feature of Afro-American experience; and insofar as it is salient, oppression has not ''caused'' but only occasioned or constrained the nature of the cultural forms black folk willed into being. Their attitudes toward their ''condition,'' he emphasized in ''The World and the Jug,'' and the strategies they styled for resolving, escaping, or surviving it, could no more be caused by oppression than their will and their imagination were ''caused'' by it: ''For even as his life toughens the Negro, even as it brutalizes him, sensitizes him, dulls him, goads him to anger, moves him to irony, sometimes fracturing and sometimes affirming his hopes; even as it shapes his attitudes toward family, sex, love, religion; even as it modulates his humor, tempers his joy—it *conditions* him to deal with his life and with himself . . . He must live it and try consciously to grasp its complexity until he can change it; must live it *as* he changes it.'' Rather than the product of unmediated victimization, ''he is a product of the interaction between his racial predicament, his individual will, and the broader American cultural freedom in which he finds his ambiguous existence. Thus, he, too, in a limited way, is his own creation'' (*S&A*, 119–20).

Because even the struggle to destroy those limits took place within the context of a life that had to be lived—and might be lost—during the process of ever contested change, it was crucial, Ellison argued, to celebrate values of endurance and transcendence as well as those of revolt. For black people's ''resistance to provocation, their coolness under pressure, their sense of timing and their tenacious hold on the ideal of their ultimate freedom are indispensable values in the struggle'' and at least as characteristic as the rebelliousness militant ideology glorifies (*S&A*, 121). As such, in encompassing life's inevitable flux and agony, the strategic values of endurance, fortitude, and forbearance are not a skin to be shed but a vital legacy to be preserved, by everyone, in a violent and divided plural society where change and struggle are pervasive and survival always at issue.

The pluralist society Ellison celebrates, then, is no utopian construct predicated on the elimination of group conflict and the achievement of absolute democracy. It is, rather a living, evolving, *improvised* social order struggling toward stability, coping—and sometimes failing to cope—with the fact of its radical heterogeneity, through the principles of democratic process, on the one hand, and the hard realities of a racial and cultural ''battle royal,'' on the other. In the wake of the Negro Renaissance, Alain Locke, who in Ellison's eyes stood always for the ''conscious approach to American culture'' (''Symposium,'' 20), had elaborated, in a series of philosophical essays written between 1935 and 1944, his own theory for reintegrating into a cultural pluralist ideal the problematic facts of social diversity. Locke proposed to make the historically subordinate goal of ''unity through diversity'' the active social philosophy of American democracy. He claimed that it was, after all, our values and value systems that have divided us, ''apart from and in many cases over and above our material issues of rivalry and conflict.'' And he insisted that ''ideological peace'' could be achieved between America's contending ethnic cultures only through the pervasive diffusion of a relativistic perspective which might discover among the competing values some ''harmony in contrariety, some commonality in divergence.''[8]

As Ellison acknowledged in a 1975 commemorative symposium at Harvard, for him ''Locke was to act as a guide'' in assessing the pluralistic condition of American culture and projecting an end to ethnic antagonisms. Ellison's conviction, however, was to be the tougher, more pragmatic view that conflict is inevitable but potentially creative as well as destructive; that because ''the basic unity of human experience'' moderates social fragmentation and assures us some organic possibility of identifying with those of other backgrounds, a proud assertion of cultural personality rather than a relativistic weakening of cultural loyalties is the richest form of cultural reciprocity; and that the principles of constitutional democracy—when used strategically even by democracy's victims—are the most effective mediators of conflict. In ''The World and the Jug,'' after chiding assimilated Jewish intellectuals for writing guiltily as though Jews were responsible for slavery and segregation, Ellison suggested that ''passing for white'' through a facile identification with the power elite is where their real guilt lay, and that, in the interest of historical and social clarity, and in order to understand the specific political and cultural boons flowing from the Jewish presence, the positive distinctions between whites and Jews should be maintained. To deny or fail to make such distinctions, he asserted, ''could be offensive, embarrassing, unjust or even dangerous'' (*S&A*, 132).

The danger, he conceived, in part, to be the possible loss of the balancing forces which plural perspectives on reality provide: ''it is to forget,'' he warned very soon after in ''Hidden Name and Complex Fate,'' ''that the small share of reality which each of our diverse groups is able to snatch from the whirling chaos of history belongs not to the group alone, but to all of us. It is a property and a witness which can be ignored only to the danger of the entire nation'' (*S&A*, 167). Similarly, bound together in conflict and interdependence, *no* group within the United States, he contends, ''achieves anything without asserting its claim against the counterclaims of other groups. . . . As Americans we have accepted this conscious and ceaseless struggle as a condition of our freedom'' (*S&A*, 262). His often-reiterated term for this process, wherever it operates in private or public life, is ''antagonistic cooperation''—a dramatic and oxymoronic naming of social ambiguity rooted in Ellison's fertile strategy of infusing aesthetic concepts into social analysis, a strategy designed to yield "close readings" of the textured psychic, cultural, and political meanings in American social chaos by turning such subtle tools as poet-critic William Empson's concept of "ambiguity" into a multiform structural principle able to encompass intricacy, tragedy, dramatic irony, and progressive disorder in social spheres of buried meanings and tense contradiction.

With all its encoded ambiguities, Ellison's celebration of the one-and-the-many in American culture, then, is ultimately a dialectical pluralism, which envisions America's unprecedented polyglot and inescapably agonistic "culture of cultures" moving from lesser to greater forms of freedom only through an historical process of unending struggle. And the peculiarities of American history have made this developing social synthesis as mysterious and unpredictable as the forms of our emblematic vernacular traditions. Here, ethnicity rather than class has been the fundamental schism dividing humanity against itself—though that fact, too, is being slowly reversed by change—and the guiding teleology in the nation's arduous evolution is, in Ellison's terms, the common search for "that condition of man's being at home in the world, which is called love, and which we term democracy" (*S&A*, 114). "The diversity of American life," he reasons, "is often painful, frequently burdensome and always a source of conflict, but in it lies our fate and our hope" (*S&A*, 133).

The tragic optimism that this blues-tinged credo reveals is—in accord with how Ellison sees the marvelous and the terrible distributed through American life—necessarily contingent on his faith in the broadly regenerative social potential of Afro-American values. The wisdom distilled from three centuries of unique American experience has an ineluctable role to play in the conquest of American reality and in the expansion of American freedom that Ellison sees, like the conquest of the frontier, as a necessarily cooperative and competitive venture in which no single group has a premium on truth. The tribal achievement Afro-American values represent is, he suggests, part of an inadvertent and mysterious division of cultural labors among the nation's tense tribal confederation—and all the more significant for that. Most of Ellison's observers, of course, have acknowledged what he has made explicit—that he locates that achievement, first, in music; that his own "basic sense of artistic form" is musical ("Completion," 275); and that his love for the blues and jazz, on the one hand, and the European classics, on the other, weaves a complex design through the fabric of his literary ideas and social philosophy. But only glancing attention has been paid to larger political and cultural meanings conveyed in his celebration of Afro-American musical creativity. It is clear enough that jazz and the blues offer Ellison a model of technical excellence, discipline, tradition, and creative ethos; clear also that he sees a potential rectification of social democracy in the forms of black folk music. But it has been less apparent that jazz, in particular, *as a form of conscious-*

ness, provides him a living metaphor both for the vernacular process he idealizes as the cutting edge of cultural democracy in America and for the dynamics of the Freedom Movement, whose secular politics embody black hopes and hold the shape of future freedoms for the entire nation.

About the potency of the black achievement in sound, Ellison is unequivocal: "the most authoritative rendering of America in music is that of American Negroes," he argues; and he theorizes that "it would be impossible to pinpoint the time when they were not shaping . . . the mainstream of American music" (*S&A*, 248). The source of this specialized authority in sound, he stressed in the review of LeRoi Jones's *Blues People*, is not "racial genius" but, first, *cultural* inheritance—"it was the African's origin in cultures in which art was highly functional which gave him an edge in shaping the music and dance of this nation"; and, second, social constraint—"art—the blues, the spiritual, the jazz, the dance, was what we had in place of freedom" (*S&A*, 247–48). Elsewhere, Ellison has often argued that the creative edge came also from the "freedom of experimentation" open to those who, at the bottom of the social hierarchy, could be innovative and daring because the strictures of "good taste" and aristocratic tradition were not imposed on them save in ridicule.[9] The main agency of black musical achievement, though, in his view, is what he calls "the vernacular process"—that diffusive, adaptive, assimilative, unsuppressible flow of ideas, styles, images, attitudes, and techniques across all lines of caste, class, region or color: "In the United States," he insists, "when traditions are juxtaposed they tend, regardless of what we do to prevent it, irresistibly to merge" ("Territory," 22–23). As he describes it, the random and the regular social contacts between the disparate social segments of our hierarchically shifting society make this process inevitable on the interpersonal level; and the magic of human symbol systems makes it accessible to all but the most solitary victims of the most absolute repression.

The vernacular process is the basis of the American revolutionary tradition, Ellison believes (*S&A*, 24), as he believes it was the vernacular process which enabled slave musicians to realize themselves in music, as human beings, by appropriating any and all sound within hearing and then, impervious to the censure and ridicule of their masters, transmuting it into self-expression so aesthetically appealing as to fashion for themselves the ironic triumph "of enslaved and politically weak men successfully imposing their values upon a powerful society through song and dance" (*S&A*, 249). And in Ellison's recollections in *Shadow and Act* of his Oklahoma boyhood, it was the vernacular process exemplified in jazz that best represented a profound regional amalgam that was simultaneously confusing, liberating, tense, and omnipresent: "Culturally everything was mixed, you see, and beyond all question of conscious choices there was a level where you were claimed by emotion and movement and moods which you couldn't put into words" (*S&A*, 30). Operating below the level of conscious culture, the vernacular process infiltrated churches, schoolyards, barbershops, drugstores, poolrooms, and streetcorners. Through jazz, Ellison suggests, it became an unavoidable "third institution," complementing the churches and schools into whose official attitudes its eclecticism and unfettered imaginativeness did not fit. More than any other cultural force, the vernacular is Ellison's model of uncensored Mind freely acting—transcending time, space, geography, and social structure and offering in its fragmentary, chaotic simultaneity a populist, pluralist traditional reservoir of the cultural unconscious to supplant T.S. Eliot's repressive neoclassic tradition of the consciously supereminent.

"Consider," Ellison noted in his essay on the Charlie Parker legend, "that at least as early as T.S. Eliot's creation of a new aesthetic for poetry through the artful juxtapositioning of earlier styles, Louis Armstrong, way down the river in New Orleans, was working out a similar technique for jazz" (*S&A*, 221). From Ellison's perspective, Louis Armstrong—trumpeter supreme, trickster, clown, scapegoat, and wearer of masks—is a kinsman of his boyhood's imaginary, roguish Renaissance Man, a live vernacular hero who helped make jazz a paradigm for liberating cultural processes in America by masterminding the fusion of popular and classical traditions. The music of Armstrong and Charlie Christian and Charlie Parker, Ellison contends, grew out of the tension the black musician feels "between his desire to master the classical style of playing and his compulsion to express those sounds which form a musical definition of Negro American experience" (*S&A*, 233). The aesthetic counterpart of this tension is the relatively unrecognized conflict between "two separate bodies of instrumental techniques: the one classic and widely recognized and 'correct'; and the other eclectic, partly unconscious, and 'jazzy' " (*S&A*, 233). Crucial for Ellison's literary aesthetic and his theory of social democracy, this conflict of techniques and ways of experiencing the world had given rise to "a fully developed and endlessly flexible technique of jazz expression, which has become quite independent of the social environment in which it developed, if not of its spirit" (*S&A*, 234).

For in codifying the subterranean conflicts, unconscious drives, random associations, and unrecorded history of American culture, jazz and the vernacular constituted the alternate reality required by Ellison's growing awareness as a novelist "that the forms of so many of the works which impressed me were too restricted to contain the experience which I knew" (*S&A*, 111). He rejected the "rather rigid concepts of reality" at the heart of the tight, well-made Jamesian novel and the understated forms of Hemingway's "hard-boiled" fiction for a fluid vernacular reality "far more mysterious and uncertain, and more exciting, and still despite its raw violence and capriciousness, more promising" (*S&A*, 112). Stirred by the aesthetic possibilities of American culture's radical forms of alienation, contradiction, and disorder—as Richard Chase suggests is characteristic of many of the best and most representative American writers—Ralph Ellison rejected the forms of realism for the "bright magic" of a marvelous and terrible existential fabling. The American tendency, when embracing the looser reality of fable and romance, has been to rest in contradiction, to leave moral problems unreconciled or equivocally so. But the vernacular gave Ralph Ellison a mode of consciousness that indeed reconciled the moral with the cultural order; and he used it to absorb all the contradictions and extremes into a normative view of American life as a "delicately poised unity of divergencies," tragicomic, transcendent, and protean.

As synthesized in jazz, the vernacular process presents reality through an elastic sense of time, a deperspectivized space, and a language Langston Hughes had described as one of conflicting changes, sudden nuances, sharp and impudent interjections, broken rhythms, riffs, runs, breaks and hyperbolic distortions. In the terms of Erich Auerbach's summation of the West's mimetic tradition for representing reality,[10] jazz is a *paratactical* mode, part of that recessive but periodically resurgent strain in Western thought and art which rejects the linguistically organized mind's *syntactical* coding of reality into dominative relationships of subordination and stress. In rejecting the orderly but provisional reality Western science and mimetic art have built upon, jazz tradition's paratactical consciousness maps the chaos of experience not through syntactical strategies of hierarchical combination but, as Walt Whitman's free verse "ensembles" attempted, by arranging them together, side by side in a sequential "democracy of lateral coexistence." The paratactical mode, though, has historically been linked with archaic, myth-dominated, authoritarian societies or with movements of reaction during periods of crisis: that T.S. Eliot's royalist resurrection of myth and religious certitude adopted a paratactical style akin to jazz modulation was part of Ellison's original attraction to *The Waste Land*. But what differentiates Whitman's parataxis and Ellison's from that of Eliot, and what suggests a new historical function in American culture for the paratactical consciousness, is its turn from the fall back into authoritarian myth toward the quest for a particularized and unified humanity. Ellison's rendering of the jazz metaphysic located in it a kaleidoscopic, communalistic, vernacular rebellion against the art, history, and ethics of a dominative, dis-integrative tradition—jazz consolidated a counterconsciousness whose subversive and liberating powers Americans had readily intuited if only ambivalently embraced.

Although Ellison's jazz mythos is antireactionary and embodies a submerged political record of the Afro-American struggle for freedom, it does postulate a "golden age" when gods mingled with humans and set the course of history. In a 1959 essay, "The Golden Age, Time Past," Ellison turned a retrospective look at jazz history's famed Minton's Playhouse into a celebration of communal myth, ritual, and revolt—all bound up in the birth of "bop" and the accompanying "revolution in culture" sounded by such resident deities at Minton's as Dizzy Gillespie, Kenny Clarke, Charlie Christian, Charlie "Bird" Parker, Thelonius Monk, Lester Young, Ben Webster, and Coleman Hawkins. As hallowed ground in a time now dead, gone, and misremembered, Minton's in the early forties was, as Ellison painted it, a festive wartime sanctuary for jazz musicians, its significance obscured in the sweep of the war effort, the urban riots, the industrial tensions, and the continuing disregard of cultural critics. But it became host nonetheless to an exceptional musical moment when "the world was swinging with change" (*S&A*, 199).

The music made at Minton's then Ellison described as a study in controlled fury—"a texture of fragments, repetitive, nervous, not fully formed; its melodic lines underground, secret and taunting; its riffs jeerings . . ., its timbres flat or shrill. Its rhythms were out of stride and seemingly arbitrary, its drummers frozen-faced introverts dedicated to chaos" (*S&A*, 201). To the young Europeans who made pilgrimages years later to Minton's in a steady stream, it was, he remarked, a shrine of legendary heroes and events associated emotionally "with those continental cafes in which great changes, political and artistic have been plotted" (*S&A*, 204). But Ellison insisted that the proper context for understanding Minton's is as "part of a total cultural expression"—as representing the national pattern of black cabarets, dance halls, and nightclubs, on the one hand, and, on the other, as a ritual ground for the apprenticeships, ordeals, initiation ceremonies, and rebirths effected in jazz musicians' jam sessions. A people's complex history came to a focus in jazz, he maintained, and beyond offering the now famous portrait of the jam session as "the jazzman's true academy" (*S&A*, 206), he treated the Minton phenomenon as the locus of a subterranean dialogue about the politics of culture, carried on between an older generation of jazz lyricists and a younger generation seeking new identities in the undanceable discord of bebop.

For Ellison the achievement of personal identity and cultural self-expression free of defensiveness and alienation has always been the ultimate objective of the political struggle whose point, he states in Du Boisian terms, is "to be both Negro and American and to bring about that condition in American society in which this would be possible" (*S&A*, 262). In "Harlem is Nowhere," ten years before the essay on Minton's and directly astride the bebop movement, Ellison had seen the lyrical, ritual elements of southern folk jazz as the embodiment of that dreamed of "superior democracy in which each individual cultivated his uniqueness and yet did not clash with his neighbors," while he perceived in "the near-themeless technical virtuosity of bebop" the musical equivalent of "slum-shocked" anomie (*S&A*, 287). "In the perspective of time," he wrote, however, in "The Golden Age, Time Past," "we now see that what was happening at Minton's was a continuing symposium of jazz, a summation of all the styles, personal and traditional" (*S&A*, 208). Bop had not been birthed out of aimlessness at all but out of a brooding recapitulation of the past which, in the terms Ellison now provided, almost bespoke a "blueprint" in music akin to Richard Wright's manifesto in literature that theme for black artists would emerge when they had "begun to feel the meaning of the history of their race as though they in one lifetime had lived it themselves throughout all the long centuries" (Wright, 47).

And in the developments at Minton's, Ellison identified a pattern of generational tensions and external commercial exploitation that might stand for the problems of historical continuity and tactical constraint that confronted every phase of the Freedom Movement and the arts at midcentury: Introspectively subdued younger jazzmen, often formally trained, their formative years shaped by post-Depression developments, warred for mastery and recognition with exuberant older men whom they mistakenly labeled—as they did Louis Armstrong—Uncle Toms and minstrel men, not artists. And in misunderstanding their forebears, they misinterpreted themselves and their art through new myths and misconceptions: "That theirs was the only generation of Negro musicians who listened to or enjoyed the classics; that to be truly free they must act exactly the opposite of what white people might believe, rightly or wrongly, a Negro to be; that the performing artist can be completely and absolutely free of the obligations of the entertainer, and that they could play jazz with dignity only by frowning and treating the audience with aggressive contempt; and that to be in control, artistically and personally, one must be so cool as to quench one's liquid fire" (*S&A*, 209). Ellison imagined the birth of bop energized in part by the despair that "after all, is ever an important force in revolutions"; and he pictured the bopsters, "like disgruntled conspirators meeting fatefully to assemble the random parts of a bomb," confronting the musical piracy of the white instrumentalists and big bands with an aggressive style fashioned from intricate chord progressions and melodic inversions that for a while at least were to be a shield against the white music industry's predatory imitators. But the lessons Ellison wanted readers to understand from his celebration of this moment of "momentous modulation" involved not just the names, the place, the mood, or the musical mode, but the significance of jazz as a form of historical consciousness and the ways the meaning of such a phenomenon becomes victim to the selectivity of memory, the arbitrariness of the historical record, and the fragile idealism of tradition and innovation.

And implicit in his exposure of how Minton's golden age had succumbed to the process which makes history "ever a tall tale told by inattentive idealists," was that relentless questioning of formulaic thinking that has been the central characteristic of Ellison's dialectical style. Although rejecting Marxian dogma, he has remained Hegelian enough in spirit to believe that error resides in incompleteness and abstraction, and that it can be exposed through the contradictions they create. And he has devoted much of his literary and cultural criticism to singling out the absurdities and non sequiturs latent in the fragmentary and one-dimensional theories generated by "that feverish industry dedicated to telling Negroes who and what they are, and which can usually be counted upon to deprive both humanity and culture of their complexity" (xviii). "Since we are more complex than we think we are," he insists, "we are constantly making blunders." This, together with his uncompromising assertion that human experience is of a whole, that in the mind as in nature, "the heel bone is connected to the head bone," has fueled his war on those partial and abstract views which reduce the dynamic gestalts of personality, culture, history, and art to stereotype. When imposed on any of these, the concept of race especially, from Ellison's perspective, has bred a logic of illusion rooted in social expediencies and psychic repression—and he has confronted it everywhere he has found it. Dialectic has been his "coping-stone," and like Plato's dialectician, he is a man who knows how to ask and answer questions. In the published exchanges with friends, foes, and interviewers, Ellison has most commonly engaged them with the nearly psychotherapeutic tactic of forcing a confrontation between their racial half-truths or facile abstractions and the general human truths which racist assumption has suppressed or kept out of consciousness. Or he has pressed and accentuated the contradictions in oversimplified formulations by showing their helplessness before the concrete and particular.

* * *

It is his sense of a black cultural tradition independent of political ideology, subtle, subterranean, and diffused throughout the social structure, for example, which gave the dialectical animus to Ellison's 1964 review of LeRoi Jones's (Imamu Baraka's) *Blues People*. Ellison, like Baraka, has always seen the blues tradition as a special repository and focus of a collective history, as embodying a "total way of life." And Ellison lauded the effort to so treat the music in Baraka's "strictly theoretical" exegesis of the journey in sound from slavery to citizenship. Ellison's final evaluation, however, was that Baraka's theory "flounders before that complex of human motives which makes human history, and which is so characteristic of the American Negro."

And as is so characteristic of Ralph Ellison, he armed his critique of Baraka's militant abstractions with pointed particularities the former could not contain. Where Baraka's theory attempted to simplify the historical bifurcation of the blues into "country" and "city/classic" forms by imposing E. Franklin Frazier's pejorative class anatomy of the rise of a self-eviscerating black bourgeoisie, Ellison confronted the resulting "rigid correlation between color, education, income and the Negro's preference in music" with the unruly instance of "a white-skinned Negro with brown freckles who owns sixteen oil wells sunk in a piece of Texas land once farmed by his ex-slave parents who were a blue-eyed, white-skinned, red-headed (kinky) Negro woman from Virginia and a blue-gummed, black-skinned, curly-haired Negro male from Mississippi, and who not only sang bass in a Holy Roller church, played the market and voted Republican but collected blues recordings and was a walking depository of blues tradition" (*S&A*, 245).

Where Baraka asserted categorically, that "a slave cannot be a man," Ellison countered, "But what, one might ask, of those moments when he feels his metabolism aroused by the rising of the sap in spring? What of his identity among other slaves? With his wife? And isn't it closer to the truth that far from considering themselves only in terms of that abstraction, 'a slave,' the enslaved really thought of themselves as *men* who had been unjustly enslaved?'' (*S&A*, 247). The implication that the test of theory is its ability to cope with concrete and idiosyncratic experience is the heart of Ellison's dialectic; and the idea of a culture of survival and transcendence built from the possibilities for maneuvering in the face of the inevitable, from affirmative roles and identities irrepressible even in bondage, and from excellences forged under limitation, is the heart of his uncompromising embrace of Afro-American traditions.

Nor is this an evasion of the problems of power and freedom or the necessity for social reconstruction. Ellison believes, with Hegel, that ''consciousness is all,'' that ''human life is a move toward the rational'' (O'Brien interview, 70, 75), and that freedom is a creation not of political institutions but of mind: ''Simply to take down a barrier doesn't make a man free,'' he insists. ''He can only free himself'' (Geller interview, 168). He does so, Ellison believes, as he discovers and pushes against the extreme limits of his own possibilities, which happens in the context of societies that are not God-constructed worlds but man-made and improvisational ''arrangements,'' inevitably hierarchical through the inheritance of power or talent, and always, tragically, productive of victimization, guilt, and scapegoats, ''whether it's in a democracy, a socialistic society, or a communistic one'' (O'Brien, 69–70). In contemporary America where, Ellison believes, the lines of color caste are blurring, class lines grow more rigid, offering the prospect not of an end to the need for victims and scapegoats but perhaps to the practice of designating them by race. Realistically, the human challenge, he contends, is to moderate injustices and inequalities that sometimes may be ineradicable; and this can only be done by ''keeping the ideal alive'' as a conscious discipline (O'Brien, 72). And for those individuals and groups who, like Afro-Americans, bear disproportionately the human costs of human systems, that keeping of ideals seems, in his view, to be simultaneously a pragmatic strategy of social reform and a mode of transcendence.

The role of art here, for Ellison, is crucial. Richard Wright, in the often cited passage in *Black Boy* where he broods upon the ''cultural barrenness of black life,'' had wondered whether such human values as tenderness, love, honor, and loyalty were native to man or whether they were in fact ''fostered, won, struggled and suffered for, preserved in ritual from one generation to another.'' Ellison, interpreting Wright's comment as an oblique affirmation of black men's struggle against alienation, visualized the conflict between Afro-Americans and white society as a ritual confrontation of willed values in which ''Western culture must be won, confronted like the animal in a Spanish bullfight, dominated by the red shawl of codified experience and brought heaving to its knees'' (*S&A*, 103). The arena for this imposition of a black vision on the world was, most properly, in the rituals of art; for, as

Malraux had helped make clear to Ellison, "the organized significance of art is stronger than all the multiplicity of the world; . . . [and] that significance alone enables man to conquer chaos and master destiny" (*S&A*, 94). When the three volumes of Malraux's *The Psychology of Art* were published in the late 1940s, Ellison paid twenty-five dollars apiece and walked around with holes in his shoes in order to possess what then "was more important than having dry feet" ("Essential," 149)—a revelation, fused in Malraux's art history, philosophy, and politics, of a secret and almost satanic path to power, freedom, and salvation.

Malraux's opulent and exacting multivolume tribute to artistic genius vouchsafed the liberating possibility that, here in the middle of the twentieth century, artists for the first time drew on the whole continuum of the world's art. Art works thereby achieved "a kind of ubiquity," and all men became both potential "heirs of the entire world" and, more important, creators and conquerors of what had profound social implications—"the first universal artistic culture."[11] This looming, inalienable world of art, in its detachment from the social order, Malraux maintained, does not imitate life but rather imitates art and reveals life—is in its origins an aggressive negation of the material world and all values opposing its own, so that it is actually allied with whatever denies, destroys, transcends ordinary human reality. Yet art is, Malraux agreed with Hegel, a vehicle for the perpetuation of spirit and hence a guardian of human values. So the artist, as creator, engages in both negation and human salvation, in the mastery of art and the deliverance of humanity. Critics imagined an embarrassing contradiction here, not comprehending Malraux's artist as in fact a rebel demiurge, a re-creator god who is neither the originator of the world nor an object of worship, but the Artisan who turns chaos into cosmos, rectifying and reorganizing the elements of the universe. And in its alliance with the forces of negation, it becomes a gnostic lord of the lower powers, envisioning the rise to sovereignty of forces the surface world would subordinate. It wants no escape from the world into aestheticism but instead a planned conquest of that world which will compel us to see that the "sustaining, enriching, transforming" image of itself humanity has inherited through art is the justification of the mystery of human life.

As such, Malraux's vision helped canalize Ellison's own demiurgic impulses, helped guide his efforts to interpret and use the cultural inheritance of the slave past and the repressive present as keys for transforming servant into sovereign. What Malraux's conception yielded when Ellison trained it on the Afro-American cultural predicament, and on his own sense of the American national experience, was the opportunity to convert the traditionally constrained and compensatory art Locke and Du Bois described into an art of redemptive conquest.The rise of a universal artistic culture accessible to any literate person with the energy and will to appropriate it had special implications for people socially submerged in an American society whose pluralism, fluidity, and relative absence of stable traditions gave literature and the arts, and the novel particularly, an unprecedented role in the development of the nation. In the 1955 *Paris Review* session, Ellison concluded by insisting that his devotion to the novel afforded him the possibility of contributing not only to the growth of the literature but to the shaping of the culture as he should like it to be: the novel was literally a conquest of the frontier, creating the American experience in the process of describing it.

* * *

The power to dominate reality, social and aesthetic, has never been for Ralph Ellison a mere matter of a field of force acting on inert human objects, nor a matter merely of ''positive thinking.'' It has always been predicated on a relationship, a confrontation of active wills, somewhere on the continuum from antagonism to cooperation, between a wielder of power and those who value the things he or she controls. Power, influence, domination, in life and in art, are always, for Ellison, directed by will and effected by the mastery of organizing techniques. On one level of the social struggle for power in America, the answer to the riddle of black political impotence rests for Ellison in the failure of black leaders to recognize their true source of power—''which lies, as Martin Luther King perceived, in the Negro's ability to suffer even death for the attainment of our beliefs'' (*S&A*, 37). On another, the political potency of a Booker T. Washington and the comparative inability of a W.E.B. Du Bois to effect his political will are measures, to Ellison, not so much of the values the two men espoused, however close or conflicting, but of their technical mastery over structured possibilities (''Indivisible,'' 53). Conversely, Ellison eschews organized violence as a means to black freedom and power in the United States because, first, ''we are outnumbered and . . . the major instruments of destruction are in the hands of the whites,'' but second, and most important, because black people have collectively *willed* neither political goal—separation or seizure of the government—which would make orchestrated violence ''something to think about'' (Geller interview, 163–64).

But then, political violence and the ideologies that seek to wield it as an instrument of power are in Ellison's vision largely aspects of the chaos and illusion that life-affirming acts of self-definition must somehow reduce to redemptive form. On the level of aesthetics, the violence the demiurge does to provisional reality is, at the same time, an act of regeneration and deliverance. Such violence seeks no throne or ideology but only to re-energize the forces of life. Its power is an initiating vision that creates human desire, overcomes human resistances, redirects human actions by reshaping what people perceive their interests and possibilities to be. For Ellison as artist and wielder of the Word, this power to dominate human minds lies in the capacity of technique—the ingenious, guileful, symbolic structuring of emotions and perceptions—to do violence to our "trained incapacity" to perceive the truth. And the revelation of truth—never mere reportage or "telling it like it is"—is always a function of style, whose test is not so much beauty as power.

Ellison's awareness, however, of the ambivalence of both experience and our perception of experience extends to power and the word as well. Power, his Invisible Man learns, can be an anodyne or an illusion as well as an instrument of the rational will—and the will itself is never completely free or inviolable but always limited by recalcitrant necessity and always vulnerable to injury or deflection. And the Word, magical and Janus-faced, has the potency not only to revive and make us free, but to "blind, imprison, and destroy" (*IM*, 42). "During the sixties," Ellison recently observed in the interview with Ishmael Reed,

> "the myth of the redeemed criminal had a tremendous influence on our young people, when criminals guilty of every crime from con games, to rape, to murder, exploited it by declaring themselves political activists and black leaders. As a result, many sincere, dedicated leaders of an older generation were swept aside. . . . I found it outrageous. Because not only did it distort the concrete historical differences between one period of struggle and another, it made heroes out of thugs and self-servers out of dedicated leaders. Worse, it gave many kids the notion that there was no point in developing their minds. . . . Years ago Du Bois stressed a leadership based upon an elite of the intellect. During the Sixties it appeared that for many Afro-Americans all that was required for such a role was a history of criminality, a capacity for irresponsible rhetoric, and the passionate assertion of the mystique of 'Blackness.' " ("Essential," 150)

Here clearly, and in the accumulating excerpts of the rumored multivolume novel he has labored meticulously over these past years, Ralph Ellison remains outspokenly absorbed in the problems of power and leadership in "a land most strange." As ever, the mysticism and militancy that mask political naiveté, personal opportunism, and an ignorance of the past are to him mirages of power and leadership in the social arena, mirages whose counterparts in the rituals of the Word are the self-pitying sentiment and vapid propaganda of the defensively illiterate writer. If black writers are to sustain a place in American literature and to become more influential in the broader community, he asserted in 1969 when the war of invective against him was still intense, "they will do it in terms of style: by imposing a style upon a sufficient area of American life to give other readers a sense that this is true, that here is a revelation of reality" ("Indivisible," 49). His hesitancy, then, to predict future popularity and impact for black wordsmiths rested in his observation that "so many of them seem to be still caught up at the point of emphasizing *inwardness*," when in his view mastery of the rhetoric of fiction requires also an intricate awareness of the world outside the self and one's immediate community. No quarter given here in Ellison's continuing guerrilla action against the forms of illusion. And no easy target offered by this one-time hornblower and quail hunter turned literary grenadier, this streetcorner activist and pamphleteer turned minister of culture, this prideful danceman and raconteur for whom "eclecticism is the word" and "playing it by ear" the mode, this artificer of masks and names and comic chaos, and whose shifting guises as synthesizer, celebrant, dialectician, and demiurge make any manhunt fixed on this mind in motion as quixotic as wingshooting at shadows.

NOTES

1. See Ralph Ellison, "Study and Experience: An Interview with Ralph Ellison," with Michael S. Harper and Robert Stepto, *Massachusetts Review* 18 (1977): 426.

2. Ralph Ellison, "On Bird, Bird-Watching, and Jazz," in *Shadow and Act*, 218–27. All further references to *Shadow and Act* are cited parenthetically in the text.

3. Ellison, "A Completion of Personality: A Talk with Ralph Ellison" with John Hersey, in *The Writer's Craft*, 267–69. The Ellison-Hersey interview is included in this volume, pp. 285–307.

4. Ellison, "Ralph Ellison: Twenty Years After," an interview with David Carson, *Studies in American Fiction*, 22.

5. Ellison, in "The Essential Ellison," an interview with Ishmael Reed, Quincy Troupe, and Steve Cannon, 148.

6. Sterling Brown, *Negro Poetry and Drama* and *The Negro in American Fiction* (Washington, D.C.: Associates in Negro Folk Education, 1937). A later edition was published in 1969 by Atheneum.

7. Ellison, from "The Alain Locke Symposium," 27.

8. Alain Locke, "Pluralism and Intellectual Democracy," in *Second Symposium*; "Cultural Relativism and Ideological Peace," in *Approaches to World Peace*; and "Pluralism and Ideological Peace," in *Freedom and Experience*.

9. See Ellison, "Alain Locke Symposium," 21, and "Study and Experience," 431.

10. See Erich Auerbach, *Mimesis: The Representation of Reality in Western Literature*.

11. André Malraux, *The Psychology of Art*, originally published in three volumes, 1947–50, was adapted as *The Voices of Silence* in 1951.

WORKS CITED

Auerbach, Erich. *Mimesis: The Representation of Reality in Western Literature*. Garden City, N.Y.: Doubleday & Co., 1957.

Brown, Sterling. *Negro Poetry and Drama* and *The Negro in American Fiction*. Washington, D.C.: Associates in Negro Folk Education, 1937.

Burke, Kenneth. "The Negro's Pattern of Life." *The Philosophy of Literary Form*, 3rd ed. Berkeley: University of California Press, 1973.

Ellison, Ralph. "The Alain Locke Symposium." *Harvard Advocate* 107 (Spring 1974): 9–28.

______. "A Completion of Personality: A Talk with Ralph Ellison." Interview with John Hersey. *The Writer's Craft*, ed. John Hersey. New York: Knopf, 1974.

______. "The Essential Ellison," Interview with Steve Cannon, Ishmael Reed, and Quincy Troupe. *Y-Bird Reader* (Autumn 1977): 126–59.

______. "Going to the Territory." *Carleton Miscellany* 18 (1980): 9–26.

______. "Indivisible Man." Interview with James Alan McPherson. *Atlantic Monthly* 226 (December 1970): 53.

______. "An Interview with Ralph Ellison." With Allen Geller. *Black American Writer* 1, ed. C. W. E. Bigsby. Baltimore: Penguin Books, 1969.

______. "An Interview with Ralph Ellison." With John O'Brien. *Interviews with Ten Black Writers*, ed. John O'Brien. New York: Liveright, 1973.

______. "Study and Experience: An Interview with Ralph Ellison." With Michael S. Harper and Robert Stepto. *Massachusetts Review* 18 (1977): 417–435.

______. "Ralph Ellison: Twenty Years After." With David L. Carson, *Studies in American Fiction* 1 (1973): 1–23.

______. *Shadow and Act*. New York: Signet Books, 1966.

Locke, Alain. "Cultural Relativism and Ideological Peace." *Approaches to World Peace*, ed. Bryson, Finkelstein, and MacIver. New York: Conference on Science, Philosophy and Religion, 1944, 609–18.

______. "Pluralism and Ideological Peace." *Freedom and Experience: Essays Presented to Horace Kallen*. New York: Cornell University Press, 1947, 63–69.

______. "Pluralism and Intellectual Democracy." *Second Symposium*, ed. Bryson, Finkelstein, and MacIver. New York: Conference on Science, Philosophy and Religion, 1942, 196–209.

Malraux, André. *The Psychology of Art*, 2 vols. New York: Pantheon Books, 1949.

Wright, Richard. "Blueprint for Negro Writing," in *Richard Wright Reader*, ed. Michel Fabre and Ellen Wright. New York: Harper & Row, 1978.

PART THREE

The Art of Ambiguity

MYTH, IDEOLOGY, AESTHETICS

Through a Writer's Eyes

HOLLIE WEST

Q: What's the status of your second novel?

A: Well, it's going well and I've begun to work with my editor.

Q: Have you set a deadline for yourself?

A: No. I won't discuss the novel. There is a part of it published in the current *New American Review*.

Q: You do not publish frequently, but I have been told you write a great deal. Why do you publish infrequently?

A: Well, I publish infrequently because most of my writing energy has gone into this novel and I have a desire to have as much of an impact of the total book at a given time as possible rather than in published pieces.

At the moment I am not so strapped for money that I have to publish those pieces. You see, I don't take myself as seriously as a writer as some people do. For me it's the most serious thing that I do. But I don't think it's important for me to publish just to publish. Too many writers publish things they might well forget, and maybe when this damn big book is done, that might be the verdict about it.

Q: You could publish because you have something important to say and I can look at this from a very personal standpoint. I recall when *Invisible Man* was published in 1952. I was in high school and an English teacher of mine pushed it on me.

A: Oh, my God—in Oklahoma?

Q: Yes. I rejected it, saying, "No, I don't want to read it." But once I got to college it became a pivotal book in my life. I can say that you had a great deal to do with inspiring me to become a journalist. At least I felt I could make some impact on the world as a writer of sorts. So I see writers having that kind of impact or making that kind of impact on people.

A: Well, of course, writers certainly have had their impact on me. I certainly would not have been a writer had I not read a lot and finally begun to meet writers and had a chance to work on the Writers Project. That was very important.

Well, so much of what I'd like to write about or what I think about is problematical. It seems important to me, and then it turns out that I doubt whether it's important. It's still a matter for me of stumbling along finding my way and doing it slowly.

I do write all the time, but to try to express what I'm trying to get at is a little bit difficult for me. It might not be for others, but it's not easy [for me] because it is against all the simplistic descriptions of experience which I hear over and over again. I know that mine has not been that way, you see. It seems more wonderful, more complex, more full of unexpected surprises, and to try to make a structure, to make a narrative, takes a bit of doing. I write things and leave them for a year or two and then go back, and sometimes they stand up but very often they don't. At least, they don't as far as what I set out to say is concerned.

Q: How long have you been working on the novel?

A: Well it's hard to say. I conceived the novel about 1955 and then reconceived it, lost about 365 pages of it in a fire when we lost a home up in Massachusetts, and have been since then continuing the writing while restructuring that which was lost.

Q: You once wrote this: "If Negro writers ever become the mainstay of American literature it will be because they have learned their craft and used the intensity, both emotional and political, of their group experience to express a greater area of American experience than the writers of other groups." And at another point you said: "I suspect I have annoyed a few people by insisting upon the mastery of craft. Craft to me is an aspect of morality." What does that latter statement mean?

A: It just means that the writer's morality is one which expresses a vision of human life. It contains a sense of what is right and wrong—what is life-preserving against that which is life-destroying. If he's a writer, his most serious way of expressing his sense of life and his identity is through his writing, and thus if he's a moral man he will try to do that as well as he can.

Now craft is the instrumentality and the body of technique through which he projects himself and his sense of life. The morality of a jazz musician, like the morality of any musician, is one based upon his strictness with himself, his discipline—the way he masters his instrument in order to project whatever it is he has to say.

I think it is a very, very important point when you tell me that you are a writer and that you have a vision of life, that you are prescribing a better way of life. If you describe a more viable and ethical way of living and denounce the world or a great part of society for the way that it conducts its affairs and then write in a sloppy way or present issues in a simplistic or banal way, then you're being immoral as an artist.

One way of achieving some sort of rectitude is to learn how to do what you are supposed to be doing as well as you can do it. If we'll switch from writers to a physician to say that a physician who insists that you patronize him because he is a black physician and then he has not mastered his craft, then he is immoral and he leads to the destruction of life—like the man who caused my mother's death, when she went to him after falling off a porch and, without x-raying her, he decided that she had arthritis—but she died of tuberculosis of the hip. That was immoral and life-destructive.

Writers who are supposed to present visions of the human condition which will lead to some sort of wisdom in confronting the existence of experience and who do not do that in a disciplined and informed way are immoral.

Q: At exactly what point did you decide to forego music and decide to become a writer?

A: Well, I came here in 1936 hoping to get the money to go back to Tuskegee, because I couldn't get a job there which would have paid anything more than my keep for the summer, and I didn't make it. I worked at the "Y" and the food bar and held on working at odd jobs but reading all the time and going around.

I had read some things of Richard Wright in the *New Masses*. I asked (Langston) Hughes about him, and Hughes wrote Wright saying that [there was] this young writer who was interested, and it turned out that Wright was coming to New York. So I met him—he came here to edit *New Challenge*—and he asked me to do a book review; then he asked me to write a short story, and I had never thought of that. So I wrote a short story which he accepted and sent to the printer—and I have the galley still—but then the magazine broke up because he and the girls who had the magazine reached a disagreement.

After that I began to think seriously about writing. It was exciting. I had been reading about technique and reading criticisms. Then I went out to Dayton where I'd lost my mother. I stayed seven months, and during that time I did a lot of writing and started a novel. Part of that was published, unfortunately. But when I came back I got on the Writers Project and this gave me a chance to work at writing.

One reason I went into writing was that conditions were so bad. This was the Depression still, or the recession, and there was just too much musical talent in New York, and I couldn't raise enough money to join the union. I played only one public engagement. I played the trumpet parts for a modern-dance performance conducted by Alex North and danced by his wife, Anna Sokolow.

I also took some lessons in composition from Wallingford Reigger, but once I decided that I was going to write I wouldn't touch the horn. I wouldn't go to a concert because I was afraid of being diverted, of being torn.

Q: Do you ever regret not having become a musician?

A: There are nostalgic moments when I would wish at least that I had kept up some level of efficiency of the trumpet so that I could play with groups, not professionally, but just because I like the instrument.

Ralph Ellison and Afro-American Folk and Cultural Tradition

GEORGE E. KENT

Ralph Ellison stressed connections between Afro-American folk and cultural tradition and American culture, since "The heel bone is, after all, connected, through its various linkages, to the head bone," and not to be ignored is "the intricate network of connections which binds Negroes to the larger society."[1] Mindful of this pronouncement I shall sketch in some of Ellison's ideas concerning the value of the folk tradition, explore representative techniques in *Invisible Man*, and offer comments concerning the value and limitations of his method.

Pressed toward a bag of pure blackness, Ellison was capable of minimizing folk tradition's value for the self-conscious writer, as he does in "Change the Joke and Slip the Yoke," an essay in response to Stanley Edgar Hyman's attempt to create archetypes of blackness.[2] In "Change the Joke," he contended that the black writer was "heir to the human experience which is literature, [an inheritance which might] be more important to him than his [own] living folk tradition" (*S&A*, 58). As for himself, black folklore became important through literary discovery. Seeing the uses to which folklore is put in the works of James Joyce and T. S. Eliot, Ellison saw the folk tradition, the spirituals, blues, jazz, and folk-tales as a stable factor in "the discontinuous, swiftly changing, and diverse American culture. . . ." (*S&A*, 58). It expresses qualities needful in a world which exemplifies to a considerable degree a blueslike absurdity. It offers much to the writer, who can "translate its meaning into wider, more precise vocabularies" (*S&A*, 59).

Actually, Ellison usually gave greater emphasis to folk traditions, and some allowance should be made for the fact that the primary goal of "Change the Joke" is to correct Stanley Edgar Hyman's concept of black folklore. Since 1940, Ellison had been stressing its *ultimate* importance. In "Stormy Weather," a review of Langston Hughes's *The Big Sea*, which was critical of Hughes on other grounds, Ellison commended him for developing the national folk sources of his art (20–21). Ellison's essay "Recent Negro Fiction" praised Hughes and Wright: Hughes for taking note of folklore and seeing the connection between his efforts and symbols and images of Negro forms and Wright for attention to the southern Negro folk (22–26). In 1944, Ellison's short story, "Flying Home," made elaborate use of the black folklore motif of the black character who comes to grief in heaven for flying too imaginatively with his angel's wings. The main character, a black aviator, finds peace only when he comes to terms with the survival values of folk tradition.

In 1945, Ellison's essay entitled "Richard Wright's Blues" (*S&A*, 77–94), revealed a profound understanding of the *blues* as a folk cultural form and the value of its *forms* of response to existence for the self-conscious writer. He also analyzed the oppressive weight of American culture upon the folk, argued their complexity, and made a widely publicized definition of the *blues*:

> The blues is an impulse to keep the painful details and episodes of a brutal experience alive in one's aching consciousness, to finger its jagged grain, and to transcend it, not by the consolation of philosophy but by squeezing from it a near-tragic, near-comic lyricism. As a form, the blues is an autobiographical chronicle of personal catastrophe expressed lyrically. (*S&A*, 78–79.)

Later in the same essay, he points out that the blues express "both the agony of life" and the possibility of overcoming it through sheer toughness of spirit. The blues are a valuable form, also, in that they emphasize self-confrontation.

Comments upon the folk tradition are scattered among several essays in *Shadow and Act*. Perhaps the most emphatic occurs in Ellison's responses during the 1955 Paris interview (*S&A*, 167–86). He called attention to several functions of folklore and described some ways in which folklore worked dramatically in *Invisible Man*. Offering the first drawings of a group's character, preserving situations repeated in the history of the group, describing the boundaries of thought and feeling, projecting the group's wisdom in symbols expressing its will to survive, embodying those values by which it lives and dies, folklore seemed, as Ellison described it, basic to the portrayal of the essential spirit of black people. In general, Ellison noted that great literature of France, Russia, and Spain was erected upon the humble base of folklore. Folk symbols serve Picasso as an annihilator of time through the use of simple lines and curves, and, for the viewer, a whole culture "may resound in a simple rhythm, an image." But most important, in its relationship to black experience is Ellison's belief that the black's folklore "announced the Negro's willingness to trust his own experience, his own sensibilities as to the definition of reality, rather than to allow his masters to define these crucial matters for him" (*IM*, 172). Black American folklore, nonetheless, represents for Ellison an American and Western experience—"not lying at the bottom of it, but intertwined, diffused in its very texture" (*IM*, 172).

Ellison also emphasizes the special qualities of a black tradition in confronting reality, and describes them at some length in his essay, "The World and the Jug" (*S&A*, 127–43 passim). Suffice it here to say that they cover the gamut of attitudes for defining life positively, surviving oppression, and extracting from existence many of its joys.

* * *

In *Invisible Man*,[3] the whole gamut of Ellison's descriptions of the functions of folklore find their place. However, to be fully suggestive of their power is to bear in mind some specifics concerning the total reach of the novel. In the first place the novel's title is *Invisible Man*, not THE *Invisible Man*. In relationship to its nameless protagonist, the story delivers itself through at least three wavelengths, none in the form of the novel, completely separable from another: the hero as cosmic man, with the inescapable duty to gather up and affirm *reality*, despite social oppression; the hero as victim, struggling with a cultural machinery that would reduce him to negative sign; and the hero as an allegory of black struggle in American history.

Black cultural and folk tradition frequently involves more than one of the wavelengths. In simplest form, we may see the interaction through several characters, who, in varying degrees, are folk figures or are a part of cultural tradition. In more complex form, the interaction of folk and cultural tradition ranges from motifs to situations, symbols, and strategic appearances of folk art forms: blues, spirituals, and folk rhymes.

The characters contrast with the lostness of the invisible narrator, since they represent reality confronted. Thus the slave woman who is envisioned singing spirituals in the prologue is used to comment upon the pain of victimization, but she and her sons also define *freedom*, a basic theme of the novel, as the ability to articulate the self, and as a question that can be answered only by each individual's confrontation with the self. Louis Armstrong and his jazz reflect both an articulated self and a mode of breaking through the ordinary categories of Western clock time. The grandfather who appears at strategic points throughout the novel is a reflector of bitter past and continuing victimization. Yet he is, in Ellison's words, the "ambiguity of the past," a sphinxlike riddle which must be approached creatively and not in the literal-minded fashion which actually makes of the invisible narrator an accessory to the Brotherhood's crime of provoking a riot in Harlem. Yet the destruction of whites by yessing and confirming their false sense of reality, which the invisible narrator has imitated with nearly fatal consequences, was a solid survival technique of his grandfather and the folk.

Trueblood and Mary, who have assimilated both folk and general black cultural tradition, play the most powerful dramatic roles among the folk figures. Trueblood, with whom the invisible narrator inadvertently confronts philanthropist Norton, is several roles. On the simple folk level, he is a person who can face the results of his humanity: becoming an expectant father by both his wife and his daughter.

He achieves a conclusion, which the brainwashed and pragmatic invisible narrator requires most of the novel to grasp: "I ain't nobody but myself." His achievement is dramatized through the rituals of first singing spirituals—and then the blues. Singing the spirituals dramatizes his struggle and pain. But it is the singing of the blues, the folk form which Ellison has celebrated for its ritual of self-confrontation, that enables Trueblood to get himself together. In chapter 9, the blues *forms of response* to existence become meaningful to the invisible narrator as a street singer celebrates the *absurdity* of a self committed passionately to a woman with "feet like a monkey" and "legs like a frog," and the narrator, realizing how Bledsoe has duped him, can laugh bitterly at himself by singing, "they picked poor Robin clean." But it is Trueblood who exemplifies the real toughness of the tradition, and also the racy humor, the folk storytelling tradition, the highly flavored speech, and the capacity for enjoyment of life.

But Trueblood is also interconnected with American and Western tradition. He is, on one hand, the testimony to the density of reality that Western rationalism evades. And he is, on the other, American and Western scapegoat, frankly admitting the sins of the flesh, the full acknowledgment of which the philanthropist Norton dodges by platonic and puritanical sublimation. For Norton too has committed incest with his daughter but mentally, rather than physically. And the white southern community acknowledges its secret sexual longings and Trueblood's role as their substitute bearer of sin by dropping coins into his pocket.

But more broadly still, Trueblood connects finally with Western incest tradition and with Freud.[4] Like Oedipus he has invaded unaware the zone of taboo. For he cohabited with his daughter while dreaming. So, was he guilty? Selma Fraiberg argues persuasively that in Freudian terms he was, since he was the author of the dream which his being conjured up for the purpose of allowing the sexual act. At any rate, Trueblood must bear up while the gods deliberate indefinitely concerning the sins of mortal man.

It will be remembered that Mary Rambo is the southern migrant—now New York mistress of a boarding house—into whose hands the invisible narrator falls after barely surviving the allegorically represented attempt of the industrial system to eliminate all potential for individuality and reduce him to anonymity. The elaborate role that Ellison had designed for Mary may be examined in the fragment published in Herbert Hill's anthology of contemporary black literature, *Soon, One Morning*.[5] Mary is the warmth, wit, coping power, and humanity of the folk tradition as it survives in the modern industrial city. And she is the integration of the bitter past with the present, as can be seen by her possession of such purely survival items as the bank topped by a minstrel figure, "a very black, red-lipped and wide-mouthed Negro . . . his face an enormous grin, his single large black hand held palm up before his chest'' (*IM*, 241–42). In chapter 15, where he appears, the invisible narrator tries unsuccessfully to drop the symbols of the past, which must be integrated into his being. Unlike Trueblood, Mary is not merged with Western symbols independent of her, a fact of dramatic significance since the hero's recovery from the industrial onslaught is managed through complete, though temporary, retreat into blackness. Also, unlike Trueblood, Mary makes a strong positive impact upon the invisible narrator, although he must symbolically leave her and become powerless to return, as he mounts higher into the abstractions of rationalism through the Brotherhood and as he retreats into the freely imaginative self.

Another folk figure is Dupre, the leader of Harlem rioters who burn down a tenement building. The dramatic and symbolic function of Dupre and his followers is to reflect the folk ability to move with poise amidst chaos and in contradiction to the flat rational assumptions of the Brotherhood concerning its mission as planners for others. The rioters move with a plan that directly confronts reality.

The discussion of the foregoing characters illustrates, rather than exhausts, the role of folk or folkish characters. We must turn now to scenes that are informed with folk motifs. Ellison himself has commented upon the early battle-royal scene as one that he lifted from living rituals and placed in a context of larger meaning (*S&A*, 174). It and the invisible narrator's speech comprise on one wavelength the ultimate in oppression and self-victimization, as the invisible protagonist tries to be pragmatic and economic man. In the highest sense, the scene is both horrible and wildly comic.

It involves several motifs from folk tradition, a full explanation of which would constitute a separate essay. On the level of blackness, there is the manipulation of blacks to fight each other blindly, education as brainwash, the general white manipulation of reality, and the shaping of misleaders of the people. The narrator himself embodies the sardonic folk concept that ''what's white is right.''

But one of the powerful folk motifs is the racial joke of black man and tabooed white woman. The unwritten folk joke, from which the scene derives, is concerned with a black looking at a white woman and expressing sexual desire while a white man stands by and replies.

> Black: Oh man, will I ever, ever!
> White: No Nigger, you will never, never!
> Black: As long as there's life there's hope!
> White: Yeah Nigger, and as long as there's trees there's rope.

In the battle-royal scene, it will be recalled, the black boys are forced to watch the nude white woman dance, and are abused if they look and abused if they do not look. In terms of blackness, the ritual is to stamp upon them the symbolic castration they are supposed to experience in the presence of a white woman.

Ellison, however, makes his connections. He dramatizes the perverted responses of the white men, and the American flag tattooed upon the nude woman's belly as a satire upon American corruption of sexuality. He unites the invisible narrator and the nude blonde as victims and makes out of her a symbol implying the mystery of freedom, similar to James Joyce's use of woman in *A Portrait of the Artist as a Young Man*: "She seemed like a fair bird-girl girdled in veils calling to me from the angry surface of some gray and threatening sea" (*IM*, 23).

Perhaps enough attention has been given to the unconstrained density of reality represented by people, folk and nonfolk, of the Golden Day, the sporting house where the philanthropist Norton is faced with all the reality that his rational categories have suppressed. I focus instead upon the vesper scene in chapter 5, a poem, really, in which black folk cultural tradition, in general, and Western mythology merge. Ellison, in this chapter, is not without humor, but he extracts, at times tenderly, a deep pathos for the uplift dreams that somehow ought to be true. The narrator looks upon them as his investment in identity. The folk motif is the remembered coming of a Moses to bring freedom and richness to the barren land, a ritual and myth delivered in the rich rhetoric of the black speech tradition. Of course, Homer Barbee, the priest who summons up pictures of ancestors to validate the myth, is blind—a device for undermining his credibility.

Ellison combines the black Moses myth with the biblical Moses and the rituals traditionally describing the miraculous birth and survival of the hero. For good measure, the students are also involved in the rites of Horatio Alger. The combination carries the chapter to one of the memorable intensities of the novel. And adding still more to the pathos is the ex-slave matron, Susie Greshman, who brings the warmth and tragic knowledge of the folk—and their high hopes—to this colorful but ineffectual ritual. Anyone who has sat through ceremonies that achieve such a high sense of group communion and shared memories will identify briefly with the invisible narrator, despite his terrible delusion.

Such folkish scenes appear also at strategic points in the section of the book devoted to the narrator's northern experiences, and Ellison exacts from them, at will, humor, pathos, and philosophy. The hero's transition to the impersonal northern experience evokes memories of folklore deriving from the southern black's initiation into northern urban life. The black-man–white-woman motif arises in a comic scene where the crush of subway traffic jams the narrator against a white woman: "I wanted desperately to raise my hands, to show her it was against my will" (*IM*, 121). I have already referred to the pivotal confrontation with Mary, symbol of all that is positive and something of the negative in folk tradition.

I shall briefly mention additional scenes—all of which function mainly in the exemplification of blackness. In chapter 11, the highly symbolic section which portrays the tendency of industrialism to reduce men to a programmed zero, the Brer Rabbit motif emphasizes the toughness of the black experience, the indestructibility of a fiber, which is later restored through the care of the folkish Mary Rambo. The numerous folk symbols appearing in different scenes within chapter 13 range in significance from the hero's *elementary* awakening to his heritage through the evoking of the entire black tradition in the eviction of the ex-slave couple, Mr. and Mrs. Primus Provo, a couple who also embody the bitter fruits harvested by blacks since securing freedom.

The self-contained and bitter pride of the Provos has an affinity with the feelings evoked in chapter 13 by Brother Tarp, a man who spent nineteen years on the chain gang for opposing white authority before escaping to New York. Tarp passes on to the invisible narrator a link from the chain broken to secure his freedom. Symbolically, it is a bitter link in the chain of black tradition, meant to serve as a reminder of roots and inescapable contours in the profile of black reality. Other images of blackness appear as warnings, as the invisible narrator moves deeper into the Brotherhood: the minstrel fascism of the Brother Wrestrum, who provokes the Brotherhood trial of the narrator; the minstrel dolls manipulated ritualistically to express the youth organizer Tod Clifton's deep sense of betrayal, and the allied image of the zoot-suited black boys playing their bitter, hip satire upon "history" in chapter 20; and perhaps we may include Ras the Exhorter whose existence and strength (Tod Clifton: "It's on the inside that Ras is strong . . . dangerous" [*IM*, 285.]) are based first upon the urban folk's hunger for identity and nationhood and second, at least latently, in the breast of every black conscious of loss and of deep and sustained betrayal. With Rinehart, symbol of possibility through imagination and masking, we are back to Western tradition.

However, Ellison has a deep sense of the beauty, as well as the terror of black tradition. Therefore, acknowledgment of his rendering the rich folk language of the South, the salty speech of the northern urban areas, and the joyful myth making of urban narrators in the Harlem riot scene is probably the proper note on which to draw toward conclusions.

The first conclusion is that, along with other devices, the folk tradition affords the black writer a device for instant movement into the privacy, tensioned coherence, toughness, terror, and beauty of black experience—a method for conjuring up instant blackness. It is to be noted that Ellison tends to use folk tradition without making outside connections, in some scenes emphasizing the height of betrayal of blackness (as in the Primus Provo eviction), in those portraying dramatic recoil of the narrator from illusions, or in those especially emphasizing a reverential treatment of folk value. But the principle is not fixed: the overriding guide is utility to theme and dramatic structure. The vespers scene at the southern college, it will be recalled, derives from black folklore and Western mythology.

Folklore does not appear, then, at any point for its own sake, nor is folk vision sentimentalized. As reverently as the folk Mary Rambo is treated, she is not seen as useful to the highest abstract reaches of personality. This view is in line, by extension, with Ellison's concept of southern folk community as a "pre-individual" community (*S&A*, 90). So it is not surprising that, once having absorbed what he can from her and having reached for more abstract levels of personality, the invisible narrator cannot return. Another example of the nonsentimental approach is the invisible narrator's newly gained appreciation of soul food, a passage which has been widely quoted for its humor and evidence of acceptance of identity. But the narrator realizes that identity on this level is really too simple. Further, as he continues to eat yams, one turns out to be frostbitten—not mere sweetness.

Yet there is something of the great performance, the *tour de force*, in Ellison's use of the folklore and cultural tradition that makes for both enlightenment regarding the literary potential of folklore and a certain unease. This response, I think, is inspired by the elaborate system of interconnection with Western symbols and mythology, and our awareness that blackness is more in need of definition than Western tradition, which has had the attention of innumerable literary masters. It has to do with the degree of faith that one has in the West, and the suspicion that major literary documents from Melville through Faulkner have been whispering to us of its death. And, in the black tradition, there have been so frequently an ambivalence and a questioning of the West that go deeper than casting a critical eye upon its technology and rationalism.

The questions raised by Larry Neal regarding Ellison's relationship to the West in his critical essays may well be raised regarding the interconnection system in *Invisible Man*, since there is almost a mathematical consistency between Ellison's critical pronouncements and his creative performance. Writing in *Black Theatre*, Neal credited Ellison with a broad theoretical sense of black folklore tradition and culture, and an awareness of the "explosive tensions underlying the Black man's presence in the United States," but criticized him for overlaying "his knowledge of Black culture with concepts that exist outside it" (10).

Certainly, the result in *Invisible Man*, if one commits himself to a grasp of the depths of the book, is sometimes simultaneously an awe at sheer brilliance of conjunctions and a hunger for further depths of definition of blackness, which this wily genius obviously has the capacity to make. For make no mistake about it, anyone who could throw in those images of blackness with such rapidity and apparent ease, who could tone their depths as a gifted musician would do, has, as a pressure behind his imagination, an almost godlike knowledge of blackness. Make no mistake, Ellison paid his dues to culture. At no time does one run into a blackness that is rhetorical only, as one still frequently does in even very radical writing. But Ellison, himself, admits that the book would have been better if it had had more of Mary Rambo.[6] We would add to Mary, more of Bledsoe, more of the campus dreamers, more of the Harlem rioters, and more even of B. P. Rinehart and Ras, the Destroyer. And we would suppose that it is possible to sound the depths of the universe by a fine excess in the examination of blackness. A William Faulkner, for example, in making us feel the American and Western aspects of his universe, simply asserts himself as the deepest of southerners, and communicates through symbols most deeply associated with the South. Perhaps the Faulknerian way is one of the future, since neither the spirit of the 1950s nor the temperament and sensibility which Ellison has frequently and emphatically expounded suggest that earlier, in dealing with blackness, a black focus would have been successful or that it would have found an audience.

In the end, it is the great fruits at hand which Ellison harvested that must be seized upon. For the young writer, his use of folk tradition provides a veritable textbook which can be adapted, according to one's own sensibility and outlook. For, more than any other writer, Ellison grappled with its power, its cryptic messages, its complexity. Particularly noteworthy is his realization that folk tradition cannot seem, in a self-conscious artist, to be an end in itself. That is, the writer cannot simply enclose himself within the womb of folkness or content himself with simple celebration of folkness. True folk forms have already celebrated folk life better than the self-conscious artist can hope to do. But the basic *attitudes* and *forms* of response to existence evolved by the folk are abandoned by us only at our peril. These attitudes and forms of response are then of greatest service as flexible instruments for confronting a darkness that is always changing in its complexity. Ellison exemplified a profound knowledge of all such ramifications.

NOTES

1. Ralph Ellison, *Shadow and Act*, 253. Subsequent citations in text appear as *S&A*.

2. Both authors' essays first appeared in *Partisan Review* (Spring 1958). Ellison's essay is reprinted in *Shadow and Act*, Hyman's in *The Promised End* (Cleveland: World Publishing Company, 1963).

3. Citations from Ellison's *Invisible Man* appear in text as *IM*.

4. See Selma Fraiberg, "Two Modern Incest Heroes," 646–61. In this section, I am very much indebted to her essay.

5. See "Out of the Hospital and Under the Bar" in *Soon, One Morning*, 240–90.

6. See unused section of hospital scene in "Out of the Hospital and Under the Bar."

WORKS CITED

Ellison, Ralph. "Flying Home." *Dark Symphony*. Ed. James A. Emanuel and Theodore L. Gross. New York: Free Press, 1968.

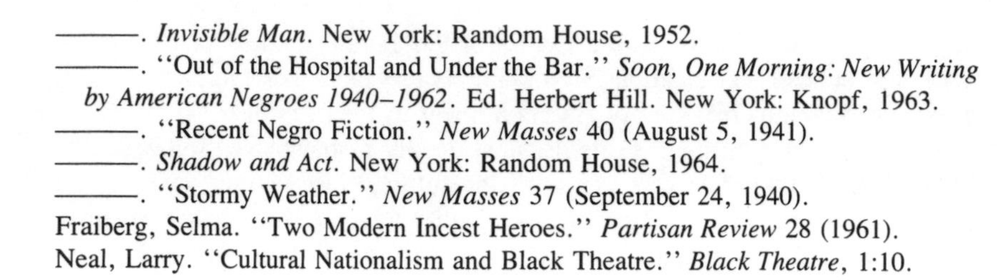

———. *Invisible Man*. New York: Random House, 1952.
———. "Out of the Hospital and Under the Bar." *Soon, One Morning: New Writing by American Negroes 1940–1962*. Ed. Herbert Hill. New York: Knopf, 1963.
———. "Recent Negro Fiction." *New Masses* 40 (August 5, 1941).
———. *Shadow and Act*. New York: Random House, 1964.
———. "Stormy Weather." *New Masses* 37 (September 24, 1940).
Fraiberg, Selma. "Two Modern Incest Heroes." *Partisan Review* 28 (1961).
Neal, Larry. "Cultural Nationalism and Black Theatre." *Black Theatre*, 1:10.

Ellison's Zoot Suit

LARRY NEAL

Well, there is one thing that you have to admit. And that is, dealing with Ralph Ellison is no easy matter. It is no easy task to fully characterize the nature of Ellison's life and work. He cannot be put into any one bag and conveniently dispensed with. Any attempt to do so merely leads to aesthetic and ideological oversimplifications. On the surface, oversimplifications may appear pragmatic and viable but, in the long run, they weaken us. To overlook the complex dimensions of a man's ideas, character, and personality is to do great disservice to the righteous dissemination of knowledge.

Much of the criticism directed against Ellison is personal, oversimplified, and often not based on an analysis of the man's work and ideas. A great deal of the criticism emanates from ideological sources that most of us today reject.

To be concise, much of the anti-Ellison criticism springs from a specific body of Marxian and black neo-Marxian thought. The literary term used to designate this body of thought is called "social realism." Some of Ellison's most virulent critics have been social realists.

One of the most famous of social realists' attacks was the subject of a literary exchange between Ellison and Irving Howe, a liberal left-winger and former editor of *Dissent* magazine. In an essay published in the Fall 1963 issue of *Dissent*, Howe accused Baldwin and Ralph Ellison of abandoning the task of the Negro writer. That task Howe proposed to be the militant assertion of Negro freedom. In his assault upon Baldwin and Ellison, Howe evoked Richard Wright as the embodiment of the truest, most relevant exponent of black freedom in fiction. Howe, the knowing white boy, praised Wright for his penchant toward what is termed "protest" literature and castigated both Ellison and Baldwin for their failure to carry on the "protest" tradition as exemplified by Wright's *Native Son*.

Ellison wrote an excellent rebuttal to Howe's piece, titled "The World and the Jug."[1] Ellison attacked Howe's attempt to rigidly circumscribe the role of the black writer. He asserted the essential differences in outlook between himself and Richard Wright. Where Wright, in *Black Boy*, saw black life "void of hope" and bare of tradition, Ellison countered with a very positive vision of Afro-American life. For Ellison, black people did not exhibit a tradition void of hopes, memories, and personal attachments. They were, instead, profoundly human and blessed with a strong, spiritually sustaining culture. "The World and the Jug" is a finely balanced essay, mean, but eloquently controlled.

Underlying this exchange between Ellison and Howe is the recurring question of the writer's role, especially in the context of the struggle for human liberation. Marxism puts forth the idea that all literature is propaganda, or becomes propaganda when it enters the social sphere. And, as propaganda, it is implicitly a reflection of class attitudes. The role of the revolutionary writer in the Marxist context is, therefore, to extol the virtues of the proletariat, to sharpen their class consciousness in order that they may overthrow the ruling classes and finally take control of the "means of production."

Richard Wright was especially influenced by the Marxist ideas he encountered in the thirties. As a young writer he had joined the John Reed Club in Chicago and was very active in Communist cultural activities. Coming from Mississippi, where he had seen and experienced racial oppression, he sincerely believed that it was his duty to use his writing as a weapon against that oppression. All of his writing, up to and including his masterwork, *Native Son*, is informed by his belief in social revolution. Following Lenin's idea that the revolutionary vanguard must expose the corruption in the capitalist system, all of Wright's fictional landscapes, with the exception of *The Long Dream*, tend to be very bleak and humorless. Excellent social realist that he was, he was skillful at depicting in exact detail the impact of the material world on both the oppressed and the oppressors alike. Now Wright has gone the way of the ancestors, but he is still a major influence in contemporary black writing. At least we are still feeling the influence of a certain kind of "protest" writing that appears highly reminiscent of Wright, even though most of it does not begin to approach Wright's high level of artistic achievement.

What Ralph Ellison was doing in his exchange with Irving Howe was defending his right to his (Ellison's) own personal vision, while trying not to fall into the bag of depreciating Wright: "Must I be condemned because my sense of Negro Life was quite different?" (*S&A*, 119). Ellison asks this question, fully aware that there is an ideological contingent lying in wait to pounce on him for not carrying on in the tradition of Wright. But, ironically, it was Wright himself who rejected the sectarian Marxism of the American Communist party. Dig his essay in Arthur Koestler's book, *The God That Failed*. And in the foreword to George Padmore's *Pan-Africanism or Com-*

munism, Wright implies that the black man operates on the premise of a personal nationalism, and not along fixed ideological lines:

> The Negro's fundamental loyalty is, therefore, to *himself*. His situation makes this inevitable. [Am I letting awful secrets out of the bag? I'm sorry. The time has come for this problem to be stated clearly so that there is no possibility of further misunderstanding or confusion. The Negro, even when embracing Communism or Western Democracy, is not supporting ideologies; he is seeking to use *instruments* (instruments owned and controlled by men of other races!) for his own ends. He stands outside of those instruments and ideologies; he has to do so, for he is not allowed to blend with them in a natural, organic and healthy manner.] (13)

Like Wright, Ellison was also active in the literary Left of the late thirties and early forties. And also like Wright, Ellison rejected sectarian Marxism. As far as I can perceive, Ellison had never really internalized Marxism in the first place. This appears to be the case even when he was writing in the left-wing *New Masses*. His work appears always to have been striving for a penetration into those areas of black lifestyle that exist below the mere depiction of external oppression. He had read Marx, though, as should anyone who is interested in those ideas operative in today's world. But luckily for us, his work never took on the simplistic assertions of the literary Marxist.

Therefore, Ellison's clearly articulated break with naturalism must also be seen in light of his previous awareness that hard-core ideologues, particularly Communists, represented an awesome threat not only to his artistic sensibility, but to his "national" sensibility as well. And it is amazing how fantastically true Ellison's initial impulses have been. If Harold Cruse's *Crisis of the Negro Intellectual* has any one theme that demands our greatest attention, it is his clear analysis of the detrimental role that the left wing has played in our struggle for self-determination and liberation. Ellison himself is also aware, and this awareness underlies the following remarks he made in an interview that was published in the March 1967 issue of *Harper's* magazine. He is speaking to several young black writers:

> They fostered the myth that Communism was twentieth-century Americanism, but to be a twentieth-century American meant, in their thinking, that you had to be more Russian than American and less Negro than either. That's how they lost the Negroes. The Communists recognized no plurality of interests and were really responding to the necessities of Soviet foreign policy and when the war came, Negroes got caught and were made expedient in the shifting of policy. Just as Negroes who fool around with them today are going to get caught in the next turn of the screw. ("Stern Discipline," 88)

Ellison has not been forgotten by his enemies both in the white Left and the black Left. The Communists were the first to lead the attack against Ellison when *Invisible Man* appeared in 1952. Since then, we have read or heard a number of attacks emanating from black writers who trace their literary lineage from the so-called progressive movements of the thirties and forties. In this connection, the interested reader should dig Harold Cruse's section on Ellison in *The Crisis of the Negro Intellectual*. Cruse's book seems theoretically out of focus in many instances, because it walks such a precarious line between a weakly defined nationalism and a strained neo-Marxism. But, in my opinion, he is strictly on the case when he enters the "debate" between Ellison and his detractors. Here I refer to Cruse's account of the anti-Ellison attack that occurred at a writers' conference at the New School in 1965. Leading the charge against Ellison were Herbert Aptheker, a leading theoretician of the Communist party; John Henrik Clarke, the editor of several significant anthologies; and John O. Killens, the novelist. Cruse asserts that the writers gathered at the conference were not properly prepared to cope with the questions posed by Ellison's critical and aesthetic methodology. Further, he asserted that "the radical left wing will never forgive Ellison for writing *Invisible Man*" (Cruse, 505–511).

Why? The answer is quite simple. The literary Left, both white and Negro, were fuming over Ellison's rejection of white-controlled left-wing politics, his harsh depiction of the Communists (called the "Brotherhood" in Ellison's novel), and the novel's obvious rejection of the aesthetics of social realism. The Communist *Daily Worker* of June 1, 1952, for example, published a review of the book under the following headline:

RALPH ELLISON'S NOVEL "INVISIBLE MAN" SHOWS
SNOBBERY, CONTEMPT FOR NEGRO PEOPLE

The review which followed was written by a Negro left-winger named Abner N. Berry, who opened his piece by stating:

> Written in vein of middle class snobbishness—even contempt—towards the Negro people, Ellison's work manipulates his nameless hero for 439 pages through a maze of corruption, brutality, anticommunism slanders, sex perversion and the sundry inhumanities upon which a dying social system feeds.

And on the aesthetic level he asserted:

> There are no *real* characters in *Invisible Man*, nor are there any *realistic* situations. The structure, the characters and the situations are *contrived* and resemble *fever fantasy*. . . . In effect, it is 439 pages of contempt for humanity, written in an *affected, pretentious*, and *other worldly* style to suit the king pins of world white supremacy. (Emphasis mine, naturally.)

Therefore, along with making the unpardonable sin of obliquely attacking the Party through his characterization of the "Brotherhood" in his novel, Ellison was also being attacked for having developed a new aesthetic universe, one that was seeking to develop its own laws of form and content. Social realism, particularly Marxist socialist realism, does not allow for the free play of fantasy and myth that Ellison was attempting in his novel. Marxist social realism essentially posits the view that the details of a work of art should be predicated on fairly simple structural lines. A work should extol the virtues of the working classes; but, the extolling should take place along Party lines. Hence, not only is the writer's aesthetic range controlled, but his political range as well. And to further worsen matters, this aesthetic ideology is nearly Victorian in the extreme. It seems to emanate from a very square vision of social realities.

Here is John O. Killens in the June, 1952 edition of the newspaper *Freedom*, commenting on *Invisible Man*:

> Mix a heavy portion of sex and a heavy, heavy portion of violence, a bit of sadism and a dose of redbaiting (Blame the Communists for everything bad) and you have the making of a bestseller today.
>
> Add to this decadent mixture of a Negro theme with Negro characters as Uncle Toms, pimps, sex perverts, guilt-ridden traitors—and you have a publisher's dream.
>
> But how does Ellison present the Negro people? The thousands of exploited farmers in the South represented by a sharecropper who made both his wife and daughter pregnant. The main character of the book is a young Uncle Tom who is obsessed with getting to the "top" by pleasing the Big, Rich White folks. A million Negro veterans who fought against fascism in World War II are rewarded with a maddening chapter [of] crazy vets running hogwild in a down home tavern. The Negro ministry is depicted by an Ellison character who is a Harlem pastor and at the same time a pimp and a numbers racketeer.
>
> The Negro people need Ralph Ellison's *Invisible Man* like we need a hole in the head or a stab in the back.
>
> It is a vicious distortion of Negro life.[7]

It is remarkable how similar were Berry's and Killens's reactions to this novel. They easily could have been written by the same person. But this is supposed to be 1970. And I would like to believe that we can read *Invisible Man* with more intellectual freedom than is apparent in Abner Berry's and John O. Killens's presumably sincere, but extremely flaccid critical remarks. Especially today, when the major concerns ramified throughout Ellison's life and work are still very relevant to our contemporary search for new systems of social organization and creative values. Ellison's vision, in some respects, is not that far removed from the ideas of some of the best black writers and intellectuals working today. That's why I wince somewhat when I reread the following statement that I made in the afterword to *Black Fire*: "The things that concerned Ellison are interesting to read, but contemporary Black youth feel another force in the world today. We know who we are, and are not invisible, *at least not to each other*. We are not Kafkaesque creatures stumbling through a white light of confusion and absurdity. . . ." (652).

My statements represent one stage in a long series of attempts, over the past several years, to deal with the fantastic impression that Ellison's work has had on my life. It is now my contention that of all the so-called older black writers working today, it is Ralph Ellison who is the most engaging. But the major issue separating many young black writers from a Ralph Ellison appears to have very little to do with creative orientation, but much more to do with the question of political activism and the black writer. Ellison's stance is decidedly nonpolitical "[The novel] is *always* a public gesture, though not necessarily a political one" (*S&A*, 110). (We'll come back to this later.) And further, there is a clearly "aristocratic" impulse in his stance, an understandable desire not to be soiled by the riffraff from all kinds of ideological camps. As we have already noted, Ellison, like Wright, was active in left-wing literary circles in the late thirties and early forties. There must have been some psychological torments for him then, since we can glean, even from his early writings, a distinctly "nationalistic" orientation that must have, at times, been at odds with the Party line. Why should this have caused problems?

The answer is very simple. Most serious writers should understand it: The left wing, particularly the Communist party, represented one of the main means by which a young black writer could get published. There were perhaps other routes through the Establishment. But for a young black writer checking out the literary happenings in 1937 (Ellison was about twenty-eight years old when he wrote his first piece for *New Challenge*, a black, left-oriented magazine), the Party was very attractive. After all, was not Richard Wright on that side of the street? And did not the Communist party seem very amenable to young black talent? I hope that I am not exaggerating, but it seems that, from this perspective, the whole literary atmosphere, for a black writer, seems to have been dominated by the Left.

Never having been a hard-core ideologue in the first place, Ellison appears to have been exceedingly uncomfortable as a leftist polemicist. Some of his journalistic writing for the Communist-oriented *New Masses* strains for political and social relevancy, just as some of ours does. But you can perceive another kind of spirit trying to cut through the Marxist phrase-mongering, another kind of spirit trying to develop a less simplistic, more viable attitude toward not only the usable content of Afro-American culture in America, but more important, a sense of the *meaning* of that culture's presence and its manifestations as they impinged upon "white culture." One isolatable political tendency that begins to emerge at the end of Ellison's Marxist period is a nascent, loosely structured form of black nationalism.

But Ellison was always clever. As Ellison himself notes in the *Harper's* interview quoted earlier, he never wrote the "official type of fiction." "I wrote," he says, "what might be called propaganda—having to do with the Negro struggle—but my fiction was always trying to be something else: something different even from Wright's fiction. I never accepted the ideology which the *New Masses* attempted to impose on writers. They hated Dostoevski, but I was studying Dostoevski. . . . I was studying [Henry] James. I was also reading Marx, Gorki, Sholokhov, and Isaac Babel. I was reading everything, including the Bible. Most of all, I was reading Malraux. . . . This is where I was really living at the time . . . . Anyway, I think style is more important than political ideologies'' (''Stern Discipline,'' 86).

But there is even a counter-Marxian thrust below the surface of his early political writings. This counterthrust manifests itself in Ellison's concern with folk culture and lifestyle. So that in the midst of his political writings, it is possible to see him groping for a unique cultural theory, one that is shaped on the basis of cultural imperatives integral to the black man's experience in America. For example, 1943 found Ellison managing editor of the *Negro Quarterly*. The editor was Angelo Herndon, a black intellectual of the radical Left. Herndon had been arrested in the South for engaging in union activities. The *Negro Quarterly* appears to have been the last attempt on the part of black intellectuals of that period to fashion an ideological position that was revolutionary but not totally dominated by the white Marxist Left.

But there was a war going on in 1943. When the war began, America found herself on the side of the Allied Forces, Britain and France. She was also allied with the Russians against the fascist German state. Now that socialist Russia was under attack, American Communists began to concentrate on the war effort. In the interim between the Russo-German Pact of 1939 and the formal entry of Russia into the war, there had been a significant shift in Party policy with respect to the ''Negro question.'' Now that Russia was under attack, the Nonaggression Pact abrogated, the Communist party was urging its American chapter to de-emphasize the struggle for Negro liberation and instead to concentrate on the war effort. They correctly reasoned that excessive political activism among black people would only slow down the industrial war machinery, thus endangering Russia by impeding the progress of the Allied struggle in Europe. All of this put left-wing black intellectuals in a trick.

Their international perspective forced them to acknowledge the awesome threat that fascism posed to human progress. But they were also acutely aware that an atmosphere of racism and fascism also existed here in America. Then there was the question of Japan. Many black people felt a vague sense of identification with the powerful Asian nation and secretly wished that she would overcome the white Western powers. And there were other attitudes which grew out of the specific situation of racism in America.

A significant item in this regard is an unsigned editorial that appeared in the *Negro Quarterly* in 1943 which, from the import of its style and content, is believed to have been written by Ralph Ellison. The editorial addresses itself to the conflicting attitudes held by black people toward the war effort. Black people were being segregated in the armed services, and, because of racism, were not even getting an opportunity to make some bread in the war-related industries. It was the latter situation which had led to A. Philip Randolph's 1941 threat to march on Washington for jobs and fair employment. Under Randolph's pressure, President Franklin D. Roosevelt was forced to sign Executive Order 8802, which was supposed to guarantee black people equal access to jobs in the war industries. Under these circumstances, it is easy to understand why there were, among black people, such conflicting attitudes toward the war.

Ellison's writings enumerated these attitudes. They ranged from apathy to all-out rejection of war. Addressing himself to this attitude of rejection in the editorial mentioned earlier, Ellison stated that it sprang from a "type of Negro nationalism which, in a sense, is admirable; it would settle all problems on the simple principle that Negroes deserve equal treatment with all other free human beings. . . ." But Ellison concluded that this attitude of total rejection of the war effort was too narrow in scope. It was not just a case of "good white men" against "bad white men." The Negro, he strongly asserted, had a natural stake in the defeat of fascism, whether it was national or international. He further proposed that there was another manifestation of "Negro nationalism" that was neither a "blind acceptance" of the war nor an "unqualified rejection" of it. This attitude is

> broader and more human than the first two attitudes; and it is *scientific* enough to make use of *both* by *transforming* them into *strategies of struggle*. It is committed to life, it holds that the main task of the Negro people is to work unceasingly toward creating those democratic conditions in which it can live and recreate itself. It believes the historical role of Negroes to be that of integrating the larger American nation and compelling it untiringly toward true freedom. And while it will have none of the slavishness of the first attitude, it is imaginative and flexible enough to die if dying is forced upon it. (Emphasis mine.)

Somehow we are involved here with an attempt at ideological reconciliation between two contending trends in Afro-American thought, that is, the will toward self-definition, exclusive of the overall white society, and at the same time the desire not to be counted out of the processes of so-called American democracy. This is the precarious balancing act that Ellison is forced to perform while he tries to cut through the ideological prison in which he finds himself encased. He attacks Negro leaders for not having group consciousness, and calls for a "centralization" of Negro political power.

But as we proceed to read the editorial, we begin to encounter the Ellison who would be himself and write one of the most important novels in history. Toward the end of this editorial, with its carefully balanced blend of Marxism and Negro nationalism, we find Ellison making the following blatantly non-Marxist statement:

> A third major problem, and one that is indispensable to the centralization and direction of power, is that of learning the meaning of the *myths* and *symbols* which abound among the Negro masses. For without this knowledge, leadership, no matter how correct its program, will fail. Much in Negro life remains a *mystery*; perhaps the *zoot suit conceals* profound political meaning; perhaps the symmetrical frenzy of the Lindy-hop conceals clues to great potential powers—

> if only Negro leaders would solve this *riddle*. On this knowledge depends the effectiveness of any slogan or tactic. For instance, it is obvious that Negro resentment over their treatment at the hands of their allies is justified. This naturally makes for a resistance to our stated war aims, even though these aims are essentially correct; and they will be accepted by the Negro masses only to the extent that they are helped to see the bright start of *their own* hopes through the *fog* of their daily experiences. The problem is *psychological*; it will be solved only by a Negro leadership that is aware of the psychological attitudes and incipient forms of action which the black masses *reveal* in their emotion-charged *myths*, *symbols*, and wartime *folk-lore*. Only through a skillful and wise manipulation of these centers of repressed social energy will Negro resentments, self-pity and indignation be channelized to cut through temporary issues and become transformed into positive action. This is not to make the problem simply one of words, but to recognize . . . that words have their own vital importance. (Emphasis mine.)

There is a clear, definite sense of cultural nationalism at work here. These statements represent an especial attempt on the part of Ellison to get past the simplistic analysis of folk culture brought to bear on the subject by Marxist social realists. For rather than locating the mechanisms for organizing political power totally in an analysis of the black man's class structure, Ellison turns Marxism on its head, and makes the manipulation of cultural mechanisms the basis for black liberation.[3] Further, these statements set into motion a host of themes which are elaborated upon in his later work, particularly his cultural criticism. Here also we get snatches of a theory of culture. And some aspect of this theory seems to imply that there is an unstated, even noumenal set of values that exists beneath the surface of black American culture.

These values manifest themselves in a characteristic manner, or an *expressive style*. The Lindy-hop and the zoot suit are, therefore, in this context not merely social artifacts, but they, in fact, mask deeper levels of symbolic and social energy. Ellison perceives this theory as the instrumental basis for a new kind of Negro leader:

> They [the leaders] must integrate themselves with the Negro masses; they must be constantly alert to new concepts, new techniques and new trends among peoples and nations with an eye toward appropriating those which are valid when tested against the reality of Negro life. By the same test they must be just as alert to reject the faulty programs of their friends. When needed concepts, techniques or theories do not exist they must create them. Many new concepts will evolve when the people are closely studied in action. . . ."

To some extent, this kind of perception shapes many of the characters in *Invisible Man*. Rinehart comes to mind in this connection. However, there is a specific allusion to the ideas enunciated in this 1943 editorial in the following passage from Ellison's novel:

> What about those fellows waiting still and silent there on the platform, so still and silent they clash with the crowd in their very immobility, standing noisy

> in their very silence; harsh as a cry of terror in their quietness? What about these three boys, coming now along the platform, tall and slender, walking stiffly with swinging shoulders in their well-pressed, too-hot-for-summer suits, their collars high and tight about their necks, their identical hats of black cheap felt set upon the crowns of their heads with a severe formality above their conked hair? It was as though I'd never seen their like before: Walking slowly, their shoulders swaying, their legs swinging from their hips in trousers that ballooned upward from cuffs fitting snug about their ankles; their coats long and hip-tight with shoulders far too broad to be those of natural western men. These fellows whose bodies seemed—what had one of my teachers said of me?—"You're like one of these African sculptures, distorted in the interest of design." Well, what design and whose?[4]

To the protagonist, they seem like "dancers in a funeral service." (This episode follows the death of Tod Clifton.) Their black faces are described as being "secret." They wear "heel-plated shoes" and rhythmically tap as they walk. They are said to be "men outside of historical time." That is to say, no current theory of historical development accurately describes them. Yet there is a gnawing and persistent feeling, on the part of the unnamed protagonist, that the boys may hold the key to the future liberation. And as he grasps the implications of this idea, he is emotionally shaken:

> But who knew (and now I began to tremble so violently I had to lean against a refuse can)—who knew but they were the *saviors*, the *true leaders*, *the bearers* of something precious? The *stewards* of something uncomfortable, burdensome, which they hated because, living outside of history, *there was no one to applaud their value* and they themselves failed to understand it. (*IM*, 333; emphasis mine.)

Ellison's 1943 remarks in the *Negro Quarterly* concerning black cultural compulsives were cloaked in the language of politics. But they implicitly penetrate way beyond the sphere of politics. It is obvious from the foregoing passage that he thought enough of the concept of hidden cultural compulsives in black American life to *translate* them into art. Further, as we have noted, the concept is rather non-Marxist in texture and in substance. It probably represents, for him, a "leap" not only in political consciousness but in aesthetic consciousness as well. As a result of his experiences with hard-core ideological constructs, Ellison came to feel that politics were essentially inhibiting to an artist, if they could not be subsumed into art. Perhaps, this is what he means when he says in the *Harper's* interview: "Anyway, I think style is more important than political ideologies" ("Stern Discipline," 86).

I am not sure whether I fully concur with Ellison on this point. But there is something in his stance that specifically relates to the current black arts movement. The current movement is faced with some of the same problems that confronted Ellison. Only the historical landscape has changed, and the operational rhetoric is different.

I don't think I am exaggerating when I say that some form of nationalism is operative throughout all sections of the black community. The dominant political orientations shaping the sensibilities of many contemporary black writers fall roughly into the categories of cultural nationalism and revolutionary nationalism. That is to say, as writers, we owe whatever importance we may have to this current manifestation of nationalism. I, for one, tend to believe this is a good situation in which to be. It provides an audience to which to address our work, and also imports to it a certain sense of contemporaneity and social relevance.

But we are going to have to be careful not to let our rhetoric obscure the fact that a genuine nationalist revolution in the arts will fail, if the artistic products of that revolution do not encounter our audiences in a manner that demands their most profound attention. I'm talking about a black art that sticks to the ribs, an art that through the strength of all of its ingredients—form, content, craft, and technique—illuminates something specific about the living culture of the nation, and, by extension, reveals something fundamental about man on this planet.

Therefore, we have to resist the tendency to "program" our art, to set unnatural limitations upon it. To do so implies that we ultimately don't trust the intelligence of the national laity, and consequently feel that we must paternally guide them down the course of righteous blackness. So very often we defuse the art by shaping it primarily on the basis of fashionable political attitudes. There is a tendency to respond to work simply on the sensation it creates.[5] If black art is to survive, in the national sense, it's gonna need more supporting it than a cluster of new clichés.

Translating Politics into Art

There is quite a discussion about the nature of history in Ellison's *Invisible Man*. Along with the obvious theme of identity, the nameless narrator is constantly in search of a "usable past." In order to arrive at an understanding of the complex dimensions of his American experience, Ellison plunged deep into the murky world of mythology and folklore, both of which are essential elements in the making of a people's history. But Ellison's history is non-dialectical. The novel attempts to construct its own universe, based on its own imperatives, the central ones being the shaping of a personal vision, as in the blues, and the celebration of a collective vision as is represented by the living culture. And it is the living culture, with all of its shifting complexities, which constitutes the essential landscape of the novel. The unnamed narrator questions the "scientific" history of the Brotherhood and, in one of the most intense sections of the novel, asks the following question: "What if Brother Jack were wrong? What if history was a gambler, instead of a force in a laboratory experiment, and the boys his ace in the hole? What if history was not a reasonable citizen, but a madman full of paranoid guile . . . ?'' (*IM*, 333)

This discourse follows the death of Tod Clifton, a man who had previously been described as having fallen ''outside of history.'' Tottering between contending political forces, that is, the rigid dogmas of the Brotherhood and the emotionally compelling rhetoric of Ras the Exhorter, Tod attempts to leap outside historical time altogether. And he ultimately leaps to his death.

Churning way beneath the surface of the novel's narrative is a fantastically rich and engaging mythic and folkloristic universe. Further, this universe is introduced to us through the music of Louis Armstrong, whose music, then, forms the overall structure for the novel. If that is the case, the subsequent narrative and all of the action which follows can be read as one long blues solo. Critic Albert Murray, a close associate of Ellison's, put it this way:

> *Invisible Man* was *par excellence* the literary extension of the blues. Ellison had taken an everyday twelve-bar blues tune (by a man from down South sitting in a manhole up North in New York, singing and signifying about how he got there) and scored it for full orchestra. This was indeed something different and something more than run-of-the-mill U.S. fiction. It had new dimensions of rhetorical resonance (based on lying and signifying). It employed a startlingly effective fusion of narrating realism and surrealism, and it achieved a unique but compelling combination of the naturalistic, the ridiculous, and the downright hallucinatory. (*Omni Americans*, 167)

What is important about Murray's observation here is that it isolates, in *Invisible Man*, a unique aesthetic. There has been much talk of late about a ''black aesthetic,'' but there has been, fundamentally, a failure to examine those elements of the black experience in America which could genuinely constitute an aesthetic. With no real knowledge of folk culture—blues, folk songs, folk narratives, spirituals, dance styles, gospels, speech, and oral history—there is very little possibility that a black aesthetic will be realized in our literature.

Ellison, however, finds the aesthetic all around him. He finds it in memories of Oklahoma background. He finds it in preachers, blues singers, hustlers, gamblers, jazzmen, boxers, dancers, and itinerant storytellers. He notes carefully the subtleties of American speech patterns. He pulls the covers off the stereotypes in order to probe beneath the surface where the hard-core mythic truth lies. He keeps checking out style. The way people walk, what they say, and what they leave *un*said. If anyone has been concerned with a ''black aesthetic'' it has certainly got to be Ralph Ellison. And even if you disagree with Ellison's political thrust these days, you have to dig his consistent concern for capturing the essential truths of the black man's experience in America.

And where are these essential truths embodied, if not in the folk culture? Do not Stagalee, High John the Conqueror, John Henry, Shine, and the Signifying Monkey reveal vital aspects of our group experience? Or has the current "rediscovery" of African culture obscured the fact that however disruptive slavery must have been to our original African personalities, our fathers and mothers intuitively understood what aspect of it could be rescued and reshaped? And did not this reshaping indicate a *willed* desire to survive and maintain one's own specific outlook on life? Didn't it exhibit a willed desire to survive in the face of danger? What kind of people were they in their weaknesses and their strengths? Haven't we read their slave narratives and listened carefully to their songs? And hasn't the essential spirit that they breathed into these expressions continued to manifest itself in all meaningful aspects of our struggle? We must address ourselves to this kind of humanity because it is meaningful and within our immediate reach. To do so means understanding something essential about the persistence of tradition, understanding the manner in which values are shaped out of tradition, and—what's more important—understanding the values whose fundamental function was to bind us together into a community of shared feelings and memories in order that we might survive.

Ellison's protagonist, when confronted with possible expulsion from his southern Negro college, suffers deeply at the thought of losing his regional roots. In his longing for a sustainable image of the world that has created him, he transforms an "ordinary" housemother into a ritual goddess. Dig. Here is your black aesthetic at its best:

> *Ha! to the gray-haired matron in the final row. Ha! Miss Susie, Miss Susie Gresham, back there looking at that co-ed smiling at that he-ed—listen to me, the bungling bugler of words, imitating the trumpet and the trombone's timbre, playing thematic variations like a baritone horn. Hey! old connoisseur of voice sounds, of voices without messages, of newsless winds, listen to the vowel sounds and the crackling dentals, to the low harsh gutturals of empty anguish, now riding the curve of a preacher's rhythm I heard long ago in a Baptist church, stripped now of its imagery: No suns having hemorrhages, no moons weeping tears, no earthworms refusing the sacred flesh and dancing in the earth on Easter morn. Ha! singing achievement. Ha! booming success, intoning. Ha! acceptance, Ha! a river of word-sounds filled with drowned passions, floating, Ha! floating, Ha! with wrecks of unachievable ambitions and stillborn revolts, sweeping their ears, Ha! ranged stiff before me, necks stretched forward with listening ears, Ha! a-spraying the ceiling and a-drumming the dark-stained after rafter, that seasoned crossarm of torturous timber mellowed in the kiln of a thousand voices; playing, Ha! as upon a xylophone; words marching like the student band, up the campus and down again, blaring triumphant sounds empty of triumphs. Hey, Miss Susie! the sound of words that were no words, counterfeit notes singing achievements yet unachieved, riding upon the wings of my voice out to you, old matron, who knew the voice sounds of the Founder and knew the accents and echo of his promise; your gray old head cocked with the young around you, your eyes closed, face ecstatic, as I toss the word-sounds in my breath, my bellows, my fountain, like bright-colored balls in a water spout—hear me, old matron, justify now this sound with your dear old*

> *nod of affirmation, your closed-eye smile and bow of recognition, who'll never be fooled with the mere content of words, not my words, not these pinfeathered flighters that stroke your lids till they flutter with ecstasy with but the mere echoed noise of the promise. And after the singing and outward marching, you seize my hand and sing out quavering, ''Boy, some day you'll make the Founder proud!'' Ha! Susie Gresham, Mother Gresham, guardian of the hot young women on the puritan benches who couldn't see your Jordan's water for their private steam; you, relic of slavery whom the campus loved but did not understand, aged, of slavery, yet bearer of something warm and vital and all-enduring, of which in that island of shame we were not ashamed—it was to you on the final row I directed my rush of sound, and it was you of whom I thought with shame and regret as I waited for the ceremony to begin.* (*IM*, 88–89)

This poetic narrative is the prelude to the ceremony in which Rev. Homer Barbee, taking the role of tribal poet, ritually consecrates the memory of the Founder. His speech is permeated with myth. The Founder's image is not merely locked into legitimate history, it bobs and weaves between facts, half-remembered truths, and apocrypha. The Founder is perceived by Barbee as a culture hero bringing order out of chaos, bringing wisdom to bear upon fear and ignorance. He is compared to Moses, Aristotle, and Jesus. He is called, by Homer Barbee, ''prophet,'' ''godly man,'' ''the great spirit,'' and ''the great sun.'' In his hardships and moments of danger, he is helped by strange emissaries, one of whom, Barbee says, may have come ''direct from above.'' Another of the Founder's helpers is an old slave who is ridiculed by the town's children:

> He, the old slave, showing a surprising knowledge of such matters—*germology* and *scabology*—ha! ha! ha!—he called it, and what youthful skill of the hands! For he shaved our skull, and cleansed our wound and bound it neat with bandages stolen from the home of an unsuspecting leader of the mob, ha! (*IM*, 94)

Barbee makes his audience, composed primarily of black college students, identify with the Founder. No, in fact, under the spell of the ritual sermon, they must *become* the Founder. They must don the mask of the god, so to speak. All of these details are said to be remembered by the students, yet Barbee has a compulsive need to reiterate them, to recharge them with meaning by reconsecrating them. His essential role, as ritual priest, is to keep before them the ''painful details'' of the Founder's life. These are memories that his young audience must internalize, and share fully, if they are to ever realize themselves in the passage from adolescence into maturity. And this is the function of folk culture. This is what Ellison sensed in the blues. In an essay entitled, ''Richard Wright's Blues,'' he notes:

> The blues is an impulse to keep the painful details and episodes of a brutal experience alive in one's aching consciousness, to finger its jagged grain, and to transcend it, not by the consolation of philosophy but by squeezing from it

> a near-tragic, near-comic lyricism. As a form, the blues is an autobiographical chronicle of personal catastrophe expressed lyrically . . . . (*S&A*, 78–79)

In "Blues People," a review of Imamu Baraka's (LeRoi Jones's) book, he makes this statement about the role of the blues singer:

> Bessie Smith might have been a "blues queen" to the society at large, but within the tighter Negro community where the blues were part of the total way of life, and a major expression of an attitude toward life, she was a priestess, a celebrant who affirmed the values of the group and man's ability to deal with chaos.[6]

Blues represent a central creative motif throughout *Invisible Man* from the hero's "descent" into the music at the beginning of the novel. The blues allow Trueblood to face up to himself after the disastrous event of making his daughter pregnant. The blues inform the texture of much of the novel's prose:

> My stomach felt raw. From somewhere across the quiet of the campus the sound of a guitar-blues plucked from an out-of-tune piano drifted towards me like a lazy, shimmering wave, like the echoed whistle of a lonely train, and my head went over again, against a tree, and I could hear it splattering the flowering vines. (*IM*, 122)

And at another point the hero contemplates the meaning of this blues lyric:

> *She's got feet like a monkey*
> *Legs*
> *Legs, Legs like a maaad*
> *Bulldog . . . .*
> (*IM*, 134)

"What does it mean?" he thinks.

> And why describe anyone in such contradictory words? Was it a sphinx? Did old Chaplin-pants, old dusty-butt, love her or hate her; or was he merely singing? What kind of woman could love a dirty fellow like that, anyway? And how could even *he* love her if she were as repulsive as the song described? . . . I strode along, hearing the cartman's song become a lonesome, broad-toned whistle now that flowered at the end of each phrase into a tremulous, blue-toned chord. And in its flutter and swoop, I heard the sound of a railroad train highballing it, lonely across the lonely night. He was the Devil's son-in-law, all right, and he was a man who could whistle a three-toned chord, . . . God damn, I thought, they're a hell of a people! And I didn't know whether it was pride or disgust that suddenly flashed over me. (*IM*, 134–35)

Why this emphasis on folklore and blues culture? In a recent issue of the *College Language Association* (CLA) *Journal*, George Kent supplies an answer which many of those who consider themselves nationalists should well consider:

> Offering the first drawings of a group's character, preserving situations repeated in the history of the group, describing the boundaries of thought and feeling, projecting the group's wisdom in symbols expressing its will to survive, embodying those values by which it lives and dies, folklore seemed, as Ellison described it, basic to the portrayal of the essential spirit of black people.[7]

Ellison's spiritual roots are, therefore, deep in the black American folk tradition. I think that this awareness of specifically black contributions to the so-called mainstream of American life gives him a fundamental certainty that no matter how much he praises the writers of the white West, he is still himself: Ralph *Waldo* Ellison. Much of Ellison's concern with the major literary figures of Europe and America emanates from his sincere belief that it is the duty of every writer, black or white, to be fully aware of the best that has ever been written. For Ellison that has never meant *becoming* a white man. It meant bringing to bear on literature and language the force of one's own sensibility and modes of feeling. It meant learning the craft of fiction, even from white artists, but dominating that craft so much that you don't play like the other feller any more. That trumpet you got in your hand may have been made in Germany, but you sure sound like my Uncle Rufus whooping his coming-home call across the cotton fields. But you got to master the instrument first, Ellison might say. I would agree to that, but add this: you got to somehow master *yourself* in the process.

If there is any fundamental difference I have with Ellison, it is his, perhaps unintentional, tendency to imply that black writers should confine their range of cultural inquiry strictly to American—and European—subject matter. For a man who was not exactly parochial about his search for knowledge to subtly impose such attitudes on young writers is to deny the best aspects of his own development as an artist.

Young writers, on the other hand, should not fall for any specious form of reasoning that limits the range of their inquiry strictly to African and Afro-American subject matter. A realistic movement among the black arts community should be about the *extension* of the *remembered* and a *resurrection* of the *unremembered*; should be about an engagement with the *selves* we know and the *selves* we have forgotten. Finally, it should be about a synthesis of the conglomerate of world knowledge; all that is meaningful and moral and that makes one stronger and wiser, in order to live as fully as possible as a human being. What will make this knowledge ours is what we do with it, how we color it to suit our specific needs. Its value to us will depend upon what we bring to bear upon it. In our dispersal, we can "dominate" Western culture or be "dominated" by it. It all depends on what you feel about yourself. Any black writer or politician who does not believe that black people have created something powerful and morally sustaining in their four hundred or so years here has declared himself a loser before the war begins. How would we create, even fight, denying the total weight of our particular historical experience *here* in America.

I must emphasize the word "total" because, as Ellison and Albert Murray often explain, there is a tendency among American sociologists and black creative intellectuals to perceive our history in purely pathological terms. For example, Don L. Lee makes a statement in *Ebony* magazine to the following effect: If you don't know about rats and roaches, you don't know about the black experience. Why define yourself in purely negative terms, when you know that your very life, in its most profound aspects, is not merely a result of the negative? We are not simply, in *all* areas of our sensibilities, merely a set of black reactions to white oppression. And neither should our art be merely an aesthetic reaction to white art. It has finally got to exist as good art also, because in terms of the development of a national art, excellent art is, in and of itself, the best propaganda you can have. By now, we should be free enough to use any viable techniques that will allow us to shape an art that breathes and is based essentially on our own emotional and cultural imperatives.

Ellison, however, almost overwhelmingly locates his cultural, philosophical, and literary sensibility in the West. That's his prerogative, and that prerogative should be protected. But being so-called free individuals, at least on the question of whom one accepts as "literary ancestors," it is possible to extend one's vocabulary and memory in any manner one chooses. It's already being done in music; Coltrane, Sun Ra, Pharaoh Sanders, and Leon Thomas indicate devices, procedures, functions, attitudes, and concerns that are not vividly indicated in Euro-American culture. They indicate a synthesis and a rejection of Western musical theory at the same time, just as aspects of Louis Armstrong's trumpet playing indicated, in its time, a respect for the traditional uses of the instrument, on the one hand, and, on the other, to the squares, it indicated a "gross defilement" of the instrument. I recall once reading an article about a son of A. J. Sax, the Belgian instrument maker, who said something to the effect that he didn't believe his father intended for the instrument to be played the way jazz musicians were playing it. Yeah, you can take the other dude's instruments and play like your Uncle Rufus's hog callings. But there is another possibility also: *You could make your own instrument*. And if you can sing through that instrument, you can impose your voice on the world in a heretofore-unthought-of manner.

In short, you can create another world view, another cosmology springing from your own specific grounds, but transcending them as your new world realizes itself.

All black creative artists owe Ellison special gratitude. He and a few others of his generation have struggled to keep the culture alive in their artistic works. We should not be content with merely basking in the glow of their works. We need what they have given us. But the world has changed. Which is as it should be. And we have changed in the world. Which is quite natural. Because everybody and everything is change. However, what Ellison teaches us is that it is not possible to move toward meaningful creative ends without somehow taking with you the accumulated weight of your forebears' experiences.

What I think we have to do is to understand our roles as synthesizers: the creators of new and exciting visions out of the accumulated weight of our Western experience. We must also deeply understand the specific reasons, both historically and emotionally, that cause many of us to *feel* that there is a range of ideas beyond those strictly of the West. To be more precise, no philosophical, political, or religious attitude in the world today, Western or Eastern, fully provides the means of mankind's spiritual and psychic liberation. No one system of ethics, oriental or occidental, exists in harmony with the social world from which it springs. Why?

Perhaps it is because the one central component of man's sensibility which would allow him to survive on human terms has never been allowed to flower. And that is the artistic sensibility which essentially defines man as a spiritual being in the world. That is because politicians have never accepted the idea that art was simply a public gesture, hence not political. Therefore, Ellison is incorrect when he says to Irving Howe: "I would have said that it [the novel] is always a public gesture, though not necessarily a political one." This statement is only half-true. The novel is *both* a public gesture *and* a political gesture. As Ellison knows, burning a Cadillac on the White House lawn[8] is a public gesture, but it is amusingly political also. The minute a work of art enters the social sphere, it faces the problem of being perceived on all kinds of levels, from the grossly political to the philosophically sublime. It just be's that way, that's all. And Marx hasn't a thing to do with it. But Marxists implicitly understand the relationship between a work's public character and its political character, however minute a work's political characteristics might be. And that is why totalitarian and fascist regimes must suppress all genuine art. "Who is that fool babbling all kinds of ghosts and chimera out of his eyes, ears, hands, feet, and mouth? We can't understand him. He must certainly be enemy."

In a system of strategies, of statement, and counterstatement, art is just one other element in the ring, even when it dons an elaborate mask and pretends not to be saying what it really says. *Invisible Man* is artistically one of the world's greatest novels; it is also one of the world's most successful "political" novels. It is just that Ellison's politics are ritualistic as opposed to secular. Ellison's manipulation of rhetorical imagery in *Invisible Man* is enough to blow the average politician off the stand.

The poet, the writer, is a key bearer of culture. Through myth, he is the manipulator of both the collective conscious and unconscious. If he is good, he is the master of rhetorical imagery. And, as such, he is much more psychically powerful than the secular politician. And that is why he is, to some extent, in some societies, feared and suppressed by secular politicians. Sometimes, he is suppressed even by the laity who must finally embrace his art, if it is to live. But the suppression of art, whether it occurs in the West or in the East, whether it occurs under capitalism or socialism, is detrimental to man's spiritual survival. Without spirit, the substance of all of his material accomplishments means essentially nothing. Therefore, what we might consider is a system of politics and art that is as fluid, as functional, and as expansive as black music. No such system now exists; we're gonna have to build it. And when it is finally realized, it will be a conglomerate, gleaned from the *whole* of all of our experiences.

Later now:
A cool *asante*
in the hey y'all,
habari gani to yo' mamma,
this has been your sweet Poppa Stoppa
running the voodoo down.

NOTES

1. Ralph Ellison, "The World and the Jug," in *Shadow and Act* (New York: Random House, 1964). Quotations from this essay and others in *Shadow and Act* are cited in the text as *S&A*.

2. John O. Killens, *Freedom*, June 1952, 7. Killens's comments are reprinted in Harold Cruse, *The Crisis of the Negro Intellectual* (New York: William Morrow & Co., 1967), 235.

3. See Maulana Karenga's seven criteria for culture in *The Quotable Karenga* (US), 1967. Note that Maulana makes one of the seven criteria for culture Mythology, and another important one Creative Motif. See also Cruse, *Crisis of the Negro Intellectual*.

4. Ralph Ellison, *Invisible Man* (New York: Random House, 1952), 332–33. Subsequent references are cited in the text as *IM*.

5. For example, Sam Greenlee's novel, *The Spook Who Sat by the Door* (New York: R. W. Baron, 1969), is an atrocious novel. It lacks style and conscious sense of craft. It is clearly more of a "manual" than a "revolutionary" novel. Its major premise is excellent, but flawed by Greenlee's inability to bring it off. Its "revolutionary content" is never firmly rooted in a form that is sustaining below the mere surface of graphic detail. Where Greenlee could have written a "great" novel, one both excellently written and revolutionary in stance, he blew the challenge by a glib adherence to militancy.

6. Ellison's review of *Blues People* (*Shadow and Act*, 257) is stringently critical, and at times a little beside the point. What he really seems to be doing here is castigating LeRoi Jones for not writing the book that he (Ellison) would have written. The specific thrust of *Blues People* was never really analyzed. Of course Ellison is capable of analyzing the specific ideas in *Blues People*, but he just wanted to write his own essay on the blues. And his essay is worthwhile and meaningful, too.

7. See George E. Kent, ''Ralph Ellison and Afro-American Folk and Cultural Tradition,'' *College Language Association (CLA) Journal* 13 (1970): 256–76. Kent's essay is included in this volume, pages 95–104.

8. See Ellison's short story ''It Always Breaks Out,'' *Partisan Review*, Spring 1963: 13–28.

WORKS CITED

Berry, Abner N. Review of *Invisible Man* by Ralph Ellison. *Daily Worker*, June 1, 1952.

Cruse, Harold. *The Crisis of the Negro Intellectual*. New York: William Morrow & Co., 1967.

Ellison, Ralph. *Invisible Man*. New York: Random House, 1952.

______. ''It Always Breaks Out.'' *Partisan Review*, Spring 1963: 13–28.

______. *Shadow and Act*. New York: Random House, 1964.

______. ''A Very Stern Discipline.'' Interview with Steve Cannon, Lennox Raphael, and James Thompson. *Harper's* 234 (March 1967): 76–95.

Karenga, Maulana. *The Quotable Karenga*. (US: n.p.), 1967.

Murray, Albert. *The Omni Americans*. New York: Random House, 1970.

Neal, Larry. Afterword in *Black Fire: An Anthology of Afro-American Writing*. Edited by LeRoi Jones and Larry Neal. New York: William Morrow & Company, 1968.

Wright, Richard. Foreword to George Padmore's *Pan-Africanism or Communism*. New York: Roy Publishers, 1956.

Chaos, Complexity, and Possibility: The Historical Frequencies of Ralph Waldo Ellison

JOHN F. CALLAHAN

In recent years critics have shared with politicians a strange fixation with history, as if the word itself were an incantation. This may be simply a guise learned from public men. One of the tests on the stump these days is whether a presidential candidate has a sense of history. Once in office, a president's mere mention of American history seems to ward off criticism, like a charm keeping away evil spirits. Even Gerald Ford's bicentennial misquotation of Paul Revere—"one if by day and two if by night," I think he said—didn't offend people very much. Like presidents, writers, particularly novelists and critics of the novel, are often prepared to take advantage of the spell of history. Now there is an explanation, if not an excuse for this; after all, the novel emerged as a response to changing social and economic relationships in the eighteenth century, and its form has continued to change with society's changing patterns. Yet in our time a certain posturing often accompanies invocations of history. Mailer did it in *The Armies of the Night*, titling Book One *History as a Novel*, Book Two *The Novel as History*. Critics, in their aversion for declarations of self, frequently tend to mix abstraction with incantation.

Behind the use of history as incantation lies an understandable human desire to magnify the self through identification with larger forces and realities: the big picture. The danger is twofold. First is the mumbo-jumbo syndrome; that is, everyone uses history and tacitly agrees not to question another's meaning. Second, true believers of all persuasions pin down history to such an extent that it's pinioned to ideology, its complexities reduced to formulas and stereotypes. I am afraid the handiest example of the merging of these dangers is Walter Cronkite's patented line: *That's the way it is, such and such a day, such and such a month, nineteen hundred and so and so*. No matter what's happened, that's the way it is. Who knows what that means? All we know

From *Chant of Saints: A Gathering of Afro-American Literature, Art, and Scholarship*, eds. Michael S. Harper and Robert B. Stepto, 1979.

is that what we've watched during the past half-hour is supposed to cover all bets. With what's happened to point of view in this century, it's a wonder of the world that Walter keeps saying his line night after night, and greater wonder that for his pains he is regarded as the most trusted man in America.

The foregoing is by way of counterpoint to Ralph Ellison's use of history. Though deadly serious about the meaning and the use of history in his work, Ellison approaches the subject partly from a comic perspective. Like all incongruities, history, no less than posturings of history, is comic in the sense that it opens up the field of possibility. On one occasion Ellison irreverently told the Southern Historical Association: "I don't think that history is Truth. I think it's another form of man trying to find himself, and to come to grips with his own complexity, but within the frame of chronology and time."[1] Earlier in his remarks he had claimed that American historiography and American fiction are "both artificial; both are forms of literature, and I would suggest further that American history grows primarily out of the same attitudes of mind, and attitudes toward chronology, which gave birth to our great tall stories" (*SLJ*, 62). This is a comic clue to Ellison's quarrel with American history as written. A little later he narrows the focus to those "realities of American historical experience ruled out officially," that "stream of history which is still as tightly connected with folklore and the oral tradition as official history is connected with the tall tale" (*SLJ*, 69). "Stream of history"—the words telegraph Ellison's sense that, taken in all its forms, This republic's history lives up to its motto, *e pluribus unum*, even as the Mississippi is composed of countless independent, related tributaries.

Alongside chaos, a name for raw, uncharted experience, is the making of history—the forms we come up with when consciousness goes to work on what's happened and what's happening. Ellison never loses sight of the elusive play between the past and attitudes and circumstances behind human attempts to order the past. Here are two illustrations of how Ellison works, the first involving Irving Howe, the second, Imamu Baraka (then known as LeRoi Jones). In response to Howe's essay "Black Boys and Native Sons," Ellison wrote Part 1 of "The World and the Jug," to which Howe replied, and to which Ellison wrote Part 2. The following exchanges are sad and funny and devastating insights into the frequencies of American consciousness:

> ELLISON: Well, it all sounds quite familiar and I fear the social order which it forecasts more than I do that of Mississippi.[2]
>
> HOWE: This sentence seems to me shocking, both as it links me with a cultural authoritarianism I have spent decades in opposing and as it declares the state of Ross Barnett more palatable than what I am alleged to represent. ("Reply," 13)
>
> ELLISON: . . . Ross Barnett is not the whole state, . . . there is also a Negro Mississippi which is more varied than that which Wright depicted. ("Rejoinder," 20)

Given America's peculiar fluidity and diversity, historical consciousness depends on a well-honed sense of nuance and complexity. To use a metaphor, Ellison threw Howe a round-house curve on a three-two pitch when the latter thought he had every right to expect a fastball. Howe, in the assurance that he knows Ellison's stuff inside and out, fails to realize that one's best pitch depends on the circumstances. Fooled and made a strikeout victim, Howe looks to the umpire, and, finding none, appeals to the crowd. Ellison, however, is defiantly in control of his stuff, and when Howe hollers, he points out that the stereotype is in Howe's mind and not in the word Mississippi.

Similar in what it reveals of the quality of Ellison's mind is his response to a statement made by Jones in *Blues People*:

> "A slave," writes Jones, "cannot be a man." But what, one might ask, of those moments when he feels his metabolism aroused by the rising of the sap in spring? What of his identity among other slaves? With his wife? And isn't it closer to the truth that far from considering themselves only in terms of that abstraction, "a slave," the enslaved really thought of themselves as *men* who had been unjustly enslaved?[3]

It is one of Ellison's great strengths that his sense of everlasting relationship between chaos and possibility steels him against the superficialities of passing vogues. For him an individual is not wholly defined by history and ideology; always there is some act of will; always possibilities of an unforeseen, unpredictable nature intervene. Yet Ellison is finely scrupulous about his own point of view. After destroying Jones's absolute assertion, he writes that slavery was not a state of absolute repression. He does not say that no such state could exist, but rather calls attention to fluidities which for his purposes are even more important than the injustices and oppressions of slavery.

* * *

Over the years Ralph Waldo Ellison has issued an eloquent call to citizenship. In the process he has become a pre-eminent American moral historian. In his essays as well as in his novel, he combines the myth-maker's imagination with the historian's instinct for specific acts of the past. While in Rome, he tells us in "Tell It Like It Is, Baby" (135) he dreamed of Lincoln's body defiled by the mob—Lincoln as coon, picked clean like poor Robin of folklore. Like Hawthorne's "My Kinsman, Major Molineux," it is a tale of fatherhood and nationhood, and Ellison is explicit about the role of his father, who died when he was three. The dream also resonates with images of democratic affirmation and denial as old as the Republic—and as new. Specifically, Lincoln's stand for freedom and democracy and the mob's desecration of those principles is Ellison's working out of "the horror generated by the Civil War" and contained in the contemporary situation—explicitly, the Supreme Court's 1954 desegregation decision and the 1956 Manifesto of Southern Congressmen against the Court.

For Ellison the ''moral predicament of the nation'' is revealed everywhere in American life as essential baggage destined to accompany the ''American experiment.'' His sense of American history involves a chronology, but the chronology's form follows the trajectory of a boomerang: ''(Beware of those who speak of the *spiral* of history; they are preparing a boomerang).''[4] The words and promises hurled at the Republic's beginning return over and over again to startle, injure, and, certainly, to challenge those who speak for the country and those who hold it accountable for its democratic promises and traditions. In the Epilogue to *Invisible Man*, Ellison's character speaks of ''the principle on which the country was built'' (*IM*, 433). He does not mention explicitly the Declaration of Independence, the Bill of Rights, Lincoln's Gettysburg Address or Second Inaugural, or any of the documents of state on which Ellison builds his case in the essays. Nevertheless, there emerges a notion of history as a name for the process by which man shapes his destiny out of the chaos of circumstances. Everywhere in Ellison's work chaos appears as the front man for possibility. It is, Ellison believes, man's fate to defy the formlessness of chaos and the abyss, and at the same time to recognize that possibility flows from chaos. Ellison's parable comes down to the myth of creation reworked by the historical mind—in a battle royal of consciousness and circumstances. He doesn't crow about it—much—but Ellison plays out a defiant, richly independent variation on the romantic myth of Eden so often and so simplistically associated with America. His bent is historical, perhaps because his mind listens to what his experience is telling him: to ignore history (''To ignore, however,'' as he says of the racial issue, ''is not to nullify'' *S&A*, 98) is to miss out on the world of possibilities inherent in the interplay between the individual and society. In any case, Ellison's version of the beginnings of the American nation is secular, sacred too, but he uses that word with a twist. For him the responsibilities citizens have to one another and to society in a democracy are no less than sacred—that is, involving dedication and sacrifice and charged with the ultimate concerns that were once reserved for religion and the gods.

Therefore, in his version of the beginning, Ellison concentrates on the shaping of the nation. Circumstances—grievances against the crown—provided an occasion to articulate fully and put to the test principles which hitherto had existed in men's minds. As Invisible Man puts it in the Epilogue—really a Bill of Rights (and responsibilities), just as the Prologue acts as a fictional Declaration of Independence—this nation was the expression of the ''principle, which they themselves had dreamed into being out of the darkness and chaos of the feudal past'' (*IM*, 433). Notice the mixing of history and myth. The feudal past is alluded to as an almost primal state of formlessness; the founders' dream is a dream of creation but not of Eden or any private Utopia. Instead, they dream of government, of society, of the rights and duties of citizenship and of the public happiness John Adams felt would exist in such a society.

In "Society, Morality, and the Novel," a 1956 essay critics neglect at great peril, Ellison writes eloquently about what was set in motion by those who founded the nation. "In the beginning was not only the word but the contradiction of the word."[5] Affirming the novel, he affirms also the country as a field of change and possibility—and absurdity, another of Ellison's characteristic words. In the beginning was the assertion of equality and the contradiction of slavery. In the beginning was the declaration of the right to life, liberty, and the pursuit of happiness and the contradiction of the right. But—and this is Ellison's magnificent point—in the state of contradiction lay a world of democratic possibilities. "For in no other country was change such a given factor of existence; in no other country were the class lines so fluid and change so swift and continuous *and intentional*. In no other country were men so conscious of having defined their social aims or so committed to working toward making that definition a reality" (*LN*, 66–67). These possibilities of self Ellison grounds in public moral and social commitments. "The major ideas of our society," he observes, were "all grounded in a body of the most abstract and explicitly stated conceptions of human society and one which in the form of the great documents of state constitutes a body of assumptions about human possibility which is shared by all Americans—even those who resist most violently any attempt to embody them in social action" (*LN*, 69).

Form is the heart of the matter. Like Frederick Douglass, when he broke with Garrison, does Ellison have in mind the Constitution whose open form invites social and political change? Clearly, Ellison both accepts and rejects contradictions of the early Republic, "for man cannot simply say, 'Let us have liberty and justice and equality for all,' and have it; and a democracy more than any other system is always pregnant with its contradiction" (*SLJ*, 70). The central contradiction, of course, involved slavery and democracy, a contradiction whose tensions erupted in the Civil War eighty-five years after Americans had declared themselves free. During the war years President Lincoln leavened his sense of fated tragic necessity with a quality of leadership both stoical and tender, and therefore was able to reconcile the inevitable with the possible. For Lincoln the word was as sacred as the deed—an enabling force. In the Gettysburg Address and Second Inaugural he committed the nation to resolve its contradiction in favor of freedom and equality. What is uttered is the word, and the fulfillment of the word. Yet, as Ellison reminds us, and Lincoln warned, the Gettysburg Address, once hallowed, became unhallowed (the contradiction again). But not entirely. Because how many Americans, reading and memorizing its words, like Ellison "pondered its themes of sectional reconciliation and national rebirth many times long since, as the awareness grew that there was little about it that was simple and that it was profoundly implicated both in my life and in the failure of my promised freedom" ("Tell It," 135). In this case the destiny of the word was tied up with the destiny of the man: hallowed in death, Lincoln's memory and accomplishment were soon unhallowed by violations of the principles he gave his life for. In a judgment both measured and passionate, Ellison suggests that "all the material progress released after the war" made Americans "evasive and given to compromise on basic principles." As a result, in his words, "we have the interruption of moral continuity symbolized in the failure of Reconstruction and the Hayes-Tilden Compromise" (*LN*, 70–71).

Ellison develops this theme of the nation's exchange of "moral predicament" for "moral evasion" in a 1960 essay called "Stephen Crane and the Mainstream of American Fiction." "To put it drastically," he observes, "if war, as Clausewitz insisted, is the continuation of politics by other means, it requires little imagination to see American life since the abandonment of the Reconstruction as an abrupt reversal of that formula: a continuation of the Civil War by means other than arms." He writes of an "unceasing state of civil war," characterizing the "America into which Crane was born" as "one of mirrorlike reversals in which the victors were the defeated and the defeated the victors; with the South, its memory frozen at the fixed moment of its surrender, carrying its aggression to the North in the form of guerrilla politics, and with the North, compromising as it went, retreating swiftly into the vast expanse of its new industrial development, eager to lose any memory traces of those values for which it had gone to war" (*S&A*, 67). Given the submergence of these reversals in national consciousness, it is small wonder Ellison links official American history to the tall tale.

* * *

I have called Ellison a moral historian. Unlike the conventional historian, who he claims is dedicated to chronology, he explores a great issue which, because of its abiding human qualities and specific national circumstances, informs chronology and prevents official history from imposing too false an order on American life. To put it positively, the pursuit of history provides a form and a frame for self-discovery. For Ellison the crucial point is that time and chronology offer cover to the historian, whereas the novelist, as he sees the craft, has nowhere to hide from the requirements of the moral imagination. Even Hemingway, whose narrator in *A Farewell to Arms*, according to Ellison, "denied the very words in which the ideals were set down," "affirms the old American values by the eloquence of his denial; makes his moral point by stating explicitly that he does not believe in morality; achieves his eloquence through denying eloquence; and is most moral when he denies the validity of a national morality which the nation has not bothered to live up to since the Civil War" (*LN*, 72, 74). For Hemingway, too, the boomerang is a metaphor for the inescapable presence of morality and history in a writer's craft. In the denials is the contradiction of denial; with the reversals comes a sharpened consideration of human values, not the least of which is history.

Diversity, fluidity, absurdity, complexity, chaos, swiftness of change—the words stand out in Ellison's mind like tablets announcing the conditions of American life. One cannot overestimate the extent to which he derives his point of view from the experience of growing up in Oklahoma, a state admitted to the Union as late as 1907, just seven years before Ellison's birth. It was the place, as he is fond of pointing out (bragging a little), that Twain had in mind when Huck Finn talks about lighting out for the territory. Oklahoma—a dream world.

"Geography is fate," Ellison recently told those present at the dedication of the Ralph Ellison Branch Library in Oklahoma City.

> The outcome of that national tragedy the Civil War brought the parents of many of us, both black and white, to the Oklahoma territory, seeking a new beginning. This I see as their enactment of a strongly held American proposition that men make their own fate through the humanization of geography and by the concerted assertion of their human will. At any rate, our forefathers collected here, and strove anew to make manifest the American Dream. They came from many places, with many philosophies, and with conflicting interpretations of the democratic compact which our nation's founding fathers had made with history. ("Profile," 94–96)

During Ellison's youth, Oklahoma was segregated and becoming more so under the thumb of the notorious Alfalfa Bill Murray. Yet there were openings. He writes movingly that "my father had many white friends who came to the house when I was quite small, so that any feelings of distrust I was to develop toward whites later on were modified by those with whom I had warm relations" (*S&A*, 12). There was enough fluidity in race relations for Ellison and a half-dozen of his friends to project themselves as Renaissance Men. "Renaissance Men, indeed!" he writes in retrospect, thinking that he and his companions were "but two generations from that previous condition" of slavery (*S&A*, xviii).

Behind the mask of irony and self-mockery Ellison is deadly serious. In reality, he has absorbed the qualities and the learning of the Renaissance Man and reinforced the concept with the style and traditions of black American experience. He is fiercely proud of his people; doubtless, this accounts for his refusal to let anything go that might deny or diminish the heroic scale of slavery. Here is his evocation of the indomitable past which lies behind his complex, independent imagination: "Any people who could endure all of that brutality and keep together, who could undergo such dismemberment and resuscitate itself, and endure until it could take the initiative in achieving its own freedom is obviously more than the sum of its brutalization. Seen in this perspective, theirs has been one of the great triumphs of the human spirit in modern times. In fact, in the history of the world" ("Stern Discipline," 84). There it stands: Ellison's heritage and his consciousness of its moral and historical meaning. He is a man who carries on the traditions of which he speaks and writes, a man who, in James McPherson's words, "doggedly affirms his identity as a Negro American, a product of the blending of both cultures" ("Indivisible," 46).

"I recognize," he told McPherson, "no American culture which is not the partial creation of black people. I recognize no American style in literature, in dance, in music, even in assembly-line processes, which does not bear the mark of the American Negro" ("Indivisible," 46). It goes way back, this matter of race and personality in American society. One thinks of landmarks along the way, of Du Bois's assertion at the beginning of the century that "the problem of the Twentieth Century is the problem of the color line" (*Souls*, 23). Bound up with this are his metaphors of double-consciousness and the Veil, both of which Ellison picks up and tests in *Invisible Man* as he explores the dream of personality. Again, Du Bois: "The history of the American Negro is the history of this strife—this longing to attain self-conscious manhood, to merge his double self into a better and truer self" (*Souls*, 17). Of course this is a universal longing, but the specific circumstances of race and their location at the center of the American experiment put the dream in the marrow of Ralph Ellison's experience and tradition. Maybe this is what he means when he says, "I don't think that history is Truth," and when he says that the craft of novelist in the United States "offers me the possibility of contributing not only to the growth of the literature but to the shaping of the culture as I should like it to be" (*S&A*, 183). When all is said and done (and written), there remains the process of self-creation, that transforming passage to a "better and truer self." Because of democracy, this is, has been, and shall be for the individual and for the nation a matter of urgent, utmost craft.

* * *

Well, what is the use of history in *Invisible Man*? In the novel as well as in essays it is through form that Ellison reveals his approach to history. Obviously, there are both chronology and a reality beyond chronology. For Ellison, the historian and the historical method operate "within the frame of chronology and time," but for the novelist, consciousness is all. The making of self and fiction are, however, linked to the making of history. Both processes are continuous, and so it is that in *Invisible Man* Ellison aims for a time frequency that I'll call the continuing present.

Consciousness and chronology constitute the paradox Ellison explores. Consider the form of *Invisible Man*. Formally, the Prologue comes before the narrative. Chronologically, it comes after. And in terms of consciousness the narrative follows the Prologue because, *as he "writes,"* Invisible Man's sense of himself and his story deepens and changes. The last piece, the Epilogue, follows the Prologue and the narrative in the sense of carrying forward both chronology and Invisible Man's consciousness. In the Epilogue, chronology and consciousness come together in the word and act of the present moment.

Even if there were no Prologue or Epilogue, the novel would open alluding not to what has happened, but to what continues to happen. "It goes a long way back, some twenty years" (*IM*, 13) is the first sentence of the narrative, and Ellison concludes the opening paragraph with Invisible Man's declaration "That I am nobody but myself. But first I had to discover that I am an invisible man!" *Invisible Man*, above all, is a novel about the process of consciousness, and about how the passage to one's root self is a passage through and beyond versions of self prepared by others. Invisible Man, the writer he becomes, is able to see himself three ways: as he was, as his present self sees that former self retrospectively, and, finally, as the person he is in the present. He rarely judges. Instead, he observes and reflects, recognizing that selfhood, like nationhood ("and the novel," Ellison has written, "is bound up with the notion of nationhood"—*LN*, 61), is a continuing process, and that the game is kept open by a fluid and tolerant as well as a rigorous sensibility.

For a novelist like Ellison the relationship between history and imagination is necessarily complex, and it is no surprise that there are some principles fluidly yet scrupulously at work in *Invisible Man*. The Prologue makes chronology wholly a matter of consciousness, and it is not until the beginning of the narrative that Ellison begins to make clear the principle of his allusive/elusive, explicit/implicit approach to historical time and chronology. When, for example, Invisible Man speaks of "it" going back "some twenty years," he is signaling that this is his time, and that it depends on frequencies of consciousness. In the next breath he speaks of having been in the cards "about eighty-five years ago"—a veiled reference to the public chronology of the Civil War–Reconstruction Era. Clearly, the intent is to link consciousness to a definite historical chronology, yet the reference is indefinite and inexplicit; Invisible Man deliberately does not particularize the situation.

Jefferson, Lincoln, Douglass, Booker T. Washington, Garvey; the Civil War, Emancipation, Reconstruction, World War I—these are presences on Invisible Man's historical landscape. Yet during his twenty-some years' experience in the narrative, he avoids even implicit reference to matters of history. Concerning the twenty years in question, presumably from *about* 1930 to *about* 1950, all is veiled and metaphoric. It's as if Ellison holds Invisible Man to a distinction between historical and imaginative consciousness. And the principle is that history (factual matters of chronology and identity) is free to occupy space during the time previous to the fictional experience, but, at that point, imagination assumes full responsibility for the word (and the world).

It is a dilemma, this relationship between history and imagination. Ellison tries to unriddle it by explaining the differing traditions of history and fiction:

> The moment you say something explicit about history in a novel, everybody's going to rise up and knock the Hell out of you, because they suspect that you are trying to take advantage of a form of authority which is sacred. History is sacred, you see, and no matter how false to actual events it might be. But fiction is anything but sacred. By fact and by convention fiction is a projection from one man's mind, of one man's imagination. (*LN*, 64)

Having made the distinction, Ellison affirms the connection between historian and novelist, and suggests that each is responsible for keeping the other honest.

Throughout the narrative Ellison's strategy is one of connotation. He seeks to open up associations and extend significance. For example, although times are tough when Invisible Man, recently arrived in Harlem, accidentally (and fatefully) gets involved in a tenement eviction, there is no mention of the Great Depression. Needless to say, it was for some purpose Ellison resisted the pull to get some explicit mileage from the thirties. He seems unwilling to restrict the Provos' dispossessed condition to one point in time, perhaps because of the danger that, if he did so, what has been archetypal in black experience might be laid simply at the door of hard times. Likewise, despite the one-to-one associations critics have made between the Brotherhood and the Communist party, it seems obvious Ellison invented the Brotherhood precisely in order *not* to limit his portrayal to the Communist party. Surely, the Brotherhood derives a measure of significance from its similarity in *some* respects to the relation between American blacks and the Democratic and Republican parties, not to mention the Progressive party of 1948.[6] The same thing is true of the race riot near the end of the book. It bears some relation to the Harlem riot of August 1943, as well as to the Harlem riot of March 1935.[7] But the point is that the race riot is Ellison's archetypal projection, in fiction, of an American form of violence by no means limited to any particular time and place.

Keeping to his theory, Ellison puts as much distance as possible between events of history and the imagined situations in his novel. With historical figures it is the same. Ras the Exhorter partakes of but is not Marcus Garvey. As a fictional character, he is compelling and lasting in a different way, again because he evokes black nationalism as a powerful archetype in American experience. As if to underscore this point, Ellison includes allusions to Marcus Garvey alongside the living fictional presence of Ras. Clearly, he is making distinctions in order to play out differences *and* associations between history and fiction.

One of the most complex historical presences in Ellison's novel is Booker T. Washington. From Invisible Man's speech in the South—"In these pre-invisible days I visualized myself as a potential Booker T. Washington" (*IM*, 15)—to his impromptu first speech in the North—" 'How would you like to be the new Booker T. Washington?' " (*IM*, 231)—his public self is as haunted by Washington as his private self is by his grandfather. Yet, by emphasizing Washington so explicitly and frequently, Ellison plays him off against other veiled but important presences in black American experience. For example, Invisible Man's speech after the battle royal recapitulates differing forms as well as differing points of view. His memorized oration takes its form and content from Booker T. Washington's Atlanta Exposition Address. But the improvisational impulse, his slip if you want, derives its form and substance from the improvising tradition represented by Douglass and countless others, by the black preacher, the blues musician. At any rate, the two phrases—''social responsibility'' and ''social equality''—express both sides of an old debate in the black community. In the novel both the white men and Invisible Man are so shocked by his substitution that they mutually write it off as wholly an accident having no significance. Yet a few months after Washington delivered his Atlanta Address, a young black scholar named John Hope said this in Nashville in public repudiation of Washington's stance: ''Now, catch your breath, for I am going to use an adjective: I am going to say we demand social equality. In this republic we shall be less than freemen, if we have a whit less than that which thrift, education, and honor afford other freemen.''[8] Consciously, Invisible Man invokes one tradition, unconsciously, another—between the lines of contradiction lie the pain and possibility of his passage to identity.

There is more to be said on Booker T. Washington. Despite Ellison's creation of an unnamed Founder of an unnamed Negro college, critics perversely persist in one-to-one correspondences. The Founder, some say, is Booker T. Washington; the college, Tuskegee Institute. Never mind that Ellison knew the names and chose not to use them. Never mind that the novel distinguishes—''You hear a lot of arguments about Booker T. Washington, but few would argue about the Founder'' (*IM*, 232). But there is a larger question. Why should the Founder evoke only Booker T. Washington? Why not other founders as well? Not only the founders of Negro colleges, but also figures like George Washington, Frederick Douglass, and Abraham Lincoln are evoked by the composite character of the Founder. For in these episodes Ellison recapitulates in a tragicomic way the founding of a social order after the Civil War. The reality is historical and mythic—archetypal. The circumstance is that unspoken compact arrived at by certain northern and southern interests, a compact institutionalized in some of the Negro colleges founded in the South. Doubtless, the college in the novel partakes of Tuskegee, but it is not contained by the association. And that is purposeful. Ellison's elusive allusions parallel the themes of his essays. Mr. Norton, proud of being one of the original founders, is called a ''trustee of consciousness.'' He evokes those New Englanders who thought freedom and Abolition a transcendent goal but who, caught up in Gilded Age materialism, offered money in place of moral commitment and whose money often upheld the new order of white supremacy.

This fictional reversal of transcendent (Transcendental) American principles is climaxed by Mr. Norton's appearance at the Golden Day. The name evokes a contemporary affirmation and repudiation similar to the pattern of the nineteenth century. With the First World War and America's promise to "make the world safe for democracy" came renewed hopes that long-denied promises would be honored at home. Instead, the parades were hardly over, the troops shortly home, before these hopes were dashed by a decade of reaction epitomized by the resurgence of the Klan.

Ellison's Golden Day is a raunchy sporting house which serves as a weekly release for a bunch of black veterans who have been consigned to a quasi insane asylum for transgressions of Jim Crow rules after their return from France. Again, the interplay is between history and consciousness. The heroism of black regiments is well known; perhaps less well known are the humiliations and terrors these soldiers faced back home, especially in the South. The power of consciousness is such that Invisible Man tries, without success, to blot out the chaos and contradictions these veterans represent. "Whenever I saw them I felt uncomfortable. They were supposed to be members of the professions toward which at various times I vaguely aspired myself; and even though they never seemed to see me I could never believe that they were really patients" (*IM*, 57). Of course he is right; they are not patients but prisoners.

The key episode involves Invisible Man, Mr. Norton, and a vet who has been a brilliant surgeon, a man gifted enough to be only the second doctor able to diagnose Norton's condition—and this in a sporting house room. Flabbergasted, Norton demands to know more:

> "Oh, yes, and how long were you in France?" Mr. Norton asked.
> "Long enough," he said. "Long enough to forget some fundamentals which I never should have forgotten." (*IM*, 70)

The conversation drags on, Norton asking foolish questions, the vet giving cryptic answers which presuppose that to understand truly, a person has to develop an authentic historical consciousness. A whore interrupts, distracting the vet from his strategy. Suddenly, he challenges Norton directly: " 'To some, you are the great white father, to others the lyncher of souls, but for all you are confusion and chaos come even into the Golden Day' " (*IM*, 72). Partly through the complicity of the Mr. Nortons, a social order came into being which destroyed the vet's creative social potential. " 'Ten men in masks drove me out from the city at midnight and beat me with whips for saving a human life. And I was forced to the utmost degradation because I possessed skilled hands and the belief that my knowledge could bring me dignity—not wealth, only dignity—and other men health' " (*IM*, 72). During the encounter Invisible Man experiences ambivalent feelings akin to those two contradictory phrases, *social responsibility* and *social equality*. He realizes the vet's performance may be spoiling his game at the college, yet he receives "a fearful satisfaction from hearing him talk as he had to a white man" (*IM*, 71).

There is no question about who holds the power. Dr. Bledsoe, the amoral, cynical, complex, fascinating president of the college, has both the vet and Invisible Man out of the state the next day. But what of the power of consciousness? The power to keep the act of personality open? In a last encounter on the bus taking each away, the vet gives Invisible Man some curious advice. ''Be your own father, young man,'' he tells him. ''And remember, the world is possibility if only you'll discover it'' (*IM*, 120). In the person of Invisible Man, Ellison plays out the psychological urgency of leaping back to one's grandparents in order to discover origins and therefore possibilities of identity. Because of his situation, Invisible Man has little choice but to be his own father in the sense of fathering (looking after, making) himself.

In New York City, Brother Jack gives what looks like similar advice. Characteristically, the words are portentous—like a pronouncement by the voice of time in the old newsreels. ''*History* has been born in your brain,'' Jack tells Invisible Man, hoping to persuade him that individuals (''agrarian types, you know. Being ground up by industrial conditions'') don't count (*IM*, 221, 220). Invisible Man, however, connects these old folks and their imagery to the power of the word. Strewn on the street, the Provos' belongings become a succession of images evoking ancestral kinship ties. Free papers/ knocking bones/a curling iron/nuggets of High John the Conqueror/a small Ethiopian flag/a tintype of Abraham Lincoln/lapsed life insurance policies/a newspaper photo captioned: ''MARCUS GARVEY DEPORTED''—these fragments evoke the texture of a people's experience. Invisible Man suddenly feels so deeply part of these folks and his own grandparents that he has no need to contest Jack intellectually. His source of energy is not science but the blues. ''Seeing them like that made me feel pretty bad,'' he tells Jack. ''. . . They're folks just like me, except that I've been to school a few years.'' Listening to Jack's paradigm of rebirth, reminiscent of the company hospital's attempt to erase consciousness and make his brain blank, Invisible Man becomes, if Jack could see him, visibly angry. ''I made that speech,'' he insists, ''because I was upset over seeing those old folks put out in the street, that's why. I don't care what *you* call it, I was angry'' (*IM*, 220–21). Here and elsewhere in *Invisible Man* there is a kinetic flow between experiencing what has been handed down for generations and the capability of action in the present. Acting for Invisible Man is, of course, speaking (''I *like* to make speeches'' [*IM*, 222]), for it is Ellison's purpose to show how Invisible Man has the gift of speech but cannot shape the people's response because, during his career as an orator, he fails to see the possibilities inherent in their simultaneous embrace of form and chaos. Even so, Invisible Man's public consciousness is heightened by the past merging with present moments; his gift is tied to the oral tradition—where the act of improvisation attains force through the old themes, the familiar struggle.

The point is that while the Brotherhood works to instill a rational, scientific view of history in Invisible Man's brain, those powerful images he suppresses on his journey north come to consciousness. It's as if geographically he had to go north to feel the coherence of southern experience, and likewise, intellectually, he has to get involved with scientific politics to discover the power of feeling and intuition—the heart's territory. For a true sense of history he has to leave familiar environments and hear truly that "whole unrecorded history . . . spoken" in "gin mills and the barber shops and the juke joints and the churches, Brother. Yes, and the beauty parlors on Saturdays when they're frying hair" (*IM*, 356). And on the deepest private level he has to hate Tod Clifton, regard him as an enemy, and see him die in the street before he knows the love he bears, before he can ask the question he (and his countrymen) have long repressed: "And could politics ever be an expression of love?" (*IM*, 341) rather than of fear and guilt, of self-absorption, self-justification. We do not know, but we do know that in the world of Ellison's novel knowledge and the transformations that follow depend on some principle of reversal.

Perhaps Ellison holds his character to the same standard against which he tests American identity in the essays. Namely, he argues that "we are a people who, while desiring identity, have been reluctant to pay the cost of its achievement. We have been reluctant since we first suspected that we are fated to live up to our sacred commitments or die, and the Civil War was the form of that fateful knowledge" (*LN*, 72). Invisible Man is driven by internal and outside forces to seek his American identity in the riddle spoken by his grandfather in words he hears as a boy, words his father seems too surprised and frightened by to heed. "I never told you," the old man says on his deathbed, "but our life is a war and I have been a traitor all my born days, a spy in the enemy's country ever since I give up my gun back in the Reconstruction" (*IM*, 13).

This is the language of reversal, and Ellison makes Invisible Man look for the act preceding the shadow of metaphor. The act's the gun and its surrender. It's left to succeeding generations to dig out the history of Reconstruction, especially to those like Invisible Man whose dreams make them vulnerable to Dr. Bledsoe's question: "My God, boy! You're black and living in the South—did you forget how to lie?" (*IM*, 107). The grandfather's imperative is urgent enough today—how much more so a generation ago when, as a matter of course, schoolbooks wrote up Reconstruction along straight *Birth of a Nation* lines. Without stating it, he both veils *and* reveals the opinion that he and other freedmen were damn fools to give up their guns. We know that some two hundred thousand Negroes fought for the Union Army. We know that President Lincoln in his Second Inaugural Address made freedom and justice for freedmen a sacred moral imperative. We know too of promises made and hopes raised high by the Thirteenth, Fourteenth, and Fifteenth Amendments, by the Freedmen's Bureau and the Freedmen's Bank. Finally, we know of the betrayal orchestrated in the Hayes-Tilden Compromise of 1877, formalized as the law of the land by the Plessy vs. Ferguson decision of 1896, and not revised until 1954, two years after *Invisible Man* was published. Again Ellison's metaphor—life as an "unceasing state of civil war":

> What is the meaning of music?
> What is the meaning of war?
> What is the meaning of oppression?
> (Harper, "*Bird Lives*," 80)

There is a world of history behind the assertion that "our life is a war"; there is also a terrible question: how does a minority, having long since given up its guns, fight such a war? The strategy the old man hands down is based on the complexity of the minstrel tradition. "Overcome 'em with yeses, undermine 'em with grins, agree 'em to death and destruction, let 'em swoller you till they vomit or bust wide open" (*IM*, 13–14). After Reconstruction was overthrown, the war became a guerrilla war fought with tactics of pretense, concealment, masking: tactics going back to complex folk techniques of survival during slavery.

Invisible Man comes slowly to an understanding of his grandfather's human complexity. Late in the novel he articulates the essential role metaphor plays in the drama of historical consciousness. His language goes underground and flows internally, unspoken, as he begins to see how he has mirrored the Sambo image society keeps flashing at him. He sees the Brotherhood version of history not as an absolute but instead as one of many possible metaphors—and not a very good one at that. "What if history was a gambler," he muses, "instead of a force in a laboratory experiment . . .?" Or a "madman full of paranoid guile" instead of "a reasonable citizen" (*IM*, 333)? He spoofs the progressive spiral conception of history, conjures up "grooves" of history, and suggests that any number of people may pass their lives outside history. As if to complement the reversals, he begins to see history in the form of a boomerang. Best of all, while he meditates, some small boys run by dropping looted candy bars, a man from the store in pursuit. Confused by the sudden chaos, Invisible Man stifles an impulse to trip the man "and was confused all the more when an old woman standing further along threw out her leg and swung a heavy bag" (*IM*, 335). Again, action arises from some undeclared tradition of consciousness. During the riot the same thing happens on an articulate level, when Invisible Man watches several men execute a long-held desire to burn down their squalid tenement. "Capable of their own action . . ." (*IM*, 414; Ellison's ellipsis), he muses, meditating again as history gets made before him, improvisationally, in variations going back to the profound double meanings of the sorrow songs and the complex ruses of the underground railroad.

Where is Invisible Man in all this? Escaping down a manhole, he finds refuge in a coal cellar and dreams a nightmare of castration. But in the dream his generations stand not for manhood but instead for the illusions fed him by almost everyone he has encountered. Free of these illusions, he nevertheless feels ''*painful and empty*'' (*IM*, 430). Meanwhile, his testicles, thrown over a bridge, give the inanimate structure the mobility of a robot, and Invisible Man awakens vowing action to stop the mechanical, man-created monster. Here, raised one more time, is the fearful specter which haunts him. Over and over he has been confronted with the likelihood that unless he makes a stand in the world, he will be reduced to a ''cog,'' an ''automaton,'' a ''mechanical man,'' a ''walking zombie.'' Finally, by bringing the nightmare into the forefront of consciousness, he exorcizes the robot in him and prepares to resist society's turn in that direction.

* * *

The novel stops at this point—the novel as narrative. What follows is an Epilogue on the process of self-realization in America. It is in the form of a memoir or fictional essay, and Ellison's strategy is similar to that employed in the narrative. There is no mention of historical persons, events, or dates, but unmistakably, the Epilogue bears the mark and resonance of the late 1940s and early 1950s—the continuing American present.

The novel's trajectory follows the path of a boomerang. A boomerang returns—that much we can say, predictably. But the precise point of return is unpredictable, erratic, uncyclical. From the Prologue through a careening ride out, and back to the Epilogue, Ellison takes his chances with open form. In the case of Invisible Man, the metaphor is trenchantly apt. Returning, he sees things from a different perspective because he has turned around. One starting point he boomerangs back toward is his grandfather, whose image grows larger and clearer because now Invisible Man travels toward it. In the beginning, his grandfather's words presented fearful dangers to his dream of individuality, whereas now he interprets those same words as a command of nationhood. ''I'' has become ''we'' in the testamental way of black experience.

> Could he have meant—hell, he *must* have meant the principle, that we were to affirm the principle on which the country was built and not the men, or at least not the men who did the violence. Did he mean say ''yes'' because he knew that the principle was greater than the men, greater than the numbers and the vicious power and all the methods used to corrupt its name? Did he mean to affirm the principle, which they themselves had dreamed into being out of the chaos and darkness of the feudal past, and which they had violated and compromised to the point of absurdity even in their own corrupt minds? Or did he mean that we had to take the responsibility for all of it, for the men as well as the principle, because we were the heirs who must use the principle because no other fitted our needs? (*IM*, 433)

He (and we) are back at the beginning, back to democracy's form of diversity and oneness, its promise of equality. But not quite at the same point. The principle affirmed is other than that expressed by Invisible Man's former belief in the gospel of "hard work and progress and action" (*IM*, 435), and different from his grandfather's strategy of "agree 'em to death and destruction" (*IM*, 13). Free at last from the bondage of absolute idealism, absolute oppression, absolute ideology, all states of mind, Invisible Man affirms a reality of "infinite possibilities." For him historical consciousness comes to stand for the endless range of complexity between chaos and possibility:

> —diversity is the word. . . .
> America is woven of many strands. . . .
> Our fate is to become one, and yet many—.
> (*IM*, 435)

Like consciousness the acts of personality are inclusive. "So I denounce and I defend and I hate and I love" (*IM*, 438).

In the Epilogue, memoir becomes history as Invisible Man affirms America as a metaphor for possibilities that are democratic, provided individuals take personal responsibility for the country's principles. Affirming his complex history, Invisible Man transforms his sense of himself from everybody's stereotype to an indivisible person. Perhaps most important, the man who began by asserting his invisibility, ends by asserting his connection with every last American one of us. No, he does more than that. He suggests he is speaking for us: "Who knows but that, on the lower frequencies, I speak for you?" (*IM*, 439). Who knows? We do, if we've tuned into the frequency of his life. Not to mention the other essential frequencies of American life, the lower frequencies—the bass line from which independent, individual melodies soar.

Of the great nineteenth-century American novels, Ellison has written: "The moral imperatives of American life that are implicit in the Declaration of Independence, the Constitution, and the Bill of Rights were a part of both the individual consciousness and the conscience of those writers who created what we consider our classic novels—Hawthorne, Melville, James, and Twain" (*LN*, 67). Aware of the novel as an experimental form with stress on both permanence and variation, he asks of the craft of his time: "How does one in the novel (the novel which is a work of art and not a disguised piece of sociology) persuade the American reader to identify that which is basic in man beyond all differences of class, race, wealth, or formal education?" He asks: "How give the reader that which we do have in abundance, all the countless untold and wonderful variations on the themes of identity and freedom and necessity, love and death, and with all the mystery of personality undergoing its endless metamorphosis?" (*LN*, 91). The questions are wonderful and profound, especially as they grant the possibility of making one culture out of many individuals, many peoples, many traditions, many idioms and styles—all the contradictions and possibilities of American life. If novelists and readers are faithful to first principles, we and those who follow will be able to repeat Invisible Man's transformations in endless variation.

Certainly, Ralph Ellison could pose these questions, confident that he had met the test of a prose "flexible, and swift as American change is swift, confronting the inequalities and brutalities of our society forthrightly, but yet thrusting forth its images of hope, human fraternity and individual self-realization" (*S&A*, 105). Certainly, *Invisible Man* modulates history, self, and form to a frequency that is unique, complex, and accessible, a frequency embodying the high democratic standards Ellison sets for American fiction.

NOTES

1. Ellison's address, "The Uses of History in Fiction," was published in the *Southern Literary Journal* 1:2 (1969): 69. Subsequent references to this source are cited in text as *SLJ*.

2. Part 1 of Ellison's "The World and the Jug," was printed in the *New Leader* 46 (December 9, 1963): 26, in response to Irving Howe's essay "Black Boys and Native Sons," in the August 1963 issue of *Dissent*. Howe's "A Reply to Ralph Ellison," along with Ellison's second response, "A Rejoinder," were both printed in the February 3, 1964 issue of the *New Leader*. The two Ellison pieces are combined as "The World and the Jug" in Ellison's *Shadow and Act*, 107–43.

3. "Blues People" in *Shadow and Act*, 254. Quotations from this and other essays printed in *Shadow and Act* are cited in text as *S&A*.

4. Ellison, *Invisible Man*, 5. Further quotations from this work are cited in text as *IM*.

5. "Society, Morality, and the Novel," *The Living Novel*, ed. Granville Hicks, 62. Further references to this source are cited in text as *LN*.

6. James Baldwin's "Journey to Atlanta," reprinted in *Notes of a Native Son*, is a powerful exposition of the contradiction between theory and practice in the Progressive party's relation to blacks.

7. See Baldwin's *Notes of a Native Son* and Russell G. Fischer's "*Invisible Man* as History," in *College Language Association (CLA) Journal* 17 (1974): 338–67.

8. John Hope quoted by Edgar A. Toppin in *A Biographical History of Blacks in America Since 1528*, 165.

WORKS CITED

Baldwin, James. *Notes of a Native Son*. Boston: Beacon Press, 1955.

DuBois, W.E.B. *The Souls of Black Folk*. New York: Fawcett, 1961. Originally published in 1903.

Ellison, Ralph. "Indivisible Man." Interview by James Alan McPherson. *Atlantic Monthly* 226 (December 1970): 46.

———. *Invisible Man*. New York: Random House, 1952.
———. Quoted by Jervis Anderson in "Profile." *New Yorker* 52 (November 2, 1976): 94–96.
———. *Shadow and Act*. New York: Random House, 1964.
———. "A Rejoinder." *New Leader* 47 (February 3, 1964): 15–22.
———. "Tell It Like It Is, Baby." *Nation* 201 (September 20, 1965).
———. "A Very Stern Discipline." Interview with Steve Cannon, Lennox Raphael, and James Thompson. *Harper's* 234 (March 1967): 76–95.
———. "The World and the Jug." *New Leader* 46 (December 9, 1963): 22–26.
Fischer, Russell G. "Invisible Man as History." *College Language Association (CLA) Journal* 17 (1974): 338–67.
Harper, Michael S. "*Bird Lives*: Charles Parker in St. Louis." *History Is Your Own Heartbeat*. Urbana: University of Illinois Press, 1971.
Hicks, Granville, ed. *The Living Novel: A Symposium*. New York: Macmillan & Co., 1957.
Howe, Irving. "A Reply to Ralph Ellison." *New Leader* 47 (February 3, 1964): 15–22.
Toppin, Edgar A. *A Biographical History of Blacks in America Since 1528*. New York: David McKay, 1971.

Ellison's "Usable Past": Toward a Theory of Myth

HORTENSE SPILLERS

The occasion that invites this piece recalls for me certain decisive memories. Prof. Elizabeth Phillips, my first instructor in American literature at Memphis State University, returned one of my student themes one afternoon with this comment: "Why be content with the lightning bug when you can have the lightning?" I have no idea what I had written—lame, I suppose, in any case—but I stored the comment, might have even stored it in my dreams, and now, well over a decade later, I know precisely what she meant. These notes on an American theme are written with Professor Phillips and the lightning in mind.

One of the critical strategies of that first course was to determine to what extent the American idiom had been driven toward precision since *Sister Carrie*. That nearly half a century separates Dreiser's first novel and *Invisible Man* is not so impressive an observation, except that between Dreiser and Ellison a radically new literary reality asserts itself, basically combative toward the strategies of the past. Gass's notes on Borges's prose—its leanness, excision, lack of ornamental dress[1]—define in part the canon of taste that impresses modernist practice with the persistence of dogma. Accompanying these profound changes in aesthetic surface was the broader implication of shifts of angle in the very vision of art, or more precisely, the philosophical bases for a technology of text (perhaps most eloquently expressed in Borges's fictions of intangibility) conduced toward another kind of artistic performance which Ortega y Gasset locates in the theme of alienation:

> Analyzing the new style, one finds in it certain closely connected tendencies: it tends toward the dehumanization of art; to an avoidance of living forms; to ensuring that a work of art should be nothing but a work of art; to considering art simply as play and nothing else: to an essential irony; to an avoidance of

Reprinted by permission of the author from *Interpretations: Studies in Language and Literature*, IX, No. 1, 1977.

> all falsehood, and finally, towards an art which makes no spiritual or transcendental claims whatsoever.[2]

We have no exact name yet for "dehumanization" as a systematic mode of expression; perhaps "modernism" is the best we can do, but for sure, this deviant attitude toward the human problematic—this flight from it that Ortega determines as the goal of modernism—pursues a structural reality, even anticipates it, that consigns language itself to an area of phenomenology, unprivileged among other things. If language is an act of concealment, condemned to obfuscation, then we should not be surprised, even if disappointed, that it talks to itself, about itself, imprisoned in an appropriate logological status.[3]

Ellison apparently saw what was coming at the end of the forties, when he completed *Invisible Man*, and responded in his acceptance speech of the National Book Award with characteristic rebellion. Wishing to avoid the "hard-boiled" idiomatic understatement of Hemingway—its "clipped, monosyllabic prose"—he found

> that, when compared to the rich babble of idiomatic expression around [him], a language full of imagery, gesture, and rhetorical canniness, it was embarrassingly austere.[4]

His decision, then, to cast the grammar of the text in a mode contrastive to understatement is complemented by his refusal of the naturalist disposition:

> Thus to see America with an awareness of its rich diversity and its almost magical fluidity and freedom, I was forced to conceive of a novel unburdened by the narrow naturalism which has led after so many triumphs to the final and unrelieved despair which marks so much of our current fiction. (Bone, 198)

In repudiating the doctrine of naturalism, Ellison turned away from the influence of Richard Wright, the dominating presence of his apprenticeship, (Bone, 198) and Dreiser, who had fathered the naturalist tradition among U.S. writers.

While Ellison would be the last to deny that his own literary procedure has been influenced by the dogmatizers of European modernism, he would also insist that his American experience, his Negroness, has mandated a literary form virtually unique in its portrayal of pluralistic issues. In order to capture the multiplicity of American experience, Ellison turned to the nineteenth century, toward Melville and Twain's "imaginative economy," where "the Negro symbolized both the man lowest down and the mysterious, underground aspect of human personality" (Bone, 201). This turning, which we view with unrelieved interest, is a remarkable decision because it reinforces a notion of the dialectic at a time when it is all but being driven out by theories of artistic objectivity. But Ellison feels too keenly, one imagines, the requirements of his own imposed alienation to raise it to an act of form and chooses, instead, the "ancestral imperative"[5] as the eminent domain of his own creative concern. The upshot is *Invisible Man* that remains, to my mind, one of the most influential American novels of the past twenty-five years. I can say with confidence that it would constitute a "first" on my own list of teachable subjects for reasons which, though obvious, may bear repeating: (1) Following a line of American fictions that had rendered "black" an item of sociological data or the subject of exotic assumptions, or yet, the gagline of white mischief, at best, its ambiguous "bi-play," *Invisible Man* addresses the issue as an exposition of modern consciousness. (2) Frustrating the tendency to perceive a coterminous relationship between the symbolic boundaries of black and the physical, genetic manifestation named black, *Invisible Man* recalls *Moby Dick* that stands Manichean orientation on its head. (3) Insisting that black American experience is vulnerable to mythic dilation, Ellison constructs a coherent system of signs that brings into play the entire repertory of American cultural traits. In order to do this, Ellison places the unnamed "agonist" on an historical line that reaches back through the generations and extends forward into the frontiers of the future. Thus, (4) the work withdraws from the modernist inclination to isolate issues of craft from ethical considerations. For Ellison, language does speak, and it clarifies selective experience under the auspices of certain figures-of-thought, unexpectedly applied to received opinions. My primary concern in these notes is to try to trace propositions three and four to some tentative conclusions.

Northrop Frye defines myth as "the union of ritual and dream in a form of verbal communication."[6] The term, however, has achieved such flexibility that it is menaced by meaning everything and nothing in particular, though Frye traces its origins and inflections from biblical and classical sources through the modern period (Frye, 131–223). Any contemporary usage is haunted by the echo of specific mythic structures and Roland Barthes's caricature of contemporary mythologies in a dazzling display of linguistic demystification.[7] But Barthes's definition of myth as a "type of speech" releases us, at least for the moment, from certain inherited or monolithic notions of mythic form.

> Myth is not defined by the object of its message, but by the way in which it utters this message: there are formal limits to myth, there are no "substantial" ones. (*Mythologies*, 109)

Myth, then, is a form of selective discourse since its life and death are governed by human history: "Ancient, or not, mythology can only have an historical foundation, for myth is a type of speech chosen by history: it cannot possibly evolve from the 'nature' of things" (*Mythologies*, 110). Not confined to oral speech, myth can be constituted of other modes of signification, including written discourse, photography, cinema, reporting, sports, shows, publicity. Myth as form does not only denote the sacred object or event, but may also be viewed as the wider application of a certain linguistic status to a hierarchy of motives and mediations. Pursuing Saussure's well-known paradigm of signification (*Mythologies*, 115), Barthes differentiates the semiological and ideological boundaries of myth in a way that can only be suggestive for our immediate purposes, for I am primarily concerned with *Invisible Man* as a literary countermyth of *good* intentions. Though from my own point of view, any countermyth is preferable to prevailing myth and is, therefore, *good*, I still emphasize the word to denote the particular difficulty there is in accepting Barthes's definition of myth as a type of speech, expressed by its intentions. Inevitably, some intentions are "more good" than others to the group wishing to appropriate them, and as Barthes's orientation leads into the ideological category of myth as an impoverishment of history, its nullification at the hands of the bourgeoisie, I would have to agree with him. Recognizing, then, the high danger of applying a term laden, a priori, with valuation that justifies it on the one hand and condemns it on the other, I can only proceed with caution.

What I find most suggestive in Barthes's argument is the distinction he enforces between the form of myth and the concept it borrows from particular historical order. We could say, following his lead, that mythic form is a kind of conceptual code, relying on the accretions of association that cling to the concept—"a past, a memory, a comparative order of facts, ideas, decisions" (*Mythologies*, 117). A French army general, pinning a medal on a one-armed Senegalese, is not my idea of a joke, nor is it Barthes's, for that matter, and he uses it to illustrate an act of attenuation wherein the subject has become an item in the "store of mythical signifiers." In short, the visual image becomes a code of French imperial procedure and the biographical/historical implications of its subjects. It is a mode of shorthand in that the mythical signifier conceals as much as it reveals. In fact, in Barthes's example, the signifier cheats, for it tells far less than it shows. This spontaneous equation of form and concept occurs also in the literary myth whose extension, like the oral myth, is linear and successive. Barthes describes the process of identification:

> The elements of the form . . . are related as to place and proximity: the mode of presence of the form is spatial. The concept, on the contrary, appears in global fashion, it is a kind of nebula, the condensation, more or less hazy, of a certain knowledge. Its elements are linked by associative relations: it is supported not by an extention but by a depth (although this metaphor is perhaps still too spatial): its mode of presence is memorial. (122)

It is this integrative paradigm of form and concept that is most interesting for specific application.

Returning to an initial metaphor which I used in one of my four propositions—Invisible Man standing on an historical line reaching back and forth—I think we can establish the central reason why the novel qualifies as myth. In Ellison's case, I would suggest that myth becomes a tactic for explanation and that the novel may be considered a discourse on the biographical uses of history. The preeminent element of form, Invisible Man's narrative unfolds through a complicated scheme of conceptual images that refer to particular historical order, but the order itself localizes in the metaphysical/personal issues of the narrative, which is then empowered to reveal both the envisioned structure of history and its fluid continuity. It seems to me that the themes of diachrony and synchrony properly apply here in that Invisible Man embodies the diachronous, spatial, continuing subject of particular historical depth or memory. In history, the individual is the key to both procedures, for he can arrest time, as the form of the novel does, and examine its related details in leisurely detachment, but he cannot escape it, either personally or historically, and is, therefore, detached only in a kind of suspended, temporary judgment. In short, through his activities, he is an image of man talking, furiously, unto death, lifting the weight of his aging flesh by the power of his tongue. Invisible Man confesses:

> So why do I write, torturing myself to put it down? Because in spite of myself I've learned some things. Without the possibility of action, all knowledge comes to one labeled "file and forget," and I can neither file nor forget. Nor will certain ideas forget me; they keep filing away at my lethargy, my complacency. Why should I be the one to dream this nightmare? Why should I be dedicated and set aside—yes, if not to at least *tell* a few people about it? There seems to be no escape. Here I've set out to throw my anger into the world's face, but now that I've tried to put it all down the old fascination with playing a role returns, and I'm drawn upward again. So that even before I finish I've failed (maybe my anger is too heavy, perhaps being a talker, I've used too many words). But I've failed . . . I have been hurt to the point of abysmal pain . . . And I defend because in spite of all I find that I love. . . [8]

Moving out of an infant inevitability toward a final one, Invisible Man embraces history as an act of consciousness. Paradoxically, history is both given to him and constructed by him, the emphatic identification of contemplative and active modes, and his refusal of the historical commitment, to remember and go forward, is certain death. *Invisible Man* charts the adventures of a black personality in the recovery of his own historical burden. This restorative act, to get well and remember and reconstruct simultaneously, is the dominating motif of the novel, and its various typological features support this central decision.

As the subject of recovery, Invisible Man must assume all, must take upon himself the haunted, questioning, troubled, even self-subversive, stance of one who insists on *telling* others. This telling fulfills a bardic task, an oracular chore, and one would do well to refuse either, but pain compels Invisible Man to talk. He calls it "nightmare" and essentially speaks to us out of his own sustained bardic trance, while as an ignorant youth, he spoke from the nightmare of others. We shall see shortly how these layers or phases of speech work. In addition, Invisible Man is "on" to something else in the quoted passages. The questions that he poses function on more than one level: Rhetorically, they hustle on the ploys and motions of argument just as the interrogative formulation has done throughout the novel. Then dramatically, the questions situate particular trouble. Uttered or held back, they are often a symptom of pride and confusion, and Invisible Man has had his share of both, but syntactically, the questions complement a principle of iteration that distinguishes both the Prologue and the Epilogue, encircling the structure. This principle of iteration, if we look closely, ratifies a decisive ambiguity beneath the surface symmetry of the text. From the Epilogue, this passage excerpted in the initial quotation is suggestive:

> The very act of trying to put it all down has confused me and negated some of the anger and some of the bitterness. So it is that now I denounce and defend, or feel prepared to defend. I condemn and affirm, say no and say yes, say yes and say no. I denounce because though implicated and partially responsible, I have been hurt . . . to the point of invisibility. . . .(*IM*, 437)

Each time a word or phrase is repeated, it comes back with a new twist of meaning, an enhancement and echo, pursuing its ambiguity with passion. This repetitive activity is one of "destructing," a flight from certainty toward systematic skepticism, in order to reconstruct the terrible complexity of decision. But enhancement is an enrichment, even though it borders on the tedious. Caring almost overmuch for linguistic entanglement, Invisible Man threatens a vision of nausea and the love of detail as neurotic indulgence, but he recalls what he has said earlier about the "possibility of action" and determines to come out of his hole:

> Thus, having tried to give pattern to the chaos which lives within the pattern of your certainties, I must come out. I must emerge. . . . (*IM*, 438)

I think we can take him at his literal word, though he is eloquently slippery, or conceptually athletic, with formulations in this passage. He must emerge: Spatially underground, he will come up into the light of day again with his dark-skinned self, a little more noble and fierce than when he entered. Sharp on punning, which has been called an "overpopulated phonetic space," Ellison recreates the illusion of a mind ordering its space, determining its motions, and this is the domain of invisibility.

The involvements of mind, its complicated calibrations in the heat of experience, point to the deeper structures of the text and, characteristically, pursue a pattern of interlocking image-clusters which emanate from the centrality of the underground. I would also impute to Ellison a circularity of influence that I think is at work in the depths of the text. The privileged geometrical version of modernist writers, circles have wrought miracles. There are rivers still flowing and young homeless boys still thumbing rides on the open road. What startles even more is that critics are still startled by these clever workings as though the repeat performance had imagined the thing on its own. Ellison, however, is not as enamored of his structures as his critics. As I recall, he doesn't mention circles or depths in interviews about the book,[9] confining himself to articulating its broad objectives, but Invisible Man cannily suggests how *he* wants his narrative read; reconciled to the chaos against which his "plan of living" has been conceived, he acquires a new sense of time:

> Under the spell of the reefer I discovered a new analytical way of listening to music. The unheard sounds came through, and each melodic line existed in itself, stood out clearly from all the rest, said its piece, and waited patiently for the other voices to speak. That night I found myself hearing not only in time, but space as well. I not only entered the music but descended, like Dante, into its depths. And *beneath the swiftness of the hot tempo there was a slower tempo and a cave and I entered it and looked around and heard an old woman singing a spiritual as full of Weltschmerz as flamenco. . . .* (*IM*, 7)

The italicized passage is unquestionably explicit about direction, and in the event that anybody misses it the first time, Dante signalizes the pit as a return to traditional configurations of the underground, but the mental location of this geography of descent places these images out of public view and restores them to their initial status of private madness. In Dante, spatial appropriation is both visual and concealed, and the latter seems to be a repressed dimension. Invisible Man, by contrast, never allows us to forget that he is dreaming, reefer-induced, and abandons himself to the irresponsibility of the induced state. Playing on the notion of vision-in-dream-brought-on-by-other-power, he expresses himself in a mode kin to the enthusiastic, and the enthusiast sees whatever fantasies are brought to him. Thus, the dreaming mind is logically decentered as Invisible Man alludes to being, but there is, of course, a mind controlling all the time. The passage proliferates, foreshadowing the specific issues of heritage that come back to the narrative in a form of discourse more suitable to linear continuity.

The dream passages are "amazing" and involved, worked around patterns of transition and contrast that yoke disparate experience in contiguous order. Since the image-flow is both acoustical and visual, Invisible Man is liberated up to a phenomenology of sensory impressions that restore the state of innocence, like dreaming, a status of freedom. He is essentially disembodied as his mind empathizes ancestral time and space.

The architectonics at work here ensure that the points-of-transition in the dream state relate to specific historical and symbolic detail whose overriding influence is religious. The preacher's text on the "Blackness of Blackness" recalls the ritualistic patterns of enthusiastic worship. The call-and-response rhythm of the black church service entangles with a dramatization of unlocalized generational conflict that is in turn overtaken by a recent scene of political challenge and revolt. What this mental survey shows are the layers of conflict and renewal that Invisible Man must work through in a reversed order of things. Above ground, the dreaming mind, intruded upon by reality, does not dominate, except at peril to the individual. By having subconscious forces confiscate, with impunity, the normal order of differentiation and succession, Ellison suggests that the "truth" for Invisible Man is mobilized in a return to racial source. This psychological economy of motives differentiates the interlocking elements of personality within a scene of temporal and spatial unfolding so that historical order or its illusion may be viewed as a survey of mental activity. But in order to actuate these mental resources or to possess the dream material beyond individual isolation, Invisible Man must submit to the dream censor, to gazing, quite consciously, at the crux of his motivations and their consequences: "It goes a long way back, some twenty years. All my life I had been looking for something, and everywhere I turned someone tried to tell me what it was" (*IM*, 13) shows not only hypotactic order and the deliberate selection of boundaries of experience that it implies. We are introduced, quickly, to the apparent orientation of his biography. But the sentences also enforce a notion of ironic detachment. In order to justify it, Invisible Man deploys the enriched details only implied from the opening lines in a systematic rehearsal of completed events. Thereafter, each syntactic gesture is a recall, increasingly full, of experience retailored in the guise of a wiser man. The first order of circularity, or return, is introduced here.

The second order is entirely memorial on the part of the "author," and we tend to forget that the place or situation of the narrative has not shifted from underground. The occasion to occupy us has been seized in an act of seduction: We were not immediately there, as the illusion suggests, when he goes over particular ground, but, instead, we have never left the scene of confession; immediacy is, therefore, borrowed and imposed for the sake of poetic complicity.

The third order of circularity, articulated through certain figures of archetype, is imposed on the second and consists of commonly identifiable symbols of authority. Maud Bodkin provides a working definition of the archetype: psychic residua inherited "in the structure of the brain, *a priori*, determinants of individual experience."[10] The specific application of Jungian theory to literary types, Bodkin's study implies the valorization of a collective unconscious which makes it possible to ascribe psychological motives of filiation and kinship to widely dispersed ancestral groups. For mythic studies, the archetype becomes an indispensable figure since the myth is ordained by a common ancestral meaning. For our immediate purposes, however, archetype may be surrounded by pairs of quotation marks, for it takes place in the midst of contrasting issues in a complementary relationship rather than a preponderant one. "Chaplain pants," Brockway, the yam-man of Harlem, and Trueblood are among the characters who conform to this general configuration, and Ellison appears to intend these "old world" characters to point to sources of a special racial gift. Even though these representatives of the archetype have receded in the dominance of urbanization, they are summoned in the narrative with the greatest clarity. This projection of folk character against an urban setting is significant: A synthesis of traditions, folk and urban, agrarian and industrial, it suggests the strategic interlarding of idioms.

This mix, however, accounts for the fusion of old and relatively new patterns of culture which make up the fundamental content of *Invisible Man*.

This content is variously expressed and repeated, and one of its most eloquent significations takes the form of phases of rhetoric itself, from Invisible Man's mimicked speech as a young boy in the opening hotel scene, to the wonderful, persistent rabble of Ras in the pre-riot scenes of the ending. Along with these patterns of rhetoric, Invisible Man assumes levels of consciousness that he takes on and off as he could articles of clothing. It is important to understand how these phases articulate moments of transition and contrast in the narrative, for it seems that Invisible Man ultimately subverts these elements of former style in the acquisition of one more apposite to his new "plan of living."

Recalling what he was like as an adolescent, he notes with ironic bitterness: What powers of endurance he had. "What enthusiasm! What a belief in the rightness of things!" (*IM*, 24). In the hotel scene that repeats an elaboration of primitive consciousness, Ellison shows the spectacular array of sexual fantasy in a perverted connection with bloodlust. As one of the victims of the scene, Invisible Man determines to speak even louder when the time comes. Whatever he said, "social equality" got into it, and he is made to apologize. His audience is, by turn, uproariously amused by him and indifferent to his trying to yell above their noise. In every particular of nuance and intention, the scene is a replication of nightmare; at the end of the ordeal, he is rewarded for having been a good boy. The cowhide briefcase gift is his sendoff to college and elsewhere. Its message, which he dreams that night, reads: "To Whom It May Concern, Keep This Nigger-Boy Running" (*IM*, 26). The shade of his grandfather had already told him as much, mocking his so-called triumph. He will run, in fact, stumble, as it were, from one adventure to the next, the victim of everybody else's notions of his own identity. His victimage is complete until he learns to manipulate various signs.

The initial college year is an extension of the naive phase, and there is a lyrical insistence in its moving Barbee sermon, set in the college chapel, and descriptions of campus landscape and iconography that expose Invisible Man's susceptibility to a rhetorical style to be fully appropriated by him in Harlem. Already a student orator of considerable power, Invisible Man watches the vesper speakers gather on the platform and recalls how, as a student leader, he had "stridden and debated . . . directing my voice at the highest beams and farthest rafters, ringing them, the accents staccato upon the ridgepole and echoing back with a tinkling, like words hurled to the trees of a wilderness, or into a well of slate-gray water; more sound than sense, a play upon the resonances of buildings, an assault upon the temple of the ears" (*IM*, 87, 88). This particular quality of metaphorical speech becomes inherent in Invisible Man's logical and syntactical disposition. He will lose the key to this impulse in the underground, but its motivation will remain instructive for him, the urge that he checks in a new-found suspicion of old affections.

The master speech of this type is given by blind Homer Barbee in an evocation of the Founder, perhaps modeled, in its symbolic import, on Booker T. Washington:

> This barren land after Emancipation . . . this land of darkness and sorrow, of ignorance and degradation, where the hand of brother had been turned against brother, father against son, and son against father; where master had turned against slave and slave against master; where all was strife and darkness, an aching land. And into this land came a humble prophet, lowly like the humble carpenter of Nazareth, a slave and a son of slaves, knowing only his mother. A slave born, but marked from the beginning by a high intelligence and princely personality; born in the lowest part of this barren, war-scarred land, yet somehow shedding light upon it where'er he passed through. I'm sure you have heard of his precarious infancy, his precious life almost destroyed by an insane cousin who splashed the babe with lye and shriveled his seed and how, a mere babe, he lay nine days in a death-like coma and then suddenly and miraculously recovered. You might say it was as though he had risen from the dead or been reborn. (*IM*, 92)

The suspension of predication in this narrative, its protracted modifiers, its unrelieved nominality and apposition, are built on a principle of composition that anticipates the climactic moment of speech, and its internal agitation of feeling induces an enthusiastic response to the word. The mode of anacoluthon, where the predicate is essentially dissolved or forgotten in the stream of modifiers, seems appropriate to oral speech, or dramatic utterance, when the speaker pursues an exact identity between himself and the words he chooses. The lexis of the passage replicates both a generalized poetic diction and the prose of King James; Barbee selects it as a manner of presentation that elevates its subject in importance. In its transcodation of one mode of figurative perception to another, Barbee's speech demonstrates that a universe of figurative relationships may be described. The ground of the metaphors actually shifts from Judaea to the American South and from Christ to the Founder. This transfer of images from their original ground of perception to a space quite distant from them points to the specific genius of *figura*[11] as a mode of historical narrative and explanation. But the key to the figurative mode is not only the way of its utterance, but also the particular world view that generates it. Essentially religious, the figurative mind perceives human history in a direct correlation with destiny: Men in their time move in a way consistent with the stars of heaven.

The inaugural, transitional, and terministic motifs of the passage inscribe a metaphorical order of language where contiguity in its passion to resolve contradiction holds sway. Whether we call Barbee's performance a speech or sermon doesn't matter, for the figures-of-perception that inform it are interchangeable along a hierarchy of forms:

> "I feel, I feel suddenly that I have become *more* human. Do you understand? More human. Not that I have become a man, for I was born a man. But that

> I am more human. I feel strong, I feel able to get things done! I feel that I can see sharp and clear and far down the dim corridor of history and in it I can hear the footsteps of militant fraternity! No, wait, let me confess . . . I feel the urge to affirm my feelings. . . . I feel that here, after a long and desperate and uncommonly blind journey, I have come home. . . . Home! With your eyes upon me I feel that I've found my true family! My true people! My true country! I am a new citizen of the country of your vision, a native of your fraternal land. I feel that here tonight, in this old arena, the new is being born and the vital old revived. In each of you, in me, in us all. . . . WE ARE THE TRUE PATRIOTS! THE CITIZENS OF TOMORROW'S WORLD! WE'LL BE DISPOSSESSED NO MORE!" (*IM*, 261–62)

The combination here of utopian images folded over a rhetoric of political revolution changes the content of Invisible Man's speeches from any apparent connection with a religious ground of perception, but in their tendencies toward a visual elaboration of ideas, we could say that the imagery belongs to a figurative extension of reality. For a time, Invisible Man is convinced that his role in the Brotherhood idea is the key to a new identity. The shock, however, is that the answer for him lies in the "plunge outside history," at least to the extent that the Brotherhood attempts to define historical role for him. His final disillusionment comes with the death of his comrade, Tod Clifton, followed by his resignation from the Brotherhood and flight into the underground.

> So there you have all of it that's important. Or at least you *almost* have it. I'm an invisible man and it placed me in a hole—or showed me the hole I was in, if you will—and I reluctantly accepted the fact. What else could I have done? Once you get used to it, reality is as irresistible as a club, and I was clubbed into the cellar before I caught the hint. Perhaps that's the way it had to be; I don't know. Nor do I know whether accepting the lesson has placed me in the rear or in the *avant-garde*. That, perhaps, is a lesson for history, and I'll leave such decisions to Jack and his ilk while I try belatedly to study the lesson of my own life. (*IM*, 432)

Various features of exclamation and delay have disappeared from the speech along with the immediate rush and excitement of words. Less visually energetic than earlier speeches, this one argues its closure in a language not intent on celebrating itself. This movement from oral to written language inscribes, precisely, Invisible Man's deliberate attempt to come into control of his own "symbol-making task," not at the behest of others, but at his own command.

The incidents that lead to perception are charted as an "analogy of experience," graced with the accoutrements of "fall." Having very little idea why things turn out so badly for him, Invisible Man is virtually used by everyone with whom he has any degree of sustained contact. He is prey, then, to evil forces, or purely arbitrary ones, in the guise of moral and institutional sanction. Having, therefore, no ego requirements of his own, obeying no ambitions or passions that he himself has generated, he is embarrassed by the least evidence of his own connection to an historical collective. Literally knocked in the head in the basement of the paint factory, he is forced to consider the impoverishment of his chosen negation. Having suppressed chitterlings and yams for the last time, he verges on a new-found freedom as the panorama of Harlem spreads before him. "I yam what I am!" is not simply a humorous dislocating of Descartian predication; it is a "re-cognitive" utterance of joy.

Invisible Man repeats the moves of the hero that Joseph Campbell illustrates in *Hero of a Thousand Faces*. Campbell's hero inhabits the center of the cycle of experience, the "nuclear unit of the monomyth," and returns to society, like Invisible Man, with a message. The contemporary hero, however, in returning with a stereo, introduces a dimension of "cool," hereafter called irony, to his return that inscribes it with more than a touch of complexity. Notably, the returned man lacks an affective dimension in the absence of women in his life, but embraces, instead, a love of people. As an orator, Invisible Man engages people as the anonymous entities of an audience. He loves them because they listen to him, but he also returns as a lover of forms, oratory included—in fact, Invisible Man meets the daimon of oratory at its source—and, somewhere along the way, he has managed to get himself some music and wire his hole for sound. Analytically, conceptually involved, he entertains himself with elaborate mental constructs, the most elaborate being the novel itself. Male, and just a little arrogant in its clutches, he is exactly "self-centered" in his world, just as Campbell's returning hero, contracted back into a status of ego.

The cycle of experience permits us to go back and forth, up and down its intersecting axes; without this versatility of motion, travel would not be possible on the globe or within the text. It is this shrewd knowledge of relationships that informs the speaker of the Prologue/Epilogue. The promise to end up somewhere other than the self compels the adventure that, for all its variety and color, leads back to the point of departure. Against this knowledge, the ideology of progression is fundamentally false and deceptive. But something does happen around the cycle of experience that lends the theme of return its particular danger. Other than cynicism, or beyond it, the return provokes an irretrievable distrust of one's own image thrown back in the mirror of language. This distrust brings us to the fourth order of circularity which introduces the ironic mode.

Invisible Man's persistent anonymity against the specifics of biographical detail is the crucial ingredient of ironic disclosure. He calls himself simply "I," and none of the other characters ever addresses him because he is, he insists, emphatically invisible—people refuse to see him. This no-name seems a contradiction at first but since he acknowledges invisibility—veritable disembodiment—why should he have a name that could confine him to orders of affection and kinship, therefore, limitation? The novel almost threatens to become an enormous hoax:

> "Ah," you say, "so it was all a build-up to bore us with his buggy jiving. He only wanted us to listen to him rave!" But only partially true: Being invisible and without substance, a disembodied voice, as it were, what else could I do? What else but try to tell you what was really happening when your eyes were looking through? And it is this which frightens me.
>
> Who knows but that, on the lower frequencies, I speak for you? (*IM*, 439)

I think that there is a precedent for Invisible Man's disembodiment from another cultural scene, and it is called the "subjectivity of freedom":

> The subject stands freely above that which must be regarded as determining him; he stands freely above it not merely at the instant of choice but at every moment, for the arbitrary will constitutes no law, no constancy, no content. . . .[12]

Since Invisible Man's task of confession has mobilized a plenitude of historical moments, laden with personal significance, we can only view his invisibility as a blazing contradiction that must stand as it is. It becomes the "modified noun," so to speak, in naming the persistently refined features of modern consciousness: We can lay hold of such consciousness both in its abstract form—the "subjectivity of freedom"—and in its concrete manifestation in the living person. "Lower frequencies" belongs to the same order of cases as invisibility. The very possibilities of the terms, their near-endless procession of implicit modification, make it virtually certain that Invisible Man's new position locates an unalterable disenchantment with words and their capacity to mean simply what they say. This sense of the overlapping contexts of meaning defies the "one-for-another" mode of expression and goes along with Invisible Man's shifting sense of identity, at least an identity that remains complicated by experience. The phases of rhetoric that he overthrows point, essentially, to fixed destiny, a notion of permanence that asserts itself against the current of experience, its enemy, but disembodiment as a way of being enters the doors of permanence by another route, backs into it, in the achieving a central allegiance to the priorities of the imagination, in directing its attention toward the theme of potentiality. In this way, lived experience is always an embarkation, returning back to the subject. The metaphorical order has folded into something else—the double intention, spying its shadows of meaning.

The ironic twist of ending is that Invisible Man discourses on invisibility as a passionately visible vocation, but more than that, he criticizes his effort as a gesture of "destructing" and remaking. He poses an ethical paradox: What is the good of talk if it finds no audience? But an audience is not better than its speaker, and the other way around. In fact, the speaker creates his audience in the remaking of their own tale, and without their consent, the speaker would have no task. This gets fairly tedious as Invisible Man knows, with his new-found sense of humor, and in irony, it appears that nobody wins. There is a nastiness in irony, an eloquent hateful passion that makes us prefer the disposition of metaphor. Ellison, however, chooses for Invisible Man an assault on metaphor in the very guise of its own terms, turning the underground and the theme of blackness into genuinely philosophical propositions. For Invisible Man, the achievement of an ironic voice—perhaps we could substitute inner for ironic—that is seen through the density of struggle and error, is a countermyth against the founders of "Sambo," the damaged humanity of an acquisitive culture, its wealth transformed into the visible evidence of status. In the realism of letters this century, *Invisible Man* insists upon the superior function of the daimon—the instrumentality of conscience—in grasping the persistently ethical idea.

At one time, the giving up of oneself to the sway of intellectual power led men to very dangerous acts; we call one of its symptoms "civil disobedience" and the victimage that flowed from it led, in all the cases we know, to the doors of the prisonhouse. In the popular examples, the man who heeds the dictates of conscience opposes to the known order a decisive threat which he asserts as his own countermyth, and it usually takes the form of a language that nobody recognizes at first, or at least doesn't admit recognition: "The individual must no longer act out of respect for the law, but must consciously know why he acts" (Kierkegaard, 249). Invisible Man, seeking the why of his acts, cuts loose from prevailing myth in a sequence of subversive moves that conjoin him with other myths of conscience—the countermythologies. What other way is open to the one who is not seen? In his acceptance of invisibility, he can only choose to undermine, systematically, all vestiges of the established order that has driven him underground. In its articulation of a figure of subversion, *Invisible Man* glitters with a notion of black disobedience. In this case, the qualifier is no necessary illumination since all disobedience, in the very force of the language, is black. The book has never called itself "revolutionary," but it begins and ends with a revolutionist determination: If "I" am to be victimized, why not let it be for good reason?

NOTES

1. William Gass, "Imaginary Borges and His Books," in *Fiction and the Figures of Life* (New York: Vintage Books, 1972), 120–34.

2. Ortega y Gasset, "The Dehumanization of Art," in *The Dehumanization of Art and Other Essays*. Trans. Alex Brown with intro. Phillip Troutman (New York: Norton, 1972), 65–84.

3. Kenneth Burke, "On Words and the Word," in *The Rhetoric of Religion: Studies in Logology* (Berkeley and Los Angeles: University of California Press, 1970).

Of the four categories to which words belong, Burke calls this class "logology," to which literary criticism, rhetoric, poetics, dialectics, grammar, etymology, philology have been relegated.

4. Robert Bone, *The Negro Novel in America* (New Haven: Yale University Press, 1965), 198.

5. The concept of the "ancestral imperative" is fully explored by Albert Murray in a study of Afro-American cultural symbols, *South to a Very Old Place* (New York: McGraw Hill, 1971).

6. Northrop Frye, "Mythical Phase: Symbol as Archetype," *Anatomy of Criticism: Four Essays* (Princeton: Princeton University Press, 1973), 106.

7. Roland Barthes, *Mythologies*. Trans. Annette Lavers (New York: Hill & Wang, 1972).

8. Ralph Ellison, *Invisible Man* (New York: Random House, 1952), 437. All subsequent references to this work are cited in text as *IM*.

9. Ralph Ellison, "The Art of Fiction: An Interview," *Shadow and Act* (New York: Random House, 1964), 169–87.

10. Maud Bodkin, *Archetypal Patterns in Poetry: Psychological Studies of Imagination* (London: Oxford University Press, 1963), 1.

11. Erich Auerbach, "Figura," in *Scenes from the Drama of European Literature* (New York: Anchor-Doubleday, 1959).

12. Soren Kierkegaard, *The Concept of Irony: With Constant Reference to Socrates*. Trans. with intro. Lee M. Capel (Bloomington: Indiana University Press, 1965), 245.

Fiction and Idea: A Note on Ellison's "Black Mask of Humanity"

WILSON HARRIS

It may be of interest to look at a series of hints in Ellison's fiction and criticism that seem to me to disclose an intuitive involvement in the philosophical nature of *coniunctio* (the ancient alchemical term for "true marriage" involving animal and psyche, male and female, earth and sky, and all the elements through which we live and whose pollution, whose debasement, endangers the mutual body of existences shared consciously and unconsciously by diverse human/animal/vegetable creatures within layers of space and time).

Coniunctio bears upon the profoundest archaeology of the muse of being. In regard to Ellison's criticism, I have in mind his article "Twentieth-Century Fiction and the Black Mask of Humanity."[1] Ellison voices a question there on "ideas," on "nonconcern with ideas," and on "myth." I interpret "ideas" in the context in which he writes, as bearing profoundly on philosophical myth whose intuitive life—within the individual artist—secretes the mysterious *conception* of a work of the imagination, a work of creation.

The nature of that "conception" (if "nature" is the term) is elusive. And since we live in a universe we tend to address as violent, violence may seem to triumph over the distinctive genius, the distinctive force, of a work of art. Distinctive force or genius may seem so close to the impact of violence that one may cease to read the blow of regenerative capacity that saves in contradistinction to *ritualized* violence that destroys.

Ellison's fascination with Hemingway's technical competence is tempered by a sensation of his (Hemingway's) incapacity in the realm of "ideas" or philosophic myth. That incapacity leads him inevitably into "ritualized violence" or rituals of violence as the absolute basis of his fiction.

> It is instructive that Hemingway, born in a civilization characterized by violence, should seize upon the ritualized violence of the culturally distant Spanish bullfight as a laboratory for developing his style. For it was, for Americans, an amoral violence (though not for the Spaniards) which he was seeking. Otherwise he might have studied that ritual of violence closer to home, that ritual in which the sacrifice is that of a human scapegoat, the lynching bee. Certainly this rite

> is not confined to the rope as agency, nor to the South as scene, nor even to the Negro as victim. (*S&A*, 37)

Ellison hints at endangered *coniunctio*, I think, when—a page or two after his comment on Hemingway—he declares, ''For man without myth is Othello with Desdemona gone: chaos descends, faith vanishes and superstitions prowl in the mind'' (*S&A*, 41).

Midway between these statements he questions assumptions by Malcolm Cowley that relate to ''myth'' and implicit *coniunctio*. Cowley misconceives these matters, Ellison implies.

> Malcolm Cowley, on the basis of the rites which he believes to be the secret dynamic of Hemingway's work, has identified him with Poe, Hawthorne and Melville, ''the haunted and nocturnal writers,'' he calls them, ''the men who dealt with images that were symbols of an inner world.'' In Hemingway's work, he writes, ''we can recognize rites of animal sacrifice. . . of sexual union. . . of conversion. . . and of symbolic death and rebirth.'' I do not believe, however, that the presence of these rites in writers like Hemingway is as important as the fact that here, beneath the dead-pan prose, the cadences of understatement, the anti-intellectualism, the concern with every ''fundamental'' of man except that which distinguishes him from the animal—that here is the twentieth-century form of that magical rite which during periods of great art has been to a large extent public and explicit. (*S&A*, 39)

One can but agree with Ellison, and yet I think he may be overlooking a complex reality in the phrase ''public and explicit'' as requisite or native to ''periods of great art.''

It is tempting to bolster one's wishes about ''periods of great art'' in the distant past, but the uncomfortable fact is that Hemingway is ''explicit'' in ways that the twentieth-century ''public,'' alas, may desire. The complexity of *coniunctio* or ''magical rite'' (as Ellison puts it) is not easily comprehensible to millions and millions of people (a great many of whom are subject to the ''illiteracy'' Ellison himself identifies with chauvinistic Bledsoe regimes in *Invisible Man*). The tastes and expectations of millions are conscripted by advertising gimmickry and uniform media, by reinforcements of appetite to consume priceless animal species around the globe within an environment of polluted landscapes, technologies of despair that plot the evacuation of cities in the event of nuclear war.

Indeed the complexity of the problem—its deviation from the ''public and explicit''—is only too manifest in Ellison's major novel, *Invisible Man*.

How does that novel counterpoint the rituals of violence that it raises to our attention? In part it does this by masterly paradox, by interpretations and reinterpretations of cliché-ridden rhetoric we take for granted, namely, ''light,'' ''darkness,'' ''visible,'' ''invisible,'' ''responsibility,'' ''equality,'' and the like. Above all, however, it is the ambiguity of myth that Ellison employs in the novel that holds out potential for the re-visionary womb of society.

Let us briefly analyze this ambiguity.

* * *

Invisible Man's odyssey immerses him in a series of metaphorical deaths and reawakenings that are not discernible, I find, to many readers who read the novel and are attracted to it as to a document of terror. It takes some time, in fact, to arouse a class of readers into the significance of the stages of dying/awakening that move in the novel from the boxing-ring cycle (where Invisible Man metaphorically dies and reawakens) into the Bledsoe cycle (where Invisible Man's expulsion from college is so shocking and demoralizing that he endures a torment akin to dying followed by reawakening as he resumes his odyssey). That odyssey ushers us into further cycles. Invisible Man "dies" in an explosion in a paint factory and reawakens under the Cyclopean eye of a doctor in a Harlem hospital. Invisible Man experiences or endures other "extinctions" of self followed by the bleakest intimations of survival.

What is remarkable about these cycles—that most readers and critics, I believe, have overlooked—is the carnival women or muses who are associated with the dying self and the capacity in that self to awaken to new life. For example, there are Ma (a shadowy muse of freedom) and the naked blonde by the boxing ring (a shadowy "white goddess" or muse of gold and ecstasy). Both are threaded into the boxing-ring cycle. I call them shadowy because they appear in the novel as terrorized and singularly disadvantaged figures which are closer to abortive freedom and false gold than to the symbols of capacity for rebirth they hint at or vaguely imply. Those hints—when read against the entire cyclical apparition of the novel—suggest to me the necessity to read through the narrative into descending formations wherein Ma's confused conception of freedom is the obverse or reverse of genuine possibility. Thus the seed or currency of freedom exists. False gold, in the terrorized white goddess of the boxing ring, is the mimicry of true gold. As such, the alchemy of true gold is obscurely alive in trials of greed and horror.

The Bledsoe phase sustains not only Invisible Man's metaphoric extinction—on being expelled from college—but surrogate metaphoric extinctions that foreshadow expulsion from college. In that foreshadowing, Invisible Man is plagued, in particular, by fear of disaster when he witnesses the fainting spells and apparent demise of the college trustee, Norton, whom he (Invisible Man) has been delegated to guide. The epicenter of those surrogate "deaths" lies in the shocking tale Trueblood tells. Invisible Man drives to the Golden Day for help, with collapsed Norton, and witnesses the inferno that exists there.

That inferno and the series of surrogate, metaphoric deaths in the Bledsoe cycle exist in concert with the tragedy of incest inflicted upon Matty Lou to inflame Matty Lou's mother, Kate, whose anger is so great that she comes close to killing her husband, Trueblood. That narrow shave Trueblood experiences is another surrogate "extinction" Invisible Man bears.

The incest, the horror, and the degradation highlight once again abused muses or carnival women of history, yet one perceives in shadowy depth, as it were, obverse or reverse currency of an inner realm or dream of ecstasy, an inner royal privilege or dream of sovereign kith and kin—associated with incest myth—a dream of flying humanity masked as birds and crowned by space.

Thus, though the myth is grossly diseased and its metaphorical significance aborted within a ghetto of poverty, it is barely active in a shadowy, ecstatic gesture that embraces all humanity to push Invisible Man into the future.

The pattern is set for the rest of the novel. Other metaphorical extinctions occur in concert with muses that tend to be swallowed by the degenerate Rinehart/Confidence Man masquerade but an impetus remains, bleakest tide of conscience-in-depth, to rescue Invisible Man from ultimate corruption of the manipulated becoming the supreme manipulator of a lost society.

* * *

The foregoing sketch of a formidable but conscripted myth brings home the difficulty of *coniunctio*. The womb of ecstasy, as we have seen, remains sealed within cruel Bledsoe and Trueblood enchantments. Thus the very nature of "public and explicit" art needs to give way to complex genius that may only sustain a "magical rite" at a depth of intuitive encounter that is inevitably complex in an age—such as the twentieth century—which is burdened by legacies of conquest and violence.

Man without myth is Othello with Desdemona gone: chaos descends, faith vanishes, and superstitions prowl in the mind.

Not only that. The vision of *coniunctio* tends to grow faint within a riddle of nightmare castration that appears toward the close of *Invisible Man*. And this tells volumes about the "Negro stereotype" of which Ellison speaks in *Shadow and Act*.

Such stereotypes may indeed seek less "to crush the Negro" and more "to console the white man" (*S&A*, 41). A deeper theme of paradox emerges when one subsumes Ellison's critical ideas within his profoundly creative imagination. Then, it seems to me, the castration nightmare is a parable and judgment, one that clothes minorities and majorities alike, against equating sex, or making sex a formula for, the games of violation and tyranny men play with men as much as with women and vice versa. In such games, sex moves away from therapeutic community into sinister enchantment, sinister manipulation, or conquest, and the mask of death-wish acquires a pertinence beyond pigmentation, whether black or white.

NOTE

1. Ralph Ellison, *Shadow and Act* (New York: Random House, 1964), 24–44. All subsequent citations of this work appear in text as *S&A*.

Notes on the Invisible Women in Ralph Ellison's *Invisible Man*

CLAUDIA TATE

Questions about the female characters in Ralph Ellison's *Invisible Man* seem to elicit two types of response: The initial one is, "What women?" since women clearly occupy peripheral roles in the novel. And then after Mary Rambo and the other female characters—that is, the old slave woman, the magnificent blonde, the rich sophisticate Emma, the anonymous seductress, and finally the prophetic and pathetic Sybil—are recalled, the second response is something like, "Oh, those stereotypes" (Sylvander, 77–79). Both replies are virtually automatic and both are legitimate, given the factual details of the narrative. But we must not be misled by what can be seen with a quick glance; we must not neglect what lies hidden behind the mask and proclaim that the mask is the face. Instead, we must remember Ellison's own witty admonition that the rind is not the heart[1] and look for the concealed truth which lies beneath the stereotyped exteriors of his female characters.

* * *

In his essay "Twentieth-Century Fiction,"[2] Ellison contends that stereotypes, though indisputably one-dimensional and therefore oversimplified, frequently hide complex aspects of human character. Moreover, he adds that "the Negro has been more willing perhaps than any other artist to start with the stereotype, accept it as true, and then seek out the human truth which it hides" (*S&A*, 43). Perhaps this is also an appropriate procedure to follow when examining the female characters in *Invisible Man*; that is "start with the [female] stereotype[s] accept [them] as true, and then seek out the human truth which [they] hide" (*S&A*, 43). Perhaps by following this example, we will not be attempting merely to define female humanity but to recognize, as Ellison suggests, broader aspects of the humanity of all of us.

* * *

That a male character dominates the novel is certainly without question. The entire story centers on an anonymous, young black man's painful acceptance of his social alienation, which is so extreme that he has virtually no control over the sequence of events that directs the course of his life. He receives so little recognition for his efforts to define a meaningful identity for himself that he assumes a new name, which characterizes his feelings of acute marginality: the Invisible Man. At first he believes that being black is responsible for his plight, but he soon learns that everyone, black and white alike, lives in a lawless, amoral, chaotic world, where honorable intentions and high moral standards have little absolute value. Painfully disillusioned by this knowledge, the young man retreats from human contact and takes up residence in an abandoned basement. There he must live in almost total isolation until he is able to discover some order, some meaning from the chaos he has unwittingly discovered.

Deriving meaning from his experiences and measuring their impact on his life are processes that the hero must complete before he can escape from the underground. At this point in the young man's development, the female characters become important beyond their obvious roles in the narrative.[3] Like the underground station masters of the American slave era, these female characters assist the Invisible Man along his course to freedom. Their associations with him force him to recognize their common plight. Through his contact with them, he comes to understand that he is the means to another's end; he is a victim, growing evermore conscious of his victimization.

At the end of the novel, we are left to ponder whether he will be successful in his attempt to escape the underground. But since Ellison has him say that he is merely hibernating and that hibernation is a covert preparation for overt action (*IM*, 16), we are inclined to believe that his retreat underground marks only a temporary period of intensive, preliminary reflection. During this time, he comes to understand that his fear and desire, guilt and innocence, the ambiguity of his experiences in general, and his resulting ambivalent feelings have propelled him along a seemingly chaotic course over which he has had so little control that he feels as though he has been boomeranged. But before he can leave the underground, he must understand the appropriateness of this analogy. He probably already knows that the course of the boomerang is, in fact, predictable, although the time of its arrival seems unexpected to those who do not witness its launching or understand the principles governing its movement. But he must apply these principles to his experiences in order to predict and understand their outcome. In so doing he will learn not to grope through his life in blind naiveté, expecting others to give him credit for his good intentions. He must nurture them to fruition, himself, with a mature strategy, based on discerning a person's genuine character without being distracted by color or gender. In this manner, he will be able to control, to some degree, the course of his future and not only map out the way to the upper world but also arrive at the method for participating, in meaningful ways, with those who inhabit the aboveground region.

But despite the optimism Ellison incites, we are not fully convinced. Doubt lurks, as we face the possibility that the young protagonist may not be successful in securing the necessary knowledge for staging his escape. Ellison does not resolve our dilemma, but I suggest the narrative does provide a method for measuring the likelihood of the young man's success. The possibility for his escape is directly related to his ability to distill meaning from his encounters with the women I have mentioned. They embody the knowledge he needs to stage his escape. If he can discern the impact that his relationships with them has on the direction and quality of his life, he will be able to abandon his polarized, black-or-white version of the world, as well as his outdated ambition to be an accommodationist race leader. Instead, he will know that power exploits color merely as a means to an end and that there is strength in manipulating one's powerlessness and in not allowing oneself always to be seen. What is most important, he will have learned that there are order and, ultimately, utility arising from accepting the ambivalence and contradictions of life. If he cannot assess the significance of his relationships with these women, he will not have learned the essential lessons, and his every effort to leave his hiding place will be aborted in fear, time and time again.

> "Old woman, what is this freedom you love so well?" I asked around a corner of my mind.
>
> "I done forgot, son. It's all mixed up. First I think it's one thing, then I think it's another. It gits my head to spinning. I guess now it ain't nothing but knowing how to say what I got up in my head." (*IM*, 14)

The old slave woman in the Prologue provides the young protagonist with the motivation for recalling his experiences which form the sequence of events for the story. She tells him about her slave master-lover, who repeatedly promised to free her but never kept his word. She also tells him that she loved her master dearly, but that she loved freedom more. She further explains her decision to assist their sons in a scheme to murder their father and secure their precious freedom. The Invisible Man responds to her story by asking that she define her understanding of freedom, which appears to have been the force that propelled her into action. Her endeavor to respond to his request incites her recollection of powerfully conflicting feelings, hence the ambiguity of her reply. As she continues her response, her head begins to ache, and she cries out in pain. Her sons come to her rescue and insist that the next time the Invisible Man has a question like that, to ask himself, instead. His effort to heed their command results in his attempting to answer this question, and he follows her example by recalling what's in his head. His recollection results in his reconstructing the events of his life, and they in turn constitute the plot of the novel.

The hero's encounter with the slave woman provides a lesson about the nature and acquisition of freedom. As we have seen, the old woman's desire to obtain her freedom was so urgent that it demanded action. The hero must learn by her example. He must learn that it is not enough for him to choose to leave the underground and articulate that choice. He must commit himself to action and thereby realize adult heroic potential. His initial steps follow her course, but whether he can exercise his determination and leave the underground remains to be seen. In any event, Ellison has the young man follow her example, and in so doing the author provides structure for the novel and gives it purpose as well.

> . . . and in the center, facing us, stood a magnificent blonde—stark naked. . . . I felt a wave of irrational guilt and fear. . . . I felt a desire to spit upon her as my eyes brushed slowly over her body. . . . I wanted at one and the same time to run from the room, to sink through the floor, or to go to her and cover her from my eyes and the eyes of the others with my own body. . . . to caress her and destroy her, to love her and murder her, to hide from her, and yet to stroke her. . . . (*IM*, 22)

The hero's encounter with the magnificent blonde marks his first direct encounter with ambivalence. On seeing the naked woman, he becomes keenly aware of his chaotic sexual responses which cannot be tempered by any social code. His every effort to control his reactions results in emotional conflict and an intense sensation of bewilderment. But she is not just any woman; she represents the forbidden white woman. Centuries of prohibition forbid his even looking upon her, but his gaze is so willfully direct that he virtually consummates their sexual union with his eyes. As a result he feels guilty, and yet he is innocent; he is bold, and yet he is afraid.

This encounter with ambivalence is not without its lesson for the young protagonist, although we cannot be certain when he learns it, if at all. When he sees the magnificent blonde, he knows immediately that he longs to possess her, but he must not touch or even look upon the forbidden white woman. Not only is she a sexual taboo; but more significantly she is the means by which the possibility of freedom is withheld from the nameless young man. In fact, she is the means by which black people in general were penalized for exercising the freedom of choice, in that the penalty was translated into the accusation of rape and the sentence was death. The symbolic linkage between the white woman and freedom, therefore, finds its origin in hundreds of years of southern race relations. And Ellison employs her as a potent vehicle for dramatizing the young protagonist's psychological journey to the region of consciousness where he can assert his new-found freedom, but only after he confronts this taboo in her various symbolic forms.

The magnificent blonde foreshadows the succession of white women who provide the circumstances for the young protagonist to realize that freedom is nothing less than the active exercise of his willful, independent choice.

Emma, the anonymous seductress, and Sybil arouse his feelings of prohibited sexuality, but, more important, they are also the means by which he realizes that freedom is first a state of mind. In order to secure it for himself, he must move beyond the need merely to conquer them sexually or to outwit the Jacks and the Rineharts of the world. He must acknowledge the humanity of these women and release them as well as himself from the sexual taboos and stereotypes that deny their acquisition of freedom. His encounters with these women provide him with opportunities to perform these tasks.

Returning to the battle royal, which is the first stage of the young protagonist's development of consciousness, we see that the magnificent blonde is elevated to such a degree that he does not realize that they share a common plight. Both are exploited objects for sensual entertainment. The blonde has learned, however, to conceal her human character behind the mask of a Kewpie doll, therefore rendering her innermost thoughts and emotions incomprehensible to the "big shots who watched her with fascination" (*IM*, 23). She has learned to use this method of concealment to her advantage. In essence, she is invisible, and she provides the young protagonist with his first lesson in invisibility.

The young protagonist manages to put on a good show at the battle royal, win the scholarship, and go off to college with the hope of becoming another Booker T. Washington. Despite his humiliation, he continues to believe that he can overcome virtually all obstacles with good intentions, conscientious effort, and self-control. At college he again encounters the intense feeling of ambivalence, which is of such proportions this time that it is entirely beyond his comprehension. He does not know how to respond to his dilemma and therefore faces peril.

The circumstances giving rise to this encounter result from his escorting one of his college's founders, Mr. Norton, around the campus. The young man is entrusted with this task precisely because he is an exemplary student. But while he is exercising his good faith and honorable intentions, he encroaches upon the unexpected and is engulfed in chaos. Rather than control the route for Norton's tour and show him evidence of racial progress, our overly zealous protagonist allows Norton to stumble upon Trueblood and his family, who are the personifications of disgrace for the local black community. Trueblood tells Norton of his incestuous relationship with his daughter. As a result Norton becomes faint and is in need of a strong stimulus to revive him. The young man eagerly takes him to the nearest tavern, the Golden Day, which is besieged by lunatics from the local state mental hospital, who both physically abuse and ridicule Norton. Upon their return to campus, the young man repeatedly says he is innocent of wrongdoing, but despite his claims of innocence, he is held responsible for his poor judgment, and the punishment is expulsion from school.

Still holding onto his dream to become a race leader, he goes to work for a paint factory in the North, deluding himself with the notion that he will earn enough money and be permitted to return to school in the fall. His continued effort in this regard results in his being seriously injured in an accident, and Ellison uses his extraordinary recovery to suggest the young man's symbolic rebirth and acquisition of a new identity. Upon regaining his consciousness, the young man finds that he must qualify his new identity and determine a course for his new life. His character is like a blank page on which some words must be written, and it is Mary Rambo who writes his new name and nurtures his new awareness of himself.

> Her eyes swept the machine and as she soothed her smashed fingers she snickered, "You must be awful strong for them to have to put you under all this pile of junk. Awful strong. Who they think you is, Jack the Bear or John Henry or somebody like that. . . . Say something, fool!"[4]

Mary Rambo's character is not fully delineated in the 1952 edition of *Invisible Man*, where she is portrayed more as a force than as an actual person (225). But by referring to a section of the original manuscript that was deleted from the 1952 edition, published in *Soon, One Morning* and titled "Out of the Hospital and Under the Bar" (247), we can see that Mary achieves complexity of character, whereas she is only briefly sketched in the novel. In this short story, from which the foregoing excerpt is taken, Mary provides the young protagonist with her tried and true folk wisdom as a means of protecting him against the irrational, unknown world. She is also the vehicle by which he departs from the world of "Keep This Nigger-Boy Running" and arrives at the threshold of a new region of consciousness where he moves toward realizing his adult, heroic potential. Moreover, Mary Rambo gives him the folk vernacular and perspective to articulate the impact of his experiences on his evolving identity. Whereas the old slave woman motivates the telling of his story, Mary provides him with the words and the narrative voice. She teaches him the folk vernacular, and it sets the tone as well as determines the idiomatic language for the novel.

Mary's physical appearance and her folksy manner may resemble the "mammy" of plantation lore, but she is not bound by this stereotype. She is the nurturer of a *black* child, not the master's white child. She is the young protagonist's surrogate mother who bears this son to fulfill a similar destiny, outlined in the old slave woman's story. He, too, is destined to grasp at freedom, and Mary is a means toward this end. She literally feeds and comforts the young protagonist, as a mother comforts her child. She nurtures his faltering vision of himself, by renaming him Jack the Bear and, thereby, announces his potential to achieve great strength but only after enduring a temporary period of hibernation. By naming him John Henry, she also announces his potential to acquire full confidence and power as a leader of his people. ("Hospital," 247)

While living with Mary, the young man is called into action by witnessing an eviction of an old couple, but rather than rely on the identity and wisdom

Mary has given him, he accepts a new name and a new program and subsequently loses his way on the course to asserting his own freedom. He becomes a pattern in Brother Jack's design and finds himself destined to repeat the lessons of the past and fight another battle royal.

The Brotherhood promotes the ultimate battle royal, but unlike the contest of his youth, this one has three preliminary dances, where the hero is not permitted simply to observe but is compelled to dance literally with one white woman, Emma, and figuratively with two others, the anonymous nude and Sybil.

> Just then Emma came up and challenged me to dance and I led her toward the floor as the piano played, thinking of the vet's prediction and drawing her to me as though I danced with such as her every evening. (273)

Dance number one is with Emma. Unlike her predecessor, the magnificent blonde, she provides the young protagonist with his first opportunity to approach the white woman, the sexual taboo, on presumably equal footing. She therefore represents stage two of his development, which is apparent when he tries to convince himself that he is not intimidated by her, but the fact that he overcompensates for his past feelings of racial anxiety makes us believe the contrary. Even though he witnesses Jack's act of defining Emma as the financial means for the Brotherhood's activities, the young protagonist does not realize that he shares Emma's fate. Both are instruments for the exercise of another's control and assertion of power, but he must finish the next two dances before he can recognize his own as well as another's exploitation.

> She was a small, delicately plump woman with raven hair in which a thin streak of white had begun almost imperceptibly to show, and when she reappeared in the rich red of a hostess gown she was so striking that I had to avert my somewhat startled eyes. (355).

Dance number two is with the anonymous, rich white woman who seems to be a real-life replica of the pink Renoir nude hanging on the wall in her penthouse apartment. She coaxes the young protagonist to her home under the pretext of discussing the woman question. His initial response to her is one of prohibition and desire (359), like his response in the earlier incidents with her symbolic predecessors—the magnificent nude and Emma. But in this case his anxiety subsides, and he succumbs to the desire of the flesh, not as a black man who is trying to prove his equality but as a man who has been sexually aroused by a woman.

His encounter with this woman represents stage three of his development. Through his relationship with her he recognizes that, like her, he is an instrument operating in a plan not of his own design. As he realizes that a third party controls and debases both himself and this woman, his perception of their common exploitation moves into focus. But before he can clearly see his relationship with the magnificent blonde, Emma, and the anonymous seductress and acknowledge their respective marginality, alienation, and ultimately their respective invisibility, he must dance his third and final dance, in which his partner is Sybil.

> "Oh, I know that I can trust you. I just knew you'd understand; you're not like other men. We're kind of alike." (450)

Sybil is not the magnificent blonde Kewpie doll of the battle royal; neither is she the "gay and responsive Emma. . . with the hard, handsome face" (446); nor is she "the small, delicately plump woman" (355) who "glows as though consciously acting out a symbolic role of life and feminine fertility" (354). To the contrary, Sybil is a "leathery old girl with chestnut hair" (448), who "would soon be a biddy, stout, with a little double chin in a three-ply girdle" (449). Sybil is a virtual parody on the magnificent blonde of the battle royal; Sybil is a pathetic buffoon, who is, nevertheless, humanly vulnerable and intensely sensitive to those who share her plight of invisibility.

Sybil, like Mary, is another surrogate mother who comes to deliver the young protagonist from the deception of his false identity with the Brotherhood. She is also another symbolic blonde, who ushers him to the threshold of the final battle royal. In addition, she is his last teacher, who propels him along the course to freedom by making him aware that invisibility is not necessarily a liability but possibly a valuable asset.

"Come to mama, beautiful" (447), she chides the young man, as she sexually entices him. Although she is a consenting adult, she regards the desired consummation as rape, fantasizing that rape by a black male is some type of ultimate sexual "high" that can release her from years of sexual frustration. She believes that the young protagonist possesses some sexual magic that can restore her vitality. And although he only "rapes" her in symbolic fashion, her request forces him to confront the taboo that has meant fear, death, and destruction for generations of black people. By confronting her, he realizes that possessing her sexually is not identical to possessing some vague sense of freedom. His confrontation also forces him to acknowledge his complicity with his exploiters, in that he has willingly allowed them to reorder his priorities and to force him to lose sight of his original ambitions. He sees that he has imitated the Brotherhood's tactics and interpreted freedom as the exercise of power over another. As a result he refuses to exploit Sybil sexually but instead reveals his genuine concern for her well-being. Once she realizes that his is not the conventional reaction, she responds by telling him that "[he] is not like other men" (450), that he is beautiful, and that he is capable of genuine compassion and understanding. Like the magnificent blonde, Sybil enables him to approach the threshold of the final battle royal, but not before she has had the opportunity to dispel his misplaced ambition and revive his faltering sense of responsibility, first to himself and then to others.

In each instance stereotype confronts stereotype, as the young protagonist confronts the succession of minor female characters. Each of the four white women represents the other's prohibition, and by confronting the taboo, the young man is slowly and painfully liberated from illusion until he reaches the story's climax. At this point he realizes that he is responsible for his own spiritual death as well as the senseless murder of countless black people. He realizes that by saying yes to the Brotherhood, he has, in effect, been saying no to his own survival as well as to that for black people in general. He is responsible for mobilizing the forces of death and destruction that exploded into the Harlem battle royal. He is guilty, and the knowledge of his guilt is so devastating that he is compelled to seek refuge at Mary's.

> I was trying to get to Mary's (484).
>
> I was going for Mary's but I was moving downtown through the dripping street rather than up. . . (485).
>
> To Mary, I thought, to Mary (485).
>
> But I was never to reach Mary's (490).

The young protagonist desperately seeks Mary—he needs her once again to provide a nurturing refuge from the pain of his disillusionment. He needs her once again to deliver him from the world of "Keep This Nigger-Boy Running" and to foster his folk identities as Jack the Bear and John Henry. He needs her to name him, but his need is unfulfilled, and he remains nameless. Instead of finding Mary, he finds himself "whirling on in the blackness, knocking against the rough walls of a narrow passage, banging [his] head and cursing. . . coughing and sneezing, into another dimensionless room. . ." (492). He is lost in the inanimate womb of the underground.

So we end where we began, which is not surprising, inasmuch as Ellison told us in the Prologue that "the end is in the beginning and lies far ahead" (*IM*, 9). The central question that motivated this study, therefore, confronts us again: Will the Invisible Man be successful in his attempt to escape the underground? I admit that Ellison supplies no easy answer; he gives us only the riddle of the text. But I offer my answer nevertheless. I predict that the Invisible Man's efforts to leave the underground, though valiant, will be aborted time and time again, since he has no mother to give him birth. The womb that encases him cannot deliver him to the aboveground region. As a result, not only is he without recognizable substance and, thus, invisible; he is, as Ellison says in the Epilogue, "a disembodied voice" (503) without a face. He is an idea, an abstraction, a painful memory of a wasted life full of disillusionment. He is knowledge without matter; he is a child unborn, suspended between the fact of his conception and the impossibility of his birth. And he haunts us with the truth that the fate of utter and devastating disillusionment is not reserved for him alone. "Who knows," as Ellison admonishes, "but that, on the lower frequencies, [the Invisible Man] speak[s] for [us all]" (503).

NOTES

1. A twist on a phrase Ellison repeatedly uses throughout the narrative of *Invisible Man*. Citations from this work appear in text as *IM*.

2. Ralph Ellison, "Twentieth-Century Fiction and the Black Mask of Humanity," *Shadow and Act* (New York: Vintage Books, 1972), 24–44. Further references appear in text as *S&A*.

3. See Sylvander, 77–79; Overmeyer, 13–15; and Waniek, 7–13.

4. Ellison, "Out of the Hospital and under the bar" 247.

5. Also see Melvin Dixon, "O, Mary Rambo, Don't You Weep."

WORKS CITED

Dixon, Melvin. "O, Mary Rambo, Don't You Weep." *Carleton Miscellany* 18: 3 (1980): 98–104.

Ellison, Ralph. *Invisible Man*. New York: New American Library, 1952.

______. "Out of the Hospital and Under the Bar." *Soon One Morning: New Writing by American Negroes 1940–1962,* ed. Herbert Hill. New York: Alfred A. Knopf, 1963.

______. *Shadow and Act*. New York: Vintage Books, 1972.

Overmeyer, Janet. "*The Invisible Man* and White Women." *Notes on Contemporary Literature* 6: 3 (1976).

Sylvander, Carolyn W. "Ralph Ellison's *Invisible Man* and Female Stereotypes." *Black American Literature Forum* 9: 3 (1975).

Waniek, Marilyn Nelson. "The Space Where Sex Should Be: Toward a Definition of the Black American Literary Tradition." *Studies in Black Literature* 6: 3 (1975).

Improvising America: Ralph Ellison and the Paradox of Form

C.W.E. BIGSBY

Writing in 1937, Richard Wright insisted that "black writers are being called upon to do no less than create values by which the race is to struggle, live and die."[1] In 1941 Ellison echoed this sentiment. His responsibility, he felt, was "to create the consciousness of his oppressed nation."[2] It was a stance he was later to be accused of abandoning by those who, in the 1960s and 1970s, proposed their own prescriptions for cultural and political responsibility and who found his determined pluralism unacceptable. For although he undeniably concentrated on the black experience in America, he tended to see this experience in relation to the problem of identity, the anxieties associated with the struggle for cultural autonomy, and the need to define the contours of experience. His central concern was with the relationship between raw experience and the shaping power of the imagination. And, for him, the "imagination itself is *integrative*," in that it is essentially involved in the process of "making symbolic wholes out of parts."[3] Such a stance plainly has implications on a moral and social level no less than on an artistic one.

He has, indeed, always been fascinated, politically, ethically, and aesthetically, with the struggle to discover form in diversity. To his mind this was equally the problem of the Negro in America, of the individual in a democracy, and of the artist confronted with the sheer contingency and flux of events. The imaginative linking of these experiences, indeed the metaphoric yoking of the processes of invention in life and art, is a characteristic of Ellison's artistic strategy and of his moral assumptions. But it is a process which, from the beginning, he acknowledged to be fraught with ambiguity, for he was not unaware that form could imply entrapment as well as release. Thus, he argued that "for the novelist, of any cultural or racial identity, his form is his greatest freedom and his insights are where he finds them," while acknowledging that that form potentially defines the limits of his freedom.[4] To use story or myth to control experience is also, potentially, to imprison oneself in the prison house of myth. Archetype too easily becomes stereotype. To deploy language as a means of inducing coherencies is to subordinate oneself to the constraints of that language, which is, at the very least, historically stained. Thus for the writer, as for the American pioneer, "the English language and traditional cultural forms served both as guides and as restraints, anchoring Americans in the wisdom and processes of the past, while making it difficult for them to perceive with any clarity the nuances of their new identity" (*MR* 431). It is a paradox that lies at the heart of all of his work. For Ellison, the act of writing is an act of shaping inchoate experience into moral meaning no less than aesthetic form. But it is an act that implies its own coercions. It implicates the imagination in the process of control.

This tension between chaos and form, this recognition of a profound ambivalence, is a fundamental trope of Ellison's work. He seems captivated by paradox, fascinated by apparent contradictions, drawn to the polarities of American experience, simultaneously attracted and repelled by the nervous energy of the unformed and the compelling grace of coalescence. Even his prose style seems often to turn around sets of dualities that are fused together by the writer, contained by the imagination, and exemplified in the linguistic structure, as he believes they can be so fused in the world beyond the page.

Thus, while he readily identified the metonymic reductivism implied in white attempts to mythologize Negro life, insisting that "the Negro stereotype is really an image of the unorganized, irrational forces of American life, forces through which, by projecting them in forms of images of an easily dominated minority, the white individual seeks to be at home in the vast unknown world of America," he nonetheless asserted that without myths, "chaos descends, faith vanishes and superstitions prowl in the mind" (*S&A*, 41). The same process contains a generative and a destructive potential.

So, too, with language. We are, Ellison insists, "language using, language misusing animals–beings who are by nature vulnerable to both the negative *and* the positive promptings of language as symbolic action."[5] He addresses this ambivalence directly in an essay called, "Twentieth-Century Fiction and the Black Mask of Humanity," where he suggests, "Perhaps the most insidious and least understood form of segregation is that of the word. And by this I mean the word in all its complex formulations, from the proverb to the novel and stage play, the word with all its subtle power to suggest and foreshadow overt action while magically disguising the moral consequences of that action and providing it with symbolic and psychological justification. For if the word has the potency to revive and make us free, it also has the power to blind, imprison and destroy." Indeed, to him "the essence of the word is its ambivalence" (*S&A*, 24–25), more especially in a society in which the nature of the real is problematic for reasons of racial ideology. This suspicion marks all of his work, from the nonfunctional articulateness of his protagonist in the early short story "Flying Home," through the deceptive speeches and documents of *Invisible Man*, to the uncontrolled rhetoric of the narrator of his later short story, "A Song of Innocence," who observes,

"They say that folks misuse words but I see it the other way around, words misuse people. Usually when you think you're saying what you mean you're really saying what the words want you to say. . . . Words are tricky. . . . No matter what you try to do, words can never mean meaning."[6]

Melville had made much the same point and addressed the same ambivalence with respect to the urge to subordinate chaos to form. He, too, was aware that language itself constitutes the primary mechanism of the shaping imagination and it was not for nothing that Ellison chose to quote from *Benito Cereno* as an epigraph to his own novel. For Captain Delano, in that story, uses language as an agent of power and control, albeit a language rendered ironic by his moral and intellectual blindness; while Benito Cereno, imprisoned by a cunning and dominant black crew, who for the most part remain potently silent, deploys a language which is willfully opaque, hinting at truths that language cannot be entrusted to reveal. And yet language is the only medium through which the novelist can attempt to communicate his own truths. It was a familiar conundrum of nineteenth-century American writing and one to which Ellison was compulsively drawn.

The strict discipline and carefully sustained order of Delano's ship is an expression of his fear of an anarchy that he dare not imagine and cannot confront. And the image of that anarchy, for Delano and Cereno alike, is the Negro, whose shadow they see as falling across American history. But Melville suggests that just as their own ordered world contains its virus of moral anarchy, so what Delano takes for anarchy is perhaps a coherence he is afraid to acknowledge; the hieroglyphs of action that he chooses to translate as pure chaos can be decoded in a wholly different way. Indeed, Melville's story turns precisely on this ambiguity. So does much of Ellison's work.

Chaos and order constitute the twin poles of experience, promising, simultaneously, vital energy and destructive flux, necessary form but threatening stasis. Indeed, he is quite capable, in a single paragraph, of presenting both order and chaos as promise and threat. Speaking of the process whereby national identity coalesces from its constituent elements, he asserted, in 1953, "Our task then is always to challenge the apparent forms of reality—that is, the fixed manners and values of the few, and to struggle with it until it reveals its insights, its truth . . . . We are fortunate as American writers in that with our variety of racial and national traditions, idioms and manners we are yet one. On its profoundest level, American experience is of a whole. Its truth lies in its diversity and swiftness of change" (*S&A*, 106). The task for the writer would seem to be to inhabit these ambiguities and thereby to cast light not merely on processes endemic to art but also on the struggle that the individual and the race wage with contingency. Irresistibly drawn to the primal energy of flux, the writer, nonetheless, is inevitably committed to the creation of coherent form, thereby offering himself as a paradigm of the processes of self-invention and the distillation of cultural identity.

It is a theme that echoes throughout Ellison's work. Thus, he quotes approvingly André Malraux's observation that "the organized significance of art . . . is stronger than all the multiplicity of the world . . . that significance alone enables many to conquer chaos and to master destiny" (*S&A*, 83), while in an introduction to Stephen Crane's *Red Badge of Courage* he chose to stress "the shaping grace of Crane's imagination," whereby "the actual event is reduced to significant form . . . each wave and gust of wind, each intonation of voice and gesture of limb combining to a single effect of meaning . . . the raging sea of life" (*S&A*, 86) thereby being contained by an act of imaginative economy. He even insists that "in the very act of trying to create something there is implicit a protest against the way things are—a protest against man's vulnerability before the larger forces of society and the universe . . . a protest against that which is, against the raw and unformed way that we come into the world . . . to provide some sense of transcendence over the given."[7] And yet he equally acknowledges that it is precisely the fear of anarchy that leads to the creation of coercive models that express nothing more than a fear of the uncontrolled and the unknown. Thus, when Leslie Fiedler identifies a homoeroticism in the relationship between Twain's Huck Finn and the Negro slave Jim, he is, according to Ellison, in reality simply shouting out "his most terrifying name for chaos. Other things being equal he might have called it 'rape,' 'incest,' 'patricide' or 'miscegenation' " (*S&A*, 51). Order has no preemptive rights. It requires a moral as well as an aesthetic elegance.

The history of Ellison's creative life, from his early days as a putative musician throughout his career as a novelist and essayist, has in effect been concerned with exploring this paradox and identifying a way, at least on a metaphoric level, in which it could be resolved. To some degree he found it in music. He began his career as a would-be composer, and music has always provided a central source of imagery for him. Thus, in describing the reaction of the reader of fiction, he suggests that "his sensibilities are made responsive to artistic structuring of symbolic form" through "the rhetorical 'stops' " of his own "pieties—filial, sacred, racial"(*AS*, 30). The writer, meanwhile, is described as playing upon these sensibilities "as a pianist upon a piano" (*AS*, 31). But, what is more significant, he found in jazz and the blues a powerful image of the struggle to imprint meaning on experience, to reconcile the apparently contradictory demands of order and freedom. Like Richard Wright, he saw the blues as an attempt to "possess the meaning of his life" (*S&A*, 7), while jazz offered a model for the act of improvisation that lies at the heart of personal experience. Indeed the key word becomes "improvisation," which is made to stand for the act of self-invention that is the essence of a private and a public drive for meaning and identity. It is an integrative metaphor that links his sense of racial distinctiveness to what is essentially a pluralist position: "The delicate balance struck between strong individual personality and the group during those early jam sessions was a marvel of social organization. I had learned too that the end of all this discipline and technical mastery was the desire to express an affirmative way of life through its musical tradition and that this tradition insisted that each artist achieve his creativity within its frame . . . and when they expressed their attitude toward the world it was with a fluid style that reduced the chaos of living to form'' (*S&A*, 189–90).

Thus, it is characteristic that in his account of growing up in the Southwest he chose to stress what he calls ''the chaos of Oklahoma,'' as he elsewhere spoke of ''the chaos of American society'' (*C*, 57), but set this against his own growing fascination with the ordered world of music and literature. It is characteristic, too, that through an extension of this logic he should identify that same tension first with the nature of the American frontier experience (still recent history for the Oklahoma of his birth), then with the jazz which emerged from that same region, and then with the nature of artistic creativity itself. The move is one from the real to the metaphoric, from the pure tone to its significant resonances. Thus, he insists, ''ours was a chaotic community, still characterized by frontier attitudes and by that strange mixture of the naive and sophisticated, the benign and the malignant, which makes the past and present so confusing'' (*C*, 57), only to go on to suggest that it is possible to ''hear the effects of this in the Southwestern jazz of the 30s, that joint creation of artistically free and exuberantly creative adventurers, of artists who had stumbled upon the freedom lying within the restrictions of their musical tradition as within the limitations of their social background, and who in their own unconscious way set an example for any Americans, Negro or white, who would find themselves in the arts.''[8]

And this was a key to Ellison's attempts to square the circle, to resolve the paradox. The problem for the jazz musician, as for any artist, was how to celebrate versatility and possibility in a form that seemingly denied both. The key is seen by Ellison as lying precisely in improvisation, the exercise of a personal freedom within the framework of the group, an act of invention that builds on but is not limited by inherited forms. This becomes both his metaphor for the process of artistic invention and the means whereby individual and group identity coalesce. In terms of writing this tended to be translated into an instinctive existentialism, at the level of theme, a picaresque narrative drive, and a prose style that could prove as fluid and flexible, and yet as controlled and subject to the harmonies of character and story, as the jazz musician is free and yet responsive to the necessities of rhythm and mood. In terms of social process it became a description of the means whereby diverse elements are harmonized. Thus, speaking of the origins of American national identity, Ellison remarked, ''Out of the democratic principles set down on paper in the Constitution and the Bill of Rights they were improvising themselves into a nation, scraping together a conscious culture out of the various dialects, idioms, lingos, and mythologies of America's diverse peoples and regions.'' Similarly, in describing the relationship between black and white cultural forms, he observed that "the slaves . . . having no past in the art of Europe . . . could use its elements and their inherited sense of style to improvise forms through which they could express their own unique sense of African experience . . . and white artists often found the slaves' improvisations a clue to their own improvisations" (*MR*, 431).

As a boy he had been taught the rudiments of orchestration, the blending, the integration, of different instruments to form an harmonic whole. It was offered to him as a lesson in the deconstruction of a score which was to enable him to "attack those things I desired so that I could pierce the mystery and possess them"; but in retrospect it becomes a lesson in civics. True jazz, he insists, "is an act of individual assertion within and against the group. Each true jazz moment . . . springs from a contest in which each artist challenges all the rest; each solo flight, or improvisation, represents . . . a definition of his identity: as individual, as member of the collectivity and as a link in the chain of tradition. Thus, because jazz finds its very life in an endless improvisation upon traditional materials, the jazzman must lose his identity even as he finds it" (*S&A*, 234). And, beyond this, jazz becomes an image of America itself, "fecund in its inventiveness, swift and traumatic in its resources" (*S&A*, 233).

The parallel between jazz and his own social circumstances, growing up in postfrontier Oklahoma, seems clear to Ellison in retrospect. "It is an important circumstance for me as a writer to remember," he wrote in 1964, "because while these musicians and their fellows were busy creating out of tradition, imagination, and the sounds and emotions around them, a freer, more complex, and driving form of jazz, my friends and I were exploring an idea of human versatility and possibility which went against the barbs and over the palings [pickets] of almost every fence which those who controlled social and political power had erected to restrict our roles in the life of the country" (*C*, 57).

And as a boy, he and his friends had constructed their heroes from fragments of myth and legend, from the movies ("improvising their rather tawdry and opportunistic version of a national mythology" [*AS*, 42]), from music and religion, from anything "which violated all ideas of social hierarchy and order" and "which evolved from our wildly improvisatory projections" (*C*, 58). In a sense this can stand as a model of Ellison's fictive and moral strategy, as of his conception of cultural identity and American pluralism. A complex eclecticism is presented as a moral necessity as much as a natural product of American circumstances. And "complexity" is a favorite word—sometimes "a stubborn complexity." For his is a sensibility that reaches out to absorb the variegated realities of American life, rejecting those who see the process of self-invention as necessitating a denial of that complexity.

The problem is to discover a means of rendering that complexity without reducing it through the sheer process of transmuting experience into art. Pure energy has no shape. The challenge confronting the artist, no less than that confronting the uncodified, free-floating sensibility of the American individual, is to sustain some kind of creative tension between a liberated and liberating imagination and the aesthetic and moral demands of an art and a life which require the subordination of random energy and an anarchic imagination to the constraints of order. For just as the artist operates ''within the historical frame of his given art'' (*AS*, 29), so the individual is located within the triangulation of time, space, and cultural inheritance. Thus the writer's responsibility in America is to define the diversity of American experience in such a way as to bring to bear the ''unifying force of its vision and its power to give meaningful focus to apparently unrelated emotions and experience'' (*AS*, 31).

The problem is that the democratic ideal of ''unity-in-diversity and oneness-in-manyness'' (*AS*, 36) creates a vertigo which he sees as sending too many plunging into the reassurance of simplified cultural models, preferring fragment to complexly formulated whole. There is a clearly positive and negative model of chaos in his mind. On the one hand, there is a fructifying interaction of differing cultural traditions, ''always in cacophonic motion. Constantly changing its mode . . . a vortex of discordant ways of living and tastes, values and traditions, a whirlpool of odds and ends'' (*AS*, 36) which inspires a profound unease but which is the source of a creative flux. On the other hand, there is a negative chaos, a fearful splintering into component elements. And this is how he saw the black aestheticians of the 1960s. ''In many ways,'' he insisted, ''the call for a new social order based upon the glorification of ancestral blood and ethnic background acts as a call to cultural and aesthetic chaos.'' Yet, ''while this latest farcical phase in the drama of American social hierarchy unfolds, the irrepressible movement of American culture toward the integration of its diverse elements continues, confounding the circumlocutions of its staunchest opponents'' (*AS*, 37).

For Ellison, strength lies precisely in diversity, in the sustained tension between chaos and form, the Apollonian and the Dionysian, and this is no less true of a racial identity which he refuses to grant the simple self-evident contours demanded by some of his contemporaries. To his mind, that identity can only express itself multivocally. And so in his essay ''The Little Man at Chehaw Station,'' which is a crucial statement of his artistic and social principles, he recalls seeing a black American who seemed to combine a whole kaleidoscope of cultural influences: and whatever sheerly ethnic identity was communicated by his costume depended upon the observer's ability to see order in an apparent cultural chaos. The essence of the man, his complex identity, existed less in the apparent clashing of styles than in the eclectic imagination, the unabashed assertion of will, which lay behind it—''not in the somewhat comic clashing of styles, but in the mixture, the improvised form, the willful juxtaposition of modes'' (*AS*, 38–39). But, as ever, Ellison is not content to leave it there for, he insists, ''his clashing of styles . . . sounded an integrative, vernacular note—an American compulsion to improvise upon the given,'' and the freedom he exercised was ''an American freedom'' (*AS*, 39).

It is not hard to see what infuriated the cultural nationalists of the 1960s. Ellison seems to be appropriating supposedly unique and definitional aspects of black life to an American cultural norm. Since America was diverse, loose-limbed, disparate, self-displaying, free-wheeling and concerned with the question of identity, with delineating its own cultural boundaries, with negotiating a relationship with its own past which would give it space for its own critical act of self-invention, the black American was apparently simply an expression of this process, one component of the American diorama. But such an assumption ignored Ellison's central conviction—the basis, indeed, of his whole aesthetic and social theory—namely, that the American identity he described was as it was precisely because of the presence of the Negro. While rigidly subordinating and segregating the black American, the whites had been shaped by what they had tried so hard to exclude. Their imagination had been penetrated, their sensibility infiltrated, by those whose experience of adjusting to a strange land and whose necessary cultural improvisations were more intensely, more deeply scarring, more profoundly disturbing than their own. As the victims of violence, as the evidence of a failure of American idealism, as an extreme case of adjustment to a hostile environment, they represented not merely a constant reminder of the poles of American moral experience but a model of possibility, a paradigm of those acts of desperate self-creation that were at the heart of the American myth. The shadow of the Negro does indeed fall across American history but not merely as promise and threat. His existence defines the nature of the American experience.

Ellison was less inclined than many to abandon the notion of the ''melting pot,'' though he saw the image less as a promise of homogeneity than as a metaphor of ''the mystery of American identity (our unity-within-diversity),'' and as a symbol of those who ''improvised their culture as they did their politics and institutions'' (*AS*, 40). The potency of the image lay in its acknowledgment of the fact that, in America, cultural traditions were brought into violent contact, that past and future were made to interact, that ideals, and the evidence of the failure of those ideals, were placed in intimate and ironic counterpoint. And, as a consequence, a series of adjustments were enforced, a process of action and reaction which, to his mind, was the very essence of Americanness. It was precisely on the level of culture that such interactions operated. Cultural appropriation and misappropriation were, to Ellison, the essence of an American development that would scarcely stand still long enough for confident definition. Indeed, since America was to him more a process than an isolable set of characteristics, such definitions carry the threat of a menacing stasis. The essence of improvisation lies in the energy released by the pure act of invention in process. In *Invisible Man* the protagonist is at his most vulnerable when he allows himself to be contained and defined by simple racial or political models. He radiates the energy of pure possibility (like the light bulbs with which he illuminates his darkness) when he abandons these restrictive definitions for the sheer flux of being—a state controlled only by the imagination, and those moral commitments that lead him out of his isolation and into the dangerous interactions of the outside world and the complex symbols of the novel, with which he seeks to address that "variegated audience" for whom the little man at Chehaw Station was Ellison's image. As he himself insists, "it is the very *spirit* of art to be defiant of categories and obstacles. . . . They [the images of art or the sound of music] are, as transcendent forms of symbolic expression, agencies of human freedom" (*AS*, 44). For Ellison, "the work of art" itself "is . . . an act of faith in our ability to communicate symbolically" (*AS*, 53).

Invisible Man opens and concludes with references to jazz. At the beginning the protagonist sits in his cellar and "feels" rather than listens to the music of Louis Armstrong who has "made poetry out of being invisible."[9] High on drugs, he responds to the off-beats, seeing meaning in the unheard sounds, the resistances to simple rhythmic structure. Music becomes a clue to his past and future. The music pulls him back to his origins, conjuring up an image of his slave past; but it also offers him a clue to his future, outside the determined structures of social life. The music, like the novel the protagonist writes, emerges from "an urge to make music of invisibility," to set it down. It is a paradoxical enterprise. But, then, as we are told at the end of the novel, the music, too, is characterized by "diversity." It, too, contains an essential conflict. And that conflict mirrors the conflict of the protagonist who reminds himself that "the mind that has conceived a plan of living must never lose sight of the chaos against which that pattern was conceived." And this, he assures us, "goes for societies as for individuals" (*IM*, 438). It is the virtue of jazz that its improvisations remind us of precisely this. Improvisation has its risks. In the form of Rinehart, a protean figure (whose first name is actually Proteus) who refuses all content and all commitment, it becomes pure chaos; but for the protagonist, willing, finally, to chance his own dangerous act of self-creation in the public world outside his cellar, it becomes a commitment to sustaining the tension between the twin compulsions of freedom and order.

Jazz operates in Ellison's work as image and fact. The thematic uses he makes of it have been usefully traced by Robert G. O'Meally in *The Craft of Ralph Ellison*. Jazz exists as a constant source of reference, an ironic counterpoint to the protagonist's earnest struggles, a celebration of his growing understanding. Ellison himself has spoken of his desire to capture the "music and idiom" of American Negro speech, but in fact his concern with musical structures goes much further than this. In "A Song of Innocence" the prose owes less to idiomatic speech than to jazz rhythms, the words being of less significance than the free flow of sound. Indeed the inadequacy of language, which is in part the subject of that story, implies the need to turn to other models, other symbols as a means of explaining the conflicting demands of pattern and chaos, form and experience, tradition and innovation. And throughout his career, Ellison turned to the improvisational thrust of jazz for that symbol, finding there a clue to the commitments required of the artist, the race, and the individual concerned with developing their own identities in the face of inherited forms: ''I had learned from the jazz musicians I had known as a boy in Oklahoma City something of the discipline and devotion to his art required of the artist . . . the give and take, the subtle rhythmical sharpening and blending of idea, tone and imagination demanded of group improvisations'' (*S&A*, 189–90). And ''after the jazzman has learned the fundamentals of his instrument and the traditional techniques of jazz—the intonations, the mute work, manipulation of timbre, the body of traditional styles—he must 'find himself,' must be reborn, must find, as it were, his soul. All this through achieving that subtle identification between his instrument and his deepest drives which will allow him to express his own unique ideas and his own unique voice. He must achieve, in short, his self-determined identity'' (*S&A*, 209). Like Charlie Parker, he is involved in a struggle ''against personal chaos'' (*S&A*, 227). To Ellison, much the same could be said of the writer in America, as of the individual struggling to make sense of his racial and cultural inheritance while defining a self strong enough to stand against the centripetal pull of the chaos that could manifest itself equally as pure contingency or deceptive consonance.

In an essay titled ''Society, Morality, and the Novel,'' Ellison observed that ''the writer has an obsessive need to play with the fires of chaos and to rearrange reality to the patterns of his imagination,''[10] while the novel achieves its ''universality'' precisely through ''accumulating images of reality and arranging them in patterns of universal significance'' (*LN*, 61). Indeed, it seemed to him possible that the novel, as a form, had evolved in order ''to deal with man's growing awareness that behind the facade of social organization, manners, customs, myths, rituals, religions of the post-Christian era, lies chaos'' (*LN*, 64). But since we can live neither ''in the contemplation of chaos'' nor ''without awareness of chaos'' (*LN*, 64–65), the novel simultaneously acknowledges and seeks to transcend the fact that ''the treasure of possibility is always to be found in the cave of chaos, guarded by the demons of destruction'' (*LN* 65). The writer's responsibility, in Ellison's eyes, is to improvise a response that denies nothing of the force and power of disorder but will ''strengthen man's will to say No to chaos and affirm him in his task of humanizing himself and the world'' (*LN*, 66), without submitting to stasis. Change and diversity are, to him, the essence of the American experience. The challenge is to bring to ''the turbulence of change'' an ''imaginative integration and moral continuity'' (*LN*, 69)—to improvise America, as the individual creates the uncreated features of his face, and as the black American had struggled to ''create the consciousness of his oppressed nation.''

NOTES

1. See Richard Wright, "Blueprint for Negro Literature," *Amistad 2* (New York, 1971): 11.

2. See Ralph Ellison, "Recent Negro Fiction," *New Masses* 40 (August 5, 1941): 26.

3. "Study and Experience: An Interview with Ralph Ellison," *Massachusetts Review* 18:3 (Autumn 1977): 424. Subsequently cited in text as *MR*.

4. Ralph Ellison, *Shadow and Act* (New York: Random House, 1964), 59. Subsequently cited in text as *S&A*.

5. Ralph Ellison, "The Little Man at Chehaw Station," *American Scholar* 47 (Winter 1977–78): 35. Subsequently cited in text as *AS*.

6. Ralph Ellison, "A Song of Innocence," *Iowa Review* 1 (Spring 1970): 32.

7. Ralph Ellison, "On Initiation Rites and Power: Ralph Ellison Speaks at West Point," *Commentary* 15 (Spring 1974): 186.

8. Ralph Ellison, "On Becoming a Writer," *Commentary* 38 (October 1964): 57. Subsequently cited in text as *C*.

9. Ralph Ellison, *Invisible Man* (New York: Random House, 1952), 8. Subsequently cited in text as *IM*.

10. Ralph Ellison, "Society, Morality, and the Novel," in *The Living Novel: A Symposium*, ed. Granville Hicks (New York: Macmillan, 1957). Subsequently cited in text as *LN*.

PART FOUR

Choosing Ancestors

THE "POSSIBILITIES" OF LITERARY TRADITION

Remembering Richard Wright

RALPH ELLISON

Earlier today while considering my relationship with Richard Wright, I recalled Heraclitus' axiom "Geography is fate," and I was struck by the ironic fact that in this country, where Frederick Jackson Turner's theory of the frontier has been so influential in shaping our conception of American history, very little attention has been given to the role played by geography in shaping the fate of Afro-Americans.

For example, Wright was a Mississippian who migrated to Chicago and then to New York. I, by contrast, am an Oklahoman and by geographical origin a Southwesterner. Wright grew up in a part of what was the old Confederacy, while I grew up in a state which possesses no indigenous tradition of chattel slavery. Thus, while we both grew up in segregated societies, mine lacked many of the intensities of custom, tradition, and manners which "colored" the institutions of the Old South, and which were important in shaping Wright's point of view. Both of us were descendants of slaves, but since my civic, geographical, and political circumstances were different from those of Mississippi, Wright and I were united by our connection with a past condition of servitude, and divided by geography and a difference of experience based thereupon. And yet it was that very difference of experience and background which had much to do with Wright's important impact upon my sensibilities.

And then there was New York. I met Wright there in 1937, and it was no accidental encounter. It came about because through my reading and working in the library at Tuskegee Institute, I'd become fascinated by the exciting developments that were taking place in modern literature. Somehow in my

---

This lecture was presented at the Institute for Afro-American Culture, University of Iowa, July 18, 1971.

uninstructed reading of Eliot and Pound, I had recognized a relationship between modern poetry and jazz music, and this led me to wonder why I was not encountering similar devices in the work of Afro-American writers. Indeed, such reading and wondering prepared me not simply to *meet* Wright, but to seek him out. It led, in other words, to a personal quest. I insist upon the "seeking out" because, you see, I too have an ego and it is important to me that our meeting came about through my own initiative. For not only is it historically true, but it has something to do with my being privileged to be here on what I consider to be a very important moment in the history of our literature. Perhaps Richard Wright would have dismissed such a moment as impossible, even as late as 1957, but still, here we are, gathered in the hot summertime to pay him honor. *I* would not have been surprised, since it was my reading of one of Wright's poems in the *New Masses* which gave me a sense of his importance. I had arrived in New York on July 5, 1936—a date of no broad symbolic importance, but one highly significant to me because it made a meeting with Wright a possibility. For although the *New Masses* poem was not a masterpiece, I found in it traces of the modern poetic sensibility and technique that I had been seeking.

The morning after my arrival in New York, I encountered standing in the entrance of the Harlem YMCA two fateful figures. They were Langston Hughes, the poet, and Dr. Alain Locke, the then head of the philosophy department at Howard University. I had never seen Langston Hughes before, but regardless of what is said about the quality of education provided by the old Negro schools (ours was named for Frederick Douglass), we were taught what is now termed "Black History" and were kept abreast of current events pertaining to our people. Thus, as early as the sixth grade we were made aware of the poetry of Langston Hughes along with the work of the other Negro Renaissance writers. So I recognized Hughes from his photographs. But I recognized Dr. Locke because he had been at Tuskegee only a few weeks prior to my arrival in New York, having gone there to visit with Hazel Harrison, a teacher in the music department, and a very fine pianist who had been one of Busoni's prize pupils . . . Here I'm trying to provide a bit of historical background to give you an idea of the diverse cultural forces at play in the lives of Afro-Americans from the early 1920s to 1936.

Miss Harrison was a friend of Prokofiev, and possessed some of his scores at a time when few would have imagined that a Russian master's music was being made a part of the musical consciousness of an Afro-American college. And certainly not in such a college as Tuskegee—even though Tuskegee's musical tradition was actually quite rich and quite varied. But then, this is but another example of the contradictions of American culture which escape our attention because they are obscured by racism. And yet, thanks to Miss Harrison, I could, like any eager, young, celebrity-fascinated college junior, walk straight up to Dr. Locke and say, "Dr. Locke, do you remember me?"

And to my delight he said, "Why, of course I do." He then introduced me to Langston Hughes and told Hughes of my interest in poetry.

Langston Hughes had with him copies of Malraux's *Man's Fate* and *The Days of Wrath*, and after a few moments' conversation he said, "Since you like to read so much, maybe you'd like to read these novels and then return them to their owner"—and so I did. And the returns were tremendous. This incident and this meeting later made it possible for me to ask Langston Hughes if he knew Richard Wright, "Yes," he said, "and it so happens that he's coming here from Chicago next week." And with his great generosity, and without telling me, Hughes wrote Richard Wright that there was a young Negro something-or-the-other in New York who wanted to meet him. The next thing I knew I received a postcard—which I still have—that said, "Dear Ralph Ellison, Langston Hughes tells me that you're interested in meeting me. I will be in New York . . ." on such and such a date in July . . . signed Richard Wright. Thus I was to meet Wright on the day after his arrival in New York in July of 1937.

At the time I still thought that I would return to Tuskegee to take my degree in music, but I was not to make it. I had come to New York to earn expenses for my senior year, but it was during the Depression and I was unable to make the money. Then, in talking with Wright, my plans and goals were altered; were, in fact, fatefully modified by Wright's.

Wright had come to New York for two purposes, one of which was talked about openly, and the other quietly underplayed. The first was to become the editor of the magazine *New Challenge*. The other was to work in the Harlem Bureau of the Communist newspaper *The Daily Worker*. With Wright's presence in the *Worker*'s 135th Street office, my introduction to the craft of writing leaped ahead. For it was there that I read many of his unpublished stories and discussed his ideas concerning literature and culture.

Wright was quiet concerning his assignment to the *Worker*'s staff because he had left Chicago under a cloud. In 1936 he had been thrown out of the May Day parade—sacred to all Communists—for refusing to carry out some assignment. And the fact that he had been publicly humiliated by both white *and* black Communists had left him quite bitter. However, someone higher up in the hierarchy recognized his value and was able to persuade him to go to New York—which proved to be to my good fortune.

Being unemployed much of the time, I began to hang around the Harlem Bureau, not so much for the ideology being purveyed there—although I found it fascinating—but because of Wright and the manuscripts of a sheaf of novelettes (later published as *Uncle Tom's Children*) that lay in an open desk drawer. Of all those who visited the office, I was the only one who bothered to read those now-famous stories. Perhaps this was because his comrades looked upon Wright as an intruder. He was distrusted not only as an "intellectual" and thus a potential traitor, but as a possible "dark horse" in the race for Harlem party leadership; a "ringer" who had been sent from Chicago to cause them trouble. Wright had little sense of humor concerning their undisguised hostility, and this led, as would be expected, to touchy relationships. Despite his obvious organizational and journalistic abilities—the *Worker* featured his reportage—the members of the Communist rank and file sneered at his intellectuality, ridiculed his writings, and dismissed his concern with literature and culture as an affectation. In brief, they thought him too ambitious, and therefore a threat to their own ambitions as possible party functionaries.

Being a true outsider, I was amused by this comedy of misperception, for Wright seemed anything but a threat to their petty ambitions. Besides, I was absolutely intrigued by his talent and felt privileged to read his writings. I'd never met anyone who, lacking the fanfare of public recognition, could move me with the unpublished products of his fictional imagination. Of course, I read Wright's work uncritically, but there was no doubt in my mind that he was an exceptional writer. Even better, he was delighted to discuss the techniques, the ideological and philosophical implications of his writings, and this with one who'd never attempted to write anything beyond classroom assignments and a few poems. Evidently Wright wished to exchange ideas with someone of his own general background, and I was fortunate in being able to contribute more than curiosity to our discussion. For I had studied with creative musicians, both classical and jazz, and had been taught to approach the arts analytically. I had also read fairly widely on my own. But to encounter the possessor of such literary talent and have him make me his friend and confidant—that was indeed an exciting and inspiring experience.

Nor did it end with mere talk. As editor of *New Challenge*, Wright asked me to contribute a book review in its first issue. To one who had never attempted to write anything, this was the wildest of ideas. But still, pressed by his editorial needs, and sustained by his belief that an untapped supply of free-floating literary talent existed in the Negro community, Wright kept after me, and I wrote a review and he published it. But then he went even further by suggesting that I write a short story!

I said "But I've never even tried to write a story . . ."

He said, "Look, you talk about these things, you've read a lot, and you've been around. Just put something down and let me see it . . ."

So I wrote a story, titled "Hymie's Bull," that was based upon experiences that I'd had a few years before when riding freight trains from Oklahoma to Alabama. I was dubious over the outcome, but to my delight Wright accepted the story and sent it to the printer.

Ah, but fate, as they say, was in the wings and *New Challenge* was not to appear again. I hasten to add that this was not a disaster created by my first attempt at fiction. Rather, it had to do with an aspect of Afro-American cultural history and involved certain lingering echoes of the Negro Renaissance, a movement which "ran out of gas" with the Crash of 1929. As the period ended, a number of figures important to the movement had died, and with the Great Depression upon them, those members of the white community who had sponsored the Renaissance were unable to continue. The money was no longer available, and so the movement languished. However, with the deepening of the Depression there came a significant development in the form of the federal projects for the arts that were organized by the Works Progress Administration. These projects were most important to the continuing development of Afro-American artists. For although a reaction to a national disaster, they provided—as have most national disasters—the possibility for a broader Afro-American Freedom. This is a shocking thing to say, but it is also a very *blues*, or tragicomic, thing to say, and a fairly accurate description of the manner in which, for Negroes, a gift of freedom arrived wrapped in the guise of disaster. It is ironic, but no less true, that the most tragic incident of our history, the Civil War, was a disaster which ended American slavery.

Wright himself worked on both the Chicago and the New York Federal Writers Projects, and I could not have become a writer at the time I began had I not been able to earn my board and keep by doing research for the New York project. Through Wright's encouragement, I had become serious about writing, but before going on the project I sometimes slept in the public park below City College because I had neither job nor money. But my personal affairs aside, the WPA provided an important surge to Afro-American cultural activity. The result was not a "renaissance," but there was a resuscitation and transformation of that very vital artistic impulse that is abiding among Afro-Americans. Remember that our African forefathers originated in cultures wherein even the simple routines of daily living were highly ritualized and that even their cooking utensils were fashioned with forms of symbolism which resonated with overtones of godhead. And though modified, if not suppressed, by the experience of American slavery, the tradition of artistic expressiveness has infused the larger American culture. Afro-American cultural style is an abiding aspect of our culture, and the economic disaster which brought the WPA gave it an accelerated release and allowed many Negroes to achieve their identities as artists.

* * *

But now, back to Wright and *New Challenge*. *New Challenge* was organized by people active in the Negro Renaissance and whose outlook was in many ways at odds with Wright's. Thus, according to Wright, *New Challenge* ended publication because the two young women who were in charge before he came on the scene were afraid that his connection with the Communist party would lead to its being taken over. So rather than lose control, they got rid of Wright.

History has no vacuum. There are transformations, there are lesions, there are metamorphoses, and there are mysteries that cloak the clashing of individual wills and private interests. *New Challenge* faded, but Wright went on to publish *Uncle Tom's Children*, and shortly afterward, *Native Son*. When Richard Wright came to New York, his talents as a writer were, to a large extent, already formed. Indeed, even before 1927, when he migrated to Chicago, he had published fiction in Robert S. Abbott's magazine *The Bronzeman*. So it isn't true, as has been said, that the Communist party "discovered" his talent. Wright was literary in an informed way even in Jackson, Mississippi. But what happened to him in Chicago resulted from his coming into contact with an organized political group which possessed a concept of social hierarchy that was a conscious negation of our racially biased social system. Thus, through his political affiliation Wright was able to identify his artistic ambitions with what was, for him, a totally new conception of social justice. In the discussions that took place in the Chicago John Reed Club he sharpened his conception of literary form and the relationship between fictional techniques and the world view of Marxism. And he came to see art and society in terms of an ideology that was concerned with power, and willing to forgo racial differences in order to take over the world. I realize that this is all rather abstract, but I am trying to suggest the tenor of our discussions. Fortunately, Wright's interest in literary theory was not limited to areas prescribed by the party line.

For instance, I was very curious as to how one could put Marx and Freud together. No real problem now, I suppose. But coming from where I did, it was puzzling. And I was to discover that it was also a problem for Communist intellectuals and for many of their opponents. Either Marx was raised up and Freud put down, or Freud raised up and Marx put down. So for me, all of this was pretty strange. But at least with Richard Wright, I could discuss such matters. This was very important for a young writer (and of course I became a young writer, for I soon realized that I wasn't going back to Tuskegee and to music). And since Wright had assured me that I possessed a certain talent, I decided that writing was the direction I would take. I don't know whether he was satisfied with my talent or not; I suspect not. This was interesting, for while I possessed more formal education, it was he who encouraged me and gave me a sense of direction. I'd like you to appreciate the irony of this development: Here was a young Afro-American who had gone only to grade school, but who had arrived in Chicago possessing a certain articulateness and an undeveloped talent for writing. He had no further formal education—although he was aware of the University of Chicago and came to associate with a number of its intellectuals—but he gave himself over to the complex reality of late 1927 Chicago and made it his own. Chicago, the city where after years of Southern Negro migration the great jazz was being played and reinvented, where the stockyards and railroads, and the steel mills of Gary, Indiana, were transforming a group of rural, agricultural Americans into city people and into a *lumpenproletariat*, a class over whom we now despair.

Wright found the scene challenging. He learned that in this country wherever one wanders one must pay his dues to change and take advantage of possibility by asserting oneself. You'll recall my saying earlier that "geography is fate"; now let me say that one's fate is also determined by what one does and by what one does *not* do. Wright set out to come into a conscious possession of his experience as Negro, as political revolutionary, as writer, and as citizen of Chicago.

Somehow, in getting into the John Reed Club, Wright had learned the techniques of agitprop art—which he came later to despise—and before he went to Harlem he had been a contributing editor of the original *Partisan Review* and a founder of such magazines as *Anvil*. He had been poor in accepting discipline and had had his political troubles in the Communist party, but when I knew him he was not shrinking from the challenges of his existence. Nor complaining that he'd been " 'buked and scorned." Nor did he feel that he had handicaps that could not be overcome because of his identity as a Negro writer. Instead, he was striving to live consciously—at least artistically and intellectually—at the top of his times. Wright's spirit was such, and his sense of possibility was such, that even during the time when he was writing *Native Son* he was concerned with learning the stylistic and dialectical fine points found in the work of Steinbeck, of Hemingway, of Malraux, and of Thomas Mann; for these he viewed as his competitors. I warn you that this is only *my* interpretation, but it was as though Wright was thinking, "I have a finer sense, a more basic knowledge of American reality than Hemingway, or Steinbeck, or anybody else who is writing." He had the kind of confidence that jazzmen have, although I assure you that he knew very little about jazz and didn't even know how to dance. Which is to say that he didn't possess the full range of Afro-American culture. But having the confidence of his talent, having the sense (which he gained from Marxism) that he was living in a world in which he did not have to be confused by the mystifications of racism, Wright harnessed his revolutionary tendencies to a political program which he hoped would transform American society. Through his cultural and political activities in Chicago he made a dialectical leap into a sense of his broadest possibilities, as man and as artist. He was well aware of the forces ranked against him, but in his quiet way he was as arrogant in facing up to them as was Louis Armstrong in a fine blaring way.

To a young Oklahoman this attitude of Wright's was affirmative—and again, "geography is fate." For out there our people fought back. We seldom won more than moral victories, but we fought back—as can be seen from the many civil rights victories that were initiated there. And as can be heard in the Southwestern jazz and in the performances of the Jimmy Rushings, the Hot Lips Paige, the Count Basies, the Bennie Motens, and Charlie Christians. We were an assertive people, and our mode of social assertion was artistic, mainly music, as well as political. But there was also the Negro church, wherein you heard the lingering accents of nineteenth-century rhetoric with its emphasis upon freedom and individual responsibility; a rhetorical style which gave us Lincoln, Harriet Tubman, Harriet Beecher Stowe, and the other abolition-preaching Beechers. Which gave us Frederick Douglass and John Jasper and many other eloquent and heroic Negroes whose spirit still moves among us through the contributions they made to the flexibility, the music, and the idealism of the American language. Richard Wright was a possessor of that tradition. It is resonant in his fiction and it was a factor in his eager acceptance of social responsibility.

But now I should add that as far as Negroes in New York were concerned, Wright was for the most part friendless. Part of this was due to the fact that he kept to Communist circles and was intensely involved with writing and political activities. But as far as his rapid development as a writer is concerned, it would not have been possible but for the Chicago John Reed Club. This required an intellectual environment, and in Negro communities such were few and far between. Thus, given his talent and driving ambition, it was fortunate that he found the necessary associations among other young writers, many of whom were not Communists. Within such integrated groups he could question ideas, programs, theories. He could argue over philosophical interpretations of reality and say, if he chose, "Well, dammit, I'm black, and this concept of this program doesn't seem valid to me." This was most important for Wright, and since he affirmed many impulses which I felt and understood in my own way, it proved important to me. And no less important was his willingness to discuss problems encountered within the Communist party, and especially his difficulty in pursuing independent thought.

Because there, too, he was encountering a form of intellectual racism. It was not couched in the rhetoric of Negro inferiority *à l'americain*, but in the form of an insistence upon blind discipline and a constant pressure to follow unthinkingly a political "line." It was dramatized in the servile attitudes of certain black Communist functionaries who regarded Wright—with his eloquence and his tendency toward an independence of thought—as a dangerous figure who had to be kept under rigid control.

And, of course, Wright's personality would not allow him to shun a battle. He fought back and was into all kinds of trouble. He had no interest in keeping silent as the price of his freedom of expression. Nor was he so dazzled by his freedom to participate in the councils of newspapers and magazines as to keep his mouth shut. Instead, he felt that his experience, insight, and talent were important to the Party's correct assessment of American reality. Thus he fought to make his comrades understand that *they* didn't know a damn thing about the complexities of the South, whether black or white, and insisted that they could not possibly understand America's racial situation by approaching it through such facile slogans as "Black and White Unite and Fight." Not when the white workingman was doing us the greatest face-to-face damage, and when the unions were practicing policies of racial exclusion.

In trying to get this across, in saying, as it were, "Your approach is too simple," Wright met all kinds of resistance, both ideological and personal. But at least he made the fight, and I bring it up here by way of offering you something of the background of emotional and intellectual conflict out of which *Native Son* was written.

I read most of *Native Son* as it came off the typewriter, and I didn't know what to think of it except that it was wonderful. I was not responding critically. After all, how many of you have had the unexpected privilege of reading a powerful novel as it was, literally, ripped off the typewriter? Such opportunities are rare, and being young, I was impressed beyond all critical words. And I am still impressed. I feel that *Native Son* was one of the major literary events in the history of American literature. And I can say this even though at this point I have certain reservations concerning its view of reality. Yet it continues to have a powerful effect, and it seems to me a mistake to say, as was said not long ago in *Life* magazine, that *Native Son* is a "neglected" novel. And here I should remind those of you who were too young to remember, that *Native Son* was such a popular work that the dust jacket of the Book-of-the-Month Club edition could consist of a collage made of accolades written by critics and reviewers from throughout the country. It was a financial as well as a critical success, and with its publication Wright became a famous man.

But its success was by no means to still his burning passion—not simply for justice, but to become the author of other compelling works of literature. His response to the reception of *12 Million Black Voices*, which is, I think, his most lyrical work, is an example. He was much bemused by the fact that this work could move his white readers to tears, and saw this as an evasion of the intended impact of his vision. Thus he began to talk over and over again of forging such hard, mechanical images and actions that no white reading them could afford the luxury of tears.

But here I must turn critic. For in *my* terms, Wright failed to grasp the function of artistically induced catharsis—which suggests that he failed also to understand the Afro-American custom of shouting in church (a form of ritual catharsis), or its power to cleanse the mind and redeem and rededicate the individual to forms of ideal action. Perhaps he failed to understand—or he rejected—those moments of exultation wherein man's vision is quickened by the eloquence of an orchestra, an actor or orator or dancer, or by anyone using the arts of music or speech or symbolic gesture to create within us moments of high consciousness; moments wherein we grasp, in the instant, a knowledge of how transcendent and how abysmal and yet affirmative it can be to be human beings. Yet it is for such moments of inspired communication that the artist lives. The irony here is that Wright could evoke them, but felt, for ideological reasons, that tears were a betrayal of the struggle for freedom.

I disagreed with his analysis, for tears can induce as well as deter action.

Nevertheless, it is imperative that I say that through his writings Richard Wright achieved, here in the social and racial chaos of the United States, a position of artistic equality. He insisted upon it. And not only in his own political party—with which he eventually broke—but internationally. He was never at peace. He was never at rest. The restlessness which sent our forefathers hurtling toward the West Coast, and which now has us climbing up all sorts of walls, was very much within him. In 1956, in Paris, when we were leaving the headquarters of the magazine *Presence Africaine* (and this is the first time I've revealed this and I hope he won't mind, since it might be meaningful to some scholar), he said to me, "Really, Ralph, after I broke with the Communist party I had nowhere else to go . . ." This was said in resigned explanation of his continued presence in Europe. And I think he was telling me that his dedication to communism had been so complete and his struggle so endless that he had had to change his scene, that he had had to find a new ground upon which to struggle. Because as long as he stayed within the framework of his political party, he had to struggle on two fronts: asserting on one the principles of equality and possibility (which the Communists stood for, or *pretended* to stand for), and on the other, insisting upon the fact *not* that it took a Negro to tell the truth about Afro-American experience, but that you had to at least get down into the mud and live with its basic realities to do so. And that you could not deal with its complexities simply from a theoretical perspective. *Black Boy* was an attempt to depict some of those complexities.

So much of *Black Boy* (originally entitled *American Hunger*) is exaggerated, I think, precisely because Wright was trying to drive home, to dramatize—indeed, because of its many fictional techniques he could with justice have called it a "nonfiction" novel—the complexity of Negro American experience as he knew it and had lived it. The fictional techniques were not there in order to "con" anyone, but to drive home to Americans, black and white, something of the complexity and cost in human terms, in terms of the loss to literature and to art, and to the cause of freedom itself, imposed by racial discrimination; the cost, that is, of growing up in a society which operated on one side of its mind by the principle of equality while qualifying that principle severely according to the dictates of racism. Wright was thinking and fighting over these issues at close quarters—fighting with the Communists especially because he had thought that they offered a viable solution. Instead, he discovered that they were blind.

But now to more delightful relationships with Wright. He had as much curiosity about how writing is written as I had about how music is composed, and our curiosity concerning artistic creation became the basis of our friendship. Having studied music from the age of eight, and having studied harmony and symphonic form in our segregated school, I was also interested in how music related to the other arts. This, combined with my growing interest in literary creation, made my contact with Wright's enthusiasm an educational and spirit-freeing experience. Having read Pound and Eliot and Shaw and the criticism of Harriet Monroe and I. A. Richards—all available in Tuskegee's excellent little library—it was important that in Wright, I had discovered a Negro American writer who possessed a working knowledge of modern literature, its techniques and theories. My approach to literature was by no means racial, but Wright was not only available, he was eager to share his interests, and it gave me something of that sense of self-discovery and exaltation which is implicit in the Negro church and in good jazz. Indeed, I had found it in baseball and football games, and it turns up in almost any group activity of Afro-Americans when we're not really thinking about white folks and are simply being our own American selves.

I'm reminded of a discussion that another Tuskegeian and I were having with a group of white friends. The discussion had to do with our discovery of Hemingway (whom I discovered in a Negro barbershop), and Conrad (another writer I often discussed with Wright), and suddenly the Tuskegee graduate said to me, "Aren't you glad that we found those guys on our own at Tuskegee?"

Now, that was not Negro chauvinism, but a meaningful observation about the relationship between social scene and experience, and I concurred. Because I had had the same reaction when I first talked with Wright about fictional techniques, and we had gone on to discuss some of the complications and interconnections between culture and society that claimed our conscious attention despite the fact that we were segregated. The question reminded me of how wonderful it was to have read T. S. Eliot in the context of Tuskegee. The question was not raised to celebrate a then-segregated college in a violently segregated state, but to inform our white friends that racism aside, there are other important relationships between scenes, ideas, and experience. Scene and circumstance combined to give ideas resonance and compel a consciousness of perspective. What one reads becomes part of what one sees and feels. Thus it is impossible for me to reread certain passages from Joyce or Eliot or Sir Thomas Browne without seeing once again the deep magenta skies that descend upon the Tuskegee campus at dusk in summer. The scene, then, is always a part of personality, and scene and personality combine to give viability to ideas. Scene is thus always a part, the ground, of action—and especially of *conscious* action. Its associations and implicit conflicts provide the extra dimension which anchors poetry in reality and structures our efforts toward freedom.

Richard Wright was trying to add to our consciousness the dimension of being a black boy who grew up in Jackson, Mississippi (a scene that was not always so rugged, even for him, as he pictured it artistically), but a boy who grew up and who achieved through his reading a sense of what was possible out there in the wider world. A boy who grew up and achieved and accepted his own *individual* responsibility for seeing to it that America become conscious of itself. He insisted that it recognize the interconnections between its places and its personalities, its act and its ideals. This was the burden of Richard Wright and, as I see it, the driving passion of Richard Wright. It led to his triumphs as it led, inevitably, to some of his defeats. But one thing must be said of Richard Wright: In him we had for the first time a Negro American writer as randy, as courageous, and as irrepressible as Jack Johnson. And if you don't know who Jack Johnson was, I'll tell you that when I was a little boy that early heavyweight boxing champion was one of the most admired underground heroes. He was rejected by most whites and by many respectable Negroes, but he was nevertheless a hero among veterans of the Spanish-American War who rejoiced in the skill and élan with which Johnson set off the now-outrageous search for a "White Hope."

This suggests that we literary people should always keep a sharp eye on what's happening in the unintellectualized areas of our experience. Our peripheral vision had better be damned good. Because while baseball, basketball and football players cannot really tell us how to write our books they *do* demonstrate where much of the significant action is taking place. Often they are themselves cultural heroes who work powerful modification in American social attitudes. And they tell us in nonliterary terms much about the nature of possibility. They tell us about the cost of success, and much about the nonpolitical aspects of racial and national identity, about the changing nature of social hierarchy, and about the role which individual skill and excellence can play in creating social change.

In this country there were good Negro writers before Wright arrived on the scene—and my respects to all the good ones—but it seems to me that Richard Wright wanted more and dared more. He was sometimes too passionate, I think now as I offer you the memories of a middle-aged man. But at least Wright wanted and demanded as much as any novelist, any artist, should want: He wanted to be tested in terms of his talent, and not in terms of his race or his Mississippi upbringing. Rather, he had the feeling that his vision of American life, and his ability to project it eloquently, justified his being considered among the best of American writers. And in this crazy, mixed-up country, as is witnessed by this conference dedicated to his works and to his memory, it turns out that he was right.

From *Native Son* to *Invisible Man*: Some Notes on Ralph Ellison's Evolution in the 1950s

MICHEL FABRE

Perhaps the ideal approach to the work of literature would be one allowing for insight into the deepest psychological motives of the writer at the same time that it examined all external sociological factors operating within a given milieu, for while objectively a social reality, the work of art is in its genesis a projection of a deeply personal process and any approach that ignores the personal at the expense of the social is necessarily incomplete.

Ralph Ellison
"Note to Twentieth-Century Fiction"

The emotional and intellectual itinerary that led Ralph Ellison from his sympathies as a Communist fellow traveler in the early 1940s to his essentially aesthetic and cultural interests in the 1950s has been competently documented in, among other works, chapter 3 of *The Craft of Ralph Ellison* by Robert G. O'Meally. As Ellison moved from left-wing political perspectives to non-partisan cultural pronouncements, he appeared to dissociate himself from Richard Wright—not from Wright as a friend and fellow writer (although the exchange between them became less intense after Wright's move to Paris), but from Wright's stance as a writer, especially from his basically sociological view of black life. After Wright's death the public image of the Wright-Ellison relationship was further confused by the polemics started by Irving Howe's essay in the Autumn 1963 issue of *Dissent*, "Black Boys and Native Sons." Not without reason, Ellison felt unfairly challenged. As a result he began, among other things, to emphasize what distinguished him from Wright, both as a literary contemporary (he claimed the right to choose his literary "ancestors," if not his literary "relatives") and as a militant who now refused "the much abused idea that novels are weapons."[1] A few years later, Ellison's defensive attitude was compounded by the attacks directed against him by black nationalist critics. Ellison's later pronouncements concerning his relationship with Wright, if they accurately reflect his recent concerns, interests, and directions, shed little light on his ideological and artistic dilemma during the crucial transitional period between his career as a reporter, essayist, and short-story writer and his career as a full-fledged novelist. To understand this dilemma and his response to it, it may thus be fruitful to re-examine the political and artistic situation both Wright and Ellison faced during the 1940s and how they happened to diverge, although less than has been believed, in the light of contemporary texts and correspondence that have, to a degree, remained untapped.[2] These documents may not radically alter our picture, yet they make it more precise and reliable.

From 1937 to 1940 Wright and Ellison had their most fruitful exchanges, sharing their conceptions of literary commitment and craft, as well as advising each other about writers they might profitably read. But they rarely corresponded at that time (the only exception being during Ellison's stay in Ohio at the time of his mother's death in 1937). But in late 1940 and 1941 Ellison wrote to Wright revealingly about his preoccupations as a writer, militant, and Negro intellectual.

Evidently, the two men shared the same enthusiasm for the Communist party, U.S.A., in the late thirties and the same distrust of its policies by 1940, both as American Negroes and as serious writers. Although Ellison published little throughout the 1940s (mostly scattered short stories and essays for left-wing magazines), he considered himself, as did Wright, a full-fledged fellow writer, not a protégé. Ellison's concern with technique and ideas was equal to and somewhat fresher than Wright's. In Ellison's view the two men stood out somewhat, not only from other black writers like Langston Hughes, Chester Himes, William Attaway, and Roi Ottley, but also from Communist Negro leaders and cultural commissars. Ellison thus had staunch faith in himself and a good deal of loyalty to Wright's controversial principles.

When Wright left for his honeymoon in Cuernavaca shortly after the publication of *Native Son*, Ellison agreed to collect for him the many reactions to the novel. Ellison thus paid close attention to the reviews, which revealed, as he saw it, not only the foreseeable ideological slant of the black bourgeoisie and the pervasive racism of white critics but also the prejudices of Communists of either race.

At this stage, Ellison's reactions to *Native Son* illuminate his own ideological and aesthetic concerns: he responded consistently both as a black man and as a Marxist.

He had always been contemptuous of the paternalistic, so-called friends of the Negro race,[3] and Wright's book had uncovered a lot of chauvinism: Jewish prejudice against blacks and the Negro middle-class denial of their emotional kinship with Bigger Thomas. But the novel also challenged the assumptions of Communist party members regarding Negroes: some saw Max's plea as an appeal to class collaboration and thundered disapproval; others saw it as something akin to a NAACP [National Association for the Advancement of Colored People] speech; some did not even see the necessity of defending Bigger, rejecting the humanistic implications of his portrayal. Here, Ellison reacted as a thoroughly logical Marxist in his declaration that Communist party leaders, still clinging to their Christian ethics, worried about how Wright "justified" Bigger because they failed to see his revolutionary significance:

> What was bad in Bigger from the point of view of bourgeois society is good from our point of view. . . . He, Bigger, has what Hegel called "the indignant consciousness" and because of this he is more human than those who sent him to his death, for it was they, not he, who fostered the dehumanizing conditions which shaped his personality. When the "indignant consciousness" becomes the "theoretical consciousness," indignant man is aware of his historical destiny and fights to achieve it. Would that *all* Negroes were psychologically as free as Bigger and capable of positive action! (April 22, 1940)

Indeed, the murder and the trial were not matters of justice: for the bourgeoisie, who heard the voice of doom through the symbol of Bigger, the answer was revenge. For Max, any attempt at moral justification has to be discarded in the realm of ideas just as Bigger had brushed it aside in the field of action: "It is not a matter of 'justice' but of necessity. In failing to see Bigger's necessity, they do not see their own and for the Marxist, *freedom* is the recognition of necessity" (ibid.). Instead of being horrified by Bigger's murder of Mary, Communist critics should sweep their Christian and bourgeois taboos from their minds. Here Ellison certainly proved a more thorough Marxist theoretician than Wright himself. In order to be able to quote Marx until he was "blue in the face" to counter Communist critics, he studied the works of Marx assiduously, noting that in "The German Ideology and the Holy Family," Marx had dealt with similar problems in his criticism of Eugène Sue for making his proletarian characters models of bourgeois morality.

Eager to discuss aesthetic issues in a broad perspective, Ellison was already delving into more general problems of characterization:

> From a literary standpoint, however, the book has raised several interesting problems for me. . . . One is: how far can the Marxist writer go in presenting a personalized, humanist version of his ideology? Both Gorky and Malraux attempted this and both ran into mysticism and criticism from the politicians and theoreticians. Then again, does the writer who accepts Marxism have the freedom to expound a personalized philosophy? As I study Max's speech, it seems to me that you were struggling to create a new terminology, i.e., you were trying to state in terms of human values certain ideas, concepts, implicit in Marxist philosophy but which, since Marx and later Lenin were so occupied with economics and politics, have not been stated in humanist terms of Marxist coloring. This lack I am trying to get at is indicated by the almost total failure on the part of Marxist-Leninist literature to treat human personality. Am I shooting up a blind alley in this? (April 14, 1940)

Here, indeed, lay the root of Ellison's disagreement with social realism and naturalism, what he called "writing from an ideological perspective." Not being so defiant of Party discipline as Wright (he half-jokingly declared that he might accept the idea of submitting his manuscripts for inspection before publication if the inspectors could be respected), he still found dialectical materialism incapable of depicting psychology and the human soul. On May 11, 1940, he wrote his friend: "You told me I would begin to write when I matured emotionally, when I began to *feel* what I understood. I am beginning to understand what you meant. I suppose that's why my experience of the [National Negro] Congress was almost mystical in its intensity. *When will the Marxist psychologists explain the material-dialectical meaning of the mystical experience?*" (Emphasis Mine.)

At the time, Ellison was covering the National Negro Congress in Washington for *New Masses*. Impatient as he may have been with obtuse Communist party leaders, he still had faith in the revolutionary potential of the masses. He found in the gathering "the real basis for *faith*." Harking back to Wright's *12 Million Black Voices*, which retraced black exultation after Joe Louis's victory over Schmelling, he celebrated in comparable terms in "A Congress Jim Crow Didn't Attend" the emotional current of pent-up folk consciousness swelling toward revolution. He noted that the leaders would be "awakened from their Marxist fog by the people who think they are carrying out God's wishes when they fight for freedom" (May 11, 1940). This belief in imminent social unrest, which one finds expressed again in the idea that social consciousness among southern Negroes was rising so rapidly that they might make alliances with whites in order to resist joining the war effort, may seem somewhat naive. Yet Ellison's belief that the black folk are sustained by religious faith when struggling for social equality is akin to Wright's handling of Christian symbolism in "Fire and Cold" or "Bright an Morning Star." It hints at the fictional use of a "personalized, humanist version" of Marxist ideology.

After the American entry into World War II and the accompanying patriotic propaganda for unity in the war effort, Ellison bitterly remarked on "the indiscriminate rights of Negroes to die in the Army." He was further disillusioned by what he saw as the "tragedy of the period: Negroes acting as the tools of fascism and the Negro middle class utterly helpless" (April 12, 1942). In spite of what he had described earlier as expressions of Marxist "necessity" when alluding to the 1939 Soviet-German pact and consequent shifts in the Communist political line, which he had expected, Ellison, like Wright, was incensed by the Communists' unconditional support of Roosevelt's war presidency, because such support meant soft-pedaling the racial struggle. Although he publicly denounced "the New Deal Administration's perpetuation of a Jim Crow Army and the shamefaced support of it given by the Communists," he still refrained from speaking of duplicity or "Red" perfidy, claiming that "regardless of their long-range intentions, they (parties) are guided not by humanism so much as the expediencies of power" (*S&A*, 296), and that one should not expect sincerity even from revolutionary political parties.

However, when dealing with Communist bankruptcy in 1944, Ellison did not speak of "political necessity," as he had in 1940, or of "political expediency,'' as he would in 1946, when recalling that in 1942, it had been essential for him to ''change the direction of [his] fictional efforts at the expense of much wrenching of emotions and intellectual convictions'' (August 28, 1946). He simply spoke of downright lack of morality.

By that time, Wright had published ''I Tried to Be a Communist,'' condemning the Communists' manipulation of people and totalitarian tactics. Accordingly, the party leveled attacks against him, labeling him psychologically deranged or a ''politically confused sadist'' (to quote Shirley Graham Du Bois). Disgusted with these smear tactics, Ellison began losing hope of being able to deal positively with such moral bankruptcy. He was preoccupied with an accurate, dispassionate reading of Wright's intentions, not only for the edification of his fellow Communists but because he shared Wright's position. In his mind, it was evident that Wright had not attacked, but supported, the Trotskyite trials, and that Wright was mostly concerned with the motivating forces behind the confessions, repudiating only dehumanizing Party tactics. Like Wright, Ellison was ''concerned with the morality of American Communism and how it took its form from the nature of race relationships in our [the American] society'' (September 5, 1944). A year later, Wright's and Ellison's break (Ellison never was a card-carrying member) was consummated, and Ellison's correspondence reveals as much disillusionment as indignation. Corruption was rampant, the Left was bankrupt and the Party could no longer help the Negroes.[4] What could Negro intellectuals do?

Much later, in 1961, Ellison contended that instead of writing propaganda, he felt it ''important to explore the full range of Negro American humanity'' (*S&A*, 35). He saw the blacks' insistence on achieving social goals both as a strength and a weakness ''because the terms with which we have tried to define ourselves have been inadequate'' (i.e., largely social and economic and not cultural). He added: ''So when I came to write I felt moved to affirm and explore all this—not as a social mission but as the stuff of literature and as an expression of the better part of my own sense of life' (*S&A*, 36). If by ''social mission'' Ellison meant ''political/partisan militancy,'' one would have to agree with him, but it seems that ''the better part of [his] own sense of life'' in 1945 meant undertaking a role of intellectual leadership. This does not mean that *Invisible Man* is the deliberate result of this sense of responsibility, but it was one among many factors. Ellison told Wright that he felt he had reached what he called the stage of ''feeling what one understands'' (May 11, 1940). This time, however, he experienced no mystical mingling with the great current of the black struggle toward freedom but felt sheer indignation at seeing the blacks betrayed.

After the explosion of the atomic bomb, Ellison went even further:

> We've got to do something to offset the [Communist party's] sell-out of our people; and I mean by this both Negroes and labor. With such power in the

> world there is no answer for Negroes certainly except some sort of classless society. . . . What could we do with cosmic forces, unless we concern ourselves with power? (August 5, 1945)

He had already started writing *Invisible Man* at John and Amelia Bates's farm in Vermont when he thought of devising ways to counter Communist corruption in America. After confessing their ideological "corruption," several Communist leaders had again accepted positions of political leadership. They were dangerous because they still pretended to "speak in the name of the only possible future." And Ellison told Wright:

> I would like very much to talk with you about independence of thought. I believe we should serve them notice that they are responsible to the Negro people at large even if they spit in the faces of their members and that they must either live up to their words or face a relentless fire of mature, informed criticism. . . . If they want to play ball with the bourgeoisie, they needn't think that they can get away with it. . . . Maybe we can't smash the atom but we can, with a few well-chosen, well-written words, smash all that crummy filth to hell. . . . What the hell do you and I care about their hate, they hated us all the time. I'm prepared for their hate. The moment that I begin to speak and write like a man they'll use all their energy to jam me off the airways, because, like you, I'll be speaking on the wavelength of the human heart on a station getting its power from the mature ideological dynamo of France and the continent. . . . A few good men *could* change that picture, but it would be folly to try to do it from the inside.
>
> I see it this way: they have no conscience, being Americans, and the only force capable of awakening a conscience within them and the only force politically capable of keeping them in line until that happens, are the Negroes. It is our job, as Joyce put it, "to create the uncreated conscience of the Negroes." And as for the Davises, Fords, Wilkersons, Yergans, yes, and Robesons, we can laugh those clowns to death. (August 18, 1945)

Like Ellison's generous indignation (which I construe as a form of militancy), his falling back upon the formula, "to create the uncreated conscience of the Negroes," is all the more remarkable since by "conscience" he means not primarily social and political consciousness but a democratic, nationalistic, sense of ethics.

Here I am claiming two things: first, that Ellison was far more of an ideological writer at the time than he later acknowledged; and second, that his perspective already emphasized the Negro's, as opposed to the Party's, point of view. But "Negro" should not be taken in a restrictive sense for, even then, Ellison stressed that parochial nationalism could offer no solution, that nothing would do short of a "perspective considering the Negro in a Western, world situation."[5]

Examining some plans for writing Ellison had earlier drawn up may illuminate what is meant here by "ideological writing" or "a novel of ideas" (the structuring of a novel upon concepts rather than developing characters) and by Ellison's "democratic concern." Both ideas are to be found in an application for a fellowship to write a novel Ellison sent to the Julius Rosenwald Fund in the early 1940s.[6]

The story was to be set in a German camp for prisoners of war. The Nazis had appointed the highest-ranking American officer as camp leader; a black American pilot was thus given tremendous power over his countrymen, among them southerners. In such a situation, giving rise to clashes of personality and ideologies, the protagonist must overcome

> the deep feelings of humiliation which have led to his intellectual development and create within the camp a functioning democracy. In other words the account of his administration of the camp is the story of his progress from humiliation to humanity. For he realizes that the idea of democracy is implicit in the Negro situation, and here for the first time in his life he is given an opportunity to define and create the society he needs.

At this stage, at least, episodes were less important to Ellison than guiding concepts in this "novel of ideas dramatized through a series of incidents in the life of the central character and revealed principally from his point of view"—a definition which, by the way, also fits *Invisible Man.*

This was to be a psychological novel insofar as the inner forces that moved the black pilot were explored and the action revolved around changes in his personality and human relationships within the camp. Yet it was also to be a novel of ideas insofar as it attempted "to determine what type of democratic relationships are necessary for a highly conscious Negro to function with white men and at the same time exercise the fullest potentialities of his personality." Again, this could be considered a fair definition of the hero's quest in *Invisible Man.* The term *democratic*, which recurred a number of times in Ellison's proposal, was not an empty allusion to the American system but was a synonym for "free and equal," his ideal of the relationship to be built among citizens of different ethnic backgrounds in order to achieve a definition of "Americanness" for all. The hint at the parable of black life in the United States at the time is unmistakable:[7] "For the democrat, life in a prison camp is a forced regression and a form of death, thus he *must* be killed off. The novel in effect will be an ironic comment upon the ideal and realistic images of democracy." Clearly, Ellison was tackling the question of the role of the responsible Negro intellectual or leader, especially in the United States.

In his projected novel, Ellison's black protagonist dies after refraining from participating in an escape he had helped plan for his fellow prisoners. But he had triumphed, especially over southern racists, not by crushing his opponents through use of Nazi power, but by evolving "a broader concept of freedom"—this was democracy.

At the close of World War II the feeling that America had become morally and even culturally bankrupt was widespread among U.S. intellectuals, among them Wright and Ellison. Wright, in a letter to Gertrude Stein, for instance, said that "in this great free land, money is fairly easy to get hold of. What is hard to get is freedom. . . . We are wonders when it comes to making machines, we are marvels when it comes to selling things. But when it comes to just talking to each other we are scared and reach for our guns."[8] Ellison expressed similar feelings. He found a square-dance session he attended in Waitsfield depressing, not so much because the dancers were poor but because they lacked "a people's expression of its sense of life" (August 18, 1945). Significantly, he alluded to Thoreau's own rejection of the New England cultural pattern (now in ruins) when it was still promising, and concluded that an artist should never hesitate to reject so-called traditions. Yet the question remained: whose mission was it to recreate America, when the Yankees had failed and the Marxists were failing?

Ellison had never been a black nationalist in the parochial sense. Aware of how important the Negro's unacknowledged contribution to American culture and history had been, he was confident, as his contemporary review of *An American Dilemma* shows, that many of the features of Afro-American culture were not pathological adaptations to the dominant Western culture but rejections of it. Nevertheless, he was convinced that the Afro-American could define himself only within the national context. There occurred at the time a gradual double shift in his ideology, not in its political coloring, since he remained a Marxist, but in the change of emphasis: first, from the narrowly political and economic toward the cultural, and second, from racial definition to American identity.

Admittedly the evolution of his attitudes corresponded to changing political circumstances: the authority of politicians in all groups of the Negro population was crumbling, along with the coalitions created by World War II. People were looking to well-informed intellectuals for objective answers to the problems of minority relationships and national identity which had been ignored for half a decade. They also looked for guidance in the face of the approach of an atomic age that threatened the very existence of civilization. In such a situation of ambivalence, the double vision of the Negro (who was both in and out of the system) allowed him a more accurate perspective. At about the time that Wright was declaring that the Negro was an American metaphor (probably thinking of the historical leap into urbanization and modernization achieved by that least industrialized sector of the rural population), thereby revealing his socioeconomic bias, Ellison asserted that the Negro was the conscience of America, thereby revealing a more socioethical, "democratic" bias. He associated himself with Wright as an intellectual and wrote: "Now people are looking for someone who can answer questions and they are looking in our direction. Your prestige should rise by leaps and bounds now. And the wonderful thing is, I feel, that this will be because you dared to be simply what you are, an *artist*" (July 22, 1945). Clearly, in Ellison's mind the serious writer who was not a servant of politicians could not only "create the conscience of his race'' but could serve as their leader and as an explicator of the national dilemma. This is expressed in a letter of July 22, 1945:

> Most Americans seem to have no capacity for consciously accepting ambivalent situations. . . . Can it be our responsibility to remind them over and over again that to be naïve is to be self-destructive? The more I think and try to understand[,] the more I tremble before the colossal responsibility we have as Negroes. Nevertheless it won't be the first time in history that the slaves and sons of slaves have risen to positions of intellectual leadership. . . . I'm beginning truly to understand the greatest joke, the most absurd paradox in American history: that simply by striving consciously to become Negroes we are becoming and are destined to become Americans, and the first truly mature Americans at that. Just as the biggest joke I know on you is that after all the struggle to become a responsible Communist writer and spokesman, you became instead something much more important: an artist and articulator of the most vital possibilities of American life. . . .

And on August 18, 1945, he claimed:

> We are, we were born and became through our experience the ''conscience'' of the Negro people although they don't fully recognize it yet. But our destiny is something more than that: it is to become the conscience of the United States. I know that now. . . . This is *our* country to an extent no one has yet set down. We might as well quit evading the issue and get busy breathing the breath of real life into its half-alive form.

By reaffirming the priority of the artist's vision, Ellison was essentially keeping close to Wright's position, as expressed in the latter's answer to Antonio Frasconi in November 1944:

> It is imperative that we artists seek and find a simpler, a more elementary, and a more personal guide to the truth and experience of events than those contained in the mandates of frenzied politicians; and I say that we shall find it . . . in the visions which our eyes create out of the insistent welter of reality, and out of the surging feelings which those visions evoke in our hearts.[9]

Nor was Ellison moving away from Wright's criticism of the Communists but followed eagerly in the tracks of the author of *Black Boy* when hoping ''to do a surgical job on the repressive effect that CP sectarianism had on [his] sensibilities, along with the quickening effects of Marxism.'' He recognized: ''I was amorphous as hell, literally; and after my discovery of Marx too many questions, nebulous emotions and moods were left waiting breathlessly behind the doors of dogma. Was any of this true with you?'' (August 18, 1945). Yet, this was ''I Tried to Be a Communist'' with a major difference. Though private, Ellison's verbal violence toward the Communist party was certainly more strident than Wright's, at the time, and possibly more long-lasting: as late as 1948 he said he wished more power to Chester Himes (whose *Lonely Crusade* he did not like much) because he had perhaps ''accomplished the task of showing what a Negro writer could do when really striking back'' at the Communists. And he steadfastly refused a request to reprint an early short story of his in one of their anthologies. ''To hell with associating closely with any kind of politicians,'' he wrote on February 1, 1948, including liberals from the *Partisan Review* group. Although he gave Wright a knowledgeable account of the impact of Henry Wallace's third party upon the American political scene, and judged that the Communist party might become a force again, he no longer even read the papers.

In Ellison's mind, again, his major quarrel with the Communist party was literary, to a degree that Wright probably had never experienced. As a result, his early work on *Invisible Man* was slow and difficult, probably because his vision of it was not clearly in accord with his changing preoccupations. The ''surgical job on the repressive effects of CP sectarianism,'' which he later superbly achieved in the depiction of the Brotherhood's attempts to control his protagonist, took time to attain. But the scope of the novel had definitely widened during the course of its composition. As Ellison remembered in ''The Art of Fiction,'' he had thought out the symbols and their connections and had a conceptual frame, even a chart of the three-part division, with most of the ideas and some of the incidents indicated: ''The three parts represent[ed] the narrator's movement from, using Kenneth Burke's terms, purpose to passion to perception'' (*S&A*, 177). Yet, Ellison experienced difficulties in creating a form which would bring together all the manifold purposes and lines of the novel. To Wright he confessed: ''The one stable thing I have in this sea of uncertainty is the raft of concepts on which I lie as I paddle my way towards the shore'' (August 18, 1945).

Indeed, Ellison was launching out into the open, after having long been held back by his own view of his writing and education as being clumsy and inadequate. Now, the newly acquired, self-imposed responsibility as a definer both of the Negro conscience and of the American conscience had given him not only purpose but passion:

> I find that when I have the broadest range for my passion it improves my writing, although that is still sadly lacking. We almost always feel more than we are able to express; the break with the [Communist party] has allowed me to come alive to many things of which I was becoming aware during my bitterly isolated college experience. I'll reclaim that now—with the stimulation of *Black Boy* I might add—and forgotten passages of literature and repressed moods are becoming the wedges of insights. (August 18, 1945)

That Ellison found *Black Boy* stimulating is noteworthy here because it suggests more than the ''antagonistic cooperation'' with Wright that Ellison later indicated in his response to Irving Howe (*S&A*, 107–43). At the same time, it is doubtful that the things of which he had become aware in college and which he now wanted to reclaim were similar to those Wright had reclaimed from his own youth in his autobiography.

By mid-1945 Ellison had completed "Richard Wright's Blues," his defense of *Black Boy* against black left-wingers like Eugene Holmes and W. E. B. Du Bois, who were incensed at Wright's depiction of "the essential bleakness of black life in America." Significantly, Ellison praised the book for reasons corresponding to his own concerns: he felt *Black Boy* should do much to redefine the problem of the Negro and American democracy; it was the result both of "the specific folk-art form which helped shape the writer's attitude towards his life" (*S&A*, 90), namely, the blues, as well as the influence of Joyce, Dostoevski, George Moore, and other Western writers; finally, "the American Negro impulse towards self-annihilation and 'going underground' had been converted into a will to confront the world" (*S&A*, 104) which was clearly positive.[10]

Ellison was loyal to his friend when tackling the touchy subject of Wright's brooding upon "the cultural barrenness of black life" (*S&A*, 103). He accurately restricted the scope of that statement to the symbolic use Wright had made of it in order to counter the Aren't-the-Negroes-Happy trend of thinking. He analyzed the preindividualistic quality of southern black life whose group imperatives had to seem stifling to the ascending individual: "it was the negative face of the Negro community upon which he [Wright] looked most as a child" (*S&A*, 103), Ellison remarked, again restricting Wright's view to his special case. Bravely, Ellison rhetorically countered the charge to which Wright was most open:

> Far from implying that Negroes have no capacity for culture, this is the strongest affirmation that they have. Wright is pointing to what should be obvious (especially to his Marxist critics): that Negro sensibility is socially and historically conditioned: Western culture must be won. . . . Wright knows perfectly well that Negro life is a by-product of Western civilization and that in it . . . are to be discovered all the impulses, tendencies, life and cultural forms to be found elsewhere in Western society. The problem arises because the special conditions of Negroes in the United States including the defensive character of Negro life itself . . . so distorts these forms as to render their recognition difficult as finding a wounded quail against the brown and yellow leaves of a Mississippi thicket. (*S&A*, 103–04)

Here Ellison also reaffirmed his own beliefs: the paramount importance of environmental as opposed to racial theories of culture; the essential Westernness of the American Negro; and the usual misinterpretation and disregard of Negro cultural forms because they were "in disguise."

Why did Ellison defend Wright in matters relating to Negro culture? Perhaps he was simply being loyal to his friend, because later, in 1961, he declared that he felt there was "more complexity" and "a larger area of possibility" in Negro life than Wright ever expressed. It was not so much that Wright was so committed to ideology, although Ellison recognized that they both "wanted many of the same things for our people" (*S&A*, 34–35), but that he and Wright had widely differing conceptions of the individual. Yet, he also remarked that "knowing Wright himself and something of what he was doing increased [my] sense of the possible" (*S&A*, 34).

Now, this sense of the possible could have been increased by *Native Son* only in terms of flinging black violence and resentment at whites. But Ellison was clearly alluding to other possibilities, which he finally characterized as a will to confront the world instead of going underground. Moreover, he qualified his praise of Wright's novel by declaring that "in order to translate Bigger's complicated feelings into universal ideas, Wright had to force into Bigger's consciousness concepts which his intellect could not formulate. Between Wright's skill and knowledge and the potentials of Bigger's mute feelings lay a thousand years of conscious culture" (*S&A*, 100). Ellison later repeatedly contrasted Wright's rich personality to Bigger's stunted responses, well aware that in *Black Boy* there resided the articulate self that lay behind *Native Son*.

Indeed, Ellison trusted Wright's appreciation of the positive aspects of Negro culture so thoroughly because he had already been able to see the black nationalist potential of his novel: "No one here is aware of how really nationalistic *Native Son* happens to be. It is NEGRO American lit.; this aspect has been ignored" (April 22, 1940). Above all, he had earlier responded to the cultural-racial panorama of *12 Million Black Voices* in a moving, lyrical statement of enthusiastic admiration which goes a long way toward defining his ethnic militancy:

> Each little critical thing I try to say is . . . but a stroke, no matter how feeble, in the battle. And, Dick, when I see the whole thing summed up as you have done it, I am rendered incapable for the moment of that controlled kind of fighting we must carry on. For *12 Million Black Voices* calls for exaltation—and direct action. My emotional drives are intensified and reorganized in such a manner that the only relieving action would be one through which all our shame and wrongs would be wiped out in blood. But this is not all. After reading your history—I knew it all already, all in my blood, bones, flesh; deepest memories and thoughts; those which are sacred and those which bring the bitterest agonies and most poignant remembrances and regrets—after reading it and experiencing the pictures, the concrete images, I was convinced that we people of emotion shall land the most telling strokes, the destructive-creative blows in the struggle. And we shall do it with books like this! (November 3, 1941)

Seldom had Ellison bared his heart and soul so completely, describing parts of his life as lacerating experiences. Yet he stresses how he had disciplined himself into not becoming another Bigger by rechanneling his pent-up anger "which could so easily become criminal" into something "socially useful" (ibid.). He was thus prompted by the book to acknowledge those destructive tendencies he had kept caged within himself. Alluding to what Wright characterized as a numbness of feeling due to the oppression of the black soul (a foreshadowing of the ''bleak landscapes'' of Negro life in *Black Boy*), Ellison remarked that he had never felt numb himself but ''had to rigidly control my thawing; allowing the liquid emotion to escape drop by drop through the trap doors of the things I write, lest I lose control, lest I be rendered incapable of thawing our frozen brothers—which all good writing must do'' (ibid.). He defined writing as an act of self-salvation. Presumably he meant that the act of writing transmutes murderous impulses (not unlike the ''Clay'' syndrome of Imamu Baraka's *Dutchman*). Or perhaps he meant that writing can be an act of communal salvation by reconsidering and redefining the ethnic experience. Following this reasoning, Ellison arrived at his definition of the blues and of *Black Boy* in ''Richard Wright's Blues'' in 1945.

As early as 1941, Ellison read *12 Million Black Voices* as Negro blues (although he did not use the term).

> I felt so intensely the fire of our common experience . . . that I felt myself opened up and crying over the painful pattern of remembered things. Not tears of self-pity . . . they were tears of impatience and anger. When experiences such as ours are organized as you have done it here, there is nothing left for a man to do but fight. (November 3, 1941)

Ellison felt that Wright's folk history of the Negro helped black readers assert their essential brotherhood and oneness of experience, their historical and cultural heritage. The book could be a good start toward a reconciliation of the different levels of Negro life, if only those Negroes who ''arrived'' did not reject their roots. At this point, Ellison stressed his personal kinship with Wright: they were both what he would later call ''the conscience of their race,'' having painfully acquired truths from comparable psychological trials:

> I have known for a long time that you have suffered many things which I know, and that the truths which you have learned are Negro truths. (That's one reason I have always been amazed by those who distrust you.) . . . Of this, however, I am now sure more than ever; that you and I are brothers. Back when I first knew you, remember, I often speculated as to what it was that made the difference between us and the others who shot up from the same region. . . . I think it is because this past which filters through your book has always been tender and alive and aching within us. We are the ones who had no comforting amnesia of childhood, and for whom the trauma of passing from the country to the city of destruction brought no anesthesia of consciousness, but left our nerves peeled and quivering. We are not the numbed but the seething. God! It makes you want to write and write and write, or murder. Like most of us, I am shy of my naked personal emotions, they are too deep. Yet one gets strength when he shares his deepest thoughts and emotions with his brother. And certainly you could have found no better way to share your experience with the rest of us. (November 3, 1941)

Bearing the foregoing sentiment in mind, Ellison's trust in Wright at the time *Black Boy* was published seems less surprising. And his contemporary faith in militant writing cannot be doubted, no more than his visceral involvement in the struggle of his race. The terms he used, alluding to the book as a ''weapon''—a *cultural* one—are more indicative of his mood at the time than are later statements, which are sometimes misinterpreted as disclaimers of his earlier commitment.

Ellison told Wright of his resolve to strike a cultural blow:

> Not strange to us who have a sense of the tragic, the book makes me feel a bitter pride which springs from the realization that after all the brutalization, starvation and suffering, we have begun to embrace the experience and master it. And we shall make of it a weapon more subtle than a machine-gun, more effective than a fighter-plane. It is like Joe Louis knocking their best men silly in his precise, impassive, alert Negro way. I think it significant that I can feel pride in a Negro *book*. (November 3, 1941)

Here lay the source of Ellison's subsequent conviction that he had a distinct literary path to follow:

> It gives me something to build upon, my work is made easier, my audience brought a bit closer. I'm a better man for having read it. (Ibid.)

Thus Ellison was assuming that his audience would be primarily black, and not, as Wright had assumed in *Native Son*, white liberals who were supposed to embody America's conscience.[11] In contrast to *Native Son*, *12 Million Black Voices* for Ellison was a clear, positive, collective affirmation of black cultural resilience and political consciousness:

> While in the novel you sliced deep and twisted the knife to open up the psychic wound, *12 Million Black Voices* seizes hold to epochs and a continent and clears them of fog. And it squeezes out of us what we leave unspoken. Some could deny *Native Son*. But all but a few have come along the path set down here. (Ibid.)

Clearly, Ellison's sense of racial community was not based on color but on common historical experience. The conceptual framework he shared with Wright was definitely Marxism, not black nationalism or negritude.[12] But he reverted to the (for him) essential problem of confronting social realism or naturalism—a problem Wright had partially solved (or bypassed) in his folk history of the Negro:

> I hope our political leaders will realize what is made available for them. Here [are] their statistics given personality. Here, I believe, is the essence of what they must work with; all Marx and Engels, Lenin and Stalin won't help them unless they understand this part of *the theoretical word made flesh*. (Ibid., italics mine.)

In 1941 Ellison perceived that Wright would write his autobiography and that he would, of necessity, emphasize the specific factors that made up his life. Now, however, he deemed it more important to make Negroes aware of features of group solidarity. Ellison and Wright both saw shared cultural forms and historical experiences of oppression and resistance to it, and the trauma of the great migration was oriented toward a positive phase of the struggle. Thus ''Men in the Making''—the last, militant section of Wright's book—Ellison reprinted when he was editor at the *Negro Quarterly*.

One now better understands how Ellison could support *Black Boy* as Wright's narrative of ascent (which Robert Stepto defines as launching the ''enslaved,'' semiliterate figure on a ritualized journey toward a symbolic North, the quest ending with the figure situated in the least oppressive social structure and free, as an articulate survivor, to forsake familial and communal postures).[13] *12 Million Black Voices* had reassured Ellison by demonstrating the possibility of an immersion narrative ''in which the protagonist seeks those aspects of tribal literacy that ameliorate, if not obliterate the conditions imposed by solitude'' (Stepto, 167). Wright had not embodied that immersion narrative in fiction, and in many ways he could not perform the part of an ''articulate kinsman'' on an individual level—*Black Boy* made that clear in 1945—although the narrator did so on a communal level in the folk history of the Negro in the United States.

In 1945, while working assiduously on his novel, Ellison cast about for a type of protagonist which would help achieve his several aims: to treat of the problem of ''American democracy,'' to treat of the Negro-white situation, to debunk Communist totalitarianism, and to explore the cultural and historical oneness of the black experience. One means would be to take his protagonist along the road from the rural South to the urban North through a symbolical great migration, as Wright had done in *12 Million Black Voices*. But how could one protagonist embody racial contradictions? Ellison wrote to his friend Kenneth Burke, whose philosophical and literary theories he admired, asking him to set up a theoretical formula ''for a Negro character who would incorporate all of the contradictions present in the Negro-white situation in this country and yet be appealing to whites'' (August 26, 1946). Burke arrived at a ''Dostoevskian *Idiot*, but clinging to the spiritual element of the Spirituals'' (ibid.). Although Ellison had expressed his preference for more rebellious types, like Ivan Karamazov, his eventual delineation of the narrator in *Invisible Man* would make him closer, at the start, to an Alyosha, but one who, in the course of the story, slowly comes to adopt the stance of a trickster in preparation for overt action.

Still at work on what he now called his ''interminable novel'' on February 1, 1948, Ellison was gaining confidence through the very favorable reactions to the battle-royal episode, which had appeared separately in the British magazine *Horizon* and the American, *'48*.[14] Ellison was a bit annoyed at Wright's remark, after reading ''Richard Wright's Blues,'' that he (Ellison) was possibly better suited for the essay than for fiction. But Ellison now felt more self-confident, although he wanted to make it clear that he was not competing with Wright:

> Attaway said that if the rest of my book was anything like the excerpt, the rest of the Negro writers would have to go out and find jobs. You would think that by now they would have learned that no one but themselves can write their stories and that writing is not a game of competition—unless with the great writers who came before us—and certainly I'm not interested in writing *better* than anyone; only in writing as well as I can with my own talent and my own intelligence. (February 1, 1948)

With his "tension building up at supersonic speed" during the weeks before publication, Ellison was agreeably surprised by the reception of *Invisible Man*. It sold very well for a first novel and was favorably and intelligently reviewed—in spite of leftist sniping from people like Ben Burns and Roi Ottley;[15] even black Communists could not "completely deny the book" because some of the material in the early sections meant too much to them individually as Negroes (January 21, 1953). Ellison was apparently never worried about his decision to "explore the whole range of Negro humanity and to affirm those qualities which are of value beyond any question of segregation, economics or previous condition of servitude" (*S&A*, 36). He was also aiming to rebut Gunnar Myrdal's sociology and to show that in Negro culture there was much of value for America as a whole, that helping to create a more human America was also the Negro's burden.[16]

When Ellison was awarded the 1952 National Book Award for Fiction, he was not only justifiably proud but glad of the "opportunity to say a few things which have a chance of being heard, about both our [Negro] shortcomings and promises" (January 1, 1953). He accepted the award in these words:

> I think there is such a rapid change in our status, with money being more plentiful and racial restrictions giving slowly but steadily way, that more and more Negroes are coming to grips with their problems as members of Western Civilization and are seeing the broader problems behind their racial dilemma. Therefore they are looking for books which relate them to the larger problem and though they might gag at the medicine they accept it in the end.

Significantly, Ellison had already become just as interested in the evolution of the novel in America as he was in the Negro's change of status. Very early, he had been held back from writing by his exacting conception of the writer's craft and by what he considered his poor performance. Even in 1945 when he had resisted Wright's suggestion that he might not be primarily a novelist, he was worried not by problems of prose but of form:

> It isn't the prose per se, that worries me; it is the form, the learning how to organize my material in order to take the maximum advantage of those psychological and emotional currents within myself and in the reader which endow prose with meaning; and which, in the writer, releases that upsurge of emotion which jells with conceptions and makes prose magical. It's an uncertain battle

> on a dark terrain but, as you know, brother, the victory is the best, most satisfying thing a writer could achieve. (August 5, 1945)

Now, having achieved recognition, he could turn to literature unimpeded by his sense that he had to satisfy a commitment to his race. Even to Wright, to whom he once had spoken of using the book as a weapon more "subtle than a machine-gun," he pointed out that in his speech accepting the National Book Award he was striking a blow, not primarily against racism, but against the "overpraised style of writing that had gripped [him] for years." In his aesthetic reaction he was not alone, but part of a new generation of American writers, white *and* black. "Watch out," he added, "for Bellow's novel, by the way. It is the first real novel by an American Jew, full of variety, sharp characterization and sheer magical prose" (ibid.). By consistently seeking "a broader scope," Ellison had thus matured as an American novelist and established his view of himself as being an artist first.

NOTES

1. Ralph Ellison, *Shadow and Act* (New York: Signet, 1966), 121. Subsequently cited in text as *S&A*.

2. Quotations immediately followed by a date are from letters Ellison wrote to Wright, now in the Wright Archive at Yale University. Quoted by permission of Mr. Ellison.

3. As early as 1937, he reported to Wright the illusions and desires of white women he had met in liberal or left-wing circles, whose sexual advances probably provided inspiration for the episodes on "the woman question" and the character of Sybil in *Invisible Man*.

4. "This sickness, this inability to face reality[,] grows, widens, deepens with each new development; each new authoritative statement reveals new termite borings of easy, sheep-like beliefs, vacuity and lack of thought. . . . Browder ran the nag down a cliff, broke its legs and left it moaning in the shallow water; Forster has told it the bones have mended, shot it full of dope and God knows what'll happen now" (August 5, 1945).

5. Ellison was already combating the conception of "negritude" found in the writings of Dr. Robert E. Park, the influential leader of the Chicago School of Sociology, who felt that the Negro had always been more interested in expression and life than in action and reformation, and characterized him as "primarily an artist, loving life for its own sake. His *métier* is expression rather than action. He is, so to speak, the lady among the races." See *S&A*, 294.

6. Richard Wright Archive, Yale University, unpublished, 2. All quotations are from this manuscript.

7. Just as ideas were dramatized through dramatic incidents in the career of the

protagonist, so were characters in the book used as projections of concepts, attitudes, and principles: the Nazi commander, for instance, was, objectively, a psychologist given to intrigue, hoping to prod the Negro into plotting the death of whites; symbolically, he was "a 'Satan' principle, a projection of the accumulated hate and humiliation against his (the airman's) experience at home and in the Army, and of his own inferiority feelings."

8. Richard Wright to Gertrude Stein, March 15, 1946, and May 27, 1945. See Michel Fabre, *The Unfinished Quest of Richard Wright* (New York: William Morrow & Company, 1973), 307, 591–92.

9. See *Richard Wright Reader* (New York: Harper, 1978), 73.

10. Again, this could apply to the narrator's hibernation and preparation for overt action in *Invisible Man*.

11. In "Some Questions and Some Answers" (*Preuves*, May 1958), he declared: "my work is addressed primarily to those who have my immediate group experience, for I am not protesting, not pleading my humanity; I am trying to communicate, to articulate, and define a group experience" (*S&A*, p. 258).

12. "It is not culture which binds the peoples who are of partially African origin now scattered throughout the world, but an identity of passion . . . we are bound by our common suffering more than by our pigmentation" (*S&A*, 255).

13. See Stepto's *From Behind the Veil: A Study of Afro-American Narrative* (Urbana: University of Illinois Press, 1979), 167.

14. Ellison acknowledged that the piece had been "somewhat censored" but was essentially the same in the American magazine *'48*. (February 1, 1948).

15. Ellison to Ellen Wright, March 26, 1952.

16. See Ellison's review of *An American Dilemma* in *S&A*, 302.

The Wright Interpretation: Ralph Ellison and the Anxiety of Influence

JOSEPH T. SKERRETT, JR.

That which we do is what we are. That which we remember is, more often than not, that which we would like to have been; or that which we hope to be. Thus our memory and our identity are ever at odds; our history ever a tall tale told by inattentive idealists.

Quoted by Ralph Ellison in *Shadow and Act*,
author unidentified

In *The Anxiety of Influence*, Harold Bloom argues that the feeling of major writers regarding their imaginative predecessors can be as powerful, as primary, as the psychodynamics of the family which Freud described. The literary relationship between the influencer and the influencee is a kind of father-son relationship, and the history of that relationship across the centuries is essentially "the story of how poets as poets have suffered other poets, just as any true biography is the story of how anyone suffered his family—or his own displacement of family into lovers and friends" (*Anxiety*, 94).

The new writer, contemplating the work of some beloved predecessor, conceives an anguishing anxiety, a dread that he will not be able to achieve a significant, immortalizing, and freedom-granting sense of originality, because, in the course of nature, the predecessor has, like a father, not only authority, but also priority; he got there first. The influencee must resent and reject his authority *and* this priority if he is to avoid the debilitating feeling of being an addendum or qualification to the predecessor's work. The strategy by which the writer meets the challenge of his influences Bloom calls "poetic misprision": the new writer misreads his powerful predecessor "so as to clear

Reprinted from *The Massachusetts Review*, © 1980, The Massachusetts Review, Inc.; from *The Massachusetts Review*, XXI, No. 1, Spring 1980.

imaginative space for himself'' (*Anxiety*, 5). Bloom puts this central point of his general theory most forcefully:

> Poetic Influence—when it involves two strong, authentic poets—always proceeds by a misreading of the prior poet, an act of creative correction that is actually and necessarily a misinterpretation, the history of fruitful poetic influence, which is to say the main tradition of Western poetry since the Renaissance, is a history of anxiety and self-saving caricature, of distortion, of perverse, willful revisionism without which modern poetry as such could not exist. (30)

The writer's creative misreading of his predecessor goes beyond intellectual revisionism. It takes on a much more personal cast. Rethinkers are not essentially disturbed by the priority of those they revise. Like children with their fathers, the influenced artist-son is involved in a complex, necessary, and compulsive emotional and imaginative as well as intellectual relationship with his influencing artist-father. As Bloom describes the operation of the poetic tradition, the acts of misreading are embodied in poems themselves, acts of the imagination which publicly imitate, reject, transform, subsume, or transcend the predecessor's style, stance, or thought.

Bloom is at pains to demonstrate that his theory is relevant to the great tradition of English poets from Milton to Yeats. He does not apply the theory to the imaginative relationships between prose writers, but nowhere does he suggest that poetic misprision is a strategy unavailable to the prose writer in his efforts to deal with artistic anxiety regarding a predecessor. Indeed, Bloom uses a prose writer as example in noting ''the frantic dances of Norman Mailer,'' in *Advertisements for Myself*, ''as he strives to evade his own anxiety that it is, after all, Hemingway all the way'' (*Anxiety*, 28). Other authors come readily to mind. Angus Wilson's fascination with his predecessor Dickens is revealed not only in his characterization—the sweetly malevolent Mrs. Curry in *Hemlock and After*, the grotesque Ingeborg Middleton in *Anglo-Saxon Attitudes*—and scenes like the disastrous opening of Vardon Hall in *Hemlock and After*, but also in scholarly readings of Dickens, acts of criticism. In speaking of the personal crisis that led him, at the age of thirty-six, to begin writing fiction, Wilson reports that he used his reading to protect his ignorance of life and self:

> I had always been, and still am, addicted to the great Victorian novelists, especially to Charles Dickens. The conflicts of the novels of Dickens or Balzac, for example, so frequently clearer on the symbolic under-level than on the surface story level, seem to me to have not only remarkable social and moral insight but also a cosmic significance that is often denied to them by critics. (*Wild Garden*, 22)

The novelist's personal burden and sense of life in Wilson's case is inextricably tied up with a sense of the emotional power and deep significance that lies beneath the narrative surface of Dickens's work. In his confusion, he relished the Victorian sentimentality ''attaching to childish or childlike innocence,'' and "battled strongly on behalf of the value of this Victorian sentimentality . . . rather than making allowance for it as an inadequacy" (*Wild Garden*, 23). The recovery of mental health was for Wilson the loss of a false and sentimentally childish self-ignorance, a loss which has become a major theme in his work and which is his personal twist on the themes of his predecessor.

In American literature, the example of William Faulkner has been the dragon by the roadside for many a young writer. Flannery O'Connor voiced the case for a whole generation of southern writers faced with the priority of Faulkner:

> I think the writer is initially set going by literature more than by life. When there are many writers all employing the same idiom, all looking out on more or less the same social scene, the individual writer will have to be more than ever careful that he isn't just doing badly what has already been done to completion. The presence alone of Faulkner in our midst makes a great difference in what the writer can and cannot permit himself to do. Nobody wants his mule and wagon stalled on the same track the Dixie Limited is roaring down.[1]

This anxiety about the Dixie Limited, this dread of the priority of Faulkner has, moreover, an element that is not so much related to the psychodynamics of interacting imaginations as to the economics of literary culture. Writers "employing the same idiom" and "looking out on the same social scene" must contend for critical and popular attention in the same marketplace. So that it is not Faulkner's imaginative priority alone that engages the anxiety of the young writer, but his contemporaneity, prestige, acceptance—his proximity—as well. The fame and prestige of a near contemporary can profoundly influence the development of a new writer whose work is, for reasons intrinsic or extrinsic to that work itself, inescapably related to that of a more established figure.

Which is exactly the situation in which Ralph Ellison found himself as he began his career. For Ellison, Richard Wright was more than a mere contemporary. Although Wright was only ten years older than Ellison, he was a presence, an image as well as a person, a reality that had to be dealt with both in the imagination and in the marketplace. Whatever place a young black writer might make for himself in the critical public attention would be a place won, to some degree and in some fashion, from Richard Wright.

Ralph Ellison grew up in Oklahoma, at some distance, both geographically and psychologically, from the violently charged racial atmosphere experienced by Richard Wright in Mississippi. Ellison was from an early age deeply interested in music, and when he came East to college it was to study under William Levi Dawson, the black symphonist whose "Negro Folk Symphony" was premiered by the Philadelphia Orchestra during Ellison's first semester at Tuskegee. But Ellison's father had intended him to be a poet, had named him Ralph Waldo for that very reason, and though his father died when Ralph was only three, Ellison's mother fostered and supported his interest in language, literature, the human imagination, and human relations.[2]

Stimulated by an impressive young teacher with an idealistic vision of the potential Negro contribution to American letters, this literary curiosity developed rapidly. Ellison dabbled in poetry after careful reading in Millay, Jeffers, Eliot, and Pound, and read heavily in classic British fiction, from Defoe to Hardy. He applied himself with great discipline to understanding artistic expression generally, and slowly lost his exclusive focus on music. After his junior year, he went up to New York, in part to earn money for his last year of music study, in part to continue experimenting with sculpture, in part to experience what he could of the New York literary scene that he had glimpsed in the journals recommended by his professor friend.[3] Someone arranged for an introduction to Langston Hughes, and, through Hughes (and during Ellison's first week in Harlem in the summer of 1937), he met Richard Wright.

Wright was then just about to come into success. The appearance of "Big Boy Leaves Home" in 1936 had brought Wright considerable status among his peers. He was now editing a journal, *New Challenge*, with Marian Minus and Dorothy West, and he was therefore eager to meet and promote new black talent. Ellison had read some of Wright's poems and liked them. Wright was impressed with Ellison's broad reading and critical acumen, and quickly gave him a new book to review for *New Challenge*. When the review was accepted for publication, Wright persuaded Ellison to try writing fiction.[4] Ellison read Wright's unpublished manuscripts and discussed modern literature and Wright's work in progress, *Native Son*, with his new friend, thus broadening and deepening their relationship. When Wright moved from the defunct *New Challenge* to the Federal Writers Project, Ellison went with him; in off-hours "they would get together at someone's house to attend the theater, a party, or political meeting" (*Unfinished Quest*, 168). In August 1939, Wright got married and chose Ellison for his best man (*Unfinished Quest*, 200).

A personal relationship was thus established between the two men that lasted over ten years, until Wright sailed for France in the late 1940s. By that time, Wright no longer fully trusted Ellison and did not confide in him, and Ellison had already made significant progress on the work that would, ultimately, dethrone his old friend and mentor.

During those two or three palmy years at the beginning of their friendship, Ellison was an eager and apt pupil in Richard Wright's informal school of writing. Wright guided Ellison to James's and Conrad's prefaces and other useful criticism, and pointed out how the great writers had achieved their effects. Though Ellison was grateful to Wright for showing him how Joyce and Dostoevski attained their artistic ends, it was Wright himself that Ellison first honored by imitation.

"Birthmark," Ellison's earliest story (published in *New Masses* in 1940), reveals the undeniable presence of Wright in Ellison's literary imagination.

The story reads like an addendum to *Uncle Tom's Children*. It has the dramatic immediacy of Wright's rural southern setting. Moreover, the story imitates Wright's dialectal style in dialogue; when Ellison came through to an independent sense of self as a writer, he would avoid this orthographic approach to black speech and adopt an idiomatic style for black dialogue.

Ellison's aborted novel of this period, *Slick Gonna Learn*, also reveals the influence of the manuscripts on Wright's desk. His model here was Wright's then unpublished novel, *Lawd Today*. Ellison's Slick Williams, like Wright's Jake Jackson, is a poor, uneducated urban black who is frustrated by difficulties arising from the responsibilities of marriage. In the brief excerpt from the book that appeared in *Direction* in September 1939, Slick is more mature emotionally than Jake Jackson. He loves his wife and children; his desperation is motivated by that love. But Ellison is incapable of bringing the story to life because he has no understanding of what such a person might seem to think about his predicament. Slick's psychology eluded his creator. He felt helpless before the chaos of psychological reality—"the images, symbols and emotional configurations" that seethed under the veneer of "apparently rational human relationships."[5]

Ellison's next stories marked a steady progress away from the specific and almost singular influence of Wright toward a more diverse and individualized style and manner. "Afternoon" (*American Writing*, 1940), "Mister Toussan" (*New Masses*, 1941) and "That I Had the Wings" (*Common Ground*, 1943) owe as much to Twain as to the Wright of "Big Boy Leaves Home"—and perhaps more. Further, Ellison here draws together literary models and personal experience in ways that his more direct imitations of Wright had not done. He pulls back from the public themes and typical black protagonists and situations to deal with a limited but familiar universe, the world of young boys. In these stories Ellison overcame Wright's social analysis and the resultant aesthetic imperatives insofar as they directly shaped Ellison's efforts to write fiction. But also, perhaps more significantly, he achieved the mastery of narrative structure and point of view that had blocked his first attempt at a novel. In his next stories, he moved into greater artistic maturity; "Flying Home" and "King of the Bingo Game," both published in 1944, marked Ellison's graduation from his apprenticeship.

But the apprentice achieved his journeyman's status, as it were, just as his mentor became a master. Wright, who respected Ellison's critical talents enough to discuss the structural problems of Book 3 of *Native Son* with him before sending it off to the publishers in the fall of 1939, came into fame and fortune with the novel's publication in March of 1940. The critical reception was excellent, and popular interest was high. "In many bookstores stock was depleted in a matter of hours. The novel sold 200,000 copies in under three weeks, breaking a twenty-year record at Harper's." Wright gave interviews, appeared at luncheons, visited universities, received fan mail, even had his name engraved on a wall at the New York World's Fair, "next to those of Phyllis Wheatley, Paul Laurence Dunbar, James Weldon Johnson, W. E. B. Du Bois, Marian Anderson and Ethel Waters'' (*Unfinished Quest*, 180). Now Wright became a seemingly permanent and formidable presence, not only a private teacher to be admired and imitated while one learned the techniques of the art of writing, but rather, now, a public eminence which any writer working in the same tradition and ''looking out on the same social scene'' would have to deal with.

Ellison's recognition of this fact was explicit. In his critical articles of the early forties, he uses Wright and *Native Son* as touchstones of excellence for black writers. In ''Recent Negro Fiction,'' Ellison dismisses the Harlem Renaissance writers, for the most part because their work was not firmly grounded in reality. He praises Hughes and Wright as the only mature black writers because their work expressed both ''an awareness of the working class and socially dispossessed Negro and his connection with the international order of things'' and the ability to draw upon folklore with advanced literary techniques. Wright is singled out for portraying, in *Uncle Tom's Children*, Negro men and women at bay in the oppressive southern environment and for delineating ''the universals embodied in Negro Experience.''[6] In Ellison's estimation, Wright's contrasting sharecroppers and rebel youths and revolutionary ministers possessed ''an emotional complexity never before achieved in American Negro writing.'' And this achievement, he thought, was only a preface to the greatness of Wright's novel.

> In Wright's *Native Son* we have the first philosophical novel by an American Negro. This work possesses an artistry, penetration of thought, and sheer emotional power that places it into the front ranks of American fiction. Indeed, except for its characters and subject matter, it seems hardly identifiable with previous Negro fiction; but this however, only in a superficial sense concealing factors of vital importance to the understanding of Negro writing. (''Recent,'' 22)

Ellison saw Wright's exposure to the great prose writers of the European tradition and to his contemporaries in America as a freedom-granting experience that made Wright a mature writer in ways never achieved by his Negro predecessors of the Harlem Renaissance. This intellectual and artistic maturity, manifested in thought and technique, and coupled with ''the tensions and disciplines'' built up in Wright as the result of his social activism, had made of Wright a new kind of black writer, one possessed of ''a new sensibility.'' As a result, Wright's novel was a monumental cultural achievement:

> *Native Son*, examined against past Negro fiction, represents the take-off in a leap which promises to carry over a whole tradition, and marks the merging of the imaginative depiction of American Negro life into the broad stream of American literature. For the Negro writer it has suggested a path which he might follow to reach maturity, clarifying and increasing his social responsibility. The writer is faced with the problem of mastering the culture of American

civilization through the techniques and disciplines provided by his art. (''Recent,'' 25)

These high claims for the impact of Wright's work are capped by Ellison's insistence that for the aspiring black writer ''there must be no stepping away from the artistic and social achievements of *Native Son*'' if the writer seeks, through his work in art, to help black Americans ''to possess the conscious meaning of their lives'' (''Recent,'' 26).

But, of course, it was necessary for Ellison—and for other black American writers in the forties and fifties—to get past Wright, to ''step away from'' *Native Son* in some freedom-granting direction of their own. The danger was twofold: they might either be swallowed up in the priority of Wright's imaginative manner, or suffer for lack of audience and critical attention because their work was ''irrelevant.'' Ellison's own aim in writing, presented here as a prescription for all his contemporaries and fellow successors, veers away from Wright's powerful but essentially apocalyptic address to current social conditions and out toward more prophetic expressions of what Ellison calls, here and elsewhere, ''unlimited intellectual and imaginative possibilities'' (''Recent,'' 22).

Ellison's movement away from Wright during the forties was accompanied by changes in the nature of their personal relationship as well. Langston Hughes has noted that during the last years of the thirties Ellison was very close to Wright; in a letter to Michel Fabre, Hughes, who had introduced Ellison to Wright, said that for the young man ''Wright became a sort of literary god for a time.''[7] As the relationship deepened, Ellison became involved in Wright's personal matters. He was the best man at Wright's first marriage, to Dhima Rose Meadman, in August of 1939. But the warm friendship cooled slightly as Ellison became entangled in the dissolution of the marriage as well. In the late spring of 1940, when the hullabaloo over *Native Son* had somewhat abated, Wright and his bride honeymooned in Mexico for three months, quarreled, and returned to New York separately. Dhima moved into an apartment with the Ellisons (who gave up a comfortable place to accommodate her plans), in hope that ''Richard's friendship with them would give them more chances to see each other and become reconciled'' (*Unfinished Quest*, 206). But Wright wanted nothing more to do with Dhima, and, despite Ellison's encouragements to the contrary, he divorced her. Meanwhile, Wright resented the apartment expenses that he felt he was paying for, and when he married Ellen Poplar in 1941, he did not invite Ellison and his wife to the wedding, though Ellison knew and liked Ellen. Ellison reports that it was only through ''stray remarks'' that he deduced they had wed. Ellison did not long stand in the shadow of Wright's disapproval—Wright deeply involved himself in Ellison's efforts to avoid conscription into a Jim Crow army during 1944 and 1945—but the intensity of their relationship lessened permanently.[8] And as Ellison had less and less personal contact with Wright, his own literary career found sustenance outside the circle of Wright's contacts. He never became a member of the Party, and even publications like *New Masses* paid him for his contributions.

Such essentially circumstantial differentiations, of course, make little difference in the kind of battle with a predecessor's priority and proximity that I mean to trace here. Ellison's "situation," in Kenneth Burke's terms, was a complex one—partly biographical (i.e., personal and circumstantial), partly intellectual and ideological, partly aesthetic. Toward the resolution of this complex of relationships with Wright and what Wright stood for, Ralph Ellison would have to bring to bear "strategies" of symbolic action in his imaginative and in his personal life that would deal not only with the literal proximity of Wright, but with his threatening imaginative priority as well.

In *The Anxiety of Influence* Bloom speaks of one of the possible relationships between writers and their predecessors as an antithetical one. Like the initiate in one of the ancient mystery religions, the artist must, to be recognized, supply a completing fragment or *tessera* which, taken in conjunction with his predecessor's work, makes a satisfactory whole, redeeming the incompleteness of the predecessor's vision (*Anxiety*, 67). By thus laboring to "complete" his predecessor, the new writer establishes his absolute necessity—his real priority—for his is by implication the larger vision. To make this "strategy" work for him, the influenced writer must impose an interpretation on his predecessor's work so that he can see it as requiring fulfillment or completion.

Now Ralph Ellison's career as a writer, begun and fostered by the influence of Richard Wright, has been maintained upon Ellison's efforts to supply *tessera* to Richard Wright's *Black Boy*. Both his critical and imaginative writing turn around Wright's posture in this now famous passage in *Black Boy*:

> (After I had outlived the shocks of childhood, after the habit of reflection had been born in me, I used to mull over the strange absence of real kindness in Negroes, how unstable was our tenderness, how lacking in genuine passion we were, how void of great hope, how timid our joy, how bare our traditions, how hollow our memories, how lacking we were in those intangible sentiments that bind man to man, and how shallow was even our despair. After I had learned other ways of life I used to brood upon the unconscious irony of those who felt that Negroes led so passional an existence! I saw that what had been taken for our emotional strength was our negative confusions, our flights, our fears, our frenzy under pressure. Whenever I thought of the essential bleakness of black life in America, I knew that Negroes had never been allowed to catch the full spirit of Western Civilization, that they lived somehow in it but not of it. And when I brooded upon the cultural barrenness of black life, I wondered if clean, positive tenderness, love, honor, loyalty and the capacity to remember were native with man. I asked myself if these human qualities were not fostered, won, struggled and suffered for, preserved in ritual from one generation to another.) (33)

Ellison's works provide contrast to Wright's expression here of the spiritual limitations of black American experience. *Invisible Man* asserts again and again the crucial role of both folk personalities (Trueblood and Mary, for example) and folk culture (the blues, the yams) in the development of a spiritually acute black leader. The hero is not, however—as Rufus Scott in Baldwin's *Another Country* is—a negation of Wright's Bigger; rather, he is *tessera* to Wright's "representative" image of his self, the "Richard" of *Black Boy*.

Ellison's opportunity to interpret his predecessor came timely to him. In the summer of 1945, very shortly after *Black Boy* appeared, Ellison published a long essay called "Richard Wright's Blues" in the *Antioch Review*. The essay is a brilliant review piece and an excellent and useful exploration of aspects of Wright's book. But I am not concerned with that here. In considering "Richard Wright's Blues" as part of Ellison's strategy for escaping Wright's priority, I am concerned with what the essay is doing for its author, and not with what it is doing for its subject. If anything, what it is doing *to* its subject must be brought into focus.

In the essay Ellison argues Wright over into his own territory. Attempting to place *Black Boy* among associated art forms and works, he asserts that the cultural form which most significantly shapes the narrative is the blues, which he defines as "an impulse to keep the painful details and episodes of a brutal experience alive in one's aching consciousness, to finger its jagged grain, and to transcend it, not by the consolation of philosophy, but by squeezing from it a near-tragic, near-comic lyricism" (*S&A*, 90). *Black Boy* is then to be interpreted as a blues, "an autobiographical chronicle of personal catastrophe" that represents the flowering of the folk form into full artistic potential (*S&A*, 91).

The question is not whether Wright's book is or is not an elaboration of the blues, but why Ralph Ellison says so. Wright nowhere expressed such an understanding of the potential usefulness of lyric forms for prose compositions. And in another context Ellison has only scorn for Wright's imaginative relationship to the blues tradition. Almost twenty years later, defending himself against Irving Howe's charge that he had stepped too far away from the protest tradition and the challenge of Wright's work, Ellison quite specifically denied Wright's influence in defining the emotional or blues tone of his work. Here he names Hemingway his father-as-artist, praising him for "a spirit beyond the tragic with which [he] could feel at home, for it was very close to the feeling of the blues," while denying Wright any communion with that spirit: "And if you think Wright knew anything about the blues, listen to a 'blues' he composed with Paul Robeson singing, a *most* unfortunate collaboration!; and read his introduction to Paul Oliver's *Blues Fell This Morning*" (*S&A*, 145).[9]

This is, of course, having your cake and eating it, too. Ellison's interpretation of Wright's life-story begins with a palpable misreading, a displacement of Ellison's own literary/cultural concerns into his predecessor's work, the better to antithetically "develop" and "complete" and "fulfill" them. Ellison constructs, for his own purposes, a version of Wright's psychology as artist that he can use to explain the limited vision of the passage from *Black Boy* quoted earlier. He argues that whatever positive values, supportive of poetic sensibility and nurturing artistic interest, Wright's Mississippi environment may have contained, they "had as little chance of prevailing against the overwhelming weight of the child's unpleasant experiences as Beethoven's Quartets would have of destroying the stench of a Nazi prison" (*S&A*, 94). Such values and elements were rightly omitted from the image of the black community in *Black Boy* on the grounds of the selectivity of art. The core of Wright's experience was violence; violence was "inflicted upon him by both family and community," and his response as artist had been to shape and thus give significance to that violence (*S&A*, 94). Wright was thus not able to express in his work moral and cultural attitudes that had played no significant roles in his development, though they may have existed in the community. Here Ellison is willing to grant Wright his given that they did not, and forms his generalization around that given.

> Man cannot express that which does not exist—either in the form of dreams, ideas or realities—in his environment. Neither his feelings, his sensibility nor his intellect are fixed, innate qualities. They are processes which arise out of the interpenetration of human instinct with environment, through the process called experience, each changing and being changed by the other. (*S&A*, 98)

But Ellison's use of this idea is ambivalent. On the one hand, it explains Wright's image of himself struggling for identity without contact with personal models or artifacts to inspirit his poetic sensibility as an historical/cultural peculiarity of Wright's experience, beyond which he would himself be carried by reading and, later, ideology. On the other hand, it seems also to account for Wright's weaknesses as an artist. He uses it to explain why Wright's major fictional creation, Bigger Thomas, is, as far as Ellison is concerned, inadequately achieved. The *lacunae* of Wright's biography are reflected in his image of Bigger struggling to express thoughts essentially philosophical in nature with a vocabulary limited to sensual counters:

> Here lies the source of the basic ambiguity of *Native Son*, wherein in order to translate Bigger's complicated feeling into universal ideas, Wright had to force into Bigger's consciousness concepts and ideas which his intellect could not formulate. Between Wright's skill and knowledge of Bigger's mute feeling lay a thousand years of conscious culture. (*S&A*, 100)

This "conscious culture," denied Wright by his Southern environment, was what Wright looked for and could not see in his black community. In asking whether qualities like love, honor, loyalty and remembrance were not "fostered, won, struggled for and suffered for," he is affirming the black American's capacity for culture, knowing that "Western culture," in Ellison's terms, "must be won, confronted like the animal in a Spanish bullfight, dominated by the red shawl of codified experience and brought heaving to its knees'' (*S&A*, 103).

But Ellison's idea of the black American's relationship with Western culture is in fact very different from Wright's precisely because his sense of personal, biographical history in relation to Afro-American culture and North American culture generally was far more complex than Wright's. If Wright conceptualizes Afro-American culture in terms of its absence from his life, its nonsupportiveness, Ellison's images of the Afro-American community in his essays show it in a more positive light, as available to a youth inspired to attempt its codification. By reading Wright's autobiography as a ''blues,'' Ellison imputes Wright a dim, uncertain, and inadequate vision of the black American's necessarily complex relationship with his community and culture, and accepts—in Wright's name, as it were—the limitations of Wright's environment as an explanation of his vision. Wright is thus encompassed, encapsulated by his own life-story, which Ellison need not feel representative of his own. ''Richard Wright's Blues'' is an act of definition, a misreading of the father-as-artist that clears the way for antithetical assertion of the ways in which Afro-American experience, Ralph Ellison's experience in particular, functions in the shaping of an artist.

The projection of an encompassing vision of that experience in Ellison's autobiographical writing is closely tied to Ellison's alternative version of his birth into art. In ''Hidden Name and Complex Fate,'' Ellison invents for himself a literary paternity that excludes Richard Wright and holds the origins of his authorship within his family circle. As I have already noted, Ellison's biological father died when Ellison was a three-year-old. In the essay, and elsewhere, Ellison grants his father a gift of prophecy which the normal course of events in his Oklahoma youth, so different from Wright's Mississippi youth and early manhood, allowed to come to fruition.

Attempting to explain his experience as an American writer, Ellison pointedly sidesteps ''the details of racial hardship'' which have, he insists, too often been evoked when writers of his ''cultural background'' have ''essayed their experience in public.'' Without denying their validity, he means to suggest that they are, ''at least in a discussion of a writer's experience as *writer*, as artist, somewhat beside the point'' (*S&A*, 148). Again, there is here an implicit rejection of the connection Wright draws between his environment and his artistic expression. Ellison sees Wright's ideas as inadequate, ''beside the point,'' and thus in need of completion.

But when Ellison stands *on* the point, it is with a view in an entirely different direction. He projects his father's action in naming him after Ralph Waldo Emerson a conferral of a destiny. The first step in achieving a sense of control in relation to the world, Ellison argues, is coming to terms with the destiny implied by one's own name. The enigmatic world, he says, is like Tar Baby in the folktale, who is ''utterly noncommittal under our scrutiny'' and once we have begun to struggle with him demands that we ''perceive the necessity of calling him by his true name as the price of our freedom.'' Coming to grips with the Tar Baby requires more than will; it requires composition, technique, self-consciousness:

> It is unfortunate that he has so many many ''true names''—all spelling chaos; and in order to discover even one of these we must first come into possession of our names. For it is through our names that we first place ourselves in the world. Our names, being the gift of others, must be made our own. (*S&A*, 151)

Charging our names with meaning—''hopes, hates, loves, aspirations''—so that they become ''our masks and our shields and the containers of all those values and traditions which we learn and/or imagine as being the meaning of the familial past'' is the way the individual completes the destiny set for him by his ancestors. For Ellison, coming to terms with ''Waldo'' involved a long process of learning something of his dead father's love for literature and for Emerson in particular, a process which only began during his adolescence. Later in his life—''much later, after [he] began to write and work with words''—he came to suspect that his father had been aware of ''the suggestive powers of names and of the magic involved in naming'' (*S&A*, 154).

In suggesting, however metaphorically, the efficacy of his father's naming him after a writer, Ellison is realigning his artistic paternity, denying the central agency of Wright that I have herein attempted to demonstrate. Ellison's artistic sensibility is not approached by him with the idea that it ''just grew,'' unsupported and even opposed by familial and communal forces, as in Wright's version of *his* development in *Black Boy*. Ellison carefully accounts for familial, environmental and artistic elements that entered his consciousness through his experience of the black community in frontier Oklahoma. His catalogues of these cultural stimulants stand in strong contrast to Wright's very Whitmanesque catalogue in *Black Boy*. In Wright's version of his childhood sensibility, nature is the dominant stimulus; it is nature that inspires him to feeling—''nostalgia'' in a string of southward-bound geese, ''melancholy'' in the odor of burning hickory, ''alarm'' in the glaring redness of the sun mirrored in windowpanes. When Wright catalogues his responses to human culture it is to note irrelevancies, superstitions *that* he used as a child to redeem through imagination his ''bare and bleak'' environment, but *which* played no role in his recomposition of the world's image in his art.[10]

In contrast, Ellison's memories of his Oklahoma environment are rich with images of human culture. While nature—''all kinds of weather . . . catalpa worms and jack rabbits . . . sunflowers and hollyhocks''—is not ignored, the greater part of the storehouse of imagery that Ellison claims for his own is filled with human stock—all manner of language, ceremony, manners, and music. Things which in Wright's childhood world were threatening are in Ellison's only a rich freight of potent value:

> I was impressed by expert players of the ''dozens'' and certain notorious bootleggers of corn whiskey. By jazz musicians and fortunetellers and by men who

> did anything well; by strange sicknesses and by interesting brick or razor scars; by expert cussing vocabularies as well as exalted praying and terrified shouting, and by transcendent playing or singing of the blues. (*S&A*, 160)

All of this, of course, went into Ellison's writing, but only after he had succumbed to the "fatal suggestions" of Richard Wright that he try his hand at it. Perhaps, as Ellison asserts, the more literature and criticism he read, under Wright's guidance and beyond it, the more the details of his background were transformed in his thinking, revealing the profound extent of their value and thus fulfilling his father's intention and his communal experience. But none of that was possible, it seems to me, until after Ellison had composed, in "Richard Wright's Blues," a theory of his mentor that enabled him to assert his own imaginative priority. If Wright had caught a sense of freedom and "glimpses of life's possibilities" only as an adolescent and through the agency of literature, Ellison's relationship is more primary—fated by family, nurtured by community, enriched by culture. And in projecting, after Wright's death, the image of his own father as his most necessary literary progenitor, Ellison closes the loop; in making that gift of his name his own, in asserting the activity of living up to the potential destiny foisted upon him by tradition and culture, Ellison reduces the importance of his apprenticeship under Wright and becomes his own major influence, his own father-as-artist.

NOTES

1. See Flannery O'Connor, *Mystery and Manners*, 45.

2. Ellison discusses in some detail the influence of his mother, in an interview with John Hersey that serves as Introduction to Hersey's *Ralph Ellison: A Collection of Critical Essays*, 2–5 in particular. The Ellison-Hersey interview is also included in this volume, pp. 285–307.

3. Albert Murray, a friend of Ellison's from the Tuskegee days, notes the impact of Professor Morteza Drexel Sprague on both of them in his *South to a Very Old Place*, 112–13. Ellison dedicated *Shadow and Act* to Professor Sprague.

4. See Michel Fabre, *The Unfinished Quest of Richard Wright*, 146.

5. Ralph Ellison, *Shadow and Act*, 175. This work is subsequently cited in text as *S&A*.

6. See Ellison, "Recent Negro Fiction," 22. This work is subsequently cited in text as "Recent."

7. Quoted in Keneth Kinnamon, *The Emergence of Richard Wright*, 72.

8. See Constance Webb, *Richard Wright: A Biography*, 408 (n.22) and 227–30.

9. Judging by Ellison's sources, he is right. Fabre gives the text of the blues collaboration with Robeson in his biography, and it is more Red than Blue. Wright seems never to have understood or accepted the deep-down personal funkiness of blues, their raucous, sensual, ornery and celebratory qualities.

10. Richard Wright, *Black Boy*, 7. Ellison quotes this same passage in "Richard Wright's Blues."

WORKS CITED

Bloom, Harold. *The Anxiety of Influence: A Theory of Poetry*. New York: Oxford University Press, 1973.

Ellison, Ralph. "Recent Negro Fiction." *New Masses* 40:6 (August 5, 1941).

———. *Shadow and Act*. New York: New American Library, 1966.

Fabre, Michel. *The Unfinished Quest of Richard Wright*. New York: William Morrow & Company, 1973.

Hersey, John. *Ralph Ellison: A Collection of Critical Essays*. Englewood Cliffs, N.J.: Prentice Hall, 1974.

Kinnamon, Keneth. *The Emergence of Richard Wright*. Urbana: University of Illinois Press, 1972.

Murray, Albert. *South to a Very Old Place*. New York: McGraw-Hill, 1971.

O'Connor, Flannery, *Mystery and Manners: Occasional Prose*, ed. Sally and Robert Fitzgerald. New York: Farrar, Straus and Giroux, 1969.

Webb, Constance. *Richard Wright: A Biography*. New York: G. P. Putnam's Sons, 1968.

Wilson, Angus. *The Wild Garden, or Speaking of Writing*. Berkeley and Los Angeles: University of California Press, 1963.

Wright, Richard. *Black Boy: A Record of Childhood and Youth*. New York: Harper & Brothers, 1945.

Ralph Ellison and a Literary "Ancestor": Dostoevski

JOSEPH FRANK

When I was invited not long ago to contribute to this volume of essays honoring the achievements of Ralph Ellison, I very much wanted to add my voice to the tributes being assembled for an old friend and a writer of major stature. But I hesitated at first because, in the years since *Invisible Man* had been published, I had lost touch with the new wave of Afro-Amcrican literature in which Ellison now takes so prominent a place. But then, remembering his love for, and familiarity with, the writings of Dostoevski, it occurred to me that I could perhaps combine my knowledge of the Russian author with the desire publicly to express all my admiration for Ellison's achievement. With this idea in mind, I began to reread his book, and was delighted to discover (or rediscover what had probably been forgotten) that my choice of subject was not so arbitrary as I had feared it might be. For in focusing on the relation between the two writers, I was only following a lead given by Ellison himself.

In his essay "The World and the Jug," Ralph Ellison makes an important distinction between what he calls his "relatives" and his "ancestors." Irving Howe had criticized him for not being enough of a "protest writer" to satisfy Howe's conception of what a Negro writer should be—Howe's ideal at the time being the highly politicized Richard Wright. In explaining why Wright had not influenced him in any significant fashion, despite his great respect for Wright's achievement, Ellison discriminates between various types of influence. "Relatives" are those with whom, by accident of birth, one is naturally associated. Negro authors like Wright and Langston Hughes, not to mention many others, are Ellison's "relatives." But, he remarks, "while one can do nothing about choosing one's relatives, one can, as an artist, choose one's ancestors." And among such "ancestors," among those who had truly stimulated his own artistic impulses and ambitions, he lists T. S. Eliot, Malraux, Hemingway, Faulkner—and Dostoevski.

Reprinted by permission of the author, from *New Criterion*, September 1983

The most obvious connection between Ellison and Dostoevski, which has often been pointed out, is that between *Invisible Man* and *Notes from Underground*. Indeed, the resemblances between the two works are self-evident, although they should not be pushed too far. Both are written in the first-person confessional form; in both the narrator is filled with rage and indignation because of the humiliations he is forced to endure; in both he explodes with fury against those responsible for subjecting him to such indignities; and both characters finally retreat to their "underground." The Underground Man retreats symbolically, back to the squalid hole-in-the-corner where he lives; the Invisible Man retreats literally, first to the coal cellar into which he falls accidentally during the Harlem race riot, and then to the abandoned basement of the Prologue, where he hibernates and meditates. (It should be remarked that, in the Underground Railway, the metaphor of the underground has an indigenous American meaning far richer than anything that can be found in nineteenth-century Russia, and Ralph Ellison did not have to read Dostoevski to become aware of its symbolic resonances; but his reading of Dostoevski no doubt gave him a heightened sense of its literary possibilities.)

What stands out for me, however, is not so much the "underground" imagery of the two books, or the many similarities between the Underground Man's rejection of the world in which he lives and the Invisible Man's rejection of his. Much more fundamental is Ellison's profound grasp of the ideological inspiration of Dostoevski's work, and his perception of its relevance to his own creative purposes—his perception, that is, of how he could use Dostoevski's relation to the Russian culture of his time to express his own position as an American Negro writer in relation to the dominating white culture. Despite the vast differences in their two situations, Ralph Ellison was able to penetrate to the underlying structural similarities beneath the obvious surface disparities.

What, after all, motivates the revolt of Dostoevski's Underground Man against his world? It is the impossibility he feels of being able to live humanly within categories that, although he has learned to accept them about himself, have been imposed on him by others. As Dostoevski saw them, these categories had been imported into Russia from European culture. (Dostoevski was far from being the only prominent Russian to take such a view; the revolutionary Alexander Herzen, for one, shared exactly the same idea.) As a result, they are categories that the Underground Man finds to be profoundly in contradiction with his moral being. The revolt of the Underground Man is a refusal to accept a definition of himself, a definition of his own nature, in terms imposed by the alien world of European culture. At the same time, like all other educated Russians, he has assimilated and accepted the ideas and values of this alien world (accepted them, that is, with the rational and self-conscious part of his personality) because of their superior authority and prestige.

This is the very situation in which the Invisible Man finds himself all through Ellison's book. The Invisible Man stands in relation to white American culture and *its* ideas and values as Dostoevski's Underground Man stands in relation to West European culture. For the Invisible Man discovers that all of its definitions of himself, all the structures within which it wishes to place him as a Negro, violate some aspect of his own integrity. No more than the Underground Man is he willing to accept such a situation passively; and he rejects each of these structures in turn the moment he realizes their true import.

The form of *Invisible Man*, as an ideological novel, is essentially the same as that of *Notes from Underground*, though Ellison's work is conceived on a much larger scale. Each major sequence dramatizes the confrontation between the Invisible Man and some type of social or cultural trap—a road opens up before him only to end in a blind alley, a possibility of freedom tempts him but then only imprisons him once again. Similarly, each of the two episodes in Dostoevski's work unmasks the morally detrimental consequences of the two dominating ideologies that, because of the force of European ideas on the Russian psyche, had ensnared the Russian intelligentsia. (The materialism and ethical utilitarianism of the 1860s is parodied in Part 1 of *Notes from Underground*; the "humanitarian" and "philanthropic" utopian socialism of the 1840s is the butt of Part 2.)

The Invisible Man, too, is a member of the American Negro intelligentsia, or has at least been chosen to be educated as one; and his adventures reveal the bankruptcy of all the doctrines that this intelligentsia has accepted up to the present from the hands of the whites. Such doctrines include the assimilationism of the carefully tailored and prettified Negro college that the Invisible Man attends; the Africanism of Ras the Exhorter, which is finally only a mirror image of white racism despite the dignity and purity of the passion at its source; and the radical politics embodied in the Brotherhood. When the Brotherhood provokes a race riot, it is employing the very tactics of the-worse-the-better that Dostoevski understood very well, and had dramatized in *The Devils*—a novel that, among many other things, is a handbook of extremist politics.

Notes from Underground and *Invisible Man* thus undertake essentially the same task, and both perform it superbly. But one should not press the comparison too hard. Ellison took from Dostoevski what he needed, but used it in his own way. Actually, *Invisible Man* is more an extrapolation than an imitation of *Notes from Underground*. Ellison portrays the *process* through which the Invisible Man becomes disillusioned with his previous conceptions, while this process is more or less taken for granted by Dostoevski. We do not really follow the Underground Man stage by stage in his development; we never see him in that state of innocent acceptance typical of the Invisible Man. *Invisible Man* ends where *Notes from Underground* begins; the two works overlap only in the framing sections of *Invisible Man*, the Prologue and Epilogue. Here Ellison's narrator directly expresses the conflict in himself between his refusal *entirely* to abandon the ideals he has accepted up to this point (in the hope of fashioning some *modus vivendi* with the white world), and his rejection of all the forms in which this *modus* has presented itself to him. Dostoevski's character is caught in exactly the same sort of conflict: his acceptance of European ideas is at war with his moral instincts. "Who knows but that, on the lower frequencies, I speak for you?" (*IM*, 439) the Invisible Man suggests to his (white) reader, who is incapable of seeing him for what he truly is but nonetheless shares with him the same tragic dilemma. The Underground Man addresses himself to *his* scornful and mocking readers in exactly the same way at the conclusion of *Notes from Underground*. "We are even so tired of being men, men of real, *our own* flesh and blood, that we have reached the point of being ashamed of it," he says; "we consider it a disgrace, and aspire to dissolve into some sort of abstract man who has never existed." He does not exclude himself from this accusation, and speaks, at the same time, for all those who will sneer at his words.

Dostoevski's novella is primarily a lengthy interior monologue of inner conflict, expressed in both ideological and psychological terms. *Invisible Man* is a negative *Bildungsroman*, in which the narrator-hero learns that everything he has been taught to believe by his various mentors is actually false and treacherous. His experiences can thus be considered to be those of a black Candide. There is, to be sure, very little of Candide in the Underground Man, but even when Ellison swerves from Dostoevski, he instinctively moves in a direction Dostoevski wished to take himself. For one of Dostoevski's cherished literary projects—one that he never got around to realizing—was to write what he called in his notes "a Russian *Candide*."

A work of Dostoevski's that bears a much less explicit connection with Ellison's *Invisible Man* is *House of the Dead*, Dostoevski's sketches of life in the Siberian prison camp where he served a term of four years. There is certainly no obvious literary similarity between the two books; but Ellison himself points toward a connection by remarking, in *Shadow and Act*, on "Dostoevski's profound study of the humanity of Russian criminals." For my part, I am convinced that the effect of *House of the Dead* on Ellison's sensibility was more profound than has ever been suspected. It affected him strongly and personally, and provided him with a powerful precedent for entering into a positive relation with the Negro folk culture he had imbibed from the cradle.

One of the outstanding characteristics of *Invisible Man* is its use of Negro folk culture, not as a source of quaint exoticism and "folksy" local color, but as a symbol of a realm of values set off against the various ideologies with which the narrator becomes engaged. What these values are is expressed in Ellison's famous definition of "the blues": "an impulse to keep the painful details and episodes of a brutal experience alive in one's aching consciousness, to finger its jagged grain, and to transcend it, not by the consolation of philosophy but by squeezing from it a near-tragic, near-comic lyricism.'' It is this quality of American Negro folk sensibility that Ellison embodies in such a character as Peter Wheatstraw, who arouses the admiration of the still naive Invisible Man even though the latter has been taught, in accordance with the standards of educated white society, to look down on Wheatstraw's punning speech style and versifying idioms as primitive and demeaning. ''God damn, I thought, they're a hell of a people!'' writes the Invisible Man after this encounter. ''And I didn't know whether it was pride or disgust that suddenly flashed over me.''

This uncertainty represents the clash within the narrator of his instinctive response to the indigenous forms of cultural expression of his people, with all the toughness and resilience of spirit that they embody, and the response instilled by his education: ''I'd known the stuff from childhood, but had forgotten it; had learned it *back of school*.'' Part of what he discovers in the course of the book is the value of what he had been taught to discard.

This is where *House of the Dead* enters the picture. For while it would be nonsensical to imagine that Ralph Ellison needed Dostoevski to make him aware of the richness and depth of Negro folk culture, Dostoevski could (and did) serve as an invaluable and prestigious literary ''ancestor'' who had had to fight the same battle on behalf of the Russian peasant culture of his own time.

American readers will find it difficult to imagine that Russians could once have looked down on their own peasant culture as American whites (and Negroes wishing to conform to white cultural standards) looked down upon the Negro folk culture developed in the slave society of the American South. But such was the rage for Europeanization in Russia, such the rejection of all vestiges of the Russian past as ''barbarous'' and ''regressive,'' that exactly the same prejudice prevailed. Anything not conforming to the standards of Europeanization was scorned and ridiculed. This situation reached such a degree of self-negation that the Russian upper class hardly any longer spoke their own language. (It will be recalled that, at the beginning of *War and Peace*, a discussion of the threat of Napoleon at an aristocratic gathering is conducted not in Russian, but in French.) One of the most important works that broke the grip of this prejudice was *House of the Dead*, in which Dostoevski not only depicts for the first time the ''humanity'' of ''criminals'' (the men he wrote about were criminals technically, but a good many had landed in Siberia only because they had reacted violently to the prevailing injustice and ill-treatment of their class), but also uncovers the hidden treasures of Russian peasant culture.

Dostoevski managed to keep a notebook while in prison camp in which he wrote down peasant expressions, proverbs, songs, and anecdotes. These revealed to him an independent, strong-willed, tough-minded outlook on life that he came to admire and even to think superior, in some of its moral aspects, to the advanced, ''progressive'' views he had once accepted. *House of the Dead* is really a story of his re-education along such lines, which finally allowed him to recognize the riches of the way of life of his own people. Could not this be said as well to be one of the major thematic aims of *Invisible Man*? One can only speculate on the effect that reading such a work had on the young Ralph Ellison, wrestling with the problem of reconciling what he had learned in school (his first ambition, after all, had been to become a *classical* composer) with what he had picked up "back of school." We do know that he later became a writer who, while measuring himself by the highest standards of the great modern masters, refused to see any contradiction between his exalted literary ambitions and his admiration for the far from classical world of American Negro folk music and folk life.

Dostoevski's book would thus unquestionably have helped Ellison to find his own way. And if we read *House of the Dead* from this angle, it is not too difficult to spot passages that might have had particular importance for him. Would he not have been struck, for example, by Dostoevski's suggestion that, so far as the Russian educated class is concerned, the Russian peasant is really *invisible*? "You may have to do with peasants all your life," he tells his educated readers, "you may associate with them every day for forty years, officially for instance, in the regulation and administrative forms, or even simply in a friendly way, as a benefactor or, in a certain sense, a father—you will never know them really. It will all be *an optical illusion*, and nothing more. I know that all who read will think I am exaggerating. But I am convinced of its truth. I have reached this conviction, not from books, not from abstract theory, but from reality, and I have had plenty of time to verify it."

One can go through the whole book in this way and pick out episode after episode that could have impressed the young Ellison as being directly relevant to his own creative problems. There is the incident where Dostoevski, who had formerly believed that the backward *muzhik* was a bungling and incompetent worker, suddenly discovers, because he is now a member of the work convoy himself, that the supposed "incompetence" is really a form of sabotage. When the peasant-convicts get the conditions they want, "there was no trace of laziness, no trace of incompetence . . . . The work went like wildfire. Everyone seemed wonderfully intelligent all of a sudden." And there was the revelation of the peasant-convict orchestra "playing the simple peasant instruments," some of them homemade. "The blending and harmony of sounds, above all, the spirit, the character of the conception and rendering of the tune in its very essence were simply amazing. For the first time I realized all the reckless dash and gaiety of the gay dashing Russian dance songs." The spirit of the people emerged and could be felt in their own music, which for the first time Dostoevski—who had previously been an inveterate concertgoer—was able to estimate at its true worth. Such a passage would surely have strengthened Ralph Ellison's determination to win for the folk music of his own people (jazz, the blues, spirituals) the recognition it deserved as a valid artistic expression of their own complex sense of life.

Many other instances of the same kind could be adduced as Dostoevski undergoes that transvaluation of values—the same transvaluation undergone by the Invisible Man—in favor of the peasant-convicts and against the "enlightened" and "civilized" standards of educated Russian society. The representatives of that society constantly speak of "justice" but assume that they have the right to a leading place in the world. How different from the peasant-convicts at the prison theatricals, who give Dostoevski a front-row seat because they feel it "just" to do so. Dostoevski is a connoisseur of the theater, who could appreciate all the nuances of the performance; therefore he "deserves" a better place. "The highest and most striking characteristic of our people," Dostoevski writes of this incident, "is just their sense of justice and their eagerness for it. There is no trace in the common people of the desire to be cock of the walk on all occasions and at all costs, whether they deserve to be or not. . . . There is not much our wise men could teach them. On the contrary, I think it is the wise men who ought to learn from the people."

What is most important, however, is Dostoevski's clear-eyed and unblinking ability to look the facts about the Russian peasant in the face; not to sentimentalize or gild or touch up their benightedness, backwardness, and sometimes terrible cruelty. And his ability to understand, at the same time, that these repulsive aspects of their lives were the result of the age-old oppression in which they had been forced to survive. He was capable of discerning whatever spark of humanity continued to exist under such conditions, and he believed that such a spark *must* exist somewhere no matter how much surface appearances might suggest its extinction. This same capacity is condensed in the observation of Ralph Ellison's that "the extent of beatings and psychological maiming meted out by southern Negro parents rivals those described by nineteenth-century Russian writers as characteristic of peasant life under the Czars. The horrible thing is that the cruelty is also an expression of concern, of love." Such a remark could only have come from Ellison's intimate identification with the spirit in which Dostoevski had portrayed Russian peasant life, and Ellison's awareness of the extent to which it had helped him enter into a genuinely creative relation with his own world.

House of the Dead stands out from Dostoevski's other books by its descriptive and plotless character. It is a series of sketches focusing on a milieu and a collectivity, which resembles a piece of reportage more than a novel. One would hardly think it written by the same author who gives us such febrile and tightly wound dramatizations of the philosophical and ideological dilemmas of the Russian intelligentsia. Its effect on Ralph Ellison is much more in the realm of attitudes and idea-feelings than in that of artistic technique. Yet there is one point at which *Invisible Man* and *House of the Dead* come together artistically in a remarkable fashion, and where a direct, artistic influence may be inferred. Or if not, the parallel is all the more worth mentioning because it reveals how close the two are in their grasp of human existence.

One of the high points of Ellison's narrative is Jim Trueblood's story about the violation of his daughter, with whom, while half-asleep and dreaming, he unwittingly commits incest. Its parallel in *House of the Dead* is a narrative entitled "Akulka's Husband." Both are written in the form of what is called a *skaz* in Russian criticism, that is, a first-person oral tale strongly colored by the speech-style of the teller. In Ellison's story, the speaker is a southern Negro tenant farmer; in Dostoevski's, it is a Russian peasant. Both recount what is, in fact, a criminal transgression of the laws of God and man—in the first case incest, in the second, the deliberate murder of an innocent wife by a craven, resentful, sadistic husband who has already beaten his victim half to death.

What unites these stories—and Dostoevski's is by far the more frightful—is the unsparing way they depict the unforgivable and unredeemable, and yet manage to do so in a manner that affirms the humanity of the people involved rather than negating it. Jim Trueblood's deed is not an act of lust or animal passion but an accident caused by being forced through poverty to sleep with his wife and grown-up daughter in the same bed. He tells what occurred as a deeply moral man, bewildered and disturbed by his own transgression, even ready to let his outraged wife chop off his head with an ax (though she is finally unable to bring herself to the act). He goes through a period of mortification ("I don't eat nothin' and I don't drink nothin' and caint sleep at night"). One night, looking up at the stars, he starts to sing, and "*ends up* singin' the blues." He then returns to his family to begin life anew and shoulder the burden of what he has done—and yet not *really* done.

In Dostoevski's tale, it is not the narrator whose ineradicable human quality emerges in this way, although we are made to realize that he kills because of intolerable personal humiliation—which at least saves him from being taken only as a bloodthirsty sadist. It is rather the murdered wife and the man she loves, Filka Morozov, who suddenly reveal a depth of sentiment that one would not have suspected. Until this happens, the wife has been only a piteous victim, Filka only a headstrong and reckless scoundrel who had slandered the girl unmercifully in order to take revenge on her domineering father with whom he had quarreled. It is Filka who is responsible for all the torments she has had to endure, including a forced marriage to her weak-willed husband. But then, just before he is taken away for military service (which meant that he would probably never return), Filka proclaims her innocence to the entire village, bowing down at her feet; and she forgives him, declaring her love in the same ritual manner and in heightened poetic speech. The tale is suddenly lit up by a flash of the purest feeling and the tenderest human emotion, only to sink back into darkness again with the murder. But we do not forget, after this flash, that the participants are *people*, not inhuman monsters; and we derive this same knowledge from the narrative of Jim Trueblood. Ellison drives home to us as Americans the same point Dostoevski had driven home to his Russian readers a hundred years earlier.

There is still another important relation between Ralph Ellison and Dostoevski worth discussing: the convergence of the two writers when they defend the integrity of art and the independence of the artist from ideological dictates and constraints imposed by the guardians (unofficial in both cases, but not to remain so in Dostoevski's homeland) of the collective conscience.

Most of the incidental journalism in which Dostoevski defended his position has not been translated at all, or has been put into English rather recently. But Ralph Ellison did not have to read Dostoevski's journalism to find himself confronted with the same problems. The attitude about art against which Dostoevski had fought in the early 1860s has become, through the triumph and worldwide influence of Russian Communism, the dogma automatically imposed on artists anywhere who become involved with radical politics. Ralph Ellison, like so many others (and like Dostoevski himself in the 1840s), went through such a phase. Finding himself subject to the authority and censure of the cultural commissars, he reacted against them exactly as Dostoevski had done.

Very early in Dostoevski's career, he ran into efforts to influence and control the nature of his literary production. The host of the radical circle whose meetings he attended, Mikhail Petrashevsky, criticized him for not writing overt social propaganda that would further the cause of progress. The best critic of the time, V. G. Belinsky, who had hailed Dostoevski's first novel, *Poor Folk,* as a masterpiece, also thought that Dostoevski's later work in the 1840s was deficient in social content. But Dostoevski resisted the criticism of both men. He even told Belinsky that the influential critic "was giving literature a partial significance unworthy of it, degrading it to the description, if one may so express it, *solely of journalistic facts,* or scandalous occurrences."[1]

What is important about Dostoevski's opposition to such views is that he did *not* defend the autonomy of art in the terms that have come to be known as "art for art's sake." He did not argue that, since art was its own supreme value, a writer could legitimately neglect the social arena in pursuit of its perfection. Dostoevski accepted the premise of the radical critics that art had an important moral and social function to fulfill. But it was exactly for this reason that the artist was obliged never to sacrifice the standards of art in the interest of social utility. For even in the terms of social utility, Dostoevski insisted, "a production without artistic value can never and in no way attain its goal; indeed, it does more harm than good to the cause. Consequently, in neglecting artistic value the Utilitarians take the lead in harming their own cause."

There is then, in Dostoevski's view, no conflict between the belief that art has a supremely important moral and social mission and a determination not to turn art into a medium of propaganda. This is exactly the position that an embattled Ralph Ellison has defended so eloquently and staunchly in his criticism. No contemporary American writer has made out a stronger case for the moral function of art than Ralph Ellison in such essays as "Twentieth-Century Fiction and the Black Mask of Humanity" and "Stephen Crane and American Fiction." These critical pieces locate the greatness of such writers as Twain and Melville in their incessant moral preoccupation with the basic injustices of American life (pre-eminently slavery and, more generally, the race problem). Ellison admires their attempts to cope with such injustices, not politically but morally. Among his own contemporaries, only Faulkner, in Ellison's view, has taken up this task, accepting and transcending the southern stereotypes of his Negro characters and exploring the deep wounds inflicted on the southern white psyche by the tangled history of its relations with the Negro.

While himself engaged in wrestling artistically with these very themes, Ralph Ellison has energetically rejected all efforts to confuse the function of art with that of social agitation. In an important exchange with Irving Howe, Ellison draws a clear line between the obligations of art and those of social action. "In his effort to resuscitate Wright," Ellison points out, "Irving Howe would designate the role which Negro writers are to play more rigidly than any Southern politician—and for the best of reasons. We must express 'black' anger and 'clenched militancy'; most of all we should not become too interested in the problems of the art of literature, even though it is through these that we seek our individual identities. And between writing well and being ideologically militant, we must choose militancy." To which Ellison retorts: "I think that the writer's obligation in a struggle as broad and abiding as the one we are engaged in, which involves not merely Negroes but all Americans, is best carried out through his role as a writer. And if he chooses to stop writing and take to the platform, then it should be out of personal choice and not under pressure from would-be managers of society."

I had read this exchange when it first appeared—in *Dissent* and the *New Leader* in 1963—and had written about it, upholding Ellison's position, in a review of *Shadow and Act* commissioned and accepted by *Partisan Review*. The piece, for some reason, was never published. I suspect that its disappearance may have had something to do with an idea expressed in the epigraph from Malraux that Ellison had appended to his reply to Howe: "What runs counter to the revolutionary convention is, in revolutionary histories, suppressed more imperiously than embarrassing episodes in private memoirs. . . ." In any case, it is impossible for me to read Ellison's words now without thinking of Dostoevski's remarks on the advice given by the radical critic Dobrolyubov to the Russian poet I. S. Nikitin.

The descendant of a lowly merchant family, Nikitin was an admirer of Pushkin and an imitator of his lyrical style. Dobrolyubov found this taste deplorable, especially in view of Nikitin's class background; and the gist of his comments is summarized by Dostoevski in the following fashion: " 'Write about your needs' Nikitin is told, 'describe the needs and necessities of your condition, down with Pushkin, don't go into raptures over him, but go into raptures over this and over that and describe this and nothing else'—'But Pushkin has been my banner, my beacon, my master' cries Mr. Nikitin (or me for Mr. Nikitin). 'I am a commoner, he has stretched out his hands to me from where there is light, where spiritual enlightenment exists, where one is not stifled by outrageous prejudices, at least not like those in my milieu; he has been my spiritual food'—'You've gone wrong, and that's too bad! Write about the needs of your class,' " etc. This is the same sort of advice that Irving Howe was giving to Ralph Ellison: forget about T. S. Eliot, Malraux, Hemingway, Faulkner, Dostoevski; write about the struggle of the Negro for civil rights, and look at Negro life *only* in relation to that all-important struggle.

What is involved here is much more than a quarrel over the role and function of art; it is really a disagreement about the range and dimension of human experience. No one knew this better than Dostoevski, who refused to accept the reduction of possibility, the shrinking of the horizon of human concern, that lay at the root of the Russian radical doctrine of art. "The imagination builds castles in the air" Chernyshevski had written with heavy sarcasm "when the dreamer lacks not only a good house, but even a tolerable hut." Hence a preoccupation with whatever transcends immediate physical and material need, or at best the concrete social issues of the moment, must be rejected as illusory and reprehensible. Dostoevski replied to this position with a satirical skit in which he portrays a new contributor to a radical journal receiving instructions on how to toe the party line from the editors: "If a person," he is told, "says to you: 'I want to think, I torment myself with age-old problems that have remained unsolved; or, I want to live, I aspire to find a faith, I search for a moral ideal, I love art, or anything of this kind,' always reply immediately, clearly, and without a moment's hesitation, that all this is stupidity, metaphysics, that all this is a luxury, childish dreams, senselessness. . . ."

Ralph Ellison again joins Dostoevski at this point, but of course in the terms of his own special situation as a Negro American writer. The white cultural world—especially those "friends" of the Negroes strongly influenced by Marxism-Leninism—has a tendency to insist that Negro experience, in particular, remain fixed within the confines laid down for human nature, as a whole, by Russian radical thought. But the Ralph Ellison who had written so touchingly about the ideal of "Renaissance man," cherished by himself and a few friends while they were growing up in Oklahoma, refused very early to accept any such limitations; and he has protested again and again when attempts have been made to impose it, or, even worse, when it has been accepted voluntarily. Indeed, Ellison's criticism of his close friend and erstwhile literary comrade-in-arms, Richard Wright, is precisely that after a certain point in his career Wright had tailored his creative imagination to such a pattern. Wright, Ellison remarked in an interview, "was committed to ideology—even though I, too, wanted many of the same things for our people.'' Fundamentally, he goes on, he and Wright had differed in their concept of the individual. ''I, for instance, found it disturbing that Bigger Thomas (in Wright's *Native Son*) had none of the finer qualities of Richard Wright, none of the imagination, none of the sense of poetry, none of the gaiety. And I preferred Richard Wright to Bigger Thomas.''

Ellison makes the same sort of argument in an article on Wright's *Black Boy,* where he directs his polemical fire against those critics who had wondered in print how a mind and sensibility such as Wright's could have developed amidst the appalling conditions of life, and the searing personal history, that he describes. These critics felt it to be a weakness in the book that no explanation was offered for this anomaly. Ellison replies ''that the prevailing mood of American criticism has so thoroughly excluded the Negro that it fails to recognize some of the most basic tenets of Western democratic thought when encountering them in a black skin. They forget that human life possesses an innate dignity and mankind an innate sense of nobility; that all men possess the tendency to dream and the compulsion to make their dreams reality; that the need to be ever dissatisfied and the urge ever to seek satisfaction is implicit in the human organism, and that all men are the victims and beneficiaries of the goading, tormenting, commanding and informing activity of that imperious process known as the Mind—the Mind, as Valery describes it, 'armed with its inexhaustible questions.' ''

The final connection between Ralph Ellison and Dostoevski that I wish to make concerns a certain similarity in the public status of their work and its relation to its audience. Dostoevski has for so long been accepted as one of the dominating figures of world literature that it comes as something of a shock to realize how much hostility he encountered during his lifetime. His major novels were published in Russia at a time when liberal and radical opinion dominated among the intelligentsia; and each of his great works was ferociously attacked. (The inferior *A Raw Youth,* published in a left-wing journal, escaped such censure, while *Notes from Underground* was simply ignored.) For conservatives, who wished only to let sleeping dogs lie and to defend the existing regime at all costs, Dostoevski's books were hardly consoling either; they were too probing and raised far too many fundamental questions. His novels really satisfied nobody's politics; but they imposed themselves by the sheer power and force of their art and the profundity of their vision.

Today, the spiritual descendants of the Russian radicals of the 1860s form the ruling class of Dostoevski's homeland. The very ideas against which he fought lie at the heart of the social and cultural ideology they have imposed. The guardians of official Soviet culture are perfectly aware that the later Dostoevski undermines all their most cherished dogmas. They would dearly like to get him out of the way, and even tried to do so during the heyday of Stalin. But Dostoevski adds too much glory to Russian literature to be lightly discarded. The Soviets are now in the process of publishing a splendid collected edition of his works in thirty volumes, whose completion will constitute a remarkable achievement of Soviet scholarship. But most of the copies are sent abroad immediately, and those remaining in the Soviet Union are extremely difficult for the average citizen to procure. Until recently the later novels were rarely republished, although the earlier (socialist-influenced) work came out in editions of several hundred thousand. On my last visit to a Russian bookstore, however, I became aware that the later novels are now also being republished in cheap editions and in hundreds of thousands of copies. Dostoevski is still a thorn in the flesh of the Soviet establishment, but he cannot simply be plucked out and thrown aside; his work refuses to be ignored or suppressed.

The position of Ralph Ellison in the United States is, happily, very different, and yet certain parallels exist all the same. *Invisible Man* was hailed as a masterpiece immediately on its publication, and Ralph Ellison's reputation has maintained its high stature through the intervening years. Yet, as the controversy with Irving Howe indicates, Ellison has come under fire for some of the same reasons that Dostoevski was also assailed. During the turbulent 1960s, these attacks, launched by left-wing spokesmen for the new upsurge of black nationalism, mounted in frequency and ferocity. Ralph Ellison became the hated enemy against whom the new black nationalist literati felt it necessary to discharge their long pent-up resentment and rage. While he maintained a quiet dignity in the face of the storm, even managing to jest about it in conversation, he was deeply wounded by the unfair and intemperate charges leveled against him in print and in person when he appeared on the lecture platform.

The storm seems happily to have abated recently, though, and the wind to have shifted, if I am to judge by a thoughtful and informative article of John Wright in an issue of the *Carleton Miscellany* largely devoted to Ellison's work.[2] Exactly as in the case of Dostoevski, the power and profundity of his art have imposed themselves despite the onslaught of his ideological foes. It even appears that some of those who had assailed Ellison most ferociously—not all, to be sure—have now begun to realize that the foundation of the new black American culture they are seeking has been laid down in his pages. In an excellent formulation, John Wright speaks of Ellison as "approaching Afro-American life through a psychology of survival and transcendence rather than through a psychology of oppression." Even Ellison's former opponents, he points out, now recognize him as providing "the new black literary radicals with a positive vision of black lifestyles as profoundly human and spiritually sustaining."

It is good to know that at least some of "Uncle Tom's children" (to borrow a phrase from Richard Wright), much more refractory and rebellious than Richard Wright could possibly have believed, have begun to see what they can learn about themselves from Ellison's clear-eyed and vibrantly appreciative vision of Negro American life and culture. As happened with Dostoevski, this vision proved too impressive to be discarded or neglected; it simply had to be assimilated, and the process of re-evaluation seems to be proceeding apace. As a result, a possibility once broached by Ellison is now well on its way to becoming a reality. ''Perhaps,'' he remarked in his controversy with Howe, ''if I write well enough the children of today's Negroes will be proud that I did, and so, perhaps, will Irving Howe's.'' The classic status now unanimously accorded to *Invisible Man* indicates that this generous hope has come true.

NOTES

1. Later, in the 1860s, the idea that literature should serve only as an auxiliary in the battle for a better social world was codified into an aesthetic theory by N. G. Chernyshevski. Chernyshevski's theory became the basis of what is now considered the Marxist conception of art. Actually, it is the Russian radical conception; nothing in Marx himself required such a subordination or regimentation of art in the exclusive service of social struggle.

2. See John Wright's essay, ''Shadowing Ellison,'' in this volume, 63–88, which is an abridged version of the longer essay ''Dedicated Dreamer, Consecrated Acts: Shadowing Ellison.'' That longer version originally appeared in *Carleton Miscellany* 18, No. 3 (Winter 1980): 142–99.

The Rules of Magic: Hemingway as Ellison's "Ancestor"

ROBERT G. O'MEALLY

We get changes of identity, often symbolized—in strict obedience to the rules of magic—by the changing of one's name, as the new synthetic character is felt to require a corresponding verbal change; or there is a formal choice of "ancestors," as one in meeting the exigencies of his present, *proposes to coerce the* future *by a quasi-mystical revising of the* past.

Kenneth Burke
Attitudes Toward History

True jazz is an art of individual assertion within and against the group. Each true jazz moment (as distinct from the uninspired commercial performance) springs from a contest in which each artist challenges all the rest; each solo flight, or improvisation, represents (like the successive canvases of a painter) a definition of his identity: as individual, as member of the collectivity and as a link in the chain of tradition.

Ralph Ellison
Shadow and Act

There has been much ado about Ralph Ellison's complex debt to Richard Wright. Ellison himself shifts back and forth uncomfortably. He comes closest to explaining his own uneasiness in the face of any simplistic formulation of his literary paternity when he reminds his readers of his own father's untimely death and of his ambivalent feelings about the stepfathers that took his place. When he met Wright the last thing Ellison wanted was another father.[1] But then again it is Ellison who calls the name of father when invoking the images of certain favorite "ancestors," notably William Faulkner and Ernest Hemingway.[2] In some ways, the Faulkner example is as easy to see as the Wright: in Ellison's fiction one hears a voice as deeply southern as Faulkner's—a voice as rich and as quick with exalted southern lies, told with conversational jam-session style as well as with poetic eloquence. In both writers, too, one finds the shared impulse for technical experimentation along with a shared vision of the human plight, and of man's capacity to overcome.

Yet it is Ernest Hemingway whom Ellison most emphatically chooses as his own, even pitting him against Wright. Why was Wright "family" and Hemingway a chosen "ancestor?" In 1964 Ellison wrote:

> Not because he [Hemingway] was white or "accepted." But because he appreciated the things of this earth which I love and which Wright was too driven or deprived or inexperienced to know: weather, guns, dogs, horses, love *and* hate and impossible circumstances which to the courageous and dedicated could be turned into benefits and victories. Because he wrote with such precision about the processes and techniques of daily living that I could keep myself and my brother alive during the 1937 Recession by following his descriptions of wing-shooting; because he knew the difference between politics and art and something of their true relationship for the writer. Because all that he wrote—and this is very important—was imbued with a spirit beyond the tragic with which I could feel at home, for it was very close to the feeling of the blues, which are, perhaps, as close as Americans can come to expressing the spirit of tragedy. . . . But most important, because Hemingway was a greater artist than Wright, who although a Negro like myself, and perhaps a great man, understood little if anything of these, at least to me, important things. Because Hemingway loved the American language and the joy of writing, making the flight of birds, the loping of lions across an African plain, the mysteries of drink and moonlight, the unique styles of diverse peoples and individuals come alive on the page. Because he was in many ways the true father-as-artist of so many of us who came to writing during the late thirties.[3]

The essay from which this excerpt comes tries to refute the "segregated" idea that black artists must depend on other black artists as prime models and teachers. Ellison brings home his rhetorical point by preferring Hemingway, in whose work one finds no admirable Afro-American characters: instead one finds wisecracks about background "niggers" with flashing smiles. But Ellison's point is not "merely" rhetorical. Ellison has changed his mind about Hemingway, and then changed it again. In his essays and fiction, one finds the younger writer steadily conjuring with Hemingway-like forms and ideas. Although his writing "voice" has remained his own since 1944, throughout his career Ellison has played Hemingway riffs, somewhat like a jazz player improvising on blues chords—or playing with and then against a jam session "gladiator." Sometimes the Hemingway influence on Ellison is obvious, sometimes not. But for Ellison, Papa Hemingway never completely disappears.

To point out that segregation, particularly in Oklahoma, was neither absolute nor, ironically, without certain benefits, Ellison recalls that as a youngster he read Hemingway while waiting his turn in Negro barbershops in Oklahoma City.[4] Probably what he first saw were the feature stories and "letters" which Hemingway wrote for *Esquire* almost every month during the thirties: dispatches from Europe, Africa, and the West Indies concerning, for the most part, war, bullfights, hunting, boxing, fishing, and, inevitably, the struggle to create good art.[5] But by 1933, when Ellison left Oklahoma to study music at Tuskegee, Hemingway also had published his greatest stories and novels[6] as well as *Death in the Afternoon*. It seems likely that in the local library (also segregated) or in the homes of friends, young Ellison saw some of this Hemingway work, too. In Hemingway's writing, Ellison would easily recognize the frontierlike Michigan, not so unlike the territory just beyond the limits of Oklahoma City. Both places had Indians, vast open spaces, and good areas to fish and hunt. And like Hemingway, Ellison played high school football and could readily identify with the undefeated sportsmen of *Men Without Women* (1927) and *Winner Take Nothing* (1933).

In the beginning, Ellison, a fledgling trumpet player, was claimed by the music of Hemingway's sentences. When the literal meanings escaped him, Ellison could get a sense of what Hemingway was up to by the sheer pitch and rhythm of his writing.[7] And later he related Hemingway's understated but allusive style to jazz:

> Jazz was eclectic . . . at its best. . . . It made the whole world of music, of sound, its own. And it took what it needed from those areas. You hear references to opera, to church music, to anything, in something by Louis Armstrong or any other jazzman of the thirties, forties, or fifties. So this acquaintance with jazz made me quite aware that allusions to ideas and to other works of art were always turning up in Hemingway. (Garrett, 224)

Although he has said that while he was in college Eliot's *Waste Land* "initiated the search" for the sources of literature, Ellison also found that Hemingway's style, especially "the what-was-not-stated in the understatement, required study" (Garrett, 223). Like the blues, Hemingway's style implied a great deal more than was expressed outright (*S&A*, 245).

In Hemingway's fiction what was implied was an heroic attitude toward life's troubles and changes, a resiliency and steadfastness which as an adult Ellison also would connect with the blues. He would not spell it out, but Hemingway could make his reader feel "that some great crisis of courage had occurred and just was not said," notes Ellison. "And I related this to jazz" (Garrett, 223–24). In 1945, Ellison wrote of the blues: "Their attraction lies in this, that they at once express both the agony of life and the possibility of conquering it through sheer toughness of spirit. They fall short of tragedy only in that they provide no scapegoat but the self" (*S&A*, 94). In this spirit, Hemingway's heroes endure with stoicism so much unmeaning agony and terror that Albert Murray calls Hemingway not just a blues writer but "an honorary Negro," a title Hemingway once chose for himself (Murray, "Storyteller," 14). Indeed, what Ellison has written about the blues is also true of certain heroes in Hemingway: "The blues voice . . . mocks the despair stated explicitly in its lyric, and it expresses the great human joke directed against the universe, that joke which is the secret of all folklore and myth: that though we be dismembered daily we shall always rise up again.''[8] Ellison describes Jake Barnes, the wounded survivor and narrator of *The Sun Also Rises* (a novel Murray says could just as well be called ''Jake's Empty Bed Blues,'' ''Blues for Lady Brett,'' or even ''Rocks in My Bed'' [''Storyteller,'' 16]), in terms that express an extreme version of the blues hero's plight and challenge: ''Ball-less, humiliated, malicious, even masochistic, he still has a steady eye upon it all and has the most eloquent ability to convey the texture of his experience.''[9]

In the late 1930s, Ellison reached around those writers of the New Negro Renaissance, much of whose work he felt was stained by the ''moribund'' influence of Carl Van Vechten, and chose Hemingway as a model. Hemingway was simply a ''greater writer than the participants in the Negro Renaissance,'' said Ellison in 1967.[10] Hemingway had spotted the ''so-called 'Jazz Age' [as] a phony, while most Negro writers jumped on the illusory bandwagon when they, of all people, should have known better'' (''Stern Discipline,'' 90). Ellison perceived the Hemingway hero's feeling of being at odds with American society to be quite similar to the feeling of blacks. The Hemingway hero held ''an attitude springing from an awareness that they lived outside the values of the larger society, and *I* feel that their attitudes came closer to the way Negroes felt about the way the Constitution and the Bill of Rights were applied to us'' (93). In this context Hemingway again evokes for Ellison the world of jazz:

> I believe that Hemingway in depicting the attitudes of athletes, expatriots, bullfighters, traumatized soldiers, and impotent idealists, told us quite a lot about what was happening to that most representative group of Negro Americans, the jazz musicians—who also lived by an extreme code of withdrawal, technical and artistic excellence, rejection of the values of respectable society. They replaced the abstract and much betrayed ideals of that society with the more physical values of eating, copulating, loyalty to friends, and dedication to the discipline and values of their art. (93)

Looking back from the vantage point of the sixties (and taking a shot at any black nationalist critics who might be listening), Ellison was quoted as overstating the case by saying that Hemingway ''tells us more about how Negroes feel than all the writings done by those people mixed up in the Negro Renaissance'' (90).

In the mid-1930s, when he first put his trumpet aside and began writing ''in earnest,'' he chose Hemingway (along with Wright) as a principal guide. In 1937, Ellison started reading Hemingway with a writer's eye, trying to learn his sentence structure and his means of organizing a story. He went about the task of learning to write with Hemingway-like intensity and singleness of purpose, and refused for a time even to attend musical performances for fear of being sidetracked (Ellison and Hersey interview). Like a young musician practicing *etudes* (or like an apprentice photographer learning to compose a picture by looking at a master's photographs through a camera lens), Ellison would copy certain Hemingway stories in longhand, "in an effort to study their rhythms, so as not just to know them but to possess them."[11]

A member of the Federal Writers Project (1936–39), Ellison interviewed many black New Yorkers and tried to get their stories on paper. Here Hemingway proved useful. Ellison would listen to his Harlem informants' talk and "very often," he recalls, "I was able to get it on paper by using a kind of Hemingway typography, by using the repetitions. I couldn't quite get the tone of the sounds in, but I could get some of the patterns and get an idea of what it was like." Thus he could avoid "falling into the transcription of dialect," which he had found unsatisfactory in Wright's fiction ("Indivisible," 59). Quite unlike Wright, who, in a typical piece of dialogue in *Uncle Tom's Children* (1938) has Aunt Sue say, "Ahma ol woman n Ah wans yuh t tell me the truth."[12] Project Worker Ellison records the words of a Harlem yarn spinner in this way:

> I hope to God to kill me if this aint the truth. All you got to do is to go down to Florence, South Carolina, and ask most anybody you meet and they'll tell you it's the truth. . . .
>
> Florence is one of these hard towns on colored folks. You have to stay out of the white folks way; all but Sweet. That the fellow I'm fixing to tell you about. His name was Sweet-the-monkey. I done forgot his real name, I caint remember it. But that was what everybody called him. He wasn't no big guy. He was just bad. My mother and my grandmother used to say he was wicked. He was bad all-right. He was one sucker who didn't give a dam bout the crackers. Fact is, they got so they stayed out of *his* way. I caint never remember hear tell of any them crackers bothering that guy. He used to give em trouble all over the place and all they could do about it was to give the rest of us hell.
>
> It was this way: Sweet could make hisself invisible. You don't believe it? Well here's how he done it. Sweet-the-monkey cut open a black cat and took out its heart. Climbed a tree backwards and cursed God. After that he could do anything. The white folks would wake up in the morning and find their stuff gone. He cleaned out the stores. He cleaned up the houses. Hell, he even cleaned out the dam bank! He was the boldest *black* sonofabitch ever been down that way. And couldn't nobody do nothing to him. . . .[13]

In this passage Ellison was obviously practicing how to capture the sounds of vernacular speech without distracting the reader with a thicket of misspellings and apostrophes.

Impressed particularly by the Oklahoman's ability to talk about Hemingway, Wright had invited Ellison to contribute to *New Challenge* magazine in 1937. Ellison's first review, which pinpointed the need for "greater development in technique" ("Creative and Cultural Lag," 91), and his short story,

"Hymie's Bull" (which did not appear because the magazine folded), were both stamped in the Hemingway mold. With poetic directness and rhythmic style, the young reporter Hemingway had written in 1922 about fishing the Rhone Canal:

> It is a good walk in to Aigue. There are horse chestnut trees along the road with their flowers that look like wax candles and the air is warm from the heat absorbed from the sun. The road is white and dusty, and I thought of Napoleon's grand army, marching along it through the white dust on the way to the St. Bernard pass and Italy. Napoleon's batman may have gotten up at sun up before the camp and sneaked a trout or two out of the Rhone Canal for the Little Corporal's breakfast. And before Napoleon, the Romans came along the valley and built this road and some Helvetian in the road gang probably used to sneak away from the camp in the evening to try for a big one in one of the pools under the willows. In the Roman days the trout perhaps were not as shy. (*By-Line*, 35)

And in a feature story entitled "A Congress Jim Crow Didn't Attend" (1939), Ellison's report for *New Masses* on the National Negro Congress, one overhears Hemingway's cadences and deadpan tone in the face of dramatic action which is deliberately detailed. Ellison writes:

> Outside of Baltimore we began passing troupes of cavalry. They were stretched along the highway for a mile. Young fellows in khaki with campaign hats strapped beneath their chins, jogging stiffly in their saddles. I asked one of my companions where they were going and was told that there was an army camp near by. Someone said that I would find out "soon enough" and I laughed and said I was a black Yank and was not coming. (5)

Later in the same piece, Ellison describes the conference meeting hall in Hemingway terms:

> The auditorium had that overwhelming air usually associated with huge churches, and I remembered what André Malraux once said about the factory becoming for the workers what the cathedral was, and that they must come to see in it not ideal gods, but human power struggling against the earth. (7)

In 1932 Hemingway wrote: "If a writer of prose knows enough about what he is writing about he may omit things that he knows and the reader, if the writer is writing truly enough, will have a feeling of those things as strongly as though the writer had stated them" (*Death*, 192). Hemingway's famous use of understatement intrigued young Ellison, but early on he had serious doubts that it was a style he wanted to incorporate into his own writing. In his 1940 review for *New Masses* of Langston Hughes's first autobiography, *The Big Sea*, Ellison takes Hughes to task for understating the meanings of too many experiences. Radical Ellison's objections were not just political but artistic:

> In his next book . . . we hope that besides the colorful incidents, the word pictures, the feel, the taste, and smell of his experiences, Langston Hughes will

> tell us more of how he felt and thought about them. For while the style of *The Big Sea* is charming in its simplicity, it is a style that depends upon understatement for its most important effects. Many *New Masses* readers will question whether this is a style suitable for the autobiography of a Negro writer of Hughes's importance; the national and class position should guide his selection of techniques, and method should influence his style. In the style of *The Big Sea* too much attention is apt to be given to the esthetic aspects of experience at the expense of its deeper meanings. Nor—this being a world in which few assumptions may be taken for granted—can the writer who depends upon understatement to convey these meanings be certain that they do not escape the reader. To be effective the Negro writer must be explicit; thus realistic; thus dramatic. . . . When Hughes avoids analysis and comment, and, in some instances, emotion, a deeper unity is lost. This is that unity which is formed by the mind's brooding over experience and transforming it into conscious thought. Negro writing needs this unity, through which the writer clarifies the experiences of the reader and allows him to recreate himself. (''Stormy Weather,'' 20)

Contrast this appraisal of Hughes's self-portrait with an early statement (preceding the novel's publication by four years) by Ellison of his intentions for *Invisible Man*'s hero: ''I am attempting to create a character who possesses both the eloquence and the insight into the interconnections between his own personality and the world about him to make a judgment upon our culture.''[14] He did not want his book to be narrowly topical, but rather he wanted it to state its case explicitly and to draw fairly definite conclusions about the state of the nation. He did not want to ''explain his book away'' (*à la* the naturalists), but he did want his ideas made clear. And although Invisible Man is a simple man (even a naive simpleton) during most of Ellison's novel, eventually he wakes up and is more able than Hughes of *The Big Sea*, or virtually any Hemingway character, to express what he's gone through, and to do so in precise, comprehensive terms.

In 1940, Ellison went so far as to declare that although the ''hardboiled'' Hemingway style was successful for conveying American violence (''a quality as common to Negro life as to the lives of Hemingway characters''),[15] it nonetheless had a ''negative philosophical basis'' (''Prize Fighter,'' 26–27). This was Ellison's most stinging criticism of work by the writer he had idealized. Even after starting on *Invisible Man*, Ellison's dissatisfaction with Hemingway seemed to center on what went unstated or understated in Hemingway's prose. In the mid-1940s Ellison expressed concern about the fact that no fully drawn blacks appear in Hemingway's work; how did he feel then about black freedom, and about the black American's tragic quest for equality? Ellison had begun to feel that the concern for the Negro and for the values which his presence connoted in American fiction were not just *unspoken* by Hemingway, they were *nonexistent*. ''It is not accidental'' wrote Ellison in 1946, ''that the disappearance of the human Negro from our fiction coincides with the disappearance of deep-probing doubt and a sense of evil'' (*S&A*, 35). Perhaps Hemingway was not so much the spokesman for the

1920s Lost Generation as he was "a product of a tradition which arose even before the Civil War—that tradition of intellectual evasion for which Thoreau criticized Emerson in regard to the Fugitive Slave Law and which has been growing swiftly since the failure of the ideals in whose name the Civil War was fought" (*S&A*, 36). Rather than probing "the roots of American culture" Hemingway "restricted himself to elaborating his personal style." This narrow naturalist explored neither society nor morality, but instead indulged in "working out a personal problem through the evocative, emotion-charged images and ritual-therapy available through the manipulation of art forms." If freedom was still at issue, it was solely *personal* freedom; and if the writing involved rituals, they were cynical rituals of defeat:

> Beneath the dead-pan prose [wrote Ellison] the cadences of understatement, the anti-intellectualism [lies] the concern with every "fundamental" of man except that which distinguishes him from the animal. . . . Here is the twentieth-century form of that magical rite which during periods of great art has been to a large extent public and explicit. Here is the literary form by which the personal guilt of the pulverized individual of our rugged era is expiated: not through his identification with the guilty acts of an Oedipus, a MacBeth or a Medea, by suffering their agony and loading his sins upon their "strong and passionate shoulders," but by being gored with a bull, hooked with a fish, impaled with a grasshopper on a fishhook; not by identifying himself with human heroes, but with those who are indeed defeated. (*S&A*, 39–40)

Flashing technique for its own sake, this writing, like the stereotype in literature, conditions the reader to complacent inaction, said Ellison. "And when I read the early Hemingway," wrote Ellison, "I seem to be in the presence of a Huckleberry Finn who . . . chose to write the letter which sent Jim back into slavery" (40).

Ellison's own fiction since 1944 shows that he has remained dissatisfied with understatement as a technique to express his own sense of the American scene. In addition to its other problems, the clipped phrases of the understated speaker did not compare, he wrote in 1953, with "the rich babel of idiomatic expression" which he heard in New York, and which he had known in the South. Robert Penn Warren has written that Hemingway's "short, simple rhythms, the succession of coordinate clauses, the general lack of subordination—all suggest a dislocated and ununified world. The figures who live in this world live a sort of hand-to-mouth existence perceptually, and conceptually. Subordination implies some exercise of discrimination—the shifting of reality through the intellect. But in Hemingway we see a Romantic anti-intellectualism."[16]

The author of *Invisible Man* sifts through reality in sentences which, in their driving complexity, often echo Faulkner or Wright more than they do Hemingway. The reality Ellison wished to project in fiction was so "mysterious and uncertain and . . . exciting," he said, that it would "burst . . . the neatly understated forms of the novel asunder" (*S&A*, 104). In 1955,

Ellison told a symposium of writers that his former mentor's laconic characters may have expressed the disillusionment of the postwar era, but when the Depression hit and "reality was ripping along," Hemingway's images no longer were adequate as a guide for confronting experience.[17] Hemingway had produced fiction that was ultimately too provincial to escape its particular setting and time. Yet, surprisingly, in the same discussion, Ellison also spoke up in defense of Hemingway: He "links up pretty close to Twain," he said ("What's Wrong," 495).

This linkage with Twain, which, for Ellison, spells adherence to the American novel's greatest themes and most characteristic forms—this sense of belonging to the national literary canon encompassing nineteenth-century prose masters along with contemporary stylists—is the theme of most of Ellison's literary essays from the fifties on.[18] And his connection of Hemingway with Twain signaled that Ellison had begun again to change his mind about what was implied "beneath the dead-pan cadences" of Hemingway's prose. By 1957 he was back squarely in Hemingway's corner. "Neither the American fiction of the twenties nor of the fifties," wrote Ellison in 1957, "can be understood outside the perspective provided by the nineteenth century."[47] For it was in the nineteenth century that Emerson, Thoreau, Whitman, Melville, Twain, James, and Crane (among others, of course, but this is the line of nineteenth-century writers that Ellison usually marshalls) wrote explicitly about American democracy and the lingering problem of freedom and unfreedom as it centered on the man beneath the social hierarchy, the Negro. With the great nineteenth-century themes in mind, Ellison now read *A Farewell to Arms* as an ironic comment upon, and ultimately a ringing affirmation of, the "sacred assumptions" of American life:

> For as I read Hemingway today [1957] I find that he affirms the old American values by the eloquence of his denial; makes his moral point by stating explicitly that he does not believe in morality; achieves his eloquence through denying eloquence; and is most moral when he denies the validity of a national morality which the nation has not bothered to live up to since the Civil War. ("Society," 74)

The confusion about Hemingway's motives—about what went unsaid in his fiction—stemmed not from a failure on the author's part, Ellison now argued, but on the part of his readers and his less skilled and less moral imitators. "For although it is seldom mentioned," wrote Ellison, "Hemingway is as obsessed with the Civil War and its aftermath as any Southern writer" (74). When Hemingway's Nick or Jake took to the woods for a round of fishing or hunting (and when Frederic declared his separate peace), they turned their backs on a society whose ideals had become so tarnished that they preferred to set up frontier outposts (like Huck and Jim's raft) where the values of freedom and friendship could be upheld, if only in a short space and time. What went unstated in Hemingway then was a firm belief in the American social ideals of liberty and democracy.

Obviously, Ellison's changed view of Hemingway's content was linked with a changed view of his style. What in the forties Ellison had begun to put down as Hemingway's decadent ''morality of craftsmanship,'' he now described as Hemingway's fineness of technique. This was not dry gear-shifting for kicks, but careful maneuvering of the reader into full and moral perspective on life in our time. True enough, most of Hemingway's readers and imitators forgot all about the moral dimension of American life and literature, misreading Hemingway and using his work as a model for their own escapist and self-indulgent fantasies. But the writer's technique itself, said Ellison in 1957, has moral implications, despite all abuses by poor writers. Even when ''the question of the Sphinx was lost in the conundrums'' of perfectly turned phrases, the Hemingway-inspired emphasis on the value of technique reminded readers that ''literature, to the extent that it is art, is *artificial*'' (''Society,'' 78). This reminder that literature is man-made is a moral reminder insofar as it helps the reader recall that language can be seductive, therapeutic, even magical. However beckoning it may be, though, it can express falsehood as well as truth. This awareness of literature as rhetoric serves as a warning for all readers to remain on guard as critics, ever aware that the most alluring fictions—be they novelistic, historical, or religious—are skillful acts of word-magic, brightly inviting castles of language. It is up to the reader to read with enough perspicuity to decide what is true and right, and to set the rest aside.

By the 1960s and 1970s, Ellison would extend this metaphor of ''morality of craftsmanship'' (now an encomium)[19] in important ways. For the writer, he said, ''craft under the pressure of inspiration'' is the crucial formula:

> It's one thing to have a feeling, an insight, to hear in your mind's ear a rhythm, or to conceive an image. It is the *craft*, the knowledge of what other people have done, of what has been achieved by those great creators of the novel which gives you some idea of the possibility of that image, that nuance, that rhythm, that dramatic situation. It's not dry technique or craft that I'm talking about; it's craft which makes it possible for you to be more or less conscious of what you are doing and of the tools that you have to work with. (WGBH-TV interview)

Repeatedly, Ellison uses the example of the medical doctor to discuss the responsibility of the writer.[20] A physician misdiagnosed his own mother's illness and caused her untimely death. A surgeon's slip killed Bennie Moten, then at the top of his career as a jazz bandleader, and his fans wanted to lynch his careless doctor. Writers, in Ellison's view, also have lives in their hands and thus bear a social (at times Ellison uses the word *sacred*) responsibility to know what they are doing. In 1942, Hemingway had compared the writer's calling to that of the priest:

> A writer should be of as great probity and honesty as a priest of God. . . . A writer's job is to tell the truth. His standard of fidelity to the truth should be

> so high that his invention, out of his experience, should produce a truer account than anything factual can be. For facts can be observed badly; but when a good writer is creating something, he has time and scope to make of it an absolute truth. (*Men at War*, xv)

Ellison elaborates on this insight, observing that not only must the moral writer always do the best work he can; but when "you [writers] describe a more viable and ethical way of living and denounce the world or a great part of society for the way it conducts its affairs and then write in a sloppy way or present issues in a simplistic or banal way, then you're being amoral as an artist" (*Washington Post*, B3). Since writers provide "disastrously explicit" images, ones which influence readers in their search for the meanings of their lives, then false images, or images faultily projected by inadequate craft, can cause confusion, dismay, and even death.

The writer's task, Ellison has said, is to do nothing less than to help create reality. "While fiction is but a form of symbolic action," he wrote in 1981, "a mere game of 'as if,' therein lies its true function and its potential for effecting change. For at its most serious . . . it is a thrust toward a human ideal. And it approaches that ideal by a subtle process of negating the world of things as given in favor of a complex of manmade positives."[21] Isn't that just wishful thinking, though? Aren't you "expressing your own hopes and aspirations for Negroes, rather than reporting historical reality?" he was asked in an interview in 1967. "But hope and aspiration are indeed important aspects of the reality of Negro American life, no less than that of others," he replied. "Literature teaches us that mankind has always defined itself *against* the negatives thrown it by society and the universe. . . . Let's not forget that the great tragedies not only treat of negative matters, of violence, brutalities, defeats, but they treat them within a context of man's will to act, to challenge reality and to snatch triumph from the teeth of destruction" ("Stern Discipline," 84). The writer imbued with the proper sense of his craft's "sacredness" knows that his job is to provide readers with strategies for confronting the chaos of the contemporary world—or, in Kenneth Burke's phrase often quoted by Ellison, to provide the reader with necessary "equipment for living."[22]

Which brings us to *Invisible Man*—Ellison's most comprehensive piece of "equipment for living." How does Hemingway figure there? Invisible Man, like most of the heroes of Ellison's short stories, is an intelligent and sensitive youngster, a brown-skinned cousin of Nick Adams, straining toward manhood in a world full of the blues. And certain of *Invisible Man*'s controlling metaphors mirror images and actions in Hemingway's work: notably the metaphors of life as a war, a game or a fight (or a prizefight, or even a bullfight)—life as an encounter between the individual and the forces set against him. Like the old waiter of "A Clean, Well-Lighted Place," Invisible has been through a lot, and needs plenty of light (in the case of Ellison's character, 1,369 filament bulbs) to feel secure in the threatening world. Furthermore,

Invisible Man itself comprises a classic defense of art that recalls defenses by Aristotle, Plato, and Shelley; but more specifically it is framed in terms that bring to mind Hemingway's descriptions of fighters, sportsmen, and writers as artists who assert their values and skills against encroachments by fakers, fools, and unfeeling power brokers, and sometimes by killers. Invisible Man, like Hemingway's apprentice heroes, learns at last to confront his experience directly, and he earns the perspective that it takes to do what Jake Barnes can do—to tell his troubling tale with the force and eloquence of an artist. Ellison informs his reader that almost as soon as he first heard, in his mind's ear, the words "I am an invisible man," the voice sounded "with a familiar timbre of voice": unmistakably black American, ringing with blues-toned irony.[23] Just as *The Sun Also Rises* makes us wonder how Jake achieves his ironic voice, his truce with his grim reality, this novel traces Invisible Man's achievement of a voice with which to state (and thus to overcome) the trouble he has seen.

In one of the novel's key passages, Invisible Man hears his grandfather's deathbed words, spoken to Invisible's father:

> "Son [the old man said], after I'm gone I want you to keep up the good fight. I never told you, but our life is a war and I have been a traitor all my born days, a spy in the enemy's country ever since I give up my gun back in the Reconstruction. Live with your head in the lion's mouth. I want you to overcome 'em with grins, agree 'em to death and destruction, let 'em swoller you till they vomit or bust wide open. . . . Learn it to the younguns," he whispered fiercely; then he died. (*IM*, 13–14)

To unlock the full meaning of these magic words, the puzzled grandson must journey through hundreds of pages of hard and contradictory living. What he finally discovers is that life *is* a war, and it is a war wherein to be a good soldier, snapping to attention and obeying all orders, is to work against one's people and oneself. In this cosmic war the first step toward victory involved more than learning the techniques of warfare; it involved getting oriented by realizing that things "ain't what they used to be," and that they are not even what they seem now. It involved having a mature perspective on oneself, on one's ideals, and on one's enemies, in whose very camp one must dwell. In short, the key was to become *conscious* in a profound sense: resigned like a bluesman to a life of war.

Significantly, the war the grandfather refers to is linked, in his dying speech, with the American Civil War.[24] Although he has long since given up his gun, he tells his son to "learn it to the younguns," the grandchildren a generation removed from the War Between the States. The point, as Ellison has said repeatedly from beyond the text, is that the Civil War continues in America. The issues of property versus human rights; individual, state, and sectional autonomy versus the power of the union; and a sheaf of other definitively American political and economic issues—centering on the abiding problem of Negro freedom—remain unresolved. American life, to paraphrase the old man, is a civil war in which the black man (and everyone) must fight, over and over again, to be free. Part of becoming conscious involves seeing, as Invisible eventually does, that his problem is not unique: "It goes a long way back, some twenty years." And it goes back still further, at least back to the nineteenth century when the Civil War was fought and when, for a brief moment during Reconstruction, Americans tried to live up to the implications surrounding that clash. "The writer is forged in injustice as a sword is forged," wrote Hemingway.[25] And a war, especially a civil war, can make or break a writer, he said. His own code heroes are often soldiers at war who must test themselves not just in theory but in the real world of intense, dangerous action. The Civil War in the background of *Invisible Man* (surfacing especially in allusions to Douglass and to other nineteenth-century writers and erupting in the riot at the novel's climax) helps to forge Invisible's consciousness as a man of eloquence who is able "to make a judgment about our culture."

Conditioning by the mass media blinds today's readers to the fact that *Invisible Man* is an extraordinarily violent novel, so violent that Ellison wondered if antiviolence commentators would snipe at the book. Fights occur in scene after scene—hand-to-hand battles, which rehearse the background struggle of the continuing Civil War. Invisible's fight with the "blind" white man in the Prologue, the yokel's fight with the prizefighter of scientific method, the battle-royal free-for-all, the Golden Day fisticuffs, Invisible against Lucius Brockway, Tod and Invisible versus Ras, and Tod versus the cops are just some of the novel's main fights. Several allusions are made to the Johnson and Jeffries fight—that symbolic encounter between the races. At one point Bledsoe promises to help Invisible because the young man shows ire and "the race needs smart, disillusioned fighters."

> Therefore [Bledsoe goes on] I'm going to give you a hand—maybe you'll feel that I'm giving you my left hand after I've struck you with my right—if you think I'm the kind of man who'd lead with his right, which I'm most certainly not. (*IM*, 112)

Up North, the Brotherhood meetings were generally as noisy and smoky as smokers or prizefights, the reader is told; in fact, Invisible's first speech is made in the very auditorium where, significantly enough, a popular fighter had lost his vision in the ring. Each of these physical fights, brawls, and prizefights has its own symbolic meaning. But one can say that in the world of *Invisible Man* the struggle for meaning and endurance is not only metaphysical but physical. The would-be hero must put his own body on the line, and only if he has the resiliency, the strength, and the technical skill can he avoid a whipping—or, if he cannot avoid a whipping, he can at least know what it's for. Lacking science and quickness, the Prologue yokel prevails through sheer strength and inspired timing:

> The fighter was swift and amazingly scientific. His body was one violent flow of rapid rhythmic action. He hit the yokel a hundred times while the yokel held

> up his arms in stunned surprise. But suddenly the yokel, rolling about in the gale of boxing gloves, struck one blow and knocked science, speed and footwork as cold as a well-digger's posterior. The smart money hit the canvas. The long shot got the nod. The yokel had simply stepped inside of his opponent's sense of time. (*IM*, 7)

The Invisible Man, the comic yokel for most of the novel, is battered by swift and scientific battlers in scene after scene. In time, of course, he learns that to prevail he must have science *and* power—and an alert sense of what time it is; he must be both *hare* and *bear*. But he finds out that either way, life will give him a thrashing to remember.

What he learns, too, is the Hemingway lesson: that he is caught up in a violent game which, like the fight game, attains a certain grace when played well. The banished Golden Day inmate (one of the crazy war veterans) gives some advice on how life's game is played:

> "For God's sake, learn to look beneath the surface," he said. "Come out of the fog, young man. And remember you don't have to be a complete fool in order to succeed. Play the game, but don't believe in it—that much you owe yourself. Even if it lands you in a strait jacket or a padded cell. Play the game, but play it your own way—part of the time at least. Play the game, but raise the ante, my boy. Learn how it operates, learn how you operate. . . . You might even beat the game. . . . Down here they've forgotten to take care of the books and that's your opportunity. . . ." (*IM*, 118)

Here Ellison defines the "they" against which Invisible's most strenuous fight must be waged: "They?" says the vet. "Why the same *they* we always mean, the white folks, authority, the gods, fate, circumstances—the force that pulls your strings until you refuse to be pulled any more. The big man who's never there, where you think he is" (*IM*, 118). To an extent it is the "*nada y pues nada*"[26] that Hemingway's heroes struggle against; the sense of dissolution and meaninglessness and the excruciating pain threatening the prizefighter Jack in Hemingway's "Fifty Grand" (*Fifth Column*, 398–424), the ever-ready opponent that threatens to sock you blind. Then, too, more than for Hemingway, Ellison's "big man who's never there" is Clio, he is *History*.

Ellison's "they" is nonetheless comparable to the bull which Hemingway's matadors must confront, and which, in the symbolic language of *Invisible Man*, the "youngun" from the South must learn to bring down. Hemingway's *Death in the Afternoon* comprises a handbook of bullfighting and a prose-poem on the poetics of the *toreo*. It teaches that the bullfight is not so much a game (or fair contest between equals) as it is a tragedy and a ritual. It is the tragedy of the bull which, whether goring or even killing its opponent or not, is doomed to die. (A bull that bests its matador has no more value as a fighter because the experience of winning makes it too skillful an opponent for the next matador to have the slightest chance against, so successful bulls also meet "death in the afternoon" of their first and last bullfights.) This tragic drama celebrates the doomed bull's best qualities. With the exuberance of the aficionado, Hemingway describes the magnificence of the fighting bull:

> Bulls in Spain have been known to charge a motor car and even, getting onto the tracks, to stop a train, refusing to back up or leave the track when the train stopped and when, with much blowing of the whistle the train finally advanced, charging the engine blindly. A really brave fighting bull is afraid of nothing on earth. . . . [He] can turn on his feet almost as a cat does. (Hemingway, *Death*, 109)

And furthermore:

> The bravery of a truly brave bull is something unearthly and unbelievable. The bravery is not merely viciousness, ill-temper, and the panic-bred courage of a cornered animal. The bull is a fighting animal and when the fighting strain has been kept pure and all cowardice bred out he becomes often, when not fighting, the quietest and most peaceful acting in repose, of any animal. It is not the bulls that are the most difficult to handle that make the best bullfights. The best of all fighting bulls have a quality, called nobility by the Spanish, which is the most extraordinary part of the whole business. The bull is a wild animal whose greatest pleasure is combat and which will accept combat offered to it in any form, or will take up anything it believes to be an offer of combat. (*Death*, 113)

It takes a good bull for the matador to do his job well. Slow or cowardly bulls, or bulls that have poor eyesight including, Hemingway specifies, one-eyed bulls (*tuertos*) (488), make dull and difficult killing. For the drama to attain the level of tragedy, the bull must have heroic parts; otherwise its death can seem cruel or even savagely comic.

Of course, the matador is the other leading character in the tragedy of the bull. Not only is Hemingway's ideal matador brave, aggressive, quick, highly skilled, and intelligent; he is an artist. In his stances, approaches, gestures, and in his style of luring and evading and then killing the bull, the bullfighter demonstrates his art. Though his creations are unpreservable, the matador's work still has lasting value and his medium is not unlike a sculptor's. Indeed, Hemingway claims to "know no modern sculpture, except Brancusi's, that is in any way the equal of the sculpture of modern bullfighting" (*Death*, 99). Furthermore, "it is impossible to believe the emotional and spiritual intensity and pure, classic beauty that can be produced by a man, an animal and a piece of scarlet serge draped over a stick" (207).

For the aficionado the ultimate meaning of the bullfight devolves from the ritual of life and death reenacted in the *toreo*. Hemingway calls the graceful action of a master bullfighter so deeply moving

> that [it] takes a man out of himself and makes him feel immortal while it is proceeding . . . . [It] gives him an ecstasy, that is, while momentary, as profound as any religious ecstasy; moving all the people in the ring together and increasing in emotional intensity as it proceeds, carrying the bullfighter with it, he playing on the crowd through the bull and being moved as it responds in

> a growing ecstasy of ordered, formal, passionate, increasing disregard for death that leaves you, when it is over, and the death administered to the animal that had made it possible, as empty, as changed and as sad as any major emotion will leave you. (206–07)

In language again quite effectively incongruous for a description of a blood and bones bullfight, Hemingway explains:

> The essence of the greatest emotional appeal of bullfighting is the feeling of immortality that the bullfighter feels in the middle of a great faena [maneuver] and that he gives to the spectators. He is performing a work of art and he is playing with death, bringing it closer, closer, closer to himself, a death that you know is in the horns because you have the canvas-covered bodies of the horses on the sand to prove it. He gives the feeling of his immortality, and, as you watch it, it becomes yours. (213)

Conditioned by a long apprenticeship, gored at least once so he knows how to come back from a horn wound, the ideal matador dominates his bull with courage, know-how, and quick reflexes. He stands at the center of a ritual in which man's "grace under pressure," even in the face of violent death, is tested. For Hemingway, he is not just *an* artist; the matador is the prototype of the artist, the idealized human. "Nobody," says Jake in *The Sun Also Rises*, "ever lives their lives all the way up except bullfighters" (10).

Bulls and bullfighting figure in *Invisible Man* in crucial ways. Metaphors that bring to mind the tragedy of the bull, as Hemingway glosses it, are, in fact, central to the novel's meanings. Waking on the morning before he takes his last Bledsoe letter to Emerson (whose son, true to this extent to the nineteenth-century Emerson's ideals, tries to tell him not to be naïve), Invisible feels a wave of nostalgia for the campus he has left behind. Ironically enough, what he recalls about the southern wasteland is a scene of sexual vibrancy in which the bull plays a part: "What were they doing now on campus? Had the moon sunk low and the sun climbed clear? Had the breakfast bugle blown? Did the bellow of the big seed bull awaken the girls in the dorms this morning as on most spring mornings when I was there—sounding clear and full above bells and bugles and early workaday sounds?" (*IM*, 131). Invisible does not, of course, comprehend the irony in this scene. He could not connect his vision of a wasteland and a bull with the world of *The Sun Also Rises*, wherein the wastelanders move aimlessly from scene to scene, unregenerated by the ceremony—the fiesta of the *bull*.[27]

Before long, Invisible and Tod Clifton are tested as they fight for political power against Ras the Exhorter/Destroyer, or, if you will, Ras the Bull. In a variation on the Prologue encounter between the yokel and the scientific fighter, Ras tries to use bull strength against Tod, who maneuvers with speed and fine technique:

> Clifton's arms were moving in short, accurate jabs against the head and stomach of Ras the Exhorter, punching swiftly and scientifically, careful not to knock

> him into the window or strike the glass with his fists, working Ras between rights and lefts jabbed so fast that he rocked like a drunken bull, from side to side to side. And as I came up Ras tried to bull his way out and I saw Clifton drive him back and down into a squat, his hands upon the dark floor of the lobby, his heels back against the door like a runner against starting blocks. And now, shooting forward, he caught Clifton coming in, butting him, and I heard the burst of breath and Clifton was on his back and something flashed in Ras's hand and he came forward, a short, heavy figure as wide as the lobby now with the knife, moving deliberately . . . [Ras was] panting, bull angry. . . . "Mahn," Ras blurted, "I ought to kill you. Godahm. . . ." (*IM*, 279)

Tod's science is not enough to bring down this thick bull, whose strong and well-timed charge brings him temporary victory. But racial loyalty won't let Ras kill Tod. "You *my* brother mahn. . . . We sons of Mother Africa, you done forgot?" (278) he says, releasing Tod. But again Invisible (who, in this scene, is less a participant than a witness, like Jake in *The Sun Also Rises*) sees what he's up against. He and the Brotherhood may command science, but the bull sometimes can rush science and bring the house crashing down.

The most capricious and powerful "bull" in *Invisible Man* is not so much a toro as such as he is a "toy bull terrier," or some sort of bull*dog*. Waiting to give his first speech as a member of the Brotherhood, Invisible recalls his childhood days and a neighborhood bulldog.

> A huge black-and-white dog, log-chained to an apple tree. It was Master, the bulldog; and I was the child who was afraid to touch him, although, panting with heat, he seemed to grin back at me like a fat good-natured man, the saliva roping silvery from his jowls. And as the voices of the crowd churned and mounted and became an impatient splatter of hand claps, I thought of Master's low hoarse growl. He had barked the same note when angry or when being brought his dinner, when lazily snapping flies, or when tearing an intruder to shreds. I liked, but didn't trust old Master; I wanted to please, but did not trust the crowd. Then I looked at Brother Jack and grinned: That was it; in some ways, he was like a toy bull terrier. (255–56)

He had seen it earlier, Jack's resemblance to "a lively small animal, a fyce" (219). But by naming him a *bull*dog, the narrator heightens the irony of the situation. Fyce or toy or terrier—however petite or petty he may be—this bull is muscular, tenacious, and capable of as much quick violence as apparent good humor. That Invisible connects him with "Master" of his childhood increases the irony's tension by yet another notch. When Invisible finally sees through Jack (an unpredictably dangerous one-eyed bull), the black man turns on him saying, "Who are you, anyway, the great white father? . . . Wouldn't it be better if they called you Marse Jack?" (357) Typical of Ellison, no easy equation works here: Jack is fyce, toy bull terrier, bulldog, bull, patron, and slavemaster (and many other things: bear, rabbit, money ["jack"] are just a few). But in this context the important point is that he is Invisible Man's opponent with the bullish power to turn and kill. Invisible's task is to learn how to confront him with style and effectiveness.

Jack takes Invisible to a place in Spanish Harlem ''where the neon-lighted sign of a bull's head announced the El Toro Bar'' (269). Suddenly Invisible finds himself in a bar from the world of Hemingway. But this is not quite a ''clean, well-lighted place'' or a muffled ''Killers'' lunchroom; Ellison fills the room with loaded talk and symbols—even the music is significantly titled. Four beer drinkers argued here in Spanish while ''a juke box, lit up green and red, played 'Media Luz' '' (269). As Invisible wonders about the purpose of Jack's bringing him to El Toro, he considers the picture behind the bar. Here the allusions to Hemingway become most explicit, as Invisible thinks:

> Before me, in the panel where a mirror is usually placed, I could see a scene from a bullfight, a bull charging close to the man and the man swinging a red cape in sculptured folds so close to his body that man and bull seemed to blend in one swirl of calm, pure motion. Pure grace, I thought, looking above the bar to where, larger than life, the pink and white image of a girl smiled down from a summery beer ad on which a calendar said April One. . . .
>
> ''Here, come back,'' he said, nudging me playfully. ''She's only a cardboard image of a cold steel civilization.''
>
> I laughed, glad to hear him joking. ''And that?'' I said, pointing to the bullfight scene.
>
> ''Sheer barbarism,'' he said, watching the bartender and lowering his voice to a whisper. (271)

A moment later, as Jack and Invisible discuss the ideological training session Invisible has just completed, he notices another bullfight scene farther down the bar. In this one ''the matador was being swept skyward on the black bull's horns.'' (271)

''The aficionado, or lover of the bullfight,'' writes Hemingway, ''has this sense of the tragedy and ritual of the fight so that the minor aspects are not important except as they relate to the whole. Either you have this or you have not, just as, without implying any comparison, you have or have not an ear for music'' (*Death*, 9). Invisible, who has never been to a bullfight (and whose ear for music also starts out faulty and improves), is by no means an aficionado. But his instincts seem right. He sees the sculptural beauty of the work of the matador close to the bull—so close they ''seemed to blend in one swirl of calm, pure motion.'' And he uses one of Hemingway's key words, ''grace,'' to describe the climaxed moment of artistic perfection, the moment Hemingway has said brings spiritual and emotional ''ecstasy,'' the moment when man's immortality seems, for an instant, achieved. If these flashes of insight place Invisible on the side of tragic ritual and art, his sighting without comment of the other image, that of the upended matador, shows he still has more naiveté than *aficion*. Presumably he doesn't know what to make of this other side of the bullfighter's art. Hemingway tells us that all bullfighters got gored—it is part of their initiation as seasoned fighters; how one comes back from the injury (tempered and tested or defensive and cowardly) determines one's true mettle as a matador. Seeing the goring scene as a *separate* frame—not part of the continiuum in the life of a bullfighter—marks

Invisible as a novice: he praises one aspect of the scene but does not see that aspect in relation to the whole bullfight. Nor does he see that this Hemingway bar, with its coded messages against the wall (''where a mirror is usually placed''), is another warning to him. Art and grace are achievable, yes, but there is no way to avoid the slashing test of the horns.

Another twist is that he's sitting at the bar right next to his opponent, One-Eyed Bull Jack. Jack is blind to the art and ritual of the bullfight, terming it ''sheer barbarism.'' He's more perceptive in interpreting the picture of the white girl on the beer ad as ''a cardboard image of a cold steel civilization.'' In fact, his suddenly cleared mood (''as though in an instant he had settled whatever had been bothering him and felt suddenly free'' [*IM*, 270]) and his laughter suggest that he perceives in the scene a joke richer than Invisible Man does, a joke reflected by the juxtaposition of the images and the April Fool's Day calendar. In this setting of the El Toro, Jack names Invisible the chief spokesman of the Harlem district. And, as the reader finds out at the novel's end, he's about to set up the Invisible Man as a betrayer of his people, as a chief sacrificial victim, number one dupe. In a sense, this seasoned bull is trying to turn the tables on the would-be matador, making him a comic butt for the bull's secret horns. As the hero discovers, it's a ''comic-strip world'' he's been put in, and Jack, faintly smiling and blind though he may be to tragedy and rituals, manipulates Invisible, using lures, fakery, and force. It's a world where Jack seems to turn gracefully with Invisible one moment but shifts as quickly as a bull to ''sweep him skyward'' in the next.

Symbolically, Invisible Man duels not just with Jack (or the others that try to bull and bully him); in a profound sense he also must confront and master history.[28] ''Western culture,'' wrote Ellison about the challenge of Wright's *Black Boy*, ''must be won, confronted like the animal in a Spanish bullfight, dominated by the red shawl of codified experience and brought heaving to its knees'' (*S&A*, 93). This confrontation with all of Western culture makes up Invisible's great challenge; and it is directly connected to his quest for identity. In 1973 Ellison spoke of Invisible's situation this way: ''His problem is to create an individuality based on an awareness of how it relates to his past and the values of the past'' (O'Brien, *Interviews*, 75). Speaking more generally of modern Americans' lack of historical and self-awareness, later in 1973 Ellison said:

> We still do not know who we are. . . . What I have found is that these strings of continuity, these linkages on the basis of ideas and of experiences were automatically—arbitrarily, it seems to me—thrown overboard. And this is disastrous for writers; it's disastrous for *bootleggers*, even. It's disastrous for any sort of human enterprise, because we live one upon the other. We follow, we climb up the shoulders of those who had gone before. (''Locke Symposium,'' 25–26)

In this book the Invisible Man learns to climb the shoulders of those who have gone before, and to fight off the series of imposed misconceptions of what he has been, and thus of who he is. He rejects not only misstatements of the "facts of the case," but of theoretical schemes in which the facts assume meaning. While theories of "history" abound in *Invisible Man*, Jack and the Brotherhood present the most complete and seductive idea of the way the world turns—the idea whose rejection by Invisible paves the way for his own freedom. Like certain Marxists (but not only them), the Brotherhood sees history as a predictably repeating pattern, a design whose turnings can be precisely charted by proper science. This view of history explains why the "brothers" strive for a style of speech and deduction that is free of emotional charges, mechanical in its accuracy. The "brother with the pipe" loses patience with Jack's figurative speech, saying: "I only wish to point out that a scientific terminology exists. . . . After all, we call ourselves scientists, let us speak as scientists" (232). Jack tells Invisible to take the scientific jargon with a grain of salt. Master ideology, he warns the young man, "but don't overdo it. Don't let it master you. There is nothing to put the people to sleep like dry ideology. . . . Remember too, that theory always comes after practice. Act first, theorize later, that's always a formula, a devastatingly effective one!" (271). Jack's success as a leader depends upon his knowing the dry ideology, and upon his ability to manipulate it to support his larger motive, personal power. "And you don't have to worry about the brothers' criticism," advised Jack. "Just throw some ideology back at them and they'll leave you alone—provided, of course, that you have right backing and produce the required results" (271). The Brotherhood theory of history is an intricate one; but what Invisible learns from Jack (part of whose seductive strategy is to mingle his lies shrewdly with bits of truth) is that political power is the name of the Brotherhood's real game.

History as defined by the Brotherhood is an upwardly spiraling tunnel: one dwells either "inside" or "outside" the irrevocably turning historical chamber. Not without religious overtones, Brotherhood history is also a kind of spirit that can be "born in your brain"; it is a stormy moment that can choose special people for special tasks and "transform" them into servants of history's high calling. Where exactly "the people" figure in this formulation of history is ambiguous. In one scene, the Brotherhood defends them as the righteous soul bearers of history, those who raise up new leaders as they need them, and even reach back into the past and name fallen heroes to direct new turns in history's path; in the next scene, the brothers speak of the people as ignoramuses who need only to be prodded, like cattle. Which simplistic formula Jack uses depends on which ideological point he is throwing out and at whom. But in any case Brotherhood history is a cynical twister which uses, if necessary, or destroys such innocent people as the ones Invisible sees evicted in Harlem. Explaining the scene in merciless terms, Jack describes history as an immutable force, this time as a storm:

> "These old ones," he said grimly. "It's sad, yes. But they're already dead,

> defunct. History has passed them by. Unfortunate, but there's nothing to do about them. They're like dead limbs that must be pruned away so that the tree may bear young fruit or the storms of history will blow them down anyway. Better the storm should hit them. . . . These people are old. . . . So they'll be cast aside. They're dead, you see, because they're incapable of rising to the necessity of the historical situation.'' (*IM*, 220)

This godlike history is no respecter of persons, guilty or innocent; it just *moves*, lifting some for a glimpse of salvation, blasting others. With this pseudo-religious, ''scientific'' formula for history as a cover, Jack targets Harlem for trouble.

Experience eventually teaches Invisible another view of history. ''Beware of those who speak of the *spiral* of history,'' he warns. ''They are preparing a boomerang. Keep a steel helmet handy. I have been boomeranged across my head so much that I now can see the darkness of lightness'' (5). History repeats, he learns, but not in a neat geometric circle, and if history moves forward or upward, the meaning of the sweep is nonetheless contradictory. ''Contradiction,'' says Invisible, ''that . . . is how the world moves: Not like an arrow, but a boomerang'' (5). Boomeranging history slashes in unpredictable parabolic patterns, and it can hit and kill others or even blindside its own unsuspecting thrower. Significantly, the boomerang is an instrument of war and of sport. (''Life,'' we are again reminded that Grandfather says, ''is a war''; and as the compulsively talking vet says, it is a game.) It is important too that the boomerang is made and thrown by human hands. In *Invisible Man*, history is revealed as a tale told not by a god or a computer, but by human beings.

Tod Clifton's death brings the message home. This zealot for Brotherhood discovers that the Party's conception of history is a malicious lie, that he's been betrayed, used against his people and himself. Unable to face the implications of his discovery, he recoils in despair, he ''plunged outside history,'' as he puts it. Having depended so much on the vision and the values (the view of history) expressed by the Brotherhood, Tod becomes a cynic who ''commits suicide'' rather than confront a world effaced of meaning. The shock of his cohort's ''suicide'' makes Invisible realize that the event's significance is open to interpretation and to misinterpretation:

> History records the patterns of men's lives, they say: Who slept with whom and with what results; who fought and who won and who lived to lie about it afterwards. All things, it is said, are duly recorded—all things of importance, that is. But not quite, for actually it is only the known, the seen, the heard and only those events that the recorder regards as important that are put down, those lies his keepers keep their power by. But the cop would be Clifton's historian, his judge, his witness, and his executioner, and I was the only brother in the watching crowd. And I, the only witness for the defense, knew neither the extent of his guilt nor the nature of his crime. Where were the historians today? And how would they put it down? (*IM*, 332)

Not just the cop who shoots Clifton, but the newspapers and the Brotherhood members decide that Clifton is guilty. The Brotherhood even judges that his selling of Sambo dolls makes him a hotheaded fool, a sellout to his people, and a traitor to Brotherhood. But Invisible, who has begun to learn something of the complexity of events and the power of language and ritual, decides to honor Tod at a public funeral. "All right," he thinks, "so we'll use his funeral to put his integrity back together." The funeral oration (not just Invisible's words themselves but "the pattern of my voice upon the air") along with the spontaneous outburst of "Many Thousand Gone" assert that Tod's death was not meaningless. "It was hot downtown and he forgot his history," says Invisible. "He forgot the time and place. He lost his hold on reality." To an extent the death was bleakly comic: "The blood ran like blood in a comic-book killing, on a comic-book day in a comic-book world." But it was also a tragic loss: "Such," says Invisible Man, echoing Hemingway, "was the short bitter life of Brother Tod Clifton" (346).

The presence of some quiet and faddishly dressed black boys on a platform makes Invisible meditate still more on the true design of history:

> What if Brother Jack were wrong? What if history was a gambler, instead of a force in a laboratory experiment, and the boys his ace in the hole? What if history was not a reasonable citizen, but a madman full of paranoid guile and these boys his agents, his big surprise! His own revenge? For they were outside, in the dark with Sambo, the dancing paper doll; taking it on the lambo with my fallen brother, Tod Clifton (Tod, Tod) running and dodging the forces of history instead of making a dominating stand. (*IM*, 333)

Rinehart is "outside history," too. The logical Brotherhood has no place for him in its calculations; it would see him "simply as a criminal." Yet Rinehart not only suggests to Invisible a survival strategy, but his style of living contains yet another lesson about history:

> My God, what possibilities existed! And that spiral business, that progress goo! Who knew all the secrets; hadn't I changed my name and never been challenged even once? And that lie that success was a rising *upward*. What a crummy lie they kept us dominated by. Not only could you travel upward toward success but you could travel downward as well; up *and* down, in retreat, as well as in advance, crabways and crossways and around in a circle, meeting your old selves coming and going and perhaps all at the same time. How could I have missed it for so long? (*IM*, 385)

With this lesson in mind, Invisible sees that the Brotherhood historians were writing a history that ignored the real experiences of blacks, among others. Not taking into account the essential ambiguity (the Rinehartness) of experience—that, for instance, the ones lowest down in the social hierarchy might be snide tricksters or even "the bearers of something precious"—Brotherhood's formulas were too spare and simple for Harlem. Nor did they take into account that even painful experiences can be interpreted in a positive light: "And now," Invisible finally sees, "all past humiliations became precious parts of my experience, and for the first time, leaning against that stone wall in the sweltering night, I began to accept my past and, as I accepted it, I felt memories welling up in me. It was as though I'd learned suddenly to see around corners" (383).

"To see around corners," says Kenneth Burke, "is to gain perspective on one's self and one's situation, to grasp enough of the true pattern of events to have a handle on the future" (*Attitudes*, 268). More Burke: Invisible Man gains, at last, "perspective by incongruity,"[29] signaled by Invisible's cryptic words concerning Rinehart's rascality. "It was unbelievable," thinks Invisible, "but perhaps only the unbelievable could be believed. Perhaps the truth was always a lie" (*IM*, 376). Incongruous as it seems, Invisible Man sees the truth of his predicament only when he sees that, "highly visible" as he is, he is *unseen*. Hence the ironic laughter in his first report to Ellison: "I am an invisible man." Much "boomeranging" of his expectations taught him the comic nature of things; his laughter is earned by his encounters with bull-necked experience.

At the novel's end, the hero has also earned the heroic title, even if he is more a comic than a tragic hero. In his memoirs he looks back on his experience and sees it in ritual terms which recall the rites of initiation, purification, and rebirth one encounters in *The Sun Also Rises* (the English edition of which was entitled *The Fiesta*), *Men Without Women*, *In Our Time*, and in Hemingway's essays about hunting and bullfighting. Like many Hemingway characters, Invisible is transformed by witnessing and suffering great violence and caprice. Like the audience at a good bullfight (as reported by Hemingway), readers of *Invisible Man* feel "changed" by Invisible's dances with death. Like a Hemingway bullfighter, Invisible has come close to the bull's horns, he has been upended; and despite his scars, he has come back battling. The novel itself is his act of supreme "grace under pressure," the ultimate Hemingway laurel. By the Epilogue he has confronted his tormentors, figured out the magic words and symbols (his grandfather's and those in his suitcase) and he has endured the wounds of his tragic knowledge. Finally he is freed of his illusions—freed of his imposed names and the imposed schemes of how the world moves. In time, he has stared down fake versions of history. Having learned that history is no more than a fiction, a "lie,"[30] he pieces together his own history, his own "exalted lie."

To Ellison, Hemingway was a guide and a "father-as-artist" in part because he was a worthy sparring partner, a "cooperative antagonist." (Like Hemingway, Ellison has said that he must go toe to toe with the best writers of his time and—to keep the stakes high—with the best writers of all time.) But Ellison also chose Hemingway as his true "ancestor" because he insisted on telling his "lies" as he himself saw them, despite all precedents and influences, political and otherwise, to tell them any other way. Over and over again his heroes make their forthright stands as artists whose integrity and talent and craft were all they either had or needed to clear a place where they could feel at home in an embattled world. One of his most gifted sons, Ellison, creates in *Invisible Man* a novel as at variance from the Dreiser-Howells-Wright naturalists and realists' work as is *The Sun Also Rises*. In Ellison's book, signs and symbols are presented and meditated upon, but they are never explained away, as Wright's images sometimes are. In this sense Ellison "understates" his case, *à la* Hemingway; the metaphor of invisibility, for instance, retains its rich mystery. But more like Wright and Faulkner than like Hemingway he is also careful not to be misunderstood, and adds his essaylike Epilogue to drive his fictional point home. Invisible Man is not a laconic Hemingway tough guy; he is a talker who says his piece in language more extroverted and southern than Hemingway's characters used. Ellison, in other words, took what he needed from Hemingway without merely copying his style. Still, Invisible Man, much more like Hemingway's Jake and Nick than like Bigger Thomas, takes on the world, body and soul. And at the novel's end, he only wants to last, as Hemingway put it, and to get his work done: to tell his story truer than the facts.

NOTES

1. See Steve Cannon, Ishmael Reed, and Quincy Troupe, "The Essential Ellison," 126–59; and Michael S. Harper and Robert B. Stepto, "Study and Experience, an Interview with Ralph Ellison," 417–35.

2. See Albert Murray, *South to a Very Old Place*. When Ellison first met Faulkner in 1953, he introduced himself as one of his sons.

3. Ralph Ellison, *Shadow and Act*, 140–41. All in-text references to the essays in this work appear as *S&A*.

4. Ellison interview, "Introduction: A Completion of Personality," in *Ralph Ellison, a Collection of Critical Essays*, edited by John Hersey, 1–19. The Ellison-Hersey interview is included in this volume, pp. 285–307.

5. See William White, ed. *By-Line: Ernest Hemingway*. Further references in text appear as *By-Line*.

6. I refer to *In Our Time* (1925) and *Men Without Women* (1927); *The Sun Also Rises* (1926) and *A Farewell to Arms* (1929); and *Death in the Afternoon* (1932).

7. See George Garrett, "Ralph Ellison," in *The Writer's Voice*, 224.

8. Ellison, "Introduction to Flamenco," 38. Note that this comment on the blues is framed in the context of a discussion of Flamenco music and dance.

9. See "Ralph Ellison," *Interviews with Ten Black Writers*, ed. John O'Brien, 68.

10. Ellison interview, "A Very Stern Discipline," 90. Further references in text appear as "Stern Discipline."

11. See Robert G. O'Meally, *The Craft of Ralph Ellison*, 29.

12. Richard Wright, "Bright and Morning Star" (1938), reprinted in Sterling A. Brown, et al., *The Negro Caravan*, 110.

13. Ellison, "Folklore," an interview for the Federal Writers Project with Leo Gurley, June 14, 1939, Library of Congress Folklore Archives, Washington, D.C.; reprinted in Ann Banks, *First-Person America*, 244.

14. Ellison, "Ralph Ellison Explains," 145.

15. Ellison, "Negro Prize Fighter," 26–27. Further references cited in text as "Prize Fighter."

16. Robert Penn Warren, "Introduction" to *A Farewell to Arms*, xxvii.

17. See Ellison et al. "What's Wrong with the American Novel?" in *American Scholar* 24: 472. Further references in text cited as "What's Wrong."

18. See Ellison: "Twentieth-Century Fiction and the Black Mask of Humanity," *Confluence* (December 1953): 3–21; "Society, Morality, and the Novel," *The Living Novel: A Symposium*, ed. Granville Hicks, 58–91; "The Novel as a Function of American Democracy," *Wilson Library Bulletin* (June 1967): 1022–1027. For an excellent analysis of stylistic linkages between Twain and Hemingway, see Richard Bridgman's *The Colloquial Style in America* (New York: Oxford University Press, 1966).

19. Ellison has, through the years, however, remained suspicious of fine technique alone. In 1967 Ellison wrote: "The state of our novel is not so healthy at the moment. Instead of aspiring to project a vision of the complexity, the diversity of the total experience, the novelist loses faith and falls back upon something which is called 'black comedy,' which is neither black or comic. It is a cry of despair. Talent and technique are there; artistic competence is there; but a certain necessary faith in human possibility before the next unknown is not there." *Wilson Library Bulletin* (June 1967): 1027.

20. See Ralph Ellison, "Through a Writer's Eyes." *Washington Post* (August 21, 1973), B3.

21. Ellison, "Introduction," *Invisible Man*, 30th Anniversary Edition (New York: Random House, 1952, 1982), xix. Further references in text are cited as *IM*.

22. See Kenneth Burke, *Philosophy of Literary Form*, 253–62.

23. See Ellison, *Invisible Man*: The Author's Introductions in the 30th Anniversary Edition and the Franklin Library Edition (New York: Franklin, 1979).

24. See John F. Callahan, "The Historical Frequencies of Ralph Waldo Ellison," in *Chant of Saints*, 33–52.

25. Quoted by Ellison, *Shadow and Act*, 144.

26. See Ernest Hemingway, "A Clean, Well-Lighted Place," in *The Fifth Column and the First Forty-Nine Stories*, 477–81.

27. See Albert Lee Murray, "The Waste Land and the Sun Also Rises: A Comparative Study," M.A. thesis.

28. Note Kenneth Burke's definition of history as more than a report of past events, but as "man's life in political communities" or the "characteristic responses of people in forming and reforming their communities," *Attitudes Toward History*, i.

29. Ibid.; see also Burke, *Permanence and Change, An Anatomy of Purpose*, 146.

30. See Ellison, "The original 2nd epithet," in "The Uses of History in Fiction," 69.

WORKS CITED

Burke, Kenneth. *Attitudes Toward History*, 2nd ed. Boston: Beacon, 1959.

Burke, Kenneth. *Permanence and Change, An Anatomy of Purpose*. New York: Republic Books, 1935.

Burke, Kenneth. *Philosophy of Literary Form*, rev. ed. New York: Vintage, 1957; original edition, 1941.

Callahan, John. "The Historical Frequencies of Ralph Waldo Ellison." *Chant of Saints*, ed. Michael S. Harper and Robert B. Stepto. Urbana: University of Illinois, 1979.

Ellison, Ralph. "Alain Locke Symposium." *Harvard Advocate* (Spring, 1974): 9–28.

———. "A Congress Jim Crow Didn't Attend." *New Masses* 35 (May 14, 1940): 5–8.

———. "Creative and Cultural Lag." *New Challenge* 2 (Fall, 1937): 90–91.

———. "The Essential Ellison." Interview by Steve Cannon, Ishmael Reed, and Quincy Troupe. *Y'Bird Reader* (Autumn 1977): 126–59.

———. "Folklore." Interview for the Federal Writers Project with Leo Gurley, June 14, 1939. Library of Congress Folklore Archives. Reprinted in Ann Banks. *First-Person America*. New York: Knopf, 1980.

———. "Introduction: A Completion of Personality." *Ralph Ellison, a Collection of Critical Essays*, ed. John Hersey. Englewood, N.J.: Prentice-Hall, 1974, 1–19.

———. "Introduction to Flamenco." *The Saturday Review of Literature* 37 (December 11, 1954): 38–39.

———. *Invisible Man*. New York: Random House, 1982.

———. "Negro Prize Fighter." *New Masses* 37 (December 17, 1940): 23–27.

———. "The Novel as a Function of American Democracy." *Wilson Library Bulletin* (June 1967): 1022–27.

———. "Ralph Ellison Explains." *'48 Magazine of the Year* 2 (May 1948): 145.

———. "Ralph Ellison." *Interviews with Ten Black Writers*, ed. John O'Brien. New York: Liveright, 1973, 63–77.

———. *Shadow and Act*. New York: Random House, 1964.

———. "Society, Morality, and the Novel." *The Living Novel: A Symposium*, ed. Granville Hicks. New York: Macmillan, 1957, 58–91.

______"Stormy Weather." *New Masses* 37 (September 24, 1940): 20–21.

______. "Study and Experience, an Interview with Ralph Ellison." Michael S. Harper and Robert B. Stepto. *Massachusetts Review* 18 (Autumn 1977), 417–35.

______ "Through a Writer's Eyes." *Washington Post* (August 21, 1973), B3.

______. "Twentieth-Century Fiction and the Black Mask of Humanity." *Confluence* (December 1953):3–21.

______. "The Uses of History in Fiction." *Southern Literary Journal* 1 (Spring 1969): 57–90.

______. "A Very Stern Discipline." Interview with Steve Cannon, Lennox Raphael, and James Thompson. *Harper's* 234 (March 1967): 76–95.

______. "What's Wrong with the American Novel?" *American Scholar* 24 (Autumn 1955): 464–503.

______. WGBH interview. "Interview with Ralph Ellison." Boston, April 12, 1974.

Garrett, George. "Ralph Ellison." *The Writer's Voice*. New York: Morrow, 1973.

Hemingway, Ernest. "A Clean, Well-Lighted Place." *The Fifth Column and the First Forty-Nine Stories*. New York: Scribner's, 1938.

______. *Death in the Afternoon*. New York: Scribner's, 1932.

______. *A Farewell to Arms*. New York: Scribner's, 1929.

______. "Fifty Grand." *The Fifth Column and the First Forty-Nine Stories*. New York: Scribner's, 1938.

______. *In Our Time*. New York: Scribner's, 1930.

______. "Introduction." *Men at War*. New York: Crown, 1942.

______. *Men Without Women*. New York: Scribner's, 1927.

______. *The Sun Also Rises*. New York: Scribner's, 1926.

Murray, Albert. *South to a Very Old Place*. New York: McGraw-Hill, 1971.

______. "The Storyteller as Blues Singer." *American Journal* (April 10, 1973): 14.

Murray, Albert Lee. "The Waste Land and the Sun Also Rises: A Comparative Study." M.A. thesis, New York University, September 1948.

McPherson, James A. "Indivisible Man." *Atlantic Monthly* 206 (December 1970): 45–60.

O'Meally, Robert G. *The Craft of Ralph Ellison*. Cambridge: Harvard University Press, 1980.

Warren, Robert Penn. "Introduction." Hemingway, *A Farewell to Arms*. New York: Scribner's 1919, 1949.

White, William, ed. *By-Line: Ernest Hemingway*. New York: Scribner's, 1967.

Wright, Richard. "Bright and Morning Star." *The Negro Caravan*. New York: Dryden, 1941.

The Mixed Heritage of the Modern Black Novel: Ralph Ellison and Friends

CHARLES T. DAVIS

Friendship is where we begin. Once upon a time there were three friends, Wright, Ellison, and Baldwin, and Wright, it was, who served as the central person in the relationship, extending the arm of affection to his two younger colleagues, Ellison and Baldwin. They were not friendly at the same time. Ellison was close to Wright until Wright's departure for France and permanent exile in 1947, just at the time that Ellison was beginning to write *Invisible Man*, and Baldwin sought out Wright in Paris during the early years of his residence there. Friendship is not always a pact made in heaven; it resembles at times an insurance policy. That is to say, there are terms, and if the terms are ignored, the friendship is strained, frequently to the breaking point.

Now the accepted element in the Wright-Ellison-Baldwin alliance was that Wright was the dominant father figure, offering advice to his younger associates, directing their reading. As everyone knows, fathers, in the course of things, are destined to be rejected—indeed, in suffering such rejection, some attain unexpected heights. The young associate, seeking distance from an all-embracing arm that has become too confining, can manage his rejection with discretion or with rudeness.

Ellison was discreet. We might expect that he would be, since he was well brought up in Oklahoma and has paid in his autobiographical pieces respect for his elders, especially to a Mr. Randolph, his adopted grandfather, who served as the learned caretaker of the library of the Oklahoma legislature. Ellison, in an interview published in the *Massachusetts Review*[1] in Autumn 1977, voiced his rejection in a measured way:

> Most friendships have their vague areas of mystery and the older member of a relationship between writers might himself project the younger in a role which obscures the extent of his intellectual maturity or the extent and variety of his

Reprinted by permission of Jeanne Davis from *Black Is the Color of the Cosmos*, 1982.

> experience. One of my early experiences with Dick Wright involved such an underestimation, with him assuming that I hadn't read many books with which I was, in fact, quite familiar. . . . Well, among others, he assumed that I hadn't read any of Marx . . . Conrad . . . Dostoevski . . . Hemingway—and so on. I was somewhat chagrined by his apparent condescension, but instead of casting him in the role of misunderstanding "father," I swallowed my pride and told myself, "Forget it, you know what you know, so now learn what he thinks of in terms of his Marxism and the insights he's gained as a developed writer of fiction." And that was the way it went.

In contrast, Baldwin was a good deal less discreet. After all, he came from a background charged by evangelical religion, and his long suit, if you forgive the mixed metaphor, was conversion, not cultivation. Baldwin attacked Wright in a famous essay written in the mid-1950s titled "Everybody's Protest Novel," in which he lumped together *Native Son* and *Uncle Tom's Cabin* and asserted, with some pretension, that both failed to qualify as high art. Baldwin said then that the novel should have to do not with society but rather with "the power of revelation," the "journey toward a more vast reality which must take precedence over all other claims." It matters little now that Baldwin was wrong, fuzzily wrong. He was mistaken about the relationship between the novel and society, about the worth of *Native Son*, even about the artistic value of that extraordinary fusion of sentiment and propaganda that is *Uncle Tom's Cabin*. What does matter in our context is that the Wrights (Richard and Ellen) never forgave him, even though they realized that he was reflecting, simply, the pressures of a singularly smug and complacent decade. I say Wrights, by the way, because Ellen, Richard's second wife, still remembers the assault upon her husband and the objectionable piety that accompanied it. I should add that the last word on this controversy has yet to be printed. There exists now in the Beinecke Library, where the whole Richard Wright Archive now rests, a completed novel, *The Island of Hallucinations*, the second work in a projected trilogy begun by *The Long Dream*, which presents a particularly unpleasant character named "Mr. Mechanical." Some of us, including Michel Fabre, see a striking resemblance between that character and a former intimate associate of Wright's. Ellen Wright, at the moment, will not permit the publication of the novel because it contains matter damaging to the reputations of people still living.

We are not essentially interested really in the flow and ebb in friendship, but in a moment in the history of Afro-American literature when these interests of Wright, Ellison, and Baldwin converged. This would be in the years 1952 and 1953, when *Invisible Man* by Ellison, *The Outsider* by Wright, and *Go Tell It on the Mountain* by Baldwin appeared. The dominant force in the literary ferment created by this convergence was exercised by Ellison, not Wright, the distant master.

Ellison is the writer who comes to mind when we retrace the beginnings of a truly modern tradition in black fiction. Indeed, Ellison's is the achievement that black critic Addison Gayle must reject when he wishes to replace a complex and perhaps perverse heritage with a simple art of straightforward expression and black pieties. Happily, such a replacement is impossible as well as unthinkable, and the dream of it is destined to go the way of the philistine complaint against Henry James, that James's fiction would somehow be stronger, healthier, and more American if he had tended the flame of his genius at Washington Square. The fact is that Ellison for all of his readers, his admirers as well as his detractors, created a new thing in the black novel, shaped a new climate, and forced upon his audience a new pattern of expectations for the art of black fiction. And he did so not by denying the Western tradition in a foolish gesture that would cost him half of the resources of his imagination and his language, but by using it and combining an essentially "white" heritage with the matter and the manner of a rich black oral culture.

Though everyone admits that a break of some kind in the continuity of black fiction occurs with Ellison, few critics, especially those so passionately opposed to his malign influence, can say exactly what it is. Certainly, there is nothing unique about stirring into the same pot white art forms and black folklore, soup stock and exotic herbs. Charles Chesnutt had done this with some commercial success in the 1890s, notably in *The Conjure Woman*; but there is a great difference here in both ingredients and cuisine. Chesnutt used the fictional forms from the conservative genteel tradition, the short narrative carefully tailored for the reading audience of *Scribner's*, *Century*, *Harper's*, the *Critic*, and the *Dial*, which respected a cultivated middle-class sensibility that welcomed titillation but not trauma. Nothing ever really changes in the psychic life of the retired couple who listen to the yarns of Uncle Julius in *The Conjure Woman*. It costs the husband a few dollars now and then and rather more time, but the exposure to black folklore is managed at a proper distance and with a display of civilized tolerance that survives quite easily the odd happenings among lesser black folk. True, Chesnutt's style at its best approaches an irony that might unsettle the most sensitive. The folklore center within the genteel envelope of a typical Chesnutt tale has vitality, but this matter is tempered, too. All of the attention to "goophering" and transformation tended to sustain conventional moral standards and values, if not in blacks directly, indirectly in the whites, punishing excess in human appetites, and rewarding, at times in odd ways, fidelity and endurance. The precedent for handling folk matter in this way was established, no doubt, by George Washington Cable in the decade preceding the emergence of Chesnutt as a writer, when the quaint ways of the Creoles in Louisiana charmed Eastern audiences, not entirely to the satisfaction of the residents of New Orleans, Plaquemine, and Natchitoches.

The comparison of Chesnutt and Ellison is a device for measuring Ellison's achievement, providing the terms for a proper evaluation. Ellison does not rely upon the more conservative models provided by the mainstream of the American narrative, which would be in the late 1940s a still vigorous naturalism. Now, "conservative" in this context has nothing to do with politics. The reality is that the American political Left applied the formulas of naturalism with a new rigor and a new intensity, giving to the achievement of James Farrell and Richard Wright an authority not to be lightly dismissed. A writer of this school practiced exact, detailed representation and looked to the social sciences, at times to Marxist notions of history, for ways of structuring human behavior. The emphasis was always upon the society, not upon the rare individual who dropped out of a well-defined place or a well-clocked time; the challenge for the naturalistic hero was inevitably adjustment, not psychic trauma that might be magnified in proportion to the character or sensitivity of an individual consciousness. The naturalist was always about the business of Man, with a capital M, and it helped little to make him Common and to claim that his low state came from a pathological environment. The consequence is an art of constraints: more, indeed, for Wright than there were for Dreiser, since Wright bore consciously and deliberately, but with much turmoil, a commitment to the Communist party.

I suppose that Wright's inner doubts and his frequent questions were as much responsible as his continuing faith in the Party for the fact that he wrote the finest proletarian novel ever written in America, *Native Son*. But a complete break with his naturalistic models was unthinkable for Wright while he was a Party member and while he remained in America. Not so for Ellison, who stood at the periphery of the New York political scene in which Wright was a central actor, and who came from a background dominated by an interest in several of the arts rather than a single one. He was also southern in a way that Wright was not. Ellison was prepared, in short, to turn his back on both American naturalism and the American Left and to welcome aspects of a southern exposure not recognized by Wright, or Chesnutt either, for that matter.

Ellison tells us that *Invisible Man* had its beginnings on a farm in Vermont in the summer of 1945 when he read *The Hero* by Lord Ragland and speculated on the nature of black leadership in the United States. Ellison never intended to construct an odyssey of a representative man, a standard exercise in naturalism, given its direction by an inflexible social milieu. From the start, he was concerned with a hero with especially endowed characteristics and possibilities, perhaps even with talents not unlike his own. Ellison had read Conrad, Henry James, and Dostoevski even before Wright in New York guided the younger writer to James's "Prefaces," the letters of Dostoevski and the critical commentary of Joseph Warren Beach. He admits now to "playing possum" with Wright, simulating an innocence of knowledge that he did not possess when they talked in the early forties. After all, T.S. Eliot, whose imprint upon *Invisible Man* is to be seen everywhere, especially on the early pages and in the conclusion, was a Tuskegee discovery, like the fine black woman pianist Hazel Harrison. Ellison had a talent for sculpture, too, as well as for music, and he was able to recognize a certain naiveté and unsophistication in the sculptor Richmond Barthé, with whom he studied briefly. As a consequence, he adopted a style that was always eclectic, changing to reflect the psychological shifts within his unnamed narrator. He has associated in "The Art of Fiction," an interview published in the *Paris Review* in 1955, a particular and distinctive style with each of the three sections of the novel: naturalism with the adventures in the South, though it is naturalism of a highly symbolic kind, when we move away from the well-manicured lawns of the black college; impressionism for the early efforts of the hero to establish himself in the North; and surrealism with the documentation of the hero's fall from grace in the Brotherhood. We may quibble, as I do, with the accuracy of these labels, but not with the presence of a staggering virtuosity in technique that brought into being *Invisible Man*. The point is that Ellison casts off the shackles of naturalism, both in matter and in manner.

Nowhere is the departure from naturalism more evident than in the way that environment is rendered, the always richly documented background demanded by that form of the novel extended by Norris and Dreiser, one which devoted attention to the central forces that shape life. Even in the more naturalistic pages of *Invisible Man*, we find a Melvillian duality, a delight in playing with two equally valid but opposed physical realities—the gleaming and orderly campus of the college, with its suggestions of New England and the triumphs of Christian faith and hard work, and the unsightly cabins of Trueblood and his brothers, sisters, and children, reminding us and Mr. Norton, the trustee from the North, of unattended back alleys of the spirit, unmistakably black and recalling an instinctive life that cannot be forgotten.

This duality is to be found wherever background is sketched in *Invisible Man*; in the Liberty Paint Factory, in the domains of Kimbro and Brockway; in upper Manhattan itself, with a topside of apartments and stores, and a bottom equipped with the most elaborately illuminated basement ever rendered in literature or in life. It is clear that the essentially fictional problem is not adjustment, since no one knows to what he might adjust; rather, the more desperate question is ordering one's tradition, history, and psyche, best put by one of Ellison's favorite authors at the time, Eliot, at the conclusion of *The Waste Land*: "These fragments I have shored against my ruins." No more. And the unnamed narrator confesses that he is only half prepared to emerge from his hole. A little like Louis Armstrong, who would "Open the window and let the foul air out," knowing all the time that the "Old Bad Air" was responsible for the good music.

Perhaps the plainest indication of Ellison's reliance upon the rich tradition in experimental Western art is the title itself. "Invisibility" is not simply a characteristic first given visual expression by the fine British actor Claude Rains in a horror movie, nor even first used as a metaphor for blackness in 1948 by George Orwell. It is a concept that owes something to European expressionism, in which the dominant idea in a complex whole of a community of values or of a social system or a culture or a human relationship is extracted, magnified, distorted, and allowed to stand for the whole. For precedents of this kind, we do not need to look to the dramatists Kaiser or Capek with their experiments in Europe, but closer at hand to O'Neill in *The Hairy Ape*, or, indeed, to Eliot, in "The Hollow Men." What is exaggerated, of course, is what some of us still remember from the bad days before the black revolution, the tendency of whites to ignore or to make easy generalizations about blacks; this is not so prevalent since the publication of *Invisible Man* and the parade of liberated individualized black psyches that followed in print.

We are dealing in halves here, since the break with naturalism constitutes only one-half of the meaning of Ellison's achievement. The flip side of the coin that represents his contribution to the modern black novel is all black and connected directly with a black oral tradition. Chesnutt, we must recall, used only that folk matter that could be absorbed with comparative ease by a genteel reading audience. He wrote about conjurers, mostly women, who restricted their practice of the black arts to blacks, in general, and blacks in a reasonably remote community in North Carolina at that. Zora Hurston knew much more than Chesnutt did about the black folk tradition, especially the animal tales, the boasts and jokes, and the rituals in folk medicine, but in her fiction she tended to separate the white world and the black, following Chesnutt's pattern, but often rendering black life with more dignity, fullness, and wonder. It was Ellison who suggested a subversive dimension for the black arts.

Ellison uses the matter and the style of a black folk culture with a new broadness and with an incredible range, from music through the spoken word to the icon. His blackness is much more accessible and much more threatening. Trueblood demonstrates this early on when Norton, the college trustee, has the temerity to stray away from the neatly landscaped grounds of the narrator's institution. But there is much more. Louis's trumpet blues complain eloquently about the unchanging condition of blackness in white America, played off the beat, of course, and making marvelous art from "bad air." The characters from beast fables, Buckeye Rabbit and Jack the Bear, appear as symbols representing the narrator's psychological states, documenting the measure of his submission to or evasion of inhuman white authority. Cryptic folk rhymes stir racial memories that would moderate somewhat the narrator's headlong pursuit of conventional goals within the context of commercial New York. The extraordinary Prologue contains, along with snatches of blues and other bits of folk matter, an irreverent folk sermon on the text "Blackness of Blackness," and it offers a summary description of the action which is hard to improve upon:

> Black will make you . . .
>
> . . . .
>
> . . . or black will un-make you.

And the response of the assembled congregation in this dream sequence seems wholly appropriate: "Ain't it the truth, Lawd?" An object, not simply a musical line or a phrase, has the power in *Invisible Man* to link past and present. We think of Brother Tarp's leg chain, a device associating two kinds of bondage: chattel slavery in the South and absolute allegiance demanded by the Brotherhood. The chain, though not folk art in any true sense, has the effect of an icon in that it arouses memories of almost unbreakable intensity of the cruelty of black servitude in the South. Illustrations accompanying the slave narratives when they appeared in the North during three decades of appeal to the American conscience just before the Civil War frequently presented a black and his leg chain.

To give a proper estimate for what Ellison has accomplished we must record it in black and white, that is to say, within the framework of a vital and comprehensive black folk culture and within the emerging tradition of the experimental modern novel. He breaks decisively, on both counts, from the practice of his immediate predecessors, and such is the power of his genius that he leaves the impression that by his efforts alone he has prepared the way for the bold achievements in black fiction that are to come.

To believe so would be to attribute too much to Ellison, great as his work is, and to ignore the time. The crucial period of gestation and formation of the modern black novel is the late forties and early fifties. Indeed, the culminating years for these pioneer efforts are 1952 and 1953, a two-year period during which not only *Invisible Man* appeared, leading the way in 1952, but *Go Tell It on the Mountain*, and also *The Outsider* by Richard Wright, which appeared a year later in 1953.

We tend to ignore *The Outsider* in this context, probably because of the false assumption that his self-imposed and widely advertised exile in France had deprived Wright of the nourishment of American society. It is the old provincialism again, underestimating, as it always did, the power of a really strong imagination. In fact, *The Outsider* is a new departure for the old master of naturalistic fiction, demonstrating that Wright in his own way had shared the same road with Ellison, not too unexpected given that they were firm friends in the early forties.

The Outsider has a protagonist who is also extraordinary and who very early in the action seeks to shape his own life by assuming a new identity: Cross Damon becomes Lionel Lane; the black postal worker in Chicago becomes an important, though unofficial, member of a local cell of the Communist party in New York. We sense in both Ellison's hero and Wright's that they have the potential for leadership, though circumstances of life are not favorable. What is important, finally, for both is not success but coming to terms with themselves. The Invisible Man must develop, first, an awareness of his needs as a person; Cross makes what he considers, at last, to be the wrong decision about his need, and faces, in his dying moments, the human consequences of a freedom gained by violating accepted moral standards and living outside of society. Both protagonists drop out of time; for Ellison, such an escape is short-term therapy that works, for Wright it is ultimately disastrous, destroying the connection, the "bridge from man to man," which is, Cross maintains, all we have: "starting from scratch every time is . . . is no good."

Despite a certain identity in theme and in fictional strategies, the two works are remarkably different. Ellison's is a personal odyssey that leads to the discovery of a rich black folk heritage, which accompanies the acquisition of a psychological equilibrium at the end, almost sufficient to face a chaotic and often senseless world. There are few such positive assurances in *The Outsider*, singularly devoid of allusions to a racial heritage or to psychic traumas that oppress the Invisible Man. Wright's novel is, instead, a form of fable in which personal relationships and their exploration count for little. What matters is a philosophical point: the power and the cost of the condition of conscious alienation debated with brilliance by Cross and Ely Houston, the district attorney of New York City, two outsiders, one a black criminal evading capture and the other a hunchback lawman with the capacity to reconstruct the motivation of the man whom he hunts and about whom he can speak, at his death, with the voice of a brother. Raskolnikoff and Porfiry, we think, in *Crime and Punishment*, and we are not far off. Wright's fable, relying on reason and philosophical discussion rather than upon psychological development, makes a powerful statement about the human condition, which is clear and unqualified: "Alone a man is nothing." The narrative, despite its lean, even ascetic technique, manages to view the future in a hopeful light, assuming, indeed, the presence of an audience that might learn from a well-told lesson. Beyond the horror, Cross's four murders, rests a promising prospect: "Man is returning to the earth finding himself in a waking nightmare. . . . The real men, the last men are coming." Nothing so hopeful as this emerges from *Invisible Man*, though Ellison's hero, despite temptation, is never moved to resort to such violent means to achieve his ends.

One critic has called Wright a birthright existentialist, which is an affirmation that criticism will use any science or pseudo-science to make its point, even dialectics. I prefer to think of Wright as a home-grown existentialist, made so by his traumatic childhood in Mississippi, his reading of the more libertarian naturalists like Dreiser, who scorned moral conventions and inhibitions supported by religion, and his trials in the Communist party.

What is inescapable, with both Ellison and Wright, is that the discovery of blackness and its meaning represents a starting point for the artists; Wright's experience, as we have seen, leads to an existential view of reality. Ellison best states his notion of what constitutes a beginning in a remarkable article on the art of his friend Romare Bearden:[2]

> I refer to that imbalance in American society which leads to a distorted perception of social reality, to a stubborn blindness to the creative possibilities of cultural diversity, to the prevalence of negative myths, racial stereotypes and dangerous illusions about art, humanity and society. Arising from an initial

> failure of social justice, this anachronism divides social groups along lines that are no longer tenable while fostering hostility, anxiety and fear; and in the area to which we now address ourselves it has had the damaging effect of alienating many Negro artists from the traditions, techniques and theories indigenous to the arts through which they aspire to achieve themselves.

Ellison practices what he counsels: he addresses "social imbalance," using the full range of the techniques available to him from contemporary fiction, music and the plastic arts, and the folk tradition.

James Baldwin, like Ellison and Wright, explored in *Go Tell It on the Mountain* the problems of a potential leader, though of a special kind. The intellectual context for the coming of John, to echo Du Bois for a moment, is religious and psychological, not political or philosophical. John, Baldwin's protagonist, has the talent and the temperament to become a preacher, a wise and compassionate shepherd for a black congregation; but he lacks the spirit, the sense of mission that comes from the experience of conversion. John's difficulty rests not with the attraction to sin, which he resists without real conflict, but in the hatred of his stepfather, Gabriel, once a powerful preacher in the South, now brought low because he has yielded to lust and pride. John must moderate his antipathy for Gabriel before he can join the community of the saints of the Temple of the Fire Baptized in Harlem. He does so by absorbing the testimonies, "prayers" Baldwin calls them, of his aunt, his stepfather, and his mother. We know that John in this way has acquired an understanding of, if not a complete sympathy for, the adults of his family, because snatches from their statements, their responses to the call of the preacher to come to God, appear in the remarkable record of his conversion. The family's collective guilt, as well as its collective memory, weighs him down as he approaches the agony and the light on the threshing-floor. This necessity to reckon with a black past, to learn it and to accept it, follows the pattern of Ellison's nameless hero who eats a yam in public as a step toward establishing his racial identity.

Though the essential fictional problem owes little to naturalism, the description of the background in Harlem, with its dirt, smells, rats, and harlot cries, displays an indebtedness that is quite clear. It is firm until John slips off into Central Park and we discover ourselves suddenly upon a hill in Judea with a view of a sinful city below. Baldwin's South has even less the shape of a readily identifiable land; the terrain is rather the mountains and the valleys of the Old Testament prophets. By the time we reach the threshing-floor, the landscape is wholly surrealistic.

Certainly one of the great triumphs of *Go Tell It on the Mountain* is the imaginative use of a folk art form, specifically the folk sermon. Ellison was ingenious, too, in the way that he absorbed folk materials within the structure of *Invisible Man*, but he did not take Baldwin's longer step in this respect. The entire novel is a response to a folk sermon, culminating indeed in a conversion scene. The black preacher's call to "Come" results first in "Telling,'' the testimonies of members of the Grimes family and then the descent of God's grace upon John. At the end of the narrative John is saved, but he has yet to be tried. His faith will be tested when he himself goes forth to spread the Word, risking the hazards to the psyche that will afflict him when he struggles to ascend the steep side of the mountain, as Gabriel had attempted to do. I can think of no other example in modern fiction in which a form derived from folk art exercises such commanding authority.

It is time now to take stock, to sum up the most visible consequences of this artistic revolution in the early fifties. We know now that it is not simply Ellison that we must thank or damn, but Wright and Baldwin, too, whose more modest participation must be counted. This new literature is a record of an exceptional sensibility as it copes not so much with a hostile world but with the terrors of its own creation. What is prized more than anything else is an understanding of one's black self, and this requires a reconciliation of some sort with the black heritage, family and folk, in America. Almost in his dying words, Cross Damon warns: ''Starting from scratch every time is . . . is no good.'' No good it is for any of these writers.

Ellison, Wright, and Baldwin depart from naturalistic techniques to render the turmoil of the psyche. Ellison uses dream sequences and violent distortions of reality, both clocked to a remarkable sense of place and of pace. Wright constructs a morality tale, a modern fable permitting a naked and a full discussion of such issues as freedom, power, and human connection. Baldwin fashions what might be called a countersermon, fleshing out what rests behind the audience's ''Amen'' and ending in a description of a convulsive transcendence that is one of the extraordinary achievements in modern literature. For all three, the old verities no longer work. Theirs are now the realities beyond success, freedom, and salvation, and we inherit a house of black fiction that has yet to settle securely on a foundation so recently reclaimed from the marshes of the psyche.

If we look more closely at *Native Son*, we can observe that the signs of change are already in the air in 1940. I refer to the third book of the novel, still often criticized for being inconsistent with the brilliant naturalism of the first two books. We recall that Bigger, after his conviction for murder, throws the crucifix out of his cell when he is visited by a black preacher bringing the chance to repent and to acquire, at the last moment, divine grace, and we listen with astonishment to the rejection of the Marxist vision of his lawyer, Max, when Bigger insists that his murders were not the consequence of society's pathology but the result of his own will. And to Max's dismay, Bigger asserts that the murders were good since they gave him a human dimension that he never possessed before. Bigger, after his resurrection in the final act, may be a phenomenon that is premature; but with the perspective of literary history, we can say that he has brothers in the heroes of novels published more than a decade later, in the fifties.

NOTES

1. See ''Study and Experience, an Interview with Ralph Ellison,'' with Michael S. Harper and Robert B. Stepto, *Massachusetts Review* 18 (Autumn, 1977): 417–35.

2. Ralph Ellison, ''Romare Bearden: Paintings and Projections,'' *Crisis* (March 1970): 81–86.

PART FIVE

Speaking for You

REINTERPRETATIONS OF *INVISIBLE MAN*

"A Completion of Personality": A Talk with Ralph Ellison

JOHN HERSEY

I

One of the most significant views of the work of Ralph Ellison happens to be his own. He is, as he himself says, a slow worker, and over the course of the years, while he was writing away at his second novel—and while Invisible Man *paradoxically refused to drop out of sight—Ellison granted a number of interviews, each of which offered some telling comments on the situation of a novelist who had been thrust into more gnawing fame than most writers would want in their own time. He reproduced three of the interviews in* Shadow and Act. *Two other valuable ones are noted in the bibliography of this book, and the vivid picture of Ellison by a younger writer, James Alan McPherson, also in this collection, originally included an exchange of letters between the two authors, in which Ellison further elaborated his predicament.*

For predicament it has been, and what is forced upon a reader of these interviews is a sense that the polemic-versus-artistic argument—the argument, as old as art itself, over the question: "What use has art?"—hounds Ellison perhaps more than any other first-rank novelist of our time, unless it be Alexander Solzhenitsyn. That argument dominates several of the essays in this book, and it hums in harmonic overtones over the rest of them.

It occurred to me as I assembled and read these various views that in the din of this argument we had never had a chance to hear much from Ellison about his attitude toward the actuality of his craft, about the processes of his creative ordeal, about what he thinks actually happens *when he writes, about the deep familial sources of his ways of being and doing, about how his mind works through problems of shape and dream and sound, and about the particular, idiosyncratic inner workings of his art which may have been molded by his existential past. Although it is entitled "The Art of Fiction," not even*

Part I of this interview served as the Introduction to *Ralph Ellison: A Collection of Critical Essays* (1974), editor John Hersey. Part II was undertaken in 1982 and appears here for the first time.—Ed.

the Paris Review *interview, reprinted in* Shadow and Act, *goes beneath the surface of his struggle to achieve an art worth arguing about as much as his has been.*

And so, on a weekend that Ellison and his wife spent in my home, we talked late into one night about all these matters, and in the cool light of the next morning we had a conversation in which Ellison, with extraordinary finish and economy, and yet with a fabulist's deceptive randomness, too, synthesized and compressed his views of his labor of choice. Here is what we said:

HERSEY. You were talking about your mother last night, and as you talked I wondered how much she had been a force in moving you toward your calling as a writer, and even in supplying materials that you have drawn on.

ELLISON. She certainly had something to do with encouraging my interest in reading. She had no idea that I was going to become a writer, or if she did, she had more insight into me than I had into myself, because I thought I was going to be a musician. My mother always encouraged me to do *something*, and to be good at it—she insisted upon that.

It was my father who wanted me to be a writer. I didn't discover that until many years later—he died when I was three—until after I had written *Invisible Man* and talked with an older cousin, who told me that my father had used to say, "I'm raising this boy to be a poet." Of course he had given me the name [Ralph Waldo].

But my mother did feed my passion for reading. She brought home books and magazines. My concern with the Picassos and Stravinskys of this world started at an earlier age than usual because she brought home *Vanity Fair*. Here was a world so far from Oklahoma City, in any expected sense, yet it was shaping my sense of what was possible. And she understood that that was what was going on.

And what I did get from my mother was an understanding of people. I was very quick-tempered and impatient, and things began to happen when I reached adolescence—and she would just talk about how people acted, what motives were, and why things were sometimes done. I remember being so outraged by something one of her friends had said that I didn't want to see her or her husband anymore. At thirteen I went to work as the husband's office boy, and this close friend of my father was so delighted with having me around that his childless wife was upset. Her reaction was to spread the word around that she suspected that I was actually her husband's child—Oh, boy! When the gossip reached me I was outraged—and not only over what it implied about my mother, but because of my love for my father. I had learned to walk at six months and had been his companion from that time until his death, and I was so far from accepting the reality of his death that I was still telling myself that any day he would reappear to take his place as the head of our family. Now I suspect that my fondness for my employer-friend and my vague awareness that he was, in fact, something of a father-figure added to my shock and outrage. At any rate, when I went to my mother about this matter she proceeded to calm me down.

"Well now," she said, "you should understand what's happening. You remember your daddy and you've been around and seen a few people and have some idea how they act. You've been working in drugstores and barbershops and at that office and since you've been around . . . and . . . as much as you have, you must know that she's crazy. So use your head. She doesn't have to be put in an institution, but you have to understand and accept the fact that she isn't responsible."

It was a rather shocking notion for me and I didn't want to surrender my anger, but I realized that my mother was right. What's more, I realized that very often I could save myself a lot of wear and tear with people if I just learned to understand them.

Beyond that, although she was religious, my mother had a great tolerance for the affairs of the world which had nothing to do with religion, and I think that that helped me to sort of balance things out, so to speak. The great emphasis in my school was upon classical music, but such great jazz musicians as Hot Lips Paige, Jimmy Rushing, and Lester Young were living in Oklahoma City, and through her allowing me to attend public dances and to maintain a certain friendship with some of them, even though she watched what I was doing, she made it possible to approach the life of the Negro community there with some sense of its wholeness instead of trying to distort it into some hoped-for religion-conceived perfection. As it turned out, the perfection, the artistic dedication which helped me as a writer, was not so much in the classical emphasis as within the jazz itself.

She also helped me to escape the limitations of trying to impose any in-group class distinctions upon the people of my community. We were very poor, but my father had been a small businessman who sold ice and coal to both whites and blacks, and since he and my mother were pioneers in a young state, my mother knew some of the city's leaders; they were my father's friends and remained as my mother's after his death. So she didn't strive to be part of the social leadership of the black community; that was left to the wives of professional men, to teachers and preachers. Her background and attitudes were such that all kinds of people came into the house, or we visited their houses. That was one of the enriching parts of my experience, because I knew people who went right back to the farm and plantation, along with those who had gone to college and medical school. Thus my sense of their stories and life-styles, and so on, was never very far from mind. My mother had grown up on a Georgia plantation herself, she was a farm girl; and then she left and went to live in Atlanta. It gave me a sense of a past which was far from narrow.

She liked to talk. She never allowed me to lose the vividness of my father, and she told me all kinds of things that he had done—that he had run away from his own father in South Carolina when he was quite young, and had become a professional soldier, and had been in Cuba and in the Philippines and in China. He was with our troops that fought against the Boxer Rebellion. Afterwards, he and his brother had operated a candy kitchen in Chattanooga. He had also operated a restaurant—always trying to get at something—and then had become a construction foreman; that was how they came West to Oklahoma.

There was also her overt and explicit concern with political conditions. There was never a time when I was not aware of what these were all about. When I was in college, my mother broke a segregated-housing ordinance in Oklahoma City, and they were throwing her in jail, and the NAACP would get her out, and they'd come back and throw her in jail again. This went on until my brother beat up one of the white inspectors, then she decided that it was about time to get out of that situation before he got himself shot. She had that kind of forthrightness, and I like to think that that was much more valuable than anything literary that she gave me.

HERSEY. The creative drive seems always to have been strong in you, ever since childhood. You said once that you couldn't remember a time when you hadn't wanted to make something—a one-tube radio, a crystal set, a toy; a little later you had an urge to compose music. Where do you think this drive came from?

ELLISON. I don't know where it comes from. Maybe it had something to do with my father's working as a construction foreman, building buildings. It certainly came from some of the boys that I grew up with, as a child. They were always *doing* things. I always admired the guys who could make things, who could draw. This was something that gave me a great deal of pleasure.

But maybe the desire to write goes back to a Christmas gift. One Christmas my mother gave me—I must have been five—a little roll-top desk and a chair, not a swivel chair but a little straight chair, oak, and a little toy typewriter. I had forgotten that. We were living in the parsonage of the old A.M.E. Church, Avery Chapel, which the leaders of the congregation turned over to my mother after the new minister turned out to have his own home. "Why don't you be the janitress of the church and live in the parsonage?" they said. And we did, and that's where I got the desk and the little typewriter. I was also given a chemistry set. Now this might have been unusual in such relatively uneducated families—I think my mother went to the eighth grade in school—but she felt that these were the kinds of things that her boys should have. She was also very explicit, as we grew older, about our economic condition. We knew why we could not have a bicycle, why we could not have this, that, or the other. She explained that we could not have such things because she didn't have the money, and we had to accept that fact. So what did we do? We learned to do other things. Instead of playing with store-bought toys, you made your own. You fished and hunted, you listened to music, you danced and you spent a great amount of time reading and dreaming over books.

When Mr. Mead, next door, taught me the fundamentals of playing an old brass alto horn, my mother bought me a pawnshop cornet. She could afford that, and owning the instrument made it possible for me to acquire enough skill to get into the school band. So she did what she could, and in addition to encouraging my interest in reading she encouraged my interest in music, and so on.

But the desire to make something out of my imagination and to experiment was constant. In one story of mine there is an incident taken from life, where my brother and I took baby chickens and made little parachutes and got up on top of the chicken house and dropped them down. The lady next door told my mother, and we caught hell for that. We didn't kill the chickens, understand, we just floated them down. We did that, you see, because we had learned to take iron taps and tie strings to them and then attach the strings to pieces of cloth. When we threw these into the air we'd get a parachute effect and imagine that the taps were parachutists. We just took it a step further.

HERSEY. What would you say was the starting point for your new novel?

ELLISON. I guess it started with the idea of an old man being so outraged by his life that he goes poking around in the cellar to find a forgotten coffin, which he had bought years before to insure against his possible ruin. He discovers that he has lived so long that the coffin is full of termites, and that even the things he had stored in the coffin have fallen apart. Somehow, this said something to my imagination and got me started. You can see that it could go in *any* direction. But then it led to the other idea, which I wrote first, of a little boy being placed in a coffin, in a ritual of death and transcendence, celebrated by a Negro evangelist who was unsure whether he was simply exploiting the circus sideshow shock set off by the sight of a child rising up out of a coffin, or had hit upon an inspired way of presenting the sacred drama of the Resurrection. In my mind all of this is tied up in some way with the significance of being a Negro in America and at the same time with the problem of our democratic faith as a whole. Anyway, as a product of the imagination it's like a big sponge, maybe, or a waterbed, with a lot of needles sticking in it at various points. You don't know what is being touched, where the needles are going to end up once you get them threaded and penetrated, but somehow I kept trying to tie those threads together and the needle points pressing home without letting whatever lies in the center leak out.

HERSEY. How soon after *Invisible Man* was published [1952] did you start working on the new novel?

ELLISON. I was pretty depleted by *Invisible Man*, so I didn't start on another book immediately. I played around with various ideas and spent some time trying to salvage material I had edited out of *Invisible Man*. It was in Rome, during 1956, that I began to think vaguely about this book and conceived the basic situation, which had to do with a political assassination; this was involved with the other patterns—the coffin business.

HERSEY. This was before the Kennedys and King were assassinated, of course.

ELLISON. Yes, this was before. Almost eight years before. One of the things which really chilled me—slowed down the writing—was that eruption of assassinations, especially the first. Because, you see, much of the mood of this book was conceived as comic. Not that the assassination was treated comically, but there is humor involved, and that was rather chilling for me, because suddenly life was stepping in and imposing itself upon my fiction. Anyway, I managed to keep going with it, I guess because there was nothing else to do. I know that it led me to try to give the book a richer structuring, so that the tragic elements could contain the comic and the comic the tragic, without violating our national pieties—if there are any left. Americans have always been divided in their pieties, but today there is such a deliberate flaunting of the pieties and traditions—of others, anyway—that it's become rather difficult to distinguish what is admissible from that which is inadmissible. Even the flag and motherhood are under attack.

HERSEY. With such fast-moving reality so close at hand, how much in control of your fictional characters can you feel that you are?

ELLISON. Once a logic is set up for a character, once he begins to move, then that which is implicit within him tends to realize itself, and for you to discover the *form* of the fiction, you have to go where he takes you, you have to follow him. In the process you change your ideas. You remember, Dostoevski wrote about eight versions of a certain scene in *The Brothers Karamazov*, and in some instances the original incidents were retained but the characters who performed them were changed. I find that happens with me. I get to the point where something has to be done and discover that it isn't logical for the character who started out to do it, to do it; and suddenly another character pops up. In this book there is an instance wherein McIntyre has to interview the man who burns his Cadillac. This man is being held in the observation cell of a hospital because the authorities believe that a Negro who burns his own Cadillac has to be crazy. So for McIntyre to see the man there has to be an intermediary—so suddenly I found myself dealing with a new character, a Negro employed by the hospital, who gets McIntyre past the barriers and to the car-burner. This fellow wasn't foreseen; he simply appeared to help me get on with the form.

HERSEY. About motive—what gives you the psychic energy to take on a massive work and keep at it for a very long time?

ELLISON. I guess it is the writing itself. I am terribly stubborn, and once I get engaged in that kind of project, I just have to keep going until I finally make something out of it. I don't know what the something is going to be, but the process is one through which I make a good part of my own experience meaningful. I don't mean in any easy autobiographical sense, but the matter of drawing actual experience, thought, and emotion together in a way that creates an artifact through which I can reach other people. Maybe that's vanity; I don't know. Still I believe that fiction does help create value, and I regard this as a very serious—I almost said "sacred"—function of the writer.

Psychic energy? I don't know, I think of myself as kind of lazy. And yet, I do find that working slowly, which is the only way I seem able to work—although I write fast much of the time—the problem is one of being able to receive from my work that sense of tension, that sense of high purpose being realized, that keeps me going. This is a crazy area that I don't understand—none of the Freudian explanations seem adequate.

HERSEY. As to the short range, you used a phrase last night that interested me. You said you wanted to keep the early morning free "in case the night before had generated something that could be put to good use." What did you mean by that?

ELLISON. I never know quite what has gone on in my subconscious in the night, I dream vividly, and all kinds of things happen; by morning they have fallen below the threshold again. But I like to feel that whatever takes place becomes active in some way in what I do at the typewriter. In other words, I believe that a human being's life is of a whole, and that he lives the full twenty-four hours. And if he is a writer or an artist, what happens during the night feeds back, in some way, into what he does consciously during the day—that is, when he is doing that which is self-achieving, so to speak. Part of the pleasure of writing, as well as the pain, is involved in pouring into that thing which is being created all of what he cannot understand and cannot say and cannot deal with, or cannot even admit, in any other way. The artifact is a completion of personality.

HERSEY. Do you experience anything like daydreaming or dreaming when you are writing? Do you feel that the writing process may involve a somewhat altered state of consciousness in itself?

ELLISON. I think a writer learns to be as conscious about his craft as he can possibly be—not because this will make him absolutely lucid about what he does, but because it prepares the stage for structuring his daydreaming and allows him to draw upon the various irrational elements involved in writing. You know that when you begin to structure literary forms you are going to have to play variations on your themes, and you are going to have to make everything vivid, so that the reader can see and hear and feel and smell, and, if you're lucky, even taste. All that is on a conscious level and very, very important. But then, once you get going, strange things occur. There are things in *Invisible Man*, for instance, that I can't *imagine* my having consciously planned. They materialized as I worked consciously at other things. Take three of the speeches: the speech made at the eviction, the funeral address in Mount Morris Park, and the one that Barbee made in chapel. Now, I realized consciously, or I *discovered* as I wrote, that I was playing variations on what Otto Rank identified as the myth of the birth and death of the hero. So in the rewriting that conscious knowledge, that insight, made it possible to come back and add elements to the design which I had written myself into under the passion of telling a story.

What should also be said in this connection is that somewhere—it doesn't have to be right in the front of the mind, of the consciousness—writers, like other artists, are involved in a process of comparative culture. I looked at the copy of *The Lower Depths* on the table there this morning, and I remembered how much of Gorki I had read, and how I was always—not putting his characters into blackface, but finding equivalents for the experience he depicted; the equivalents for turns of phrase, for parables and proverbs, which existed within the various backgrounds that I knew. And I think that something of that goes on when a conscious writer goes about creating a fiction. It's part of his workshop, his possession of the culture of the form in which he works.

HERSEY. You once said that it took you a long time to learn how to adapt myth and ritual into your work. Faulkner speaks of a "lumber room in the subconscious," where old things are kept. How do you get at the sources of these things deep down in your mind?

ELLISON. I think I get at them through sheer work, converting incidents into patterns—and also by simply continuing at a thing when I don't seem to be getting anywhere. For instance, I wrote a scene in which Hickman is thinking about the difficulty of communicating with someone as constituting a "wall"; he thinks this as he is drifting off to sleep. Well, later in my work I suddenly realized that the damn wall had turned up again in another form. And that's when that voice in my unconscious finally said, "Hey, *this* is what you've been getting at." And looking back, I saw that I had worked up a little pattern of these walls. What the unconscious mind does is to put all manner of things into juxtaposition. The conscious mind has to provide the logical structure of narrative and incident through which these unconscious patterns can be allowed to radiate by throwing them into artful juxtaposition on the page.

HERSEY. Do you, as some writers do, have a sense of standing in a magic circle when you write?

ELLISON. To the extent that unexpected things occur, that characters say things or see things which, for all my attempts to be conscious and to work out of what I call a conceptual outline, are suddenly just *there*. That *is* magical, because such things seem to emerge out of the empty air. And yet, you know that somehow the dreams, emotions, ironies, and hidden implications of your material often find ways of making themselves manifest. You work to make them reveal themselves.

HERSEY. Do you, when you are writing, sometimes find yourself so totally engaged by a character that you are carried away outside yourself by *his* feelings—are literally beside yourself?

ELLISON. I find myself carried away and emotionally moved, sometimes quite unexpectedly, and my tendency is to distrust it, feeling that perhaps I'm being sentimental, being caught in a situation which I am not adequately transforming into art. So I put it aside and wait awhile, maybe months, and then go back, and if it still works after I've examined it as well as I can, as objectively as I can, I then perhaps read it to Fanny, and if she doesn't indicate that it's slobbering sentimentality, in bad taste, or just poorly achieved—then I leave it in.

HERSEY. Would you say that, by and large, when you have had these surges of feeling the writing does hold up in the long run?

ELLISON. Sometimes it does, sometimes it doesn't. I won't be able to say about this book until it has been read by enough objective readers. I won't be able to judge until then because it has some crazy developments.

I found myself writing a scene in which Hickman and Wilhite, his deacon, go into a strange house in Washington, and find a bunch of people in the hallway who are very upset because the police won't tell them what has happened in the apartment of one of their neighbors. Then one of the women goes hysterical and pretty soon she's outraging the crowd by talking about the most personal matters as she addresses herself to a bewildered Wilhite and Hickman. Not only was I shocked to discover myself writing this unplanned scene, but I still have questions about how it functions. Yet, for all its wild, tragicomic emotion—there it is! Now when your material takes over like that you are really being pushed. Thus, when this woman started confessing, she forced *me* to think about Hickman's role as minister on a different level; I mean on the theological level, which was something I hadn't planned, since I wasn't writing an essay but a novel. Finally, Hickman came to my aid by recognizing that the woman had been unfolding a distorted and highly personalized dream-version of the immaculate birth. To me she sounded merely irrational and comic, but Hickman, being a minister, forced himself to look beneath her raving, even though she is without question a most unacceptable surrogate for the Virgin. After that, I was forced to realize that this crazy development was really tied in with the central situation of the novel: that of an old man searching throughout the years for a little boy who ran away. So I guess it sprang from that magic circle you referred to, from that amorphous level which lies somewhere between the emotions and the intellect, between the consciousness and the unconscious, which supports our creative powers but which we cannot control.

HERSEY. I have wondered about the ways in which your musical experience has fed into your writing.

ELLISON. My sense of form, my basic sense of artistic form, is musical. As a boy I tried to write songs, marches, exercises in symphonic form, really before I received any training, and then I studied it. I listened constantly to music, trying to learn the processes of developing a theme, of expanding and contracting and turning it inside out, of making bridges, and working with techniques of musical continuity, and so on. I think that basically my instinctive approach to writing is through *sound.* A change of mood and mode comes to me in terms of sound. That's one part of it, in the sense of composing the architecture of a fiction.

On the other hand, one of the things I work for is to make a line of prose *sound* right, or for a bit of dialogue to fall on the page in the way I hear it, aurally, in my mind. The same goes for the sound and intonation of a character's voice. When I am writing of characters who speak in the Negro idiom, in the vernacular, it is still a real problem for me to make their accents fall in the proper place in the visual line.

HERSEY. Which comes first for you in writing, hearing or seeing?

ELLISON. I might conceive of a thing aurally, but to realize it you have got to make it vivid. The two things must operate together. What is the old phrase—"the planned dislocation of the senses"? That *is* the condition of fiction, I think. Here is where sound becomes sight and sight becomes sound, and where sign becomes symbol and symbol becomes sign; where fact and idea must not just be hanging there but must become a functioning part of the total design, involving itself in the reader as idea as well as drama. You do this by providing the reader with as much detail as is possible in terms of the visual *and* the aural, *and* the rhythmic—to allow him to involve himself, to attach himself, and then begin to collaborate in the creation of the fictional spell. Because you simply cannot put it all there on the page, you can only evoke it—or evoke what is already there, implicitly, in the reader's head: his sense of life.

HERSEY. You mentioned "making bridges" a minute ago. I remember that you once said that your anxiety about transitions greatly prolonged the writing of *Invisible Man*.

ELLISON. Yes, that has continued to be something of a problem. I try to tell myself that it is irrational, but it is what happens when you're making something, and you know that you are *making* something rather than simply relating an anecdote that actually happened. But at the same time you have to strike a balance between that which you can imply and that which you must make explicit, so that the reader can follow you. One source of this anxiety comes, I think, from my sense of the variations in American backgrounds—especially as imposed by the racial situation. I can't always be certain that what I write is going to be understood. Now, this doesn't mean that I am writing for whites, but that I realize that as an American writer I have a problem of communicating across our various social divisions, whether of race, class, education, region, or religion—and much of this holds true even within my own racial group. It's dangerous to take things for granted.

This reminds me of something that happened out at a northwestern university. A young white professor said to me, ''Mr. Ellison, how does it feel to be able to go to places where most Negroes can't go?'' Before I could think to be polite I answered, ''What you mean is: 'How does it feel to be able to go places where most *white* men can't go?'' He was shocked and turned red, and I was embarrassed; nevertheless, it was a teaching situation so I told him the truth. I wanted him to understand that individuality is still operative beyond the racial structuring of American society. And that, conversely, there are many areas of black society that are closed to *me* while open to certain whites. Friendship and shared interests make the difference.

When you are writing fiction out of your individual sense of American life it's difficult to know what to take for granted. For instance, I don't know whether I can simply refer to an element of decor and communicate the social values it stands for, because so much depends upon the way a reader makes associations. I am more confident in such matters than I was when writing *Invisible Man*, but for such an allusion—say, to a certain type of chair or vase or painting—to function, the reader must not be allowed to limit his understanding of what is implied simply because the experience you are presenting is, in its immediate sense, that of blacks. So the writer must be aware that the reality of race conceals a complex of manners and culture, because such matters influence the shaping of fictional form and govern, to a large extent, the writer's sense of proportion, and determine what he feels obligated to render as well as what he feels he can simply imply.

I had to learn, for instance, that in dramatic scenes, if you got the reader going along with your own rhythm, you could omit any number of explanations. You could leave great gaps, because in his sense of urgency the reader would say, ''Hell, don't waste time telling me how many steps he walked to get there, I want to know what he *did* once he got there!'' An ellipsis was possible and the reader would fill the gap.

Still, I have uncertainty about some of the things I'm doing, and especially when I'm using more than one main voice, and with a time scheme that is much more fragmented than in *Invisible Man*. There I was using a more tidy dramatic form. This novel is dramatic within its incidents, but it moves back and forth in time. In such a case I guess an act of faith is necessary, a faith that if what you are writing is of social and artistic importance and its diverse parts are presented vividly in the light of its overall conception, and if you *render* the story rather than just tell it, then the reader will go along. That's a lot of "ifs," but if you can involve him in the process his reading becomes a pleasurable act of discovery.

HERSEY. Do you have in mind an image of some actualized reader to whom you are communicating as you write?

ELLISON. There is no *specific* person there, but there is a sort of ideal reader, or informed persona, who has some immediate sense of the material that I'm working with. Beyond that there is my sense of the rhetorical levers within American society, and these attach to all kinds of experiences and values. I don't want to be a behaviorist here, but I'm referring to the systems of values, the beliefs and customs and sense of the past, and that hope for the future, which have evolved through the history of the Republic. These do provide a medium of communication.

For instance, the old underdog pattern. It turns up in many guises, and it allows the writer to communicate with the public over and beyond whatever the immediate issues of his fiction happen to be. That is, deep down we believe in the underdog, even though we give him hell; and this provides a rhetoric through which the writer can communicate with a reader beyond any questions of their disagreements over class values, race, or anything else. But the writer must be aware that that is what is there. At the same time, I do not think he can manipulate his readers too directly; it must be an oblique process, if for no other reason than that to do it too directly throws you into propaganda, as against that brooding, questioning stance that is necessary for fiction.

HERSEY. How do literary influences make themselves felt concretely in your work? You have spoken often of Joyce, Eliot, Dostoevski, Hemingway, Stein, Malraux, and others as having influenced you early. How do the influences manifest themselves? How have you transformed them for your own ends?

ELLISON. It is best, of course, when they don't show themselves directly, but they are there in many ways. Joyce and Eliot, for instance, made me aware of the playful possibilities of language. You look at a page of *Finnegans Wake* and see references to all sorts of American popular music, yet the context gives it an extension from the popular back to the classical and beyond. This is just something that Joyce teaches you that you can do, and you can abstract the process and apply it to a frame of reference which is American and historical, and it can refer to class, it can refer to the fractions and frictions of color, to popular and folk culture—it can do many things.

A writer makes himself present in your work through allowing you to focus upon certain aspects of experience. Malraux's concern with the individual caught up consciously in a historical situation, a revolutionary situation, provided insights which allowed me to understand certain possibilities in the fictional material around me. From him I learned that the condition of that type of individual is essentially the same, regardless of his culture or the political climate in which he finds his existence.

Or again, some writers—say, Dostoevski, or even Tolstoy—will make you very much aware of what is possible in depicting a society in which class lines either are fluid or have broken down without the cultural style and values on either extreme of society being dissipated. From such writers you learn to explore the rich fictional possibilities to be achieved in juxtaposing the peasant's consciousness with that of the aristocrat and the aristocrat's with the peasant's. This insight is useful when you are dealing with American society. For years, white people went through Grand Central Station having their luggage carried by Ph.D.'s. They couldn't see the Ph.D.'s because their race and class attitudes had trained them to see only the uniforms and the dark faces, but the Ph.D.'s could see them and judged them on any number of levels. This makes for drama, and it is a drama which goes right to the core of the democratic faith. So you get your moral perception of the contradictions of American class and personality from such literature, even more, perhaps, than from psychiatry or sociology, because such novelists have always dealt with the drama of social living.

HERSEY. You once had some very interesting things to say about the similarities and differences of the stances of black and Jewish writers in this country. It seems clear that Russian novelists have had a special kind of access to the deeper resources we were talking about earlier, access to primary feelings. Do you think there are particular ways in which Negro writers have had a corresponding access to those deeper resources—different in kind or degree from that of the Jewish writer, or the white Protestant writer in America, say, or the Russian writer, or the English writer?

ELLISON. You will have to be very careful about that, because writers are individuals, each unique in his own way. But I would think that the access to primary feelings that the great Russian novelists had grew out of the nature of their society and the extreme disruption of hierarchal relationships which occurred during the nineteenth century. Then you had a great declassed aristocracy, with the Tsar still at the top, and an awakening peasantry at the bottom. On one hand, society was plunging headlong into chaos, and on the other there was a growing identification on the part of many declassed aristocrats with the peasantry, an identification across traditional hierarchal divisions which was sustained by the unifying force of Russian Greek Orthodox Christianity. The friction generated by these social unities and divisions in that chaotic scene made possible all kinds of intensities of emotion and aggravations of sensibility. The belief in the Tsar as a sacred "Little Father" remained a unifying force, but was no longer strong enough to rationalize and impose order upon the expression of primary emotions—class hate, greed, ambition, and so on. Such disruption of the traditional ordering of society, as in our own country since 1954, made for an atmosphere of irrationality, and this created a situation of unrestrained expressiveness. Eyeballs were peeled, nerves were laid bare, and private sensibilities were subjected to public laceration. In fact, life became so theatrical (not to say nightmarish) that even Dostoevski's smoking imagination was barely able to keep a step ahead of what was actually happening in the garrets and streets. Today, here in the United States, we have something similar, but there's no point in my trying to explain Russian extremism, or the genius of the great nineteenth-century Russian novelists. Not even Dostoevski was able to do that.

Anyway, for all its expressiveness and chaos, the Negro American situation is something else, both in degree and source. Except for the brief period of Reconstruction, when we helped create the new constitutions of the southern states and attempted to restructure society so as to provide a more equal set of relationships between the classes and races, we were *below* the threshold of social hierarchy. Our social mobility was strictly, and violently, limited—and in a way that neither our Christianity nor belief in the principles of the Constitution could change. As the sociologists say, we were indeed disadvantaged, both by law and by custom. And yet, our actual position was ambiguous. For although we were outside the social compact, we were existentially right in the middle of the social drama. I mean that as servants we were right in the bedroom, so to speak. Thus we saw things, and we understood the difference between ideal assertions and crude realities. Much of the rhetorical and political energy of white society went toward proving to itself that we were not human and that we had no sense of the refinement of human values. But this in itself pressured you, motivated you, to make even finer distinctions, both as to personality and value. You *had* to, because your life depended upon it and your sense of your own humanity demanded that you do so. You had to identify those values which were human and preserving of your life and interests as against those which were inhuman and destructive. So we were thrown upon our own resources and sense of life. We were forced to define and act out our own idea of the heights and depths of the human condition. Because human beings cannot live in a situation where violence can be visited upon them without any concern for justice—and in many instances without possibility of redress—without developing a very intense sense of the precariousness of all human life, not to mention the frailty and arbitrariness of human institutions. So you were forced to be existential in your outlook, and this gives a poignancy and added value to little things and you discover the value of modes and attitudes that are rejected by the larger society. It also makes you terribly brutal and thick-skinned toward some values while ultrasensitive to others.

Now this background provides the black writer with much to write about. As fictional material it rivals that of the nineteenth-century Russians. But to the extent that other American writers, writers of different backgrounds, understand this material, or can implicate it in their own experience, they too have a way into what is currently known as "the black experience"—which I prefer to call "the *Negro* American experience"—because for it to be worthy of fictional treatment, worthy of art, it has to be meaningful to others who do not share in its immediacy. I'll add that since it is both my own and an irrevocable part of the basic experience of the United States, *I* think that it is not only worthy but indispensable to any profoundly *American* depiction of reality.

To repeat myself, this society has structured itself so as to be unaware of what it owes in both the positive and negative sense to the condition of inhumanity that it has imposed upon a great mass of its citizens. The fact that many whites refuse to recognize this is responsible for much of the anger erupting among young blacks today. It makes them furious when whites respond to their complaints with, "Yes, but *I* had nothing to do with any of that," or reply to their demands for equal opportunity in a racially rigged society with, "We're against a quota system because *we* made it on our individual merits"—because this not only sidesteps a pressing reality, but it is only partially true. Perhaps they *did* make it on their own, but if that's true the way was made easier because their parents did not have to contend with *my* parents, who were ruled out of the competition. They had their troubles too, but the relative benevolence of democracy shared by their parents, and now by them, was paid for by *somebody* other than themselves, and was being paid long before many of them arrived on these shores. *We* know that as the nation's unwilling scapegoat we paid for much of it. Nor is this knowledge a matter of saying, "Pay us off," or saying, in the words of the old joke, "Your granddaddy kicked my granddaddy a hundred years ago, so now I've come to collect the debt, bend over." That's not the point. The point is one of moral perception, the perception of the wholeness of American life and the cost of its successes and its failures. What makes for a great deal of black fury is the refusal of many Americans to understand that somebody paid for the nation's peace and prosperity in terms of blood and frustrated dreams; that somebody now denied his proper share helped convert the raw materials into the sophisticated gadgetry. I don't mean to imply that only the blacks did this; the poor southern whites, the Irish, numbers of peoples did. They, too, underwent the crudities and inequities of democracy so that the high rhetoric could retain some resonance of possibility and truth.

HERSEY. How much is anger a motive force for novelists of all kinds? Does the artist start with anger more than with other emotions?

ELLISON. I don't think that he necessarily starts with anger. Indeed, anger can get in the way, as it does for a fighter. If the writer starts with anger, then if he is truly writing he immediately tranlates it through his craft into consciousness, and thus into understanding, into insight, perception. Perhaps, that's where the morality of fiction lies. You see a situation which outrages you, but as you write about the characters who embody that which outrages, your sense of craft and the moral role of your craft demands that you depict those characters in the breadth of their humanity. You try to give them the density of the human rather than the narrow intensity of the demonic. That means that you try to delineate them as men and women who possess feelings and ideals, no matter how much you reject their feelings and ideals. Anyway, I find this happening in my own work; it humanizes *me*. So the main motive is not to express raw anger, but to present—as sentimental as it might sound—the wonder of life, in the fullness of which all these outrageous things occur.

HERSEY. Have you felt some defiance of death as a writer—in the sense that what you are making may possibly circumvent death?

ELLISON. No, I dare not. (*He laughs*) No, you just write for your own time, while trying to write in terms of the density of experience, knowing perfectly well that life repeats itself. Even in this rapidly changing United States it repeats itself. The mystery is that while repeating itself it always manages slightly to change its mask. To be able to grasp a little of that change within continuity and to communicate it across all these divisions of background and individual experience seems enough for me. If you're lucky, of course, if you splice into one of the deeper currents of life, then you have a chance of having your work last a little bit longer.

II

Ellison and I resumed this conversation, some time later, in Key West, where he and I are off-and-on next-door neighbors in small "conch" houses. This time I began asking him to tell me about his formative years.

HERSEY: Could we talk a bit about your fledgling years in writing? Would you tell about how you got started?

ELLISON: Well, it was kind of play, at first. I had begun to read Eliot and Pound and Hemingway and others—I think I read my first Hemingway in *Esquire* in barbershops in my home city, but it was Eliot's *Waste Land*, with its footnotes, that made me become fascinated with how writing was written. I always read a lot; I took a course in the nineteenth-century English novel at Tuskegee.

HERSEY: Who put *The Waste Land* in your way?

ELLISON: It was in the library at Tuskegee—a good library, even though it wasn't enough used. In fact, you could find most of the anthropological and geological references in that library. I worked in the library one year, just prowling the stacks, and reading. No one taught Eliot there. I think I got one professor interested in that area, although he was a very good man with a very good mind.

HERSEY: You've told me in the past about Richard Wright's taking you under his wing when you moved to New York. When did you meet him?

ELLISON: When I got to New York, I happened to have seen a copy of the *New Masses*, which had a poem by Wright. I was interested, because I did not see the techniques of modern poetry in the work of Afro-American poets. I happened to meet Langston Hughes the first morning that I was in New York. Staying at the Harlem Annex of the YMCA, I went across the street to get breakfast, and he was talking there with Alain Locke who was professor of philosophy at Howard, one of the theorists of the Negro Renaissance. I had read Locke's work, and I had met him a few weeks before, when he had been at Tuskegee to visit Hazel Harrison. So I introduced myself to him, and he introduced me to Hughes. Hughes put me to work immediately to return some books to the library. They happened to be Malraux's *Days of Wrath* and *Man's Fate*. He said, "You can read these before you return them, if you like," and of course I read them. I had read some Marxism even at Tuskegee—that, too, was in the library! I was quite excited by these books of Malraux's, and I asked Hughes if he knew a Negro writer by the name of Wright. He said, "Yes, he'll be here next week," and he dropped Wright a card. When Wright got to New York, he sent me a card telling me where I could meet him. We hit it off, because I was, I guess, one of the few Afro-Americans at that point who could talk about writing. At that time I had no thought of becoming a writer myself—my world was music. I had tried to write some poetry at Tuskegee, but just for myself, just playing around with it. One poem was published; my first publication was a poem, which I wrote after a friend of mine died. He hadn't attended Tuskegee but had gone to some other university, and coming home, he had had an attack of appendicitis; they wouldn't accept him at a white hospital and peritonitis had set in.

One of Wright's reasons for coming to New York was to work in the Harlem bureau of *The Daily Worker* and to edit a magazine which they were trying to resuscitate. It had been called *Challenge* during the Harlem Renaissance; they now called it *New Challenge*. He was editing this with two women, and he wanted a book review, so I wrote my first book review—not a very good one. I later reviewed the same book for the *Times*, and I think I did a *little* better! And then as he planned his next issue, he didn't have any short fiction, and he asked me to write a story. I said, "I don't know anything about writing a story." He said, "You talk well about stories. Why don't you try? You've had some experiences." I had ridden freight trains, so I wrote a story about an incident occurring on a hobo trip. He accepted it. I still have the galleys somewhere. But the magazine folded; the girls didn't get along. But by that time, I was caught, hooked. I began to write little stories, and the *New Masses* published them; and I began to write book reviews for them. In some of the issues I wrote most of the unsigned reviews. They encouraged me. Some of the people there didn't particularly care for Wright. I guess he was rising too fast. They told me, "Oh, you're going to be a better writer than he is.'' I said, ''You're crazy.'' I just let that go. But I kept writing.

There's something of a misunderstanding about Wright and my fiction. I met him in 1936 and I was writing a lot of fiction, but I approached writing as I approached music. I'd been playing since I was eight years old, and I knew you didn't just reach a capable performance in whatever craft without *work*. I'd play one set of scales over and over again. In Tuskegee I'd get up early in the morning—and this was required of brass instrument players—and I'd blow sustained tones for an hour. I knew the other students used to hate it, but this developed embouchure, breath control, and so on. And I approached writing in the same way. I wrote a hell of a lot of stuff that I didn't submit to anybody. At first I showed some of my things to Wright, and then by 1940 I wrote a story which had to do with some fight that broke out between a chef and a hallboy in a club, basing it upon a club where I had worked in Oklahoma City; I'd worked there as a bread-and-butter boy and then as an extra waiter—and I showed this to Dick, and he kept it and kept it and didn't say anything. I let a few weeks go by and then finally said, ''Well, what *about* it? What *about* it?'' And he said, ''This is *my* stuff.'' And I said, ''O.K., but what do you expect? I thought I was taking your advice.'' So after that I never showed him another piece of fiction.

HERSEY: What kind of advice had he been giving you?

ELLISON: Well, he'd suggest how to tighten, that kind of thing. Wright did not have the kind of experience I'd had and was not familiar with it; but generally he gave me suggestions on structure. I was struggling with the problem of how to render Afro-American speech without resorting to misspellings—to give a *suggestion* of the idiom. Of course I had a musician's ear; and I kept working with that. Some of the first things were embarrassing. You go from something that you've read, until you find out about how *you* really feel about it. But after 1940, I'd show him some of my essays and book reviews, and very often he felt that I had too many ideas in the pieces, and I told myself, ''Well, there may be too many ideas, but I guess the real problem is in articulating them''—because by then I was reading a hell of a lot of Malraux, and I knew that I didn't have enough ideas to cause confusion; it was a matter of writing with clarity. So I kept working for that. I started to come in contact with writer-intellectuals in New York—on the [New York Federal] Writers Project and because Wright introduced me to people in the League of American Writers. I began to meet people. They were so available during those days! And, you know, you began to *measure* yourself. In trying to learn something I talked to very well-known Afro-American writers, and I found that they did not know consciously what was going on in literature. I could not discuss technique with them, and even though we shared some points of ideology, because a number of them were leftists, they couldn't talk to me about technical matters.

HERSEY: Who might some of them have been?

ELLISON: Well, Hughes was one, Claude McKay was another, and there were lesser writers, some newspapermen. But they were all on the Project. Some of the stuff I worked on back then has recently been published.

HERSEY: What sorts of things did you do with the Project?

ELLISON: I did several things. But the main thing was a book to be titled *Negroes in New York.* When I got into the research, I realized I was dealing with American history. It was an education in itself. I also worked on a projected book of folklore—B. A. Botkin was at the top somewhere, I didn't work directly under him; I collected kids' rhymes and game songs and so on, but I'd take the opportunity to question old people and get them to tell me stories. It was a rich harvest. It was just tremendous. And it fitted right into some of the things I was reading. By this time I was rereading Mark Twain, and I'd started reading Henry James. And it was this kind of thing where Wright was important. He introduced me to the Henry James prefaces, which were edited by Dick Blackmur. I used to repunctuate James's prose, so that I could get the most out of it! I had to teach myself to read him. And I was reading Conrad's essays—any writer who wrote about the craft. The Goncourt brothers, the Russians. I was also reading essays on the cinema by Eisenstein and Pudovkin. I would collect old copies of *Hound and Horn*, copies of *International Literature*; and I had a hell of a lot of Gorki's works; and the pamphlets on literature which were published by the Communists. And I was reading *Partisan Review*, even though I disagreed with the politics. Hell, I could read Eliot in the *Partisan Review*; I used to say, "I wonder why these guys are publishing people whose politics disagree with theirs." But I was glad that they did, because what Eliot had to say was far more interesting than what Philip Rahv had to say.

HERSEY: There is one other thing about those early days I'd like to explore with you. In my previous interview with you, we talked about family influences, and you told me how your mother and your father had helped to shape what you have become. You've often talked about Fanny's role in your literary life. Would you talk about that a little? She must have come into your life about that time.

ELLISON: As I said in the introduction to the thirtieth-anniversary edition of *Invisible Man*, when I met Fanny, she had a steady job. I had been working on the *Negro Quarterly*, and sometimes you got paid, and sometimes you didn't. Angelo Herndon had set up the *Negro Quarterly* and wanted someone who was familiar with literature to work with him. I was doing very well on the Writers Project—it wasn't much money, but it *came* on payday. And finally I said, "All right, Angelo, if you'll pay me what I make on the Writers Project, I'll come on there." I'd gone on the Project in 1938, and this was

1942; and of course the money was not always there. I guess I should say that I had been married once before.

HERSEY: Yes, I know.

ELLISON: By the time I met Fanny I was going to sea—in 1944. She worked for the Urban League. Of course I had money from my voyages; you got a bonus whenever you went into the war zone. So that was fine, but by the time we were married in 1944, the war was still on, and I was going to sea. In 1945, I started *Invisible Man*. I had come back from the sea and had no job. She was working. I began building high-fidelity amplifiers and installing sound systems with a friend of mine who knew more about such things than I did. And I took photographs and sold a few pieces, and so on. But the main—and secure—financial support was Fanny. Beyond that, she would read the damn stuff—and type it!—and correct the spelling! We laugh now, because I've become a much better speller, just by giving my attention to it.

HERSEY: Does she still help in these ways?

ELLISON: She still types final drafts; I type my rough stuff. I read aloud to her, over and over again.

HERSEY: Do her responses make a difference to you?

ELLISON: Yes, they do, very definitely. I don't always agree, because in an oral reading, you don't always get the nuances, you don't get the visual rhythm. But she knows quite a bit. Fanny studied drama and speech at the University of Iowa; so she's had her training. She directed a little in Chicago. before she was married. I think one of the reasons we became attracted to each other was that we both liked books. We combined our libraries. One of the things which always struck me is that we both had the same copy of *Vanity Fair*, which we'd kept; it had a cover with a Balinese woman by Covarrubias. I'd begun reading *Vanity Fair* when I was a kid; when I was able, I'd buy it. What you were exposed to in the magazine was the avant-garde. I was familiar with names that didn't turn up in college courses until many years later—even if it had been at Harvard! That's what I mean when I speak of "free-floating educational possibilities." If you're attuned, the stuff is there.

HERSEY: And then, of course, in 1952 you published *Invisible Man*, and everything must have changed in your life; all your relationships must have changed. What about your relationship with your former mentor, Wright, for instance?

ELLISON: Dick and I remained friends, although of course it had not been so close after he had gone to live in Paris. Fanny and I went over to Europe first in 1954, when I lectured at the Salzburg Seminars; then in 1955 when we went to Rome, we stopped in Paris and saw him; then I think I saw him again in 1956 when I went to Mexico for a conference and went by to see him as we passed through. There was some correspondence; a lot of the letters are in the collection at Yale. Our relationship changed, of course. After all, I had read books, and all kinds of books, most of my life, and Wright was self-taught, without even any structured instruction.

HERSEY: More than thirty years have passed since *Invisible Man*. You've grown and changed. America has changed. How will the big book you've been working on all this time differ in tone and purpose and method from *Invisible Man*?

ELLISON: You see, John, *Invisible Man* took on its own life, and has more or less gone its own way. I am identified with it. I haven't read the book in years and years. I've read sections. It's out there, and I certainly appreciate the fact that it lives. But the main thing is to make a rounded form out of the material I'm dealing with *now*. The book uses comic effects; maybe ultimately what I write always turns out to be tragicomedy, which I think has proved to be the underlying mode of American experience. We don't remember enough; we don't allow ourselves to remember events, and I suppose this helps us to continue our belief in progress. But the undercurrents are always there. You and I were speaking the other day about how we turn our eyes away from the role that religion has continued to play in American life. It has re-emerged recently as a very potent and, in some ways, dangerous force, and it has taken on the danger because we were not paying attention to its significance in all those earlier years. And this is not just to take a negative view of it. Negro religion has been a counterbalance to so much of the inequality and the imposed chaos which has been the American Negro experience. When Martin Luther King [Jr.] emerged as an important American figure, there was an instance of the church making itself visible in the political and social life and fulfilling its role in the realm of morality. So that the kinds of things which are involved in this book seem to have grown out of what has been happening all along.

HERSEY: The religious element in these intervening years operates in the book, then?

ELLISON: Yes. I guess with all my work there is an undergrounding of American history, as it comes to focus in the racial situation. One of the characters is a Negro minister who was once a jazz musician, a jazz trombonist; and he underwent an experience which turned him from his wild life as a musician into a serious minister, but one who also brought with him his experience as a showman. He isn't always sure when he's using religious methods, even though his motives are religious, or when he's allowing the devices of his old past to intrude.

HERSEY: Is this a metaphor for the tour of Ralph Ellison from jazz musician to another kind of performer in the moral realm?

ELLISON: No, I don't think of it that way. So much of American life evolves around the dedication toward a religious outlook, but religion always runs into the limitations of politics. Many of our politicians were ministers. We had a recent instance of a Catholic priest, Father Drinan, who had to be ordered out of Congress by Rome. This book was conceived before Martin Luther King became such a figure, but he, too, had to enter the realm of politics, while trying to stay outside it. When he began to connect the struggle for racial justice with Vietnam, he made himself quite vulnerable; that might well have played a role in his being killed. This fellow Hickman developed, as I worked on the book, from a musician who adopted the more folkish ways of ministers into something fairly sophisticated. He was always capable with words. He was the son of a preacher and thus inherited that kind of eloquence from his own family. The other part of it has to do with a little boy of indefinite race who looks white and who, through a series of circumstances, comes to be reared by the Negro minister. They used to go around, and the little boy preached; there have been plenty of examples of pairings like this, too, in actual life. One of the devices used was to bring the little boy into a service in a white coffin, and, at a certain point, when the minister would preach of Christ's agony on the cross, saying "Lord! Lord! Why hast thou forsaken me?" the little boy would rise up from the coffin!

HERSEY: Can you recall a little of the history of the development of the book?

ELLISON: I started working on it in 1958. Some of what I just told you appeared in the *Noble Savage*, for which Saul Bellow was one of the editors. It was the same period when, at Saul's urging, I started teaching at Bard College. That was an unsettled period for us. We had spent two years in Rome, and Fanny was working, having gone back to the job she had had before we went to Rome—where incidentally she had worked, too. The Catholic Church had set up something called La Lampada della Fraternita, which was a veterans organization, and they needed someone to set up a clerical system, and she went in there with her Berlitz Italian . . . it was quite admirable the way she went about it. When I came back, I didn't have a job. I was trying to stay out of activities in New York, so Bellow suggested that I live in his house in Tivoli, as he and his wife and baby were spending most of the year in Minnesota, at the university. I got started on the book and wrote quite a lot of it, but was never satisfied with how the parts connected. The sections I have published have gotten good responses, and I've given public readings of other sections, always with satisfaction. I'm finding myself having to try first-person narration, and then try it again as third-person, in an effort to stay out of it as narrator myself. It's exasperating, but at the same time I've come to feel that one of the challenges for a writer who handles the kind of material I'm working with is to let the people speak for themselves, in whatever way you can. Then you draw upon more of the resources of

American vernacular speech. One of the narrators is a newspaperman, a white, who had had some radical experiences during the thirties and had had an affair, which didn't end well, with a Negro girl.

HERSEY: What sort of time span do you cover?

ELLISON: Roughly from 1954 to 1956 or 1957. That is time present in the novel, but the story goes back into earlier experiences, too, even to some of the childhood experiences of Hickman, who is an elderly man in time present. It's just a matter of the past being active in the present—or of the characters becoming aware of the manner in which the past operates on their present lives. Of course, this gets into the general history, because one of the characters is a senator—he, too, is a trickster!

HERSEY: In our earlier talk you said: "I believe that fiction does help create value, and I regard this as a very serious—I almost said 'sacred'—function of the writer." I know you have very strong views about the moral fabric of the country. To what extent does fiction have a bearing on that fabric?

ELLISON: At its best, fiction allows for a summing up. The fiction writer abstracts from the flow of experience certain abiding patterns, and projects those patterns as they affect the lives and the consciousnesses of the characters. So fiction allows for a summing up. It allows for contemplation of the moral significance of human events. We don't always live up to the broader implications of this aspect of fiction, I think, because sometimes, out of a sense of frustration or disgust, we don't consider what a powerful effect vividly projected images of symbolic actions can have upon readers. If you think of the popularization of drugs and the let-it-all-hang-out syndrome—these are very suggestive; and I believe writers might think a little bit about the implications of what they project, and of the kinds of heroes or antiheroes they project. Of course I'm not offering formulas. Everyone has to work out his writing for himself, but the things he writes do have consequences. Sometimes you touch upon forces which are implicit, and you establish moods and give forms to attitudes. These are not always for the best. Someone asked me about all the burnings of tenements which occurred during the period after *Invisible Man* had been published, and I had to point out that I had covered the Harlem Riot of 1943 for the *New York Post*, and I certainly wasn't recommending that people burn buildings but was suggesting that that was a negative alternative to more democratic political action. When it was impossible to be heard within the democratic forum, people would inevitably go to other extremes. There was always somebody to suggest that we live in an era of revolutions. In any case, it is that aura of a summing up, that pause for contemplation of the moral significance of the history we've been through, that I have been reaching for, in my work on this new book.

Luminosity from the Lower Frequencies

LEON FORREST

I should like to discuss certain intellectual, cultural and historical influences upon Ralph Ellison's sense of the hero's character-in-process and the structure of the major chapters throughout his monumental novel, *Invisible Man*. Several influences come to mind: Kenneth Burke, Lord Raglan, Dostoevski and Faulkner, as well as the artistic and jazzlike rendering of folkloric sources.

From the literary critic Burke, Ellison came to see the possibility of using a formula to structure a chapter. Burke held that a pattern could be employed to achieve character-in-process progression through the formula of *purpose*, *passion*, and *perception*: each chapter begins with a *purpose* for the hero, but then much of the action of the middle section involves a struggle, or *passion*, over this *purpose*, or quest. Out of this mix or confrontation with others and the self, the hero comes away with a heightened *perception*, a keener awareness about his life, so that a metamorphosis, or rebirth, is implied. But these moments are stages of his processing into life, and the cycle, once completed, unleashes new problems and struggles.

Another literary influence on *Invisible Man* came from Lord Raglan, whose seminal book *The Hero* argues that a constant pattern of biographical data defines the lives of the heroes of tradition. The heroes Raglan calls forth run a gamut from Oedipus Rex to Elijah, Zeus, Orpheus, and Robin Hood. The pattern traces some twenty-two steps from birth to death. But the central constant in Raglan's pattern of heroic dimension is this: that the hero dies, goes through a life underground, and is reborn. Raglan's concept meshes neatly with Burke's formula of *purpose*, *passion*, and *perception*. For instance, the passion, or conflict, is quite similar to the turmoil in the mental underground and all of the attendant agonies. The idea of a heightened *perception* can be linked to Raglan's concept of rebirth, or even redemption in

Reprinted by permission of the author from *Carleton Miscellany* 18, No. 3 (Winter 1980), 82–97.

the Christian sense, and to discovery and self-recognition in the Aristotelian sense.

In the major chapters of his novel, Ellison—a jazz trumpeter who studied musical composition—orchestrates and improvises upon an introductory theme raised through a character at the beginning of a chapter. And he ends the chapter on an upbeat thematic moment (sometimes with an enriching, elusive literary statement, that speaks for the chapter and the intelligence of the novel as a whole "at the lower frequences") which stands in opposition to the opening thematic idea. Our sense of luminosity is heightened with the hero's, because of the sweeping poles or polar distances traversed from the beginning to the end. These are mini-odysseys of purpose, passion, and perception, we might say.

Ellison's arrangement of characters and themes standing in during confrontational moments forms a constant source of instruction, as we see the hero's character-in-process evolve and the novel evolve; and it helps the reader to see how these apparently oppositional forces are really quite closely connected. This device recalls anthropologist Levi-Strauss's concept of *thesis, counterthesis, synthesis*. And it is related to Dostoevski's uses of *doubling* and of character. One way of looking at doubling is to see it as a blending of opposites—characters who stand in sharp opposition to each other and yet have much in common.

The novel abounds with instances of this Dostoevskian doubling. There is for example the Norton/Trueblood pairing—a one-to-one confrontation, with the Oedipal desire/act forging a linkage between the rich, white, blue-blood philanthropist, Norton, and the poor, black, uneducated peasant farmer, Jim Trueblood. In Trueblood's dream, we discover an abundance of underground images indicating that Trueblood lusts for power in the real world as much as the powerful Norton lusts for the body of his own daughter—behind the monument of money he has donated in her honor to the school. Another form of Dostoevskian doubling occurs in the reverberating manner in which characters in apparent oppositional quest, status, or station are paired by a theme at completely different stages and times.

For instance, the theme of *eloquence*, its manipulation, uses and misuses, links the tall, Lincoln-like Hambro, mouthpiece for the Communist-like Brotherhood, with the spokesman-versifier for the Negro college and the American white way, the blind, Founder-celebrating minister, Homer Barbee. Short and ugly like Homer, Barbee gives a high-priest choral arrangement and tribal eulogy for the Founder that sounds like Whitman praising Abe Lincoln (note Ellison's parody on the great Whitman's grand blindness to Abe's angularity, his blemishes, his body-and-soul torment over slavery, his complexity of motives). Now these two high-powered word-artists-cum-magicians, in turn, represent two power-mad, master tricksters. For Hambro illuminates the enslaving dogma espoused by the one-eyed Cyclops, Brother Jack, *Head White Man in Charge* (HWMC) of the Brotherhood. And as Hambro attempts to drop the illuminating (but really enshrouding, and blinding) veil of "understanding" over the student-hero's eyes, he also blinds himself to the pranks of public policy that enslave the individual for the public good of this most private, elite of American parties. Thus he is veiled by his own public pronouncements.

And that high priest of bamaboozlement, Odyssey-echoing Homer Barbee, eloquently drops the enslaving veil of intellectual blindness across the students' eyes, to please that manipulator of polished slave chains, the college president Herbert Bledsoe and his captive audience of white trustees, that is, overseers. For in this situation, at least, Bledsoe is not only the Head Nigger in Charge (HNIC), but he has actually reversed the plantation system so that he is slave-master on this plantation, with Barbee as slave-driver of history. And Barbee, in turn, is blinded like the statue of the Founder, as he drops the veil honoring institutional power, which is manifested in the body and soul of the Founder's epic story (not in the students' learning and intellectual development). Barbee participates in his own self-impaling ceremony: he dims the light of his own intellectual and moral vision of history, preferring the luxurious delusion of "sweet harmonies" over the reality of the chaos of African-American life. And as he extinguishes his vision with his words, Barbee recalls Oedipus, who, having seen too much, tears out his eyes with the clasps of Jocasta's gown. Barbee's physical blindness seems a fitful banishment from the lost North Star light of daring freedom and progress, or as he himself says at one point, as he recalls the declining luminosity in the Founder's life on the train:

> I remember how I looked out of the frosted pane and saw the looming great North Star and lost it, as though the sky had shut its eye. (99)

In this sense, too, the phrase-polishing Barbee becomes a kind of scapegoat for Bledsoe, as minister Homer leads the lamb-innocent Negro students to a slaughtered rendering of their history. Yet their only hope for escape is the Underground Railroad, as it were, and that too on an individual basis. For each must read his or her own way through Barbee's fabulous spiel, and the only hope for escape from reenslavement is to hold fast to the undersides of their history, beneath Barbee's words and memories, and hope that probing questions will ignite a liberating response from their fellow blacks. Indeed they must be ready to commit a kind of "treason" like that "snowy-headed man" at one of the Founder's ceremonial lectures who demands that the Founder cut the accommodationist spiel and

> "Tell us what is to be done, sir! For God's sake, tell us! Tell us in the name of the son they snatched from me last week!" And all through the room the voices arising, imploring, "Tell us, tell us!" And the Founder is suddenly mute with tears. (97)

Like Ulysses escaping the Cyclops in the cave, the students must approach

Barbee's story with cunning to match the blinding light of his language and, like Ulysses, must catch hold of the sacred and the profane aspects of their history under-the-belly, and hold on for dear life—as Ulysses says, "so I caught hold of the ram by the back, ensconced myself in the thick wool under his belly and hung on patiently to his fleece, face upwards keeping a firm hold on it all of the time." For the students would need to reverse so much of Barbee's speech and to reveal the truths from oral history handed along by the great storytellers, truths that he constantly subordinates and countermands. This is a central problem for a young Negro confronted by all of the distortions of that peasant, underground history—a fact that the Klan-beset snowy-headed man in Homer Barbee's saga-spiel knows only too well.

Ellison is concerned there in the Barbee-Founder-Bledsoe trinity, as it were, with the unquestioned reverence for leadership that still seems to haunt certain groups within the race vulnerable to the cult of the personality, especially when touched by the fires of political-religious enterprise. But there is a yeasty truth in Barbee's saga. Barbee knows the language of power, and he manipulates it as it manipulates him—and in that sense he's masking the wisdom of his peasant tongue. Similarly, it is not so much what Brother Jack says about the Party but the fact that he lost his eye which keeps him from facing his underground history. When his false eye drops out into the glass of water in a moment of confrontation with the hero late in the novel (over the Invisible Man's unauthorized speech for Tod Clifton), he must drop the Party line that covers his vision and babble back into his peasant tongue or into the obscuring language of power. The dropping out of Jack's eye recalls the revelation of Barbee's blindness at the end of his spiel, as he trips in his darkness after having maintained his verbal high-wire act with such deftness, symmetry of line, and balance of power. It recalls chaos-loving Rinehart's manipulative spiel of eloquence that extracts handouts from the blinded, lamb-innocent church ladies. Rinehart's spiel is tied to the profane eloquence of chaos-destroyed, hypersensitive Tod Clifton, whose streetcorner spiel about the Sambo doll—that it will be whatever you want it to be—reflects the gist of what the streetcorner hustler tells all slum dwellers hungry to be recognized or loved.

Even in small segments of the novel we see how these clusters, formulas, and influences operate with Ellison's materials. Chapter 9 starts off soon after the hero gets to Harlem on his way to Mr. Emerson to check out the job reference letter given to him by the powerful black president. The hero was booted out, you will recall, because quite by accident he showed the white trustee, Norton, the underground of Negro life and the black madness manifested at the riotous Golden Day, and showed him, as well, the base human passions (and by indirection Norton's own purposeful passion) revealed by Jim Trueblood's eloquent saga of incest.

Now our hero starts off with the purpose of finding a job, but early on he runs into a bluesman whose song celebrates the powerful, sexually fulfilling catharsis he achieves from his love-making lady, whose praises he sings, as follows:

> "She's got feet like a monkey
> Legs like a frog—Lawd, Lawd!
> But when she starts to loving me
> I holler Whoooo, God-dog!
> Cause I loves my baabay,
> Better than I do myself. . . ." (131)

Now this blues song celebrates the fulfilling sex life of a poor bluesman at the bottom, whose woman's beauty is questionable according to standards of beauty in the upper world. Yet their sex life is an affirming glory of life at the bottom, and it leads him to swear that he loves her better than he does himself. The second point is this: the blues singer is certain about his identity, about who he is sexually; and as it turns out, he is a fierce individualist who tries to tell the hero to be what he is, not to masquerade himself, not to deny the bluesman.

Now toward the end of the chapter the hero comes to discover and recognize his new fate, when he finds out that the masquerading trickster, Dr. Bledsoe, indeed has written the hero out of history and driven him toward the unattainable horizon, not with a job reference letter, as the hero assumed, but rather with a prank piece of paper that says, in effect—"To Whom It May Concern, Keep This Nigger-Boy Running." But now at this agony-filled, perception-sharpening junction, another kind of song comes bubbling up to the surface of the hero's consciousness, rescuing him from self-pity—a mock dirge, played traditionally in the Oklahoma area. After a burial, Negro jazz musicians would light up into this dirge once they hit the Negro business section of town. It expresses the attitudes central to the black man's memory of his history, that if he is to survive he must not allow himself to wallow in self-pity over death, or over the constant dream-shattering, death-dealing experience that is his fate, his mocked fate. The dirge goes:

> O well they picked poor Robin clean
> O well they picked poor Robin clean
> Well they tied poor Robin to a stump
> Lawd, they picked all the feathers round
>   from Robin's rump
> Well they picked poor Robin clean. (147)

The bluesman's song is filled with life, possibility, affirmation of love and identity through fundamental sexual confrontation and confirmation. The dirge stands in apparent opposition, since it comes at the time of a death; yet it is life giving and intelligence heightening, even as it is innocence destroying—mocking our hero's false pride and his naive hero worship of Bledsoe. The song mocks and thereby instructs him that each person must constantly die, or shed the skin of his innocence, in order to grow. The mock dirge comes after a moment of the hero's mock murder, through the pen of bloody Bledsoe. Finally, the song says that savage experience picks us clean of the plumagelike illusions round our baby-soft rounded rumps and leaves us picked clean to the bone of our innocence—but then, perhaps that is indeed the necessary price of eating of the forbidden fruit of experience and knowledge. Unlike the blues, "which allows no scapegoat but the self," the dirge allows us to "lighten our load by becoming one with the bird, as he symbolically takes over our bone-picked sorrow."

This pattern of death, agony, and mocking affirmation or momentary rebirth informs the entire novel, but is pointedly suggested in that marvelous skeleton of a call-and-response sermon by the black minister in the Prologue. There, in the cellar of the hero's racial consciousness where Ellison's version of Underground Man is dwelling, the preacher says, "I said black is . . . an' black ain't . . . Black will git you . . . an' black won't . . . It do, Lawd . . . an' it don't—Black will make you . . . or black will unmake you" (8). Bledsoe, the black president of the college, has undone the hero. And minister Barbee looks through a glass darkly, never face to face. But it is a black dirge that sourly surges forth from the underground racial past and it helps rescue, school, and repair the hero at the junction in chapter 9. Here again the movement from affirmation through denial to affirmation, or from thesis to counterthesis to synthesis, is treated dialectically as it was by the man at the bottom, the bluesman, Peter Wheatstraw.

The bluesman is "doubled" with the hero in the Dostoevskian sense. The streetwise bluesman knows everything about northern idiom and what it takes to get along in this here man's town and on the lower frequencies; and yet Peter Wheatstraw is lost and homeless in the world of power, unable at the higher frequencies to manipulate its symbols or to manifest his vision, and he's uneducated in the school sense. At the other end, the Invisible Man is lost in the streets of Harlem and is also homeless in the world of power; indeed, the most powerful man in his world has just kicked him out of this world (upstairs, you might say, to the North) to Harlem, which is, of course, *nowhere*. And the Invisible Man is undereducated in the street sense. Still, there is synthesis possible for the hero if he but trusts his underground peasant intelligence and memory. For as the hero reflects upon one riff in Peter Wheatstraw's spiel he thinks,

> I liked his words though I didn't know the answer. I'd known the stuff from childhood, but had forgotten it; had learned it back of school. . . [Ellipsis in original, 134]

But at this junction, too, the hero and the bluesman are tied together again because it is very important to him that this "new boy" in town not deny him. Peter Wheatstraw's concern is almost prophetic because, at the end of the chapter, the hero is to be denied by his *Peter*, Herbert Bledsoe. Bledsoe is glad to see him at first and then denies him privately. The fear of being denied by race brother, by public power, and by father figures sets the stage for the hero's next confrontation.

In the middle of chapter 9, the hero undergoes the *passion* phase of Burke's law via a confrontation with young Emerson, a man of shattered dreams, denied personal fulfillment, at the top of the economic spectrum. His sexuality is confused and so is his identity about a host of subjects, ranging from the way he really feels about blacks to the ambivalence about his powerful father, who has figuratively devoured his son, as Cronus did unto Zeus. Young Emerson, a homosexual undergoing a form of psychoanalysis which apparently brings him no affirmation, stands, then, in direct opposition to the solidly based, blues-singing, dirt-poor, black man of the streets at the beginning of the chapter, who knows who he is. Yet this pairing also recalls the Norton-Trueblood pairing and doubling.

And this pairing also recalls the old American story of the man who has everything and nothing: young Emerson is rich, white, free and twenty-one, yet he really has nothing but a world of confusion; and the bluesman has nothing but a batch of blueprints showing his dreams of powerful towns and country clubs that he will never erect. He has everything, though, in a real woman who loves him with a great sexual power, even though her beauty, at the lower frequencies, is invisible to all but the naked eye. It is young Emerson, the homosexual, who unfolds the truth of the letter to the hero, just as it is the remarkable-looking lady of the bluesman who gives him the sexual, naked truth and renders him a celebrant of her naked powers, body and soul. One recalls how it is the blind hermaphrodite, Tiresias, who bears to Oedipus the truth below the king's self-righteous existence. But the homosexual at the top and the bluesman at the bottom are also linked; for both are existential outlaws in our society, yet at the same time both are high priests from the peripheral underground, warning the hero of hidden reality. (Tangentially, we might reflect here that so many of our current musical dance patterns have their genesis in black bars, on the one hand, and gay bars, on the other, long before we all began to dance, dance to the music.) Indeed, one recalls that young Emerson tells the hero about a kind of peripheral bar, the Club Calamus:

> "You haven't? It's very well known. Many of my Harlem friends go there. It's a rendezvous for writers, artists and all kinds of celebrities. There's nothing like it in the city, and by some strange twist it has a truly continental flavor." (141)

At this point the hero has undergone a mini-motif of Lord Raglan's pattern in this chapter—he has figuratively died, undergone an underground agony, and been reborn tougher and more perceptive and able to laugh at himself. Finally the wonderful spiel delivered by the bluesman as he is advising our hero has provided the first confrontation the southern-born hero has with a northern black, and it is significant that, although they are speaking the same language, he hardly understands the bluesman's transformed tongue, at first. Migrate from one part of America to another and you are often lost in terms of idiomatic meaning. Yet in the case of the black man the genesis of language has an ancestral underground root in the old country of the Southland. To show Ellison's many dimensioned use of idiom, let me now attempt to unravel one of his bluesman's riffs:

> "All it takes to get along in this here man's town is a little shit, grit and mother-wit. And man, I was bawn with all three. In fact I'maseventhsonofaseventhson bawnwithacauloverbotheyesandraisedonblackcatboneshighjohntheconqueror andgreasygreens—" he spieled with twinkling eyes, his lips working rapidly. "You dig me daddy?" (134)

Let me suggest that here Ellison is rendering up the fusion of myth and lore which is the genesis of Negro/Black/White/Afro-American idiomatic versification. "The seventh son of a seventh son" comes from the Scottish-English influence upon the former slaves and suggests how myth-bound and haunted the slaveholders were and refers to one who is born lucky. "Bawn with a caul over both eyes" suggests one who is born with the gift of clairvoyance; and has an Ashanti linkage from the African aspect of the heritage. "Raised on black cat bones" is from the Afro-*American* version of voodoo and the context is this: in voodoo, which always reverses meaning (as does so much of Negro idiom): you throw a live black cat into a boiling pot of hot water; after the flesh has fallen away you pick out its bones and gnaw away, and if you are lucky, and gnaw down upon the right bone, you will become *invisible*. "High John the Conqueror" is a mythical hero from slavery, an invisible hero who sided with the slaves, during bad times, with good advice. And "greasygreens," of course, refers to African-American cuisine, in the old country Southland.

The hero's presence in the North at this time in the novel recalls the migration from the South to the North of blacks who came, often on the run, pursuing the dream of a peaceful kingdom, jobs, and personal fulfillment. But the hero's dream becomes a nightmare through a mocking note that, unknown to him, reads: "To Whom It May Concern: Keep This Nigger-Boy Running." It is significant, and one of the ironies of the meshing of race and class, that (while looking for employment) the hero discovers this dimension of his representative fate in the North from a rich white entrepreneur's son whose mock employment has brought him no fulfillment.

But it is even more significant that the hero first recalls the "Nigger-Boy Running" joke via a recalled dream that he has of his grandfather, at the end of chapter 1, just after he wins his scholarship to the Negro college. For in the dream, through his grandfather, the hero is ritually warned and instructed:

> He told me to open my brief case and read what was inside—and I did, finding an official envelope stamped with the state seal; and inside the envelope I found another and another, endlessly, and I thought I would fall of weariness. "Them's

> years,'' he said. ''Now open that one.'' And I did and in it I found an engraved document containing a short message in letters of gold. ''Read it,'' my grandfather said. ''Out loud!''
>
> ''To Whom It May Concern,'' I intoned, ''Keep This Nigger-Boy Running.'' (26)

And there is an underground story beneath this memory. For in the old South, a form of black-baiting which had its genesis in slavery would proceed as follows: A Negro newcomer would arrive upon the scene, looking for gainful employment; he would go to a prospective white employer. This ordinary small-town white businessman would immediately spot the fact that this was not one of the local blacks and would tell the black outsider that he did not have work at this time but that he did know of someone who might have jobs available down the road, perhaps.

The white businessman would then give the horizon-seeking black a sealed letter to take to the next prospective employer. Upon reaching the next white man, the letter would be presented, opened by the white man, read and mused over, and then the Negro would hear the same old story—''No jobs'' here but perhaps ''Up the road,'' and then the white merchant would scribble something on the note, reseal the communiqué (like the Negro's fate), and hand the letter back to the outreaching dark hand. This would happen again and again, until the black finally opened the letter and read the message, or got the message, and read out his symbolic fate (or some variation upon the theme): ''To Whom It May Concern, Keep This Nigger-Boy Running.'' This brutal joke of course had its antecedents in slavery, when many or most slaves couldn't read or write, and could only go from plantation to plantation with a note signed by the Master, or his *earthly* representative. The slave didn't in fact know what might or might not be written down on that note. And although this tortuous ritual or bad-faith convenant came from the pastoral scenes of the gallant South, actually the ''jobs'' search and its attendant mocking ceremony were often played out in the industrial North. Or more to the point, the duplicity operative at the Paint Factory in *Invisible Man*, which in fact did hire our nameless hero, but only as a scab (union strike buster), signified the way industrial bosses pitted the racial and ethnic groupings of the underclasses against each other. And when the Invisible Man's day labor was used up, he was discarded and put on tentative welfare after signing some papers which freed him from work—new slave papers meant to quiet his aggressive appetite for employment.

It is structurally salient that Ellison establishes early the ancestral tie with the grandfather's folk voice, via the underground avenue of the dream. For the grandfather's appearance and intelligence in the dream is the deeper Underground Railroad reality beneath the American Dream for the Negro. And the grandfather is the oldest ancestor within the hero's family memory. And who is the *grandfather's* authority? No doubt the oldest member of the tribe in his memory, perhaps *his* grandfather—and then we are back into slavery; so that in a highly oral culture the grandfather is the proper high priest to pass on mythical reality and survival wisdom from the battle zone. Throughout the novel, a warning or extolling voice issues forth from underground (often coming to the hero's aid, like Tarp's voice at the bottom of the Brotherhood) during moments of agony, conflict, trial, public and private passion. *And* (like the rescuing dirge, or High John the Conqueror) this intelligence informs his hard-won experience, thereby constantly presenting the reader with a hero's awareness or perception that is heightened. Not all of the underground warning voices confer benefits upon the hero as they warn him, however, as Lucius Brockway, in the underground of the paint factory, demonstrates. Brockway becomes a most trying combination of Tar Baby and Proteus for the Invisible Man.

Now in some cases the ancestral voice comes directly out of the remembering hero's own past, as did the rescuing dirge. The second kind of ancestral voice issues from the hero's consciousness when he recalls moments from his own personal history, which then leads him to racial memory, as did the dream of the grandfather. The third kind of historical-ancestral linkage comes from symbols or specific items which don't touch the hero's own past but which form a lucid part of his racial memory and the consciousness of the race, in the Joycean sense, suggesting then a duty and a task and a covenant or responsibility to the ancestral community.

Now these symbolic objects surge forth at moments of passion or trial. For instance, when the hero, late in the novel, discovers another kind of "Keep This Nigger-Boy Running" note on his desk at the Brotherhood's office, Brother Tarp, the man at the bottom of the organization, gives the hero a picture of Frederick Douglass, our man at the top of Negro leadership in the nineteenth century. Later Tarp gives the hero his own leg irons, retained from a chain gang. The hero must learn to trust those symbolic ancestral tokens, voices, or manifestations—yet he must sort out the consulting surge of past and present counselors. Indeed one of the hero's many agonies is to learn not to accept the advice from authority figures without question and to wrestle with advice until he's made it his own and understood it, or spurned it, or accepted it and by accepting it, made certain he's reshaped the advice to fit his own experience. For the other side of the most profane or the healthiest advice is that it renders the hero somebody's "running boy" and does not allow him to be his own man.

So, motifs involving power, sex, women, images of light and dark, broken taboos, Afro-American folklore, papers of importance, quests for identity and responsibility, individualism, music, violence, uses of eloquence, all come in clusters and order the improvisations of Ellison's orchestrated novel. Here we can see the influence of William Faulkner's *Light in August*, in which the major scenes are ordered by the presence of sex, women, food, and money, and are in turn connected with images of light and dark, religion and slavery, as integrating forces which undergird the associative patterns of each narrative section. In terms of power Ellison is constantly improvising upon the whole plantation system as a metaphor for understanding American institutions. This improvisation on the plantationlike hierarchy can be seen in the "descent" section of the Prologue, in the pecking order at the paint factory scene, in life at Mary Rambo's rooming house, in the Brotherhood, at the college, at the battle-royal smoker, and at the Golden Day.

Connected with this imagery of the plantation is another, deeper dimension of Ellison's metaphoric patterning in which he projects a symbolic model of American history—thereby joining the very select company of Melville, Hawthorne, and especially Faulkner in this recombining of metaphorical vision with history. All of Faulkner's major works involving the black presence, it seems to me, possess this epic design. For instance, in *Absalom, Absalom!* the "design" of metaphor can be read in the following manner: Let the French architect stand for America's "borrowed" French principles of refinement, creativity, artistry, ideals of culture, freedom, and liberty (indeed our fitful intellectual indebtedness to the French Revolution); and let Sutpen stand for American know-how, cunning, outlandish daring, bigotry, savage frontiersmanship-hustle, furious energy and industry, and white-ethnic class hatred; and let the Negro slaves of Sutpen's Hundreds stand as the enslaved bases of the American economic order.

Sutpen must reduce all others to "niggers" (blacks, women, his family, outside family, poor whites, his son) as he hacks his insanely ambitious way to the top. The new American Adam must reduce the French architect, at the other end of the social spectrum, to a subhuman, to a nigger, once he has used up the architect's expertise. And he then attempts to free his body from Sutpen's clutches. Sutpen, in turn, reenacts a mock French Revolution by bringing down the French aristocrat-artist. But the French architect only flees when he discovers that he too is enslaved—thus the synthesis between slave and aristocrat is forged by *slavery's* chains. And the French architect's flight and Sutpen's pursuit of him with hound dogs recalls that of a runaway slave and the ritual pursuit by hound dogs.

Dostoevski's hero in *Notes from Underground*, and the illumined Invisible Man of the Ellison Prologue and Epilogue, are manifestations of hyperawareness and terror concerning the inner meanness of the outer world: they observe it as a treacherous terrain. Structurally, the Prologue contains within it all of the materials needed for Ellison's invention; and the core of the work then goes on to illustrate and orchestrate these materials. In Underground Man's world, Part 1 is a presentation of the arguments, and in Part 2 we have the illustrations. *Notes from Underground* can be seen as a monologue rich with personal and political commentary. The grand sweep of the many monologues in *Invisible Man* carries a similar personal, political "doubleness." But Ellison's monologues have a kind of epic grandness that goes beyond Dostoevski. Witness, for example, Trueblood's saga and Barbee's sermon.

At every turn in *Notes*, Underground Man is out to shock the reader, to *shock* reason itself. The Invisible Man is out to shake the reader into an awareness that is streaked with a soured humor and a great gift for hyperbole. Both novels are within the tradition of the memoir, and, like *Notes, Invisible Man* is seasoned in the tradition of confessional literature of the seductive underground diary.

The Russia of Underground Man's day was highly repressive, and so for Ellison's hyperaware man there is ever the feeling of alienation and dispossession. (And you will recall that the Invisible Man's second public address treats the theme of dispossession, and he uses it in his third address at the stadium.) In Dostoevski's Russia you either accepted your socioeconomic status as your fate or you dropped out. No mobility. Faced with the fitful combination of power, race and wrenching leadership, the Invisible Man faces a comparable terrain, cut off in the cellar from upward movement. Perhaps even more in keeping with the vaulting, scorning attitude of Underground Man are the men in the Golden Day, who remain as Afro-American examples of broken men, though madness has consumed their soured brilliance.

Both narrators appear to be onto something concerning the way the normal world of power operates in a system of deceit—especially if you are highly aware, you are apt to be driven to treason. For example, after seeing too much, in an ancestral dream of the shattering past in the Prologue, the Invisible Man recalls:

> *And at that point a voice of trombone timbre screamed at me, "Git out of here, you fool! Is you ready to commit treason?"* (8)

Both narrators suggest that the mind of highly aware man contains much spite and even vengeance. Underground Man seeks revenge, not justice. But the Invisible Man would seek both. There is a sense in both works—particularly in *Notes*—that hyperconsciousness leads to paralysis. Therefore the only action issues out of a sense of willfulness and spitefulness. The Invisible Man, though, is obsessed with responsibility, and cultural enterprise, and the rage for freedom that remains a viable ancestral imperative. The Invisible Man, however, frets about overstaying his time of contemplation in the underground and knows he is bound to come up; he seeks love, and spite can only lead to disintegration of personality, as in those memorable figures in the Golden Day. Ultimately, of course, going underground is a kind of psychological going within oneself for both narrators.

Ralph Ellison starts out wanting to reverse the idea, current at the time he conceived *Invisible Man*, that the Negro was invisible. The narrator says, "I am invisible simply because you refuse to see me." But having committed himself to assaulting the current sociological metaphor of the day, Ellison turns the metaphor into a dialectic vision of modern America as a brier patch.

The metaphor of invisibility is "doubly" enriched by his constant allusions to the plantation system. The logic is as follows: *Thesis*: You (society) say I'm a slave. *Counterthesis*: but I'm not a slave in my soul, or in my mind. *Synthesis*: I'll admit that slavery is the system in which I dwell, but I see myself as slave in that system only if you'll accept the metaphor of how the system enslaves us all, Master . . . And because I've lived with this knowledge longer, I've learned how to make the plantation my brier patch; though it enslaves my body I have learned how to keep my mind and spirit free from its damnation of the spirit. And Master, economically your survival depends upon my body's productivity in the slave system that obsesses your mind and spirit. Alternatively, the Invisible Man asks himself, and us, as he weaves through the possible meanings of the grandfather's advice in the Epilogue,

> Was it that we of all, we, most of all, had to affirm the principle, the plan in whose name we had been brutalized and sacrificed—not because we would always be weak nor because we were afraid or opportunistic, but because we were older than they, in the sense of what it took to live in the world with others and because they had exhausted in us, some—not much, but some—of the human greed and smallness, yes, and the fear and superstition that had kept them running. (433–34)

Like Dostoevski's Underground Man, the Invisible Man puts down the idea of racial invisibility; he embraces the metaphor, assaults it, then reverses it. He discovers at the height of the race riots in Harlem that he cannot return to Mary's, either, that he is invisible to Mrs. Rambo as he is to Jack, Ras, and Bledsoe. For like Underground Man, he discovers that statistical computations for the collective good, or institutional asylums for the individual's good, or visions of the individual's good by powerful figures and forces constantly leave out one important impulse: man's urge and capacity to conceptualize his humanity beyond statistics and regimentation; his willfulness to do what he wants, in the underground economy of his imagination, to turn a plantation into an underground brier patch or a hostile terrain into the sources and resource points of escape via the mind's Underground Railroad.

For finally the Invisible Man is underground indeed; but he has decided that it is time to end his hibernation and come up to meet a new level of experience. And it is plain to me that at the end of the novel, our hero, reborn, is about to emerge from his womb of safety in the underground; yet it is also clear that he is trapped in a personal way between two voices. For as he acknowledges:

> Thus, having tried to give pattern to the chaos which lives within the pattern of your certainties, I must come out. I must emerge. And there's still a conflict within me: With Louis Armstrong one half of me says, "Open the window and let the foul air out," while the other says, "It was good green corn before the harvest." (438)

Now the "green corn" motif comes from a Leadbelly song and refers to a state of innocence before the harvest of experience. Innocence is beautiful but it carries dangerous naiveté with it—a naive skin that our hero sheds.

But first of all the hero hears a lyrical line from the man who makes poetry out of invisibility, Louis Armstrong, a song which suggests the sophisticated, toughened shape the hero's perception of reality has taken on out of the furnacelike bad air of passion and conflict which has been his experience throughout the life of the novel. The line refers to a song by Buddy Bolden which Louis Armstrong—also known as Dipper Mouth and Bad Air—used to sing:

> I thought I heard Buddy Bolden say,
> Funky-Butt, Funky-Butt, take it away,
> I thought I heard somebody shout,
> Open up the window and let the foul air out.

The Funky-Butt was a powerhouse jazz nightclub in New Orleans, where the solos on the horns were as furious and glorious as the sex act itself, filled with bad air and ecstatic charges, savage thrusts and stellar flourishes. Armstrong, as a kid of ten, used to stand outside the door of the Funky-Butt and listen to Bolden, the great jazz trumpeter who ended up in a madhouse, blowing and singing and wailing. Bolden would sing the song in tribute to the funkiness and the foul air in the dance hall, caused by the jelly-tight dancing.

Without the liberating bad air that riffs through the chamber of the good-bad horn of plenty (which also resembles the chamber from whence all life emerges), you can't have the real music of life, or the dance. For as the hero comments,

> Of course Louie was kidding, *he* wouldn't have thrown old Bad Air out, because it would have broken up the music and the dance, when it was the good music that came from the bell of old Bad Air's horn that counted. (438)

NOTE

1. Ralph Ellison, *Invisible Man* (New York: Random House, 1952), 99. All subsequent citations in this article are to this edition.

To Move Without Moving: An Analysis of Creativity and Commerce in Ralph Ellison's Trueblood Episode

HOUSTON A. BAKER, JR.

Them boss quails is like a good man, what he got to do he do.

Ralph Ellison
Trueblood in *Invisible Man*

In his essay "Richard Wright's Blues," Ralph Ellison states one of his cherished distinctions: "The function, the psychology, of artistic selectivity is to eliminate from art form all those elements of experience which contain no compelling significance. Life is as the sea, art a ship in which man conquers life's crushing formlessness, reducing it to a course, a series of swells, tides and wind currents inscribed on a chart."[1] The distinction between nonsignificant life experiences and their inscribed, artistic significance (i.e., the meaning induced by form) leads Ellison to concur with André Malraux that artistic significance alone "enables man to conquer chaos and to master destiny" (*S&A*, 94).

Artistic "technique," according to Ellison, is the agency through which artistic meaning and form are achieved. In "Hidden Name and Complex Fate" he writes:

> It is a matter of outrageous irony, perhaps, but in literature the great social clashes of history no less than the painful experience of the individual are secondary to the meaning which they take on through the skill, the talent, the imagination and personal vision of the writer who transforms them into art. Here they are reduced to more manageable proportions; here they are imbued with humane value; here, injustice and catastrophe become less important in themselves than what the writer makes of them. (*S&A*, 148–49)

Even the thing-in-itself of lived, historical experience is thus seen as devoid

Reprinted by permission of the Modern Language Association of America from *PMLA* 98 (1983).

of ''humane value'' before its sea change under the artist's transforming technique.

Since Ellison focuses his interest on the literary, the inscribed, work of art, he regards even folklore as part of that realm of life ''elements . . . which contain no compelling significance'' in themselves. In ''Change the Joke and Slip the Yoke,'' he asserts:

> The Negro American writer is also an heir to the human experience which is literature, and this might well be more important to him than his living folk tradition. For me, at least, in the discontinuous, swiftly changing and diverse American culture, the stability of the Negro folk tradition became precious as a result of an act of literary discovery. . . . For those who are able to translate [the folk tradition's] meanings into wider, more precise vocabularies it has much to offer indeed. (*S&A*, 72–73)

During a BBC program recorded in May 1982 and titled ''Garrulous Ghosts: The Literature of the American South,'' Ellison stated that the fiction writer, to achieve proper resonance, must go beyond the blues—a primary and tragically eloquent form of American expression:

> The blues are very important to me. I think of them as the closest approach to tragedy that we have in American art forms. And I'm not talking about black or white, I mean just American. Because they do combine the tragic and the comic in a very subtle way and, yes, they are very important to me. But they are also limited. And if you are going to write fiction there is a level of consciousness which you move toward which I would think transcends the blues.

Thus Ellison seems to regard Afro-American folklore, before its translation into ''more precise vocabularies,'' as part of lived experience. Art and chaos appear to be homologous with literature and folklore.

To infer such a homology from one or two critical remarks, however, is to risk the abyss of ''false distinction,'' especially when one is faced with a canon as rich as Ralph Ellison's. For it is certainly true that the disparagement of folk expression suggested by these remarks can be qualified by the praise of folklore implicit in Ellison's assertion that Afro-American expressive folk projections are a group's symbolically ''profound'' attempts to ''humanize'' the world. Such projections, even in their crudest forms, constitute the ''humble base'' on which ''great literature'' is erected (*S&A*, 172).

It does seem accurate, however, to say that Ellison's criticism repeatedly implies an extant, identifiable tradition of Western literary art—a tradition consisting of masters of form and technique who must be read, studied, emulated, and (if one is lucky and eloquent) equaled. This tradition stands as the signal, vital repository of ''humane value.'' And for Ellison the sphere that it describes is equivalent to the *primum mobile*, lending force and significance to all actions of the descending heavens and earth.

Hence, while the division between folk and artistic may be only discursive, having no more factual reality than any other such division, it seems to matter to Ellison, who, as far as I know, never refers to himself as a folk artist. Moreover, in our era of sophisticated "folkloristics," it seems mere evasion to shy from the assertion that Ellison's criticism ranks folklore below literary art on a total scale of value. What I argue is that the distinction between folklore and literary art evident in Ellison's critical practice collapses in his creative practice in *Invisible Man*'s[2] Trueblood episode. Further, I suggest that an exacting analysis of this episode illuminates the relation not only between Ellison's critical and creative practices but also between what might be called the public and private commerce of black art in America.

The main character in the Trueblood episode, which occupies chapter 2 of *Invisible Man*, is both a country blues singer (a tenor of "crude, high, plaintively animal sounds") and a virtuoso prose narrator. To understand the disjunctiveness between Ellison's somewhat disparaging critical pronouncements on "raw" folklore and his striking fictional representation of the folk character, one must first comprehend, I think, the sharecropper Trueblood's dual manifestation as trickster and merchant, as creative and commercial man. Blues and narration, as modes of expression, conjoin and divide in harmony with these dichotomies. And the episode in its entirety is—as I demonstrate—a metaexpressive commentary on the incumbencies of Afro-American artists and the effects of their distinctive modes of expression.

In an essay that gives a brilliant ethnographic "reading" of the Balinese cockfight, the symbolic anthropologist Clifford Geertz asserts:

> Like any art form—for that, finally, is what we are dealing with—the cockfight renders ordinary, everyday experience comprehensible by presenting it in terms of acts and objects which have had their practical consequences removed and been reduced (or, if you prefer, raised) to the level of sheer appearances, where their meaning can be more powerfully articulated and more exactly perceived. ("Deep Play," 443)

Catching up the themes of Balinese society in symbolic form, the cockfight thus represents, in Geertz's words, "a metasocial commentary . . . a Balinese reading of Balinese experience, a story they tell themselves about themselves" (448). The anthropologist's claims imply that the various symbolic (or "semiotic") systems of a culture—religion, politics, economics—can themselves be "raised" to a metasymbolic level by the orderings and processes of "ritual interactions" like the Balinese cockfight.

The coming together of semiotic systems in ways that enlarge and enhance the world of human meanings is the subject of Barbara Babcock-Abrahams's essay "The Novel and the Carnival World." Following the lead of Julia Kristeva, Babcock-Abrahams asserts that a "metalanguage" is a symbolic system that treats of symbolic systems; for example, *Don Quixote* "openly discusses other works of literature and takes the writing and reading of literature as its subject" ("Novel," 912). Both social rituals and novels, since they "embed" other semiotic systems within their "texture," are "multivocal," "polyvalent," or "polysemous"—that is, capable of speaking in a variety of mutually reflexive voices at once.

The multiple narrative frames and voices operative in Ellison's Trueblood episode include the novel *Invisible Man*, the protagonist's fictive autobiographical account, Norton's story recalled as part of the fictive autobiography, Trueblood's story as framed by the fictive autobiography, the sharecropper's own autobiographical recall, and the dream narrative within that autobiographical recall. All these stories reflect, or "objectify," one another in ways that complicate their individual and composite meanings. Further, the symbolic systems suggested by the stories are not confined to (though they may implicitly comment on) such familiar social configurations as education, economics, politics, and religion. Subsuming these manifestations is the outer symbolic enterprise constituted by the novel itself. Moreover, the Trueblood episode heightens the multivocalic character of the novel from within, acting as a metacommentary on the literary and artistic system out of which the work is generated. Further enriching the burden of meanings in the episode is the Christian myth of the Fall and Sigmund Freud's mythic "narrative" concerning incest, which are both connoted (summoned as signifiers, in Babcock-Abrahams's terms) and parodied, or inverted. I analyze the text's play on these myths later in my discussion.

For the moment, I am primarily interested in suggesting that the Trueblood episode, like other systematic symbolic phenomena, gains and generates its meanings in a dialogic relation with various systems of signs. The sharecropper chapter as a text derives its logic from its intertextual relation with surrounding and encompassing texts and, in turn, complicates their meanings. The Balinese cockfight, according to Geertz, can only tell a "metastory" because it is intertextually implicated in a world that is itself constituted by a repertoire of "stories" (e.g., those of economics and politics) that the Balinese tell themselves.

As a story that the author of *Invisible Man* tells himself about his own practice, the Trueblood episode clarifies distinctions that must be made between Ellison as critic and Ellison as artist. To elucidate its metaexpressive function, one must summon analytical instruments from areas that Ellison sharply debunks in his own criticism.

For example, at the outset of "The World and the Jug," a masterly instructive essay on the criticism of Afro-American creativity, Ellison asks:

> Why is it so often true that when critics confront the American as *Negro* they suddenly drop their advanced critical armament and revert with an air of confident superiority to quite primitive modes of analysis? Why is it that sociology-oriented critics seem to rate literature so far below politics and ideology that they would rather kill a novel than modify their presumptions concerning a given reality which it seeks in its own terms to project? (*S&A*, 115–16)

What I take these questions to imply is that a given artistic reality designed to represent "Negro American" experience should not be analyzed by "primitive'' methods, which Ellison leaves unspecified but seems to associate with sociological, ideological, and political modes of analysis. In the following discussion I hope to demonstrate that sociology, anthropology, economics, politics, and ideology all provide models essential for the explication of the Trueblood episode. The first step, however, is to evoke the theater of Trueblood's performance.

* * *

Trueblood's narration has an unusual audience, but to the farmer and his Afro-American cohorts the physical setting is as familiar as train whistles in the Alabama night. The sharecropper, a white millionaire, and a naive undergraduate from a nearby black college have arranged themselves in a semicircle of camp chairs in the sharecropper's yard. They occupy a swath of shade cast by the porch of a log cabin that has survived since the days of slavery, enduring hard times and the ravages of climate. The millionaire asks, ''How are you faring now? . . . Perhaps I could help.'' The sharecropper responds, ''We ain't doing so bad, suh. 'Fore they heard 'bout what happen to us out here I couldn't get no help from nobody. Now lotta folks is curious and go outta their way to help'' (*IM*, 52). What has occurred ''out here''—in what the millionaire Mr. Norton refers to as ''new territory for me'' and what the narrator describes as a ''desert'' that ''almost took [his] breath away''(*IM*, 45)—is Jim Trueblood's impregnation of both his wife and his daughter. The event has brought disgrace on the sharecropper and has mightily embarrassed officials at the nearby black college.

The whites in the neighboring town and countryside, however, are scarcely outraged or perturbed by Trueblood's situation. Rather, they want to keep the sharecropper among them; they warn the college officials not to harass him or his family, and they provide money, provisions, and abundant work. ''White folks,'' says Trueblood, even ''took to coming out here to see us and talk with us. Some of 'em was big white folks, too, from the big school way cross the State. Asked me lots 'bout what I thought 'bout things, and 'bout my folks and the kids, and wrote it all down in a book'' (*IM*, 53). Hence, when the farmer begins to recount the story of his incestuous act with his daughter Matty Lou, he does so as a man who has thoroughly rehearsed his tale and who has carefully refined his knowledge of his audience: ''He cleared his throat, his eyes gleaming and his voice taking on a deep, incantatory quality, as though he had told the story many, many times'' (*IM*, 53).

The art of storytelling is not a gift that Trueblood has acquired recently. He is introduced in *Invisible Man* as one who ''told the old stories with a sense of humor and a magic that made them come alive'' (*IM*, 46). A master storyteller, then, he recounts his provocative exploits to an audience that is by turns shamed, indignant, envious, humiliated, and enthralled.

The tale begins on a cold winter evening in the sharecropper's cabin. The smell of fat meat hangs in the air, and the last kindling crackles in the dying flames of the stove. Trueblood's daughter, in bed between her father and mother, sleepily whispers, "Daddy." At the story's close, the sharecropper reports his resolution to prevent Aunt Cloe the midwife from aborting his incestuous issue. At the conclusion of his tale, he reiterates his judgment that he and his family "ain't doing so bad" in the wake of their ordeal.

Certainly the content and mode of narration the sharecropper chooses reflect his knowledge of what a white audience expects of the Afro-American. Mr. Norton is not only a "teller of polite Negro stories" (*IM*, 37) but also a man who sees nothing unusual about the pregnant Matty Lou's not having a husband. "But that shouldn't be so strange," he remarks later (*IM*, 49). The white man's belief in the promiscuity of blacks is further suggested by Mr. Broadnax, the figure in Trueblood's dream who looks at the sharecropper and his daughter engaged in incest and says, "They just nigguhs, leave 'em do it" (*IM*, 58). In conformity with audience expectations, the sharecropper's narrative is aggressively sexual in its representations.

Beginning with an account of the feel of his daughter's naked arm pressed against him in bed, the farmer proceeds to reminisce about bygone days in Mobile when he would lie in bed in the evenings with a woman named Margaret and listen to the music from steamboats passing on the river. Next, he introduces the metaphor of the woman in a red dress "goin' past you down a lane . . . and kinda switchin' her tail 'cause she knows you watchin'" (*IM*, 56). From this evocative picture, he turns to a detailed account of his dream on the night of his incestuous act.

The dream is a parodic allegory in which Trueblood goes in quest of "fat meat." In this episode the name "Mr. Broadnax" (Mr. Broad-in-acts) captures the general concepts that mark any narrative as allegory. The man whose house is on the hill is a philanthropist who gives poor blacks (true bloods) sustaining gifts as "fat meat." The model implied by this conceptualization certainly fits one turn-of-the century American typology, recalling the structural arrangement by which black southern colleges were able to sustain themselves. In one sense, the entire Trueblood episode can be read as a pejorative commentary on the castrating effects of white philanthropy. Trueblood's dream narrative is parodic because it reveals the crippling assumptions (the castrating import) of the philanthropic model suggested in "Broadnax." The man who is broad-in-acts in the dream is the one who refers to the sharecropper and his daughter as "just nigguhs." Further, his philanthropy—like Mr. Norton's—has a carnal undercurrent: it is dangerously and confusingly connected with the sexuality of Mrs. Broadnax. What he dispenses as sustaining "fat meat" may only be the temporarily satisfying thrill of sexual gratification. The "pilgrim," or quester, in Trueblood's dream allegory flees from the dangers and limitations of such deceptive philanthropy. And the general exposé effected by the narrative offers a devastating critique of that typography which saw white men on the hill (northern industrialists) as genuinely and philanthropically responsive to the needs of those in the valley (southern blacks).

Instructed to inquire at Mr. Broadnax's house, Trueblood finds himself violating a series of southern taboos and fleeing for his life. He enters the front door of the home, wanders into a woman's bedroom, and winds up trapped in the embraces of a scantily clad white woman. The gastronomic and sexual appetites surely converge at this juncture, and the phrase "fat meat" takes on a dangerous burden of significance. The dreamer breaks free, however, and escapes into the darkness and machinery of a grandfather clock. He runs until a bright electric light bursts over him, and he awakens to find himself engaged in sexual intercourse with his daughter.

In *Totem and Taboo*, Freud advances the hypothesis that the two taboos of totemism—the interdictions against slaying the totem animal and against incest—result from events in human prehistory.[3] Following Darwin's speculations, Freud claims that human beings first lived in small hordes in which one strong, jealous man took all women to himself, exiling the sons to protect his own exclusive sexual privileges. On one occasion, however, Freud suggests, the exiled sons arose, slew, and ate the father, and then, in remorse, established the taboo against such slaughter. To prevent discord among themselves and to ensure their newly achieved form of social organization, they also established a taboo against sexual intercourse with the women of their own clan. Exogamy, Freud concludes, is based on a prehistorical advance from a lower to a higher stage of social organization.

From Freud's point of view, Trueblood's dream and subsequent incest seem to represent a historical regression. The sharecropper's dreamed violations of southern social and sexual taboos are equivalent to a slaughter of the white patriarch represented by Mr. Broadnax, who does, indeed, control the "fat" and "fat meat" of the land. To eat fat meat is to partake of the totemic animal. And having run backward in time through the grandfather clock, Trueblood becomes the primal father, assuming all sexual prerogatives unto himself. He has warned away "the boy" (representing the tumultuous mob of exiled sons) who wanted to take away his daughter, and as the sexual partner of both Matty Lou and Kate, he reveals his own firm possession of all his "womenfolks"—his status, that is to say, as a sexual producer secure against the wrath of his displaced "sons." Insofar as Freud's notions of totemism represent a myth of progressive social evolution, the farmer's story acts as a countermyth of inversive social dissolution. It breaks society down into components and reveals man in what might be called his presocial and unaccommodated state.

One reason for the sharecropper's singular sexual prerogatives is that the other Afro-Americans in his area are either so constrained or so battered by their encounters with society that they are incapable of a legitimate and productive sexuality. The sharecropper's territory is bounded on one side by the black college where the "sons" are indoctrinated in a course of instruction that leaves them impotent. On the other side lie the insane asylum and the veterans' home, residences of black men driven mad—or at least rendered psychologically and physically crippled—by their encounters with America. These "disabled veterans" are scarcely "family men" like Trueblood. Rather, they are listless souls who visit the whores in "the sun-shrunk shacks at the railroad crossing . . . hobbling down the tracks on crutches and canes; sometimes pushing the legless, thighless one in a red wheelchair" (*IM*, 35). In such male company Trueblood seems the only person capable of ensuring an authentic Afro-American lineage. When he finds himself atop Matty Lou, therefore, both the survival of the clan and the sharecropper's aversion to pain require him to reject the fate that has been physically or psychologically imposed on his male cohorts. He says, "There was only one way I can figger that I could git out: that was with a knife. But I didn't have no knife, and if you'all ever seen them geld them young boar pigs in the fall, you know I knowed that was too much to pay to keep from sinnin" (*IM*, 59). In this reflection, he brings forward one of the dominant themes of *Invisible Man*. This theme—one frequently slighted, or omitted, in discussions of the novel—is black male sexuality.

Perhaps critical prudery prevents commentators from acknowledging the black male phallus as a dominant symbol in much of the ritual interaction of *Invisible Man*. In *The Forest of Symbols: Aspects of Ndembu Ritual*, the symbolic anthropologist Victor Turner provides suggestive definitions for both "ritual" and "dominant symbols." He describes ritual as "prescribed formal behavior for occasions not given over to technological routine, having reference to beliefs in mystical beings or powers. The symbol is the smallest unit of ritual which still retains the specific properties of ritual behavior; it is the ultimate unit of specific structure in a ritual context" (19). For Turner, the most prominent—the "senior," as it were—symbols in any ritual are dominant symbols (20); they fall into a class of their own. The important characteristic of such symbols is that they bring together disparate meanings, serving as a kind of condensed semiotic shorthand. Further, they can have both ideological and sensuous associations; the mudyi tree of Ndembu ritual, for example, refers both to the breast milk of the mother and to the axiomatic values of the matrilineal Ndembu society (28).

Ellison's *Invisible Man* is certainly an instance of "prescribed formal behavior" insofar as the novel is governed by the conventions of the artistic system in which it is situated, a system that resides ludically outside "technological routine" and promotes the cognitive exploration of all systems of "being" and "power," whether mystical or not. The black phallus is a dominant symbol in the novel's formal patterns of behavior, as its manifold recurrence attests. In "The Art of Fiction: An Interview," Ellison writes, "People rationalize what they shun or are incapable of dealing with; these superstitions and their rationalizations become rituals as they govern behavior.

The rituals become social forms, and it is one of the functions of the artist to recognize them and raise them to the level of art'' (*S&A*, 175).

Stated in slightly different terms, Ellison's comment suggests an intertextual (indeed, a connoted) relation between the prescribed formal social behaviors of American racial interaction and the text of the novel. Insofar as Jim Crow social laws and the desperate mob exorcism of lynchings (with their attendant castrations) describe a formal pattern of Anglo-American behavior toward black men, this pattern offers an instance of ritual in which the black phallus gathers an extraordinary burden of disparate connotations, both sensuous and ideological. It should come as no surprise that an artist as perceptive as Ellison recognizes the black phallus as a dominant symbol of the sometimes bizarre social rituals of America and incorporates it into the text of a novel. In ''The Art of Fiction,'' in fact, Ellison calls the battle-royal episode of *Invisible Man* ''a ritual in preservation of caste lines, a keeping of taboo to appease the gods and ward off bad luck'' (*S&A*, 175). He did not have to invent the ritual, he says; all he had to do was to provide ''a broader context of meaning'' for the patterns the episode represents.

The black phallus, then, does seem an implicit major symbol in Ellison's text, and, prudery aside, there are venerable precedents for the discussion of male sexual symbols in ritual. For example, in ''Deep Play'' Geertz writes:

> To anyone who has been in Bali any length of time, the deep psychological identification of Balinese men with their cocks is unmistakable. The double entendre here is deliberate. It works in exactly the same way in Balinese as it does in English, even to producing the same tired jokes, strained puns, and uninventive obscenities. [Gregory] Bateson and [Margaret] Mead have even suggested that, in line with the Balinese conception of the body as a set of separately animated parts, cocks are viewed as detachable, self-operating penises, ambulent genitals with a life of their own. (417)

Certainly the notion of ''ambulent genitals'' figures in the tales of the roguish trickster recorded in Paul Radin's classic work *The Trickster*. In tale 16 of the Winnebago trickster cycle, Wakdjunkaga the trickster sends his penis across the waters of a lake to have intercourse with a chief's daughter.[4]

The black phallus as a symbol of unconstrained force that white men contradictorily envy and seek to destroy appears first in the opening chapter of *Invisible Man*. The influential white men of a small southern town force the protagonist and his fellow black boxers in the battle royal to gaze on a ''magnificent blonde—stark naked'' (*IM*, 18). The boys are threatened both for looking and for not looking, and the white men smile at their obvious fear and discomfiture. The boys know the bizarre consequences that accompany the white men's ascription of an animallike and voracious sexuality to black males. Hence, they respond in biologically normal but socially fearful (and justifiably embarrassed) ways. One boy strives to hide his erection with his boxing gloves, pleading desperately to go home. In this opening scene, the white woman as a parodic version of American ideals ("a small American flag tattooed upon her belly" [*IM*, 19]), is forced into tantalizing interaction with the mythically potent force of the black phallus. But because the town's white males exercise total control of the situation, the scene is akin to a castration, excision, or lynching.

Castration is one function of the elaborate electrically wired glass box that incarcerates the protagonist in the factory-hospital episode: "'Why not castration, doctor?' a voice asked waggishly" (*IM*, 231). In the Brotherhood, the class struggle is rather devastatingly transformed into the "ass struggle" when the protagonist's penis displaces his oratory as ideological agent. A white woman who hears him deliver a speech and invites him home seizes his biceps passionately and says, "Teach me, talk to me. Teach me the beautiful ideology of Brotherhood" (*IM*, 405). And the protagonist admits that suddenly he "was lost" as "the conflict between the ideological and the biological, duty and desire," became too subtly confused (*IM*, 406). Finally, in the nightmare that concludes the novel, the Invisible Man sees his own bloody testes, like those of the castrated Uranus of Greek myth, floating above the waters underneath a bridge's high arc (*IM*, 557). In the dream, he tells his inquisitors that his testes dripping blood on the black waters are not only his "generations wasting upon the water" but also the "sun" and the "moon"—and, indeed, the very "world"—of his own human existence (*IM*, 558). The black phallus—in its creative, ambulent, generative power, even when castrated—is like the cosmos itself, a self-sustaining and self-renewing source of life, provoking both envy and fear in Anglo-American society.

While a number of episodes in *Invisible Man* (including Trueblood's dream) suggest the illusory freedoms and taboo-induced fears accompanying interaction between the black phallus and white women, only the Trueblood encounter reveals the phallus as indeed producing Afro-American generations rather than wasting its seed upon the waters. The cosmic force of the phallus thus becomes, in the ritual action of the Trueblood episode, symbolic of a type of royal paternity, an aristocratic procreativity turned inward to ensure the royalty (the truth, legitimacy, or authenticity) of an enduring black line of descent. In his outgoing phallic energy, therefore, the sharecropper is (as we learn on his first appearance in *Invisible Man*) indeed a "hard worker" who takes care of "his family's needs" (*IM*, 46). His family may, in a very real sense, be construed as the entire clan, or tribe, of Afro-America.

As cosmic creator, Trueblood is not bound by ordinary codes of restraint. He ventures chaos in an outrageously sexual manner—and survives. Like the Winnebago trickster Wakdjunkaga, he offers an inversive play on social norms. He is the violator of boundaries who—unlike the scapegoat—eludes banishment.[5] Indeed, he is so essential to whites in his sexual role that, after demonstrating his enviable ability to survive chaos, he and his family acquire new clothes and shoes, abundant food and work, long-needed eyeglasses, and even the means to reshingle their cabin. "I looks up at the mornin' sun," says the farmer, describing the aftermath of his incestuous act, ''and expects somehow for it to thunder. But it's already bright and clear. . . . I yells, 'Have mercy, Lawd!' and waits. And there's nothin' but the clear bright mornin' sun'' (*IM*, 64–65).

Noting that most tricksters ''have an uncertain sexual status,'' Victor Turner points out that on some occasions

> tricksters appear with exaggerated phallic characteristics: Hermes is symbolized by the herm or pillar, the club, and the ithyphallic statue; Wakdjunkaga has a very long penis which has to be wrapped around him and put over his shoulder in a box; Eshu is represented in sculpture as having a long curved hairdress carved as a phallus. (''Myth,'' 580)

Such phallic figures are, for Turner, representatives par excellence of what he calls ''liminality'' (*Forest*, 93–112). Liminality describes that ''betwixt and between'' phase of rites of passage when an individual has left one fixed social status and has not yet been incorporated into another. When African boys are secluded in the forest during circumcision rites, for example, they are in a liminal phase between childhood and adulthood. They receive, during this seclusion, mythic instruction in the origin and structures of their society. And this instruction serves not only to ''deconstruct'' the components of the ordered social world they have left behind but also to reveal these elements recombined into new and powerful composites. The phallic trickster aptly represents the duality of this process. In his radically antinomian activities—incest, murder, and the destruction of sacred property—he symbolically captures what Turner describes as the ''amoral and nonlogical'' rhythms and outcomes of human biology and of meteorological climate: that is, the uncontrollable rhythms of nature (''Myth,'' 577). But the trickster is also a cultural gift bearer. Turner emphasizes that ''the Winnebago trickster transforms the pieces of his broken phallus into plants and flowers for men (580).'' Hermes enriches human culture with dreams and music. In a sense, therefore, the phallic trickster is a force that is, paradoxically, both anticonventional and culturally benevolent. The paradox is dissolved in the definition of the trickster as the ''*prima materia*—as undifferentiated raw material'' from which all things derive (*Forest*, 98). Trueblood's sexual energies, antinomian acts, productive issue, and resonant expressivity make him—in his incestuous, liminal moments and their immediate aftermath—the quintessential trickster.

In his sexual manifestation, Ellison's sharecropper challenges not only the mundane restraints of his environment but also the fundamental Judeo-Christian categories on which they are founded. As I have already noted, he quickly abandons the notion of the knife—of casting out, in Mr. Norton's indignant (and wonderfully ironic) phrase, ''the offending eye.'' His virtual parodies of the notions of sin and sacrifice lend comic point to his latitudinarian challenge to Christian orthodoxy. When his wife brings the sharpened ax down on his head, Trueblood recalls, ''I sees it, Lawd, yes! I sees it and seein' it I twists my head aside. Couldn't help it. . . . I moves. Though I meant to keep still, I moves! Anybody but Jesus Christ hisself woulda moved'' (*IM*, 63). So much for repentance and salvation through the bloody sacrifice of one's life. But Trueblood goes on to indicate why such sacrifice may not have been required of him: with the skill of a revisionist theologian, he distinguishes between ''blood-sin'' and ''dream-sin'' (*IM*, 62) and claims, with unshakable certainty, that only the dream of his encounter at the Broadnax household led to his sexual arousal and subsequent incest.

But while this casuistic claim suffices in the farmer's interaction with the social world, his earlier appraisal of the event suggests his role as a cosmically rebellious trickster. He says that when he awoke to discover himself atop Matty Lou, he felt that the act might not be sinful, because it happened in his sleep. But then he adds, ''although maybe sometimes a man can look at a little old pigtail gal and see him a whore'' (*IM*, 59). The naturalness, and the natural unpredictability, of sexual arousal implied by ''although'' seems more in keeping with the sharecropper's manifestation as black phallic energy.

Trueblood's sexual energies are not without complement in the arid regions where the sharecropper and his family eke out their existence. His wife, Kate, is an awesome force of both new life and outgoing socioreligious fury. His yard is filled with the children she has borne, and his oldest child, Matty Lou, is Kate's double—a woman fully grown and sexually mature who looks just like her mother. Kate and Matty Lou—both moving with the ''full-fronted motions of far-gone pregnancy'' (*IM*, 47)—are the first human figures that Mr. Norton sees as he approaches the Trueblood property. The two bearers of new black life are engaged in a rite of purification, a workaday ritual of washing clothes in a huge boiling cauldron, which takes on significance as the men situate themselves in a semicircle near the porch where the ''earth . . . was hard and white from where wash water had long been thrown'' (*IM*, 51). In a sense the women (who flee behind the house at Norton's approach) are present, by ironic implication, as the sharecropper once more confessionally purges himself—as he, in vernacular terms, again ''washes his dirty linen'' before a white audience. Further, Matty Lou, as the object of Trueblood's incestuous desire, and Kate, as the irate agent of his punishment for fulfilling his desire, assume significant roles in his narrative.

The reversal of a traditional Freudian typology represented by Trueblood's dream encounter at the Broadnax Big House is reinforced by an implied parody of the Christian myth of the Fall.[6] For if the white Mrs. Broadnax serves as the temptress Eve in the dream, then Matty Lou becomes an ersatz Eve, the paradoxical recipient of the farmer's lust. Similarly, if Mr. Broadnax—an inhabitant of the sanctuarylike precincts of a house of ''lighted candles and shiny furniture, and pictures on the walls, and soft stuff on the floor''—is the avenging father, or patriarch, of the dream, then the matriarchal Kate replaces him in exacting vengeance. The ''fall'' of Trueblood is thus enacted on two planes—on a dream level of Christian myth and on a quotidian level of southern black actuality. In its most intensely conscious and secular interpretation, the incestuous act is a rank violation that drives Kate to blind and murderous rage: "I heard Kate scream. It was a scream to make your blood run cold. It sounds like a woman who was watching a team of wild horses run down her baby chile and she caint move. . . . She screams and starts to pickin' up the first thing that comes to her hand and throwin' it" (*IM*, 61).

The "doubleness" of Kate and Matty Lou is felt in the older woman's destructive and avenging energies, which elevate her to almost legendary proportions. Her woman's wrath at the sharecropper's illicit violation of "my chile!" spirals, inflating Kate to the metaphorical stature of an implacable executioner: "Then I sees her right up on me, big. She's swingin' her arms like a man swingin' a ten-pound sledge and I sees the knuckles of her hand is bruised and bleedin . . . and I sees her swing and I smells her sweat and . . . I sees that ax" (*IM*, 63). Trueblood tries to forestall Kate's punishing blow but, he says, he "might as well been pleadin' with a switch engine" (*IM*, 63). The ax falls, and the farmer receives the wound whose blood spills on Matty Lou. The wound becomes the "raw and moist" scar the protagonist notices when he first moves "up close" on the sharecropper (*IM*, 50).

Kate becomes not only an awesome agent of vengeance in the sharecropper's account but also the prime mover of the parodic ritual drama enacted in the chilly southern cabin. It is Kate's secular rage that results in the substitute castration-crucifixion represented by Trueblood's wound. She is the priestess who bestows the scarifying lines of passage, of initiation—the marks that forever brand the farmer as a "dirty lowdown wicked dog" (*IM*, 66). At her most severe, she is the moral, or socioreligious, agent of both Trueblood's "marking" and his exile. She banishes him from the community that rallies to support her in her sorrow. In keeping with her role as purifier—as supervisor of the wash—she cleans up the pollution, and dirt and danger, represented by Trueblood's taboo act.

It is important to bear in mind, however, that while Kate is a figure of moral outrage, she is also a fertile woman who, like her husband, provides "cultural gifts" in the form of new life. In her family manifestation, she is less a secular agent of moral justice than a sensitive, practical parent who turns away in sick disgust at the wound she inflicts on Trueblood. And though she first banishes the farmer, she also accepts his return, obeys his interdiction against abortions for herself and Matty Lou, and welcomes the material gains that ironically accrue after Trueblood's fall from grace. The sharecropper says, "Except that my wife an' daughter won't speak to me, I'm better off than I ever been before. And even if Kate won't speak to me she took the new clothes I brought her from up in town and now she's gettin' some eyeglasses made what she been needin' for so long" (*IM*, 67).

As a woman possessed of a practical (one might say a "blues") sensibility, Kate knows that men are, indeed, sometimes "dirty lowdown wicked" dogs who can perceive a whore in a pigtailed girl. She is scarcely resigned to such a state of affairs where her own daughter is concerned, but like the black mother so aptly described in Carolyn Rodgers's poem "It Is Deep," Kate knows that being "religiously girdled in her god"[7] will not pay the bills. She thus brings together the sacred and the secular, the moral and the practical, in a manner that makes her both a complement for Trueblood and (again in the words of Rodgers) a woman who "having waded through a storm, is very obviously, a sturdy Black bridge" (12).

To freight Trueblood's sexual manifestation and its complement in Kate with more significance than they can legitimately bear would be as much a critical disservice as were previous failures, or refusals, even to acknowledge these aspects. For while it is true that sexuality burdens the content of his narrative, it is also true that Trueblood himself metaphorically transforms his incestuous act into a single, symbolic instance of his total life situation:

> There I was [atop Matty Lou] trying to git away with all my might, yet having to move *without* movin'. I flew in but I had to walk out. I had to move without movin'. I done thought 'bout it since a heap, and when you think right hard you see that that's the way things is always been with me. That's just about been my life. (*IM*, 59)

Like the formidable task of the Invisible Man's grandfather, who gave up his gun during the Reconstruction but still had to fight a war, Trueblood's problem is that of getting out of a tight spot without undue motion—without perceptibly moving. The grandfather adopted a strategy of extrication by indirection, pretending to affirm the designs of the dominant white society around him. Having relinquished his gun, he became "a spy in the enemy's country," a man overcoming his adversaries with yeses. He represents the trickster as subtle deceiver. Trueblood, in contrast, claims that to "move without movin' " means to take a refractory situation uncompromisingly in hand: "You got holt to it," he says, "and you caint let go even though you want to" (*IM*, 60). He conceives of himself in the throes of his incestuous ecstasies as "like that fellow . . . down in Birmingham. That one what locked hisself in his house and shot [with a gun that he had *refused to give up*] at them police until they set fire to the house and burned him up. I was lost" (*IM*, 60). An energetic, compulsive, even ecstatically expressive response is required:

> Like that fellow [in Birmingham], I stayed. . . . He mighta died, but I suspects now that he got a heapa satisfaction before he went. I *know* there ain't nothin' like what I went through, I caint tell how it was. It's like when a real drinkin' man gets drunk, or like a real sanctified religious woman gits so worked up she jumps outta her clothes, or when a real gamblin' man keeps on gamblin' when he's losing. (*IM*, 60)

In his energetic response, Trueblood says a resounding no to all the castratingly tight spots of his existence as a poor black farmer in the undemocratic South.[8]

The most discursively developed *expressive* form of this no is, of course, the narrative that Trueblood relates. But he has come to this narrative by way of music. He has fasted and reflected on his guilt or innocence until he thinks his "brain go'n bust," and then, he recalls, "one night, way early in the mornin', I looks up and sees the stars and I starts singin'. I don't know what it was, some kinda church song, I guess. All I know is I *ends up* singin' the blues. I sings me some blues that night ain't never been sang before" (*IM*, 65–66). The first unpremeditated expression that Trueblood summons is a religious song. But the religious system that gives birth to the song is, presumably, one in which the term "incest" carries pejorative force. Hence, the sharecropper moves on, spontaneously, to the blues.

* * *

In *The Legacy of the Blues*, Samuel Charters writes:

> Whatever else the blues was it was a language; a rich, vital, expressive language that stripped away the misconception that the black society in the United States was simply a poor, discouraged version of the white. It was impossible not to hear the differences. No one could listen to the blues without realizing that there are two Americas. (22)

On the origins of this blues language, Giles Oakley quotes the blues singer Booker White: "You want to know where did the blues come from. The blues come from behind the mule. Well now, you can have the blues sitting at the table eating. But the foundation of the blues is walking behind the mule way back in slavery time"(*Devil's Music*, 7). The language that Trueblood summons to contain his act grows out of the soil he works, a soil that has witnessed the unrecompensed labor of many thousand blacks walking "behind the mule," realizing, as they negotiated the long furrows, the absurdity of working from "can-to-caint" for the profit of others.

Born on a farm in Alabama and working, at the time of his incestuous act, as an impoverished, cold, poorly provisioned sharecropper, Trueblood has the inherent blues capacity of a songster like Lightnin' Hopkins, who asserts, "I had the one thing you need to be a blues singer. I was born with the blues" (Charters, 183). Originating in the field hollers and work songs of the agrarian South and becoming codified as stable forms by the second decade of the twentieth century, the blues offer a language that connotes a world of transience, instability, hard luck, brutalizing work, lost love, minimal security, and enduring human wit and resourcefulness in the face of disaster. The blues enjoin one to accept hard luck because, without it, there is "no luck at all." The lyrics are often charged with a surreal humor that wonders if "a match box will hold my clothes." In short, the "other America" that they signal is a world of common labor, spare circumstances, and grimly lusty lyrical challenges to a bleak fate.

In the system of the blues Trueblood finds the most symbolic code for expressing the negativity of his own act. Since he is both a magical storyteller and a blues singer par excellence, he can incorporate the lean economics and fateful intransience of the blues world into his autobiographical narrative. His metaphorical talent, which transforms a steamboat's musicians into a boss quail's whistle and then likens the actions of the quail to those of a good man who ''do'' what he ''got to do,'' reflects a basic understanding of the earthy resonances of blues. He says of his evenings listening to boats in Mobile:

> They used to have musicianers on them boats, and sometimes I used to wake her [Margaret] up to hear the music when they come up the river. I'd be layin' there and it would be quiet and I could hear it comin' from way, way off. Like when you quail huntin' and it's getting dark and you can hear the boss bird whistlin' tryin' to get the covey together again, and he's coming toward you slow and whistlin' soft, 'cause he knows you somewhere around with your gun. Still he got to round them up, so he keeps on comin'. Them boss quails is like a good man, what he got to do he *do*. (*IM*, 55)

Further, the farmer begins his story by describing his desperate economic straits, like those frequently recorded in blues—that is, no wood for fuel and no work or aid to be found (*IM*, 53)—and then traces the outcome of his plight. Matty Lou is in bed with her mother and father because it is freezing: ''It was so cold all of us had to sleep together; me, the ole lady and the gal. That's how it started'' (*IM*, 53). It seems appropriate—even natural—that blues should expressively frame the act resulting from such bitter black agrarian circumstances. And it is, in fact, blues affirmation of human identity in the face of dehumanizing circumstance that resonates through the sharecropper's triumphant penultimate utterance: ''I make up my mind that I ain't nobody but myself and ain't nothin' I can do but let whatever is gonna happen, happen'' (*IM*, 66).

The farmer's statement is not an expression of transcendence. It is, instead, an affirmation of a still recognizable humanity by a singer who has incorporated his personal disaster into a code of blues meanings emanating from an unpredictably chaotic world. In translating his tragedy into the vocabulary and semantics of the blues and, subsequently, into the electrifying expression of his narrative, Trueblood realizes that he is not so changed by catastrophe that he must condemn, mortify, or redefine his essential self. This self, as the preceding discussion indicates, is in many ways the obverse of the stable, predictable, puritanical, productive, law-abiding ideal self of the American industrial-capitalist society.

The words the sharecropper issues from ''behind the mule'' provide a moral opposition (if not a moral corrective) to the confident expressions of control emanating from Mr. Norton's technological world. From a pluralistic perspective, the counteractive patterns represented by the sharecropper and the millionaire point to a positive homeostasis in American life. In the southern regions represented by Trueblood, an oppositional model might suggest, the duty-bound but enfeebled rationalist of northern industry can always achieve renewal and a kind of shamanistic cure for the ills of civilization. But the millionaire in the narrative episode hardly appears to represent a rejuvenated Fisher King. At the close of the sharecropper's story, in fact, he seems paralyzed by the ghostly torpor of a stunned Benito Cereno or a horrified Mr. Kurtz. Thus a pluralistic model that projects revivifying opposition as the relation between sharecropper and millionaire does not adequately explain the Norton-Trueblood interaction. Some of the more significant implications of the episode, in fact, seem to reside not in the opposition between industrial technocrat and agrarian farmer but in the two sectors' commercial consensus on Afro-American expressive culture. Eshu and Hermes are not only figures of powerful creative instinct. They are also gods of the marketplace. Two analytical reflections on the study of literature and ideology, one by Fredric Jameson and the other by Hayden White, elucidate the commercial consensus achieved by Trueblood and his millionaire auditor.

Fredric Jameson writes:

> The term "ideology" stands as the sign for a problem yet to be solved, a mental operation which remains to be executed. It does not presuppose cut-and-dried sociological stereotypes like the notion of the "bourgeois" or the "petty bourgeois" but is rather a mediatory concept: that is, it is an imperative to re-invent a relationship between the linguistic or aesthetic or conceptual fact in question and its social ground. . . . Ideological analysis may . . . be described as the rewriting of a particular narrative trait or seme as a function of its social, historical, or political context. (Jameson, 510–11)

Jameson's interest in a reinvented relation between linguistic fact and social ground is a function of his conviction that all acts of narration inscribe social ideologies. In other words, there is always a historical, or ideological, subtext in a literary work of art. For, since history is accessible to us only through texts, the literary work of art either has to "rewrite" the historical texts of its time or "textualize" the uninscribed events of its day in order to "contextualize" itself. What Jameson calls the "ideology of form" White calls "reflection theory." If literary art can indeed be said to reflect, through inscription, the social ground from which it originates, at what level of a specifically social domain, asks White, does such reflection occur? How can we most appropriately view literary works of art as distinctively "social" entities?

White's answer is that ideological analysis must begin with a society's exchange system and must regard the literary work as "merely one commodity among others and moreover as a commodity that has to be considered as not different in kind from any other." To adopt such an analytical strategy, according to White, is to comprehend "not only the alienation of the artist which the representation of the value of his product in terms of money alone might foster, but also the tendency of the artist to fetishize his own produce as being itself the universal sign and incarnation of value in a given social system'' (White, 378). White could justifiably summon Ellison's previously quoted remarks on the transformative powers of art to illustrate the ''fetishizing'' of art as the incarnation of value. In Ellison's view, however, artistic value is not a sign or incarnation in a given social system but, rather, a sign of humane value in toto. What is pertinent about White's remarks for the present discussion, however, is that the relation Jameson would reinvent is for White an economic one involving challenging questions of axiology.

To apply Jameson's and White's reflections in analyzing the Trueblood episode, one can begin by recognizing that the sharecropper's achievement of expressive narrative form is immediately bracketed by the exchange system of Anglo-American society. Recalling his first narration of his story to a group of whites, the sharecropper remembers that Sheriff Barbour asked him to tell what happened:

> . . . and I tole him and he called in some more men and they made me tell it again. They wanted to hear about the gal lots of times and they gimme somethin' to eat and drink and some tobacco. Surprised me, 'cause I was scared and spectin' somethin' different. Why, I guess there ain't a colored man in the county who ever got to take so much of the white folkses' time as I did. (*IM*, 52)

Food, drink, tobacco, and audience time are commodities the sharecropper receives in barter for the commodity he delivers—his story. The narrative of incest, after its first telling, accrues an ever-spiraling exchange value. The Truebloods receive all the items enumerated earlier, as well as a one-hundred-dollar bill from Mr. Norton's Moroccan-leather wallet. The exchange value of the story thus moves from a system of barter to a money economy overseen by northern industrialists. The status of the farmer's story as a commodity cannot be ignored.

As an artistic form incorporating the historical and ideological subtext of American industrial society, the sharecropper's tale represents a supreme capitalist fantasy. The family, as the fundamental social unit of middle-class society, is governed by the property concept. A man marries—takes a wife as his exclusive ''property''—to produce legitimate heirs who will keep their father's wealth (i.e., his property) in the family. Among royalty or the aristocracy such marriages may describe an exclusive circle of exchange. Only certain women are eligible as royal or aristocratic wives. And in the tightest of all circumstances, incest may be justified as the sole available means of preserving intact the family heritage—the nobleman's or aristocrat's property. An unfettered, incestuous procreativity that results not only in new and legitimate heirs but also in a marked increase in property (e.g., Trueblood's situation) can be viewed as a capitalist dream. And if such results can be achieved without fear of holy sanction, then procreation becomes a secular feat of human engineering.

Mr. Norton reflects that his "real life's work" has been, not his banking or his researches, but his "first-hand organizing of human life" (*IM*, 42). What more exacting control could this millionaire New Englander have exercised than the incestuous domination of his own human family as a productive unit, eternally giving birth to new profits? Only terror of dreadful heavenly retribution (i.e., of punishment for "impropriety") had prevented him from attempting such a construction of life with his pathetically idealized only child, now deceased. Part of his stupefaction at the conclusion of the sharecropper's narrative results from his realization that he might have safely effected such a productive arrangement of life. One need not belabor the capitalist-fantasy aspect of Trueblood's narrative, however, to comprehend his story's commodity status in an industrial-capitalist system of exchange. What the farmer is ultimately merchandising is an image of himself that is itself a product—a bizarre product—of the slave trade that made industrial America possible.

Africans became slaves through what the West Indian novelist George Lamming describes as an act of "commercial deportation" overseen by the white West (Lamming, 93). In America, Africans were classified as "chattel personal" and turned into commodities. To forestall the moral guilt associated with this aberrant, mercantile transformation, white Americans conceptualized a degraded, subhuman animal as a substitute for the actual African. This categorical parody found its public, physical embodiment in the mask of the minstrel theatrical. As Ellison writes in "Change the Joke and Slip the Yoke," the African in America was thus reduced to a "negative sign" (*S&A*, 63): "the [minstrel] mask was the thing (the 'thing' in more ways than one) and its function was to veil the humanity of Negroes thus reduced to a sign, and to repress the white audience's awareness of its moral identification with its own acts and with the human ambiguities pushed behind the mask." Following the lead of Constance Rourke, Ellison asserts that the minstrel show is, in fact, a "ritual of exorcism" (*S&A*, 64). But what of the minstrel performance given by the Afro-American who dons the mask? In such performances, writes Ellison:

> Motives of race, status, economics and guilt are always clustered. . . . The comic point is inseparable from the racial identity of the performer . . . who by assuming the group-debasing role for gain not only substantiates the audience's belief in the "blackness" of things black, but relieves it, with dreamlike efficiency, of its guilt by accepting the very profit motive that was involved in the designation of the Negro as national scapegoat in the first place. There are all kinds of comedy; here one is reminded of the tribesman in *Green Hills of Africa* who hid his laughing face in shame at the sight of a gut-shot hyena jerking out its own intestines and eating them, in Hemingway's words, "with relish." (*S&A*, 64–65)

Trueblood, who assumes the minstrel mask to the utter chagrin of the Invisible Man ("How can he tell this to white men, I thought, when he knows they'll say that all Negroes do such things?''), has indeed accepted the profit motive that gave birth to that mask in the first place. He tells his tale with relish: ''He talked willingly now, with a kind of satisfaction and no trace of hesitancy or shame'' (*IM*, 53). The firm lines of capitalist economics are, therefore, not the only ideological inscriptions in the sharecropper's narrative. The story also contains the distorting contours of that mask constructed by the directors of the economic system to subsume their guilt. The rambunctiously sexual, lyrical, and sin-adoring ''darky'' is an image dear to the hearts of white America.

Ideologically, then, there is every reason to regard the sharecropper's story as a commodity in harmony with its social ground—with the system of exchange sanctioned by the dominant Anglo-American society. For though Trueblood has been denied ''book learning'' by the nearby black college, he has not failed to garner some knowledge of marketing. Just as the college officials peddle the sharecropper's ''primitive spirituals'' to the white millionaires who descend every spring, so Trueblood sells his own expressive product—a carefully constructed narrative, framed to fit market demands. His actions as a merchant seem to compromise his status as a blues artist, as a character of undeniable folk authenticity. And his delineation as an untrammeled and energetic prime mover singing a deep blues no to social constraints appears to collapse under the impress of ideological analysis. The complexities of American culture, however, enable him to reconcile a merchandising role as oral storyteller with his position as an antinomian trickster. For the Afro-American blues manifest an effective, expressive duality that Samuel Charters captures as follows:

> The blues has always had a duality to it. One of its sides is its personal creativity—the consciousness of a creative individual using it as a form of expression. The other side is the blues as entertainment. Someone like Memphis Slim is a professional blues entertainer. But the blues is a style of music that emphasizes integrity—so how does a singer change his style without losing his credibility as a blues artist? (Charters, 168)

As entertainment, the blues, whether classic or country, were sung professionally in theatres.[9] And their public theatricality is analogous to the Afro-American's donning of the minstrel mask. There is, perhaps, something obscenely—though profitably—gut-wrenching about Afro-Americans delivering up carefully modified versions of their essential expressive selves for the entertainment of their Anglo-American oppressors. And, as Charters implies, the question of integrity looms large. But the most appropriate inquiry in the wake of his comment is, Integrity, *as what*?

To deliver the blues as entertainment—if one is an entertainer—is to maintain a fidelity to one's role. Again, if the performance required is that of a minstrel and one is a genuine performer, then donning the mask is an act consistent with one's stature. There are always fundamental economic questions involved in such uneasy Afro-American public postures. As Ellison suggests, Afro-Americans, in their guise as entertainers, season the possum of black expressive culture to the taste of their Anglo-American audience, maintaining, in the process, their integrity as performers. But in private sessions—in the closed circle of their own community—everybody knows that the punch line to the recipe (and the proper response to the performer's constrictive dilemma) is, "Damn the possum! That sho' is some good gravy!" It is just possible that the "gravy" is the inimitable technique of the Afro-American artist, a technique (derived from lived blues experience) as capable of "playing possum" as of presenting one.

A further question, however, has to do with the artist's affective response to being treated as a commodity. And with this query, White's and Jameson's global formulations prove less valuable than a closer inspection of the self-reflexive expressivity of Afro-American spokespersons in general. Ellison's Trueblood episode, for example, suggests that the angst assumed to accompany commodity status is greatly alleviated when that status constitutes a sole means of securing power in a hegemonic system.

In the Trueblood episode, blacks who inhabit the southern college's terrain assume that they have transcended the peasant rank of sharecroppers and their cohorts. In fact, both the college's inhabitants and Trueblood's agrarian fellows are but constituencies of a single underclass. When the college authorities threaten the farmer with exile or arrest, he has only to turn to the white Mr. Buchanan, "the boss man," to secure immunity and a favorable audience before Sheriff Barbour, "the white law" (*IM*, 52). The imperious fiats of whites relegate all blacks to an underclass. In Trueblood's words, "no matter how biggity a nigguh gits, the white folks can always cut him down" (*IM*, 53). For those in this underclass, Ellison's episode implies, expressive representation is the only means of prevailing.

Dr. Bledsoe, for example, endorses lying as an effective strategy in interacting with Mr. Norton and the other college trustees. And Trueblood himself adopts tale telling (which is often conflated with lying in black oral tradition) as a mode of expression that allows him a degree of dignity and freedom within the confines of a severe white hegemony. The expressive "mask," one might say, is as indispensable for college blacks as it is for those beyond the school's boundaries. Describing the initial meeting between Mr. Norton and the sharecropper, the protagonist says, "I hurried behind him [Mr. Norton], seeing him stop when he reached the man and the children. They became silent, their faces clouding over, their features becoming soft and negative, their eyes bland and deceptive. They were crouching behind their eyes waiting for him to speak—just as I recognized that I was trembling behind my own" (*IM*, 50). The evasive silence of these blacks is as expressive of power relations in the South as the mendacious strategy advocated by Dr. Bledsoe.

When the protagonist returns from his ill-fated encounters with Trueblood and the crew at the Golden Day, the school's principal asks him if he is unaware that blacks have "lied enough decent homes and drives [got enough material advantage by lying] for you to show him [Mr. Norton]'' (*IM*, 136). When the protagonist responds that he was obeying Mr. Norton's orders by showing the millionaire the ''slum'' regions of Trueblood rather than ''decent homes and drives,'' Bledsoe exclaims, ''He *ordered* you. Dammit, white folk are always giving orders, it's a habit with them. . . . My God, boy! You're black and living in the South—did you forget how to lie?'' (*IM*, 136).

Artful evasion and expressive illusion are equally traditional black expressive modes in interracial exchange in America. Such modes, the Trueblood episode implies, are the only resources that blacks at any level can barter for a semblance of decency and control in their lives. Making black expressiveness a commodity, therefore, is not simply a gesture in a bourgeois economics of art. Rather, it is a crucial move in a repertoire of black survival motions in the United States. To examine the status of Afro-American expressiveness as a commodity, then, is to do more than observe, within the constraints of an institutional theory of art, that the art world is a function of economics. In a very real sense, Afro-America's exchange power has always been coextensive with its stock of expressive resources. What is implicit in an analysis of black expressiveness as a commodity is not a limited history of the ''clerks'' but a total history of Afro-American cultural interaction in America.

In *When Harlem Was in Vogue*—a brilliant study that treats the black artistic awakening of the 1920s known as the ''Harlem Renaissance''—David Levering Lewis captures the essential juxtaposition between white hegemony and black creativity as a negotiable power of exchange. Writing of Charles Johnson, the energetic black editor of *Opportunity* magazine during this period, Lewis says:

> [Johnson] gauged more accurately than perhaps any other Afro-American intellectual the scope and depth of the national drive to ''put the nigger in his place'' after the war, to keep him out of the officer corps, out of labor unions and skilled jobs, out of the North and quaking for his very existence in the South—and out of politics everywhere. Johnson found that one area alone—probably because of its very implausibility—had not been proscribed. No exclusionary rules had been laid down regarding a place in the arts. Here was a small crack in the wall of racism, a fissure that was worth trying to widen. (48)

''Exclusionary rules'' were certainly implicit in the arts during the 1920s, but what Lewis suggests is that they were far less rigid and explicit than they were in other domains. Blacks thus sought to widen the ''fissure,'' to gain what power they could to determine their own lives, through a renaissance of black expressiveness.

An ideological analysis of expressiveness as a commodity should take adequate account of the defining variables in the culture where this commercialization occurs. In Afro-American culture, exchanging words for safety and profit is scarcely an alienating act. It is, instead, a defining act in aesthetics. Further, it is an act that lies at the heart of Afro-American politics conceived in terms of who gets what and when and how. Making a commodity of black expressiveness, as I try to make clear in my concluding section, does entail inscription of an identifying economics. But aggressively positive manifestations of this process (despite the dualism it presupposes) result from a self-reflexive acknowledgment that only the "economics of slavery" gives valuable and specifically black resonance to Afro-American works of art.

* * *

The critic George Kent observes a "mathematical consistency between Ellison's critical pronouncements and his creative performance" (Kent, 161). Insofar as Ellison provides insightful critical interpretations of his own novel and its characters, Kent's judgment is correct. But the "critical pronouncements" in Ellison's canon that suggest a devaluing of Afro-American folklore hardly seem consistent with the implications of his Trueblood episode. Such statements are properly regarded, I believe, as public remarks by Ellison the merchant rather than as incisive, affective comments by Ellison the creative genius.

Trueblood's duality is, finally, also that of his creator. For Ellison knows that his work as an Afro-American artist derives from those "economics of slavery" that provided conditions of existence for Afro-American folklore. Black folk expression is a product of the impoverishment of blacks in America. The blues, as a case in point, are unthinkable for those happy with their lot.

Yet, if folk artists are to turn a profit from their monumental creative energies (which are often counteractive, or inversive, vis-à-vis Anglo-American culture), they must take a lesson from the boss quail and "move without moving." They must, in essence, sufficiently modify their folk forms (and amply advertise themselves) to merchandise such forms as commodities in the artistic market. To make their products commensurate with a capitalistic marketplace, folk artists may even have to don masks that distort their genuine selves. Ralph Ellison is a master of such strategies.

Ellison reconciles the trickster's manifestations as untrammeled creator and as god of the marketplace by providing critical advertisements for himself as a novelist that carefully bracket the impoverishing economics of Afro-America. For example, in "Change the Joke and Slip the Yoke" he writes, "I use folklore in my work not because I am a Negro, but because writers like Eliot and Joyce made me conscious of the literary value of my folk inheritance. My cultural background, like that of most Americans, is dual (my middle name, sadly enough, is Waldo)" (*S&A*, 72).[10] What is designated in this quotation as "literary value" is in reality market value. Joyce and Eliot taught Ellison that if he was a skillful enough strategist and spokesman he could market his own folklore. What is bracketed, of course, is the economics that required Ellison, if he wished to be an Afro-American artist, to turn to Afro-

American folklore as a traditional, authenticating source for his art. Like his sharecropper, Ellison is wont to make literary value out of socioeconomic necessity. But he is also an artist who recognizes that Afro-American folk forms have value *in themselves*; they "have named human situations so well," he suggests in "The Art of Fiction," "that a whole corps of writers could not exhaust their universality" (*S&A*, 173). What Ellison achieves in the Trueblood episode is a dizzying hall of mirrors, a redundancy of structure, that enables him to extend the value of Afro-American folk forms by combining them with an array of Western narrative forms and tropes. Written novel and sung blues, polysyllabic autobiography and vernacular personal narrative, a Christian Fall and an inversive triumph of the black trickster—all are conjoined in a magnificently embedded manner.

The foregoing analysis suggests that it is in such creative instances that one discovers Ellison's artistic genius, a genius that links him inextricably and positively to his invented sharecropper. For in the Trueblood episode conceived as a chapter in a novel, one finds not only the same kind of metaexpressive commentary that marks the character's narration to Norton but also the same type of self-reflexive artist that the sharecropper's recitation implies—an artist who is fully aware of the contours and limitations, the rewards and dilemmas, of the Afro-American's uniquely expressive craft.

In the expository, critical moment, by contrast, one often finds a quite different Ralph Ellison. Instead of the *reflexive* artist, one finds the *reflective* spokesman. Paraphrasing Babcock-Abrahams, who uses a "failed" Narcissus to illustrate the difference between the "reflective" and the "reflexive," one might say that in his criticism Ralph Ellison is not narcissistic enough ("Reflexivity," 4). His reflections in *Shadow and Act* seem to define Afro-American folk expressiveness in art as a sign of identity, a sign that marks the creator as unequivocally Afro-American and, hence, other. I have sought to demonstrate, however, that Ellison's folk expressiveness is, in fact, "identity within difference." While critics experience alienation, artists can detach themselves from, survive, and even laugh at their initial experiences of otherness. Like Velázquez in his *Las Meninas* or the Van Eyck of *Giovanni Arnolfini and His Bride*, the creator of Trueblood is "conscious of being self-conscious of himself" as artist.[11] Instead of solacing himself with critical distinctions, he employs reflexively mirroring narratives to multiply distinctions and move playfully across categorical boundaries. Like his sharecropper, he knows indisputably that his most meaningful identity is his Afro-American self imaged in acts of expressive creativity.

Ralph Ellison's bracketings as a public critic, therefore, do not forestall his private artistic recognition that he "ain't nobody but himself." And it is out of this realization that a magnificent folk creation such as Trueblood emerges. Both the creator and his agrarian folk storyteller have the wisdom to know that they are resourceful "whistlers" for the tribe. They know that their primary matrix as artists is coextensive not with a capitalistic society but with material circumstances like those implied by the blues singer Howling Wolf:

> Well I'm a po' boy, long way from home.
> Well I'm a po' boy, long way from home.
> No spendin' money in my pocket, no spare meat on my bone. (Nichols, 85)

One might say that in the brilliant reflexivity of the Trueblood encounter, we hear the blues whistle among the high-comic thickets. We glimpse Ellison's creative genius beneath his Western critical mask. And while we stand awaiting the next high-cultural pronouncement from the critic, we are startled by a captivating sound of flattened thirds and sevenths—the private artist's blues-filled flight.

NOTES

1. Ralph Ellison, *Shadow and Act*, 82–83. This work comprises the bulk of Ellison's critical canon. All subsequent references to this work are cited in text as *S&A*.

2. Ellison, *Invisible Man*, 55. All subsequent references to this work are cited in text as *IM*.

3. One of the general questions provoking Freud's inquiry into totemism is "What is the ultimate source of the horror of incest which must be recognized as the root of exogamy?" Sigmund Freud, *Totem and Taboo*, 122, 141–46.

4. Paul Radin, *The Trickster*, Tale 16. Originally published in 1955 in London by Routledge & Kegan Paul, it has been reprinted several times, the most recent by Schocken Books, Inc. in 1972.

5. For a stimulating discussion of the trickster in his various literary and nonliterary guises, consult Barbara Babcock-Abrahams's provocative essay, "'A Tolerated Margin of Mess': The Trickster and His Tales Reconsidered," *Journal of the Folklore Institute* 11 (1974): 147–86. She writes, "In contrast to the scapegoat or tragic victim, trickster belongs to the comic modality or marginality where violation is generally the precondition for laughter and communitas, and there tends to be an incorporation of the outsider, a leveling of hierarchy, a reversal of statuses" (153).

6. I had enlightening conversations with Kimberly Benston on the Trueblood episode's parodic representation of the Fall, a subject that he explores at some length in a critical work in progress. I am grateful for his generous help.

7. See Carolyn Rodgers, *How I Got Ovah: New and Selected Poems*, 11.

8. The significance of the sharecropper's incestuous progeny may be analogous to that of the broken link of leg chain given to the Invisible Man during his early days in the Brotherhood. Presenting the link, Brother Tarp says, "I don't think of it in terms of but two words, *yes* and *no*, but it signifies a heap more" (*IM*, 379).

9. Ellison introduces this claim, which contradicts LeRoi Jones's assertions on blues, in a review of Jones's book *Blues People* in *Shadow and Act*, 249.

10. The implicit "trickiness" of Ellison's claim—its use of words to "signify" quite other than what they seem to intend on the surface—is an aspect of the Afro-American "critic as trickster." In "The 'Blackness of Blackness': A Critique of the Sign and the Signifying Monkey," a paper presented at the Modern Language Association Convention, New York, December 30, 1981, Henry Louis Gates, Jr., began an analysis—in quite suggestive terms—of the trickster's "semiotic" manifestation. For Gates, the Afro-American folk figure of the "signifying monkey" is an archetype of the Afro-American critic. In the essays "Change the Joke and Slip the Yoke" and "The World and the Jug," Ellison demonstrates, one can certainly conclude, an elegant mastery of what might be termed the "exacerbating strategies" of the monkey. Perhaps one also hears his low Afro-American voice directing a sotto voce "Yo' Mamma!" at heavyweights of the Anglo-American critical establishment.

11. "Reflexivity," 4. One of the most intriguing recent discussions of the Velázquez painting is Michel Foucault's in *The Order of Things*, 3–16. Jay Ruby briefly discusses the Van Eyck in the introduction to his anthology, *A Crack in the Mirror*, 12–13.

WORKS CITED

Babcock-Abrahams, Barbara. "The Novel and the Carnival World." *Modern Language Notes* 89 (1974): 912.

———. "Reflexivity: Definitions and Discriminations." *Semiotica* 30 (1980): 4.

Charters, Samuel. *The Legacy of the Blues: Lives of Twelve Great Bluesmen*. New York: DaCapo, 1977.

Ellison, Ralph. *Invisible Man*. New York: Vintage-Random House, 1974

———. *Shadow and Act*. New York: Signet-NAL, 1966.

Foucault, Michel. *The Order of Things*. New York: Random House, 1973.

Freud, Sigmund. *Totem and Taboo*. Trans. James Strachey. New York: Norton, 1950.

Geertz, Clifford. "Deep Play: Notes on the Balinese Cockfight," *Interpretation of Cultures*. New York: Basic, 1973.

Jameson, Fredric. "The Symbolic Inference; or, Kenneth Burke and Ideological Analysis." *Critical Inquiry* 4 (1978): 510–11.

Kent, George. *Blackness and the Adventure of Western Culture*. Chicago: Third World, 1972.

Lamming, George. *Season of Adventure*. London: Allison & Busby, 1979.

Lewis, David Levering. *When Harlem Was in Vogue*. New York: Knopf, 1981.

Nicholas, A. S., ed. *Woke Up This Mornin': Poetry of the Blues*. New York: Bantam, 1973.

Oakley, Giles. *The Devil's Music: A History of the Blues*. New York: Harvest, 1976.

Radin, Paul. *The Trickster: A Study in American Indian Mythology*. London: Routledge & Kegan Paul, 1955.

Rodgers, Carolyn. *How I Got Ovah: New and Selected Poems*. New York: Doubleday, 1975.

Ruby, Jay, ed. *A Crack in the Mirror: Reflexive Perspectives in Anthropology*. Philadelphia: University of Pennsylvania Press, 1982.

Turner, Victor. *The Forest of Symbols: Aspects of Ndembu Ritual*. Ithaca: Cornell University Press, 1967.

______. "Myth and Symbol." *International Encyclopedia of the Social Sciences*, Vol. 10. New York: Free Press, 1986.

White, Hayden. "Literature and Social Action: Reflections on the Reflection Theory of Literary Art." *New Literary History* 12 (1980): 378.

Ralph Ellison's Trueblooded *Bildungsroman*

KENNETH BURKE

Dear Ralph:

The several pages I wrote you by way of first draft have vanished. One usually feels either desolate or furious about such a slip, depending upon one's inclination to think of the notes as either lost or pilfered. But in this case I am neither. For I had already decided on a new start, and my first effort hadn't seemed quite right, anyhow.

I had taken off from comments in my *Rhetoric of Motives* (1950) with reference to "the Negro intellectual, Ralph Ellison," who said that Booker T. Washington "described the Negro community as a basket of crabs, wherein should one attempt to climb out, the others immediately pull him back." I sized up the black man's quandary thus: "Striving for freedom as a human being generically, he must do so as a Negro specifically. But to do so as a Negro is, by the same token, to prevent oneself from doing so in the generic sense; for a Negro could not be free generically except in a situation where the color of the skin had no more social meaning than the color of the eyes."

I moved on from there to a related "racist" problem, sans the accident of pigment, as dramatized in the role of Shakespeare's Shylock; and then on to promises of being purely and simply a person (and visibly so) "thereby attaining the kind of transcendence at which all men aim, and at which the Negro spiritual had aimed, though there the aim was at the spiritual transcending of a predestined material slavery, whereas the Marxist ultimates allow for a material transcending of inferior status."

My job in that book was to feature the persuasiveness of such designs, be they true or false; and I went on accordingly, with variations on the theme of the special cultural (sociopolitical) problems that the inheritance from slavery imposed upon the Negro "intellectual" who would carve a "supply

---

This essay began as a short letter from Mr. Burke to Mr. Ellison and has been expanded for the present volume.—Ed.

side'' career under conditions of ''freedom and equality,'' as ambiguously developed since the explicit constitutional proclaiming of emancipation, a few years after the Czar had abolished serfdom in Russia. (It sometimes seems as though the inheritance from serfdom has also left its ambiguities.)

Those paragraphs I wrote in connection with your literary situation then were done, of course, when I had not the slightest idea of what you were to unfold in your (literally) ''epoch-making'' novel[1] (''epoch-making'' in the strict sense, as a work that, by its range of stories and corresponding attitudes, sums up an era). I had heard you read a portion of the early section on the battle royal, and had vaguely sensed the introductory nature of your narrator's fumbling acquiescence to the indignities implied in the encounter. But the actuality of your inventions was wholly beyond any but your imagining.

Recently, on rereading the book, I begin to see it differently. As I see it now, ''retrospectively,'' and in the light of your own development since it was first published, despite its (we might say ''resonant'') involvement with the cultural problems of the Negro in the United States, its ''fixation'' on that theme, I would propose to class it primarily as an example of what the Germans would call a *Bildungsroman*.

I guess the greatest prototype of such fiction is Goethe's *Wilhelm Meister*, which details the character's progressive education from ''apprenticeship'' through ''journeymanship'' toward the ideal of ''mastery'' that shows up in his name. Also, its brand of fact and fiction shows up in its fluctuations, like yours, between ''realistic detail and poetic allegory'' (I quote verbatim from the resources most available to me now, namely, my copy of the *Encyclopaedia Brittanica*, eleventh edition). Yes, you have written the story of your Education. And the details of your life since then, with that most charming helpmeet-helpmate of yours in attitudinal collaboration, testify clearly enough to your kind of mastery, in these mussy times when who knows where to turn next?

With regard to your book and its ingenious ways of dealing with the black-white issue, my notes didn't seem to be getting anywhere. Then I gradually came to realize: Your narrator doesn't ''solve'' that problem. For it's not quite the issue as implicitly presented in that opening ''traumatic'' incident out of which your plot develops. The whites were superciliously condescending to reward your ''apprentice'' for being able to be educated (and never forget that the literal, but obsolete meaning of ''docile'' is ''teachable''). And they were right. According to the book itself, your boy was teachable. It tells step by step how he got taught, in the most astute of realistic terms, plus the sometimes even fun-loving twists of what the encyclopedia article would call ''poetical allegory.''

At least half a century has passed since I read Goethe's novel which, by its subtitles, likens the acquiring of an education in the art of living to the stages of development among the members of such craftsmanship as was exemplified in the kinds of sodality operant among the masons that build the cathedrals (as per the etymological interchangeability of ''edifice'' and ''edification''). So my memory of Goethe's book is much on the fuzzy side—and I don't have the time or opportunity now to hurry back and verify my notions. In any case, even if my recollections happen to be a bit wrong, my observations will serve accurately for present purposes with regard to your, in its way, superb enterprise, if it is viewed as such a story. Viewed thus, your book shows us, page by page, the author in the very act of using as ''spokesman'' a fictive narrator and putting him through the transformations needed to present the entire inventory of the ''ambiguities'' the author had to confront in the process of growing up when that author was your comprehensive kind of black man.

First, we should note, the character's step from apprenticeship to journeymanship is as clear as could be. His apprenticeship (his emergence out of childhood) concerns the stage of life when a black man at that time in our history was confronting strong remembrances from the days of the plantation from which ''your kind of humans'' had not long ago by constitutional amendment been ''emancipated.'' And your narrator's ''grandfather'' (who remembered being a slave) introduces the whole unfolding, with admonitions that will figure to the end. As your spokesman-narrator puts it: ''The mind that has conceived a plan of living must never lose sight of the chaos against which that pattern was conceived'' (*IM*, 438). He says this when he's about to ''emerge'' from his ''hibernation.'' And his author's book did help its author to do precisely that, superbly.

Obviously, the step from apprenticeship to journeymanship takes place when your narrator comes North. Goethe's word for that stage in one's career is *Wanderjahre*, from the root of which we get our word ''wander'' in the sense of ''travel,'' the second half of the word meaning ''years.'' Your story takes an ironically ''perfect'' twist here. At the end of the first chapter your narrator tells of a dream involving his grandfather (who figures the very essence of the book's subsequent motivational quandaries).

> He told me to open my brief case and read what was inside and I did, finding an official envelope stamped with the state seal; and inside the envelope I found another and another, endlessly, and I thought I would fall of weariness. ''Them's years,'' he said. ''Now open that one.'' And I did and in it I found an engraved document containing a short message in letters of gold. ''Read it,'' my grandfather said, ''Out loud!''
>
> ''To Whom It May Concern'' I intoned. ''Keep This Nigger-Boy Running.'' I awoke with the old man's laughter ringing in my ears. (26)

Any time the book gets to terms like that for the withinness-of-withinness-of-withinness, and they are words by a black man's grandfather from out of the days of slavery, and it's a dream with all the prophetic quality of such, it's at the very heart of motivation. And what a ''grandfather clause'' that was!

Whoever knows your story will realize how well the incident foretells the end of chapter 9 introducing the critical step from apprenticeship in the South to his journeymanship in the North, when your spokesman finds that the supposed letters of recommendation he had brought with him were of the "Bellerophontic" sort. (Bulfinch tells us that "the expression 'Bellerophontic letters' arose to describe any species of communication which a person is made the bearer of, containing matter prejudicial to himself"); and your Invisible Man sizes up the letters as designed to give him the runaround, as though they were phrased exactly, "Please hope him to death, and keep him running" (*IM*, 147).

In any case, chapter 10 begins the turn from southern apprenticeship to northern journeymanship in a big way, we might even say allegorically. For in going to apply for his first job after being dismissed from a southern college (and via fantastic twists indeed!), when going to the plant in Long Island, he "crossed a bridge in the fog to get there and came down in a stream of workers" (*IM*, 149). Morbidities of the black-white issue had all been of a quite realistic presentation. But here the whole next phase was to be in terms of "a huge electric sign" proposing to KEEP AMERICA PURE WITH LIBERTY PAINTS that were pure white! Forty pages later, he says,

> I found the bridge by which I had come, but the stairs leading back to the car that crossed the top were too dizzily steep to climb, swim or fly, and I found a subway instead. . . .
>
> We, he, him—my mind and I—were no longer getting around in the same circles. Nor my body either. Across the aisle a young platinum blonde nibbled at a red Delicious apple as station lights rippled past behind her. The train plunged. I dropped through the roar, giddy and vacuum-minded, sucked under and out in late afternoon Harlem. (*IM*, 189–90)

Those chapters (10, 11, and 12) vigorously trace a series of such transformations as epitomize, within the conditions of the fiction, a "myth-and-ritual" of "being born again." (Incidentally, that new start comes close to the center of the book.) They are simultaneously one author's personal way of intuiting such a psychic process while doing so in ways such that, despite their localization in terms of this particular fiction, are addressed to a *general* responsiveness on the part of readers. There is a sense in which the whole book is a continual process of transformation. But here occurs the initiation of the narrator's turn from apprentice to journeyman. Henceforth his ways of being "teachable" will be correspondingly modified. Yet as I interpret the story in its entirety, despite the ideological sharpness of the black-white issue, there was not to be a resolution of a total Saul/Paul sort. Here is the tangle, when the salient details are brought together, and viewed in imagery that reflects the actions, passions, and attitudes of the narrator.

After he learns that the president of the college had given him those supposed letters of recommendation which were nothing of the sort, he starts the next phase by getting a job in a factory that was hiring black workers (suspected by the white workers as being finks) to produce white paint, with the slogan "If It's Optic White, It's The Right White." He works in a cellar that has boilers, with gauges controlled by valves. Everything comes to a focus when he gets into a furious fight with his black boss while telling himself "*you were trained*" to accept what the whites did, however foolish, angry, spiteful, drunk with power, and so on (*IM*, 171). At the height of his rage he insults the elderly man with rebukes that his grandfather taught him. The machine blows up because the quarreling had caused him to neglect the gauges. Suddenly the situation becomes clear. The boss shouts for him to turn the valve. "Which?" he yelled. Answer: "The white one, fool, the white one!" Too late. He tries to escape. Then he "seemed to run swiftly up an incline and shot forward with sudden acceleration into a wet blast of black emptiness that was somehow a bath of whiteness" (*IM*, 173–74). The gradual regaining of consciousness in a hospital after the explosion is marked by various distinguishings and confusings of white and black. And in the midst of trying to define his identity (I would make much of this sentence) he says, "But we are all human, I thought, wondering what I meant" (*IM*, 182). Two pages later we read:

> I felt a tug at my belly and looked down to see one of the physicians pull the cord which was attached to the stomach node, jerking me forward.
> "What is this?" I said.
> "Get the shears," he said.
> "Sure," the other said, "Let's not waste time."
> I recoiled inwardly as though the cord were part of me. (*IM*, 184)

Obviously, as part of a rebirth ritual, this detail figures the severing of the umbilical cord. With that expression "part of" in mind, turn to this passage in the Epilogue, five pages from the end of the book:

> "Agree 'em to death and destruction," grandfather had advised. Hell, weren't they their own death and their own destruction except as the principle ["the principle on which the country was built and not the men"] lived in them and in us? And here's the cream of the joke: Weren't we *part of them* as well as apart from them and subject to die when they died? (*IM*, 433–34)

And in this connection recall that the Saul/Paul reversal, as a paradigm of rebirth, was referred to by the grandfather thus:

> When you're a youngun, you Saul, but let life whup your head a bit and you starts to trying to be Paul—though you still Sauls around on the side. (*IM*, 288)

All told, I take it that the motivational design of the book is in its essence thus: Though "ideological" prejudices (and I would call the black-white issue a branch of such) make humans be "apart from" one another, we are all, for better or worse, "part of" one humankind—and, at least on paper, an amended U.S. Constitution holds out that same promise to us all.

I want to discuss an episode in your book which bears upon the complications implicit in all that follows. It involves the generically human (as distinguished from the ideologically divisive). For it's the story of Jim Trueblood's incest. Obviously in itself the "critical occasion" about which the anecdote is built is by sheer definition wholly black-white. But the book's ways of adapting it to your narrator's circumstantially goaded development toward graduation as a "master" can deflect attention from what I consider a major aspect of its "rightness" as a motive.

Incest is a familial motive, involving problems of identity that are variously confronted as the individual, under the incentives of sexual maturation, develops from infantile narcissism (the primary "autistic" stage) to a kind of divisiveness that comes to fruition in the taboos ("incest awe") that are featured in psychoanalysis. The whole range of perversions, neuroses, sublimations could be classed under the one head of responses to the need of modifying the sense of identity out of which human infants variously "emerge." Sibling incest was even institutionalized in the legal fictions of ancient Egyptian rule, as the pharaoh was expected to cohabit with his sister, both of the offspring being "part of" the same dynastic identity. Incest taboos, viewed from the standpoint of family identity, are seen to reflect a breach that implicitly transforms what was "a part of" into the "apart from." Trueblood (perfect name) symbolizes the all-blackness of the identity that either the narrator or his author in childhood started from by way of experiences with the sense of family identity—and the pattern gets fittingly ("perfectly") rounded out by his role as a singer of the all-black Negro spirituals (even when performance before whites introduces the black-white ideology as a motivational dimension having to do with the overall plot, a dimension also lithely exploited by references to the special attention he gets from white sociological-anthropological researchers, whose interviews with him give them data for their studies).

And all told, here is the place to sum up what I think can be gained if, when considering your book's way of carving out a career, we discuss it not just in itself, but by comparison and contrast with the Goethean pattern. Both were dealing with periods of pronounced social mobility, in Germany the kind of transitions that would come to a crisis in the French Revolution, in the United States in the aftermath of a war designed to decide whether all the states would remain part of the same Union or whether some would form a Confederacy apart from the uneasy national identity that had been bequeathed us by *our* Revolution.

There was the critical difference between Wilhelm Meister as white and your narrator as black. Whereas Goethe's father was quite well-to-do, you began with the vexations that were vestiges of life as experienced by slaves on the southern plantation. The second stage of Wilhelm's apprenticeship (the first had been a kind of Bohemianism, among people of the theater) centered in friendly relations to the landed gentry. And the theme of his *Wanderjahre* is "resignation," an attitude that is denied you so long as so many blacks are still so underprivileged. And though your book's championship is dignified by the fact that it fights not just the author's battle but the battle of your "people," its ways of doing so are not the ways of other doughty "spokesmen" for your cause, whose poetical or rhetorical methods vow them to different rules (some so different that anything a white man might say in your favor might be cited as, on its face, a charge against you).

Not long before you entered the world's unending dialogue, our amended Constitution had promised blacks and whites equal opportunities so far as color is concerned. You have clearly stated your ironic stand on that matter. You are thoroughly aware of how flagrantly it was flouted, even by condescension on the part of white philanthropists for whom your narrator presents Bledsoe as designing the "teachable-docile" kind of education he takes them to be paying for. In his *Critique of Practical Reason*, Kant says that, although we cannot scientifically prove the grounds of a belief in God, freedom, and immortality, we should harbor such beliefs and frame our conduct on such a basis. You did a Kantian "as if" by acting as if the constitutional promise has the markings of reality—and within feasible limits, it worked! And I think it worked in part because, within the ideological conflict forced upon you by the conditions local to the vestiges of black slavery in that stage of our history, there was also the more general sense of "growing up" in general. I interpret that kind of motivation as implicit in the Trueblood episode, which is formally there as a necessary stage—a process of maturing, a transition from the simplicity of a black identity in a black child's "pre-ideological" view of familial relationships.

But I should do a bit more about my ironic "matching" of Wilhelm Meister's all-white involvements and your narrator's black-white tension. A character with a name having the overtones of "Will-Helm-(Helmit)-Master" starts out under good auspices that your narrator has no share of. Also it turns out that, unbeknown to him, he had been being watched by some fellows of goodwill whose benign spying ended in his welcoming them to their sodality (a slant quite different from the conspiratorial "Brotherhood" that marked your protagonist's mode of socialization). Some years back, Goethe had gotten a resounding start by a contribution to the *storm and stress* wave of that time. Troubled by a love affair that drove him to the edge of suicide, he "creatively" solved his problem by writing *The Sorrows of Young Werther*, the story of a similarly unhappy lover who does commit suicide—and it was a success enough to launch him, to cause a rash of suicides, and to set a pattern . . . for such writers as Kleist to be self-victimized by. The first syllable of the name is English "Worth." So it would seem to be indicated that the victim chosen to be Goethe's surrogate was, prima facie, admirably endowed.

And as for Goethe's Faust, the adjective *faustus* in Latin, from the root *fav*, from which we get "favorable," has such "predestinating" meanings as "bringing good luck or good fortune, fortunate, lucky, auspicious." Faustulus was the mythic herdsman who saved and brought up Romulus and Remus, whose brotherhood became a fratricide, with Romulus surviving to become the eponymous founder of Rome. In its purely Germanic line, *Faust* means "fist," "hand," an implicit pun I was always conscious of.

I don't know whether readers whose native language-consciousness is *echt deutsch* ever hear such connotations in the term. And I tend to suspect that I am much more responsive to such accidental connotations in English than the average user and abuser of our idiom is (this side of Joyce, of course!). But here's how it turned out. The author's hand wrote of how Faust sealed a contract with the devil, selling his soul to eternal damnation in hell. Thanks to this deal, Faust was able to seduce a naive girl who loved him almost reverently and would have married him without the slightest hesitation; he killed her brother; his impregnating of her led her to kill her child in madness; but innocence incarnate, she was all set for heaven. Then the same hand wrote a sequel—and in *Faust II* things got to so turn out that the benignly predestinating connotations of the Latin adjective and the happy side of the diminutive noun for the mythic herdsman ultimately prevailed. The Faust story traditionally ends in Faust's damnation. Recall Christopher Marlowe's play, for instance, with Faust on his way to eternal hell as the clock strikes twelve. But Goethe's Faust, against all tradition, ends up among the saved. You put your boy through the mill and brought him out the other side, but you couldn't contrive a transformation like that. But Meister-Master didn't either; for neither he nor your protagonist began from a contract with the devil.

And Goethe's initiate had a "Nordic" nostalgia for the South with which your man's going North could not be quite in tune. Mignon's *Heimweh* song, the very thought of which makes me want to cry (knowest thou the land where bloom the lemon trees; *Kennst du das Land wo die Citronen blühen*?) is an example of your perceptive notions about the psychology of geography. Yet by the same token you and your narrator began their apprenticeship under unforgettably traumatic conditions. (Dr. Bledsoe, the black head of the black college, called your man a "Nigger.")

Incidentally, the nostalgic theme of Mignon's song is there, though with appropriately quite different appurtenances. I refer to your narrator's avowals that gravitate about the lines: "I'd like to hear five recordings of Louis Armstrong playing and singing 'What Did I Do to Be so Black and Blue'—all at the same time" (*IM*, 6).

But I have a hunch of this sort: I think of your Mary Rambo in the spirit of the article on her by Melvin Dixon in the *Carleton Miscellany*. He would "suggest that Mary Rambo, more than any other character, is the pivotal guide in the hero's effort to discover and to articulate the form of his identity and experience. He learns that this form is housed in a vernacular consciousness, not in the alien ideology of the Brotherhood or of industrial capitalism, or in racial absorption.'' I have not seen the text in which you wrote of her elsewhere. But I should agree with Dixon's observation, remembering my Goethe ''workmanship'' analogy (which, in the *Faust* plays, becomes striving, *Streben*): ''Rambo's full character as depicted in this episode encapsulates the major drama of self-realization at the heart of *Invisible Man*.'' (R.W.B. Lewis's article in the *Carleton Miscellany* refers to this overall development as ''the myth of initiation.'')[2]

She is in principle what I think you might be willing to call a ''vernacular'' Virgin Mary, in her wholly feminine role as nurse and mother. Like a mother, she doesn't ask for pay. She nurses the newborn journeyman. And her ''fromness'' from the South is just naturally part of her. And here comes the final twist: our hero says:

> There are many things about people like Mary that I dislike. For one thing, they seldom know where their personalities end and yours begins; they usually think in terms of ''we'' while I have always tended to think in terms of ''me''—and that has caused some friction, even with my own family. Brother Jack and the others talked in terms of ''we,'' but it was a different, bigger ''we.'' [Maybe that's why conspiratorial brother Hambro has a name that sounds so much like hers.]
>
> Well, I had a new name and new problems. I had best leave the old behind. Perhaps it would be best not to see Mary at all, just place the money in an envelope and leave it on the kitchen table where she'd be sure to find it. (*IM*, 240)

Yes, he was Ready for the Next Phase. So he had outgrown his new adolescence and had to hurry on, in effect, growing up and ''leaving home.'' Dixon quotes you as saying ''Mary Rambo deserved more space in the novel and would, I think, have made it a better book.'' Yet there's something to be gained by her role being left less pointedly so.

There's only one thing left for this time. It has to do with my salute to your book as ''epoch-making.'' It is remarkable how much your book brings together, in its two methods of bookkeeping, accounting both what it is to be growing up and what it is to be a black man growing up in one particular stage of U.S. history. At the end of your Epilogue we read:

> In going underground, I whipped it all except the mind, the *mind*. And the mind that has conceived a plan of living must never lose sight of the chaos against which that pattern was conceived. That goes for societies as well as for individuals. (*IM*, 438)

And it goes for an ''epoch-making'' book, too. There was the chaos of its unfinishedness while you hung on during the writing with what Augustine would call your *donum perseverandi*, your gift of persevering. Then, when your book constitutes the culmination of all those entanglements, the chaos out of which it emerged is there the other way around, in the memory. The epoch-making function of the book's emerging "mind" ends for the reader as a retrospective "mind." And I take the frame of your Prologue and Epilogue to be, in effect, saying so.

But an epoch-making book rules out a sequel. As I see it, technology got developed to a stage when the South could be developed by the importation of Negroes for slave labor on plantations in the South. At the same time in other parts of the country conflicting ways of using technological resources led to the abolition of slavery. That led to political conditions such that the ways of distributing the profits made by the use of technological resources brought about the epoch in which, through which, and out of which the descendants of black slaves in this country experienced such cultural developments as you have so comprehensively summed up.

But technology has moved on. "What *is* the next phase?" your man says in his Epilogue (*IM*, 435). Technology transcends race, not in the sense that it solves the problem of racial discrimination, but in the sense that technology itself *is* the problem. In that connection my compulsory (and damnably boring) *idée fixe* is along these lines:

In various ways people incline to keep asking, "What is the meaning of life? What is its purpose? And is there some attitude that offers us an overall purpose?"

There is one that makes wholly rational sense. It has been given to us by the fact that the human animal's great prowess with the resources of symbolic action has carried us so extensively far in the astoundingly ingenious inventions of technology. Now, owing to technology's side effects (not only in the hellish possibilities it now contributes to the disastrousness of war but also to the kinds of pollution and desiccation that result from its gruesomely efficient resourcefulness in the expansion of purely peaceful enterprises) the whole of humankind has now one questionable purpose. We are all part of the same threat to our destiny. So all must join together in seeking for ways and means (with correspondingly global attitudes) of undoing the damage being done by the human animal's failure to control the powers developed by that same organism's own genius. With the current terrific flowering of technology the problem of self-control takes on a possibly fatal, and certainly ironic, dimension. We must all conspire together, in a truly universal siblinghood, to help us all help one another to get enough control over our invented technologic servants to keep them from controlling us. Until we solve that problem (and the destructive powers of technology are so damnably efficient, we had better hurry!) our kind of verbalizing bodies has purpose aplenty.

Insofar as that cultural emphasis comes to take over, if it does, to that extent you will be surviving the "immediacy" of your "epoch-making" book in its sheerly "ideological" dimension. But in the universality of its poetic dimension, it will go on being what it is, namely, the symbolic constituting of an epoch, human every step of the way.

Time's about up. But I'd like to add some odds and ends in parting. Richard Lewis's recollections in the *Carleton Miscellany* document the existence of a friendly nonracial "we" that your "me" was a part of, in Bennington days when Stanley Hyman and Shirley Jackson were being very lively there. The demands local to your story ruled out that biographical strand in which not only did *we* back you, but you could and did get us to look for traces of unconscious Nortonism in our thinking (plus our not shelling out funds to a black institution in commemoration of a saintly dead daughter).

The difference between an "epoch-making" book and the day's news is this: The news ceases to be news, but the book goes on reconstituting its epoch. Whereas at the time of the writing it grew out of its background, in being read now it both reconstructs its time and takes on a universal poignancy.

Best luck, to you and Fanny both,
K. B. (Kenneth Burke)

NOTES

1. Ralph Ellison, *Invisible Man* (New York: Random House, 1952), 26. Subsequent references are cited in text as *IM*.

2. The references cited in this paragraph are to Melvin Dixon's "O, Mary Rambo, Don't You Weep" and R.W.B. Lewis's "The Ceremonial Imagination of Ralph Ellison," which appeared in the Winter 1980 issue of *Carleton Miscellany*.—Ed.

Literacy and Hibernation: Ralph Ellison's *Invisible Man*

ROBERT B. STEPTO

I'm not blaming anyone for this state of affairs, mind you; nor merely crying mea culpa. *The fact is that you carry part of your sickness within you, at least I do as an invisible man. I carried my sickness and though for a long time I tried to place it in the outside world, the attempt to write it down shows me that at least half of it lay within me.*

Ralph Ellison
Invisible Man

Anocheci Enfermo Amaneci bueno (I went to bed sick. I woke up well.)

Jay Wright
Dimensions of History

By the time we travel beyond the major work of Richard Wright, Afro-American literature's narrative tradition is still very much alive—even though the texts are rarely termed ''narratives'' by writer or reader, or consciously placed in an ongoing artistic continuum. However, after Wright it is also clear that the possibilities for significant revoicings of the ascent and immersion narratives (and their accompanying rhetorics) are virtually exhausted. This is not to say that ascent and immersion narratives do not appear in our recent literature; nor is it to say that Afro-American writers are no longer fascinated with creating rhetorics of racial soulfulness and soullessness. Indeed, in the last decade the abiding fascination with rhetorics of the former type has become so pronounced that in some quarters it is seen to be an artistic movement, and even an aesthetic.

Be this as it may, the fact remains that, after *Black Boy*, in particular, the situation is such that any actual forwarding of the ''historical consciousness''

Originally published in *From Behind the Veil: A Study of Afro-American Narrative* (Urbana: The University of Illinois Press, 1979).

of Afro-American narrative must involve some kind of escape from the lock-step imposed by the tradition's dominant and prefiguring narrative patterns. In theory, the logical first stop beyond the narrative of ascent or immersion (a stop which need not be any more generic, in a conventional sense, than were the preceding stops) is one that somehow creates a fresh narrative strategy and arc out of a remarkable combination of ascent and immersion narrative properties. In theory, attempts to achieve such remarkable combinations are possible in Afro-American letters anytime after the appearance of *The Souls of Black Folk* in 1903. In practice, however, very few Afro-American narrativists appear to have comprehended the opportunity before, let alone fashioned combinations of merit and of a certain energy.

In *The Autobiography of an Ex-Coloured Man*, for example, James Weldon Johnson clearly demonstrates that he has some idea of the symbolic journeys and spaces which the new narrative will require, but his dedication to troping the Du Boisian nightmare of immersion aborted—which, in his hands, is fundamentally a commitment to expressing a new narrative content—precludes his achieving a new narrative arc. In writing *Cane*, Jean Toomer takes further than Johnson did the idea of binding new narrative content to new narrative form; but the success of his effort is questionable, since a new narrative arc never really emerges from his aggressive yet orchestrated display of forms and voices. The absence of such an arc is a further indication of Toomer's inability to detail his persona's final posture outside the realms of ascent and immersion. Without this requisite clarification, *Cane* appears to be an inventive text that can evoke, but not advance, the historical consciousness of its parent forms.

Before *Invisible Man*, Zora Neale Hurston's *Their Eyes Were Watching God* is quite likely the only truly coherent narrative of both ascent and immersion, primarily because her effort to create a particular kind of questing *heroine* liberates her from the task (the compulsion, perhaps) of revoicing many of the traditional tropes of ascent and immersion. Of course, Hurston's narrative is neither entirely new nor entirely "feminine." The house "full ah thoughts" to which Janie ascends after her ritualized journey of immersion with Teacake into the "muck" of the Everglades (recall here Du Bois's swamp in both *The Souls* and *The Quest of the Silver Fleece*) is clearly a private ritual ground, akin in construction if not in accoutrement to Du Bois's study. And Janie's posture as a storyteller—as an articulate figure knowledgeable of tribal tropes (a feature probably overdone in the frame, but not the tale, of *Their Eyes*) and in apparent control of her personal history—is a familiar and valued final siting for a primary voice in an Afro-American narrative. Still, there is much that is new in *Their Eyes*. The narrative takes place in a seemingly ahistorical world: the spanking new all-black town is meticulously bereft of former slave cabins; there are no railroad trains, above or underground, with or without Jim Crow cars; Matt's mule is a bond with and catalyst for distinct tribal memories and rituals, but these do not include the hollow slogan, "forty acres and a mule"; Janie seeks freedom, selfhood, voice, and "living" but is hardly guided—or haunted—by Sojourner Truth or Harriet Tubman, let alone Frederick Douglass. But that world is actually a fresh expression of a history of assault. The first two men in Janie's adult life (Logan Killicks and Jody Starks) and the spatial configurations through which they define themselves and seek to impose definition upon Janie (notably, a rural and agrarian space, on one hand, and a somewhat urban and mercantile space, on the other) provide as much social structure as the narrative requires. Furthermore, the narrative's frame—the conversation "in the present" between Janie and Pheoby—creates something new in that it, and not the tale, is Hurston's vehicle for presenting the communal and possibly archetypal aspects of Janie's quest and final posture. Presentation does not always provide substantiation, and the clanking of Hurston's narrative and rhetorical machinery calls attention to itself when Pheoby offers her sole remark in the final half of the frame: "Lawd! . . . Ah done growed ten feet higher from jus' listenin' tuh you, Janie. Ah ain't satisfied wid mahself no mo'. Ah means tuh make Sam take me fishin' wid him after this. Nobody better not criticize yuh in mah hearin'."[1] But these minor imperfections do not delimit the narrative's grand effort to demystify and site the somewhat ethereal concept of group- and self-consciousness, forwarded especially by *The Souls of Black Folk* and *Cane*. Clearly, Hurston is after a treatment of Janie and Pheoby that releases them from their immediate posture of storyteller and listener, and that propels them to one in which their sisterhood suggests a special kinship among womankind at large.

The one great flaw in *Their Eyes* involves not the framing dialogue, but Janie's tale itself. Through the frame Hurston creates the essential illusion that Janie has achieved her voice (along with everything else), and that she has even wrested from menfolk some control of the tribal posture of the storyteller. But the tale undercuts much of this, not because of its content—indeed, episodes such as the one in which Janie verbally abuses Jody in public abets Hurston's strategy—but because of its narration. Hurston's curious insistence on having Janie's tale—her personal history in, and as, a literary form—told by an omniscient third person, rather than by a first-person narrator, implies that Janie has not really won her voice and self after all, that her author (who is, quite likely, the omniscient narrating voice) cannot see her way clear to giving Janie her voice outright. Here, I think, Hurston is genuinely caught in the dilemma of how she might both govern and exploit the autobiographical impulses that partially direct her creation of Janie. On one hand, third-person narration of Janie's tale helps to build a space (or at least the illusion of a space) between author and character, for the author and her audience alike; on the other, when told in this fashion control of the tale remains, no matter how unintended, with the author alone.

Despite this problem, *Their Eyes* is a seminal narrative in Afro-American letters. It forwards the historical consciousness of the tradition's narrative forms, and helps to define those kinds of narratives which will also advance the literature in their turn. The narrative successes and failures of *Their Eyes* effectively prefigure several types of narratives; but, given the problems I have just discussed, one might say that the example of *Their Eyes* calls for a narrative in which the primary figure (like Janie) achieves a space beyond those defined by the tropes of ascent and immersion, but (*unlike* Janie) also achieves authorial control over both the frame and tale of his or her personal history. In short, *Their Eyes*, as a narrative strategy in a continuum of narrative strategies, directs us most immediately to Ralph Ellison's *Invisible Man*. Janie is quite possibly more of a blood relative to Ellison's narrator than either the "male chauvinist" or "feminist" readers of the tradition would care to contemplate.

* * *

As I have suggested elsewhere, the Afro-American pregeneric myth of the quest for freedom and literacy has occasioned two basic types of narrative expressions, the narratives of ascent and immersion. The classic ascent narrative launches an "enslaved" and semiliterate figure on a ritualized journey to a symbolic North; that journey is charted through spatial expressions of social structure, invariably systems of signs that the questing figure must read in order to be both increasingly literate and increasingly free. The ascent narrative conventionally ends with the questing figure situated in the least oppressive social structure afforded by the world of the narrative, and free in the sense that he or she has gained sufficient literacy to assume the mantle of an articulate survivor. As the phrase *articulate survivor* suggests, the hero or heroine of an ascent narrative must be willing to forsake familial or communal postures in the narrative's most oppressive social structure for a new posture in the least oppressive environment—at best, one of solitude; at worst, one of alienation. This last feature of the ascent narrative unquestionably helps bring about the rise and development of an immersion narrative in the tradition, for the immersion narrative is fundamentally an expression of a ritualized journey into a symbolic South, in which the protagonist seeks those aspects of tribal literacy that ameliorate, if not obliterate, the conditions imposed by solitude. The conventional immersion narrative ends almost paradoxically, with the questing figure located in or near the narrative's most oppressive social structure but free in the sense that he has gained or regained sufficient tribal literacy to assume the mantle of an articulate kinsman. As the phrase *articulate kinsman* suggests, the hero or heroine of an immersion narrative must be willing to forsake highly individualized mobility in the narrative's least oppressive social structure for a posture of relative stasis in the most oppressive environment, a loss that is only occasionally assuaged by the newfound balms of group identity. (The argument being, that these "shared epiphanies'' were previously unavailable to the questing figure when he or she was adrift in a state of solitude.) When seen in this way, the primary features of the ascent and immersion narratives appear to call for an epiloguing text that revoices the tradition's abiding tropes in such a way that answers to all of the following questions are attempted: Can a questing figure in a narrative occasioned by the pregeneric myth be both an articulate survivor *and* an articulate kinsman? Must all such quests in the narrative literature conclude as they began, in imposed configurations of social structure? And can the literary history of Afro-American narrative forms—which is, at root, the chronicle of a dialectic between ascent and immersion expressions—become, in and of itself, the basis for a narrative form?

The whole of *Invisible Man* is a grand attempt to answer these questions, but the burden of reply falls mainly upon the narrative's frame (its Prologue and Epilogue), rather than upon its tale. I do not wish to demean the tale, for it is a remarkable invention: it presents the spatial expressions of social structure as well as the nearly counterpointing rituals of ascent (to self-consciousness) and immersion (in group consciousness) which collectively contextualize and in some sense occasion the questing narrator's progress from muteness to speech, or formlessness to form. However, what is narratively new in *Invisible Man*, and what permits it to answer the questions cited earlier, is not its depiction of a pilgrim's progress, but its brave assertion that there is a self, and form, to be discovered beyond the lockstep of linear movement within imposed definitions of reality. For this reason the inventive tale of the questing narrator's steady progression to voice and selfhood cannot stand alone as the *narrative* of Ellison's hero. The tale must be framed, and in that sense controlled, because progression as a protean literary form and progress as a protean cultural myth must be contextualized. *Invisible Man*'s success as a fresh narrative strategy depends upon its ability to formalize in the art the ''fiction'' of history expounded primarily in its frame. To the extent that *Invisible Man*'s frame controls its tale, its hero may gloss his personal history, and art may impose upon event.

With all this in mind, we may proceed to examine certain aspects of *Invisible Man*'s frame. I would like to begin with the hero's hole itself, which, in the context of the tradition, is clearly a revoicing of the private ritual ground to which Du Bois's persona retreats after his ritual of immersion in the Black Belt. Despite the fact that these ritual grounds are situated differently—the prefiguring space is a ''high Pisgah,'' while the epiloguing space is a ''warm hole'' below ground—there are many similarities between the two. In the first place, both spaces are discovered or achieved after several literal and figurative rail journeys that clearly revoice the primary episode of flight on the ''freedom train.'' I refer here on one hand to Du Bois's various symbolic rides in that social structure-in-motion called the Jim Crow car, rides which prompt his vision and hope of *communitas* in this world, and on the other hand to Invisible Man's equally conspicuous subway rides which establish the particular rhythm of immersion and ascent that guides him finally to see the people of Harlem ("They'd been there all along, but . . . I'd missed them . . . I'd been asleep"[2]) and to consider hibernation as a viable if transient state of being. In either case, the elevated study or the subterranean hole, the private space is one wherein the best thoughts occasioned by these travels may collect and linger—wherein physical motion is interrupted, body and voice are at rest, but the mind travels on.

Another point of similarity involves each space's distance from those spatial expressions of social structure (the Black Belt, Harlem) in which major acquisitions of tribal literacy are accomplished. In *The Souls*, Du Bois's study is high up on an Atlanta hill, not engulfed in the "dull red hideousness" of rural Georgia. In *Invisible Man* the hero's "warm hole" is not in "the jungle of Harlem," but in a "border area" that is, as the hero admits, a grand spatial and historical joke: it is of Harlem as far as the utility company's "master meter" is concerned, but out of Harlem according to most other conventional measurements of American reality, because it is a basement section of "a building rented strictly to whites" that was "shut off" (reconstructed?) and "forgotten during the nineteenth century" (Reconstruction?) (*IM*, 5). In either case, vertical distance—placement upon a different plane—accentuates the more apparent horizontal displacement between tribal space and private space. These distances force each questing narrator to fashion a rhetoric that earnestly seeks to minimize the distances and to portray the narrators as group-conscious as well as self-conscious figures.

Here, I think, the points of congruence between Du Bois's study and Invisible Man's hole are most pronounced; yet here we can also begin to see how Ellison's construction assumes its own integrity. When the Invisible Man speaks in the Epilogue of how his grandfather must have meant "the principle, that we were to affirm the principle on which the country was built and not the men, or at least not the men who did the violence" and also of how "we of all, we, most of all, had to affirm the principle . . . because we were older than they, in the sense of what it took to live in the world with others" (*IM*, 433–34), he clearly restates in his own terms Du Bois's persona's claim that "we the darker ones come even now not altogether empty-handed: there are to-day no truer exponents of the pure human spirit of the Declaration of Independence than the American Negroes."[3] Furthermore, both questing narrators seek to qualify or contextualize these assertions of race pride and responsibility by forwarding expressions of their abiding faith in the ideal of cultural pluralism. Certainly this is suggested when we recall the following passage from chapter 1 of *The Souls* (which is, for all intents and purposes, that narrative's prologue):

> Work, culture, liberty,—all these we need, not singly but together, not successively but together, each growing and aiding each, and all striving toward that vaster ideal that swims before the Negro people, the ideal of human brotherhood, gained through the unifying ideal of Race; the ideal of fostering and

> developing the traits and talents of the Negro, not in opposition to or contempt for other races, but rather in large conformity to the greater ideals of the American Republic. . . . (11)

and place beside it these ringing, epiloguing words from *Invisible Man*:

> Whence all this passion toward conformity anyway?—diversity is the word. Let man keep his many parts and you'll have no tyrant states. . . . America is woven of many strands; I would recognize them and let it so remain. It's "winner take nothing" that is the great truth of our country. Life is to be lived, not controlled; and humanity is won by continuing to play in face of certain defeat. Our fate is to become one, and yet many—This is not prophecy, but description. (435–36)

Amid the similarities there lies one profound discrepancy: Ellison's refusal to sustain Du Bois's Herderian overlay of racial idealism. Ellison discerns a quite substantial distinction in meaning and image between the prospect of ideal races conforming to a national ideal, and that of intact races interweaving to become a national fabric. That distinction has much to do with how he subsequently fashions his questing narrator as a group-conscious and self-conscious human being.

In *The Souls*, Du Bois's hero's group consciousness is distinctly racial in character. Ensconced in his study after his immersion journey, transported by the bits of ancient song wafting up from below, he becomes a weary traveler in a tribal song—an embodied and embodying voice or, in terms indebted to Ellison, a tribally visible man. The creation of this voice and visibility is central to *The Souls*'s narrative strategy; it provides the rationale for Du Bois's refusal to formalize his first and last chapters as framing prologue and epilogue, even though they function largely this way in the narrative. Unlike Ellison, Du Bois is not after an expression of group consciousness that bursts beyond tribal boundaries. Therefore he need not situate his hero's private ritual ground outside the geography of his hero's tale any more than he already has. Here we must recall especially that Du Bois's final siting of his hero is occasioned in part by autobiographical impulses. Through generous reference to the "master" Sorrow Songs, Du Bois binds his narrative's resulting space and his narrator's resulting self to what has come before, and in that way seeks his own visibility in the events and images his narrative has recorded. The whole machinery of *The Souls* is geared for acts of unveiling (making *visible*) the soul of a race and of a man; it lacks the components for processing such subtleties as invisible articulate heroes residing outside History and Veil alike.

The final posture of Ellison's questing narrator may be clarified in the following terms. To begin with, the hero's hole is described in a formal frame removed from the tale. That frame is, in a sense, that hole, because Ellison is indeed after expressions of group consciousness and self-consciousness that respectively transcend tribal literacy and resist the infecting germs of heroic self-portraiture. The whole of the frame (or, if you will, the whole of the hole) proclaims that the narrative distinction to be drawn between tale and frame is a trope for other distinctions central to *Invisible Man*, including those between blindness and insight, sleepfulness and wakefulness, sickness and health, social structure and nonstructure, History and history, embodied voice and disembodied voice, and acts of speech and of writing. All this occasions a second and fresh rhetoric that is not found in the framing chapters of *The Souls*, but is prefigured instead by the "why do I write" passages in slave narratives. The strategy behind Ellison's rhetoric is, however, quite different from that of the fugitive slaves. Ellison is less interested in having his hero authenticate his tale (or rather, its content) and more interested in having that tale devalorized in such a way that the principles of living (which are, at base, principles of writing or artfulness) delineated in the frame may finally take hold and control the way in which the narrative as a whole is read.

"So why do I write," the Invisible Man asks rhetorically, and again and again in the final pages of the epilogue his answers—brimming with references to release from lethargy, negation of "some of the anger and some of the bitterness," shaking off the old skin, springtime, and love—serve to minimize the distance between his private space and the "concrete, ornery, vile and sublimely wonderful" world in which, alas, the rest of us reside. Indeed, we sense that when he asks the question with which the narrative ends—"Who knows but that, on the lower frequencies, I speak for you?"—"for you" expresses that last distancing interval that remains before speech "to you." But finally it is writing or the experience of writing, not speech, that shapes whatever group consciousness Invisible Man will bring in tow upon his return. Writing has taught him much about himself—indeed, it has made him a highly self-aware invisible man. But it has also taught him that his personal history is but an arc of the parabola of human history, and that his personal tale is only a finite particle in the infinity of tale-telling. According to Ellison's vision, what group-orients Invisible Man and ends his hibernation is his marvelously robust desire to take another swing around that arc of what other men call reality: to tell, shape, and/or "lie" his tale anew. In this way, then, he becomes both an articulate survivor and an articulate kinsman.

Before we follow Invisible Man to a realm beyond hibernation, the whys and wherefores of his writing while underground should be examined further. What interests me specifically is the apparent cause-and-effect relationship between the explicit emptying of the briefcase at the end of the tale and the implicit filling of pages during hibernation, a sequence that revoices a feature of slave narratives such as Douglass's 1845 *Narrative*. The Douglass narrative tells us that, in 1835, Douglass and a few of his fellow slaves devised an escape plan that depended mainly upon each slave's possessing a "protection" or "pass," allegedly written by "Master" William Hamilton but actually composed by Douglass himself. Such a pass granted each man "full liberty" to travel to Baltimore for the Easter holidays—to celebrate, one assumes, the ancient Resurrection of the One, and the more recent ascent of each other. Unfortunately, the plan is thwarted, and each slave has to save his skin by "denying everything" and destroying his "forged" protection. But through telling the tale Douglass manages to remind us once again of the great bond between freedom and literacy, and also of the great power that comes with the ability not only to read a culture's signs (in this case, a sign that is truly a written document) but also to write them and, in that supreme way, manipulate them. In short, the *Narrative's* Easter escape or "protection" episode is a primary trope for acts of authorial control over text and context.

The lesson advanced by Douglass is one of many that Ellison's narrator is destined to learn the hard way; indeed, his remarkable innocence and gullibility regarding these matters provide a major comic strain in the narrative's tale. The perpetual sight of our valiant hero doggedly lugging his briefcase around New York, and even risking life and limb in order to retrieve it from a burning Harlem tenement, is funny enough; but the heart of the joke has to do less with Invisible Man's attachment to his briefcase than with what he has consciously and subconsciously gathered inside it. Our hero's tale is substantially that of how he accumulates a motley array of cultural signs, mostly written "protections" or "passes" (diplomas, letters of recommendation, slips of paper bearing new names, etc.) that supposedly identify him and grant him "full liberty" in the "real" world beyond "home." Ellison's double-edged joke is that none of these "protections" is worth more than the paper it's written on (they are indeed "paper protections"), and that all of them ironically "Keep a Nigger-Boy Running," but not on a path that would be recognizable to Douglass or any other self-willed hero with any control over his fate.

This is not to say that the nonwritten signs are without importance. On the contrary, part of Ellison's point is that Tarp's leg iron, Mary Rambo's "grinning darky" bank, Tod Clifton's Sambo doll, and the Rinehart-like dark glasses and "high hat" are all cultural signs of a tribal sort. Our questing narrator thinks he knows how to read them, but he knows or reads only in a very limited way. Collectively, these nonwritten signs represent Invisible Man's illiteracy *vis-à-vis* his tribe as much as the written signs betoken his illiteracy *vis-à-vis* the nontribal social structures besetting him; his unwitting act of gathering both types of signs in one bulging briefcase finally occasions the demystification of the one type by the other. Once Invisible Man *sees* this—once he comprehends that seemingly mute objects such as the dark glasses, hat, and leg iron are the only "protections" he possesses, and that the written documents from Bledsoe, Jack, and the rest are the only signs that may be *usefully* destroyed (here, burned to light his way)—he is ready to begin his life and tale again, or rather to *prepare* to begin again. The demystification and nearly simultaneous use and destruction of the cultural signs gathered in the briefcase during the tale occasion his removal to a fresh space, the "warm hole" of the narrative's frame.

All this suggests that Invisible Man is finally free in his framing hole, and that that freedom is expressed most conspicuously by his nearly empty briefcase. But this is not completely true—nor is it in keeping with the full measure of the lesson learned from an innocent but almost deadly trafficking in false "protections." Perhaps the most profound lesson our hero learns when the once-precious "protections" are demystified is that they are worthless, not because of what they do or do not say, but because they are authenticating documents over which he has absolutely no authorial control. (They impose on him and his tale much as the competing authenticating texts of white guarantors often impose upon a fugitive slave's tale.) Seen in this light, Invisible Man's frenzied movement and speech (his "sleepwalking" and "sleeptalking") in the narrative's tale are tropes for his total lack of control over that history or tale, and his relative stasis in the narrative's frame (pointedly, his "wakefulness") is a trope for his brave effort to assume control of his history or tale (*and* of tale telling) through artful acts of written composition. Thus, another aspect—perhaps *the* other aspect—of Invisible Man's newfound freedom is that he may now pursue acts of written articulateness and literary form-making, filling the empty briefcase with what are in effect "protections" or "passes" from his *own* hand. To compose such "protections" is to assert a marvelous and heroic concept of self-willed mobility, an idea of mobility that is in keeping with the narrative's definition of hibernation: "A hibernation is a covert preparation for a more overt action" (*IM*, 11). The covert filling of the satchel with the self-authored "protection" that constitutes the completed narrative (tale *and* frame) is Ellison's most convincing expression of his hero's inevitable return, partly because it revoices a primary trope inaugurated in the tradition by Frederick Douglass.

All in all, the frame in *Invisible Man* is a familiar construction in Afro-American narrative literature, primarily because it is the mechanism for authentication and authorial control in the narrative. At the beginning of the frame, the competing or imposing fictions that surface in the tale as items in the hero's briefcase are generally defined: "When they approach me they see only my surroundings, themselves, or figments of their imagination—indeed, everything and anything except me." By the end of the frame those fictive "certainties" have been subsumed by the hero's own self-authored "plan of living" or, as he calls it, his "pattern to the chaos" (*IM*, 438). Perhaps even more impressive and resilient, however, is the manner in which this trumping of fictions with fictions is occasioned and sustained by Ellison's remarkably explicit expression of one authenticating strategy overtaking and making a joke out of another. In the tale, Invisible Man's briefcase is much more than a repository of cultural signs and false "protections"; it is, most ironically and humorously, *the* trope for the strategy of self-authentication Invisible Man values during most of the tale. He carries it everywhere, never realizing that it possesses him far more than he possesses it. At the beginning of the tale, in the battle royal where he "earns" his briefcase and his first "protections" (the diploma and scholarship to Bledsoe's college), his speech full of echoes of Booker T. Washington's Atlanta Exposition Address is a signal not simply of initial rhetorical indebtedness to Washington, but (more profoundly) of an initial adherence to the Washingtonian strategy of narration and self-authentication as résumé. The briefcase substantiates this idea because it is, in effect, a résumé edited and amended by acts of sign gathering during the course of the tale. In vivid contrast to Washington, however, Invisible Man learns not only that he lacks a grand public speech to be authenticated by a tale of his life, but also that his accumulated résumé isn't his tale.

* * *

Like Johnson's *Autobiography of an Ex-Coloured Man* and Wright's *Black Boy*, *Invisible Man* presents, as part of its narrative machinery, a series of portraits—on the wall as well as in the flesh—that may be loosely termed the narrative's portrait gallery. While it can be argued that any character in any narrative is in some sense a portrait, the portraits I'm about to discuss are special. They constitute a narrative strategy by which various models of voice and action are kept before the questing narrator, and by which the full range of human possibility in the differing social structures of the narrative may be defined and seen. [Elsewhere] I describe at some length the portrait gallery in the parlor of the Ex-Coloured Man's Club; it is important to recall that gallery here, because it is our best example of a symbolic construction in which all of the models (from Frederick Douglass to the minstrel who yearns to be a Shakespearean) are valorized as heroic examples that the narrator would do well to emulate. The whole point to the construction is that the Ex-Coloured Man could have learned from these "portraits," but didn't—because he could not really see them, let alone see through them. In *Black Boy*, virtually the opposite is true. Few if any portraits are displayed on the walls of the narrative's prisonlike interiors; the major portraits are intentionally "in the flesh" and, with the exceptions of Ella (the schoolteacher who tells the story of Bluebeard), the editor of the Negro newspaper, and the Irishman who surreptitiously lends his library card to young Richard, they are all of men and women who are "warnings" rather than "examples." While the Ex-Coloured Man cannot fully see the heroic examples before him, and thus not only remains a nonhero but effectively relinquishes the narrative's space for heroic posturing to figures such as "Shiny," Wright's persona pursues a far different and aggressive course. In *Black Boy* the potential or assumed examples, especially the elder kinfolk, are systematically devalorized and portrayed as "warnings"—partly so that a hellish landscape may be depicted and peopled, but mostly so that Wright's persona, as an emerging articulate survivor, may not only control but also fill the narrative's space for heroic posturing. In this way Wright's persona, unlike Johnson's Ex-Coloured

Man, sees and aggressively *sees through* the major "portraits" in his tale. For this reason, to cite only one example, the persona "methodically" buries his father alive in the red clay of Mississippi.

Invisible Man retains certain aspects of the portrait galleries found in both *The Autobiography* and *Black Boy*. The narrative offers portraits both on the wall and in the flesh, and the portrait motif is indeed central to Ellison's strategy of keeping both examples and warnings before the questing narrator. But more significant is how *Invisible Man* bursts beyond the strategies of portraiture and gallery construction that we find in Johnson's and Wright's prefiguring texts. At first glance, the portrait gallery in *Invisible Man* is much like that in *Black Boy*, in that it is not confined to a ritual space such as the Ex-Coloured Man's Club (or the outdoor revival in which the preacher, John Brown, and the master singer, Singing Johnson, are sketched) but is dispersed throughout the narrative. Furthermore, as in *Black Boy*, the portraits in *Invisible Man* are usually dismantled or demystified—that is, the figures are usually less than heroic. But this is also where the different treatment of this motif begins in each narrative. In *Black Boy*, Wright's portraits of would-be examples, such as the father and the persona's Uncle Tom, are *always* demystified; the figures thereby plummet from their assigned (if not always earned) heights to the depths of life as it is lived by partially animate warnings. But to judge from *Invisible Man*, Ellison is perennially suspicious of such simple dichotomies, and in pursuit, therefore, of more complex and differentiated expressions. Hence we discover that while Bledsoe, Norton, and the one-eyed Jack are indeed warnings, not examples, Trueblood, Brother Tarp, and most especially the advice-giving grandfather are neither examples nor warnings, but enigmas of varying sorts. They occupy and enlarge a fresh narrative space.

While the demystification of these would-be examples is a prerequisite for Invisible Man's blossoming as a truly literate figure, the thrust of the narrative is not to replace these portraits with that of Invisible Man as a heroic example. Rather, it is to *identify* Bledsoe, Norton, and the rest as varying fictions of reality and history which must be deposed or, as we soon will see, defiled in order for the fiction that is the narrative to be imagined. The narrative and not the narrator, the "principle" and not the "men," and the frame far more than the tale collectively constitute the heroic example forwarded by Ellison's narrative and rhetorical strategies. To see this is to know a major way in which *Invisible Man* aggressively contradicts the abiding idea of the artist in *Black Boy*, and to sense as well how it assumes its place in the Afro-American narrative tradition.

One final preliminary point is that the portrait motif in *Invisible Man* is joined by, and in some sense conjoined to, what I wish to call the narrative's museum motif. There are at least three great "museum collections" in the narrative, and these are important to the narrative's machinery as contexts or syntaxes, just as the portraits are important as relatively discrete expressions.

What binds the portrait motif to the museum motif is not simply the fact that portraits frequently form an integral part of certain specific contexts or syntaxes, but that both motifs are reduced, in the narrative's frame, to being one and the same expression and sign—the collected and displayed light for which certain other people's measurements of reality cannot account. The narrator's warm hole is at once a portrait gallery of light and an exquisite museum collection of light; the light "confirms" his "reality" and "gives birth" to his "form," just as other, ostensibly more delineated, portraits and displayed objects confirm other realities and give birth to other forms—especially of a literary sort.

But perhaps, as Invisible Man says of himself at the end of the beginning (which is the beginning of the end), I am moving too fast. The frame is not visible in its full splendor of invisibility unless we can see the proud visages and precious vestiges which it both visibly and invisibly frames. We must begin with *Invisible Man*'s tale—even though it is neither the narrative's beginning nor its end—and with the portrait of the grandfather who seems, as a highly visible invisibility, to begin and end it all.

The grandfather enters the tale at its beginning, in a speech—or, rather, *as* speech: "'Live with your head in the lion's mouth. I want you to overcome 'em with yeses, undermine 'em with grins, agree 'em to death and destruction, let 'em swoller you till they vomit or bust wide open'" (*IM*, 13–14). This entrance is central to his place in the tale; he is a portrait-in-language that his grandson must learn to hear, read, and contextualize. But as the following passage from the end of the battle-royal episode instructs, the grandfather is as much a portrait on the wall (of the mind, as well as of the space called "family" or "home") as he is one in language:

> When I reached home everyone was excited. Next day the neighbors came to congratulate me. I even felt safe from grandfather, whose deathbed curse usually spoiled my triumphs. I stood beneath his photograph with my brief case in hand and smiled triumphantly into his stolid black peasant's face. It was a face that fascinated me. The eyes seemed to follow everywhere I went. (*IM*, 26)

Several things are afoot here, and one of them is certainly a radical revision of the "obituary" with which Wright's *Black Boy* persona buries his father alive by calling him a "stranger" and a "black peasant." In *Black Boy*, the implication is clearly that the father is a known quantity; that he is fixed or immobilized in a "culture's" time and space, and that his portrait has been completely and consummately read by his "civilized" questing kinsman. In *Invisible Man*, however, the grandfather is not quite so easily removed from the wall and (in that sense, among others) dismantled. As the phrase "the eyes seemed to follow everywhere I went" suggests, Ellison's narrator's grandfather is an unknown and mobile figure whose eyes are hardly "glazed" like those of the "dead" father in *Black Boy*; he will travel with and reappear before his youthful kinsman in word and image many times before the narrative's tale is finally complete. The grandfather, who provides the first portrait in the tale's portrait gallery, is neither a warning nor an example but a huge and looming question mark—an enigma. In this way his portrait prefigures those of other "peasants" in the narrative, such as Trueblood and Brother Tarp (Brother Veil? Brother Sail?), who are also enigmas. Moreover, the grandfather's portrait quite purposefully skews whatever preconceptions we might have regarding a simple system of dialectical or antipodal portraiture ("warning"/"example") in the narrative. The grandfather is, in short, a "Mr. In-Between," a Vergilian guide who occupies neither antipodal space, not because he is supposedly dead (or thought "mad" by the intervening generation—Invisible Man's parents), but because of the implicit distinction the narrative draws between the spoken and written word and, hence, between guides and artists.

Another method of debunking an antipodal system of portraiture is simply to invent situations in which examples, warnings, and the world they define are eventually and comically turned inside out. Ellison does essentially this with the portraits in the campus episodes and with the initially Edenic campus as a world within the world of the narrative. His activity differs from Wright's in *Black Boy*, mainly because Wright never allows a model to become an example before he shows it to be warning, or a space to assume paradisiacal proportions before he demonstrates that it is a circle of hell. In the campus episodes, the portraits begin with the bronze statue of the college Founder. Ellison has a lot of fun with both his narrator and the conventions of heroic portraiture while describing this work of art:

> It's so long ago and far away that here in my invisibility I wonder if it happened at all. Then in my mind's eye I see the bronze statue of the college Founder, the cold Father symbol, his hands outstretched in the breathtaking gesture of lifting a veil that flutters in hard, metallic folds above the face of a kneeling slave; and I am standing puzzled, unable to decide whether the veil is really being lifted, or lowered more firmly in place; whether I am witnessing a revelation or a more efficient blinding. And as I gaze, there is a rustle of wings and I see a flock of starlings flighting before me and, when I look again, the bronze face, whose empty eyes look upon a world I have never seen, runs with liquid chalk—creating another ambiguity to puzzle my groping mind: Why is a bird-soiled statue more commanding than one that is clean? (*IM*, 28)

Of course, there is much serious activity here that advances the narrative's discussion of what is visible and invisible, seen and unseen. The second veil of a very organic tulle joins the first, of bronze, adding a necessary complexity to the abiding question of who is the prophet, who the sheep, and what indeed can that prophet see. Furthermore, it prefigures other tropes in the narrative, such as the Liberty Paint Factory's celebrated Optic White paint. But basically this comic portrait of Founder and narrator alike achieves its humor not so much because a heroic example is draped in guano or because the youthful narrator attempts to make and unmake a philosophical puzzle out of that event. Rather, it arises from the more profound incongruities that displace the narrator as seer from the Founder who, according to one definition of history, is a Seer, but who, according to at least one other definition, is the seen.

This high comedy continues in the narrative when Homer A. Barbee, the noted blind minister, preaches on and adds further luster to the legend of the Founder's death. Indeed, the inanimate statue on the lawn and the highly animated tale or "lie" as sermon are parts of the same composite portrait of the Founder. Through a marvelous orchestration of images, reminding us of many other train rides in elegiac art (recall, for example, Lincoln's cortege in Whitman's "When Lilacs Last in the Dooryard Bloom'd"), Homer Barbee transports us on another ride, a solemn ride of sorrowful rest and joyous resurrection: "'When the train reached the summit of the mountain, he [the Founder] was no longer with us'" (*IM*, 100). But there is a new and humorous twist to all of this: Barbee and Bledsoe, like two disciples become vaudevillians, are on board. Were you there when they crucified my Lord? Yessir, as a matter of fact I was! Me and Bledsoe! Right there!

Barbee's sermon is finally less a valorization of the Founder than of A. Hebert Bledsoe. Put another way, the text of his sermon diminishes the legend of the Founder while it authenticates the supreme fiction with which Bledsoe wields power and proffers a particular construction of historical reality:

> "Oh, yes, Oh, yes," he [Barbee] said. "Oh, yes. That too is part of the glorious story. But think of it not as a death, but as a birth. A great seed has been planted. A seed which has continued to put forth its fruit in its season as surely as if the great creator had been resurrected. For in a sense he was, if not in the flesh, in the spirit. And in a sense in the flesh too. For has not your present leader become his living agent, his physical presence? Look about you if you doubt it. My young friends, my dear young friends! How can I tell you what manner of man this is who leads you! How can I convey to you how well he has kept his pledge to the Founder, how conscientious has been his stewardship?" (*IM*, 102)

With these words, Homer Barbee demonstrates how he and Hebert Bledsoe—the Preacher and the Principal—are indeed quite a team, more than likely one of the most extraordinary comedy teams in Afro-American narrative literature. Evidently they have made a long black joke out of the long black song of the Founder's long black train. Who follows in his train? The shadows do.

Another arresting portrait in the campus episodes is that of Norton's daughter. Appropriately enough, her image is not a photograph on the wall or a totem on the lawn, but a cameo of sorts which her father reverently carries on his person, as close to his waist as to his heart:

> Suddenly he fumbled in his vest pocket and thrust something over the back of the seat, surprising me.

> "Here, young man, you owe much of your good fortune in attending such a school to her."
>
> I looked upon the tinted miniature framed in engraved platinum. I almost dropped it. A young woman of delicate, dreamy features looked up at me. She was very beautiful, I thought at the time, so beautiful that I did not know whether I should express admiration to the extent I felt it or merely act polite. And yet I seemed to remember her, or someone like her, in the past. I know now that it was the flowing costume of soft, flimsy material that made for the effect; today, dressed in one of the smart, well-tailored, angular, sterile, streamlined, engine-turned, air-conditioned modern outfits you see in the women's magazines, she would appear as ordinary as an expensive piece of machine-tooled jewelry and just as lifeless. Then, however, I shared something of his enthusiasm. (*IM*, 33–34)

Of course, the business immediately at hand here is Norton's erection of a pedestal for his "biblical maiden" daughter, and Invisible Man's retrospective awareness of that. But Ellison may be up to something else as well: surely it is worth considering that Norton and his daughter trope or refigure Wright's Mr. Dalton and his virginal Mary. If so, then at least two key revisions of Wright are achieved. One is that sexual taboos as a subject for narrative are not isolated as interracial phenomena, the other is that the young black observer of all such emotions at play does not become a *participant*–observer in any readily anticipated sense. Indeed, it is the gross disparity between what constitutes his "participation" in Norton's fantasies and the punishment he nonetheless receives that renders his situation—in stark, intended contrast to Bigger Thomas's—darkly comic.

Equally interesting, regarding Ellison's demystification of this portrait, are Invisible Man's remarks about Miss Norton's costume in the miniature, and what she would have looked like in contemporary "engine-turned" dress. At this point in the tale he hasn't met the likes of her, but he is about to meet her again and again—and phrases like "an expensive piece of machine-tooled jewelry" instruct us as to where and when. The portrait of Miss Norton in her father's vest pocket is but an abiding fiction of "modern" women like Emma and other women in the Brotherhood episodes—but especially of Emma, who, like a slick magician performing an ancient trick, will pull the narrator's new name out of her otherwise empty bosom. Miss Norton, or rather her portrait, may return to New York in her father's pocket; but it is clear that, as that portrait is dismantled, it (and she) will not remain there. Indeed, one of the most remarkable contrasts offered in the New York episodes is that of Norton's "daughters" entertaining the Brotherhood at the chic Chthonian while Norton himself is lost in the subway.

But we're not yet ready to go to New York; we must return to the campus and to Bledsoe's office—which is a kind of annex to the college's museum of slavery, although no one there would dare call it that. Several aspects of this museum will be discussed shortly, but what interests me here are the "framed portrait photographs and relief plaques of presidents and industrialists, men of power'' (*IM*, 106). These portraits are redoubtable examples of heroic portraiture in which the ''men of power'' appear as heroic examples, or gods. In the process of attempting to describe their extraordinary presence in Bledsoe's *sanctum sanctorum*, Invisible Man unwittingly stumbles upon much of the symbolic space's hidden significance when he observes that these men are ''fixed like trophies or heraldic emblems upon the walls.'' He's right: the ''men of power'' *are* Bledsoe's ''trophies''—he has bagged them in many senses of the term. The phrase ''heraldic emblems'' is also apt, because these men are messengers of given sovereignties, as well as of given fictions of historical reality. As such, they are harbingers of war, morticians to the dead, and custodians of national and genealogical signs. This fits them and, indeed, destines them for positions of stewardship to constructions such as Bledsoe's college; this is much of what the narrator may finally see about them, once he is released from the pattern of their certainties and deep into the task of creating a competing fiction. In Bledsoe's office, however, wherein our hero is summarily expelled from ''nigger heaven,'' the ''men of power'' are but a mute angelic choir (to Bledsoe's St. Peter) whose collective voices and visages seem to condemn him all the more with their silence.

In the Brotherhood episodes, Ellison continues to give his portraits a comic texture, but he also seems intent on enlarging the space for enigmatic models in which the grandfather has already been situated. Quite fittingly, these portraits appear on the walls of Invisible Man's office within the Brotherhood's Harlem headquarters, constituting a significant portion of the narrative strategy by which that space is positioned (and thereby read) within a spatial dynamic that also embraces Bledsoe's ''trophy room'' and the framing warm hole. Especially in their conversation with one another, the portraits expose the hidden seams in the elaborate fiction that Invisible Man jokingly calls, in retrospect, his ''days of certainty'' with the Brotherhood. The controversial ''rainbow poster,'' for example, is described matter-of-factly, but not without a dollop of Ellisonian humor:

> It was a symbolic poster of a group of heroic figures: An American Indian couple, representing the dispossessed past; a blond brother (in overalls) and a leading Irish sister, representing the dispossessed present; and Brother Tod Clifton and a young white couple (it had been felt unwise simply to show Clifton and the girl) surrounded by a group of children of mixed races, representing the future, a color photograph of bright skin texture and smooth contrast . . . [its] legend:
>
> ''After the Struggle: The Rainbow of America's Future'' (*IM*, 290–291)

The rhetoric of heroic example offered here is at once antithetical to that put forth by Bledsoe's display of the ''men of power,'' and yet similar to that rhetoric in that it is another imposed fiction of reality. However, at this point in the narrative Invisible Man cannot see or read this rhetoric, any more than he can comprehend what certain Brotherhood members find objectionable about the poster. (Here, it is reasonable to assume that some Brothers viewed the poster as being too "racial" or "nationalistic" in its statement and, therefore, insufficient as an expression of the international class struggle.) One guesses that Invisible Man probably overheard some Harlemite in a bar telling a "lie" about Josephine Baker and her "rainbow tribe," and "ran" with the idea in his own newly ideological way. All such guesses aside, however, it is clear that the rainbow poster portrays not just a rhetoric our hero thinks he can see, but also a compromise he has made which he *can't* see.

The other portrait on the wall helps Ellison make much the same point. The first of several gifts Invisible Man receives from Brother Tarp, it is of Frederick Douglass, and it is the first portrait of a truly heroic example to be hung in the narrative's gallery. But, unlike Johnson with his Ex-Coloured Man, Ellison seeks neither to provide redoubtable examples for his confused protagonist nor to lament the sad fact that his narrator cannot see or see through Douglass. In the scene where the Douglass portrait is discussed, we receive instead another example of the Invisible Man's partial comprehension of a heroic rhetoric:

> I liked my work during those days of certainty. I kept my eyes wide and my ears alert. The Brotherhood was a world within a world and I was determined to discover all its secrets and to advance as far as I could. I saw no limits, it was the one organization in the whole country in which I could reach the very top and I meant to get there. Even if it meant climbing a mountain of words. For now I had begun to believe, despite all the talk of science around me, that there was a magic in spoken words. Sometimes I sat watching the watery play of light upon Douglass' portrait, thinking how magical it was that he had talked his way from slavery to a government ministry, and so swiftly. Perhaps, I thought, something of the kind is happening to me. Douglass came north to escape and find work in the shipyards; a big fellow in a sailor's suit who, like me, had taken another name. What had his true name been? Whatever it was, it was as *Douglass* that he became himself, defined himself. And not as a boatwright as he'd expected, but as an orator. Perhaps the sense of magic lay in the unexpected transformations. "You start Saul, and end up Paul," my grandfather had often said. "When you're a youngun, you Saul, but let life whup your head a bit and you starts to trying to be Paul—though you still Sauls around on the side." (*IM*, 287–88)

Several things stand out in this remarkable piece of writing. One is the presumably naive way in which Invisible Man convinces himself of the great truths subsumed within the fiction he is living by means of creating an authenticating fiction for his own life story. At the heart of this fiction is his questionable assertion that Douglass defined himself as an orator—as a private-become-public act of speech. Abetting this assertion are several revealing revisions of Douglass's language in the 1845 *Narrative:* "from slavery to a government ministry" is, for example, a remarkable misreading of Douglass's famous "from slavery to freedom." Of course, he has the goal all wrong; but even more disastrously wrong is the misconception of literacy and its uses that lies behind it.

In the Douglass *Narrative*, the phrase "from slavery to freedom," or more fully "the pathway from slavery to freedom," is Douglass's most felicitous expression for acts of reading and writing. He writes in chapter 6 of what he learned when Mr. Auld forbade Mrs. Auld to instruct him any further in "The A B C": "From that moment, I understood the pathway from slavery to freedom. It was just what I wanted, and I got it at a time when I the least expected it. . . . Though conscious of the difficulty of learning without a teacher, I set out with high hope, and a fixed purpose, at whatever cost of trouble, *to learn how to read*" (italics added). This is the abiding idea of literacy and its uses in the *Narrative* (and in the Afro-American tradition). Given the events of the *Narrative*, it is clear that, for Douglass, acts of literacy include acts of reading the signs and events, or "patterns of certainties," that comprise oppressive and imposing fictions of reality. Douglass didn't "talk" his way to freedom; rather, he "read" his way and, as far as the *Narrative* is concerned (it being his personal history as and in a literary form), "wrote" his way.

In the Brotherhood episode wherein Douglass's portrait is hung, Invisible Man only partially comprehends the heroic example and rhetoric captured in that usually fierce visage, mainly because he is still wrapped up in the idea of composing a fiction in which he himself is a great speaker or act or sound. Somehow he senses—perhaps because Douglass's portrait forces him to hear unwelcome echoes of his grandfather's voice—that Douglass is as much an enigma to him as the grandfather, that both images will remain looming question marks in his mind. Surely he will later sense that Douglass poses some very substantial questions about the fiction he is living, when he returns to Harlem to discover that Tod Clifton and Brother Tarp are missing and that Douglass's portrait has been torn down as well. In the meantime, however, during those days of certainty, the portraits on the walls of the narrator's bustling office only exhibit to him a full and sufficient expression of himself as a brother in the struggle—and on the make.

* * *

As I have suggested before, there is a museum as well as a portrait gallery in *Invisible Man*. That museum contains various collections that are contexts or syntaxes for certain portraits and, more to the point, certain cultural artifacts or material objects. Although given portraits and artifacts may function (and possibly resonate) in the narrative in much the same way, an essential distinction must be drawn between how the portraits as a group (the gallery) and the artifacts as a group (the museum) operate as narrative strategies, especially within the tale. The portraits present the full array of examples, warnings, and enigmas before the questing narrator; the artifacts offer the range of prescribed or preformed patterns of mobility. Of course, the collected portraits and artifacts are both at base systems of models; but in *Invisible Man* they are differing systems insofar as the portraits are prototypes for the self and the artifacts prototypes for the self-in-motion.

Returning to Bledsoe's office, described before as an unofficial annex to the college's museum of slavery, we are led to discover, amid the heavy furniture, mementos of the Founder, and collective gaze of the "men of power," an artifact of which Bledsoe as curator and custodian is very proud.

> He looked at me as though I had committed the worst crime imaginable. "Don't you know we can't tolerate such a thing? I gave you an opportunity to serve one of our best white friends, a man who could make your fortune. But in return you dragged the entire race into the slime!"
>
> Suddenly he reached for something beneath a pile of papers, an old leg shackle from slavery which he proudly called a "symbol of our progress."
>
> "You've got to be disciplined, boy," he said. "There's no ifs and ands about it." (*IM*, 108)

I quote from the text at some length because we must see the leg shackle both as an object and as language. As an object, it is *not* a charmingly rustic paperweight gracing Bledsoe's many papers, but something far more sinister and weaponlike that must be concealed—perhaps, as in this instance, by a cloak of words. As language, the leg shackle is less a silence or pause than a transitional phrase—a veritable link—between the two parts of Bledsoe's speech. For Bledsoe, the shackle is a charged rhetorical object in the present (a "symbol of our progress"), principally because it is also a rhetorical expression of the past (the "slime" which is invariably the nearly excremental quicksand of slavery; recall here, in contrast, Du Bois's swamp) and a paradigm for a fiction that may be imposed selectively on the future—in this case, the narrator's future. The half-dozen or so letters of introduction (the "protections")—which Bledsoe is able to produce so mysteriously in thirty minutes' time, and which allow Invisible Man no mobility whatsoever except a bus ride to New York (undoubtedly on the Bloodhound or North Star line)—are prefigured before, in all of their nefarious qualities, by the "pile of papers" in collusion, as it were, with the leg shackle.

Another telling aspect of Bledsoe's shackle is that it is smooth and unsullied, perhaps still gleaming as if brand new—or not yet put to its purpose. But we do not learn this until Brother Tarp presents the narrator with a very different leg iron, in the same Brotherhood episode wherein he hangs the portrait of Frederick Douglass:

> He was unwrapping the object now and I watched his old man's hands.
>
> 'I'd like to pass it on to you, son. There," he said, handing it to me. "Funny thing to give somebody, but I think it's got a heap of signifying wrapped up

> in it and it might help you remember what we're really fighting against. I don't think of it in terms of but two words, *yes* and *no*; but it signifies a heap more . . ."
>
> I saw him place his hand on the desk. "Brother," he said, calling me "Brother" for the first time, "I want you to take it. I guess it's a kind of luck piece. Anyway, it's the one I filed to get away."
>
> I took it in my hand, a thick dark, oily piece of filed steel that had been twisted open and forced partly back into place, on which I saw marks that might have been made by the blade of a hatchet. It was such a link as I had seen on Bledsoe's desk, only while that one had been smooth, Tarp's bore the marks of haste and violence, looking as though it had been attacked and conquered before it stubbornly yielded. (*IM*, 293)

With these words Invisible Man receives the first and only viable "protection" he is given in the tale. Shortly thereafter he fits the leg iron on his hand as if it were a pair of brass knuckles ("Finding no words to ask him more about it, I slipped the link over my knuckles and struck it sharply against the desk"), never dreaming that he will soon use it in this very manner in a pitched battle with Ras and his followers. Here we receive nothing less than a deft and momentous construction and ordering of the narrative as a whole. Tarp's shackle, in contrast to Bledsoe's, is worn, not just in the sense that it bears the marks of a violent attack and defeat, but also in that it has been literally worn—for nineteen years—by Brother Tarp. This suggests that Tarp is a very different kind of "curator" and, in some sense, *author* of the leg shackle and its accompanying fictions than is Bledsoe—recall here Tarp's earlier remark, "'I'm tellin' it better'n I ever thought I could'" (*IM*, 293). As an author, Tarp has been both in and out of his tale, and has thereby gained the perspectives and techniques with which to *see* the tale and *tell* it well. He—like certain other "peasants" in the narrative, such as the grandfather, Trueblood, and Frederick Douglass—is something of an artist, while Bledsoe—like certain other "uplifted" types, including Brother Jack—is not so much an artist or tale-teller as a manipulator of them. In both cases, Tarp's and Bledsoe's, the leg iron each man possesses, displays, and in varying senses gives away, portrays them as quite different "men of power," especially as far as art-making is concerned.

Related is the substantial matter of how the two leg irons prompt another review of Bledsoe's and Invisible Man's offices as contrasting symbolic spaces. I have already suggested how the portraits alone help to construct these spaces, but what is pertinent here is how they are further assembled by the beams of meaning that stretch between portrait and artifact. The heart of the matter is that once the portraits and leg irons are bound before us, we see more clearly the profound distinction between a rhetoric of progress and one of liberation. In Bledsoe's office, the "men of power" are the smooth, closed shackle—and the shackle, the men—not only because the men are a "closed circle," but also because the rhetoric of progress which they as trustees (or is it trusties?) oversee, and in that sense enclose far more than author, is as fixed or static as is their conception (and perception) of the present. Indeed, much as Bledsoe is characterized in another episode as a ''headwaiter'' and not a consummate chef (hence the continuity in his career from his college days as the best ''slop dispenser'' up to the narrative present), the ''men of power'' must be seen as figures who ''serve'' power: they dispense its prevailing fictions, yet are shackled to those fictions. The unending circle of Bledsoe's leg iron is a remarkable manifestation of a particular and prevailing uplift myth in which ''service'' is not just equated with ''progress,'' but is also its literary form.

In Invisible Man's office, the portrait of Frederick Douglass is modally bound to the violently opened leg shackle partly because Douglass, like Tarp, set himself free, and partly because Douglass, like the filed-open shackle, is an expression of human possibility. The key, as it were, to this construction is the exquisitely rude aperture that ''defiles'' the otherwise completed (or closed) form of the leg iron. On one level, that space is an exit or entrance; on another, it is a void to be filled, not once and for all, but continually. Douglass and the open shackle speak as one, not just of human but also of artistic possibility. To fill the space is less to close the form than to shape the form, and there can never be only one form. After all, hadn't Douglass written at least three *tales* of his life? Hadn't he hung a mighty door in his shackle's space and shaped his form not once but three times? Douglass's breaking of the shackle, his artful movement out and back in and out of the shackle, and his forming and *reforming* of the shackle is finally *the* trope before the questing narrator for a viable pattern of mobility and a viable system of authorial control. Once Invisible Man takes Tarp's shackle with him down into the narrative's framing warm hole and learns to *read* it, as well as to *hear* his grandfather and to *return* Douglass's gaze, he is ready to hibernate and write. Once these portraits and artifacts are removed from what Ishmael Reed has called ''Centers of Art Detention'' and displayed in that Center of Art Retention which Ellison calls the mind, he is ready to ''birth his form.''

It would appear, then, that Ellison pursues a narrative strategy in which aspects of the tale are turned inside-out in the frame, much as the narrator is transformed from an illiterate to a literate protagonist. But this is not the case. The means by which Ellison avoids such a closure—which would destroy his narrative—tell us much about the strategies by which he seeks to burst beyond the prototypical narratives of ascent and immersion provided by Frederick Douglass and W. E. B. Du Bois. Here I wish to suggest that, on a level not altogether removed from the inner workings of *Invisible Man*, Bledsoe's smooth and closed shackle is a trope for inherited and, to a degree, imposed narrative forms in the tradition (of which Douglass's and Du Bois's forms are the dominant forms), and that Tarp's rudely opened shackle symbolizes both the release from these forms and the new form which is *Invisible Man*.

Ellison appears only too aware that any step outside the shackles of what other men call reality necessitates an accompanying step outside what other men, including kinsmen, call literary form.

Douglass's 1845 *Narrative* is built upon a strategy and rhetoric of triumphant reversal: ''how a man became a slave'' becomes ''how a slave became a man.'' Furthermore, the world of the narrative reverses somehow, in accord with the reversal of the persona's condition, even though the persona is still situated in an imposed social structure. *Invisible Man* breaks with this strategy most obviously but more subtly by not completing all aspects of the reversal. Although Invisible Man does indeed ''reverse'' from visible to invisible (or invisible to visible) as well as from illiterate to literate, and although the portraits and artifacts of the tale move from the surfaces of the tale's symbolic interiors to those of the narrator's mind, the darkness or dimness that once occupied his mind is *not* transposed to the surfaces of the new symbolic space (the hole). Instead, it quite simply and profoundly vanishes. What *are* on these surfaces are expressions, if you will, not of darkness but of light; there are 1,369 light bulbs, and apparently more to come. These lights ''speak'' not of a former somnolent dimness, but of a contemporary illuminated wakefulness. And in addition to not expressing the narrator's prior ''dim-wattedness,'' the many lights are not portraits and artifacts like those in the tale. They are not competing or guiding fictions, but expressions of something that is distinctly prefiction, preform, and preart. In the warm hole of hibernation (or so Ellison's new construction informs us), what is so ''torturous'' about writing is not that one must work in the presence of already formed artworks, but that this work must be accomplished under the scrutiny of a certain radiant and self-inflicted brilliance.

The ''brilliance'' interests me principally because it is a constructed brilliance and, as such, part of the strategy by which Ellison bursts beyond the narrative model provided by Du Bois. Of course, the model as a whole is *The Souls*, but the particular feature of that model which Ellison must revise in order to achieve a new narrative expression, is the conspicuously romantic primary scene at the end of the narrative, where brilliance makes its visit to the self-conscious artist in the form of an enlightening sunshine. In *The Souls*, Du Bois's light must *enter* his persona's private space; it is a natural energy that binds him to whatever ''Eternal Good'' resides in this and other worlds. Furthermore, once these beams are entwined with those of the songs of his generations (''My children, my little children, are singing to the sunshine''), they bind him to his ''tribe'' as well, and, more specifically still, to his tribe's *genius loci*. Quite to the point, and in full accord with other romantic aspects of the model, Du Bois remarks on how these magnificent energies are ''free''; notably, there isn't even a veiled suggestion that he, too, is free. This primary scene in *The Souls* insists that a price must be paid for accomplishing immersion; it is the other side of the coin, as it were, to being self-consciously situated in an isolated space, where the windows are few and ''high'' and latticed with bars of light and song. The brilliance that enlightens Du Bois's persona as self and artist speaks as much of loss as of gain, and this brilliance and its accompanying idea of artistic compensation must be radically revoiced in order for the "shackle" of the immersion narrative form to be broken.

Ellison's deliberate positioning of the brilliance before his narrator *inside* the hole, all over the hole, and with many bulbs instead of a few high windows begins such a revision and revoicing. Of course, there is more to his expression than this: the brilliance is a constructed brilliance in that it is man-made or "tinker-made," and it is an interior brilliance most particularly in that it is mind-made or "thinker-made." Indeed, as Invisible Man informs us in the Prologue, it is the self-work of a "thinker-tinker" (*IM*, 6), an "inventor" with a "theory and a concept" who is almost anything but an embodiment of an "Eternal Good." This brilliance is "free" in a sense of the term very different from the one Du Bois advances. In *The Souls*, the entwining beams of light and voice are free *only* in the sense that they are as visible, audible, and mobile as those who reside within the shadows of the Veil are invisible, inaudible, and immobile. This is clearly Du Bois's point when he writes:

> If somewhere in this whirl and chaos of things there dwells Eternal Good, pitiful yet masterful, then anon in His good time America shall rend the Veil and the prisoned shall go free. Free, Free, as the sunshine trickling down the morning into these high windows of mine, free as yonder fresh young voices welling up to me from the caverns of brick and mortar below. . . . (263)

However, as I've suggested, these energies are not free to the persona; he has paid for them in various ways, including the undertaking of a requisite pilgrimage into more oppressive systems of social structure. For these reasons it may be said that the immersion narrative, like the narrative of ascent, is less about strategies for avoiding payment than about strategies for making payment that yield, in turn, a fresh posture within social structure which is somehow *worth* that payment—or *more than worth it*. Viewed in this way, ascent and immersion narratives are much of a piece, and so it would appear that a strategy for bursting beyond the one is also a scheme for release from the other.

* * *

Ellison achieves such a strategy when he makes it clear that his narrator has found a way not only to stop paying for his life within what other men call reality, but also to avoid paying for his enlightenment once he has fallen outside those imposing fictions. The former discovery releases him, as Du Bois and others are not, from various rhetorics of progress; the latter discovery allows him to gain as few others have a rhetoric of liberation. Above and beyond the hilarious joke of "socking it" to the power company with every socket installed (or of "screwing" them with every screw of a bulb) lies the serious point that the self-initiated and self-constructed brilliance before the hibernating narrator does not, and in fact cannot, reverse the charge: it comes free and freely without a service payment, without a loss the narrator must balance against his gain. In the narrative of hibernation—for so we must call it, because it is a new form in the tradition—what defines the new resulting posture and space for the questing narrator has nothing to do with whether he is situated in the most or least oppressive social structure of the narrative, and little to do with how much space lies between his hole and the ''ornery'' world above (after all, Invisible Man can smell the stench of Spring), but everything to do with whether it is a context in which the imagination is its own self-generating energy. The new resulting posture and space beyond those of the ascent and immersion narratives are ones in which the narrator eventually gains authorial control of the narrative text, and of the imagination as a trope subsumed within that text. (For those who have said repeatedly that Ellison ''grabbed all the marbles,'' but didn't know by what sleight of hand he did it—this is how he did it.)

I have not forgotten that Du Bois's enlightening brilliance is an exquisite commingling of light *and* song—nor apparently has Ellison. Indeed, just as Invisible Man wants more and more light, he also desires more and more machines with which to play Louis Armstrong's ''What Did I Do to Be so Black and Blue.'' This music, like the light it accompanies, does not have to waft in some high window, but emanates instead from *within* the space; it is a ''thinker-tinker'' music, a music improvised upon. Invisible Man touches on this matter when he writes:

> Sometimes now I listen to Louis while I have my favorite dessert of vanilla ice cream and sloe gin. I pour the red liquid over the white mound, watching it glisten and the vapor rising as Louis bends that military instrument into a beam of lyrical sound. Perhaps I like Louis Armstrong because he's made poetry out of being invisible. . . . And my own grasp of invisibility aids me to understand his music. . . . Invisibility, let me explain, gives one a slightly different sense of time, you're never quite on the beat. Sometimes you're ahead and sometimes behind. Instead of the swift and imperceptible flowing of time, you are aware of its nodes, those points where time stands still or from which it leaps behind. And you slip into the breaks and look around. That's what you hear vaguely in Louis' music. (*IM*, 6–7)

With these words Ellison clarifies an essential distinction between immersion and hibernation that is at root a distinction between embracing the music you hear and making the music you hear your own. The counterpointing image immediately appearing before us is one in which Du Bois is ensconced in his study, awaiting those entwined beams from above, while dear Louis is fashioning beams of a certain brilliance all his own. But of course the grand trope before us is the one with which we (and, Ellison to a degree) began: Tarp's open leg shackle. Louis Armstrong's bending of a ''military instrument into a beam of lyrical sound'' magnificently and heroically revoices Tarp's defiling of the shackle. As these brilliant images conjoin and speak as one, we see as perhaps never before the full extent to which Tarp and Louis are poets of invisibility, not because they make art out of chaos or nothingness, but because they make art out of art. As master craftsmen to whom Invisible Man is apprenticed, their master lesson for him (and us) is that while the artist must be able to burst beyond the old forms, he also must make light of the light that fills the resulting hole—"slip into the breaks and look around" (*IM*, 7). In *Invisible Man*, "making light of the light" is a rhetoric of liberation, a theory of comedy, and a narrative strategy rolled into one. Once Ellison's questing narrator becomes a hibernating narrator and finally comprehends all of this, he may truly say, "Light confirms my reality, gives birth to my form" (*IM*, 5).

NOTES

1. Zora Neale Hurston, *Their Eyes Were Watching God* (1937; Urbana: University of Illinois Press, 1978), 284.

2. Ralph Ellison, *Invisible Man* (New York: Random House, 1952), 335. All subsequent references to this source are cited in text as *IM*.

3. W.E.B. DuBois, *The Souls of Black Folk* (Chicago: A. C. McClurg, 1903), 11.

Spokesman for Invisibility

THOMAS R. WHITAKER

"I am an invisible man."[1] More than thirty years after the first publication of that famous opening sentence, some readers may find it hard to credit the notion that Americans who can claim African ancestry are in any sense "invisible." For quite a while Tom Bradley has been mayor of Los Angeles, Andrew Young mayor of Atlanta, and Coleman Young mayor of Detroit. After the more recent election of Harold Washington as mayor of Chicago, there were 224 "black" mayors, 347 "black" state legislators, and twenty-one "black" congressmen in the United States. Citing those figures, *Newsweek* declared that "blacks" have now demonstrated their ability to reach beyond "their own community" and "reshape the politics of this nation."

Though our changing politics will make it harder to read Ralph Ellison's *Invisible Man* as a sign of the times, it doesn't follow that this realistic, comic, grotesque, allegorical, and nearly apocalyptic book is outdated. Its most obvious satirical targets are still with us: racial prejudice, blind and deceptive leadership, and the betrayal of America's promise. And its most obvious positive values remain necessary for the health of our body politic: a belief in the importance of the "forms of American Negro humanity,"[2] as Ellison called them in *Shadow and Act*, and a final precarious affirmation of "the principle on which the country was built" (*IM*, 561).

That affirmation is necessary, Ellison's protagonist and narrator surmises, because "we, through no fault of our own, were linked to all the others in the loud, clamoring semi-visible world" (*IM*, 561). He knows, as the staff of *Newsweek* apparently does not, that talk of "blacks" and "their own community" can refer to no ultimate or even unambiguous categories. He recounts in his Prologue a reefer-dream shaped by ambivalence in which a preacher expounded the "Blackness of Blackness" by shouting that "*black is*" and "*black ain't*" (*IM*, 9). And he later tells us how "Optic White" is made at Liberty Paints by adding color to a base prepared underground by the Negro engineer, Lucius Brockway, and then mixing in some drops of "dead black" dope. The explosion in Brockway's engineroom sent him flying "into a wet blast of black emptiness that was somehow a bath of whiteness" (*IM*, 195, 225). Again and again he has found that "blackness" and "whiteness" are mutually defining and mutually inclusive—as ambiguous as the metaphysical "whiteness" that, a century earlier, troubled the Ishmael imagined by Melville, one of the "ancestors" to whom Ellison has paid tribute in "Hidden Name and Complex Fate" (*S&A*, 160).

Ellison's protagonist has also learned what Melville had implied through the mixed crew of the *Pequod*, and another "ancestor" through the mixed crew of Huck Finn's raft: "black" and "white" belong to the same community of ethical obligation and problematic identity. The "black" preacher Homer Barbee is as blind as the "white" sleepwalkers who don't recognize a "black" man's presence. The "white" Brother Jack, with his hypnotic glass eye, sees no more than did the "ginger colored" protagonist he was deceiving. The doomed youth leader, Tod Clifton, has "the chiseled, black-marble features sometimes found on statues in northern museums and alive in southern towns in which the white offspring of house children and the black offspring of yard children bear names, features and character traits as identical as the rifling of bullets fired from a common barrel" (*IM*, 354). And the protagonist's gropings toward identity can proceed quite appropriately from his memory of a teacher's critique of Joyce's *Portrait of the Artist as a Young Man* ("Stephen's problem, like ours, was not actually one of creating the uncreated conscience of his race, but of *creating the uncreated features of his face*" [*IM*, 345–46]) to his own reverie on the portrait of Frederick Douglass: "What had his true name been? Whatever it was, it was as Douglass that he became himself, defined himself" (*IM*, 372).

By the time he tells his story, of course, the protagonist has become disillusioned with the "faces" or "self-definitions" he had constructed in running either for or from "the Jacks and the Emersons and the Bledsoes and Nortons," and he has decided to run "only from their confusion, impatience, and refusal to recognize the beautiful absurdity of their American identity and mine" (*IM*, 546). He knows that we all, as Albert Murray has argued in *The Omni-Americans*, are hyphenated members of one multiform community. But he has also approached the darker vision of one of Ellison's recent "ancestors," André Malraux, whose protagonists often learn that any increase in consciousness entails an isolating disillusionment with the hypnotic roles men play. At the end of *Man's Fate* we doubt that a revolutionary could ever return from his deathly hell to take up again some role in daily life. At the end of *Invisible Man*, after the protagonist has burned his identifying documents, endured a nightmare of castration, and become "free of illusion," we must have a similar doubt. What "face" or "self-definition" could he now propose that wouldn't result from some new blindness or deception? And yet this isolated and nameless man can conclude his story with what he calls a frightening question: "Who knows but that, on the lower frequencies, I speak for you?" (*IM*, 557, 568).

For three decades readers have been probing the possible implications of that question, and we can abstract from their responses a remarkable gamut of opinion. Some have emphasized Ellison's apparent inability to get the protagonist out of his hole. William Barrett complained at the outset that the novel "just misses greatness" because it fails to provide any alternative to invisibility. Marcus Klein concluded that this "death-driven novel" can only "confirm again and again that the hero doesn't exist." Though accepting invisibility as a "negative metaphor" that holds together "the long experience of chaos that has met Ellison's vision," Klein dismissed the protagonist's final affirmation as a "faked" grace note. William J. Schafer then replied that the novel's negations comprise a fragmentary epic quest, leading to a state of "impotent self-knowledge" that poses for all of us the question of death or resurrection.[3]

Others have emphasized the presence of some yet more affirmative meaning. Finding a "preparation for something like redemption," Thomas A. Vogler said that the protagonist has already taken the necessary "first step" after discovering his invisibility. "He has preserved his anger and his suffering by embodying it in art, and has even more fully grasped his identity in the process." Todd Lieber concluded that "in the creative act of writing the invisible man succeeds in giving form to the pattern of his reality and in the process defines himself." The book therefore renders "the possibility of true freedom and responsibility without the surrender, assimilation or destruction of his identity." Robert B. Stepto argued that the protagonist has replaced his identifying documents with the "completed narrative," in which he "eventually gains complete authorial control of the text" and of "the imagination as a trope subsumed within that text." Earl H. Rovit had already argued in a very different vein that the protagonist's acceptance of visibility is no "resignation to chaos" but a "mask of facelessness," a comic and Zen-like version of the role Emerson had assigned to the American poet. He "becomes 'the world's eye'—something through which one sees, even though it cannot itself be seen." And more recently, undisturbed by the novel's negations and seeing no need for such sophisticated justifications of an affirmative reading, Robert G. O'Meally has described the protagonist's gradual rediscovery of a traditional "black" identity. He has been "jarred to consciousness" by folk rhymes and tales; by the blues, spirituals, and gospel music; by signifying and the dozens; and by such characters as Mary Rambo, Peter Wheatstraw, Brother Tarp, and those unnamed boys in the subway who seem "the bearers of something precious" (*IM*, 431). He has therefore realized "the value of the black masses," has accepted "the tested wisdom" of the folk as "a vital part of his experience," and understands at last that "he is, simply, who he is."[4]

Must we decide, then, whether our spokesman is an absence, a metaphor for chaos, an antihero caught between death and resurrection, an agent of responsible freedom who has now defined himself, an emergent author in control of the imagination, an Emersonian transparent eyeball, or a black man whose identity is rooted in the vernacular tradition? Perhaps not. Such diverse readings suggest an indeterminacy or plurality of meaning in the book itself. The protagonist may be all of these things, and more besides, in ways that we have yet to explore. And we might start with Ellison's own remarks in 1955 to interviewers from the *Paris Review*: "It's not an important novel," he said. "I failed of eloquence, and many of the immediate issues are rapidly fading away. If it does last, it will be simply because there are things going on in its depth that are of more permanent interest than on its surface" (*S&A*, 175).

At first glance, that is a startling confession of failure. It seems to echo the narrator's own rueful remark about his final meeting with Ras the Exhorter: "But even as I spoke I knew it was no good. I had no words and no eloquence" (*IM*, 546). For the narrator, "eloquence" often means the persuasive "magic in spoken words" (*IM*, 372) that he recognizes with admiration or uneasiness in such various styles as Homer Barbee's incantatory sermon, Peter Wheatstraw's boasts and patter, and Ras's "crude, insane" pleas—the magic he can produce only when "another self" within him has "taken over and held forth" (*IM*, 344). Eloquence for him arises from an invisible source and requires some tacit relation between speaker and hearers. Indeed, he has found that it doesn't need to be verbal. Describing his speeches downtown for the Brotherhood, he says: "I acted out a pantomime more eloquent than my most expressive words. I was a partner to it but could no more fathom it than I could the mystery of the man in the doorway" (*IM*, 410). His comparison is apt: that image of a man in the doorway, which he had seen after a wealthy white woman had tempted him into her bed, may or may not have been a dream but certainly corresponded to his own fear and desire. And such hallucinatory eloquence of appearances has pervaded his life. He has moved in a psychic field that repeatedly manifests itself in speaking objects—Tod's dancing doll, Jack's glass eye, Tarp's chain link with "a heap of signifying wrapped up in it" (*IM*, 379)—and in speakers without great talent who can express the pattern of an unconsciously shared situation. Even now he often seems unaware of the full meaning of such eloquence. When he relates Jim Trueblood's tale of incestuous dreamwork, he admits only that he had been "torn between humiliation and fascination" (*IM*, 67). We can see, however, that Trueblood's tale symbolically mirrors not only Mr. Norton's repressed relation to his daughter and compensatory relation to the black college but also the protagonist's own Oedipal entrapment by that black-and-white structure of authority. And when he finally suggests that he himself may speak "for" us, we recognize a possibility that would gather up all the participatory eloquence of his world in an inclusive instance.

Though a novel so richly concerned with eloquence might conceivably fail of eloquence, in that interview Ellison was probably using the term in yet another sense. Ever since 1937 he had been interested in Kenneth Burke's analyses of how the personal sources of art engage social meanings. And in Burke's *Counter-Statement* the symbolic and formal intensity of an artwork is called "eloquence" (165). In this sense, the eloquence of *Invisible Man* does falter, sometimes dissipating itself in overblown rhetoric, sometimes lapsing into a rather tired realism. But in what Ellison called the novel's "depth" we can see impulses that have shaped such various works as Joyce's *Ulysses*, Eliot's *The Waste Land*, Faulkner's *Absalom, Absalom!*, Aiken's *Ushant*, and Pynchon's *Gravity's Rainbow*. Its stylistic shifts involve a verbal playfulness that transcends the ostensible realism of its narrative line. Its protean and allusive voice generates a "history" that often seems mythical or even whimsical. It recounts the apparent maturing of a self while sharing the modern suspicion that "self" is always an illusory entity. And its protagonist journeys through one role after another toward a nearly apocalyptic vision of metamorphosis.

Such writings, as they engage the process that shapes and unshapes the personae we usually regard as the agents of history, necessarily become self-transforming trajectories of interpretation. They repeatedly question our certainties—postulates, facts, even the existence of individual persons. But they also tacitly affirm our ability to participate in their continuing hermeneutic endeavor. Indeed, they suggest that our life together must be constituted by some such trajectory, and that we are not atomic individuals but mutually implicated participants in a community of interpretation. That's one reason why the narrator of *Invisible Man* tells us in the Epilogue, as if he were some persona in an Eliot poem, that he has "tried to give pattern to the chaos which lives within the pattern of your certainties" (*IM*, 567). And that's also a reason why the book's opening sentence requires its closing sentence. On what Ellison called the "surface," the trope of direct address frames a novel about an alienated American Negro whose life illustrates Richard Wright's assertion in *12 Million Black Voices* that "we black folk, our history and our present being, are a mirror of all the manifold experiences of America" (146). In its "depth," however, it acknowledges the fictionality of all determinate identities and the invisibility, therefore, of all writers and readers.

The fact that the title of *Invisible Man* lacks a definite or indefinite article suggests that this condition is neither entirely remediable nor entirely to be feared. (Georg Goyert's translation into German was yet more starkly titled *Unsichtbar*.) The narrator asks in the prologue: "Could this compulsion to put invisibility down in black and white be thus an urge to make music of invisibility?" (*IM*, 13–14). His punning question, which conflates literary and social texts, almost proposes a blues doctrine of cosmic creation by some lonely and protean Jazzman. And in the Epilogue he defends his "buggy jiving" in language just as extreme: "Being invisible and without substance, a disembodied voice, as it were, what else could I do?" (*IM*, 568). Of course, he isn't the Reverend B. P. Rinehart calling us to "Behold the Invisible," though he has played that role, too. In fact, he is recalling the song of the "thin brown girl" in the college chapel, which stands as a complex image for the paradoxical aspects of his own performance—and of Ellison's:

> She began softly, as though singing to herself of emotions of utmost privacy, a sound not addressed to the gathering but which they overheard almost against her will. Gradually she increased its volume, until at times the voice seemed to become a disembodied force that sought to enter her, to violate her, shaking her, rocking her rhythmically, as though it had become the source of her being, rather than the fluid web of her own creation. (*IM*, 114)

As a "disembodied voice" speaking through and yet created by Ellison, and generated for us by this doubly "black and white" text that he ostensibly writes, he invites us to explore some of the "musical" possibilities of our shared fate.

Those possibilities are both improvisatory and conversational, as he learned when he discovered a "new analytical way" of listening to the eloquence of Louis Armstrong's music:

> The unheard sounds came through, and each melodic line existed of itself, stood out clearly from all the rest, said its piece, and waited patiently for the other voices to speak. That night I found myself hearing not only in time, but in space as well. I not only entered the music but descended, like Dante, into its depths. (*IM*, 8–9)

If we enter his own comic and desperate music, we'll find that the manifold invisibility for which he speaks will lead us toward a yet more comprehensive invisibility, whose spokesman is the conversational design of this writing.

* * *

"I was a *spokesman*," the protagonist had once insisted, "—why shouldn't I speak about women, or any other subject?" (*IM*, 397). After he has burnt up his more hopeful "names" or "self-definitions"—the eager student, the willing worker, the charismatic orator—he retains that incompletely defined function. Invisible and without substance, he may speak for us. But what can this mean? His invisibility has more leaves than the onion to which Ibsen's Peer Gynt had compared his own histrionic nonidentity.

He has been invisible, of course, because he is "black." When people of exclusively Caucasian ancestry look in his direction, they see only his surroundings, themselves, or figments of their imagination. But his invisibility has simply been exacerbated by his skin color. As a student at college, as an agent for President Bledsoe and a beneficiary of Mr. Norton, as a worker for Liberty Paints, and as a spokesman for the Brotherhood, he has also been invisible. Anyone who enters a structure of power tends not be seen by those who wield that power. Jack and Hambro, he learns, "didn't see either color or men. . . . I was simply a material, a natural resource to be used" (*IM*, 497). Because we are all members of minority groups (as Thomas Sowell has recently reminded us in *Ethnic America*), and because we are all used as means to the economic, political, and psychological ends through which others try to define themselves, the narrator speaks for us.

But he has also been invisible because, like Tod Clifton, he has fallen outside organizational or official history. Clifton had effectively foretold that fate in his wry comment on Ras ("I suppose sometimes a man *has* to plunge outside history" [*IM*, 368]), and the protagonist poignantly apprehends it, at the Faulknerian moment of Clifton's death, through a fortuitous image of flight:

> I saw a flight of pigeons whirl out of the trees and it all happened in the swift interval of their circling. . . . just as the cop pushed him, jolting him forward and Clifton trying to keep the box from swinging against his leg and saying something over his shoulder and going forward as one of the pigeons swung down into the street and up again, leaving a feather floating white in the dazzling backlight of the sun. . . . (*IM*, 425)

That image haunts his later thoughts of Clifton:

> Where were the historians today? And how would they put it down? . . . What did they ever think of us transitory ones? Ones such as I had been before I found the Brotherhood—birds of passage who were too obscure for learned classification, too silent for the most sensitive recorders of sound; of natures too ambiguous for the most ambiguous words, and too distant from the centers of historical decision to sign or even to applaud the signers of historical documents? (*IM*, 429)

Those boys seen in the subway, fresh from the South, speaking "a jived-up transitional language" and thinking "transitional thoughts, though perhaps they dream the same old ancient dreams," were such birds of passage. They were "men out of time"—but "who knew but that they were the saviors, the true leaders, the bearers of something precious?" (*IM*, 430–31) And at Tod's funeral, when the protagonist's eyes fall upon "a peanut vendor standing beneath a street lamp upon which pigeons were gathered," the birds of passage compose an implicitly Franciscan image: "and now I saw him stretch out his arms with his palms turned upward, and suddenly he was covered, head, shoulders and outflung arms, with fluttering, feasting birds" (*IM*, 443). In these images, as in the folk material that O'Meally has emphasized, the protagonist recognizes the elusive richness of ordinary people, what William Carlos Williams had called in *Paterson* a "radiant gist that/resists the final crystallization." In doing so, he anticipates the celebration in *Gravity's Rainbow* of what Pynchon calls the "preterite," those of us who have been passed over, who have dropped out of the plots of history. Because such anonymity characterizes our social identity, the protagonist speaks for us.

But it's not just a matter of the blindness of official history. More fundamentally yet, the narrator has been invisible because he doesn't conform to the patterns of reality that others have defined for themselves. "Step outside the narrow borders of what men call reality,'' he says in the Epilogue, ''and you step into chaos—ask Rinehart, he's a master of it—or imagination'' (*IM*, 563). Clinging to their certainties, refusing to exercise imagination, people blind themselves to the unique possibilities that seem to be ''chaos.'' The protagonist knows, as Emerson and Whitman did before him, that ''Our fate is to become one, and yet many—This is not prophecy, but description'' (*IM*, 564). And because the reality of each of us is always at least partly invisible to those who have defined a different reality, he speaks for us.

It follows, of course, that he has also been invisible because he too has been blind. At least ''half'' of his ''sickness,'' he says, lay within him. Exploitation depends on our willingness to accept the ''names'' or ''identities'' foisted upon us. For a long time he couldn't see beyond the hope or glamour suggested by such names. Only when taken for ''Rine the runner and Rine the gambler and Rine the briber and Rine the lover and Rinehart the Reverend'' (*IM*, 486–87) did he recognize that he moved in a society of role-playing to which the confidence-man had found one kind of solution. Frustrated now by the awareness that names designate masks, he was tempted to ''do a Rinehart'' (*IM*, 496) and gain control of the whole charade. When that boomeranged in moral revulsion during his evening with Sybil—''Such games were for Rinehart, not me'' (*IM*, 512)—he had to admit that even an invisible power tempted by possibility must, if human, acknowledge a moral obligation to another human being. Then he ran in the night, and within himself, until his moment of truth in the midst of the Harlem riot. Facing Ras without ''eloquence,'' he recognized the ''beautiful absurdity'' of the ''American identity'' compounded of ''hope and desire, fear and hate,'' that had kept him running:

> I stood there, knowing that by dying, that by being hanged by Ras on this street in this destructive night I would perhaps move them one fraction of a bloody step closer to a definition of who they were and of what I was and had been. But the definition would have been too narrow; I was invisible. . . . (*IM*, 546–47)

Because we blind ourselves to the inadequacy of the names given us by others, or exploit that inadequacy by blinding ourselves to the obligations that link us together in our invisible reality, he speaks for us.

After recognizing all this, he still remains invisible because he can't perform any action, however authentic, or formulate any self-definition, however accurate, that would disclose him as a determinate individual. In this sense, he is indeed ''non-existent,'' though Klein's pessimistic deductions from that fact are unwarranted. The immediate action makes the matter clear. Knowing that ''it was better to live out one's own absurdity than to die for that of others, whether for Ras's or Jack's,'' the protagonist let fly the spear at Ras—''and it was as though for a moment I had surrendered my life and begun to live again'' (*IM*, 547). Even what an existentialist might call an authentic action has only a momentary validity. Now, after being chased underground, he must endure the nightmare that expresses the emptiness of his freedom from illusion. And Lieber's and Stepto's optimistic belief that his artistic "self-definition" in this story will guarantee his emergence from hibernation is also unwarranted. The protagonist now knows that all definitions are too narrow: they freeze the changing reality that a Rinehart exploits. Even the most richly detailed self-definition can describe only a past trajectory through illusory or momentary selves. And yet Lieber was right to insist on the possibility of "true freedom and responsibility," for those attributes of our shared subjectivity require no self-definition, which could only fix what the narrator calls "necessity" and limit what he calls "possibility." ("Until some gang succeeds in putting the world in a strait jacket," he says, "its definition is possibility" [*IM*, 563].)

"The end was in the beginning," he tells us (*IM*, 558). And for him, as for the speaker of Eliot's *Four Quartets*, that will always be so. He has made a "decision" to emerge from his hole, but he hasn't yet emerged. Though free to take the next step, he will even then be invisible. And that situation will recur in new forms, no matter what choices he makes. That's why he says: "I'm shaking off the old skin and I'll leave it here in the hole. I'm coming out, no less invisible without it, but coming out nevertheless" (*IM*, 568). That old skin may be his story—or did you think he found a publisher? It is certainly the conflict-ridden "I" that his story has finally defined, an "I" still caught between yes and no, love and hate, denunciation and defense, the bad air and the good music it makes. If he emerges without that skin, we won't be able to see him. ". . . I've overstayed my hibernation," he says at last, "since there's a possibility that even an invisible man has a socially responsible role to play" (*IM*, 568). There is no reason to believe that note to be faked. And because, though appearing to be distinct objects, we all participate in a free and answerable subjectivity, the protagonist speaks for us.

We have arrived at part of Ellison's answer to what Kenneth Burke, in *Attitudes Toward History*, had posited as the central literary problem, that of "identity." The naturalists, Burke said, had "discovered accurately enough that identity is *not* individual" but had resisted their own discovery. He argued that the "so-called 'I' is merely a unique combination of partially conflicting 'corporate we's.'" For everyone, a "change of identity" will occur "as any given structure of society calls forth conflicts among our 'corporate we's.' From this necessity you get, in art, the various ritualizations of rebirth." Such rituals "dredge" the problem of "How much of one's past identity must be forgotten, how much remolded, as he moves from one role to the next." It followed that "Change of identity is a way of 'seeing around the corner'" (*Attitudes*, 2:139–40, 147).

Ellison told interviewers from *Y'Bird Reader* in 1977 that Burke had "provided a *Gestalt* through which I could apply intellectual insights back into my own materials and into my own life'' (148). And in fact *Invisible Man* is a ''ritual of rebirth'' in which the protagonist, after several changes of identity, remembers his earlier life with an undeniably Burkean effect: ''It was as though I'd suddenly learned to look around corners'' (*IM*, 496). But if he understands at last, as O'Meally has argued, that ''he is, simply, who he is,'' he also knows that ''isness'' to be a manifold invisibility.

* * *

Nor have we completely unpeeled this onion. A structuralist would say, in accord with Emile Beneviste's formula,[5] that we have been looking at ''story'' but not at ''discourse.'' But Ellison's answer to the ''problem of identity'' works itself out on that level, too. As the ''story'' of *Invisible Man* dissolves the protagonist's fictive identities, disclosing him to be a participatory center of responsible freedom, so its ''discourse'' proceeds to dissolve the act of narration, disclosing the narrator to be an aspect of literary conversation. Vogler, Lieber, and Stepto have variously argued that the act of narration defines an identity that can replace those identities previously imposed upon the protagonist. Quite aside from the fallacy of taking any self-definition as other than a description of the past, their arguments would be plausible only on the assumption that *Invisible Man* is a work of realistic mimesis in which protagonist and narrator constitute a single and indivisible entity. But Ellison's self-conscious fiction repeatedly undermines that assumption.

The protagonist's eloquence, we may recall, surprises him because it arises from an invisible source, ''another self'' that has ''taken over and held forth,'' and because it depends on a tacit relation to his audience that exceeds his understanding. The narrator's eloquence in addressing us depends upon just those conditions, but in ways that the protagonist's story can hardly explain. Many voices seem to speak through this ''disembodied voice.'' Its ''discourse'' manifests to a remarkable degree what M. M. Bakhtin has called the ''heteroglossia'' or ''dialogism'' toward which the novel as a genre must tend. That trait appears in its rich array of stylistic levels and rhetorical procedures, which reflect not only the various social and intellectual milieux through which the protagonist has passed but also a good many literary milieux of which he seems ignorant. We know that he took a college course dealing with Joyce, Yeats, and O'Casey. He can allude to Dante's descent into hell, and to the lives of Frederick Douglass, Booker T. Washington, and George Washington Carver. The Brotherhood has given him several crash courses in left-wing politics. But on the evidence of his story and his commentary, he is not a literary man. He quotes from folk rhymes, the blues, spirituals, and gospel hymns. His hole, so brightly lit by 1,369 light bulbs, contains no books. He does have a radio-phonograph, and he plans to have five of them. If he invokes an artistic master, it is Louis Armstrong. And yet, as he addresses us in his often quite oral style, he employs literary strategies that he seems never to have encountered, much less studied as the "sedulous ape" that Robert Louis Stevenson urged every young author to become.

That effect doesn't simply result from the movement from "naturalism" through "expressionism" to "surrealism" that Ellison mentioned to the interviewers from the *Paris Review* (*S&A*, 178). In fact, the naturalism seems mainly confined to chapter 1, on the "battle royal" though the later accounts of the Brotherhood often recall the styles of James T. Farrell and John Dos Passos. The expressionism, too, seems mainly confined to chapters 10 and 11, which deal with the experiences at Liberty Paints. (As Charles T. Davis hinted in "The Mixed Heritage of the Modern Black Novel: Ralph Ellison and Friends," included in *Black Is the Color of the Cosmos*, some images from O'Neill's *The Hairy Ape* enter here and in the prologue's "bumping" scene.) And the surrealism is most evident in chapter 25, in the nightmare of castration and in some earlier descriptions of the riot:

> Up the street there sounded the crashing of huge sheets of glass and through the blue mysteriousness of the dark the walks shimmered like shattered mirrors. All the street's signs were dead, all the day sounds had lost their stable meaning. (*IM*, 525)

Quite apart from this intermittent progression, the narrator's eloquence seems to converse with American authors whose existence the protagonist has nowhere recognized.

Sometimes, of course, the parodic effect suggests the narrator's own unadmitted knowledge, as when in chapter 2 he echoes the "Shakespeherian rag" of *The Waste Land*: "And oh, oh, oh, those multimillionaires!" (*IM*, 37). But even that echo serves to climax a description that began with a Faulkneresque setting—"Honeysuckle and purple wisteria hung heavy from the trees and white magnolias mixed with their scents in the bee-humming air" (*IM*, 34)—and then proceeded to wallow in a morass of Thomas Wolfe's nostalgic and questioning apostrophes, laced with Eliotic disillusionment:

> Oh, long green stretch of campus, Oh, quiet songs at dusk, Oh, moon that kissed the steeple and flooded the perfumed nights. . . . And why does no rain fall through my memories, soak through the hard dry crust of the still so recent past? Why do I recall, instead of the odor of seed bursting in springtime, only the yellow contents of the cistern spread over the lawn's dead grass? Why? And how? How and why? (*IM*, 36)

We understand that he can't go home again to that "flower-studded wasteland" (*IM*, 37).

More often, however, the pastiche suggests not the narrator's tacit knowledge but another voice speaking through him, which engages in an admiring competition with the special effects of some literary ancestor. In chapter 5 the narrator's meditation upon the meaning of college vespers engages, as

Michael Allen has shown,[6] the loose but resonant Ciceronian rhetoric—with its sound patterns of repetition, antithesis, and parallelism—that Faulkner has often used to render a characteristically southern consciousness. In chapter 12 the protagonist's feverish state is at first reflected in overwrought images: "Two huge women with spoiled-cream complexions seemed to struggle with their massive bodies as they came past, their flowered hips trembling like threatening flames." But then the style switches abruptly into Faulknerian absolute phrases and italicized quotations:

> And the big dark woman saying, *Boy, is you all right, what's wrong*? in a husky-voiced contralto. And me saying, *I'm all right, just weak*, and trying to stand, and her saying, *Why don't y'all stand back and let the man breathe*? . . . and the policeman saying . . . and me answering . . . and him ordering. . . . (*IM*, 245–46)

And so on for two pages.

In chapter 17, with the cooperation of the setting itself, the narrator's discourse evokes *The Sun Also Rises*:

> Before me, in the panel where a mirror is usually placed, I could see a scene from a bullfight, the bull charging close to the man and the man swinging the red cape in sculptured folds so close to his body that man and bull seemed to blend in one swirl of calm, pure motion. (*IM*, 349)

That mirror of Hemingway's "grace" at El Toro Bar is prophetic. When Clifton fights the bull-like Ras the next evening, events suddenly appear to us through the medium of Hemingway's circumstantial and often paratactic prose:

> And as I came up Ras tried to bull his way out and I saw Clifton drive him back and down into a squat, his hands upon the dark floor of the lobby, his heels back against the door like a runner against starting blocks. And now, shooting forward, he caught Clifton coming in, butting him, and I heard the burst of breath and Clifton was on his back and something flashed in Ras's hand and he came forward, a short, heavy figure as wide as the lobby now with the knife, moving deliberately. (*IM*, 360–61)

In chapter 19, as the narrator describes the "sense of both comfort and excitement" aroused by the "Puritan-with-reverse-English" who tried to seduce him, he seems haunted by the more abstract and sophisticated voice of Henry James:

> It was not merely the background of wealth and gracious living, to which I was alien, but simply the being there with her and the sensed possibility of a heightened communication; as though the discordantly invisible and the conspicuously enigmatic were reaching a delicately balanced harmony. (*IM*, 401)

That harmony suggests a conjunction not just of a man and a woman but also of *Invisible Man* and, say, *The Ambassadors*. Of course, that self-consciously literary effect, like the others, is momentary. By chapter 20 the voice of Faulkner will again emerge to narrate the slow-motion cinematic death of Tod Clifton, and chapter 25 will end with a pointed echo of Eliot's *East Coker*.

Such instability or versatility of style dissolves the narrator-protagonist into a "discordantly invisible" locus of effects. He is in this respect, as in his ambivalent optimism, quite unlike the narrators of Dostoevski's *Notes from the Underground* and Céline's *Journey to the End of the Night*—two more books that he seems not to have read but that figure here as stylistic presences. Dostoevski's underground man is an arrogant, evasive, self-lacerating, rhetorical, and paradoxical writer of a confession to himself, but with all his contradictions he is a stylistically consistent and ironic persona. (His metaphorical location becomes literal in *Invisible Man*, thanks partly to Richard Wright's tale, "The Man Who Lived Underground," and his quasi-oral style helps to shape the Prologue and Epilogue.) Céline's Bardamu is a terse, ironic, and disillusioned man who wants to enter "the depths of the darkness" and experience his "personal emptiness" but can't help revealing on occasion his suppressed compassion, indignation, and moral seriousness—a rather transparent mask for the author. (His swift, colloquial, but hallucinatory or even surrealistic style is approached here in the last few chapters.)

In *Invisible Man*, however, the narrator has no such stylistic consistency. We are entertained and informed by a bravura sleight-of-hand that openly pretends to merge, through that narrator, a limited but oratorical protagonist and an improvisatory and conversational "implied author." Responding to that effect, Stepto has argued that the protagonist "gains complete authorial control of the text." But Ellison's narrator seems ignorant of much of his text's meaning—unless he is really a deadpan ironist who has invented all of its parodic names, attitudes, and events and is merely pretending to be his own protagonist. (That assumption would fit Nabokov's *Lolita* more easily than *Invisible Man*.) It's more reasonable to assume that the narrator's unaccountable eloquence points here to an improvisatory pattern that transcends him. In fact, Ellison's gift of authorial eloquence to a limited narrator plays a bold variation on four novelistic conventions: the naive or unreliable narrator who is the vehicle of satire and allegory, as in Swift's *Gulliver's Travels*; the self-closed narrator who is unlikely to unburden himself in this way to any audience, as in Camus's *The Stranger*, or the third section of Faulkner's *The Sound and the Fury*; the untutored narrator whose oral style employs a rhetorical amplitude and finesse that would require a literary skill quite beyond him, as in Mark Twain's *The Adventures of Huckleberry Finn*; and the Jamesian "reflector" whose consciousness has become as "super-subtle" as its author's.

In reading such a self-conscious and paradoxical fiction, we ourselves must play two invisible roles. We must imagine ourselves to be what Seymour Chatman, in *Story and Discourse: Narrative Structure in Fiction and Film*, has called the "narratee." In doing so, we follow the narrator's account as if it were a more or less factual report addressed to us—even though, in this instance, that assumption renders us as unlocatable as he is. But we must also play the more inclusive role of "implied reader." In and through our response to the narrator, we respond to the implied author's more widely ranging cues, so becoming another aspect of the literary conversation in which he participates. We aren't disturbed when the narrator seems oblivious to the significance of Mr. Emerson's name or his references to the Club Calamus. We don't expect him to know, in this book searching for the grounds of a faith beyond disillusionment, that Rinehart is a twentieth-century avatar of Melville's confidence-man. Nor are we surprised when he fails to explain that Lewis Mumford's *The Golden Day* celebrates those transcendentalist ideals the decay of which was depicted by Henry James in *The Bostonians* and the further corruption of which is depicted here in Mr. Norton's visit to the disreputable house called the Golden Day.

Given the narrator's imperfect understanding of his own text, we accept the fact that to arrive at Liberty Paints he must cross "in the fog" (*IM*, 192) a bridge that he doesn't try to identify but that we can recognize as the one above which Hart Crane had seen a gull "building high / Over the chained bay waters Liberty." And if we doubt the implied author's allusion here to *The Bridge*, that doubt is dispelled when we recall that, after being directed to Liberty Paints by Mr. Emerson, the narrator had said that the "elevator dropped me like a shot" (*IM*, 189) (Crane had said, "Till elevators drop us from our day"), and when we find that, after his rebirth at the factory hospital, he doesn't return to Manhattan across the bridge because "the stairs leading back to the car that crossed the top were too dizzily steep to climb, swim or fly, and I found a subway instead." Ironically completing the gamut of *The Bridge*, he cuts from "To Brooklyn Bridge" to "The Tunnel": "The subway yawns the quickest promise home." When his train has "plunged" and he has "dropped through the roar, giddy and vacuum-minded," (*IM*, 244) he enters Crane's "hades" of vacuous and daemonic fragmentation—where he sees opposite him, as Vogler has noted, an Eve-like platinum blonde who is this book's ironic answer to Crane's vision of Helen in the subway of "For the Marriage of Faustus and Helen."

Perhaps the most strikingly ironic instance of the narrator's imperfect understanding of the rhetorical world projected by the implied author occurs when Peter Wheatstraw urges a recognition of their "Southern" complicity:

> "All it takes to get along in this here man's town is a little shit, grit and mother-wit. And man, I was bawn with all three. In fact, I'maseventhsonofa-seventhsonbawnwithacauloverbotheyesandraisedonblackcatboneshighjohnthe-conquerorandgreasygreens—" he spieled with twinkling eyes, his lips working rapidly. "You dig me, daddy?"
>
> "You're going too fast," I said, beginning to laugh. (*IM*, 172–73)

The protagonist is nudged by Wheatstraw toward an admission of his Southern roots, though a moment later he defiantly refuses to order a meal of pork chops and grits. But what he never notices is the fact that Wheatstraw's boast—which suggests the "comic triumph" of American wanderers that Constance Rourke had described in *American Humor*—hides within itself W. E. B. Du Bois's anticipatory summary of his own condition: "the Negro is a sort of seventh son, born with a veil," Du Bois had said in *The Souls of Black Folk*, "and gifted with second-sight in this American world—a world which yields him no true self-consciousness, but only lets him see himself through the revelation of the other world" (45).

The narrator's improbable and various eloquence is of a piece with such effects, part of the artistic world of *Invisible Man* rather than a realistic accomplishment of a protagonist turned author. Rovit understandably thought him a "mask of facelessness" or "world's eye" that had emerged from the American comic tradition. But those metaphors ignore his paradoxically limited status within the book's design. He is more like a series of riffs on Louis Armstrong's trumpet.

* * *

We seem to have reached the onion's invisible core. Like the protagonist and the narrator, the implied author of *Invisible Man* has no determinate identity. He supplies, of course, the title and two carefully balanced epigraphs: one evoking the "shadow" of the masked Negro that can't be dismissed by Melville's Benito Cereno, the other evoking the shadows of the past that *are* dismissed by Eliot's Harry. Benito Cereno, who perceives a darker "destiny" in Babo than the self-deceptive Mr. Norton perceives in Ellison's protagonist, follows his "leader" to death. Harry, recognizing that "all my life has been a flight / And phantoms fed upon me while I fled," moves toward an open future that puzzles his family as much as that of Ellison's protagonist has puzzled his readers. "Where are you going?" Amy asks him. And he answers:

> I shall have to learn. That is still unsettled.
> I have not yet had the precise directions.
> Where does one go from a world of insanity?
> Somewhere on the other side of despair. (Eliot, 281)

Between those two epigraphs Ellison's fiction will run its course. But after dropping those clues for the active reader, the implied author becomes the vehicle of the "disembodied voice" that speaks through him—though this voice, rather like that singing through the girl in the college chapel, is also a "fluid web" of his own creation.

Even as a supposedly determinate author speaking about "his" work, Ralph Ellison hasn't wanted to reduce that paradox of creativity. Introducing the 30th Anniversary Edition, he called this "a most self-willed and self-generating piece of fiction," which "announced itself in what were to become the opening words of its prologue" (*IM*, v). And he described his long struggle with "the voice which spoke so knowingly of invisibility," his rather Jamesian desire to endow that voice with an "eloquence" it would not otherwise have, and his need to improvise upon his materials "in the manner of a jazz musician putting a musical theme through a wild star-burst of metamorphosis" (*IM*, ix, xvi, xix). Though a good many critics have written of Ellison's interest in jazz, and Ellison himself has often told us what it means to him, no statement comes closer to our present theme than a couple of sentences from Ellison's essay, "The Charlie Christian Story." There he describes the "cruel contradiction" implicit in an art form that allows for no enduring identity to be forged even by the artist:

> Each true jazz moment . . . springs from a contest in which each artist challenges all the rest; each solo flight, or improvisation, represents (like the successive canvases of a painter) a definition of his identity: as individual, as member of the collectivity and as a link in the chain of tradition. Thus, because jazz finds its very life in an endless improvisation upon traditional materials, the jazzman must lose his identity even as he finds it. . . . (*S&A*, 234)

Like the protagonist, narrator, and implied author, the author of *Invisible Man* must be imagined as an inherently invisible but participatory presence on the edge of chaos, yet in free and responsible relation to a community, making a momentary form that simultaneously seems to make itself through him.

Ellison has amply recognized that such a form is no "object" but a nexus of conversation with ancestors, contemporaries, and readers. The "main source of any novel," he told his *Y'Bird* interviewers, "is other *novels*; these constitute the culture of the form, and my loyalty to our group does nothing to change that. . . ." He had used the first person, he claimed, "just to see what I could do with it, and by way of arguing across the centuries with Henry James, who considered the first person as contributing to formal looseness." And when asked about indebtedness to Frederick Douglass, he answered: "that's *allusion*, that's riffing" ("Essential," 156, 159, 156). In "The World and the Jug," explaining his complex relation to Richard Wright, he said that "all novels of a given historical moment form an argument over the nature of reality and are, to an extent, criticisms of each other" (*S&A*, 117). And in "Society, Morality, and the Novel," included in Granville Hicks's *The Living Novel*, he said that the novelist's reader is "a most necessary collaborator who must participate in bringing the fiction into life" (61). Amplifying that statement in his first interview with John Hersey, he pointed out that the writer must allow the reader "to involve himself, to attach himself, and then begin to collaborate in the creation of the fictional spell. Because you simply cannot put it all there on the page, you can only evoke it—or evoke what is already there, implicitly, in the reader's head: his sense of life" (Hersey, 12).

Invisible Man is therefore a conversation through and among invisibilities who are inexplicably, and inextricably, part of each other. ("And here's the cream of the joke," says the narrator: "Weren't we *part of them* as well as apart from them . . .?" [*IM*, 562].) It takes the world of role-playing into which we all are thrown, replaces it with the story of unmasking that the protagonist has experienced, and replaces that with the conversational history in which we all participate through art. As Ellison said in "The World and the Jug," such a work is a "social action in itself" (*S&A*, 137). And what has it to do with the changing shape of our politics, about which *Newsweek* has informed us with such confidence? A good deal. Only on this basis can we rightly understand Ellison's answer to the question asked by the narrator during Tod Clifton's funeral. Looking down at the assembled crowd, he had felt a "lostness":

> Why were they here? . . . Because they knew Clifton? Or for the occasion his death gave them to express their protestations, a time and place to come together, to stand touching and sweating and breathing and looking in a common direction? Was either explanation adequate in itself? Did it signify love or politicalized hate? And could politics ever be an expression of love? (*IM*, 441)

On receiving the National Book Award in 1953, Ellison translated the protagonist's struggle and his own into the mythical terms of Menelaus's bout with the shape-changer Proteus:

> For the novelist, Proteus stands for both America and the inheritance of illusion through which all men must fight to achieve reality; the offended god stands for our sins against those principles we all hold sacred. The way home we seek is that condition of man's being at home in the world, which is called love, and which we term democracy. (*S&A*, 106)

We can understand that Whitmanesque answer without sentimentality or self-deception only if we also accept the more difficult notion that the "love" invoked is a bond among those who share a manifold invisibility beyond all objective determination. For *Invisible Man* we constitute an unfolding conversational design, conditioned by necessity, open to possibility, shot through with contradictory impulses, and called to responsibility—but with nowhere a solid and visible identity to be found. To imagine otherwise is to reenter the coercive world of masks inhabited by Bledsoe, Norton, Jack, Ras, and Rinehart.

NOTES

1. Ralph Ellison, *Invisible Man*, 3. Subsequent references are cited in text as *IM*.

2. Ellison, *Shadow and Act*, 17. Subsequent references are cited in text as *S&A*.

3. On this point see Barrett, 100–04; Klein, 71–146; and Schafer, 81–93. Jacqueline Covo has surveyed the firt two decades of criticism in her wry checklist *The Blinking Eye*.

4. For contrasting views see Vogler, 64–82; Lieber, 86–100; Stepto, 163–94; Rovit, 34–42, and O'Meally, 78–104. Stepto's essay is also contained in this volume, pp. 360–385.

5. See, for example, Seymour Chatman, *Story and Discourse*.

6. See Michael Allen's essay in *The Black American Writer*, 1:143–51.

WORKS CITED

Allen, Michael. "Some Examples of Faulknerian Rhetoric in Ellison's *Invisible* Man." *The Black American Writer*. Ed. C.W.E. Bigsby. Deland, Fla.: Everett Edwards, 1969.

Barrett, William. "Black and Blue: A Negro Celine." *American Mercury* 74 (June 1952): 100–04.

Burke, Kenneth. *Attitudes Toward History*. New York: New Republic, 1937 (2 vols.).

______. *Counter-Statement*, 2nd ed. Los Altos, Cal.: Hermes, 1953.

Chatman, Seymour. *Story and Discourse: Narrative Structure in Fiction and Film*. Ithaca: Cornell University, 1978.

Covo, Jacqueline. *The Blinking Eye: Ralph Waldo Ellison and His American, French, German and Italian Critics, 1952–71*. Metuchen, N.J.: Scarecrow, 1974.

DuBois, W.E.B. *The Souls of Black Folk*. New York: New American Library, 1969.

Ellison, Ralph. "The Essential Ellison." Interview with Ishmael Reed, Quincy Troupe, and Steve Cannon. *Y'Bird Reader* (Autumn 1977): 126–59.

______. *Invisible Man*. New York: Random House, 1982.

______. *Shadow and Act*. New York: Random House, 1964.

______. "Society, Morality, and the Novel." *The Living Novel: A Symposium*. Ed. Granville Hicks. New York: Macmillan, 1957.

Hersey, John, ed. *Ralph Ellison: A Collection of Critical Essays*. Englewood Cliffs, N.J.: Prentice-Hall, 1974.

Klein, Marcus. "Ralph Ellison." *After Alienation: American Novels in Mid-Century*. New York: World, 1964.

Lieber, Todd. "Ralph Ellison and the Metaphor of Invisibility in Black Literary Tradition." *American Quarterly* 24 (1972).

O'Meally, Robert G. "Invisible Man: Black and Blue." *The Craft of Ralph Ellison*. Cambridge, Mass.: Harvard Univerity, 1980.

Rovit, Earl H. "Ralph Ellison and the American Comic Tradition." *Wisconsin Studies in Contemporary Literature* 1 (Fall 1960).

Schafer, William J. "Ralph Ellison and the Birth of the Anti-Hero." *Critique* 10 (1968).

Stepto, Robert B. "Literacy and Hibernation: Ralph Ellison's *Invisible Man*." *From Behind the Veil: A Study of Afro-American Narrative*. Urbana: University of Illinois, 1979.

Vogler, Thomas A. "*Invisible Man*: Somebody's Protest Novel." *Iowa Review* 1 (Spring 1970).

Wright, Richard. *12 Million Black Voices*. New York: Viking, 1941.

Fingering the Jagged Grains

MELVIN DIXON

The blues is an impulse to keep the painful details and episodes of a brutal experience alive in one's aching consciousness, to finger its jagged grain, and to transcend it. . . .

Ralph Ellison
''Richard Wright's Blues''

1.

Blue notes from Baltimore and Charlotte, N.C.
Albert Murray riffing on Bearden's
long vamp to his own fast train,
a whistling northbound steel-smoking hound,
and the tracks of writing tell it true:
''There were no bad trains, but everybody
used to think of passenger trains
as good trains.''

Well, right in the gallery
we almost had church!

This time in Brooklyn, before the first killing
frost or the frozen steel of subways and tenement
pipes, Teddy Wilson and son heat up on piano
and bass, fingering Ellington's A train
back through Catfish Row. Upstairs the melody
is Bearden playing Bearden: *Out Chorus, Tenor Spot,*
Stomping at the Savoy and *Carolina Shout*,
calling up J. P. Johnson and baptism in the Pee Dee.
Scooter conducts the orchestra,
Maudell Sleet takes a bow.
And Rinehart solos up from underground.

It is the elegance of ritual: Bearden, Ellison
and Murray cutting the jagged grains: patchwork
figures in silhouette, blue notes in calico
and quilting under glass. *What did I do*
to be so black and blue? Electric blue, fire
and fuchsia in the sky. Lightning, lonesome blue.
Cut out legs, fingers and bebop eyes
shape the uncreated features of face and race.
Found objects of the territory:
Mecklenberg County to Harlem and back.
Cloth and color in piano stride.

What did I do? You lived, you lived!
And the jagged grains *so black and blue*
open like lips about to sing.

2.

Everywhere women: Miss Sheba and Queen Susannah.
High butt women. Thick thigh women.
Luvernia or sweet Liza in the grass.
Maudell Sleet riffing Mary Rambo
don't you weep, don't you weep.
Faces cut from Benin masks with jaws
carved out of hunger and loss and joy.
Women in gardens, bathing from washtubs,
or just making love with those great huge hands.
Pieces of fried-chicken-tablecloths
and bedspreads waiting a long good night
of Carolina quilting and African weaves
and those wide and wrinkled hands
fingering the empty spaces.

Black Nativity:
High Cotton, Mother & Child.
Eyes like liquid marbles
in a blaze of sun.

Afro-American Gothic:
Miss Bertha & Mr. Seth.
25 X 18. Collage on board.
From a private collection.

"The last time I saw Liza," Bearden's
handwriting said, "was down at the station
when I left for Pittsburgh on the 5:13."

The Daybreak Express. The heartbreak stride
to Harlem where Rinehart played the keys.

3.

Rinehart, Rinehart, where you been?
Round the corner and back again.
Boomerang!
Jagged grains.
Boomerang!
Jagged masks:

Faceless picaro cool-strutting through collage,
you smoked glasses and high-water threads,
fedora hat and patent leather dogs, you midnight
indigo of mood and magic, act cut from sack-cloth
shadow: Ellison playing Bearden playing Ellison.

Rinehart, you fooled them all
and you sure fooled me. I know all about
the Pee Dee and Carolina yams, but not
that the grains could talk that talk:

"*Do Jesus!*"
And he did.

Yeah, Rine, we know where you been.
But baby, where you going?

4.

South. To a new old place. Back
to the track and the clickety-clack
like someone's Saturday child.

Cool Scooter, you so Louisiana sweet.
Fast-tracking Scooter, you real southern sweet.
Your daddy is Rinehart, your mama Maudell Sleet.

"When I was old enough," the handwriting said,
"I found out what Liza's mother did for a living."

And it was blue. Steel-cutting blue.
Luzanna Cholly riffing Mr. Seth,
and Murray playing Ellison playing Bearden
playing Murray on infinite multiples of three:

Tri-angular. A three-note chord.

Triptych and three part harmony.
Alto. Tenor. Bass.

Ellison on Painting:
"The problem for the plastic artist
is not one of telling but of *revealing*."

Bearden on Fiction:
Pepper Jelly Lady (1981)
"The trains in the stories she told
always ran North.
I used to look at the sky
and think of storybook dragons."

Murray on Music and More:
Stomp, stomp, stomping the blues.
"Young men who become the heroes
do so by confronting and slaying dragons.
Improvisation is the ultimate skill."

And at the Brooklyn Museum
Teddy Wilson on piano.

5.

Those hands cut from paper bag groceries and grace,
those hands opening like lips on a blues,
finger the jagged grains of a long, long, long
remembered time. Can you see it? Can you hear it?
What did I do to be so black and blue?
Rinehart, Scooter and Maudell Sleet:
Character, Consciousness and Collage.

PART SIX

Bibliography
Contributors
Index

The Writings of Ralph Ellison

ROBERT G. O'MEALLY

This bibliography, arranged chronologically and categorically, charts the career of Ralph Ellison from 1937, when his first book review appeared, until the present. Along with fiction and formal essays I have listed a miscellany of Ellison materials: book-jacket comments, letters to editors, television interviews, and unpublished (but available) memorandums.

For help with this bibliography, I wish to thank William Collins and Charlotte Hunter, skillful and persistent research assistants.

Fiction

''Slick Gonna Learn.'' *Direction* 2 (September 1939): 10–11, 14, 16.

''The Birthmark.'' *New Masses* 36 (July 2, 1940): 16–17.

''Afternoon.'' *American Writing*. Edited by Hans Otto Storm, Sidney Alexander, and Eugene Joffe, 28–37. Prairie City, Ill.: J. A. Decker, 1940.

''Mister Toussan.'' *New Masses* 41 (November 4, 1941): 19–20.

''That I Had the Wings.'' *Common Ground* 3 (Summer 1943): 30–37.

''In a Strange Country.'' *Tomorrow* 3 (July 1944): 41–44.

''King of the Bingo Game.'' *Tomorrow* 4 (November 1944): 29–33.

''Flying Home.'' *Cross Section*. Edited by Edwin Seaver, 469–85. New York: L. B. Fischer, 1944.

''Invisible Man.'' *Horizon* 16 (October 1947): 104–18; later published as the ''Battle Royal'' chapter of *Invisible Man*.

''Invisible Man: Prologue to a Novel.'' *Partisan Review* 19 (January–February 1952): 31–40.

Invisible Man. New York: Random House, 1952.

"Did You Ever Dream Lucky?" *New World Writing* 5 (April 1954): 134–45.

"February." *Saturday Review* 38 (January 1, 1955): 25.

"A Coupla Scalped Indians." *New World Writing* 9 (1956): 225–36.

"And Hickman Arrives." *Noble Savage* 1 (1960): 5–49.

"The Roof, the Steeple and the People." *Quarterly Review of Literature* 10 (1960): 115–28.

"Out of the Hospital and Under the Bar." *Soon, One Morning*. Edited by Herbert Hill, 242–90. New York: Knopf, 1963.

"It Always Breaks Out." *Partisan Review* 30 (Spring 1963): 13–28.

"Juneteenth." *Quarterly Review of Literature* 4 (1965): 262–76.

"Night-Talk." *Quarterly Review of Literature* 16 (1969): 317–29.

"A Song of Innocence." *Iowa Review* 1 (Spring 1970): 30–40; a revised version of this story was read by Ellison at the Library of Congress, March 28, 1983; a recording is available through the Library.

"Cadillac Flambé." *American Review* 16 (February 1973): 249–69.

"Backwacking: A Plea to the Senator." *Massachusetts Review* 18 (Autumn 1977): 411–16.

Literary Essays, Reviews, and Speeches

"Creative and Cultural Lag." *New Challenge* 2 (Fall 1937): 90–91.

"Practical Mystic." *New Masses** 28 (August 16, 1938): 25–26.

"Ruling-class Southerner." *New Masses* 33 (December 5, 1939): 27.

"Javanese Folklore." *New Masses* 34 (December 26, 1939): 25–26.

"The Good Life." *New Masses* 34 (February 20, 1940): 27.

"TAC Negro Show." *New Masses* 34 (February 27, 1940): 29–30.

"Hunters and Pioneers." *New Masses* 34 (March 19, 1940): 26.

"Romance in the Slave Era." *New Masses* 35 (May 28, 1940): 27–28.

"Anti-War Novel." *New Masses* 35 (June 18, 1940): 29–30.

"Stormy Weather." *New Masses* 37 (September 24, 1940): 20–21.

"Southern Folklore." *New Masses* 37 (October 29, 1940): 28.

"Big White Fog." *New Masses* 37 (November 12, 1940): 22–23.

---

*Ralph Ellison has said, in an interview that appears in this volume, that he wrote many unsigned pieces for *New Masses*. Only the signed works, however, are noted here.

"Argosy Across the USA." *New Masses* 37 (November 26, 1940): 24.

"Negro Prize Fighter." *New Masses* 37 (December 17, 1940): 26–27.

"Richard Wright and Recent Negro Fiction." *Direction* 4 (Summer 1941): 12–13.

"Recent Negro Fiction." *New Masses* 40 (August 5, 1941): 22–26.

"The Great Migration." *New Masses* 41 (December 2, 1941): 23–24.

"Transition." *The Negro Quarterly, a Review of Life and Culture* 1 (Spring 1942): 87–92.

"Native Land." *New Masses* 43 (June 2, 1942): 29.

"The Darker Brother." *Tomorrow* 3 (September 1943): 67–68.

"Boston Adventure." *Tomorrow* 4 (December 1944): 120.

"The Magic of Limping John." *Tomorrow* 4 (December 1944): 121.

"New World A-Coming." *Tomorrow* 4 (December 1944): 67–68.

"Escape the Thunder." *Tomorrow* 5 (March 1945): 91–92.

"Richard Wright's Blues." *Antioch Review* 5 (Summer 1945): 198–211.

"Beating That Boy." *New Republic* 113 (October 22, 1945): 535–36.

"Stepchild Fantasy." *Saturday Review* 29 (June 8, 1946): 25–26.

"The Shadow and the Act." *Reporter* 1 (December 6, 1949): 17–19.

"Collaborator with His Own Enemy." *New York Times Book Review* (February 19, 1950): 4.

"Twentieth Century Fiction and the Black Mask of Humanity." *Confluence* (December 1953): 3–21.

"Society, Morality, and the Novel." *The Living Novel: A Symposium*. Edited by Granville Hicks, 58–91. New York: Macmillan, 1957.

"Change the Joke and Slip the Yoke." *Partisan Review* 25 (Spring 1958): 212–22.

"Resourceful Human." *Saturday Review* 41 (July 12, 1958): 33–34.

"Stephen Crane and the Mainstream of American Fiction." Introduction to Crane's *The Red Badge of Courage and Four Great Stories*, 7–24. New York: Dell, 1960.

"The World and the Jug." *New Leader* 46 (December 9, 1963): 22–26.

"A Rejoinder." *New Leader* 47 (February 3, 1964): 15–22.

"If the Twain Shall Meet." *Washington Post Book Week* (November 8, 1964): 1, 20–25.

"Hidden Name and Complex Fate." *The Writer's Experience*, 1–15. Washington, D.C.: Library of Congress, 1964.

"The Blues." *New York Review of Books* 1 (February 6, 1964): 5–7.

''On Becoming a Writer.'' *Commentary* 38 (October 1964): 57–60.

Shadow and Act. New York: Random House, 1964.

''The Novel as a Function of American Democracy.'' *Wilson Library Bulletin* (June 1967): 1022–27.

''American Humor.'' ''Comic Elements in Selected Prose of James Baldwin, Ralph Ellison, and Langston Hughes.'' Masters thesis by Elwyn E. Breaux, 146–57. Fisk University, 1971.

Foreword. *There Is a Tree More Ancient Than Eden* by Leon Forrest, i–ii. New York: Random House, 1973.

''On Initiation Rites and Power: Ralph Ellison Speaks at West Point.'' *Contemporary Literature* 15 (Spring 1974): 165–86.

''The Alain Locke Symposium.'' *Harvard Advocate* (Spring 1974): 9–28.

''Perspective of Literature.'' *American Law: The Third Century, the Law Bicentennial Volume*. Edited by Bernard Schwartz, 391–406. Hackensack, New Jersey: Rotham, 1976.

''The Little Man at Chehaw Station.'' *American Scholar* 47 (Winter 1977–78): 25–48.

''Remembering Richard Wright.'' *Delta* 18 (April 1984): 1–13. Transcript of a lecture presented at the University of Iowa, July 18, 1971.

Going to the Territory. New York: Random House, 1986.

Essays and Speeches on Politics and Culture

''Anti-Semitism Among Negroes.'' *Jewish People's Voice* 3 (April 1939): 3, 8.

''Judge Lynch in New York.'' *New Masses* 32 (August 15, 1939): 15–16. A shortened version, ''They Found Terror in Harlem,'' in *Negro World Digest* (July 1940): 43–45.

''Camp Lost Colony.'' *New Masses* 34 (February 6, 1940): 18–19.

''A Congress Jim Crow Didn't Attend.'' *New Masses* 35 (May 14, 1940): 5–8.

''Philippine Report.'' *Direction* 4 (Summer 1941): 13.

''The Way It Is.'' *New Masses* 44 (October 20, 1942): 9–11.

''Editorial Comment.'' *Negro Quarterly, a Review of Life and Culture* 1 (Winter 1943): 295–302.

''Eyewitness Story of Riot: False Rumors Spurred Mob.'' *New York Post* (August 2, 1943), 4.

''Address at Tuskegee Institute.'' Press release issued by Division of Public Relations, Tuskegee Institute (July 1954).

"*Nôtre lutte nous proclame à la fois nègres et américains.*" *Preuves* 87 (May 1958): 33–38.

"What These Children Are Like." *Education of the Deprived and Segregated.* Dedham, Mass.: Bank St. College (1965), 44–51.

"Tell It Like It Is, Baby." *Nation* 201 (September 20, 1965): 129–36.

"Harlem's America." *New Leader* 49 (September 26, 1966): 22–35.

"What America Would Be Like Without Blacks." *Time* (April 6, 1970): 54–55.

Speech Honoring William L. Dawson. Philadelphia, Tuskegee Alumni Club, 1971.

"Ralph Ellison." *Attacks of Taste.* Edited by Evelyn B. Byrne and Otto M. Penzler, 20–22. New York: Gotham, 1971.

"Address at Harvard's Alumni Meeting." Press release issued by Harvard University News Office, June 12, 1974.

"Middle-Income Blacks Need to Find Cultural Awareness." *Los Angeles Times* (February 2, 1975), 37.

Speech at the Opening of the Ralph Ellison Public Library. Oklahoma City, June 21, 1975.

"Going to the Territory" and "A Portrait of Inman Page." *Carleton Miscellany* 18 (Winter 1980): 9–26, 18–32.

Interviews

"The Art of Fiction: An Interview." Alfred Chester and Vilma Howard. *Paris Review* 2 (Spring 1955): 55–71.

"An Interview with Ralph Ellison." Ted Cohen and N. A. Samstag. *Phoenix* 22 (Fall 1961): 4–10.

"That Same Pain, That Same Pleasure: An Interview." R. G. Stern. *December* 3 (Winter 1961): 30–32, 37–46.

"An Interview with Ralph Ellison." Allen Geller. *Tamarack Review* (Summer 1964): 3–24.

Under Pressure. Edited by A. Alvarez, 120–21, 136–37, 148–49, 160–63, 172–73, 178–79. Baltimore: Penguin, 1965.

"Dialogue." *Who Speaks for the Negro*? Robert Penn Warren, 325–54. New York: Random House, 1965.

"Ralph Ellison." Center for Cassette Studies, no. 7508. (ca. 1965).

"A Very Stern Discipline." Steve Cannon, Lennox Raphael, and James Thompson. *Harper's* 234 (March 1967): 76–95.

"Found: A NonProtester." Mike McGrady, *Newsday* (October 28, 1967), 3W, 36W.

"A Dialogue with His Audience." *Barat Review* 3 (January 1968): 51–53.

''Indivisible Man.'' James A. McPherson. *Atlantic Monthly* 226 (December 1970): 45–60.

''A Conversation with Ralph Ellison.'' Leon Forrest. *Muhammad Speaks* (December 15, 1972): 29–31.

''Ralph Ellison: Twenty Years After.'' David L. Carson. *Studies in American Fiction* 1 (Spring 1973): 1–23.

''Ellison: Exploring the Life of a Not So Invisible Man.'' Hollie West. *Washington Post* (August 19, 1973), G1–G3.

''Travels with Ralph Ellison Through Time and Thought.'' Hollie West. *Washington Post* (August 20, 1973), B1, B3.

''Through a Writer's Eyes.'' Hollie West. *Washington Post* (August 21, 1973), B1, B3.

''Growing Up Black in Frontier Oklahoma . . . From an Ellison Perspective.'' Hollie West. *Washington Post* (August 21, 1973), B1, B3.

''Ralph Ellison.'' *The Writer's Voice*. George Garrett, 221–27. New York: Morrow, 1973.

''Ralph Ellison.'' *Interviews with Ten Black Writers*. John O'Brien, 63–77. New York: Liveright, 1973.

Appendix. ''Invisibility: A Study of the Works of Toomer, Wright, and Ellison.'' Master's thesis by Arlene Joan Crewdson. Loyola University, 1974.

''Interview with Ralph Ellison.'' WGBH-TV, Boston, April 12, 1974.

''Introduction: A Completion of Personality.'' John Hersey. *Ralph Ellison, a Collection of Critical Essays*. Edited by Hersey, 1–19. Englewood, N.J.: Prentice-Hall, 1974.

News Report. KVTV-TV, Oklahoma City, June 15, 1975.

''A Talk with Ralph Ellison.'' KVTV-TV, Oklahoma City, June 19, 1975.

''Study and Experience, an Interview With Ralph Ellison.'' Michael S. Harper and Robert B. Stepto. *Massachusetts Review* 18 (Autumn 1977): 417–35. Reprinted in *Chant of Saints*. Editied by Harper and Stepto. Urbana: University of Illinois Press, 1979.

''The Essential Ellison.'' Steve Cannon, Ishmael Reed, and Quincy Troupe. *Y'Bird Reader* 1 (Autumn 1977): 126–59.

''Ralph Ellison's Territorial Vantage.'' Ron Welburn. *The Grackle* 4 (1977–78): 5–15.

''Book Essay.'' Walter Lowe, Jr. *Playboy* (October 1982): 42.

'''Invisible Man' as Vivid Today as in 1952.'' Herbert Mitgang. *New York Times* (March 1, 1982), C13.

Interview with Ralph Ellison. ''The Today Show.'' NBC-TV, New York, March 10, 1982.

Essays on Music and Art

"Modern Negro Art." *Tomorrow* 4 (November 1944): 92–93.

"Introduction to Flamenco." *Saturday Review* 37 (December 11, 1954): 38–39.

"Living with Music." *High Fidelity* 4 (December 1955): 60ff.

"The Swing to Stereo." *Saturday Review* 41 (April 26, 1958): 37, 39, 40, 60.

"The Charlie Christian Story." *Saturday Review* 41 (May 17, 1958): 42–43, 46.

"Remembering Jimmy." *Saturday Review* 41 (July 12, 1958): 36–37.

"As the Spirit Moves Mahalia." *Saturday Review* 41 (September 27, 1958): 41, 43, 69–70.

"The Golden Age Time Past." *Esquire Magazine* 51 (January 1959): 107–10.

"On Birds, Bird Watching, and Jazz." *Saturday Review* 45 (July 28, 1962): 47–49, 62.

"Romare Bearden: Paintings and Projections." *Crisis* (March 1970): 81–86.

Editorial Work

The Negro in New York. Edited with Roi Ottley et al. New York: Arno Press, 1966; originally written and edited during the 1930s by the New York Federal Writers Project.

Negro Quarterly. Ellison was managing editor, 1942–43.

Noble Savage. Ellison was contributing editor, 1960.

Transcribed Conferences, Group Discussions

"What's Wrong with the American Novel?" *American Scholar* 24 (Autumn 1955): 464–503.

Proceedings, American Academy of Arts and Letters and the National Institute of Arts and Letters, 2nd series, 15 (1965): 452–54; 17 (1967): 178–82, 192.

"Conference Transcript." *Daedalus* 95 (Winter 1966): 408–41.

"Literature and the Human Sciences on the Nature of Contemporary Man." *The Writer as Independent Spirit*, 37–44. New York, 1968.

"The Uses of History in Fiction." *Southern Literary Journal* 1 (Spring 1969): 57–90.

Profiles with Extensive Quotes from Ellison

"Inside a Dark Shell." Harvey Curtis Webster. *Saturday Review* 35 (April 12, 1952): 22–23.

''Talk with Ralph Ellison.'' Harvey Breit. *New York Times Book Review* 4 (May 1952): 26.

''Light on *Invisible Man*.'' *Crisis* 60 (March 1953): 157–58.

''Sidelights on Invisibility.'' Rochelle Gibson. *Saturday Review* 36 (March 14, 1953): 20, 49.

''A Best-Seller Starts Here.'' Jim Simpson. *Daily Oklahoman* (August 23, 1953), 3.

''En Väl Synlig Man.'' Vilgot Sjöman. *Dagens Nyheter* (January 3, 1955): 1–6.

''Five Writers and Their African Ancestors.'' Harold Isaacs. *Phylon* 21 (Winter 1960): 317–22.

''The Visible Man.'' *Newsweek* 62 (August 12, 1963): 81–82.

''An American Novelist Who Sometimes Teaches.'' John Corry. *New York Times Book Review* (November 20, 1966): 54–55, 179–80, 182–85, 187, 196.

''Ralph Ellison: Novelist as Brown Skinned Aristocrat.'' Richard Kostelanetz. *Shenandoah* 20 (Summer 1969): 56–77.

''Going to the Territory.'' Jervis Anderson. *New Yorker* 52 (November 22, 1976): 55–108.

''Alfred Ellison of Abbeville.'' Stewart Lillard. Unpublished monograph, 1976.

''Ralph Ellison, the Quiet Legend.'' Lynn Darling. *Washington Post* (April 21, 1982), B1, B5.

Miscellaneous

Writers Project Interviews, Essays. Unpublished; available at Library of Congress, Folklore Archives; parts were published as ''Leo Gurley,'' ''Lloyd Green,'' ''Jim Barber,'' ''Eli Luster,'' *First-Person America*, Edited by Ann Banks, 243–45, 250–52, 254–57, 257–60. New York: Knopf, 1980. See also ''First Person America: Voices From the Thirties'' (Part V, ''Harlem Stories''), National Public Radio Special Series SP-801214.06/06-C.

Federal Writers Project Interviews, Essays. Unpublished; available at New York Public Library, 135th Street branch.

''Ralph Ellison Explains.'' *'48 Magazine of the Year* 2 (May 1948): 145.

Book-jacket comment. *Go Tell It on the Mountain* by James Baldwin. New York: Signet Edition, 1954.

''At Home: Letter to the Editor.'' *Time* 73 (February 19, 1959): 2.

''No Apologies.'' *Harper*'s 235 (July 1967): 4ff.

Book-jacket comment. *Culture and Poverty* by Charles A. Valentine. Chicago: University of Chicago Press, 1968.

Book-jacket comment. *Hue and Cry* by James A. McPherson. Boston: Atlantic Monthly Press, 1969.

Book-jacket comment. *The Omni-Americans* by Albert Murray. New York: Outerbridge, 1970.

Advertisement comment. *The Unwritten War* by Daniel Aaron. *New York Review of Books*, Fall 1973.

Book-jacket comment. *Elbow Room* by James A. McPherson. Boston: Atlantic Monthly Press, 1977.

"A Special Message to Subscribers From Ralph Ellison." *Invisible Man*, i–iii. New York: Franklin, 1980.

"A Page in Ralph Ellison's Life." *Brown Alumni Monthly* 80 (November 1979): 40–41.

Book-jacket comment. *Drylongso* by John L. Gwaltney. New York: Random House, 1980, paperback edition.

Book-jacket comment. *This Was Harlem 1900–1950* by Jervis Anderson. New York: Farrar, Straus & Giroux, 1982.

"Introduction." *Invisible Man Special 30th Anniversary Edition*, ix–xxi. New York: Random House, 1982.

Book-jacket comment. *Our Nig; or, Sketches from the Life of a Free Black* by Harriet E. Wilson. New York: Random House, 1983.

Book-jacket comment. *One More Day's Journey: the Story of a Family and a People* by Allen B. Ballard. New York: McGraw-Hill, 1984.

"A Personal Memoir by Ralph Ellison." Written for National Medical Fellowships, New York City, August 1984.

Contributors

HOUSTON BAKER, JR., is a poet and critic whose works include the recently published *Blues Journey Home* and the forthcoming *Modernism and the Harlem Renaissance*. He is currently the Albert M. Greenfield Professor of Human Relations at the University of Pennsylvania.

ROMARE BEARDEN is an artist whose paintings and graphics appear in many exhibits and major collections, including those of the Metropolitan and Whitney museums in New York, the Philadelphia Museum of Art, and the Boston Museum of Fine Arts.

KIMBERLY BENSTON is the author of *Baraka: The Renegade and the Mask* and of many essays on Afro-American literature. He currently teaches English and drama at Haverford College.

C. W. E. BIGSBY is Professor of American Literature at the University of East Anglia, Norwich, England. He is the author of more than twenty books on subjects ranging from English and American drama to black writing and popular culture.

KENNETH BURKE is the author of many books on literature and culture, including *A Grammar of Motives*, *The Philosophy of Literary Form*, and *The Rhetoric of Religion*.

JOHN F. CALLAHAN is Professor of English at Lewis & Clark College. He is the author of a book on F. Scott Fitzgerald, *The Illusions of a Nation*, and of many articles on Afro-American literature, including essays on Ellison. His latest book, *In the African-American Grain*, is soon to be published.

CHARLES T. DAVIS was Professor of English and Chairman of Afro-American Studies at Yale University. A scholar of American poetry, he was also the author of numerous essays on Afro-American literature, many of which are collected in *Black Is the Color of the Cosmos*.

MELVIN DIXON is Professor of English at Queens College, City College of New York. A poet, novelist, translator, and critic, he is the author of a book of poetry, *Change of Territory*, and is translator of Genevieve Fabre's *Drumbeats, Masks, and Metaphors: Contemporary Afro-American Theatre*.

RALPH ELLISON is the author of the novel, *Invisible Man*, which won the National Book Award and the Russwurm Award in 1952. He is a charter member of the National Council on the Arts and Humanities. His other published works include two collections of essays, *Shadow and Act* (1964) and, most recently, *Going to the Territory* (1986).

He was the Albert Schweitzer Professor of the Humanities at New York University from 1970 to 1980.

MICHEL FABRE is Professor of American Studies at the Université de la Sorbonne Nouvelle in Paris and director of the Centre d'Etudes Afro-Americaines et des Nouvelles Litteratures en Anglais there. His written or edited volumes include *The Unfinished Quest of Richard Wright* and *The World of Richard Wright*, and a special issue of *Delta* (1983) on *Invisible Man*.

LEON FORREST is Chair of the Department of African-American Studies at Northwestern University and Professor of English. He has published three novels, *There Is a Tree More Ancient Than Eden*, *The Bloodworth Orphans*, and *Two Wings to Veil My Face*.

JOSEPH FRANK is Professor of Slavic and Comparative Literature at Stanford University and also Professor Emeritus of Comparative Literature at Princeton University. His publications include *The Widening Gyre* and three volumes of a critical biography of Dostoevsky.

MICHAEL S. HARPER is the I. J. Kapstein Professor of English at Brown University. He is author of eight books of poetry, including *Dear John, Dear Coltrane*, *Nightmare Begins Responsibility*, *Images of Kin*, and *Healing Song for the Inner Ear* and has co-edited *Chant of Saints: A Gathering of Afro-American Literature, Art, and Scholarship* with Robert Stepto, and a special edition of *The Carleton Miscellany* on Ralph Ellison, with John S. Wright.

WILSON HARRIS is the author of many novels, including *Palace of the Peacock*, *Heartland*, *The Far Room*, and most recently, *Carnival*. The four novels of his *Guyana Quartet* were recently reissued in a single volume.

JOHN HERSEY is Adjunct Professor Emeritus at Yale University. He is a novelist and journalist and a member of the American Academy of Arts and Letters.

GEORGE E. KENT was Professor of English at the University of Chicago and a prolific critic of Afro-American literature. His works included *Blackness and the Adventure of Western Culture*.

R. W. B. LEWIS is Professor Emeritus at Yale University. His many books include *The American Adam*, *Trials of the Word*, *The Picaresque Saint*, *The Presence of Hart Crane*, and *Edith Wharton: A Biography*.

JAMES ALAN McPHERSON is the author of an award-winning volume of short stories, entitled *Hue and Cry* (1969) and *Elbow Room* (1971). He currently teaches writing at the University of Iowa.

LARRY NEAL was a principal figure of the Black Arts Movement and was the author of many influential essays, poems, and plays. His works included *Black Boogaloo*, *Hoodoo Hollerin' Bebop Ghosts*, and *The Glorious Monster in the Bell of the Horn*.

ROBERT G. O'MEALLY is the author of *The Craft of Ralph Ellison* and the editor of a book of new essays on *Invisible Man*. He teaches at Wesleyan University.

JOHN M. REILLY is Professor of English at State University of New York at Albany and editor of *Twentieth Century Interpretations of Invisible Man*. He has published numerous articles on Afro-American writers, and is a contributor to the forthcoming volume, *Approaches to Teaching Invisible Man*.

JOSEPH T. SKERRETT, JR., is Associate Professor of English at the University of Massachusetts, Amherst, where he has taught since 1973. His essays on black and white American fiction have appeared in *American Quarterly*, *MELUS*, *Callaloo*, *The Massachusetts Review*, and elsewhere.

HORTENSE SPILLERS is Professor of English at Haverford College. Her articles and stories have appeared widely in journals. One of her short stories won the National Award for Excellence in Fiction and Belles Lettres in 1976.

ROBERT B. STEPTO is Professor of English, Afro-American Studies, and American Studies at Yale University. He is the author of *From Behind the Veil: A Study of Afro-American Narrative* and the co-editor of several volumes, including the anthology, *Chant of Saints: A Gathering of Afro-American Literature, Art, and Scholarship*.

CLAUDIA TATE is Associate Professor of English at Howard University and the author of *Black Women Writers at Work*. She is currently working on a book entitled, *Black Women Writers, Feminism and Literary Theory*.

HOLLIE WEST is currently a feature writer with the *Detroit Free Press*. He has served in similar capacities with *The Washington Post* and CBS News.

THOMAS R. WHITAKER is Professor of English and Theater Studies at Yale University. His books include *Swan and Shadow: Yeats's Dialogue with History*, *William Carlos Williams*, *Fields of Play in Modern Drama*, and *Tom Stoppard*.

JOHN S. WRIGHT is Associate Professor of English and Chairman of Afro-American and African Studies at the University of Minnesota. He was co-editor with Michael S. Harper of the special edition of *The Carleton Miscellany* devoted to Ralph Ellison. His forthcoming book is entitled *The Riddle of Freedom: Art, Ideas, and the Contours of Afro-American Literary Throught*.

Index